Invertebrates

Rare and Endangered Biota of Florida
Ray E. Ashton, Jr., Series Editor

Florida Committee on Rare and Endangered Plants and Animals

Ray E. Ashton, Jr.
FCREPA Chair (1989–91)
  and Series Editor
Water and Air Research, Inc.
6821 SW Archer Road
Gainesville, Florida 32608

Daniel F. Austin, Co-Chair
Special Committee on Plants
Department of Biological Sciences
Florida Atlantic University
Boca Raton, FL 33431

James W. Beever III
FCREPA Chair (1993–94)
Florida Game and
  Fresh Water Fish Commission
306 Little Grove Lane
North Fort Myers, Florida 33917

Mark Deyrup, Co-Chair
Special Committee on Invertebrates
Archbold Biological Station
Route 2, Box 180
Lake Placid, Florida 33852

Richard Franz, Co-Chair
Special Committee on Invertebrates
Florida Museum of Natural History
University of Florida
Gainesville, Florida 32611

Carter R. Gilbert
Chair, Special Committee on Fishes
Florida Museum of Natural History
University of Florida
Gainesville, Florida 32611

Stephen R. Humphrey
Chair, Special Committee on Mammals
Florida Museum of Natural History
University of Florida
Gainesville, Florida 32611

Herbert W. Kale II
FCREPA Chair (1985–86)
Co-Chair, Special Committee on Birds
Florida Audubon Society
460 Highway 436
Suite 200
Casselberry, Florida 32707

Paul E. Moler
FCREPA Chair (1992–93)
Chair, Special Committee
  on Reptiles and Amphibians
Wildlife Research Laboratory
Florida Game and
  Fresh Water Fish Commission
4005 S. Main Street
Gainesville, Florida 32601

James Rogers
Co-Chair, Special Committee on Birds
Wildlife Research Laboratory
Florida Game and
  Fresh Water Fish Commission
4005 S. Main Street
Gainesville, Florida 32601

I. Jack Stout
FCREPA Chair (1987–88)
Department of Biological Sciences
University of Central Florida
Orlando, Florida 32816

Daniel B. Ward
FCREPA Chair (1983–84)
Co-Chair, Special Committee on Plants
Department of Botany
University of Florida
Gainesville, Florida 32611

Rare and Endangered Biota of Florida

VOLUME IV.
INVERTEBRATES

EDITED BY

MARK DEYRUP &
RICHARD FRANZ

Co-Chairs, Special Committee on Invertebrates
Florida Committee on Rare and Endangered
Plants and Animals

UNIVERSITY PRESS OF FLORIDA
Gainesville, Tallahassee, Tampa, Boca Raton,
Pensacola, Orlando, Miami, Jacksonville

This volume was made possible in part by grants from Florida Power and Light Company and Save the Manatee Club.

99 98 97 96 95 94   6 5 4 3 2 1

Library of Congress Cataloging-in-Publication Data
(Revised for vol. 4)

Rare and endangered biota of Florida.

   Includes bibliographical references and indexes.
   Contents: v. 1. Mammals / edited by Stephen R.
Humphrey—v. 2. Fishes / edited by Carter R. Gilbert
—[etc.]—v. 4. Invertebrates / edited by Mark Deyrup
& Richard Franz.
   1. Rare animals—Florida.   2. Endangered species—
Florida.   3. Rare plants—Florida.   4. Endangered plants—
Florida.   I. Ashton, Ray E.
QL84.22.F6R37 1992   591.52'9'09759   91-36368
ISBN 0-8130-1127-2 (v. 1 : alk. paper)
ISBN 0-8130-1128-0 (v. 1 : pbk. : alk. paper)

The University Press of Florida is the scholarly publishing agency of the State University System of Florida, comprised of Florida A & M University, Florida Atlantic University, Florida International University, Florida State University, University of Central Florida, University of Florida, University of North Florida, University of South Florida, and University of West Florida.

Orders for books published by all member presses should be addressed to
University Press of Florida
15 NW 15th St.
Gainesville, FL 32611

Contents

Insects

Foreword

The initial six-volume Rare and Endangered Biota of Florida series has enjoyed enormous popularity (each volume was reprinted at least once, most two or three times). It has served as the definitive reference compendium on endangered and threatened species in Florida and is widely recognized as among the most authoritative and comprehensive such works in the nation. I am proud the Florida Game and Fresh Water Fish Commission was integrally involved in that initial work, and likewise proud that we were involved in producing this revised series.

In the forewords to the initial volumes, my predecessors, Dr. O. E. Frye, Jr., and Colonel Robert M. Brantly acknowledged the momentum of endangered species conservation to that point, and how the series was a significant contribution in that regard, but admonished that we must not rest on our laurels—much remained to be done. Although much has indeed been done in the interim, I am disappointed that we have not approached the level of progress I had hoped we would attain by now. As the species accounts herein clearly demonstrate, many Florida species are perilously near extinction, and many of the factors leading to that dire circumstance are still with us. The composition of the current official state lists—40 endangered, 27 threatened, and 50 special concern animals, along with 199 endangered and 283 threatened plants—is compelling evidence in and of itself that our progress has been relatively minor (by comparison, there were 31 endangered and 54 threatened species in 1978). There are several reasons for this much-less-than-hoped-for progression, but primarily it has been related to insufficient funding at both the state and federal levels. And without proper funding, the necessary manpower and other resources cannot be emplaced to address many critical needs. So we face the dilemma of either addressing the needs of only a few species so as to maximize effect, or spreading our resources thinly among many species, minimizing the effects on an individual basis.

This is not to say, however, that we have not made some substantial strides forward in the last decade or so. Through an innovative translocation strategy, we have reestablished in Florida the previously extirpated Perdido Key beach mouse and significantly expanded the range of the Choctawhatchee beach mouse; because of stringent protection and rigorous application of "Habitat Management Guidelines for the Bald Eagle in the Southeast Region," Florida's bald eagle nesting population has grown to nearly 700 pairs (as of the 1992–93 nesting season); the brown pelican and Pine Barrens tree-frog have been delisted because of increasing populations and/or because our research efforts have provided new insight into those species' true status;

nearly 50 manatee sanctuaries have been established in which boat speeds are restricted during the winter congregation period; our research over the past two decades has resulted in more knowledge about endangered species biology, habitat needs, etc., than during all previous time cumulatively; considerable endangered species habitat has been secured through CARL, (Conservation and Recreation Lands), Save Our Coasts, Save Our Rivers, Save Our Everglades, and other land acquisition programs; and various information/education programs have resulted in a significant increase in public awareness and support for endangered species conservation. These few examples demonstrate what can be done with adequate resources and commitment, but in fact represent only the proverbial drop in the bucket in light of the total needs.

I hope this revised series reinvigorates our resolve and commitment to endangered and threatened species conservation and we will be able to cite a multitude of such examples by the time a third revision is necessary. These volumes provide an authoritative and comprehensive database from which to embark on such a course, and I congratulate and personally thank each researcher, writer, editor, and individual whose committed efforts have culminated in this exemplary work.

Allan L. Egbert, Executive Director
State of Florida Game and Fresh Water Fish Commission

Preface

"Thirty years ago Florida was one of the most extraordinary states in the Union, but being flat and quite park-like in character (a large part of the country consisted of open pinelands) it was an easy state for man to ruin, and he has ruined it with ruthless efficiency." This quote from Thomas Barbour's *That Vanishing Eden, A Naturalist's Florida*, written in 1944, is ever more appropriate today. He continues his lament—"A large part of Florida is now so devastated that many of her friends are disinclined to believe that she ever could have been the Paradise which I know once existed." Barbour was talking about the loss of natural habitat in Florida from 1915 to the early 1940s. Imagine what he would think today!

Within the FCREPA volumes, the emphasis is on specific plants and animals that the committee considers to be endangered, threatened to become endangered, or species of special concern (those species apparently in danger but about which we need more information). However, as one reads through the species accounts, there is a continuing theme of habitat loss or alteration by man. Since Barbour's days of study in Florida, the loss and degradation of natural habitats have accelerated beyond human comprehension. We are faced with the possible reality that the only thing which will cause a decline in the loss is that there will soon be no land left to develop.

We are also faced with the fact that we actually know very little about the fauna and flora of this state. When challenged to protect a species or develop regulations to prevent extinction, we are inevitably confronted with the fact that we know little about their life histories, let alone what is needed to preserve a population through biological time. We are also faced with the dilemma that there probably is not enough time or money to allow us to study these organisms, let alone experiment with management techniques. Our ecological knowledge of interspecific interactions and biological communities is even less. Yet we do know that once certain biological needs are not met, we lose another species and another community. The biological communities of this state are being compromised time and again by all levels of government, simply to serve the hunger for growth and development.

We are the first generation to realize that not only do we have local or regional environmental concerns but we now have to be aware of serious global degradations of our air and water. Global warming, acid rain, increased ultraviolet radiation, and degradation of our oceans are making us realize for the first time that our species may well be jeopardizing itself as well as the lowly gopher tortoise and tree snail. We are realizing that the world's biodiversity and the biological engine that drives many of the necessities of all life are being used up or changed by our overpopulated species. If we know so little about individual species and communities, how can we be prepared to understand the complexities of the biosphere, let alone the cause and effect of our actions.

Alarms have sounded in the minds of many people around the world, including Florida. The first step toward a solution to all of this is acknowledging that we are causing problems. Loss of uplands not only means loss of wildlife but also that we affect our water supplies, river systems, and ultimately the health of our coastal systems. Our state agencies are in the fledgling stages of creating regulations on development and the organized effort of protecting biological diversity and natural communities. Hopefully these agencies and the people of Florida will begin to recognize that we must increase our efforts to protect our environment and the creatures who inhabit it, not just to use for recreation but for the sake of preserving the machinery that makes our lives as living things possible.

It is these concerns that have been the driving force behind the volunteer-biologists who have unselfishly spent so many long hours putting together the information in these volumes. We hope that through the information provided here more biologists will turn their thoughts from the test tube to the laboratory in the field, funding agencies will realize the need for this basic knowledge, and government agencies will begin to think more on the biological community level and not the species or individual organism level. Most important, we hope that these volumes serve to educate the citizens of Florida so that we may all recognize the need to learn more and work together to make prudent decisions about our "Vanishing Eden."

Ray E. Ashton, Jr.
Series Editor

A Brief History of FCREPA

The Florida Committee on Rare and Endangered Plants and Animals, FCREPA, was founded in 1973. The original group of 100 scientists, conservationists, and concerned citizens was organized by James Layne, Peter Pritchard, and Roy McDiarmid. The chairs of the Special Committees on Terrestrial Invertebrates, Marine Invertebrates, Plants, Reptiles and Amphibians, Fish, Birds, Mammals, and Liaison made up the first Endangered Species Advisory Board to the Florida Game and Fresh Water Fish Commission. These special committees were made up of concerned biologists who were living and/or working in the state of Florida. The first FCREPA meeting was called for biologists to discuss and evaluate the status of Florida's wildlife and to determine which species should be considered for special classification and concern. From this conference, five volumes—The Rare and Endangered Biota of Florida series—were produced. These were edited by Peter Pritchard of the Florida Audubon Society and Don Wood of the Florida Game and Fresh Water Fish Commission. Section editors for the first series included Roy McDiarmid, reptiles and amphibians; Herb Kale, birds; James Layne, mammals; Carter Gilbert, fish; Howard Weems, terrestrial invertebrates; Joe Simon, marine invertebrates; and Dan Ward, plants. Before its completion, the invertebrate volumes were combined under the editorship of Richard Franz.

Following the production of the FCREPA volumes by the University Press of Florida in 1976, FCREPA continued to meet and support a special section of papers at the annual meeting of the Florida Academy of Sciences. The affiliation of FCREPA was organized under the guidance of Dan Ward, director of the herbarium at the University of Florida.

In the fall of 1986, it became obvious that the original publications were becoming dated and the demand for the publication was great (the volumes had been reprinted repeatedly). Then chair, Herbert Kale, vice president of the Florida Audubon Society, convened the second FCREPA conference at the youth camp in the Ocala National Forest. The committees on each group met and deliberated on the status of the species in their charge. It was decided at that meeting to rewrite the FCREPA series since considerable changes in our knowledge and in the state of the natural environment in Florida made much of the information produced more than 13 years before out of date. Editors for each of the volumes called together those knowledgeable individuals and potential contributors to the future volumes to discuss the status of the taxa covered in their volume. Their recommendations on the status (and the criteria used) of various species were discussed by everyone present at the 1986 meeting.

Under the direction of Jack Stout, University of Central Florida, and each of the section chairs and editors, the arduous task of preparing the new manuscripts was undertaken. Each section chair served as compiler and editor for each volume. Individual species accounts were prepared by biologists who were among the most qualified to write about the status of that species.

Ray Ashton, vertebrate zoologist, Water and Air Research, Inc. was appointed by the section chairs as managing editor of the series in 1988. Four years of preparation and coordination, fund raising, and gentle prodding of the volunteer editors and contributors have produced the second FCREPA series.

Without the thousands of volunteer hours given by many outstanding Florida biologists, and the support from the Florida Game and Fresh Water Fish Commission, Save the Manatee Club, and Florida Power and Light Company, this effort would not have been possible. Royalties from the sales of these volumes and donations to the FCREPA effort are used to keep all the volumes in print and to fund future work.

Ray E. Ashton, Jr.
Series Editor

Definitions of Status Categories

Categories used to designate the status of the invertebrates included in the Florida list of rare and endangered species are defined below.

Endangered.—Species in danger of extinction or extirpation if the deleterious factors affecting their populations continue to operate. These are forms whose numbers have already declined to such a critically low level or whose habitats have been so seriously reduced or degraded that without active assistance their survival in Florida is questionable.

Threatened.—Species that are likely to become endangered in the state within the foreseeable future if current trends continue. This category includes: (1) species in which most or all populations are decreasing because of overexploitation, habitat loss, or other factors; (2) species whose populations have already been heavily depleted by deleterious conditions and, while not actually endangered, are nevertheless in a critical state; and (3) species that may still be relatively abundant but are being subjected to serious adverse pressures throughout their range.

Rare.—Species that, although not presently endangered or threatened as defined above, are potentially at risk because they are found only within a restricted geographic area or habitat in the state or are sparsely distributed over a more extensive range.

Species of special concern.—Species that do not clearly fit into one of the preceding categories yet warrant special attention. Included in this category are: (1) species that, although they are perhaps presently relatively abundant and widespread in the state, are especially vulnerable to certain types of exploitation or environmental changes and have experienced long-term population declines; and (2) species whose status in Florida has a potential impact on endangered or threatened populations of the same or other species outside the state.

Status undetermined.—Species suspected of falling into one of the above categories for which available data are insufficient to provide an adequate basis for their assignment to a specific category.

Recently extirpated.—Species that have disappeared from Florida since 1600 but still exist elsewhere.

Recently extinct.—Species that have disappeared from the state since 1600 through extinction.

*Invertebrates of concern.*We include a list of invertebrates that contributors felt are in need of recognition but that are not of the same status as those in the full accounts. We presume that many of these species will appear in other categories in future editions of this book.

Major Habitats of Florida

Invertebrates occur in every available natural and culturally derived habitat in Florida, including several very specialized ones where vertebrates and green plants are rare or absent. The ubiquitous nature of invertebrates forced us to expand the number of habitat descriptions to include nearshore marine, coral reefs, caves, and animal hosts. The basic wetlands and terrestrial community descriptions follow those of Brad Hartman, presented in the most recent FCREPA mammal and amphibian-reptile volumes, edited by Stephen R. Humphrey and Paul Moler, respectively. The aquatic community descriptions were extensively modified from the FCREPA fish volume, edited by Carter R. Gilbert. Readers wishing more detailed descriptions of Florida's freshwater habitats should consult this reference.

Major Terrestrial and Wetland Habitats
1. Coastal strand
2. Dry prairies
3. Pine flatwoods
4. Sand pine scrub
5. Longleaf pine-xerophytic oak woodlands
   (Sand and Clay Hills)
6. Mixed hardwood-pine
7. Hardwood hammocks
8. Tropical hammocks
9. Freshwater marshes and wet prairies
10. Scrub cypress
11. Cypress swamps
12. Hardwood swamps

Coastal and Nearshore Habitats
13. Mangrove swamps
14. Coastal marshes
15. Coral reefs

Freshwater Habitats
16. Rivers
17. Creeks
18. Springs
19. Ditches, sloughs, and ponds
20. Lakes

Specialized Habitats
21. Caves and interstitial groundwater
22. Animal and plant hosts

Major Terrestrial and Wetland Habitats
1. Coastal Strand

The coastal strand includes beaches and the vegetation zones of beaches and adjacent dunes or rock. This vegetation type is most commonly associated with shorelines subjected to surf and high winds, but may sometimes be found bordering calmer bays and sounds.

The vegetation of the beaches and foredunes is characterized by pioneer plants able to establish themselves in the shifting sand. Typical species include railroad vines, beach cordgrass, and sea oats. Inland from the foredune, saw palmetto and dwarf scrubby oaks are found and, in southern Florida, sea grape and other tropical vegetation as well. The vegetation tends to change from grassy to woody from the foredune inland to the more protected back dunes, and the composition of the vegetation of these back dunes is often similar to that of sand pine scrub habitat found inland on old dunes.

Strand communities are adapted to the severe stresses of shifting sands, a highly saline environment, and high winds. In some instances, salt spray plays a role similar to fire in other ecosystems by retarding succession indefinitely at a grass or shrubby stage.

Historically, impacts to coastal strand plant communities (sometimes the total loss of the community) have resulted from beachfront residential development; invasion by exotic vegetation, primarily Australian pine; and accelerated erosion of beaches due to maintenance of inlets or nearby residential and tourist development.

2. Dry Prairies

Dry prairies are vast, treeless plains, often intermediate between wet grassy areas and forested uplands. Scattered bayheads, cypress ponds, or cabbage palm hammocks often occur in prairie areas. The largest areas of dry prairies occur north and west of Lake Okeechobee.

This community is dominated by many species of grasses such as wiregrass and broomsedge. Palmettos are the most common shrubby plant over large areas, with fetterbush, staggerbush, and dwarf blueberry common in places. A number of sedges and herbs are also found on the dry prairies.

Relatively little has been published on the ecology of dry prairies. They have often been compared to flatwoods minus the overstory trees, and the similar vegetative groundcover would seem to justify this idea.

Fire is important in determining the nature of the vegetation and its suitability for different species of wildlife. Winter burning associated with cattle operations may have shifted this community from grasses and forbs to saw palmetto. Absence of fire may result in shrubby communities, while frequent growing season fires yield a more herbaceous environment.

Large areas of native dry prairies have been converted to improved pasture, and this trend is continuing. Eucalyptus plantations have also been established on some former dry prairie sites, although this does not appear to be a continuing trend. Expansion of citrus production southward is probably responsible for most dry prairie losses at this time.

3. Pine Flatwoods

Pine flatwoods are characterized by one or more species of pine as the dominant tree species and occur on level areas. The soils of flatwoods are sandy with a moderate amount of organic matter in the top few centimeters and an acid, organic hardpan 0.3-1.0 m (1-3 ft) beneath the surface.

Three major types of flatwoods occur in Florida: **longleaf pine flatwoods** found on well-drained sites and characterized by longleaf pine as the dominant overstory tree; **slash pine flatwoods** with slash pine as the dominant overstory species and usually in areas of intermediate wetness; and **pond pine flatwoods** with the pond pine as the dominant tree species and typically occurring in poorly drained areas. South Florida slash pine tends to replace both slash pine and longleaf pine in central to southern peninsular Florida.

Southern slash pine forest is found on the sand flatlands and rocklands of extreme southern Florida, and is characterized by an overstory of the South Florida variety of the slash pine. This association often has tropical components in its understory.

Considerable overlap in understory plants exists among the three major types of flatwoods, with many species found in all three communities. Generally, however, gallberry and saw palmetto dominate the understory in slash pine flatwoods; wiregrasses, blueberries, and runner oaks are especially prevalent in longleaf pine flatwoods; and several of the bay trees are characteristic of pond pine areas. Flatwoods also often include intermingled cypress domes, bayheads, and small titi swamps.

Pine flatwoods are the most widespread of major plant communities, occurring throughout the relatively level Pleistocene marine terraces in both peninsular and panhandle Florida. Their suitability for growing pine trees has resulted in vast areas being incorporated into industrial forests. Changes in both fire and moisture regimes have resulted in changes in plant species composition and wildlife values. In south Florida, residential development is rapidly eliminating this plant community (and all other upland communities).

4. Sand Pine Scrub

Sand pine scrub is a plant community found almost exclusively in Florida on relict dunes or other marine features. Sand pine scrub communities occur along the coasts on old dunes, in the Ocala National Forest, and along the

Lake Wales Ridge extending through Polk and Highlands counties. The soil is composed of well-washed, sterile sands.

This community is typically two-layered, with sand pine occupying the top layer and various scrubby oaks and other shrub species making up a thick, often clumped, understory. Little herbaceous groundcover exists, and large areas of bare sand occur frequently. Groundcover plants, when present, frequently include gopher apple and Florida bluestem grass. Deermosses are often common. Typical understory plants include myrtle oak, inopina oak, sand live oak, Chapman's oak, rosemary, scrub holly, and silkbay.

Where sand pines are absent, this community is often referred to as evergreen oak scrub. **Scrubby flatwoods** is a scrub-like association often occurring on drier ridges in typical flatwoods or near coasts. The understory species of this vegetation type are similar to those of sand pine scrub, but the sand pine is replaced by slash pine or longleaf pine.

The sand pine scrub is essentially a fire-based community. Ground vegetation is extremely sparse and leaf fall is minimal, thus reducing the chance of frequent ground fires so important in the sandhill community. As the sand pines and scrub oaks mature, however, they retain most of their branches and build up large fuel supplies in the crowns. When a fire does occur, this fuel supply, in combination with the resinous needles and high stand density, ensures a hot, fast-burning fire. Such fires allow for regeneration of the sand pine community and associated oak scrub, which would otherwise pass into a xeric hardwood community.

Sand pine scrub and its ecologically important variations are seriously threatened. Residential development and especially citrus production have eliminated much of this plant community. In addition, isolation from fire has resulted in succession to xeric hardwood hammock with a relatively closed canopy, thereby reducing its value to most endemic plants and animals.

5. Longleaf Pine–Xerophytic Oak Woodlands (Sand and Clay Hills)

Sandhill communities (the **longleaf pine-turkey oak** association being one major subtype of this community) occur on well-drained, white to yellowish sands.

Longleaf pines form a scattered overstory in mature natural stands. In many areas, xeric oaks such as turkey oak, bluejack oak, southern red oak, and sand post oak, which were originally scattered or small understory trees, now form the overstory as the result of cutting of the pines and prevention of fire. In some areas of southern peninsular Florida, South Florida slash pine replaces longleaf pine in the overstory. Although tree species diversity in sandhills is low, there is a wide variety of herbaceous plants such as wiregrass, piney woods dropseed, golden aster, partridge pea, gopher apple, bracken fern, and paw paw, which provide fairly complete groundcover.

Sandhills were second in area only to flatwoods in Florida's predevelopment landscape, occurring widely throughout the panhandle and the northern half of the peninsula. Fire is a dominant factor in the ecology of this community. The interrelationships of the sandhill vegetation types, particularly the longleaf pine–wiregrass relationship, are dependent on frequent ground fires. The longleaf pine is sensitive to hardwood competition, and wiregrass plays a major role in preventing the germination of hardwood seeds while ensuring that there is sufficient fuel buildup on the floor of the community to carry a fire over large areas.

Very little longleaf pine sandhill remains. Commercial foresters have attempted to convert large areas to slash pine with poor success, but have had better success converting sandhills to a closed canopy monoculture of sand pine. In many cases the wiregrass groundcover has been destroyed, making restoration of this community type problematic. Large areas have been converted to improved pasture or citrus. The well-drained soils make attractive development sites, and the majority of sandhill community in peninsular Florida in private ownership has either been developed, is being developed, or is platted and subdivided for future development.

6. Mixed Hardwood-Pine

The mixed-hardwood-pine community of John H. Davis (General Map of the Natural Vegetation of Florida, 1967) is the southernmost extension of the piedmont southern mixed hardwoods, and occurs in the clay soils of the northern panhandle.

Younger growth may be primarily pine, with shortleaf and loblolly pine predominant. As succession proceeds, the various hardwoods become dominant and constitute the natural climax vegetation of much of the area, especially wetter, yet well-drained sites. The overstory is characterized by a high species diversity and includes American beech, southern magnolia, white oak, sweetgum, mockernut hickory, pignut hickory, basswood, yellow poplar, white ash, and spruce pine. The understory includes many young overstory species plus dogwood, red mulberry, hop hornbeam, blue beech, and sweetleaf.

Historically, fire played a role in the function of this community by limiting its expansion into higher, better-drained sites. Later, agriculture served a similar function and limited this community to slopes and creek bottoms. The best examples, with the most diversity of tree species, tend, therefore, to occur in creek bottoms or on moist but well-drained slopes.

Residential subdivisions and other aspects of urbanization and conversion to loblolly pine plantations and agriculture are resulting in continued losses of this plant community. Locally significant losses result from stream or river impoundments, clay mining, and highway construction.

7. Hardwood Hammocks

The hardwood hammock community constitutes the climax vegetation of many areas of northern and central Florida. Hardwoods occur on fairly rich, sandy soils and are best developed in areas where limestone or phosphate outcrops occur. Hardwood forests are similar to the mixed hardwood and pine of the panhandle, but generally lack the shortleaf pine, American beech, and other more northern species, have a lower overstory species diversity, and tend to have a higher proportion of evergreen species. Southern magnolia, sugarberry, live oak, laurel oak, American holly, blue beech, and hop hornbeam are characteristic species of this association. Variations in the species composition of hardwood hammocks are partially due to differences in soil moisture.

Major variations of this vegetative association include coastal hammocks, live oak-cabbage palm hammocks, and maritime hammocks. **Coastal hammocks** are relatively wet hardwood communities that occur in narrow bands along parts of the Gulf and Atlantic coasts and often extend to the edge of coastal marshes. **Live oak-cabbage palm hammocks** often border larger lakes and rivers and are scattered throughout the prairie region of central Florida. Either the oak or palm may almost completely dominate in any one area. **Maritime hammocks** occur behind sheltering beachfront dunes and are often dominated by live oak.

Notable examples of hardwood hammocks are in public ownership, but residential development is widespread in better-drained hammocks within the ever-increasing range of urban centers. Historically, large areas of coastal hardwood hammocks have been site-prepared and planted to pine for pulpwood production. The current rate of loss due to this land use has apparently declined. Hammocks continue to be lost to agricultural conversion, although the near-surface limestone of many hammocks sometimes makes them unattractive for agriculture.

8. Tropical Hammocks

Tropical hammocks are found on many of the tree islands in the Everglades and on many of the Florida Keys. Remnants of these habitats occur north to Palm Beach on the east coast and Sarasota on the west coast.

Tropical hammocks typically have very high plant diversity, containing over 35 species of trees and almost 65 species of shrubs and small trees. Typical tropical trees are the strangler fig, gumbo limbo, mastic, bustic, lancewood, the ironwoods, poisonwood, pigeon plum, and Jamaica dogwood. Vines, air plants, and ferns are often abundant. Tropical hammocks of the Florida Keys contain a number of plants that are extremely rare in the United States, including mahogany, lignum vitae, and thatch palms.

The tropical hardwood forest is the successional climax for much of the uplands of extreme south Florida. Because of susceptibility to frequent fires, this association is largely confined to islands or slightly wetter areas, but may invade drier areas if fire is removed for any length of time.

Tropical hammocks have been largely lost to residential development in most areas of southern Florida. Relatively large areas remain on north Key Largo, where intensive efforts to buy or regulate this community have occurred.

9. Freshwater Marshes and Wet Prairies

Freshwater marshes are herbaceous plant communities occurring on sites where the soil is usually saturated or covered with surface water for one or more months during the growing season.

Wet prairies are characterized by shallower water and more abundant grasses, and usually fewer of the tall emergents, such as bulrushes, than marshes. This category also includes the wet to dry marshes and prairies found on marl areas in south Florida.

Upwards of 15 separate types of marshes or wet prairies have been described in Florida. Major ones include sawgrass marshes; flag marshes dominated by pickerel weed, arrowhead, fire flags, and other nongrass herbs; cattail marshes; spike rush marshes; bulrush marshes; maidencane prairies; grass, rush, and sedge prairies; and switchgrass prairies dominated by taller grasses. Any single marsh may have different sections composed of these major types, and there is also almost complete intergradation among the types.

Fire and water fluctuations, the two major ecosystem managers of Florida, are important in the maintenance of marshes and wet prairies. Fire, especially when combined with seasonal flooding, serves to stress plants not adapted to these conditions and reduces competition from more upland species.

Historic major marsh systems include the Everglades, Upper St. Johns River, Kissimmee River floodplain, and Lake Apopka/Oklawaha marshes. Drainage for agriculture has been the dominant factor in marsh losses. Existing wetland regulatory programs and a relatively small amount of agriculturally suitable major marsh systems remaining in private ownership have reduced past rates of loss of these large systems. Major wetland acquisition and restoration projects are underway in the examples cited. Ephemeral, isolated, smaller marshes are more vulnerable to both agricultural and urban development and drainage or use as stormwater holding basins.

10. Scrub Cypress

Scrub cypress areas are found on frequently flooded rock and marl soils in south Florida. The largest areas occur in the Big Cypress region of eastern Collier County and northern Monroe County.

Scrub cypress forests are primarily marshes with scattered, dwarfed pond cypress. Much of the vegetation is similar to other relatively sterile marshes with scattered sawgrass, beakrushes, St. John's-wort and wax myrtle occurring commonly. Bromeliads, as well as orchids and other epiphytes, are often abundant on the cypress trees.

Most scrub cypress in the Big Cypress is in public ownership and does not appear threatened.

11. Cypress Swamps

Cypress swamps are usually located along river or lake margins or interspersed through other habitats such as flatwoods or dry prairies. In addition, they also occur as strands along shallow, usually linear drainage systems. These swamps have water at or above ground level for a considerable portion of the year.

Bald cypress is the dominant tree along lake and stream margins and may be the only tree that occurs in significant numbers in these locations. Other trees that are found within bald cypress swamps include water tupelo, ogeechee tupelo, and Carolina ash. Pond cypress occurs in cypress heads or domes that are typically found in flatwoods or dry prairies. Associated trees and shrubs include slash pine, blackgum, red maple, wax myrtle, sweetbay, and buttonbush. Other plants include various ferns, epiphytes, poison ivy, greenbrier, and lizard's tail, with arrowhead, pickerel weed, sawgrass, and other marsh plants often found in the open water within cypress domes or strands.

Cypress swamps occur in submerged or saturated soils. Fire is an additional factor in drier cypress heads or domes. These factors are important in reducing competition and preventing the community from advancing to one dominated by evergreen hardwood trees (the bayhead community). There has apparently been a shift from cypress to hardwood swamps in areas where heavy harvesting of cypress has occurred in the past and the surviving hardwoods subsequently prevented cypress regeneration.

Bald cypress swamps are reasonably well protected by wetland regulations and the high cost of converting them to other land uses. Pond cypress swamps, while extremely widespread, have less protection because of their smaller size and more isolated nature. Cypress heads and ponds are susceptible to draining associated with industrial pine management, dredging for open water sites in residential development, and increased flooding when used to store stormwater runoff.

12. Hardwood Swamps

Deciduous hardwood swamps are found bordering rivers and lake basins where the forest floor is saturated or submerged during part of the year. Other names for this community include floodplain forest, bottomland hardwoods, and river swamp.

The wettest portions of these forests usually overlap with bald cypress swamps and consist largely of water tupelo, Carolina ash, and ogeechee tupelo. In slightly higher areas this community is characterized by such hardwoods as pop ash, pumpkin ash, red maple, overcup oak, sweetgum, and water hickory. On terraces or other higher portions of the floodplain, the overstory includes a variety of more mesic species such as spruce pine, swamp chestnut oak, and diamond-leaf oak. Understory trees and shrubs include dahoon holly, buttonbush, blue beech, and hop hornbeam. Groundcover is sparse in most of these swamps.

Two distinctive additions to this major category are **bay swamps** (bayheads or baygalls) and **titi swamps.** The former are broadleaf evergreen swamps occurring in shallow drainage ways and depressions, particularly in pine flatwoods. Loblolly bay, red bay, and sweet bay are the major tree species. Water levels are relatively stable, and the soil is usually an acidic peat. Titi swamps are dominated by one or more of three titi species and occur on strands or depressions in flatwoods or along the borders of some alluvial swamps in north Florida.

The periodic flooding of the river swamps is a dominant factor in the functioning of the system, and different communities will become established if these fluctuations are eliminated. All species within this community must be able to withstand or avoid the periodic stresses imposed by high water.

Hardwood swamps share common threats with cypress swamps. The wetter and the more contiguous with open waters, the stronger the regulatory protection. Bay swamps are occasionally mined for peat or lost in phosphate-mining operations and receive comparatively less wetland regulation protection than other wetlands. The rate of loss is unknown.

Coastal and Nearshore Habitats

13. Mangrove Swamps

Mangroves occur along low wave-energy shorelines on both coasts south from Cedar Keys on the Gulf and St. Augustine on the Atlantic. Some of the best examples of mangrove forests are located in the Ten Thousand Islands area of southwest Florida.

Three species of mangroves dominate the composition of mangrove swamps. The red mangrove, with its stilt root system, is typically located on the outermost fringe with the most exposure to salt water. Further inland, but usually covered by water at high tides, are the black mangroves, with white mangroves yet farther inland. Buttonwood trees are often found above the reach of salt water. Other plants commonly found among the mangroves include saltwort, glasswort, and a variety of other salt marsh species.

The mangrove community contributes to the productivity of bordering estuaries. Leaf fall from the mangroves provides food or substrate for countless organisms, ranging from bacteria to large fish such as the striped mullet. Detritus-feeding organisms support much of the estuarine trophic structure in mangrove areas including such gamefish as snook, tarpon, and spotted sea trout.

Mangrove swamps are largely in public ownership and the remainder are reasonably well protected by wetland regulations, although losses due to marina and residential developments occur on a relatively small scale.

14. Coastal Marshes

Coastal marshes occur on low wave-energy shorelines north of the range of the mangroves, and are also interspersed with mangroves in many areas. Salt marshes may also extend into tidal rivers and occur as a narrow zone between the mangroves and freshwater marshes in the southern areas of the state.

Many areas within salt marshes are dominated by one plant such as salt-grass, smooth cordgrass, or blackrush. The species existing in any one area depends largely on the degree of inundation by tides.

Smooth cordgrass typically occupies the lower areas and often borders tidal creeks and pools. Blackrush occurs over vast areas, particularly along the Gulf coast, and is inundated less frequently, while the highest areas of the marsh are vegetated by saltgrass or such succulents as saltwort, glasswort, and sea ox-eye daisy.

The functioning of salt marshes centers primarily on tides and salinity. The harsh conditions associated with daily inundation, desiccation, and high salinities contribute to a low plant and animal species diversity. Those organisms that have adapted to this environment can be very productive, however. Tides also provide a close ecological relationship with adjacent estuaries.

Coastal marshes have been affected primarily by waterfront residential development. Current wetland regulatory programs appear to be successful in preventing major losses of this community for the time being, although scattered losses continue.

15. Coral Reefs

In Florida, reef corals occur primarily on an arc-shaped shallow water limestone shelf, approximately 240 km long and about 7 km wide in extreme south Florida. Known as the Florida Reef Tract, this shelf is bounded on the seaward side by the Straits of Florida and on the shore side by the Florida Keys and south Florida. The Florida Reef Tract consists of the Outer Reefs on the seaward edge, the Patch Reefs behind them, and the numerous channels that dissect the reef structure. The Outer Reefs with the greatest variety of coral species protect the Patch Reefs from wave action of the open ocean. Some corals also occur in deep reefs off Broward County.

Reef corals are sensitive to the encroachment of silt and sand, and sometimes die as a result of being smothered by excessive amounts of sediment. Because of this, coral growth is suppressed in some parts of the reef tract. Key Largo, which acts as a barrier to sediments from Florida Bay, protects the northeastern portions of the reef tract, making it the most favorable area for coral growth.

Freshwater Habitats

16. Rivers

Thirteen major rivers occur in Florida, five of which have drainage basins greater than 3000 sq. mi (Apalachicola, 17,600 sq. mi; Suwannee, 9,640 sq. mi; Choctawhatchee, 4,384 sq. mi; St. Johns, 3,066 sq. mi; and Escambia, 3,817 sq. mi) (Livingston 1991). The largest rivers in the Florida panhandle originate in Alabama and/or Georgia (Escambia, Choctawhatchee, and Apalachicola rivers). Other smaller rivers (Black, Yellow, Shoal, Chipola, and

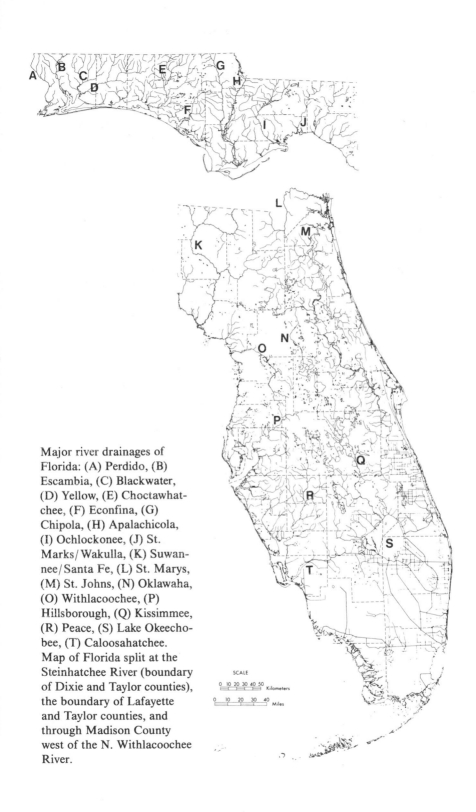

Major river drainages of Florida: (A) Perdido, (B) Escambia, (C) Blackwater, (D) Yellow, (E) Choctawhatchee, (F) Econfina, (G) Chipola, (H) Apalachicola, (I) Ochlockonee, (J) St. Marks/Wakulla, (K) Suwannee/Santa Fe, (L) St. Marys, (M) St. Johns, (N) Oklawaha, (O) Withlacoochee, (P) Hillsborough, (Q) Kissimmee, (R) Peace, (S) Lake Okeechobee, (T) Caloosahatchee. Map of Florida split at the Steinhatchee River (boundary of Dixie and Taylor counties), the boundary of Lafayette and Taylor counties, and through Madison County west of the N. Withlacoochee River.

Ochlockonee rivers) originate mostly in Florida with minor portions of their drainages in adjoining states. The Apalachicola River, the largest river system that enters Florida, has its origin in the mountainous areas of northern Georgia. The St. Johns River is the longest river that lies entirely within the state (318 mi). This river and the southern Withlacoochee River are among the few rivers of the world that flow north. The St. Marys and Suwannee rivers originate in the Okeefenokee Swamp on the Florida-Georgia state line but flow in opposite directions. The drainages in south Florida are dominated by the Kissimmee-Okeechobee-Everglades system (Livingston and Fernald 1991). Few natural streams exist in south Florida because natural drainages have been severely altered by canal construction and intensive water management since before the turn of the century. Many of these canals had opened directly into the sea in the past, allowing salt water to penetrate inland during the dry season. Now, many of these canals have salinity-control structures built near their mouths to prevent this intrusion. The main rivers along the southwest coast of Florida include the Caloosahatchee, Peace, Alafia, Manatee, Little Manatee, Myakka, and Hillsborough rivers. Most of these rivers are badly degraded from phosphate mining, agriculture, and urban runoff. Gilbert (1992) provides an excellent description of Florida rivers, notably (1) stagnant, (2) slow-flowing and deep, and (3) larger calcareous streams. The nature of these rivers is dependent on color, bottom type, amount of vegetation, and chemical composition. Aquatic invertebrates are extremely sensitive to these features, to the point that they can be extirpated by changes. Damming, siltation, and pollution seem to be the factors that have caused declines and the subsequent listing of these animals.

17. Creeks

Permanent creeks are similar to the larger rivers in general characteristics, except for size. Gilbert (1992) provides an excellent description of sand-bottomed creeks and silt-bottomed creeks. He considered the amount of vegetation important in his descriptions. Many aquatic invertebrates, as well as vertebrates, distinguish between creeks and the larger rivers.

18. Springs

Most large springs in Florida are artesian in nature. They generally flow from flooded cave systems in Eocene and Miocene limestones. As many as 27 springs are considered first-magnitude, with flow rates that average over 6 billion gallons per day. Spring water usually is high in calcium and magnesium, and maintains temperatures that reflect the average annual surface temperature of the region (69-72° F in north Florida). Upon emergence from the ground, the water is low in oxygen. This condition rapidly changes as the water passes through dense vegetation downstream from the spring. The water of Florida springs is crystal clear, cool, and definitely alkaline in nature. Because of large quantities of phosphates in the water, springs and spring runs are among the most productive aquatic habitats in the state.

19. Ditches, Sloughs, and Ponds

A large portion of Florida's surface freshwater collects in ditches, sloughs, and ponds. Many ditches and sloughs are clogged with vegetation that restricts water flow. Roadside ditches are a common sight throughout Florida, many created when road beds were constructed or for mosquito control.

Ponds in Florida are usually localized pools that seldom have surface outlets. Gilbert recognized sinkhole ponds, fluctuating ponds, temporary woodland ponds, sporadic ponds, and alligator ponds. Most of these water bodies tend to be small and shallow, although some sinkhole ponds can be exceptionally deep when there is a direct connection with sinks or solution pipes in their bottoms. Some ponds are wooded, or may have dense mats of floating vegetation or dense stands of emergent plants.

Many ditches, sloughs, and ponds are dependent on rainfall for their water supply. As a consequence, they are subject to marked fluctuations in water levels. Ditches and sloughs may flow during periods of high runoff toward more permanent water bodies and dry out completely during periods of drought. Many ponds also are subject to drying during drought periods. One of the major consequences of complete drying is that it tends to eliminate fishes that may have had an opportunity to invade particular water bodies during periods of high water. The presence or absence of predatory fishes influences the structure of the animal community of the site.

Like lakes, many of these water bodies have been invaded by exotic plants, such as alligator weed, water-hyacinth, hydrilla, wild taro, and others, which in many cases have changed not only the community's outward appearance but also its function.

20. Lakes

Nearly all of the lakes in Florida are the result of solutioning of underlying limestone; however, some such as Lake Okeechobee occupy basins that are natural depressions in the surface. Many solution-caused lakes are simple sinks that may be connected directly to underlying limestones and that never have had surface outlets. Others are part of connected wetlands and represent pooled areas in a larger wetland or riverine system.

Gilbert divided Florida lakes into sand-bottomed lakes, silt-bottomed lakes, and disappearing lakes. Most Florida lakes are fragile systems that can easily become degraded, particularly when they are exposed to urban and agricultural runoff. Few contain specialized invertebrate faunas, although lakes in the north central part of the state are inhabited by at least one mayfly that appears restricted to this habitat.

Florida lakes can be circum-neutral or acidic in nature, with clear or tea-colored water. Most lakes are shallow, usually less than 3 m (10 feet) deep, and may be ringed with cypress, black gum and/or woody shrubs, or may be surrounded by open meadows of herbaceous plants. Some lakes, such as Orange Lake, have much rooted vegetation and are exceptional in having numerous floating islands of vegetation, some supporting large trees, that change positions with wind conditions.

Specialized Habitats

21. Caves and Interstitial Groundwater

Groundwater habitats in Florida are inhabited by crustaceans, a gastropod, and a plethodontid salamander that show highly specialized morphological adaptations. Most of these blind, white animals are restricted to caves, but at least one appears to invade interstitial groundwater habitats. Most, if not all, of these troglobitic species are dependent on organic detritus that enters these specialized habitats from the surface. Some species require greater amounts and usually remain near the sources of this material, while others are free to inhabit most of the available flooded cave environment. Terrestrial cave-adapted invertebrates are rare in Florida caves, but this may be an artifact of limited collecting. Cave species are thought to be extremely sensitive to changes in both water quality and disruption in the flow of detritus into cave systems. Many species have extremely restricted ranges, and the closure of a single cave may cause the extinction of such a species.

22. Animal and Plant Hosts

Many invertebrates are associated with plants or with other animals, their dung, nests, or burrows. Frequently these associations are specific, and the parasite or commensal does not occur elsewhere. As a result, invertebrate symbionts will decline as the host becomes rare. Therefore, it seems reasonable to include these specialized animals in a volume on rare and endangered invertebrates. We have listed them at the same status classification as the host when appropriate. The inclusion of parasites and commensals on a Rare and Endangered list may be difficult for some of us to accept. These invertebrates, however, are part of Florida's natural biodiversity and play roles in the host's natural history. They also are important in their own right as products of the evolutionary process. We offer only a few examples in this volume, particularly those parasitic Mallophaga associated with threatened and endangered mammals and birds, arthropods restricted to burrows and nests of the gopher tortoise, certain pocket gophers, Audubon's caracara, and some insects tied to pitcher plants.

Introduction

Diversity of Florida's Rare and Endangered Invertebrates

Invertebrates are animals that lack backbones. There are more than 1 million described species, classified into at least 30 phyla, which makes them the most diverse group of organisms on earth. They live in every natural environment from the equator to the polar icecaps, from the deepest oceanic basins to the highest mountain tops. Their histories extend back to the very dawn of life on earth.

There are no estimates available for the actual number of invertebrates that live in terrestrial, freshwater, and nearshore marine environments of Florida, but they probably outnumber by a factor of 10 the 5,000 or so vertebrates and vascular plants reported from the state. Fifteen corals, 18 mollusks, 13 arachnids, 18 crustaceans, and 154 insects (total: 218) found in Florida were listed in the original FCREPA invertebrate volume published in 1982. This list contained 24 Endangered, 94 Threatened, 19 Rare, 34 Species of Special Concern, and 47 Status Undetermined taxa. Contributors to this original volume felt that their species lists were far from complete and that the information represented the first step in identifying rare and endangered invertebrates. They hoped by its publication the volume would serve to "stimulate public awareness of the need to conserve Florida's invertebrate fauna."

Since the appearance of the first volume, there has been a substantial surge of interest in declining invertebrates among biologists. As a result, the number of taxa in the new volume has swelled to include 20 corals, 29 bivalves, 14 snails, 26 crustaceans, 15 arachnids, 1 millipede, 19 mayflies, 33 dragonflies and damselflies, 13 orthopterans, 1 roach, 34 caddisflies, 34 mammal and bird lice, 94 beetles, 50 butterflies, 17 flies, and 11 ants, bees, and wasps. Of these taxa, two are thought to have been extirpated from the continental United States, and 149 are considered endangered or threatened. Of the remainder, 27 taxa and 2 faunas are placed in a special list, simply called "Invertebrates of Concern." Contributors that included species in this Concern list wanted them mentioned, but deemed it inappropriate at this time to give them the recognition that accompanies species with full accounts. We removed 17 taxa that were included in the original list, and the status categories for 52 taxa were changed because of new information.

Readers still need to regard the current list as only a beginning. Many large groups of invertebrates have not been championed by conservation-minded biologists and consequently are missing from this volume. Other spe-

1

cies will become threatened as environmental conditions continue to worsen in the state.

A casual review of the distributions and threats in the accompanying accounts of declining invertebrates shows some predictable patterns. The non-insect invertebrates include 105 taxa, with 60% and 18% found in freshwater and terrestrial habitats, respectively. Fifty-four taxa of non-insect invertebrates are considered either endangered or threatened.

Except for the Atlantic geoduck, all of the marine species are restricted to coral reef or mangrove habitats in extreme south Florida. As a group, inshore marine invertebrates have pelagic larvae that can easily reestablish in suitable habitats after localized populations have been depleted by overharvest or some catastrophic event. This makes them less vulnerable to extinction than many other species, although this perception may change as more species are studied. Commercially exploited species, such as queen conch, spiny lobster, blue crabs, stone crabs, etc., are already controlled by state regulations, although their placement on proposed protected lists might stimulate more concern over their conservation status. Vulnerable freshwater species, notably bivalves, snails, and crustaceans, are concentrated in large streams and rivers in the Florida panhandle and in springs and caves in north and central Florida. The patterns for terrestrial species are not as clear-cut, but obviously south Florida habitats and scrub areas in central Florida figure prominently.

Tallies for insects show a complex pattern that is dependent on whether the taxa are aquatic or strictly terrestrial. Listed aquatic species (all are freshwater inhabitants) have life cycles that include both aquatic and terrestrial/arboreal stages. The eggs and immature stages (larvae or nymphs) of mayflies, dragonflies and damselflies, caddisflies, and certain dipterous flies live in water. They emerge from the water as winged adults. Animals that need two very different habitats, such as many aquatic insect groups, may be placed in double jeopardy, as each habitat and its specialized features must be available.

Over 90 taxa of aquatic insects are listed in this volume. One is in the Endangered category; 34 are listed as Threatened. Forty species are found in the Florida panhandle and 51 are associated with clean streams and rivers. Other important habitats include ponds and lakes, bogs, springs, and cypress swamps. Six species are so poorly known that their immature stages are unknown and their larval habitat uncertain. Certain flies are restricted to the fluid inside the leaves of insectivorous pitcher plants. There are no strictly marine species of insects listed, although certain mosquitos may be associated with brackish water in the transition zones between hammocks and black mangrove areas in south Florida. The remainder of the invertebrate fauna consists of 207 terrestrial species of grasshoppers, cockroaches, lice, beetles, butterflies, flies, ants, wasps, and bees. Thirty-four species are parasitic lice that occur on endangered or threatened vertebrates. The status of lice mirrors the status of their hosts. Only 60 terrestrial insects fall within the Endangered or Threatened categories. Over 28% of the terrestrial insects are listed either as Status Undetermined or as Invertebrates of Concern. The listed terrestrial insect fauna is distributed primarily in central Florida, where

they ar ost often associated with scrub and sandhill habitats, or in south
Florid tropical hammocks. Many of the insects found in north Florida
and i anhandle also occur in upland habitats. Like the parasitic Mallo-
pha st eight beetles and several flies appear to be obligate associates
of rtebrates, notably fox squirrels, pocket gophers, caracara, and
go ses. Many listed lepidopterans have close associations with par-
ti . Loss of those plants would cause the extinction of these in-
s nately, many of the beetles and other insects are poorly known,
e habitat or host has been assigned to them.

f hundreds of invertebrates is linked to the kind of sensible
Florida needs for many reasons. The state is experiencing
h in its human population and a concomitant demand on its
resources. To maintain the state's biodiversity, we will need
tments to plan areas of human population growth, leave as
ea intact as possible, manage lands that require it, and im-
e strict environmental regulations. There also is a need for
tion concerning the nature and vulnerability of Florida's nat-
)nly through education will people recognize the value of
and champion their protection. Our challenge is best em-
following statement by Aldo Leopold in *A Sand County*
40 years ago: "We abuse land because we regard it as a com-
ng to us. When we see land as a community to which we be-
begin to use it with love and respect."

FCREPA and Invertebrate Conservation

la Committee on Rare and Endangered Plants and Animals is not
as an advocacy organization. It is not a government organization;
bers are volunteers who donate their work. FCREPA pronounce-
n rare and endangered invertebrates have no legal standing. Members
committee may share a general feeling that Floridians should be con-
about threats to their natural heritage, but it is not the role of FCREPA
)ose which species should receive official protection, or to decide what
that protection should take. Even the sections on "recommendations"
ch appear in most species accounts are intended as recommendations if a
rson or agency decides that the species should be protected. These recom-
nendations are not demands by FCREPA; they are suggestions for people,
especially land managers and community groups, who are already concerned
about rare and endangered invertebrates. Some species accounts have subjective phrases, such as, "This beautiful insect . . . ," or, "this species is particularly interesting because. . . ." The editors did not suppress such phrases
because these expressions of enthusiasm are legitimate and timely reminders
of an important truth: the study of invertebrates reveals a world of such extraordinary complexity, with such an adaptive dovetailing of myriad relationships that it is impossible to regard it closely without experiencing an
aesthetic and intellectual jolt.

Much of the value of FCREPA resides in its objectivity, an
ity is indicated by the fact that every species receives the most
erage available, given current knowledge. To many people t
volume itself would seem a symbol of scientific objectivity,
worry about the survival of various species of spiders, for ex
dung beetles, or mosquitos. This invertebrate volume, howeve
enormous effort and was expensive to publish, and would sc
while just as a symbol of the scientific evenhandedness of F
must be a serious purpose behind this work, and that pu
other FCREPA volumes, is to announce that Florida is in d
large number of its native life forms.

There are reasons why the loss of invertebrates should be
to people without any special concern for arthropods.

1. Even rare species may have ecological importance.
example, might be the pollinator of a rare plant. More com
brate is listed as rare or endangered because it inhabits a r
ened habitat, where it is an abundant and important speci
of cave crayfish may be the dominant animal within its re
localized corals may be important in the reef communit
caddisflies may be important in the food chain of cert
Florida scrub communities the most abundant spiders, be
and ants are all restricted to scrub; these rare species, ma
in this volume, have major roles as herbivores, predators,

2. Unlikely though it may seem, some invertebrates
cally valuable traits. We are on the threshold of the ne
prospecting, and it is clear that invertebrates will be a p
compounds. Many species have original and comple
others have the ability to detoxify the strongest pois
spider, which appears in this volume, shares with oth
ability to produce several different venoms. One of the
poison, which could be the basis of a whole new class
a rare poisonous spider which may have something of v

3. Invertebrates are also particularly useful indi
small size and remarkable diversity can provide high
on which habitats or microhabitats are in peril. The
mosquito that lives in a particular type of shallow
might not in itself inspire any heroic conservation eff
may share its larval habitat with a great variety of
cline has gone completely unobserved because they
that are of medical importance and are not the obje
efforts.

4. Invertebrates may also be biogeographical ind
less grasshoppers that are restricted to very small ar
there may be something special about those sites,
may be habitat islands with a long history of isola
lution of endemic species. Perhaps we should look
especially plants, with restricted habitat requirem

they are most often associated with scrub and sandhill habitats, or in south Florida in tropical hammocks. Many of the insects found in north Florida and in the panhandle also occur in upland habitats. Like the parasitic Mallophaga, at least eight beetles and several flies appear to be obligate associates of certain vertebrates, notably fox squirrels, pocket gophers, caracara, and gopher tortoises. Many listed lepidopterans have close associations with particular plants. Loss of those plants would cause the extinction of these insects. Unfortunately, many of the beetles and other insects are poorly known, and no definite habitat or host has been assigned to them.

The fate of hundreds of invertebrates is linked to the kind of sensible planning that Florida needs for many reasons. The state is experiencing dramatic growth in its human population and a concomitant demand on its existing natural resources. To maintain the state's biodiversity, we will need to make commitments to plan areas of human population growth, leave as much natural area intact as possible, manage lands that require it, and impose and enforce strict environmental regulations. There also is a need for accurate information concerning the nature and vulnerability of Florida's natural resources. Only through education will people recognize the value of these resources and champion their protection. Our challenge is best embodied in the following statement by Aldo Leopold in *A Sand County Almanac* over 40 years ago: "We abuse land because we regard it as a commodity belonging to us. When we see land as a community to which we belong, we may begin to use it with love and respect."

FCREPA and Invertebrate Conservation

The Florida Committee on Rare and Endangered Plants and Animals is not designed as an advocacy organization. It is not a government organization; its members are volunteers who donate their work. FCREPA pronouncements on rare and endangered invertebrates have no legal standing. Members of the committee may share a general feeling that Floridians should be concerned about threats to their natural heritage, but it is not the role of FCREPA to choose which species should receive official protection, or to decide what form that protection should take. Even the sections on "recommendations" which appear in most species accounts are intended as recommendations if a person or agency decides that the species should be protected. These recommendations are not demands by FCREPA; they are suggestions for people, especially land managers and community groups, who are already concerned about rare and endangered invertebrates. Some species accounts have subjective phrases, such as, "This beautiful insect . . . ," or, "this species is particularly interesting because. . . ." The editors did not suppress such phrases because these expressions of enthusiasm are legitimate and timely reminders of an important truth: the study of invertebrates reveals a world of such extraordinary complexity, with such an adaptive dovetailing of myriad relationships that it is impossible to regard it closely without experiencing an aesthetic and intellectual jolt.

Much of the value of FCREPA resides in its objectivity, and this objectivity is indicated by the fact that every species receives the most complete coverage available, given current knowledge. To many people the invertebrate volume itself would seem a symbol of scientific objectivity, as few people worry about the survival of various species of spiders, for example, or ants, dung beetles, or mosquitos. This invertebrate volume, however, demanded an enormous effort and was expensive to publish, and would scarcely be worthwhile just as a symbol of the scientific evenhandedness of FCREPA. There must be a serious purpose behind this work, and that purpose, as in the other FCREPA volumes, is to announce that Florida is in danger of losing a large number of its native life forms.

There are reasons why the loss of invertebrates should be disturbing, even to people without any special concern for arthropods.

1. Even rare species may have ecological importance. A rare insect, for example, might be the pollinator of a rare plant. More commonly, an invertebrate is listed as rare or endangered because it inhabits a restricted or threatened habitat, where it is an abundant and important species. A local species of cave crayfish may be the dominant animal within its restricted ecosystem; localized corals may be important in the reef community; rare mayflies or caddisflies may be important in the food chain of certain rivers. In some Florida scrub communities the most abundant spiders, beetles, grasshoppers, and ants are all restricted to scrub; these rare species, many of which appear in this volume, have major roles as herbivores, predators, and decomposers.

2. Unlikely though it may seem, some invertebrates may have economically valuable traits. We are on the threshold of the new world of chemical prospecting, and it is clear that invertebrates will be a prime source of useful compounds. Many species have original and complex chemical defenses, others have the ability to detoxify the strongest poisons. The red widow spider, which appears in this volume, shares with other widow spiders the ability to produce several different venoms. One of these is an unusual insect poison, which could be the basis of a whole new class of insecticides. Here is a rare poisonous spider which may have something of value to mankind.

3. Invertebrates are also particularly useful indicator species, as their small size and remarkable diversity can provide high resolution information on which habitats or microhabitats are in peril. The decline of a species of mosquito that lives in a particular type of shallow limestone depression might not in itself inspire any heroic conservation efforts, but that mosquito may share its larval habitat with a great variety of other species whose decline has gone completely unobserved because they do not belong to groups that are of medical importance and are not the objects of intensive sampling efforts.

4. Invertebrates may also be biogeographical indicators. Spiders or wingless grasshoppers that are restricted to very small areas of Florida tell us that there may be something special about those sites, which may be refuges or may be habitat islands with a long history of isolation that fostered the evolution of endemic species. Perhaps we should look carefully at other species, especially plants, with restricted habitat requirements, limited mobility, and

occurring on sites with these isolated species of invertebrates. Recently discovered (undescribed) species of upland grasshoppers on the southern Brooksville Ridge, the Trail Ridge, and the Big Scrub of Marion County indicate areas that should be explored for more endemic species.

In addition to the indirect significance of invertebrates, one might argue that they are significant in themselves. Reducing the fantastic diversity of native invertebrates may be unfair to future human generations, which may have a more refined appreciation of invertebrates than is presently prevalent. A great number of animal species whose extinction or near-extinction is widely lamented were considered vermin by our ancestors. Many people believe that other species do not need to offer humans any benefits, direct or indirect, aesthetic or intellectual, in order to have the right to share the planet. Extinction of small species is just as irrevocable as extinction of large species. A species of spider or beetle may represent as many hundred millennia of evolution as a species of bird or mammal. It may be more comfortable to remain ignorant of the great numbers of obscure species that we threaten by our activities, but it is not at all comfortable to know that our generation could go down as a purblind bull rampaging through Florida's collection of fragile treasures.

Many of the arguments used to support conservation of such organisms as wood storks or pygmy fringe trees could, with equal logic, be applied to tree snails or sand roaches. This may be an unwelcome view to politically-minded conservationists, who can easily envisage an opponent who says, "You claim the roseate spoonbill is a rare bird, and should be protected; I have a book right here that says the desert snapping ant is rare. Do you propose that we set aside large areas to protect the breeding grounds of the desert snapping ant?" To the beleaguered conservationist it is not solace to know that FCREPA is above such arguments, since FCREPA is not an advocacy organization. A reasonable response might be to offer thanks for the suggestion, with a promise to forward it to the proper authorities. In reality, governmental agencies usually choose their battles rather carefully. Official protection, in the form of actual desert snapping ant legislation, is unlikely. As in a large percentage of cases, a specific protection strategy is unwarranted, since big populations occur on sites that are likely to receive protection to preserve scrub jays and other conspicuous species that require much more extensive areas to maintain a breeding population.

This brings up one of the most important features of modern biological conservation, the realization that rare and endangered species, both large and small, tend to aggregate on certain sites. When a particular site is considered for preservation, the biotic significance of the site can often be supported by a whole list of rare and endangered species. As these lists of organisms lengthen, it is clear that entire habitats are in need of protection. It is evident that we cannot preserve Florida's biodiversity by gathering a few species and relocating them out of the path of habitat destruction, assuming an appropriate haven exists in the state. The idea that obliterated habitats can be recreated became an obvious delusion once we realized that most natural habitats include hundreds, if not thousands of species, whose culture and husbandry is a mystery, whose very identity is often unknown. FCREPA, with its original documentation of threats to a great number of formerly obscure species, contributed to the growth of the modern realization that Florida must be saved, not species by species, but ecosystem by ecosystem.

While some environmentalists might feel that publishing a volume on rare and endangered invertebrates is politically unwise, some scientists object to the volume for a different reason. They are concerned that focusing attention on these invertebrates could lead to restrictions on the study of these organisms at exactly the time when studies of distribution and biology are most crucial. Almost all studies of invertebrates involve collecting and killing some specimens. Many rare and endangered invertebrates can be positively identified only by microscopic examination. The rosemary wolf spider, the desert snapping ant, the microcaddisflies, and a number of scarab beetles are examples of this. Even for field studies of large distinctive species it is recommended practice to deposit voucher specimens in a collection, in case there is any doubt of the identity of the species.

Surveys for rare invertebrates, especially arthropods, often require the use of traps that kill and preserve the specimens. Indeed, a number of species in this volume have never even been seen alive and are known only from trapped specimens. Several beetles, for example, have only been found in flight intercept traps or light traps.

Invertebrate zoologists are not particularly fearful of universally applied state or federal regulations on the study of a species, as such regulations have been established for only a tiny number of invertebrates. They are, rather, concerned that there will be more restrictions placed on invertebrate study in state, federal, or private preserves. Specialized experts find it particularly irritating to think that they might be forbidden to work with a population of a species which only a few people in the world (not necessarily including preserve personnel) can even recognize, especially when such studies might provide information needed for the management of the population. Invertebrate zoologists point out that, as a rule, invertebrates are threatened by habitat destruction, almost never by overly avid collecting.

On the other hand, managers of preserves see that, as Florida becomes increasingly developed, they are becoming the sole custodians of unique natural ecosystems, with concomitant pressure to maintain the total diversity of these ecosystems. Managers now realize that this biodiversity includes an enormous list of invertebrates, most of which are difficult to recognize. Preserve personnel may feel, with some justification, that unregulated collecting or manipulation of any species that is "rare or endangered" is a poor policy. The less they know about the species involved, the more cautious they may become. It is not easy to manage ecosystems in the face of widespread threats such as pollution, disrupted drainage systems, great escalations in public use, the concerns of residential communities crowding around the preserve boundaries, the constant threat of becoming the path of least resistance for transportation or power corridors, and the general inadequacy of manpower and funding. Custodians of preserves tend to feel that since they are maintaining, against considerable odds, unique assemblages of organisms, these organisms should be treated with some respect, and not be needlessly killed or disturbed. If these organisms are to be studied, it should be with discretion and with a clear purpose and useful results.

Invertebrate zoologists are probably correct in expecting that extra attention will focus on some invertebrates owing to their coverage in this volume. On the whole, this should improve recognition of the work of these invertebrate zoologists, and it may even lead to study grants. More important, the extra attention may increase the chances of survival of a number of species that are particularly interesting to zoologists. In return, it does not seem too much to ask that a zoologist be able to justify his or her research in an ecological preserve, and to provide a report on the completed research. A worker who has no hypotheses and who does not expect to produce a report is not engaged in research and might not be invited to engage in destructive sampling in an ecological preserve. The managers of ecological areas are, in our experience, eager to add to the invertebrate data base of the area, and not only tolerate research, but even assist in some cases.

Selection and Documentation
of Rare and Endangered Invertebrates

A recurring theme throughout this volume is that when dealing with invertebrates the concepts of rare and endangered take on new and frustrating dimensions. With plants and vertebrates there is often room for argument about the sizes and stability of populations, but these differences in opinion are relatively subtle. Few people would claim that the gray squirrel is rare and endangered, few would contend that lignum-vitae is an abundant and ubiquitous plant. Among invertebrates, a small species that is as common as the gray squirrel may be extremely rare in collections; an invertebrate as rare as lignum-vitae is likely to have completely escaped the attention of zoologists. On the other hand, an invertebrate may be known from only a few specimens taken from a single site, but such evidence by itself reveals nothing about the rarity or vulnerability of the species. Many invertebrate species can be recognized by only a few experts, and it may be that nobody else bothers to collect specimens. Even an invertebrate that is conspicuous, distinctive, and known from only a few sites may be neither rare nor endangered. The reason is that many relatively abundant species show themselves under very specific conditions, perhaps only at night in a particular habitat at a certain time of year. These animals are unlikely to be found without a specialized search. The tremendous number of invertebrates (we estimate there are at least 50,000 species in Florida) guarantees that there will never be enough specialists to conduct appropriate searches for all the apparently rare and endangered species. In fact, among invertebrate zoologists, especially entomologists, one occasionally hears statements to the effect that "rare" invertebrates are just common invertebrates with unknown home addresses.

Even if there were no data to the contrary, the notion that there are no

rare or endangered invertebrates would be absurd. We know that invertebrates are often incredibly specialized for life in a particular habitat or microhabitat. Whenever a habitat dwindles or disappears, so goes a batch of
associated invertebrates. We know that many invertebrates have poor dispersal ability and are unable to cross barriers of only a few kilometers separating suitable habitats. Species with poor dispersal may be restricted to a
fraction of their potential geographic range. We also know that isolated populations of invertebrates, like those of vertebrates and plants, may change
through natural selection and genetic drift. This must result in many isolated, vulnerable populations that have diverged into local varieties or species. In short, the historical and environmental factors which have caused
plants or vertebrates to become rare, endangered, or extinct operate on invertebrates with comparable facility. The FCREPA volume on plants (Ward
1979) lists almost 5% of the total flora of the state; extrapolating from this,
the real number of rare and endangered invertebrates could be in the thousands. This presents the appalling vision of a potential FCREPA volume the
thickness of a couple of Miami telephone directories. Bearing in mind the
problems of documenting these numerous species, we need to consider the
kinds of evidence actually used in the present work. This does not imply that
the editors sent contributors a set of rigid rules for determining whether a
species should be included in this volume. The contributors were aware of
the problem of documentation and used their best judgment, which the editors do not question. The following paragraphs describe the various lines of
evidence that were used.

Some invertebrates are conspicuous animals that have been intensively
studied, or eagerly collected, for many years. Numerous butterflies, a smaller
number of moths, a few dragonflies, beetles, and mollusks have been studied
by so many people that their distribution and abundance are almost as well-
known as those of most Florida birds. The status of rare or endangered species in these groups may be judged from direct evidence. A subset of this type
of species is those that are of medical importance and that have been the
subjects of regular surveys; almost all of these are mosquitos.

Some invertebrates that are small, obscure species are known to be rare or
endangered because they have an obligatory association with hosts that are
themselves rare or endangered. Many of the known examples of these are associated with vertebrates, such as the various arthropods that live with gopher
tortoises, or species of lice restricted to rare and endangered birds and
mammals. There are many phytophagous species, especially Lepidoptera,
that have specific relationships with rare and endangered plants. Even arthropods and mollusks often have host-specific parasites. It might be questioned whether it is necessary to list parasites and commensals of rare and
endangered plants and animals since the hosts are already covered in other
FCREPA volumes. The editors have not made any extraordinary effort to
obtain accounts of nematodes or mites of plants, or quill mites of birds, or
the various mites associated with snakes, to say nothing of flukes, trema-
todes, tapeworms, and other internal parasites. These omissions should be
viewed as deficiencies in this volume rather than the result of premeditated

policy. It is important to realize that even individual species may support miniature ecosystems that have achieved specialization and balance over thousands or millions of years of evolution. We refrain from diatribes on the conservation of parasitic species or a discussion of the possible importance of the weird and wonderful physiological relationships between hosts and parasites. It should be enough to say that we are unlikely to understand the growth, or behavior, or morphology, or management of any species without reference to its most intimate relationships with other species.

Turning to a much larger scale, there are many invertebrates that are rare and endangered because they occur only in types of habitats that are scarce or threatened. The list of such habitats is depressingly long, ranging from caves and springs to coastal dunes, unpolluted streams, remnant uplands, and the entire coral reef system. One characteristic of the invertebrates occurring in these habitats is that they are often common within the restricted confines of the habitat. In a counter-intuitive way, this abundance may be an important indicator of rarity, as it allows the narrow geographic distribution to be mapped with some confidence. Most invertebrates do not have their habitat preferences clearly enough reflected in their morphology so that we can just look at them and conclude that a particular ant must be restricted to Florida scrub on the Lake Wales Ridge, or a particular microcaddisfly could only survive in one stream system. If a species is known from only a few specimens from a special habitat, it could possibly be a widespread species that is difficult to find, but if it is common in that habitat, the association is much clearer. The number of individuals of such a species may be in the hundreds of thousands, or even millions, but the species may be in jeopardy because one episode of stream pollution or a few extensive land-clearing projects could eradicate it.

This brings up the question of endemic versus non-endemic Florida species. There is a general feeling that rare and endangered species occurring only in Florida and nowhere else in the world should receive more attention than species that are rare and endangered only in Florida. Similarly, a species with a broad northern range and a small contiguous expansion into northern Florida seems less noteworthy than a northern species with a highly disjunct Florida population. These differing types of geographic ranges may be important for conservation strategy, but they should not affect FCREPA, whose mission is to document threats to the biodiversity of Florida. If this volume covers Florida endemics more completely than species with outlier populations in Florida, that is because the endemic species have generated more interest.

Idiosyncrasies of the Invertebrate Volume

The numbers and diversity of invertebrates have led to some unusual features in this volume. The group is so enormous that even the best educated naturalist does not aspire to know all the orders and families, to say nothing of the genera and species. For this reason we supply brief introductions to most of the orders and families. This also results in the species accounts being organized by family. Compared with other volumes, the selection of species for the invertebrate volume may seem almost random, at best incomplete. Most families of invertebrates that include rare species are not covered at all here, because nobody has the necessary information, or because the editors did not know of an appropriate expert. In a few cases we have provided lists of species that should be included, even though there is nobody available to write discussions of these species.

In contrast to other FCREPA volumes, this volume includes many minimalist species accounts because the biology of many species is unknown. Even the section on diagnosis may be curtailed; many invertebrates are almost impossible to identify without a taxonomic key, preferably bolstered by a good collection of similar species for comparison. In such cases it can be almost misleading to provide a supposedly diagnostic description, and it is more reasonable to direct the reader to an appropriate publication. All these deficiencies may seem annoying, but they should be viewed as the result of the glorious diversity of invertebrates, and our ignorance should be considered proof that the invertebrates will provide exciting new discoveries for centuries to come.

Designations of Status

Status of Florida invertebrates. * indicates species not previously listed in the 1982 FCREPA volume. FC followed by E, T, R, SSC, or Und indicates the taxon was listed by FCREPA and its former listed status. US = federal list followed by status category. Page number on which account can be found follows name.

Recently Extirpated

Corals
* Black Coral, *Antipathes pennacea*
* Black Coral, *Antipathes dichotoma*

Endangered

Corals
Elkhorn Coral, *Acropora palmata* FC-E
Staghorn Coral, *Acropora cervicornis* FC-E
Staghorn Coral, *Acropora prolifera* FC-E
Pillar Coral, *Dendrogyra cylindrus* FC-E
Flower Coral, *Mussa angulosa* FC-E
Flower Coral, *Eusmilia fastigiata* FC-E

Bivalves
* Triangle Floater, *Alasmidonta undulata*
* Apalachicola Floater, *Anodonta sp.*
* Round Ebonyshell, *Fusconaia rotulata*
* Ochlockonee Moccasinshell, *Medionidus simpsonianus*

Endangered (continued)

Snails
Stock Island Tree Snail, *Orthalicus reses reses* FC-E, US-T
Freemouth Hydrobe, *Aphaostracon chalarogyrus* FC-E
Enterprise Siltsnail, *Cincinnatia monroensis* FC-E

Crustaceans
Squirrel Chimney Cave Shrimp, *Palaemonetes cummingi* FC-T, US-T

Arachnids
Lake Placid Funnel Wolf Spider, *Sosippus placidus* FC-E
Dusky-Handed Tailless Whip Scorpion, *Paraphrynus raptator* FC-E

Lice
Florida Panther Louse, *Felicola sp.* FC-E
Wood Stork Louse, *Ardeicola loculator* FC-E
Wood Stork Louse, *Ciconiphilus quadripustulatus* FC-E
Wood Stork Louse, *Colpocephalum mycteriae* FC-E

11

Endangered *(continued)*

Lice (continued)

Wood Stork Louse,
Colpocephalum scalariforme
FC-E

Wood Stork Louse,
Neophilopterus heteropygus FC-E

Everglades Kite Louse,
Craspedorrhynchus obscurus
FC-E

Everglades Kite Louse,
Falcolipeurus quadriguttatus
FC-E

Beetles

* Florida Forestiera,
Nesostizocera floridana
* Round-Necked Romulus,
Romulus globosus

Butterflies and Moths

* Bahama Swallowtail,
Papilio andraemon bonhotei

Schaus Swallowtail,
Papilio aristodemus ponceanus
FC-E, US-E

Flies

* Central American Malaria
Mosquito, *Anopheles albimanus*

Threatened

Corals and Sea Fans

Lettuce Coral, *Agaricia agaricites*
FC-T

Starlet Coral,
Siderastrea siderea FC-T

Brain Coral, *Diploria clivosa* FC-T

Brain Coral,
Diploria labyrinthiformis FC-T

Brain Coral, *Diploria strigosa* FC-T

Giant Brain Coral,
Colpophyllia natans FC-T

* Rose Coral, *Manicina areolata*

Threatened *(continued)*

Corals and Sea Fans (continued)

Little Star Coral,
Montastrea annularis FC-T

Large Star Coral,
Montastrea cavernosa FC-T

Brain Coral, *Meandrina meandrites*
FC-T

* Sea Fan, *Gorgonia ventalina*
* Sea Fan, *Gorgonia flabellum*

Bivalves

* Fat Threeridge, *Amblema neislerii*
* Flat Floater,
Anodonta suborbiculata
* Chipola Slabshell,
Elliptio chipolaensis
* Purple Bankclimber,
Elliptoideus sloatianus
* Narrow Pigtoe,
Fusconaia escambia
* Southern Pocketbook,
Lampsilis ornata
* Gulf Moccasinshell,
Medionidus penicillatus
* Suwannee Moccasinshell,
Medionidus walkeri
* Oval Pigtoe, *Pleurobema pyriforme*
* Fuzzy Pigtoe,
Pleurobema strodeanum
* Tapered Pigtoe,
Quincuncina burkei
* Southern Creekmussel,
Strophitus subvexus
* Southern Sandshell,
Villosa australis

Choctaw Bean, *Villosa choctawensis*
FC-T

Snails

* Ridge Scrubsnail,
Praticolella bakeri

Florida Keys Tree Snail,
Orthalicus reses nesodryas FC-T

Threatened *(continued)*

Snails (continued)
Blue Spring Hydrobe,
Aphaostracon asthenes FC-T
Wekiwa Hydrobe,
Aphaostracon monas FC-T
Clifton Springs Hydrobe,
Aphaostracon theiocrenetus FC-T

Crustaceans
Orlando Cave Crayfish,
Procambarus acherontis FC-T
* Panama City Crayfish,
Procambarus econfinae
* Putnam County Cave Crayfish,
Procambarus morrisi
Mangrove Crab,
Aratus pisonii FC-T
Mangrove Crab,
Goniopsis cruentata FC-T

Spiders
Keys Cesonia Spider, *Cesonia irvingi*
FC-E
Eleuthra Orb Weaver,
Eustala eleuthra FC-T

Mayflies
Dolania Mayfly, *Dolania americana*
FC-T
Blue Sand-River Mayfly,
Homoeoneuria dolani FC-T
White Sand-River Mayfly,
Pseudiron centralis
(=*P. meridionalis*) FC-T

Dragonflies and Damselflies
Eastern Ringtail,
Erpetogomphus designatus FC-T
Cocoa Clubtail,
Gomphus hybridus FC-T
Gulf Coast Clubtail,
Gomphus modestus FC-T
Cobra Clubtail, *Gomphus vastus*
FC-T

Threatened *(continued)*

Dragonflies and Damselflies (continued)
* Diminutive Clubtail,
Gomphus westfalli
Laura's Clubtail, *Stylurus laurae*
FC-T
Yellow-Sided Clubtail,
Stylurus potulentus FC-T
Townes' Clubtail, *Stylurus townesi*
FC-T
Say's Spiketail, *Cordulegaster sayi*
FC-T
Allegheny River Cruiser,
Macromia alleghaniensis FC-T
* Robust Baskettail, *Epitheca spinosa*
Smokey Shadowtly,
Neurocordulia molesta FC-T
Treetop Emerald,
Somatochlora provocans FC-T
* Purple Skimmer, *Libellula jesseana*

Orthopterans
Big Pine Key Conehead,
Belocephalus micanopy FC-T
Keys Short-Winged Conehead,
Belocephalus sleighti FC-T
Keys Scaly Cricket,
Cycloptilum irregularis FC-T

Lice
Florida Black Bear Louse,
Trichodectes pinguis euarctidos
FC-T
Eastern Brown Pelican Louse,
Colpocephalum occidentalis FC-T
Eastern Brown Pelican Louse,
Pectinopygus occidentalis FC-T
Eastern Brown Pelican Louse,
Piagetiella bursaepelecani FC-T
Rothschild's Magnificent Frigatebird
Louse, *Colpocephalum spineum*
FC-T
Rothschild's Magnificent Frigatebird
Louse, *Fregatiella aurifasciata*
FC-T

Threatened *(continued)*

Lice (continued)

Rothschild's Magnificent Frigatebird
  Louse, *Pectinopygus fregatiphagus*
  FC-T
Southern Bald Eagle Louse,
  Colpocephalum flavescens FC-T
Southern Bald Eagle Louse,
  Craspedorrhynchus halieti FC-T
Southern Bald Eagle Louse,
  Degeeriella discocephalus FC-T
Osprey Louse,
  Kurodaia haliaeeti FC-T
Southeastern American Kestrel
  Louse, *Degeeriella rufa carruthi*
  FC-T
Audubon's Caracara Louse,
  Acutifrons mexicanus FC-T
Audubon's Caracara Louse,
  Colpocephalum polybori FC-T
Audubon's Caracara Louse,
  Falcolipeurus josephi FC-T
Florida Sandhill Crane Louse,
  Esthiopterum brevicephalum
  FC-T
Florida Sandhill Crane Louse,
  Gruimenopon canadense FC-T
Florida Sandhill Crane Louse,
  Heleonomus assimilis FC-T
American Oystercatcher Louse,
  Actornithophilus grandiceps FC-T
American Oystercatcher Louse,
  Austromenopon haematopi FC-T
American Oystercatcher Louse,
  Quadraceps auratus FC-T
American Oystercatcher Louse,
  Saemundssonia haematopi FC-T
Roseate Tern Louse,
  Quadraceps giebeli FC-T
Least Tern Louse,
  Quadraceps nychthemerus FC-T
Least Tern Louse,
  Saemundssonia melanocephalus
  FC-T
Florida Scrub Jay Louse,
  Brueelia deficiens FC-T

Threatened *(continued)*

Beetles

* Highlands Tiger Beetle,
  Cicindela highlandensis
* Gopher Tortoise Hister Beetle,
  Chelyoxenus xerobatis
Fox Squirrel Scarab,
  Ataenius sciurus FC-E
Southwest Florida Mycotrupes,
  Mycotrupes pedester FC-T
Gopher Tortoise Copris,
  Copris gopheri FC-T
Gopher Tortoise Onthophagus,
  Onthophagus polyphemi FC-T
Gopher Tortoise Aphodius,
  Aphodius troglodytes FC-T
Caracara Trox, *Trox howelli* FC-T
* Chevrolat's Stenodontes,
  Stenodontes chevrolati
* Strohecker's Eburia,
  Eburia stroheckeri
* DeLong's Aneflomorpha,
  Aneflomorpha delongi
* White-Spotted Longhorn,
  Linsleyonides albomaculatus
* Cape Sable Longhorn,
  Heterachthes sablensis

Caddisflies

Zigzag Blackwater River Caddisfly,
  Agarodes ziczac FC-T
* Gordon's Little Sister Sedge,
  Cheumatopsyche gordonae
* Wakulla Springs Vari-Colored
  Microcaddisfly,
  Hydroptila wakulla
* Okaloosa Somber Microcaddisfly,
  Ochrotrichia okaloosa
Provost's Somber Microcaddisfly,
  Ochrotrichia provosti FC-T
Dentate Orthotrichian
  Microcaddisfly,
  Orthotrichia dentata FC-T
* Changeable Orthotrichian
  Microcaddisfly,
  Orthotrichia instabilis

Threatened *(continued)*

Caddisflies (continued)
Florida Cream and Brown Mottled
  Microcaddisfly,
  Oxyethira florida FC-T
* Kelley's Cream and Brown Mottled
  Microcaddisfly, *Oxyethira kelleyi*
* King's Cream and Brown Mottled
  Microcaddisfly, *Oxyethira kingi*
* Morse's Little Plain Brown Sedge,
  Lepidostoma morsei
* Porter's Long-Horn Sedge,
  Oecetis porteri
Little Meadow Long-Horn Sedge,
  Oecetis pratelia FC-T
Little-Fork Triaenode Caddisfly,
  Triaenodes furcella FC-T
* Florida Brown Checkered Summer
  Sedge, *Polycentropus floridensis*

Butterflies
* Klots' Skipper,
  Euphyes pilatka klotsi
* Rockland Grass Skipper,
  Hesperia meskei
Maesites Hairstreak,
  Chlorostrymon maesites FC-T
Bartram's Hairstreak,
  Strymon acis bartrami FC-SSC
Florida Leafwing,
  Anaea troglodyta floridalis
  FC-SSC

Flies
* Bahamian Culex,
  Culex bahamensis
* Mulrennan's Culex,
  Culex mulrennani
* Gopher Tortoise Robber Fly,
  Machimus polyphemi

Rare

Bivalves
Atlantic Geoduck,
  Panopea bitruncata FC-R

Rare *(continued)*

Crustaceans
* Swimming Little Florida Cave
  Isopod, *Remasellus parvus*
Miami Cave Crayfish,
  Procambarus milleri FC-SSC
* Silver Glen Springs Cave Crayfish,
  Procambarus attiguus
* Big-cheeked Cave Crayfish,
  Procambarus delicatus
Santa Fe Cave Crayfish,
  Procambarus erythrops FC-SSC
Orange Lake Cave Crayfish,
  Procambarus franzi FC-SSC
Big Blue Spring Cave Crayfish,
  Procambarus horsti FC-SSC
* Coastal Lowland Cave Crayfish,
  Procambarus leitheuseri
Withlacoochee Light-fleeing Cave
  Crayfish,
  Procambarus lucifugus lucifugus
  FC-SSC
Alachua Light-Fleeing Cave
  Crayfish,
  Procambarus lucifugus alachua
  (and intergrades in Gilchrist, Levy,
  and Marion counties) FC-SSC
Woodville Cave Crayfish,
  Procambarus orcinus FC-SSC
Pallid Cave Crayfish,
  Procambarus pallidus FC-SSC
Black Creek Crayfish,
  Procambarus pictus FC-SSC
North Florida Spider Cave Crayfish,
  Troglocambarus maclanei
  FC-SSC
Apalachicola Cave Crayfish,
  Cambarus cryptodytes FC-SSC
* Red-Back Crayfish,
  Cambarus pyronotus

Spiders
McCrones Burrowing Wolf Spider,
  Geolycosa xera FC-T
* Escambia Burrowing Wolf Spider,
  Geolycosa escambiensis

Rare (continued)

Spiders (continued)
Rosemary Wolf Spider,
   Lycosa ericeticola FC-T
Little Mountain Jumping Spider,
   Habrocestum parvulum FC-R
* Workman's Jumping Spider,
   Phidippus workmani
Torreya Trap-Door Spider,
   Cyclocosmia torreya FC-SSC
Blue Purseweb Spider,
   Sphodros abboti FC-SSC
Red-Legged Purseweb Spider,
   Sphodros rufipes FC-SSC

Millipedes
* Florida Scrub Millipede,
   Floridobolus penneri

Dragonflies and Damselflies
Southeastern Spinyleg,
   Dromogomphus armatus FC-R
Hodges' Clubtail, *Gomphus hodgesi*
   FC-R
Twin-Striped Clubtail,
   Gomphus geminatus FC-R
Belle's Sanddragon,
   Progomphus bellei FC-R
Arrowhead Spiketail,
   Cordulegaster obliqua fasciata
   FC-R
Sely's Sunfly, *Helocordulia selysii*
   FC-R
Coppery Emerald,
   Somatochlora georgiana FC-RSU
Elfin Skimmer, *Nannothemis bella*
   FC-R
Gray Petaltail, *Tachopteryx thoreyi*
   FC-R
Taper-Tailed Darner,
   Gomphaeschna antilope FC-R
Elegant Spreadwing,
   Lestes inaequalis FC-R

Orthopterans
* East Coast Scrub Grasshopper,
   Melanoplus indicifer

Rare (continued)

Orthopterans (continued)
* Ocala Claw-Cercus Grasshopper,
   Melanoplus sp. 1
* Trail Ridge Scrub Grasshopper,
   Melanoplus sp. 2

Roaches
* Florida Sand Cockroach,
   Arenivaga floridensis

Beetles
* Florida Scrub Tiger Beetle,
   Cicindela scabrosa
* Simple Cebrionid,
   Selonodon simplex
* Archbold Cebrionid, *Selonodon*
   sp. 1
* Santa Rosa Cebrionid, *Selonodon*
   sp. 2
* Similar Cebrionid, *Selonodon* sp. 3
* Rusty Cebrionid, *Selonodon* sp. 4
* Scrub Ischyrus,
   Ischyrus dunedinensis
* Alachua Triplax, *Triplax alachuae*
Havana Ataenius,
   Ataenius havanensis FC-T
Panhandle Beach Scarab,
   Polylamina pubescens FC-T
Keys Green June Beetle, *Cotinus* sp.
   FC-T
Ocala Deep-digger Scarab,
   Peltotrupes youngi FC-SU
Cartwright's Mycotrupes,
   Mycotrupes cartwrighti FC-SU
North Peninsular Mycotrupes,
   Mycotrupes gaigei FC-SU
* Uneasy June Beetle,
   Phyllophaga anxia
Elizoria June Beetle,
   Phyllophaga elizoria FC-SU
Elongate June Beetle,
   Phyllophaga elongata FC-SU
* Forbe's June Beetle,
   Phyllophaga forbesi
* Horn's June Beetle,
   Phyllophaga hornii

Rare *(continued)*

Beetles (continued)

Diurnal Scrub June Beetle,
  Phyllophaga okeechobea FC-SU
Oval June Beetle, *Phyllophaga ovalis*
  FC-SU
Southern Lake Wales Ridge June
  Beetle, *Phyllophaga panorpa*
  FC-SU
* Long June Beetle,
  Phyllophaga perlonga
* Skelley's June Beetle,
  Phyllophaga skelleyi
Spiny Burrowing June Beetle,
  Gronocarus multispinosus FC-SU
Panhandle Beach Anomala,
  Anomala flavipennis okaloosensis
  FC-SU
Scrub Anomala, *Anomala eximia*
  FC-SU
Pygmy Anomala, *Anomala exigua*
  FC-SU
Scrub Palmetto Scarab,
  Trigonopeltastes floridana FC-SU
Frost's Silky June Beetle,
  Serica frosti FC-SU
Howden's Copris, *Copris howdeni*
  FC-T

Caddisflies

Peters' Little Sister Sedge,
  Cheumatopsyche petersi FC-T
* Broad Varicolored Microcaddisfly,
  Hydroptila latosa
* Llogan's Varicolored
  Microcaddisfly,
  Hydroptila lloganae
Molson's Varicolored Microcaddisfly,
  Hydroptila molsonae FC-T
Short Orthotrichian Microcaddisfly,
  Orthotrichia curta FC-R
Elerob's Cream and Brown Mottled
  Microcaddisfly,
  Oxyethira elerobi FC-T
* Setose Cream and Brown Mottled
  Microcaddisfly, *Oxyethira setosa*

Rare *(continued)*

Caddisflies (continued)

* Tavares White Miller,
  Nectopsyche tavara
Floridian Triaenode Caddisfly,
  Triaenodes florida FC-T
* Marsh Triaenode Caddisfly,
  Triaenodes helo
Daytona Long-Horn Sedge,
  Oecetis daytona FC-T
* Morse's Long-Horn Sedge,
  Oecetis morsei
* Florida Cernotinan Caddisfly,
  Cernotina truncona
* Morse's Dinky Light Summer
  Sedge, *Nyctiophylax morsei*

Butterflies

* Hoary Edge, *Achalarus lyciades*
* Textor Skipper,
  Amblyscirtes aesculapius
* Least Florida Skipper,
  Amblyscirtes alternata
* Bell's Roadside Skipper,
  Amblyscirtes belli
* Pepper and Salt Skipper,
  Amblyscirtes hegon
* Roadside Skipper,
  Amblyscirtes vialis
* Arogos Skipper,
  Atrytone arogos arogos
* Southern Dusted Skipper,
  Atrytonopsis hianna loammi
* Golden-banded Skipper,
  Autochton cellus
* Caribbean Duskywing,
  Erynnis zarucco
* Berry's Skipper, *Euphyes berryi*
* Dion Skipper, *Euphyes dion*
* Duke's Skipper, *Euphyes dukesi*
* Common Sooty Wing,
  Pholisora catullus
* Wild Rice Skipper,
  Poanes viator zizaniae
* Southern Swamp Skipper,
  Poanes yehl
* Zabulon Skipper, *Poanes zabulon*

Rare (continued)

Butterflies (continued)
* Little Glassy Wing,
  Pompeius verna
* Eastern Tailed Blue,
  Everes comyntas comyntas
* Coral Hairstreak,
  Harkenclenus titus mopsus
* Frosted Elfin, *Incisalia irus*
* Eastern Pine Elfin,
  Incisalia niphon niphon
* Hessel's Hairstreak,
  Mitoura hesseli
* King's Hairstreak, *Satyrium kingi*
* Striped Hairstreak,
  Satyrium liparops
* Martial Hairstreak,
  Strymon martialis
* Silvery Checkerspot,
  Chlosyne nycteis nycteis
* Mourning Cloak,
  Nymphalis antiopa antiopa
* Comma Anglewing,
  Polygonia comma
* Appalachian Eyed Brown,
  Satyrodes appalachia

Flies
* Keys Ochlerotatus, *Aedes thelcter*
* Antillean Psorophora,
  Psorophora johnstonii
* North American Pitcher
  Plant Mosquito,
  Wyeomyia smithii
* North American Pitcher Plant
  Midge, *Metriocnemus knabi*
* Florida Asaphomyian Tabanid Fly,
  Asaphomyia floridensis
* Little Panhandle Deerfly,
  Chrysops tidwelli

Ants and Bees
* Elegant Cone-Ant,
  Dorymrymex elegans
* Silvery Wood Ant,
  Formica subsericea

Rare (continued)

Ants and Bees (continued)
* Desert Snapping Ant,
  Odontomachus clarus
* Jamaican Fungus Ant,
  Trachymyrmex jamaicensis
* Lake Wales Ridge Velvet Ant,
  Dasymutilla archboldi
* Eastern Caupolicana Bee,
  Caupolicana electa

Species of Special Concern

Bivalves
* Purple Pigtoe, *Fusconaia succissa*
* Round Pearlshell,
  Glebula rotundata
* Round Washboard,
  Megalonaias boykiniana
* Florida Pigtoe,
  Pleurobema reclusum
* Shiny-Rayed Pocketbook,
  Villosa subangulata

Snails
Florida Tree Snail, *Liguus fasciatus*
  FC-SSC
Banded Tree Snail,
  Orthalicus floridensis FC-SSC
Dense Hydrobe,
  Aphaostracon pycnus FC-SSC
Fenney Springs Hydrobe,
  Aphaostracon xynoelictus
  FC-SSC
Ichetucknee Siltsnail,
  Cincinnatia mica FC-SSC
Clench's Goniobasis, *Elimia clenchi*
  FC-SSC

Crustaceans
Florida Cave Amphipod,
  Crangonyx grandimanus FC-SSC
Hobbs Cave Amphipod,
  Crangonyx hobbsi FC-SSC

Species of Special Concern (continued)

Crustaceans (continued)
Florida Cave Isopod,
 Caecidotea hobbsi FC-SSC

Spiders
Red Widow Spider,
 Latrodectus bishopi FC-SSC

Dragonflies and Damselflies
Tawny Sanddragon,
 Progomphus alachuensis FC-SSC
Sandhill Clubtail,
 Gomphus cavillaris FC-SSC
Maidencane Cruiser,
 Didymops floridensis FC-SSC
American Rubyspot,
 Hetaerina americana FC-SSC
* Everglades Sprite,
 Nehalennia pallidula

Orthopterans
* Rosemary Grasshopper,
 Schistocerca ceratiola

Beetles
* Small Pocket Gopher Scarab,
 Aphodius aegrotus
* Large Pocket Gopher Scarab,
 Aphodius laevigatus
Florida Deepdigger Scarab,
 Peltotrupes profundus FC-SU
* Broadspurred Pocket Gopher
 Scarab, *Aphodius hubbelli*
* Florida Hypotrichia,
 Hypotrichia spissipes

Butterflies
* Zestos Skipper,
 Epargyreus zestos zestos
* Florida Duskywing,
 Ephyriades brunneus floridensis
* Mangrove Skipper,
 Phocides pigmalion okeechobee

Species of Special Concern (continued)

Butterflies (continued)
Atala, *Eumaeus atala florida* FC-T
* Miami Blue,
 Hemiargus thomasi bethunebakeri
* Dingy Purplewing, *Eunica monima*
Florida Purplewing,
 Eunica tatila tatilista FC-SSC
* Mangrove Buckeye,
 Junonia evarete
* Florida Statira Sulphur,
 Aphrissa statira floridensis
* Florida White,
 Appias drusilla neumoegenii
* Bush Sulphur, *Eurema dina helios*
* Jamaican Sulphur,
 Eurema nise nise
* Guayacan Sulphur,
 Kricogonia lyside

Flies
* Tortoise Burrow Dance Fly,
 Drapetis sp.
* Tortoise Burrow Anthomyiid,
 Eutrichota gopheri

Status Undetermined

Bivalves
* Ochlockonee Arc-Mussel,
 Alasmidonta wrightiana
* Roundlake, *Amblema perplicata*
* Rayed Creekshell,
 Anodontoides radiatus
* Bankclimber,
 Plectomerus dombeyanus
Southern Kidneyshell,
 Ptychobranchus jonesi FC-SSC

Crustaceans
Benedict's Wharf Crab,
 Sesarma benedicti FC-SSC

Status Undetermined
(continued)

Spiders
Florida Trap-Door Spider,
Ummidia spp. FC-SSC
* Florida Trap-Door Spider,
Myrmekiaphila spp.

Dragonflies and Damselflies
Umber Shadowfly,
Neurocordulia obsoleta FC-SC
Calvert's Emerald,
Somatochlora calverti FC-SU
Slender Blue, *Enallagma traviatum*
FC-SU

Orthopterans
* Tequesta Grasshopper,
Melanoplus tequestae
Larger Sandhill Grasshopper,
Melanoplus querneus
* Pygmy Sandhill Grasshopper,
Melanoplus pygmaeus
* Broad Cercus Scrub Grasshopper,
Melanoplus forcipatus
* Volusia Grasshopper,
Melanoplus adelogyrus
* Apalachicola Grasshopper,
Melanoplus apalachicolae

Beetles
* Large-Jawed Cebrionid,
Selonodon mandibularis
* Florida Cebrionid, *Selonodon* sp. 5
* Handsome Tritoma,
Tritoma pulchra
* Red-Winged Tritoma,
Tritoma sanguinipennis
* Darkling Tritoma,
Tritoma tenebrosa
* Black-Headed Triplax,
Triplax frontalis
* Florida Pseudischyrus,
Pseudischyrus nigrans

Status Undetermined
(continued)

Beetles (continued)
* Shining Ball Scarab,
Ceratocanthus aeneus
Robinson's Anomala,
Anomala robinsoni FC-SU
Big Pine Key Ataenius,
Ataenius superficialis FC-T
Sandyland Onthophagus,
Onthophagus aciculatulus
Woodruff's Ataenius,
Ataenius woodruffi FC-T
Strohecker's Ataenius,
Ataenius stroheckeri FC-SU
Sand Pine Scrub Ataenius,
Ataenius saramari FC-SU
Florida Coast Scarab,
Ataenius rudellus FC-SU
Carolina Forest Scarab,
Aphotaenius carolinus FC-SU
Bicolored Burrowing Scarab,
Bolbocerosoma hamatum FC-SU
Red Diplotaxis,
Diplotaxis rufa FC-SU
Mat Burrowing Scarab,
Eucanthus alutaceus FC-SU
* Clemens June Beetle,
Phyllophaga clemens
* Profound June Beetle,
Phyllophaga profunda
* Yemassee June Beetle,
Phyllophaga yemasseei
Handsome Flower Scarab,
Rutela formosa FC-SU
Delicate Silky June Beetle,
Serica delicatula FC-SU
Pygmy Silky June Beetle,
Serica pusilla FC-SU
Crooked Silky June Beetle,
Serica rhypha FC-SU
Little Silky June Beetle,
Serica tantula FC-SU
Miami Chafer,
Cyclocephala miamiensis FC-SU

Status Undetermined
(continued)

Beetles (continued)

Scaly Anteater Scarab,
  Cremastocheilus squamulosus
  FC-SU
* Horn's Aethecerinus,
  Aethecerinus hornii
* Cabbage Palm Longhorn,
  Osmopleura chamaeropis
* Yellow-Banded Typocerus,
  Typocerus flavocinctus

Caddisflies

Florida Scaly Wing Sedge,
  Ceraclea floridana FC-SU
* Marsh-dwelling White Miller,
  Nectopsyche paludicola
* Florida Long-Horn Sedge,
  Oecetis floridana
* Little Long-Horn Sedge,
  Oecetis parva
* Silvery Little Black Sedge,
  Chimarra argentella

Flies

Sugarfoot Fly,
  Nemopalpus nearcticus FC-SU
* Cold-Hardy Orthopodomyia,
  Orthopodomyia alba
* North American Canopy Treehole
  Aedes, *Aedes hendersoni*
* Black-Bearded Nemomydas,
  Nemomydas melanopogon
* Panhandle Nemomydas,
  Nemomydas jonesi

Ants and Bees

* Striate Aphaenogaster Ant,
  Aphaenogaster mariae
* Yellow-Chested Cone-Ant,
  Dorymyrmex flavopectus
* Pitted Myrmica Ant, *Myrmica
  punctiventris*

Status Undetermined
(continued)

Ants and Bees (continued)

* Slave-Making Ant, *Polyergus* sp.
* Nocturnal Scrub Velvet Ant,
  Photomorphus archboldi

Additional Invertebrates of Concern

Snails
* North Florida fauna
* South Florida fauna

Mayflies
* *Cleon sp.*
* *Siphloplecton brunneum*
* *Siphloplecton fuscum*
* *Siphloplecton simile*
* *Isonychia berneri*
* *Isonychia sicca*
* *Macdunnoa brunnea*
* *Stenacron floridense*
* *Stenonema modestum*
* *Leptophlebia collina*
* *Hexagenia bilineata*
* *Attenella attenuata*
* *Dannella simplex*
* *Leptohyphes dolani*
* *Brachycercus nasutus*
* *Baetisca laurentina*

Beetles
* *Cicindela olivacea*
* *Cicindela hirticollis*
* *Cicindela dorsalis media*
* *Cicindela nigrior*
* *Cicindela striga*
* *Curtomerus fasciatus*
* *Elaphidion clavis*
* *Elaphidion tectum*
* *Heterops dimidiata*
* *Neoclytus longipes*
* *Parmenonta thomasi*

Status Changes and Removals

The following list shows the changes in status classification of Florida invertebrates between the 1982 edition of FCREPA and the current volume. These changes are based on our current understanding of the conservation status of these species. A second list shows 17 taxa that have been removed from the 1982 list because either the species is more common than previously known, or there has been a name change and the 1982 name is no longer valid.

Changes in Status Classification

Ataenius sciurus (Endangered to Threatened)

Ataenius havanensis (Threatened to Rare)

Ataenius superficialis (Threatened to Status Undetermined)

Ataenius woodruffi (Threatened to Status Undetermined)

Anomala flavipennis okaloosensis (Status Undetermined to Rare)

Anomala eximia (Status Undetermined to Rare)

Anomala exigua (Status Undetermined to Rare)

Anaea troglodyta floridalis (Species of Special Concern to Threatened)

Cyclocosmia torreya (Species of Special Concern to Rare)

Cesonia irvingi (Endangered to Threatened)

Ceraclea floridana (Status Undetermined to Species of Special Concern)

Cheumatopsyche petersi (Threatened to Rare)

Cambarus cryptodytes (Species of Special Concern to Rare)

Copris howdeni (Threatened to Rare)

Eumaeus atala floria (Threatened to Species of Special Concern)

Gronocarus multispinosus (Status Undetermined to Rare)

Changes in Status Classification (continued)

Hydroptila molsonae (Threatened to Rare)

Lycosa ericeticola (Threatened to Rare)

Mycotrupes cartwrighti (Status Undetermined to Rare)

Mycotrupes gaigae (Status Undetermined to Rare)

Neotrichia elerobi (Threatened to Rare)

Neurocordulia obsoleta (Species of Special Concern to Status Undetermined)

Oecetis parva (Status Undetermined to Species of Special Concern)

Oecetis daytona (Threatened to Rare)

Palaemonetes cummingi (Threatened to Endangered)

Peltotrupes profundus (Status Undetermined to Species of Special Concern)

Peltotrupes youngi (Status Undetermined to Rare)

Phyllophaga elizoria (Status Undetermined to Rare)

Phyllophaga elongata (Status Undetermined to Rare)

Phyllophaga okeechobea (Status Undetermined to Rare)

Phyllophaga ovalis (Status Undetermined to Rare)

Phyllophaga panorpa (Status Undetermined to Rare)

Changes in Status Classification *(continued)*

Procambarus erythrops (Species of Special Concern to Rare)
Procambarus franzi (Species of Special Concern to Rare)
Procambarus horsti (Species of Special Concern to Rare)
Procambarus lucifugus alachua and intergrade populations (Species of Special Concern to Rare)
Procambarus lucifugus lucifugus (Species of Special Concern to Rare)
Procambarus milleri (Species of Special Concern to Rare)
Procambarus orcinus (Species of Special Concern to Rare)
Procambarus pallidus (Species of Special Concern to Rare)
Procambarus pictus (Species of Special Concern to Rare)
Proserpinus gaurae (Rare to Threatened)
Polylamina pubescens (Threatened to Rare)
Ptychobranchus jonesi (Species of Special Concern to Status Undetermined)
Strymon acis bartrami (Species of Special Concern to Threatened)
Serica frosti (Status Undetermined to Rare)
Sphodros abbotti (Species of Special Concern to Rare)

Changes in Status Classification *(continued)*

Sphodros rufipes (Species of Special Concern to Rare)
Triaenodes florida (Threatened to Rare)
Troglocambarus maclanei (Species of Special Concern to Rare)
Trigonopeltastes floridana (Species of Special Concern to Rare)
Ummidia sp. (Species of Special Concern to Status Undetermined)

Removals

Ataenius brevicollis
Agarodes libalis
Aphodius haldemani
Aphodius laevigatus
Chimarra florida
Drymaeus multilineatus multilineatus
Epitheca spinosa
Hydroptila berneri
Lampsilis haddletoni
Osyethira janella
Osyethira novasota
Pseudiron meridionalis
Pseudataenius waltherhorni
Phyllophaga youngi
Phidippus xeros
Proserpinus gaurae
Tetragoneuria spinosa

Corals and Sea Fans

INTRODUCTION: Corals are a diverse group of strictly marine, attached (sessile), bottom-dwelling (benthic) organisms. Like all other members of their phylum, they possess radial symmetry, a simple sac-like cavity for digestion (gastrovascular cavity) with a single opening (mouth) encircled by tentacles, stinging cells (cnidoblasts) used for prey capture and defense, and a body wall consisting of three tissue types (epidermis and gastrodermis with a cellular or acellular mesoglea sandwiched in between). No specific structures for respiration, circulation, or excretion are present, and all have a cylindrical body form called a polyp. They may be either solitary or colonial. They protect their soft parts by secreting an internal or external skeleton of either calcium carbonate, chitin, or horny material. It is this skeleton that most of us associate with the term coral.

Reproduction in corals takes place either asexually or sexually. Asexual reproduction (budding), typical among colonial corals, involves the formation of new polyps from existing ones. As new polyps begin to grow, underlying ones die and leave behind only their skeletal remains. These remains then form the stable substrate on which the new polyps develop. Sexual reproduction also occurs. Eggs and sperm are produced by separate individuals and are expelled through the mouth into open water. The eggs, once fertilized, develop into planktonic larvae (planula) which, after a few days to several weeks, settle onto a hard substrate and form new polyps.

Two living classes of Cnidaria contain corals, the Hydrozoa and the Anthozoa. Hydrozoan corals constitute only a minor portion of the total species of coral and are considered a specialized group because, unlike most hydrozoans, they secrete an external calcareous skeleton. Two hydrozoan coral orders, Milleporina and Stylasterina, are colonial, and both are common and widespread. The shallow-water Milleporina, sometimes called fire coral, is probably best known because it inflicts a painful sting when touched.

The great majority of living corals belong to the class Anthozoa. These corals, distinguished by tentacle shapes and numbers, can be divided into two subclasses, the Octocorallia and the Zoantharia. The Octocorallia possess eight feather-like (pinnate) tentacles and contain corals within four living orders. These are the Stolonifera (organ-pipe corals), Alcyonacea (soft corals), Helioporacea (blue corals), and Gorgonacea (sea fans and sea whips). The Zoantharia, a group with more than eight tentacles which are rarely pinnate, contains two orders of corals, the Antipatharia (black or thorny corals) and the Scleractinia (stony corals).

Scleractinian corals constitute the largest order of anthozoans and are found in all oceans, particularly coastal waters. They can be divided into two ecological groups. The first, called hermatypic or mound-building corals, contain single-celled photosynthetic dinoflagellates (zooxanthellae) within their soft tissues to assimilate metabolic wastes and thus help increase secretion of the calcareous skeleton. Hermatypic corals form the framework for massive coral reefs and are restricted to clear water which permits light penetration required by their symbionts. These reefs, which typically form in shallow (less than 70 m), semitropical to tropical waters, are usually found where the average annual sea temperatures are above 23°C. The other group, ahermatypic corals, those which lack zooxanthellae, are not as light dependent and therefore can build deeper-water coral banks in partial to total darkness. Coral reefs are ecologically important, not only because they protect the coastline from erosion by dissipating wave energy, but also because they provide food and shelter for a multitude of plants and animals. Corals are adversely affected by many things, including changes in water temperature, water movement, salinity, sediment loading, chemical pollution, and private or commercial collecting. Once weakened or damaged, these typically slow-growing animals become more vulnerable to attack by many predators (e.g., fish, echinoderms, worms, sponges, and boring mollusks).

Corals are extremely vulnerable in the Florida Reef Tract. They are troubled by the synergistic effects of human-made stresses and natural pathogenic syndromes (see Antonius 1977, 1981, 1985a, 1985b). Many of these species are still taken by coral collectors, even though such collecting is illegal.

Useful general references on corals include Almy and Carrion-Torres (1963), Bayer (1961), Colin (1978), Duarte Bello (1960), Geister (1972), Opresko (1974), Roos (1964, 1971), Smith (1948), Warner (1981), Wells (1973), Wood (1983), and Zlatarski & Martinez (1982).

PREPARED BY: Roger W. Portell, Florida Museum of Natural History, University of Florida, Gainesville, FL 32611.

Coral and Coral Reef Management

The State of Florida enacted statutes to protect corals beginning in 1973. The statute (Florida Statute 370) protects the Milleporina, Scleractinia, and two species of octocorals (*Gorgonia ventalina, Gorgonia flabellum*) from harvest, sale, or from being destroyed in place. Other statutes protect all corals in John Pennekamp Coral Reef State Park. Enforcement is provided by the Florida Marine Patrol and park rangers. The federal government provides similar protection under the Magnuson Act for the same set of corals. Enforcement is provided by the U.S. Coast Guard and National Marine Fisheries Service. The Florida Keys National Marine Sanctuary (FKNMS), National Oceanic and Atmospheric Administration, protects coral from harvest and destruction in place. Sanctuary patrol officers enforce regulations. Biscayne and Dry Tortugas National Parks also have statutes protecting corals. Park rangers enforce these regulations.

The Convention on International Trade in Endangered Species of Wild Fauna and Flora (CITES), Appendix II, lists genera of Antipatharia, Octocorallia, Millepora, and Scleractinia that are prohibited in commerce. The entire order of Antipatharia (black coral) and the family Stylastridae are listed under Appendix II. Protected genera of Milleporina and Scleractinia include:

Millepora	*Heliopora*
Tubipora	*Acropora*
Euphyllia	*Favia*
Fungia	*Halomitra*
Lobophyllia	*Merulina*
Pavona	*Pectinia*
Platygyra	*Pocillopora*
Polyphyllia	*Seriatopora*
Stylophora	

The U.S. Fish and Wildlife Service enforces CITES agreements.

Collection of corals for research requires a permit from the Florida Department of Environmental Protection for state waters, from the National Marine Fisheries Service for federal waters, and from the Florida Keys National Marine Sanctuary administration within its waters. The state and federal parks have similar permitting procedures.

Coral Reef Issues

Corals and reefs in Florida waters are at risk from natural and anthropogenic disturbance. The Florida reefs are at the northern fringe of reef development in the western Atlantic. They suffer from extremes in seawater temperature, hurricanes, winter cold fronts, water-borne diseases, and competition with nutrient-tolerant organisms. The most devastating forces impacting coral reefs are hurricanes and major winter storms. The most recent examples are Hurricane Andrew (1992) and the 13 March 1993 "storm of the century." Both events dislodged organisms, rearranged sedimentary deposits, and moved large reef structures. These types of disturbances are not unusual and probably play an important role in structuring reef communities (analogous to the role of fire in certain terrestrial plant communities). Seawater temperatures below 14° C or above 31° C stress the corals, and, if conditions do not improve, the corals bleach, and in severe cases, die. An extreme polar front caused 90% mortality to *Acropora spp.* populations at Dry Tortugas in February 1977. Summer doldrums are more apt to create zooxanthellae expulsions (coral bleaching episodes). These events were unusually common during the decade of the 1980s. There is some suspicion that this increased frequency is related to ENSO events, increased UV radiation, and increased greenhouse gases in the atmosphere. The corals are often physically weakened, and there is some evidence that they do not reproduce or grow after severe bleaching episodes. Natural biological interactions are also significant. For example, prior to 1983, the black-spined sea urchin (*Diadema antillarum*) was the most important herbivore on Caribbean reefs. A water-borne pathogen extirpated virtually all the *Diadema* within an 18 month period. The consequence of this epidemic mortality has been a major increase in fleshy algae in the coral reefs. Furthermore, coral and sponge diseases occasionally run rampant on certain reefs.

Habitat destruction and exceeding sustained yields of animal populations characterize anthropogenic disturbance of reef resources. The former is very difficult and costly to correct, while the latter can be corrected if the populations are not too severely decimated. Large ship groundings are the principal habitat destructive agent on the reefs. Examples include the *Wellwood* (1983, Molasses Reef), *Elpsis* (Elbow Reef, 1988), and the *Mavro Vetranic* (Pulaski Shoal, 1988). Each vessel destroyed acres of reef habitat. The damage was severe, and virtually all the organisms in the path of the ship were crushed. More importantly, the reef framework was fractured and left in an unstable condition. This results in chronic resuspension of sediments, allowing storms to reconfigure the subsurface substrates with the result that the area is poorly recolonized because of instability.

Small boats run aground on shallow reefs routinely. The damage is not as severe in terms of magnitude or spatial area; however, the problem has become chronic and some reefs in heavy traffic areas have suffered significant loss of coral cover. Mosquito Banks and Western Sambo are two examples of reefs that experience numerous grounding incidents.

Contamination by pesticides, nutrients, trace metals, and other products of man's society influences the health of the reefs. Urbanization is a creeping menace in south Florida, where the coastal fringe is the most densely populated. Development is virtually impossible to control, and much of the resultant liquid wastes are poorly treated, if at all. For example the principal means of treating sewage in the urban settings of Monroe County are septic tanks and cesspools. The leachate gains access into the marine waters, increasing levels of nitrogen and phosphorous, nutrients that are not desirable attributes.

In areas north of the Keys, the principal human impact that destroys reef habitat is beach renourishment, a process that causes physical damage from dredges and chronic turbidity generated by the dredge and silt that washes off the beach. There are numerous cases of damage caused by dredges in Dade, Broward, and Palm Beach counties. In some cases, the dredge company has been required to mitigate the damages with restoration and monitoring programs.

Sophisticated methods of fishing remove the pinnacle of the food webs (grouper and snapper) resulting in fish communities that lack larger predators. This predator/prey imbalance is recognized, but the political will to resolve it is difficult because of the impact on the fishing community and the lack of alternative work. The most reasonable management is to limit fishing access and zone certain areas as non-fishing areas to facilitate stock replenishment.

The aquarium market is also a major harvester of reef biota, since the opulent species are desired for the aquarium trade. The destructive practice of live-rock harvest has become another concern, thanks to the popularity of saltwater aquariums with reef-like structures and organisms. The trade harvests hundreds of tons of reef limestone rocks with the attached plants and animals. The major collection areas are found off the southeast coast, off Tampa Bay, and in the area around Destin. The excessive harvest of ornamental species has caused severe reductions in some invertebrate populations.

All species of black coral, fire coral, true stony corals, and the two sea fans are protected by state and federal statute. These organisms are distributed, with few exceptions, throughout the Caribbean and Bahamas. A few taxa extend as far north as Bermuda and as far south as Brazil. The only endemic stony coral species known from Florida are *Oculina robusta* and *Oculina tennela*. While some species exhibit population declines, it is not an unusual situation in nature. For example, the decline of *Acropora palmata* at Dry Tortugas is very dramatic. Between 1883 and 1983 this species suffered a loss of 44 hectares due to natural disturbances. The congener *Acropora cervicornis* suffered a massive population die off at Dry Tortugas in February 1977 due to hypothermia and, again, in 1981 due to disease.

The process of designating individual coral species as endangered is difficult to support in the context of the federal criteria for endangered species (the species must be endangered throughout it's distributional range). Based on this criteria, there are no endangered corals. All corals are at risk as noted earlier from natural causes and anthropogenic perturbations. We have a responsibility to educate society and sustain environmental quality to perpetuate the corals and reefs for future generations.

PREPARED BY: Walter C. Jaap, Florida Marine Research Institute, 100 8th Avenue SE, St. Petersburg, FL 33701

Recently Extirpated

Black Corals

Antipathes pennacea (Pallas)
Antipathes dichotoma (Pallas)

DESCRIPTION: Black corals have tree, willow-tree, or bush-like growth forms which can be extremely variable even in the same species. There is considerable taxonomic confusion about the commercially valuable species, which are almost certainly more numerous than the two taxa listed here. However, in order to qualify as "precious coral" they must attain a certain minimum size. About 1 m (3.3 ft) in height is common, but 2 or even 3 m (6–10 ft) is not unusual.

Black Coral, *Antipathes dichotoma* (courtesy of Arnfried Antonius).

Black Coral, *Antipathes pennacea* (courtesy of Arnfried Antonius).

RANGE: Black corals occur throughout the Caribbean, the Bahamas, and Bermuda. In Florida they were restricted to the Florida Reef Tract.

HABITAT: Some species of black corals can occur under shady overhangs in shallow-water reef habitats; however, most are deep-water forms found below 20 m (66 ft) to a depth of several hundred meters. They often flourish on vertical drop-offs.

LIFE HISTORY AND ECOLOGY: White or bright colored polyps grow on a black horny skeleton that is flexible in slender branches, but quite stiff in thick (up to several centimeters in diameter) portions of the trunk. In the field, they are easily distinguished from gorgonians by the spiny feeling of their branches.

SPECIALIZED OR UNIQUE CHARACTERISTICS: The large, keratin-like skeleton grows in concentric layers around a hollow core. Larger parts of this skeletal material are used to make semi-precious jewelry.

Location of the
Florida reef tract.
Distributions of sea
fans, black corals,
and pillar corals.

BASIS FOR STATUS CLASSIFICATION: Commercial harvesting and illegal poaching since the development of SCUBA diving have depleted the population in Florida. There is no more breeding stock left in Florida, but reproduction through Caribbean larvae may make possible its reestablishment in the Florida Reef Tract.

RECOMMENDATIONS: Corals should be totally protected within Florida waters from all collecting. They also will continue to suffer from increasing pollution, even in protected areas.

PREPARED BY: Arnfried Antonius, Florida Reef Foundation, P.O. Drawer 1468, Homestead, FL 33030.

Endangered

Elkhorn Coral

Acropora palmata (Lamarck)

DESCRIPTION: Elkhorn coral forms tree-like growths with elkhorn-shaped branches. Colonies in Florida rarely reach 2 m (6.6 ft); in other areas giant elkhorn corals may get to 3 m (10 ft). Living colonies are light brown with whitish branch tips.

RANGE: Elkhorn coral is found throughout the Caribbean and the Bahamas. In Florida it occurs in the Florida Keys at Fowey Rocks, from Carysfort to Molasses Reef, and from Looe Key to the end of the Florida Reef Tract.

HABITAT: Elkhorn corals are found on crests of offshore reefs with stable water conditions. In the Florida Keys, they occur mainly on reefs that are protected from the waters of Florida Bay by large keys.

Elkhorn Coral, *Acropora palmata* (courtesy of Arnfried Antonius).

33

LIFE HISTORY AND ECOLOGY: The skeleton of elkhorn coral is extremely hard and resistant to wave action. In high-energy environments, it
forms V-shaped rods that point against or away from the prevailing waves,
but in calmer waters it occurs as broad, unoriented plates. Linear annual
growth rates up to 10 cm (4 in) are reported for Florida, but often more than
20 cm (8 in) occur in the Caribbean. They are very sensitive to cold water.

SPECIALIZED OR UNIQUE CHARACTERISTICS: The species is the
most important builder of reef crests and is often called the "*Acropora palmata* zone."

BASIS FOR STATUS CLASSIFICATION: Elkhorn coral is endangered
throughout the Florida Reef Tract due to natural forces, such as cold winters, and through man-induced stresses. This species was exterminated by
humans on Triumph, Long, Ajax, and Pacific reefs before the establishment
of Biscayne National Park, as well as in the area from Pickles to Alligator
Reef.

RECOMMENDATIONS: All corals need complete protection. No collecting should be allowed in Florida waters.

PREPARED BY: Arnfried Antonius, Florida Reef Foundation, P.O. Drawer
1468, Homestead, FL 33030.

                                            FAMILY ACROPORIDAE

Endangered
_____

Staghorn Corals

Acropora cervicornis (Lamarck)
Acropora prolifera (Lamarck)

DESCRIPTION: These corals form tree-like growths with staghorn-shaped
(or antler-shaped) branches. *Acropora cervicornis* branches are round in
cross section, while *Acropora prolifera* branches are somewhat flattened and
oval. While *A. cervicornis* colonies may reach 1 m in length and height and
form thickets of several square meters, *A. prolifera* colonies grow no higher
than 0.5 m (1.5 ft) and tend to be scattered. Color is usually a light brown.

RANGE: These corals occur throughout the Caribbean and the Bahamas,
with *A. cervicornis* generally the more common of the two. Neither species is

Staghorn Coral, *Acropora cervicornis* (courtesy of Arnfried Antonius).

Staghorn Coral, *Acropora prolifera* (courtesy of Arnfried Antonius).

found in Bermuda. In the Florida Reef Tract, they both occur at Fowey Rocks, from Carysfort to Molasses Reef, and from Looe Key to the end of the reef tract. *A. cervicornis* is much more common than *A. prolifera.*

HABITAT: Staghorn corals are found below reef crests down to several tens of meters on fore reef slopes. They also can occur in clear-water lagoon areas of offshore reefs with stable water conditions.

LIFE HISTORY AND ECOLOGY: With an annual growth rate of over 10 centimeters in Florida and up to 30 cm (1 ft) in the Caribbean, *A. cervicornis* is the fastest growing coral in the western Atlantic. Due to its antler-like shape it can colonize sandy bottoms, where the lower parts of the coral may die, but the upper parts continue to grow vigorously. Both species are sensitive to cold water.

SPECIALIZED OR UNIQUE CHARACTERISTICS: These species, particularly *A. cervicornis*, are among the most important builders of the upper reef zones.

BASIS FOR STATUS CLASSIFICATION: The staghorn corals are endangered throughout the Florida Reef Tract from natural forces, such as cold winters, and through human-made stresses. The species were exterminated by humans on Triumph, Long, Ajax, and Pacific reefs before the establishment of Biscayne National Park, and in the area from Pickles to Alligator Reef.

RECOMMENDATIONS: Corals should be completely protected and no collecting should be allowed in Florida waters.

PREPARED BY: Arnfried Antonius, Florida Reef Foundation, P.O. Drawer 1468, Homestead, FL 33030.

Order Scleractinia

FAMILY MEANDRINIDAE

Endangered

Pillar Coral

Dendrogyra cylindrus Ehrenberg

DESCRIPTION: Pillar corals are the only western Atlantic corals that form vertical columns. A single colony may consist of more than a dozen individual pillars and grow 3 m (10 ft) tall in the central Caribbean. In Florida, a colony rarely exceeds 1 m (3.3 ft) in height. Its usual color is light ochre.

RANGE: The pillar coral occurs throughout the central part of the Caribbean Sea and the Bahamas. It very rare or absent at the southern fringes of the Caribbean basin (coastline of Venezuela, Colombia, and Panama) and in Bermuda. It is found scattered throughout the Florida Reef Tract.

HABITAT: Pillar corals prefer horizontal plains or gentle slopes in reefs, from about 2 m to 20 m (66 ft) in depth. The species does not occur in extremely exposed locations, although it can colonize mobile substrates to some extent.

LIFE HISTORY AND ECOLOGY: In contrast to other Caribbean Scleractinia, the polyps of the pillar coral expand during daylight. Pillars which topple over may grow a second generation of pillars along the entire length of the fallen branch, which can topple and produce a third generation. The resulting colony then has a broad, stable base.

Pillar Coral, *Dendrogyra cylindrus* (courtesy of Arnfried Antonius).

SPECIALIZED OR UNIQUE CHARACTERISTICS: Pillar corals are extremely rare in Florida waters.

BASIS FOR STATUS CLASSIFICATION: This coral was never very abundant in Florida waters, and most colonies have been exterminated by commercial collectors.

RECOMMENDATIONS: Corals should be completely protected, and no collecting should be allowed.

PREPARED BY: Arnfried Antonius, Florida Reef Foundation, P.O. Drawer 1468, Homestead, FL 33030.

Order Scleractinia
FAMILY MUSSIDAE

Endangered

Flower Coral
Mussa angulosa (Pallas)

DESCRIPTION: These corals form colonies of distinctly separated polyps that remain in one hemispherical plane. Because of this arrangement, the polyps resemble a bouquet of flowers, hence the common name. The densely packed, colorful polyps of *Mussa angulosa* reach 3–5 cm (1–2 in), and the colonies grow up to 1 m in diameter.

RANGE: This coral is found throughout the Caribbean and the Bahamas, but does not occur in Bermuda. In Florida, it is scattered throughout the Florida Reef Tract and also in deep reefs off Broward County.

HABITAT: This species is absent from the shallowest reefs, but can occur from about 3 m (10 ft) in sheltered areas to more than 40 m (132 ft).

LIFE HISTORY AND ECOLOGY: This flower coral, along with the unrelated coral *Eusmilia fastigiata*, represents an intermediate stage of development between single polyps and colonies. *M. angulosa* is one of the most aggressive Caribbean corals and can hold its ground by attacking other corals.

SPECIALIZED OR UNIQUE CHARACTERISTICS: Flower corals have beautiful, ornamental shapes and have been highly prized by collectors.

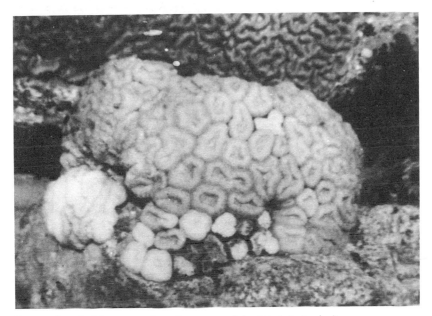

Flower Coral, *Mussa angulosa* (courtesy of Arnfried Antonius).

Distribution of flower corals.

BASIS FOR STATUS CLASSIFICATION: This coral has never been abundant in Florida, and due to its appealing appearance, its numbers have been reduced even further by coral collectors.

RECOMMENDATIONS: Corals should be completely protected.

PREPARED BY: Arnfried Antonius, Florida Reef Foundation, P.O. Drawer 1468, Homestead, FL 33030.

Order Scleractinia

FAMILY CARYOPHYLLIIDAE

Endangered

Flower Coral

Eusmilia fastigiata (Pallas)

DESCRIPTION: Like the other flower coral, *Eusmilia fastigiata* forms colonies of distinctly separated polyps that develop along one hemispherical plane and resemble a bouquet of flowers. It has loosely spaced, brown polyps 1–2 cm (less than 0.5 in) in diameter and forms colonies of up to 0.5 m (1.5 ft) in diameter.

RANGE: This coral occurs throughout the Caribbean and the Bahamas, but not in Bermuda. In Florida, it is found scattered throughout the Florida Reef Tract as well as in deep reefs off Broward County.

HABITAT: It is absent from the shallowest reefs, but can occur from about 3 m (10 ft) of water in sheltered places to depths in excess of 40 m (132 ft).

LIFE HISTORY AND ECOLOGY: Like other flower corals, this species represents a stage of phylogenetic development that is somewhat intermediate between single polyps and colonies.

SPECIALIZED AND UNIQUE CHARACTERISTICS: *E. fastigiata* is adapted to a wide variety of habitats, including crevices and overhangs where other species tend not to grow as easily.

Starlet Coral, *Siderastrea siderea* (courtesy of Arnfried Antonius).

BASIS FOR STATUS CLASSIFICATION: This coral has never been abundant in Florida, but its numbers have been reduced even further by coral collectors.

RECOMMENDATIONS: Corals should receive absolute protection, and no collecting should be allowed in Florida waters.

PREPARED BY: Arnfried Antonius, Florida Reef Foundation, P.O. Drawer 1468, Homestead, FL 33030.

Threatened

Brain Corals

FAMILY AGARICIIDAE
Agaricia agaricites (Linnaeus), Lettuce Coral.

FAMILY SIDERASTREIDAE
Siderastrea siderea (Ellis and Solander), Starlet Coral.

FAMILY FAVIIDAE
Diploria clivosa (Ellis and Solander), Brain Coral.
Diploria labyrinthiformis (Linnaeus), Brain Coral.
Diploria strigosa (Dana), Brain Coral.
Colpophyllia natans (Muller), Giant Brain Coral.
Manicina areolata (Linnaeus), Rose Coral.
Montastrea annularis (Ellis and Solander), Little Star Coral.
Montastrea cavernosa (Linnaeus), Large Star Coral.

FAMILY MEANDRINIDAE
Meandrina meandrites (Linnaeus), Brain Coral.

DESCRIPTION: The common names of these corals describe their shapes. *Agaricia agaricites* is the smallest of this group, with lettuce-shaped colonies up to 20 cm (8 in) in diameter. All other species are head- or boulder-shaped and range from 30 cm (1 ft) to over 1 m (3 ft) in diameter. The only exception is *Montastrea annularis*, which can form buttresses several meters in height and width.

RANGE: All species occur throughout the Caribbean Sea and on most of the reefs of the Florida Reef Tract.

HABITAT: Brain corals can be found in moderate water depths, and some also inhabit deep parts of the reef. They are absent from the *Acropora* crest zone.

SPECIALIZED OR UNIQUE CHARACTERISTICS: Together these corals represent the main reef-builders in all depth zones except for the reef crest itself.

BASIS FOR STATUS CLASSIFICATION: These species, like other continental benthic marine animals in the vicinity of Florida, are threatened by pollution. Corals under severe pollution stress die upon additional impacts

(Antonius 1977), as clearly demonstrated by the death of Hen and Chicken Reef.

RECOMMENDATIONS: Fighting pollution and regulating tourism in the Florida Keys should be future goals. At the present the situation could be vastly improved by prohibiting the collection of at least the mentioned species, and, even better and simpler, of all species of stony corals. In Bermuda, for example, the only permitted underwater activity is photography.

PREPARED BY: Arnfried Antonius, Florida Reef Foundation, P.O. Drawer 1468, Homestead, FL 33030.

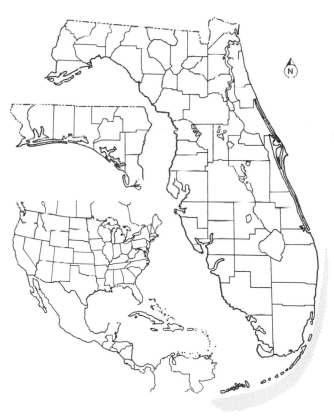

Distribution of massive, reef-building corals including *Acropora* and *Diplora*.

Brain Coral, *Diplora labyrinthiformis* (courtesy of Arnfried Antonius).

Little Star Coral, *Montastrea annularis* (courtesy of Arnfried Antonius).

Large Star Coral, *Montastrea cavernosa* (courtesy of Arnfried Antonius).

Brain Coral, *Meandrina meandrites* (courtesy of Arnfried Antonius).

Threatened

Sea Fans

Gorgonia ventalina Linnaeus
Gorgonia flabellum Linnaeus

DESCRIPTION: Fan-shaped colonies grow in one plane and have ascending branches linked together by a dense network of smaller connecting branches. These are compressed in the plane of the fan in *Gorgonia ventalina*, but are perpendicular to it in *Gorgonia flabellum*. Coloration varies widely, but usually shows shades of purple in *G. ventalina*, and variations of yellow in *G. flabellum*. In Florida, they usually grow to less than 1 m (3.3 ft) in height, but may exceed 2 m (6.6 ft) in Caribbean locations.

RANGE: Sea fans are found throughout the Florida Reef Tract, with *G. ventalina* much more frequent than *G. flabellum*. These sea fans occur throughout the Caribbean and the Bahamas. *G. ventalina* also occurs in Bermuda. *G. flabellum* appears the more tropical of the two species. They occur in similar numbers in central and southern Caribbean locations, but *G. ventalina* is predominant in the northern regions.

HABITAT: Both sea fans occur in shallow coral reef environments, preferring horizontal rather than vertical surfaces. Both are found from the shallowest reef flats or nearshore areas to 10–15 m (33-46 ft) water depth; however, whenever they compete for space, *G. flabellum* dominates the shallowest zones.

LIFE HISTORY AND ECOLOGY: Sea fans possess a horny skeleton made of gorgonin. It is deposited by polyps and coenosarc in concentric layers around a narrow, chambered axis.

SPECIALIZED OR UNIQUE CHARACTERISTICS: Thicker branches of sea fans are sometimes used for jewelry marketed as "false black coral." However, in contrast to antipatharians, the gorgonid skeleton is smooth.

BASIS FOR STATUS CLASSIFICATION: Sea fans are very popular collector items. Neither species is abundant in Florida. *G. flabellum* is more at risk than the other species since it is the rarer of the two in Florida waters.

RECOMMENDATIONS: Sea fans are protected by state and federal regulations from the high water line to 320 km (200 mi) offshore. Like other corals, sea fans are vulnerable to chemical pollution and physical damage from human activities.

PREPARED BY: Arnfried Antonius, Florida Reef Foundation, P.O. Drawer 1468, Homestead, FL 33030.

Phylum Mollusca
Class Bivalvia
Order Myoida

Marine Bivalves

INTRODUCTION: Bivalves consist of two shells (valves) and a soft body. They constitute an important element of most nearshore marine environments. One marine bivalve, the Atlantic geoduck (*Panopea bitruncata*), has been included in this volume as rare; other species probably will be included in future lists as threats to them are identified.

The majority of the bivalves are sessile as adults. There are some notable exceptions: for example, scallops (e.g. *Argopecten irradians*) are able to transport themselves by clapping their valves together and expelling water from the mantle cavity. Bivalves generally may be distinguished as either epifaunal (live above the substrate) or infaunal (live within the substrate). Epifaunal bivalves are usually free-living (e.g. scallops) or attached to solid substrates. Attachment is accomplished by cementation of one of the valves directly to the substrate or by means of a byssus, a structure usually consisting of a bundle of hairlike threads that connects to the substrate. Bivalves with these structures include mussels (e.g. *Mytilus edulis*) and pearl oysters (e.g. *Pinctada imbricata*).

Infaunal bivalves most commonly bore, burrow, or nestle into their preferred substrates. Borers typically penetrate hard material such as coral, rock, or shell by chemical or mechanical means. Another member of this group, the notorious shipworm (*Teredo navalis*), bores into wood and actually uses the cellulose as a food source. While borers are generally associated with a solid substrate, burrowers usually are found in softer, unconsolidated sediments, burrowing with musculature structure known simply as a foot. Quahogs (*Mercenaria* sp.) and the Atlantic geoduck are well-known examples. Nestling bivalves (e.g. species in the arc genus *Barbatia*) are those which inhabit previously formed spaces in a hard substrate.

Several groups of bivalves show intermediate versions and combinations of these life habits including semi-infaunal, byssally attached infaunal, etc., demonstrating the adaptability and ubiquity of the group.

PREPARED BY: Kevin S. Schindler, Florida Museum of Natural History, University of Florida, Gainesville, FL 32611.

Rare

Atlantic Geoduck

Panopea bitruncata (Conrad)

DESCRIPTION: The shell of *Panopea bitruncata* is robust, heavy, subrectangular, rounded anteriorly, and truncated posteriorly; it gapes at both ends and is about 23 cm (9 in) long. It is white, often stained light brown or gray by muds; its interior is glossy white. The exterior sculpture is of prominent concentric growth rings. The animal is far larger than the shell: two united siphons, leathery in appearance, may extend three times or more the shell length in live specimens. The body is tan or light tan.

RANGE: This species has been collected very infrequently from several areas of the Carolinian zoogeographic province (North Carolina to Texas). In various parts of its range, it occurs in depths from intertidal to as great as 48 m (158 ft). In Florida, living specimens are known with certainty only from Duval, Gulf, and St. Johns counties.

HABITAT: Except for a single specimen dredged from a depth of 22 m (73 ft) about 15 km (9 mi) northeast of St. Augustine Inlet, the few Florida specimens have been found in mud in very shallow water near inlets. C. W. Johnson (1890, 1904) reported the first Florida specimen, collected freshly dead in 1883 from a bar at Marsh Island near St. Augustine. Marsh Island had disappeared, and the bar was extensively altered on a subsequent visit (C. W. Johnson 1919). M. C. Johnson (1956) reported the habitat of a living specimen from St. Augustine as "alluvial mud typical of salt marshes of the Southeastern Coast. However, the [mud] bank which is alternately inundated and exposed by the tides is overlain with sand deposited by the fast flowing water of the main river channel and will support a man without miring." Robertson (1963) reported a specimen collected from "black, oozy mud in very shallow water at Fort George Inlet near Jacksonville." He suggested that specimens collected near an oil-drilling rig off Galveston Island, Texas, were living in mud, and he reported another living specimen from a mud lump in a depth of 48 m of water off Port Isabel, Texas. The late Mrs. Loraine Ridge of St. Augustine collected four living specimens from "soupy mud" in Matanzas Bay, St. Johns County (pers. comm.); she noted that the main area of the bar where the specimens were collected easily supported the weight of a man. The Gulf County record, questionably included in the first edition of this work on the basis of a hinged pair of valves dredged from mud in St. Joseph Bay, has since been substantiated in two instances by live specimens collected in shrimp trawls within the bay; no data on substrate are available

48

Atlantic Geoduck,
Panopea bitruncata
(courtesy of Kurt
Auffenberg). (UF
143593).

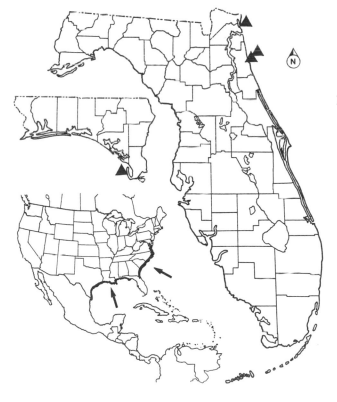

Distribution of the
Atlantic geoduck,
*Panopea
bitruncata.*

for those specimens. The few beached specimens from North Carolina and the specimen from offshore of St. Augustine may have lived in less muddy substrate.

LIFE HISTORY AND ECOLOGY: Small specimens of *P. bitruncata* are virtually unknown. In intertidal areas, living specimens have been found buried from 46 to 76 cm (18–30 in) (L. Ridge, pers. comm.) to depths as great as 122 cm (48 in) (V. Pope, in M. C. Johnson 1956) in mud. Robertson (1963) speculated that the species may usually live subtidally but that specimens rarely would be obtained alive below the tidal zone because of the depth within the substrate where they normally live. He noted that living subtidal specimens had all been obtained under exceptional circumstances. Two of the three instances of offshore collection of living *Panopea* have followed natural or human disturbances, i.e., a hurricane off northeast Florida and oil-drilling activities off Texas. The few beached specimens from North Carolina came ashore following storms. It is difficult to decide what relationship the occurrence of dead shells may have to the distribution of living animals. C. W. Johnson (1904) reported shells from North Carolina, west Florida, and Mississippi. Robertson (1963) listed numerous records of dead shells from North Carolina to Cape Canaveral, from Sanibel Island to Tampa Bay, and from Panama City to southwestern Texas. Nearly all were beach collections, but single dead pairs were reported from about 33 km north of Cape Hatteras (depth unknown) and from northeast of Port Isabel, Texas, in about 55 m of water. More recently, dead shells have been collected along the Florida west coast off Cape Romano, in Charlotte Harbor, in St. Joseph Bay, and at Pensacola. Most such shells are old and worn; none has been subjected to dating analysis. They could represent extinct populations whose shells are now being exposed by erosion associated with storms and rising sea level.

SPECIALIZED OR UNIQUE CHARACTERISTICS: This species is the largest western Atlantic bivalve. Shells of certain Pinnidae (*Pinna, Atrina*) may exceed those of Panopea in size, but the living animal of *P. bitruncata* is far larger. There are numerous fossil species of *Panopea*, ranging back in age to perhaps the mid-Jurassic. C. W. Johnson (1904, 1929) suggested that *P. bitruncata* is a relict form of a common Tertiary species from the southeastern United States, known both as *P. floridana* and *P. navicula*, and also erroneously reported under several other names. This proposed synonym of Recent and Tertiary names has been ignored by most subsequent reporters of both fossil and recent forms, but the hypothesis warrants further consideration.

BASIS FOR STATUS CLASSIFICATION: Except for one offshore specimen, all living Florida *P. bitruncata* have been collected in estuarine environments near inlets in Duval, Gulf, and St. Johns counties. Robertson's speculation that the species is more successful offshore may prove true, but the estuarine populations are the only ones now known where biology of the species can be studied. Virtually nothing is known of the life history of the species. As early as 1919, C. W. Johnson expressed concern that estuarine populations are "very apt to be destroyed by changes such as encroaching sand bars, sedimentary deposits, and harbor pollution." It is imperative that these known populations be protected from overzealous collection and habitat destruction.

RECOMMENDATIONS: Ranges and densities of estuarine populations should be determined. Future developmental planning for areas containing the few known populations must ensure that these stocks are not reduced or eliminated by habitat destruction such as industrial and domestic pollution or filling operations. Local educational programs and perhaps local regulation should be considered to protect these populations from overcollection.

PREPARED BY: William G. Lyons, Florida Department of Environmental Protection, Marine Research Laboratory, 100 Eighth Avenue SE, St. Petersburg, FL 33701.

Freshwater Bivalves

INTRODUCTION: Three families of bivalve mollusks are found in the fresh waters of Florida, two native and one exotic or nonnative. The two families of native bivalve mollusks, pea clams (family Sphaeriidae) and freshwater mussels (family Unionidae), once occurred in most freshwater habitats in the state. In many aquatic habitats they formed an important component of the benthic community. The pill clams, which inhabit small ponds, lakes, freshwater wetlands, canals, small creeks, and large rivers, are especially important food of waterfowl and, to a lesser extent, fishes. Mussels are more likely to be found in creeks, rivers, and lakes, where they may form extensive beds. Mussels are preyed upon by several species of fishes, turtles, birds, and small mammals.

The third family of bivalve mollusks in the state of Florida, family Corbiculidae, is represented by one species, the exotic Asian clam, *Corbicula fluminea*. This species was first discovered in the United States on the West Coast (Washington) in 1938 (Burch 1944) and has spread throughout the entire United States, causing economic and ecological problems. The Asian clam was first discovered in Florida in 1960 (Schneider 1967) and has now successfully invaded almost every drainage system in the state (Bass 1974). In some lakes and streams, it has reached densities of several hundred individuals per square meter of substrate. Its abundance may have contributed to the decline of certain native mussels. This point, however, is difficult to prove because unrelated environmental perturbations in most systems make cause and effect relationships nearly impossible to demonstrate.

These three families of mollusks are very distinctive in appearance and are easily distinguished on the basis of size, shape, and shell characteristics. In Florida, the pea clams (also known as pill or fingernail clams) are small, rarely exceeding 15 mm in length, and very thin shelled. Mussels or freshwater clams are usually mature at more than 25 mm and have thicker shells. The exotic Asian clam is somewhat intermediate between the two families of native clams, in both size and shell thickness. It may reach 45 mm in length, but individuals rarely exceed 32 mm. The most distinctive feature of the Asian clam is the evenly spaced concentric ridges which cover the entire shell.

In North America, the family Sphaeriidae is represented by 38 species and

4 genera (Turgeon et al. 1988). Four species are exotics, apparently introduced from Europe, but none of these occur in the state of Florida (Turgeon
et al. 1988). Twelve species are reported from Florida but none are endemic
to the state (Heard 1979). Although we are not aware of any precipitous decline in these sphaeriids, we also have no data that indicate their populations
are stable; their conservation status should therefore be considered unknown.

The family Unionidae in North America is represented by about 297 species and subspecies (Turgeon et al. 1988). Although this fauna has been studied since the early 1800s, there are unresolved questions regarding the validity
of numerous species. Problems also exist in the definition or limits of certain
genera. Very few genera and species have an adequate diagnosis and description based on anatomy of soft tissues. This information is critical to our understanding of generic and specific concepts in unionid mollusks. The identification of some species is difficult using conchological characters alone.

Several fairly extensive reports (Simpson 1900a; Walker 1905; van der
Schalie 1940; Clench and Turner 1956; Johnson 1967, 1969, 1970; Heard
1979; Butler 1989) on Florida unionids have been published during the past
century. Most addressed regional faunas, zoogeographic, and taxonomic
problems, with little or no information on basic biology. The unusual life history of unionids, a life cycle typically including a larval stage which is parasitic on the gills and fins of one or more species of fishes, presents some very
difficult problems when one considers protection and recovery actions. Conservation activities must consider ecological requirements for the unionids
and their host fish; however, neither the host fish nor other basic requirements such as temperature, dissolved oxygen, and stream flow, are known
for unionids in Florida. Research on the life history of unionids is desper-
ately needed.

We record a total of 52 species of unionids in Florida. This number is
conservative, as additional unionids, including described forms currently
placed in synonymy with other species, as well as undescribed species, will
undoubtedly be recognized in the future. *Elliptio* is one example of a genus
that may have several valid biological species that are not currently recognized
by malacologists. Five of the 52 unionid species known from Florida, *Alasmidonta wrightiana*, *Elliptio buckleyi*, *E. chipolaensis*, *Medionidus walkeri*,
and *Villosa amygdala*, appear to be restricted to the state.

Of the 52 freshwater mussels known from Florida, 28 species (54%) are
deemed worthy of a conservation category. Five species are endangered, 14
are threatened, 5 are of special concern, and 4 are of undetermined status.
Only 3 unionids were included in the 1982 FCREPA list; the increase reflects
a better understanding of the threats to these mollusks.

Most of the biological diversity in freshwater stream-dwelling organisms
in Florida is found in the panhandle and in northern peninsula regions. The
unionids are no exception, as there are only 10 species known to occur in the
peninsula south of the Suwannee and St. Johns rivers. In Florida, the most

diverse unionid fauna is in the Apalachicola River drainage, which is inhabited by 28 species. Species of unionids in other rivers are as follows: Choctawhatchee (23 species); Escambia (23 species); Ochlockonee (18 species); Suwannee (14 species); and Yellow River (12 species).

All 28 species assigned conservation status in Florida are confined to the Apalachicolan Region, defined as the drainages from the Escambia to the Suwannee River (Butler 1989). Sixteen (57%) of these species are restricted in the state to single river systems. Seven species occur in only two drainages, and the remaining five species occur in three drainage systems.

Diversity of unionid mollusks in Florida would be even greater if the Apalachicolan Region drainages were not beheaded by the state boundary, with most of the stream habitat in Alabama and Georgia. Protection of this diverse freshwater mussel assemblage depends in part on the stewardship of adjacent states since the rivers traversing the Florida panhandle originate in the states of Alabama and Georgia. Although many point sources of water pollution have been addressed by adjacent states in recent years, others continue to be a problem.

One of the most significant pollution problems for aquatic organisms involves a non-point source, silt. This pollution comes from improperly managed agricultural lands, road construction, and other development activities. These pollution problems may originate in adjacent states, but they are not confined to those areas. Florida has its share of pollution and siltation problems which need to be addressed if we are going to conserve our aquatic resources.

The only two major impoundments in the panhandle area are the Jim Woodruff Dam (constructed in the mid-1950s) on the Apalachicola River (Lake Seminole) and the Jackson Bluff Dam (constructed in the late 1920s) on the Ochlockonee River (Lake Talquin). These two dams and reservoirs drastically altered the free-flowing upstream areas they impounded as well as the riverine areas downstream. For example, the disappearance of *Alasmidonta wrightiana* in the 1930s (last known collections) may be associated with the impoundment of the Ochlockonee River. This impoundment not only destroyed riverine habitat of the mussel, but blocked the upstream movement of anadromous fishes that may have served as the host of the glochidia. The dam on Dead Lake, which further impounded a flow-through natural basin on the lower Chipola River, was removed in December 1987 because of deteriorating water quality in the shallow lake. The removal of this dam returned the river to its natural flow. However, we estimate at least two decades will be required to flush out the accumulated silt and re-establish the natural pre-impoundment littoral zone.

PREPARED BY: James D. Williams, National Biological Survey, 7920 N.W. 71st Street, Gainesville, FL 32653, and Robert S. Butler, U.S. Fish and Wildlife Service, 6620 Southpoint Drive South, Jacksonville, FL 32216.

Endangered

Triangle Floater
Alasmidonta undulata (Say)

DESCRIPTION: The triangle floater is a thin-shelled, medium-sized species, reaching lengths of about 70 mm (2.7 in). It is oval to subtriangular in shape and is inflated with high, broad umbos anterior to the center. A high and prominently angled posterior ridge ends in a point near the base. The epidermis in adults is dark greenish brown to black and is faintly rayed in transmitted light. The pseudocardinal teeth-one in the right valve, two in the left valve-are stumpy and thick. Lateral teeth are poorly developed or absent. The nacre is usually bluish white, but may be salmon to pink in some individuals.

RANGE: On the Atlantic coast *Alasmidonta undulata* occurs from the St. Lawrence River system in Canada south to the Ogeechee River system, Georgia (Clarke 1981). On the Gulf Coast, *A. undulata* is restricted to the Apalachicola River system in Alabama, Georgia, and Florida (Clench and Turner 1956; Clarke 1981). In Florida, it is reported from a few localities in the main channel of the Apalachicola and lower Chipola rivers.

HABITAT: Triangle floaters have been taken in waters ranging from large creeks to large rivers. This species is found in sand or sand and mud substrate in moderate current.

LIFE HISTORY AND ECOLOGY: There is no life history or ecological information available for the Apalachicola drainage population of this species. Although little is known about Atlantic Coast populations, they have been reported as gravid for most of the year (Ortmann 1919; Clarke 1981).

SPECIALIZED OR UNIQUE CHARACTERISTICS: The angular posterior ridge, high umbos, shell outline, and near absence of lateral teeth serve to differentiate the triangle floater from other sympatric species in Florida.

BASIS FOR STATUS CLASSIFICATION: In the past 20 years, only a single live specimen has been found (Chipola River, Scotts Ferry, Calhoun County, in 1986). The limited distribution and threat from dredging activities in the Apalachicola River are the major factors in determining the conservation status of the triangle floater.

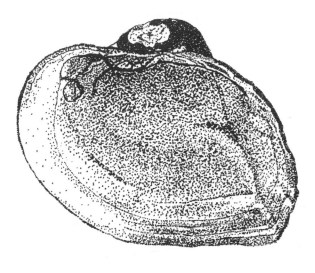

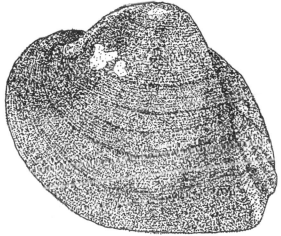

Triangle Floater, *Alasmidonta undulata*, UF 403, length 51 mm (2.0 in). Florida, Calhoun County, Dead Lake, Chipola River at Chipola Park, 32 km (20 mi) south of Blountstown (illustration by Tracy Smith).

RECOMMENDATIONS: Protection of the Chipola River is essential to the survival of this species in Florida. Current status of the species in the Apalachicola River proper should be determined to provide for its protection during maintenance dredging of the channel.

PREPARED BY: James D. Williams, National Biological Survey, 7920 N.W. 71st Street, Gainesville, FL 32653, and Robert S. Butler, U.S. Fish and Wildlife Service, 6620 Southpoint Drive South, Jacksonville, FL 32216.

Distribution of the triangle
floater, *Alasmidonta
undulata*.

FAMILY UNIONIDAE

Endangered

Apalachicola Floater

Anodonta sp. (undescribed)

DESCRIPTION: This large undescribed species of the genus *Anodonta* attains a length of at least 139 mm (5.5 in). It is oval and very inflated, almost
as wide as it is high in large individuals. The dimensions for the largest
known specimen are 139 mm long, 82 mm (3.2 in) high and 63 mm (2.5 in)
wide. In large individuals the umbos extend above the hinge line and are

sculptured with simple loops. The surface of the shell is smooth except posteriorly, where it becomes somewhat roughened. Most of the shell is yellowish olive to light brown. Dark olive to brown concentric bands are present on some individuals. Internally, the valves are completely toothless. The nacre is white with some pinkish to purplish color. A formal description of the Apalachicola floater is being prepared by Mark E. Gordon and Walter R. Hoeh.

RANGE: The total range of this species is unclear at this time, but appears to be confined to the Apalachicola River system in Florida. It has been collected from three localities in Calhoun, Gadsden, and Jackson counties. It might occur in the Chattahoochee River in Alabama and Georgia and in the Flint Fiver in Georgia, but no specimens are known from these rivers. One collection (Tanvat Pond, Jackson County, Florida), from the Chattahoochee River floodplain was reported by Clench and Turner (1956) as *Anodonta gibbosa*.

HABITAT: Like most species of the genus *Anodonta*, the Apalachicola floater inhabits waters with little or no current, such as floodplain lakes and backwater areas of the Apalachicola River in mud substrates. No other habitat information is available.

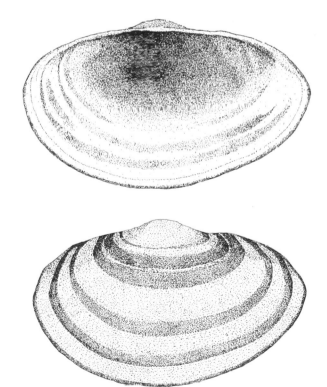

Apalachicola Floater, *Anodonta* sp., UF 1915, length 141 mm (5.5 in). Florida, Jackson County, Tanvat Pond, 4.8 km (3 mi) north of Sneads (illustration by Tracy Smith).

Distribution of the Apalachicola floater, *Anodonta* sp.

LIFE HISTORY AND ECOLOGY: Heard (1979) described various aspects of the reproductive biology of the Apalachicola floater as *Anodonta couperiana*. Females displayed early oogenesis in early August and were spent by late August. A single hermaphroditic individual was also noted in the population.

SPECIALIZED OR UNIQUE CHARACTERISTICS: As presently known, the Apalachicola floater has the most restricted distribution of all North American species of the genus *Anodonta*.

BASIS FOR STATUS CLASSIFICATION: Alteration of the habitat by impoundment and dredging activities and the rarity of the species are the bases for assigning endangered status to the Apalachicola floater.

RECOMMENDATIONS: Habitat protection for the known populations is essential to the conservation of this species. Surveys are needed in suitable habitat in the vicinity of Lake Seminole and the Apalachicola River mainstem. Biological studies to determine the current distribution, life history, and habitat requirements should be conducted to plan for the conservation and recovery of this species.

PREPARED BY: James D. Williams, National Biological Survey, 7920 N.W. 71st Street, Gainesville, FL 32653, and Robert S. Butler, U.S. Fish and Wildlife Service, 6620 Southpoint Drive South, Jacksonville, FL 32216.

FAMILY UNIONIDAE

Endangered

Round Ebonyshell
Fusconaia rotulata (Wright)

DESCRIPTION: *Fusconaia rotulata* is a medium-sized species that attains a length of approximately 65 mm (2.5 in). It has an almost circular outline and heavy, somewhat inflated, thick shell with a smooth black epidermis. Internally, the umbonal pocket is very deep and wide. The pseudocardinal teeth are low and usually double in the left valve and single in the right valve. The lateral teeth are long, slightly curved, and separated from the pseudocardinal teeth by a broad smooth interdentum. The nacre is typically white to silvery, and iridescent.

This species was originally placed in the genus *Unio* by Wright (1899). Simpson (1900b) reexamined the type specimen and assigned it to the genus *Obovaria*. Subsequent workers (Simpson 1914; Johnson 1967, 1969; Turgeon et al. 1988) have continued to recognize *rotulata* as a species of *Obovaria*. After examining several specimens of this species and making comparisons with species of *Obovaria* and *Fusconaia*, it is very clear, based on conchological characters (teeth and deep umbo pocket), that *rotulata* is a species of *Fusconaia* not *Obovaria*. *Fusconaia rotulata* most closely resembles *F. ebena*, which is widespread in the Mississippi basin and along the Gulf Coast east to the Alabama River system.

RANGE: *Fusconaia rotulata* is endemic to the Escambia River drainage in Escambia County, Alabama, and Escambia and Santa Rosa counties, Florida (Johnson 1969; Burch 1975). In Florida, it has been taken from near the Alabama border downstream to Molino.

HABITAT: This mussel is confined to the main channel of the Escambia River in areas with moderate current and a mixture of sand and gravel substrates.

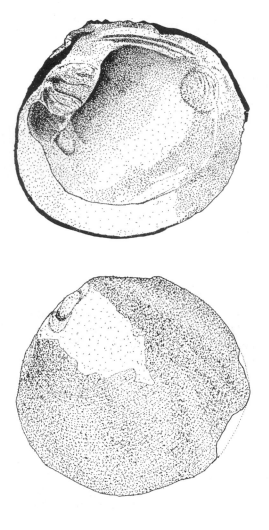

Round Ebonyshell,
Fusconaia rotulata,
USNM 159969
(type), length 45.5
mm (1.8 in). Florida,
Escambia County,
Escambia River
(illustration by
Tracy Smith).

LIFE HISTORY AND ECOLOGY: Unknown.

SPECIALIZED OR UNIQUE CHARACTERISTICS: Based on current records, the round ebonyshell has one of the most restricted distributions of any extant North American unionid. Shell morphology allows easy differentiation from other species in the Escambia River.

BASIS FOR STATUS CLASSIFICATION: The restricted distribution of *F. rotulata* and habitat degradation in the Escambia River are the basis for the endangered status of this species.

Distribution of the round
ebonyshell, *Fusconaia
rotulata.*

RECOMMENDATIONS: Protection of the Escambia River is essential to
the survival of *F. rotulata.* Efforts to reduce the silt load and other pollutants would contribute to the conservation of this species. Because most of
the Escambia River system is in Alabama, a joint effort of Alabama and
Florida will be required to improve the water quality of this system.

PREPARED BY: James D. Williams, National Biological Survey, 7920 N.W.
71st Street, Gainesville, FL 32653, and Robert S. Butler, U.S. Fish and Wildlife Service, 6620 Southpoint Drive South, Jacksonville, FL 32216.

Endangered

Ochlockonee Moccasinshell

Medionidus simpsonianus Walker

DESCRIPTION: The Ochlockonee moccasinshell is a small species, generally under 55 mm (2.5 in) in length. It is slightly elongate-elliptical in outline,
the posterior end obtusely rounded at the shell's median line and the ventral
margin broadly curved. The posterior ridge is moderately angular and covered its entire length with well developed, irregular ridges. Sculpture may
also extend onto the disk below the ridge. Surface texture is smooth. The
color is light brown to yellowish green, with dark green rays formed by a series of connected chevrons or undulating lines across the length of the shell.
Internal characters include thin straight lateral teeth and compressed pseudocardinal teeth. There are two laterals and two pseudocardinals in the left
valve and one lateral and one pseudocardinal in the right valve. The nacre is
bluish white.

Considerable confusion has clouded *Medionidus* taxonomy in the eastern
Gulf Coast region. Van der Schalie (1940) recorded *M. penicillatus* and *M.
kingi* from the Chipola River system. *Medionidus penicillatus* was the only
member of the genus recognized from the Gulf drainages east of the Mobile
basin by Clench and Turner (1956) and Burch (1975). In a list of unionids
from the Apalachicolan Region, Johnson (1970) erroneously reported both
M. penicillatus and *M. walkeri* (Wright 1897) from the Apalachicola River
system and the latter species in the Ochlockonee and Suwannee rivers as
well. In a monograph of the genus, Johnson (1977) recognized *M. penicillatus*, *M. walkeri*, and a third form, *M. simpsonianus*, the latter two species
endemic to the Suwannee and Ochlockonee river systems, respectively. These
three species of *Medionidus* are generally recognized by malacologists today
(Turgeon et al. 1988).

RANGE: *Medionidus simpsonianus* is endemic to the Ochlockonee River
system in Georgia and Florida (Johnson 1977). In Florida the species has
been recorded from the lower mainstem (Wakulla County, no specific locality) upstream in Gadsden and Leon counties to the Georgia portion of the
river and from the Little River, the system's largest tributary (Johnson 1977).
Clench and Turner (1956) erroneously synonomized *M. simpsonianus* under
M. penicillatus; their Ochlockonee River records for *M. penicillatus* were actually *M. simpsonianus*.

HABITAT: The Ochlockonee moccasinshell inhabits large creeks to medium-
sized rivers in substrates of sand with some gravel in moderate current.

LIFE HISTORY AND ECOLOGY: Unknown.

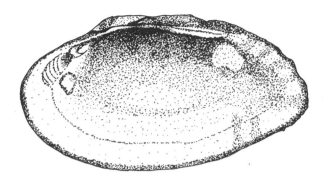

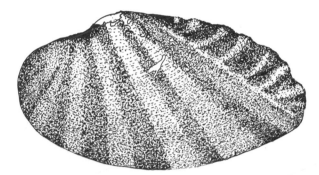

Ochlockonee Mocca-sinshell, *Medionidus simpsonianus*, UF 8399, length 34.5 mm (1.4 in). Florida, Leon County, Ochlockonee River, 11.2 km (7 mi) west of Tallahassee (illustration by Tracy Smith).

UNIQUE OR SPECIALIZED CHARACTERISTICS: The small size and characteristic sculpture distinguish *M. simpsonianus* from other species in the Ochlockonee River system. The characteristic ray pattern and the medial position of the posterior slope distinguish it from other *Medionidus* species in Florida.

BASIS FOR STATUS CLASSIFICATION: One live *M. simpsonianus* has been found since 1975 (one specimen in 1990; G. T. Watters, pers. comm.) at a site (U.S. Highway 27 crossing, Gadsden-Leon counties, Florida) where it was once fairly common. Construction of a new bridge span in the mid-1970s may have had a detrimental effect on the population (W. H. Heard, pers. comm.) A few dead shells have appeared infrequently in recent collections. Although it may have been overlooked because of its diminutive size and affinity for stream channels, endangered status is warranted for the Ochlockonee moccasinshell in Florida.

RECOMMENDATIONS: This is the second extremely uncommon mussel (see *Alasmidonta wrightiana* account) endemic to the Ochlockonee River. A thorough survey of the mainstem upstream and downstream of Lake Talquin and principal tributaries is needed to determine the present status of Florida populations of the Ochlockonee moccasinshell.

Distribution of the Ochlockonee moccasinshell, *Medionidus simpsonianus.*

PREPARED BY: James D. Williams, National Biological Survey, 7920 N.W.
71st Street, Gainesville, FL 32653, and Robert S. Butler, U.S. Fish and Wildlife Service, 6620 Southpoint Drive South, Jacksonville, FL 32216.

FAMILY UNIONIDAE

Threatened

Fat Threeridge
Amblema neislerii (Lea)

DESCRIPTION: *Amblema neislerii* is medium-sized to large, subquadrate,
inflated, solid, and heavy shelled. It reaches a length of 102 mm (4.0 in).
Older, larger individuals are so inflated that their width approximates their

height. The umbos are in the anterior quarter of the shell. The dark brown to black shell is strongly sculptured with seven to nine prominent horizontal parallel ridges. Internally, there are two subequal pseudocardinals in the left valve and typically one large and one small tooth in the right valve. The nacre is bluish white to light purplish and very iridescent.

RANGE: An Apalachicola River system endemic, the fat threeridge is restricted to the Flint River in Georgia and the Apalachicola and Chipola rivers in Florida (Clench and Turner 1956; Burch 1975). In the Apalachicola River it is known from two localities in Calhoun and Gadsden counties, Florida. Its distribution in the Chipola River extends from Scotts Ferry, Calhoun County, downstream to Wewahitchka, Gulf County, Florida.

There are two published records of *Amblema neislerii* from the Escambia River in Florida. The first was by Wright (1897), who listed it as one of several species occurring with a new species he was describing. The second re-

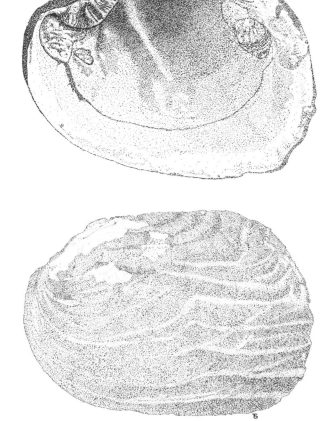

Fat Threeridge, *Amblema neisleri,* UF 229775, length 65.8 mm (2.6 in). Florida, Gulf County, Chipola River, Florida Highway 22 east of Wewahitchka (illustration by Tracy Smith).

Distribution of the fat threeridge, *Amblema neislerii.*

port was Heard (1979), who listed *A. neislerii* as occurring in the Escambia River drainage in Florida. These records are believed to be based on *A. perplicata* not *A. neislerii*. All specimens of *Amblema* from the Escambia River in Florida and Alabama that we have examined are *A. perplicata.*

HABITAT: *Amblema neislerii* inhabits the main channel of small to large rivers in slow to moderate current. Substrate varies from gravel and rocky rubble to a mixture of sand and sandy mud.

LIFE HISTORY AND ECOLOGY: Unknown.

SPECIALIZED OR UNIQUE CHARACTERISTICS: The seven to nine horizontal parallel ridges and the highly inflated appearance of larger specimens make *A. neislerii* one of the most distinctive unionids in Florida.

BASIS FOR STATUS CLASSIFICATION: The restriction of *A. neislerii* to the main channels of the Chipola and Apalachicola rivers makes it vulnerable to a variety of environmental perturbations. The most serious threat is probably maintenance dredging in the Apalachicola River. High population levels of the exotic Asian clam *Corbicula fluminea* may also be adversely affecting this species.

RECOMMENDATIONS: Habitat protection in the Chipola and Apalachicola rivers is the highest priority in the conservation of *A. neislerii*. Effects of dredging on *A. neislerii* in the Apalachicola River should be determined as soon as possible. A battery salvage operation in the Chipola drainage is now an Environmental Protection Agency Superfund site. Maintenance of water quality in this system will help protect the sizable population in the lower reach of the Chipola River.

PREPARED BY: James D. Williams, National Biological Survey, 7920 N.W. 71st Street, Gainesville, FL 32653, and Robert S. Butler, U.S. Fish and Wildlife Service, 6620 Southpoint Drive South, Jacksonville, FL 32216.

FAMILY UNIONIDAE

Threatened

Flat Floater
Anodonta suborbiculata Say

DESCRIPTION: The flat floater is a large species that reaches over 130 mm (5.0 in) in length. The shell is compressed with a suborbiculate outline. The valves are thin but strong and fit imprecisely, leaving gaps both anteriorly and posteriorly. The ventral margin is rounded. A low posterior ridge forms a rounded point medially. At each end of the straight dorsal margin, wing-like structures are present, most prominent posteriorly. The umbos are low, compressed, and do not extend above the hinge line. Beak sculpture consists of a few irregular undulations with series of small but sharp tubercles. The periostracum is smooth and shining, and pale yellowish-green with fine green rays. Older specimens may become more yellow and tend to lose the raying. Internally, the umbonal cavity is shallow and adductor scars are indistinct. The valves are completely toothless as in other members of the genus. Nacre color is silvery, but some specimens may exhibit a purplish or bluish iridescence.

RANGE: *Anodonta suborbiculata* occurs in Gulf of Mexico drainages from the Trinity River in Texas east to Florida and north in the Mississippi River basin to southeastern Minnesota (Johnson 1980). In Florida, the flat floater is restricted to two localities in the Escambia River system, which is the southeasternmost portion of its range. In the Escambia drainage in Alabama,

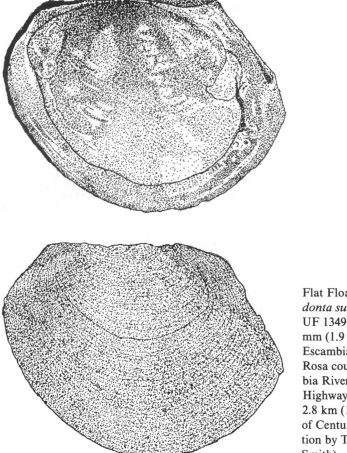

Flat Floater, *Anodonta suborbiculata*, UF 134930, length 48 mm (1.9 in). Florida, Escambia–Santa Rosa counties, Escambia River, Florida Highway 4 crossing, 2.8 km (1.4 mi) east of Century (illustration by Tracy Smith).

it is known only from Gantt Lake, an impoundment on the Conecuh River in Covington County (Johnson 1969).

HABITAT: The flat floater is generally found in medium-sized creek to large river backwaters as well as in oxbows, sloughs, and impoundments with muddy substrates (Johnson 1980; Gordon 1984). In Florida this species has been found in riverine habitat in sand with slow current (Butler 1989).

LIFE HISTORY AND ECOLOGY: Surber (1915) illustrated a glochidium of *A. suborbiculata*.

SPECIALIZED OR UNIQUE CHARACTERISTICS: The unique outline, compressed umbo below the hingeline, and the complete lack of hinge teeth

Distribution of the flat
floater, *Anodonta
suborbiculata.*

easily distinguish the flat floater from other freshwater mussels in extreme
northwestern Florida.

BASIS FOR STATUS CLASSIFICATION: *Anodonta suborbiculata* is
known in Florida from two records in the Escambia River system: Chu-
muckla Springs, Santa Rosa County, and the Escambia River near Century,
Escambia-Santa Rosa counties (Butler 1989). These two collections of single
specimens were made 70 years apart. The restricted distribution and sporadic
occurrence of *A. suborbiculata* in Florida is the basis for its threatened
status.

RECOMMENDATIONS: Thorough surveys of the sloughs, oxbows, and
backwater swamps of the extensive Escambia River floodplain are needed to
determine the status and conservation needs of *A. suborbiculata* in Florida.

PREPARED BY: James D. Williams, National Biological Survey, 7920 N.W.
71st Street, Gainesville, FL 32653, and Robert S. Butler, U.S. Fish and Wildlife Service, 6620 Southpoint Drive South, Jacksonville, FL 32216.

Threatened

Chipola Slabshell

Elliptio chipolaensis (Walker)

DESCRIPTION: This medium-sized species achieves a length of about 85 mm (3.3 in). The shell is ovate to subelliptical, somewhat inflated and with the posterior ridge starting out rounded but flattening to form a prominent biangulate margin. The surface is smooth and chestnut colored. Dark brown coloration may appear in the umbonal region and the remaining surface may exhibit alternating light and dark bands. The umbos are prominent, well above the hingeline. Internally, the umbonal cavity is rather deep. The lateral teeth are long, slender, and slightly curved; two in the left and one in the right valve. The pseudocardinal teeth are compressed and crenulate; two in the left and one in the right valve. Nacre color is salmon, becoming more intense dorsally and somewhat iridescent posteriorly.

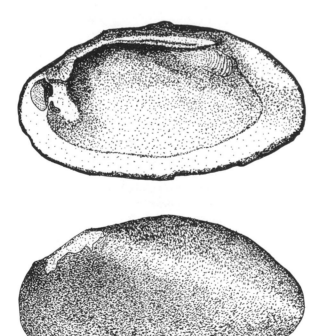

Chipola Slabshell, *Elliptio chipolaensis*, UF 4977, length 56.1 mm (2.2 in). Florida, Calhoun County, Chipola River, 3.2 km (2 mi) east of Clarksville (illustration by Tracy Smith).

Distribution of the Chipola slabshell, *Elliptio chipolaensis.*

RANGE: An endemic of the Chipola River drainage (van der Schalie 1940; Clench and Turner 1956), *E. chipolaensis* is generally distributed in the river mainstem and the lower portion of larger tributaries. The species apparently does not inhabit the river downstream from Dead Lake (Gulf County) and is also absent from most of the tributaries including the Alabama portion of the system (van der Schalie 1940).

HABITAT: *Elliptio chipolaensis* inhabits silty sand substrate of large creeks and the main channel of the Chipola River in slow to moderate current.

LIFE HISTORY AND ECOLOGY: Unknown.

SPECIALIZED OR UNIQUE CHARACTERISTICS: Among southern unionids, the Chipola slabshell is the only species that exhibits the combined characters of light and dark banded epidermis with a salmon nacre. At present, it is the only known mussel endemic to the Chipola River drainage.

BASIS FOR STATUS CLASSIFICATION: Any major habitat degradation in the Chipola drainage may seriously jeopardize the existence of *E. chipolaensis*. The restricted distribution of this endemic to a small river system also contributes to its threatened status.

RECOMMENDATIONS: Maintaining quality habitat in the Chipola River should insure the continued existence of the Chipola slabshell. An Environmental Protection Agency Superfund project on the site of a battery salvage operation near the river should help in achieving this goal.

PREPARED BY: James D. Williams, National Biological Survey, 7920 N.W. 71st Street, Gainesville, FL 32653, and Robert S. Butler, U.S. Fish and Wildlife Service, 6620 Southpoint Drive South, Jacksonville, FL 32216.

FAMILY UNIONIDAE

Threatened

Purple Bankclimber
Elliptoideus sloatianus (Lea)

DESCRIPTION: The purple bankclimber is the second largest freshwater mollusk in Florida, attaining a length of 203 mm (8.0 in). Its brownish black to black shell is subrhomboidal, moderately inflated, heavy, and strongly sculptured. A well developed posterior ridge extends from the umbos to the posterior ventral margin of the shell. The posterior slope and the disk just anterior to the posterior ridge are sculptured by several irregular ridges that vary greatly in development. Umbos are low, extending just above the dorsal margin of the shell. Internally, there is one pseudocardinal tooth in the right valve and two in the left valve. The lateral teeth are very thick and slightly curved. Nacre color is whitish near the center of the shell, becoming deep purple toward the margin, and very iridescent posteriorly. *Elliptoideus sloatianus* was considered a species of the genus *Elliptio* until Frierson (1927) erected the subgenus *Elliptoideus* based on the presence of glochidia in all four gills instead of two gills as is characteristic of the genus *Elliptio*.

RANGE: *Elliptoideus sloatianus* is known only from the Apalachicola River system in Alabama, Georgia, and Florida and from the Ochlockonee River in Florida (Clench and Turner 1956; Burch 1975). Historically, it occurred in the Chattahoochee River upstream to Columbus, Georgia, but has not been collected in that river since the mid-1800s. It has been collected, however, in the Flint River, an Apalachicola River tributary, in Georgia in recent years.

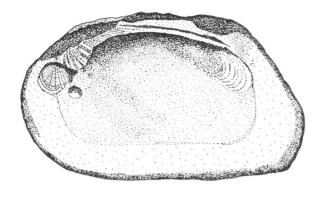

Purple Bankclimber, *Elliptoideus sloatianus*, UF 360, length 113 mm (4.4 in). Florida, Gadsden County, Apalachicola River (east bank) at Chattahoochee (illustration by Gina Collins).

In Florida, it occurs in the Apalachicola River below Jim Woodruff Dam downstream in the vicinity of the U.S. Highway 90 crossing at Chattahoochee, Gadsden County. Records from the Chipola River are from Dead Lake, Calhoun County. In the Ochlockonee River, it is known from three localities west and northwest of Tallahassee, in Gadsden and Leon counties. Heard (1979) reported one shell of *Elliptoideus* from the Escambia River near Century. In the absence of other records from the Escambia River and the intervening drainages, we believe this record is probably based on the conchologically similar *Plectomerus dombeyanus*.

HABITAT: The purple bankclimber inhabits small to large rivers in slow to moderate current over sand or sand mixed with mud or gravel substrates.

LIFE HISTORY AND ECOLOGY: The biology of *E. sloatianus* is essentially unknown. Lea (1863a) briefly described the soft anatomy based on three male specimens. Heard and Guckert (1971) included *Elliptoideus* in a group of unionid mollusks which were characterized by having all four gills serve as marsupial demibranchs and a tachytictic (short term breeders carrying glochidia only during summer) reproductive strategy.

Distribution of the purple
bankclimber, *Elliptoideus
sloatianus.*

SPECIALIZED OR UNIQUE CHARACTERISTICS: *Elliptoideus* is a
monotypic genus and represents one of the two largest freshwater mollusks
in the state of Florida.

BASIS FOR STATUS CLASSIFICATION: This species is confined to the
Apalachicola and Ochlockonee river systems. In the Apalachicola River it is
known only from the area below Jim Woodruff Dam downstream for a distance of about 1.5 km (1 mi). While it has been found living in this area in
recent years, the population is dominated by very large, old individuals. It
has not been found in the Chipola River since the 1950s so its current status
in this system is unknown. In the Ochlockonee River the purple bankclimber
appears to be confined to the upper reaches of the river, above Lake Talquin
in Gadsden and Leon counties. Based on observations during the past 15
years, populations in this area appear stable. Continued success of the Ochlockonee population depends mostly on good water quality from the headwaters in southwest Georgia. Habitat alteration resulting from maintenance
dredging in the Apalachicola River is a threat to the purple bankclimber.

Threatened status for *Elliptoideus* is based on its restricted distribution, uncertainty of the Chipola River population, and the age structure of the population in the Apalachicola River.

RECOMMENDATIONS: A thorough survey to determine the current status of *Elliptoideus* in the Apalachicola and Chipola rivers is needed before conservation actions can be initiated in these rivers. The survey should also determine the reproductive status of the population below Jim Woodruff Dam. In the Ochlockonee River, protection of the existing population and actions to prevent deterioration of riparian habitat and water quality are the highest priority conservation activities. A survey of the Ochlockonee River below Lake Talquin should be undertaken to determine whether population might exist there.

PREPARED BY: James D. Williams, National Biological Survey, 7920 N.W. 71st Street, Gainesville, FL 32653, and Robert S. Butler, U.S. Fish and Wildlife Service, 6620 Southpoint Drive South, Jacksonville, FL 32216.

FAMILY UNIONIDAE

Threatened

Narrow Pigtoe
Fusconaia escambia (Clench and Turner)

DESCRIPTION: *Fusconaia escambia* is a small species, rarely exceeding 50 mm (2.0 in) in length, and subcircular in outline. It has a smooth, moderately heavy shell, somewhat inflated and with broad, full, and high umbos. The posterior ridge is well developed and ends in a point (angle slightly more than 90°) posteriorly. The posterior slope is slightly concave. Color of *F. escambia* varies from dark reddish brown to blackish. Internally the hinge plate is broad, heavy, and slightly arcuate. There is one large pseudocardinal tooth in the right valve and two in the left valve. The nacre is highly iridescent and white to salmon colored.

RANGE: The narrow pigtoe was first discovered in the Escambia River near Century, Escambia-Santa Rosa counties, Florida, which was designated the type locality (Clench and Turner 1956). Subsequently, it was found to occur upstream in the Conecuh River below Gantt Lake, Covington County, Alabama. Johnson (1969) reported the first record of *F. escambia* from the Yellow River, Okaloosa County, Florida.

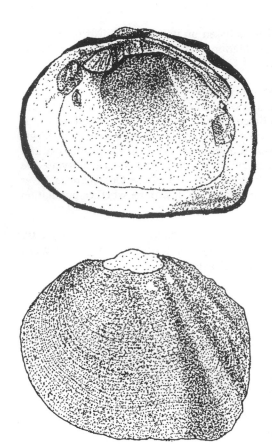

Narrow Pigtoe, *Fusconaia escambia*, UF 4997 (paratype), length 41 mm (1.6 in). Florida, Escambia County, Escambia River, 4.8 km (3 mi) southeast of Century (illustration by Tracy Smith).

HABITAT: *Fusconaia escambia* inhabits the main channel of small to medium-sized rivers with slow to moderate current over gravel, gravel mixed with sand, or a silty sand substrate.

LIFE HISTORY AND ECOLOGY: Unknown.

SPECIALIZED OR UNIQUE CHARACTERISTICS: *Fusconaia escambia* appears to be the southeasternmost representative of the *F. flava* species group, which is more widespread in the western Gulf Coast drainages and the Mississippi River system.

BASIS FOR STATUS CLASSIFICATION: The limited distribution of *F. escambia*, restricted habitat and paucity of collections, and deterioration of water quality in the Escambia River are the major reasons for assigning threatened conservation status.

Distribution of the narrow
pigtoe, *Fusconaia escambia.*

RECOMMENDATIONS: Protection of habitat in the Escambia and Yellow
rivers is crucial to the conservation of *F. escambia.* Of these two rivers the
Escambia River is probably the most important since it potentially supports
the largest population. A thorough survey of the Escambia and Yellow rivers
to determine current distribution and population levels of *F. escambia* is also
needed.

PREPARED BY: James D. Williams, National Biological Survey, 7920 N.W.
71st Street, Gainesville, FL 32653, and Robert S. Butler, U.S. Fish and Wildlife Service, 6620 Southpoint Drive South, Jacksonville, FL 32216.

Threatened

Southern Pocketbook

Lampsilis ornata (Conrad)

DESCRIPTION: *Lampsilis ornata* is a large mussel that reaches about 125 mm (4.9 in) in length. The shell is inflated and broadly oval with an angular posterior ridge. Umbos, appearing high and full, are located anterior to the center of the shell. The epidermis is smooth and shining on the disk, becoming somewhat roughened and wrinkled on the posterior slope. *Lampsilis ornata* is yellow to brownish yellow with narrow light to dark green rays. There are two compressed pseudocardinal teeth in the left valve; the larger anterior tooth is triangular in outline. The two small lateral teeth are located near the middle of the hinge plate. In the right valve there are two moderately compressed pseudocardinals and a single, high lateral tooth. Internally, the nacre is white or bluish white to pale salmon and somewhat iridescent.

Distribution of the southern pocketbook, *Lampsilis ornata*.

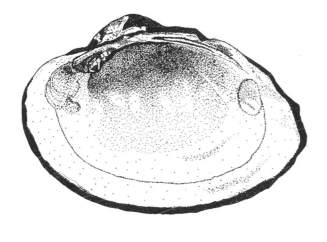

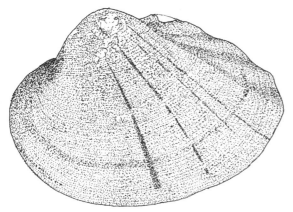

Southern Pocket-book, *Lampsilis ornata*, UF 20740, length 78.6 mm (3.1 in). Florida, Escambia County, Escambia River, 4.8 km (3 mi) southeast of Century (illustration by Tracy Smith).

RANGE: The southern pocketbook occurs in eastern Gulf drainages from the Amite River of Louisiana (Vidrine 1985) eastward to the Escambia River system of Alabama and Florida (Clench and Turner 1956; Burch 1975). In Florida, it is known only from the main channel of the Escambia River near the Alabama border downstream to McDavid in northern Escambia and Santa Rosa counties.

HABITAT: *Lampsilis ornata* is typically found in large creeks to rivers where it inhabits sand and gravel substrates with slow to moderate current. It has also been found in pools and backwater areas where there is little current and the substrate is predominantly mud.

LIFE HISTORY AND ECOLOGY: There is very little published information on the life history of *L. ornata*. Lea (1874) briefly described and figured the glochidia, but provided no information on the reproductive period. Ortmann (1924) reported a gravid female from the Black Warrior River, Alabama, collected 15 October 1912, and briefly described the soft anatomy of the female and the glochidia.

SPECIALIZED OR UNIQUE CHARACTERISTICS: In Florida, *L. ornata* is the only unionid with a high umbo, angular posterior ridge, and yellowish color with green rays.

BASIS FOR STATUS CLASSIFICATION: The conservation status of this species is based on its restricted distribution in Florida and its low population levels in the Escambia River.

RECOMMENDATIONS: Action should be taken to protect the remaining habitat of *L. ornata* in Florida. The states of Alabama and Florida should address the pollution problems in the Escambia drainage which potentially degrade the Florida portion of the river.

PREPARED BY: James D. Williams, National Biological Survey, 7920 N.W. 71st Street, Gainesville, FL 32653, and Robert S. Butler, U.S. Fish and Wildlife Service, 6620 Southpoint Drive South, Jacksonville, FL 32216.

FAMILY UNIONIDAE

Threatened

Gulf Moccasinshell
Medionidus penicillatus (Lea)

DESCRIPTION: *Medionidus penicillatus* reaches a length of about 55 mm (2.2 in) and is elongate-elliptical or rhomboidal and fairly inflated, and has relatively thin valves. The ventral margin is nearly straight or slightly rounded. The posterior ridge is rounded to slightly angled and intersects the end of the shell at the base line. Females tend to have the posterior point above the ventral margin and are somewhat more inflated. Sculpturing consists of a series of thin, radially oriented plications along the length of the posterior slope. The remainder of the surface is smooth and yellowish to greenish brown with fine, typically interrupted green rays. The left valve has two stubby pseudocardinal and two arcuate lateral teeth. The right valve has one pseudocardinal and one lateral tooth. Nacre color is smokey purple or greenish and slightly iridescent at the posterior end. (See the DESCRIPTION section of *Medionidus simpsonianus* Walker for a discussion of the taxonomic history of eastern Gulf Coast drainages of *Medionidus*).

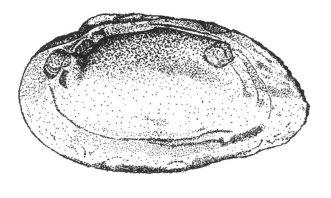

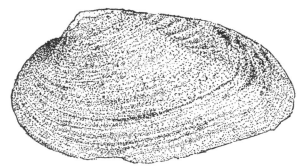

Gulf Moccasinshell, *Medionidus penicillatus*, UF 4161, length 45.4 mm (1.8 in). Florida, Jackson County, Spring Creek, 4.8 km (3 mi) southeast of Marianna (illustration by Tracy Smith).

RANGE: The gulf moccasinshell is reported from the Yellow River in Alabama and Apalachicola River system in Alabama, Georgia, and Florida. It has also been found in the Econfina Creek drainage (Johnson 1977), and the Choctawhatchee River system (Butler 1989), both in Florida. Florida records are from Walton (Choctawhatchee River system), Bay (Econfina Creek drainage), Jackson and Calhoun (Chipola River drainage), and Gadsden (Apalachicola River) counties.

HABITAT: The gulf moccasinshell inhabits medium-sized creeks to large rivers with sand and gravel substrates in slow to moderate currents.

LIFE HISTORY AND ECOLOGY: Very little is known about *M. penicillatus*. Lea (1858) figured the subspatulate glochidium and later discussed the soft anatomy (Lea 1863a).

UNIQUE OR SPECIALIZED CHARACTERISTICS: This species is not easily confused with any other species in its range, except *Quincuncina burkei* in the Choctawhatchee River system.

BASIS FOR STATUS CLASSIFICATION: Although known from several stations in the Chipola River drainage (van der Schalie 1940) and single sites on the Apalachicola River and Econfina Creek, recent material from Florida

Distribution of the Gulf
moccasinshell, *Medionidus
penicillatus.*

drainages is scarce. The gulf moccasinshell has recently been found live in
Econfina Creek, Bay County (two specimens in 1987), and the lower Chipola
River mainstem above Dead Lake near Scotts Ferry, Calhoun County (one
specimen in 1988). The population reported from Chattahoochee on the
Apalachicola River in Gadsden County (Clench and Turner 1956; Johnson
1977) is most likely extirpated. The present status of *M. penicillatus* in the
Yellow and Choctawhatchee river systems is unknown.

RECOMMENDATIONS: Protecting the nearly pristine Chipola and Econfina watersheds will aid in the perpetuation of *M. penicillatus* in Florida.
Abundance (1,000+ per square meter) of the Asian clam *Corbicula fluminea*
(Müller) has drastically altered the substrate microhabitat at the Chattahoochee site, making it unlikely that *M. penicillatus* could inhabit that area.
Research on negative effects of *C. fluminea* on native unionids is needed to
determine future conservation strategies of this and other species.

PREPARED BY: James D. Williams, National Biological Survey, 7920 N.W.
71st Street, Gainesville, FL 32653, and Robert S. Butler, U.S. Fish and Wildlife Service, 6620 Southpoint Drive South, Jacksonville, FL 32216.

Threatened

Suwannee Moccasinshell

Medionidus walkeri (Wright)

DESCRIPTION: The Suwannee moccasinshell is a small species rarely exceeding 50 mm (2.0 in) in length. The shell is subrhomboid and moderately inflated, and the valves are relatively thick. The high, angular posterior ridge and slope have a series of coarse, radially-curved corrugations that sometimes extend onto the disk. The umbos are high and located on the anterior third of the shell. The periostracum is greenish to black with inconspicuous broad green rays. Females are longer than males and have postbasal swelling and posterior point above the ventral margin. Internally, the left valve has two compressed pseudocardinal and two short lateral teeth. The right valve has single pseudocardinal and lateral teeth. Nacre color varies from bluish white to light pinkish. (See the DESCRIPTION section of *Medionidus simpsonianus* for a discussion of the taxonomic history of *Medionidus* species in eastern Gulf Coast drainages).

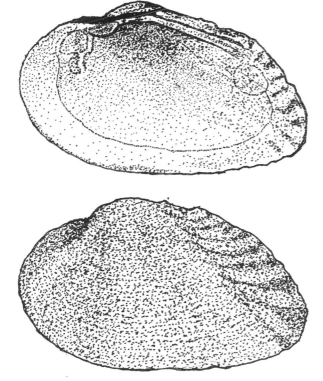

Suwannee Moccasinshell, *Medionidus walkeri*, UF 133932, length 41.5 (1.6 in). Florida, Suwannee County, Suwannee River at Branford (illustration by Tracy Smith).

Distribution of the Suwannee
moccasinshell, *Medionidus
walkeri.*

RANGE: *Medionidus walkeri* is endemic to the Suwannee River system in
Florida (Johnson 1977) and recorded from sites along the mainstem from
Fanning Springs (Levy County) upstream to the Withlacoochee River con-
fluence at Ellaville (Madison-Suwannee counties), at Blue Spring on the
Withlacoochee River (Madison County), and in the Santa Fe River drainage
above the Santa Fe Sink (Alachua, Bradford, and Union counties). Records
for *M. penicillatus* from the Suwannee River system (Clench and Turner
1956; Burch 1975) are actually *M. walkeri*. At present, no records are available in the Georgia portions of the Withlacoochee or Alapaha rivers, the major northern tributaries of the Suwannee River system.

HABITAT: Clear medium-sized creeks to rivers with muddy sand or sand
with some gravel in slow to moderate current.

LIFE HISTORY AND ECOLOGY: Unknown.

SPECIALIZED OR UNIQUE CHARACTERISTICS: The sharp posterior
ridge and generally dark and rayless shells distinguish *M. walkeri* from other

Medionidus species in the Gulf drainage. The Suwannee moccasinshell is apparently one of the few unionids endemic to the state of Florida.

BASIS FOR STATUS CLASSIFICATION: Johnson (1977) stated that *M. walkeri* was abundant at the type locality (Suwannee River, Ellaville, Madison County), but uncommon at other localities. Although the New River (Santa Fe River drainage) has yielded numerous specimens in the past 15 years, it is presently rare in the drainage. Large series were collected 55 years ago, but the present status of the population at the Santa Fe River Sink (Alachua County) is unknown. Phosphate mining has affected the Suwannee River system upstream of Ellaville and may have contributed to the decline of the once large population known from the type locality. These adverse effects and the restricted distribution of the low density populations are the basis for the threatened status of the Suwannee moccasinshell in Florida.

RECOMMENDATIONS: The most pristine refugium for this diminutive species remains the upper Santa Fe River drainage. The population in the New River must be protected by ensuring good water quality and protection of riparian areas. Lack of development in the watershed should aid in the perpetuation of the Suwannee moccasinshell. Thorough inventories of known localities, particularly in the Santa Fe watershed, and upper Suwannee and Withlacoochee rivers, are required to determine the present status of *M. walkeri*.

PREPARED BY: James D. Williams, National Biological Survey, 7920 N.W. 71st Street, Gainesville, FL 32653, and Robert S. Butler, U.S. Fish and Wildlife Service, 6620 Southpoint Drive South, Jacksonville, FL 32216.

FAMILY UNIONIDAE

Threatened

Oval Pigtoe
Pleurobema pyriforme (Lea)

DESCRIPTION: *Pleurobema pyriforme* is a small to medium-sized species that attains a length of about 60 mm (2.4 in). The shell is suboviform compressed, with a shiny smooth epidermis. The periostracum is yellowish or chestnut, rayless, with distinct growth lines. The posterior slope is biangulate and forms a blunt point on the posterior margin. The umbos are slightly elevated above the hingeline. As is typical of the genus, no sexual dimorphism is displayed in shell characters. Internally, the pseudocardinal teeth are fairly large, crenulate, and double in both valves. The lateral teeth are somewhat shortened, arcuate and double in each valve. Nacre color varies from salmon to bluish white and is iridescent posteriorly.

RANGE: The oval pigtoe is an Apalachicola River system endemic, with a Florida range restricted to the Chipola River drainage. Earlier records of *Pleurobema* east of the Apalachicola River (Ochlockonee and Suwannee rivers) by Clench and Turner (1956), Johnson (1970), Burch (1975) and Heard (1979) refer to *P. reclusum*, which those authors considered a synonym of *P. pyriforme* (see DESCRIPTION section of the *P. reclusum* account). We recognize records of the oval pigtoe from headwater tributaries in Jackson County and sites along the lower river mainstem downstream to Dead Lake, Calhoun County.

HABITAT: *Pleurobema pyriforme* occurs in medium-sized creeks to small rivers where it inhabits silty sand to sand and gravel substrates, usually in slow to moderate current. Stream channels with clean substrates appear to offer the best habitat for the oval pigtoe.

LIFE HISTORY AND ECOLOGY: Unknown.

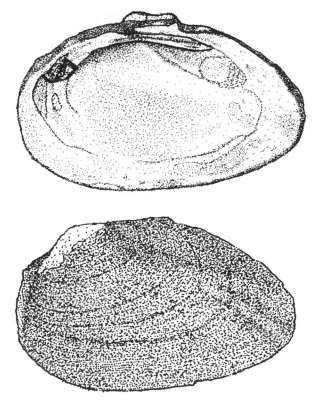

Oval Pigtoe, *Pleurobema pyriforme*, UF 413, length 43.1 mm (1.7 in). Florida, Jackson County, Chipola River, 1.6 km (1 mi) north of Marianna (illustration by Tracy Smith).

Distribution of the oval pigtoe, *Pleurobema pyriforme*.

SPECIALIZED OR UNIQUE CHARACTERISTICS: In Florida, *P. pyriforme* is restricted to the Chipola River drainage.

BASIS FOR STATUS CLASSIFICATION: Recent collections have located
a population at a lower mainstem site and a tributary, Dry Creek. However,
any drastic changes in water quality in the Chipola River drainage could eradicate *P. pyriforme* from Florida waters. The restricted range and potential
water quality problems in the Chipola River are the basis for threatened conservation status for the oval pigtoe.

RECOMMENDATIONS: An inventory of the poorly surveyed lower Chipola mainstem and the larger tributaries in the system is needed to determine
the extent of Florida populations.

PREPARED BY: James D. Williams, National Biological Survey, 7920 N.W.
71st Street, Gainesville, FL 32653, and Robert S. Butler, U.S. Fish and Wildlife Service, 6620 Southpoint Drive South, Jacksonville, FL 32216.

FAMILY UNIONIDAE

Threatened

Fuzzy Pigtoe

Pleurobema strodeanum (Wright)

DESCRIPTION: *Pleurobema strodeanum* is a small to medium-sized species that reaches a length of approximately 61 mm (2.4 in). The outline of
the shell is subtriangular or subcircular with a broadly rounded ventral margin. The posterior margin is obtusely angular, resulting from the broad, bi-
angulated, and flattened posterior slope. The surface is usually slightly
roughened, appearing satiny or clothlike, although some specimens may appear smooth. Surface color is dark green to black and rayless. The umbos
are somewhat pointed and barely extend above the hingeline. The pseudocardinal teeth are prominent and double in each valve. The lateral teeth are
well developed, arcuate and also double in each valve. The color of the nacre
is white, oftentimes with a bluish tint, and slightly iridescent marginally.

Distribution of the fuzzy
pigtoe, *Pleurobema
strodeanum.*

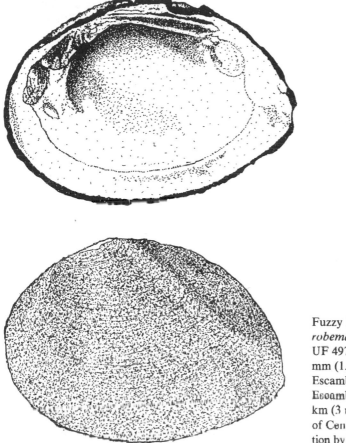

Fuzzy Pigtoe, *Pleurobema strodeanum*, UF 4973, length 38.4 mm (1.5 in). Florida, Escambia County, Escambia River, 4.8 km (3 mi) southeast of Century (illustration by Tracy Smith).

RANGE: The fuzzy pigtoe occurs in the Escambia and Choctawhatchee river systems of Alabama and Florida and in the geographically intermediate Yellow River in Alabama (Clench and Turner 1956; Burch 1975). There are several Florida collections from the Choctawhatchee mainstem and from several of its tributaries in Walton and Holmes counties. Two records are known for the Escambia River, Escambia and Santa Rosa counties, Florida.

HABITAT: An inhabitant of medium-sized creeks to rivers, *P. strodeanum* occurs in sand and silty sand substrates in slow current.

LIFE HISTORY AND ECOLOGY: Unknown.

BASIS FOR STATUS CLASSIFICATION: The fuzzy pigtoe is known from several localities in the Choctawhatchee River system. However, material from elsewhere in Florida is scarce. Recent material from Florida localities in general is scant and most records are 35 to 55 years old. For these reasons, Florida populations of this species should be considered threatened.

RECOMMENDATIONS: Sites that historically sustained populations of *P. strodeanum*, particularly the Choctawhatchee River system, need to be resurveyed to determine the present status of populations in Florida.

PREPARED BY: James D. Williams, National Biological Survey, 7920 N.W. 71st Street, Gainesville, FL 32653, and Robert S. Butler, U.S. Fish and Wildlife Service, 6620 Southpoint Drive South, Jacksonville, FL 32216.

FAMILY UNIONIDAE

Threatened

Tapered Pigtoe
Quincuncina burkei Walker

DESCRIPTION: The tapered pigtoe is a small to medium-sized mussel that attains a length of 71 mm (2.8 in), but generally is less than 50 mm (2.0 in) in length. Subelliptical to subtriangular in outline, the shell has a fairly sharp posterior ridge that intersects the posterior end near the base line, which is nearly straight. Series of radial plications appear in rows down the posterior slope and, when present on the disk, appear as chevron shaped sculpture. The degree of sculpture is sometimes reduced, particularly on the disk. The surface is uniformly dark brown and shiny, but roughened anteriorly and posteriorly. Young individuals may appear light brown with faint green rays. The pseudocardinal teeth are fairly strong and well developed; two in the left and one in the right valve. The lateral teeth are fairly thick and somewhat arcuate; two in the left and one in the right valve. The color of the nacre is bluish white.

RANGE: *Quincuncina burkei* is an endemic of the Choctawhatchee River system of Alabama and Florida (Clench and Turner 1956; Burch 1975). In Florida it has been found in the mainstem sites and in several of the tributaries in Holmes, Jackson, Walton, and Washington counties.

HABITAT: An inhabitant of medium-sized creeks to large rivers, *Q. burkei* lives in stable sand with some gravel to silty sand substrates in slow to moderate current.

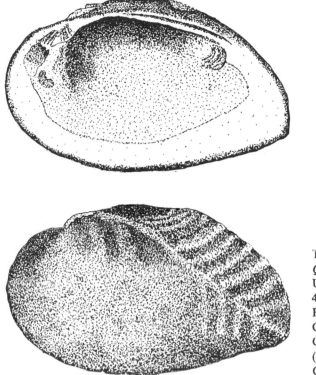

Tapered Pigtoe, *Quincuncina burkei*, UF 64976, length 44.8 mm (1.8 in). Florida, Jackson County, Holmes Creek near Graceville (illustration by Gina Collins).

LIFE HISTORY AND ECOLOGY: Unknown.

SPECIALIZED OR UNIQUE CHARACTERISTICS: The shell sculpture and size of *Quincuncina burkei* readily separate it from other Florida unionids with the possible exception of *Medionidus penicillatus*.

BASIS FOR STATUS CLASSIFICATION: Collections of *Q. burkei* along the Choctawhatchee River mainstem in Florida are generally over 50 years old. Its current status in that system is not known. Good populations apparently remain in a few tributaries in Holmes and Walton counties. Restriction to large stream habitat in a single drainage system increases the vulnerability of this species.

RECOMMENDATIONS: Mainstem Choctawhatchee River sites are in need of surveys to ascertain the status of the tapered pigtoe in river habitat. Preservation of good water quality in tributaries should aid in the preservation of *Q. burkei* in Florida.

Distribution of the tapered
pigtoe, *Quincuncina burkei.*

PREPARED BY: James D. Williams, National Biological Survey, 7920 N.W.
71st Street, Gainesville, FL 32653, and Robert S. Butler, U.S. Fish and Wildlife Service, 6620 Southpoint Drive South, Jacksonville, FL 32216.

FAMILY UNIONIDAE

Threatened

Southern Creekmussel

Strophitus subvexus (Conrad)

DESCRIPTION: The southern creekmussel is a moderately large species
that attains a length of 181 mm (7.1 in), although a length of less than 125

mm (4.9 in) is more common. It is suboval to elliptical in outline and moderately inflated. The anterior end is rounded and the posterior end is subtruncate to rounded. The dorsal margin is short and broadly rounded. The ventral margin is nearly straight to slightly arcuate in larger individuals. Umbos, located near the anterior third of the shell, have low concentric ridges and are slightly inflated and usually raised above the hinge line. Shell thickness varies from thin to moderately thick. Periostracum color varies from greenish yellow to brownish with green rays often present on the posterior slope. A single low, stumpy, pseudocardinal tooth is present in each valve; lateral teeth are absent. Color of the nacre is typically bluish white and iridescent.

The generic and specific recognition of *S. subvexus* has varied during the past century. It was reported by Clench and Turner (1956) as *Anodontoides Elliotti*, and by van der Schalie (1940) as *Strophitus spillmani*. Johnson (1967) reexamined the systematic and taxonomic questions and recognized one species on the Gulf Coast, *Strophitus subvexus*, a decision that is currently followed by most researchers.

RANGE: *Strophitus subvexus* occurs in most Gulf Coast drainages from the Sabine River in Louisiana (Vidrine 1985) east to the Apalachicola River system in Florida and Georgia (Johnson 1967; Burch 1975). In Florida the southern creekmussel is known from several localities in the Chipola River system and one locality in the Choctawhatchee River system (White Creek,

Southern Creekmussel, *Strophitus subvexus*, UF 4996, length 47 mm (1.8 in). Florida, Jackson County, Chipola River, 1.6 km (1 mi) north of Marianna (illustration by Tracy Smith).

Distribution of the southern
creekmussel, *Strophitus*
subvexus.

Walton County). The Florida records are based on collections made prior to
1957 except for a recent (1988) live collection of a single specimen from Dry
Creek, a Chipola River tributary.

HABITAT: The southern creekmussel, as its vernacular name implies, typically inhabits small to large creeks, but individuals have been found in small
to large rivers. Substrate varies from sand to sandy mud in slow or no
current.

LIFE HISTORY AND ECOLOGY: Unknown.

SPECIALIZED OR UNIQUE CHARACTERISTICS: *Strophitus subvexus*
is one of two Florida mussels (see *Anodontoides radiatus* account) with a
single pseudocardinal tooth in each valve and no lateral teeth.

BASIS FOR STATUS CLASSIFICATION: The paucity of records and the
fact that only one of these is recent suggest that the survival of this species in
Florida is in jeopardy. The single known collection from the Choctawhatchee

River system was taken in 1933. It is possible that the only Florida population presently surviving is in the Chipola River drainage. While the main channel of the Chipola River has experienced periodic water quality problems, some tributaries have remained in fair condition.

RECOMMENDATIONS: Actions to prevent deterioration of the remaining habitat are needed immediately. A survey of the Chipola River system is needed to determine the extent and number of populations in that system. The Choctawhatchee River system needs to be surveyed to determine whether populations of the southern creekmussel are extant there.

PREPARED BY: James D. Williams, National Biological Survey, 7920 N.W. 71st Street, Gainesville, FL 32653, and Robert S. Butler, U.S. Fish and Wildlife Service, 6620 Southpoint Drive South, Jacksonville, FL 32216.

FAMILY UNIONIDAE

Threatened

Southern Sandshell

Villosa australis (Simpson)

DESCRIPTION: *Villosa australis* is a medium-sized species that attains a length of about 72 mm (2.8 in). The shell is subelliptical, moderately inflated with a low rounded posterior slope, and the bluntly pointed posterior end is above the longitudinal axis. The surface is smooth and shiny, generally dark brown or black over much of the shell except portions of the margins, which may abruptly appear greenish yellow with green rays of variable width. Young shells lack the dark brown or black coloration. Sexual dimorphism is not as pronounced in *V. australis* as in several other *Villosa* species. Female shells, however, are more inflated in the postbasal area and appear less pointed than male shells. Internally, the umbonal cavities are moderately deep, the hinge teeth thin and slightly arcuate whereas the pseudocardinal teeth are rather thick and well developed; two in the left valve and one in the right valve. The nacre is bluish white and moderately iridescent posteriorly.

Previous investigators have generally placed this species in the genus *Lampsilis* (Simpson 1900a,b, 1914; Clench and Turner 1956; Athearn 1964; Burch 1975; Turgeon et al. 1988). However, for this report the species has been placed in *Villosa* following Heard (1979), who made the designation based on the absence of mantle flaps, and presence of branchial villi, characters typical of the genus *Villosa*. Species of the genus *Lampsilis* are defined, in part, by the presence of well defined mantle flaps.

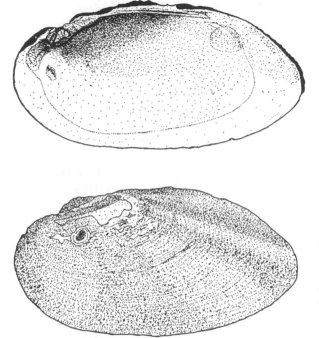

Southern Sandshell, *Villosa australis*, UF 2600, length 74.9 mm (2.9 in). Florida, Walton County, White Creek (illustration by Tracy Smith).

RANGE: The southern sandshell is found in the Escambia, Yellow, and Choctawhatchee river systems in Alabama and Florida (Fuller and Bereza 1973; Burch 1975). At present, however, no records are known for the Florida portions of the Escambia or the Yellow river systems. This presumably limits its distribution in Florida to tributaries of the Choctawhatchee River system and possibly the mainstem in Holmes, Jackson, Walton, and Washington counties.

HABITAT: *Villosa australis* generally occurs in clear medium-sized creeks to rivers. It inhabits sand substrates with woody debris in channels with slow to moderate current.

LIFE HISTORY AND ECOLOGY: Nothing has been published on the biology of *V. australis*. However, it may be unique among unionids in discharging the entire contents of the gravid inner pair of marsupial gills into a single glochidial mass or "super" conglutinate. This phenomenon was observed by one of the authors (RSB) and W. R. Hoeh in Limestone Creek, Walton County, Florida, on 25 June 1988. The "super" conglutinate was found in a long gelatinous strand dangling from woody debris below a female mussel partially buried in the sand. The glochidial mass resembles a caterpillar or grub and, when tangled in sticks in flowing water, presumably presents itself as an easy meal to potential host fish.

Distribution of the southern
sandshell, *Villosa australis.*

SPECIALIZED OR UNIQUE CHARACTERISTICS: The dark shell, abruptly margined by greenish yellow, is unique among southern unionids. Fuller and Bereza (1973) suggested that this species belonged to a yet undescribed genus, but failed to note specific reasons for its distinctiveness. *Villosa australis* may be deserving of generic status based on its unique mode of expelling glochidia.

BASIS FOR STATUS CLASSIFICATION: Records of *V. australis* in Florida are limited to a few localities. Generally uncommon, it appears to be thriving only in Limestone Creek, the only sizable tributary of the Pea River (Choctawhatchee River system) in the state. Siltation may preclude the continued existence of this clean water species in the Choctawhatchee River mainstem in Florida.

RECOMMENDATIONS: Preserving the water quality of streams in the Choctawhatchee River system is paramount in the protection of the southern sandshell. High quality streams should be surveyed to locate additional populations of this interesting mussel.

PREPARED BY: James D. Williams, National Biological Survey, 7920 N.W.
71st Street, Gainesville, FL 32653, and Robert S. Butler, U.S. Fish and Wildlife Service, 6620 Southpoint Drive South, Jacksonville, FL 32216.

FAMILY UNIONIDAE

Threatened

Choctaw Bean

Villosa choctawensis Athearn

DESCRIPTION: The shell of this small species measures no more than 42 mm (1.6 in). Subelliptical in shape, it is fairly inflated with a slightly thickened margin. The posterior ridge is low and rounded. The surface is chestnut to brownish black with fine green rays of variable extent. Shell texture is shiny smooth on the disk, but may be roughened to varying degrees, particularly ventrally and posteriorly. Female shells are truncate to broadly rounded posteriorly, whereas male specimens display a more evenly rounded or bluntly pointed posterior margin. Umbo sculpture consists of a few thin undulating ridges. The umbonal cavities are somewhat deep, whereas the anterior adductor scar is well defined. The left valve has two moderately thickened, nearly straight lateral teeth and two well developed pseudocardinal teeth. The right valve has one prominent and a vestigial secondary lateral tooth and one large and one or two poorly developed pseudocardinal teeth. Nacre color varies from white to a blotched smokey brown, and is somewhat iridescent posteriorly.

RANGE: According to Athearn (1964), Johnson (1967), and Burch (1975) the Choctaw bean is endemic to the Choctawhatchee River system in Alabama and Florida. Butler (1989) extended its range to include the Yellow River system in Alabama and Florida as well as the Escambia River system in Alabama. Records for the Florida portion of the Escambia, however, were unknown until a specimen was recently located in the Smithsonian Institution from the Escambia River, near Century, Escambia and Santa Rosa counties. In Florida, this species is also reported from the mainstem Choctawhatchee River from the vicinity of the FL Highway 20 crossing upstream to the U.S. Highway 90 crossing and Yellow River near the Alabama border in Okaloosa County.

HABITAT: *Villosa choctawensis* inhabits small to medium-sized rivers with sand to silty sand substrates in moderate to swift current (Athearn 1964).

Choctaw Bean, *Villosa choctawensis*, UF 18868, length 34.7 mm (1.4 in). Florida, Holmes County, Choctawhatchee River, 3.2 km (2 mi) southwest of Caryville (illustration by Tracy Smith).

LIFE HISTORY AND ECOLOGY: Unknown.

BASIS FOR STATUS CLASSIFICATION: Because of its apparent rarity and restriction in Florida to several sites along the mainstem of the Choctawhatchee River and single sites on the Escambia and Yellow rivers, *V. choctawensis* is deserving of threatened status.

RECOMMENDATIONS: The maintenance of high water quality in the Escambia, Yellow, and Choctawhatchee rivers should safeguard populations of this threatened species.

PREPARED BY: James D. Williams, National Biological Survey, 7920 N.W. 71st Street, Gainesville, FL 32653, and Robert S. Butler, U.S. Fish and Wildlife Service, 6620 Southpoint Drive South, Jacksonville, FL 32216.

Distribution of the Choctaw
bean, *Villosa choctawensis.*

FAMILY UNIONIDAE

Species of Special Concern

Purple Pigtoe

Fusconaia succissa (Lea)

DESCRIPTION: *Fusconaia succissa* is a medium-sized species that attains a length of about 60 mm (2.4 in). The shell is subcircular in outline and has a poorly developed posterior ridge. Specimens in the western portion of its range tend to be thicker shelled than those in eastern drainages. Olivaceous brown to nearly black in older specimens, the periostracum is rayless and generally smooth in appearance. The umbos, anterior of center, are broad but not full and high. Internally the hinge plate is arcuate and broad and produces a well-defined umbonal cavity. The pseudocardinal teeth are heavy. The lateral teeth are slightly arcuate. The adductor muscle scars are pronounced both anteriorly and posteriorly. Nacre color is generally purplish but specimens may display a white center with age.

RANGE: *Fusconaia succissa* ranges from the Escambia to Choctawhatchee river systems in Alabama and Florida (Clench and Turner 1956; Burch 1975). Collections from Florida include localities in the Escambia and Yellow rivers and several sites in the Choctawhatchee River system.

HABITAT: *Fusconaia succissa* inhabits medium-sized creeks to rivers with substrates of mud to silty sand in slow to no current.

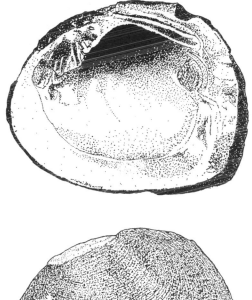

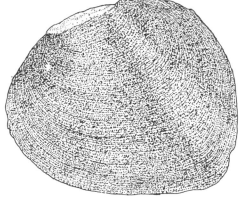

Purple Pigtoe, *Fusconaia succissa*, UF 3452, length 48.5 mm (1.9 in). Florida, Escambia County, Escambia River (illustration by Tracy Smith).

Distribution of the purple
pigtoe, *Fusconaia succissa.*

LIFE HISTORY AND ECOLOGY: Unknown.

SPECIALIZED OR UNIQUE CHARACTERISTICS: The purple pigtoe is
the southeasternmost species of the genus *Fusconaia* in Gulf of Mexico
drainages.

BASIS FOR STATUS CLASSIFICATION: Restricted to three river systems, *F. succissa* is generally known from scattered localities. Suitable non-
mainstem habitat is practically nonexistent in the Escambia and Yellow river
systems. In the Choctawhatchee system, where it was historically abundant
and widespread, *F. succissa* now appears to be declining. Recent Florida collections have generally been small and sporadic. A status of special concern
appears appropriate for this species.

RECOMMENDATIONS: Establishing guidelines for water quality and
stream maintenance in the three drainage systems where *F. succissa* occurs
are imperative to its continued existence. Surveys, particularly in the Chocta-

whatchee River system, are needed to ascertain the present Florida distribution of this species.

PREPARED BY: James D. Williams, National Biological Survey, 7920 N.W. 71st Street, Gainesville, FL 32653, and Robert S. Butler, U.S. Fish and Wildlife Service, 6620 Southpoint Drive South, Jacksonville, FL 32216.

FAMILY UNIONIDAE

Species of Special Concern

Round Pearlshell
Glebula rotundata (Lamarck)

DESCRIPTION: *Glebula rotundata* is a medium-sized to large species reaching 107 mm (4.2 in) in length. The shell is moderately inflated, with an elliptical or oval outline. The valves are solid but not heavy. The umbos are relatively low. A moderately prominent posterior ridge separates the disk from the flat or slightly concave posterior slope. The posterior end is either rounded or slightly pointed. Females display some post-basal swelling. The periostracum appears satiny on the disk and becomes more clothlike along the shell margins. Color varies from dark brown in the young to nearly black in older individuals. Internally, the pseudocardinal teeth are radially laminate with serrate edges. Nacre color is generally purplish but may appear bluish white in some individuals. The posterior region is highly iridescent.

RANGE: *Glebula rotundata* occurs primarily in the lower Mississippi River basin in Louisiana and southern Mississippi and along the Gulf Coast in drainages from east Texas to Florida (Burch 1975). Disjunct localities are known from the Rio Grande River (Simpson 1900a), Oklahoma (Branson 1969), Arkansas (Gordon 1983), and Kentucky (Schuster 1988). It has been reported in Florida from the Escambia River (Escambia County, no specific locality data, thus this record is not on distribution map), Chipola and Apalachicola rivers (Clench and Turner 1956; Heard 1979). Butler (1989) reported it from the lower Choctawhatchee River system in Florida.

HABITAT: The round pearlshell is most frequently found in the lower portions of rivers in Florida. It inhabits small to large rivers and associated sloughs, oxbows, and backwaters. Typical substrates of the round pearlshell are mud and silt in slack current. Collections in the Apalachicola River were in silty sand with slow current.

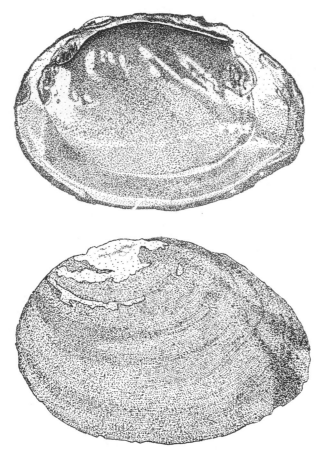

Round Pearlshell,
Glebula rotundata,
UF 229776, length
57 mm (2.3 in). Flor-
ida, Gulf County,
Dead Lake at Gates
Fish Camp (illustra-
tion by Tracy Smith).

LIFE HISTORY AND ECOLOGY: Little is known about *G. rotundata*. The marsupia occupy the posterior portion of the outer demibranchs (Burch 1975).

SPECIALIZED OR UNIQUE CHARACTERISTICS: The structure of the pseudocardinal teeth set this monotypic genus apart from all others.

BASIS FOR STATUS CLASSIFICATION: *Glebula rotundata* in Florida is known from a few localities in the main channel of three rivers. Although it may occur commonly in localized areas, such as Dead Lake (Chipola River) and the lower Apalachicola River (Butler 1989), records from the Escambia and Choctawhatchee rivers are several decades old.

RECOMMENDATIONS: Surveys of the Escambia and Choctawhatchee rivers are crucial in determining the present status of *G. rotundata*. The termination of barge channel maintenance activities in the Apalachicola would

Distribution of the round
pearlshell, *Glebula
rotundata.*

aid in the perpetuation of *G. rotundata* in this river, the easternmost drainage in its range.

PREPARED BY: James D. Williams, National Biological Survey, 7920 N.W.
71st Street, Gainesville, FL 32653, and Robert S. Butler, U.S. Fish and Wildlife Service, 6620 Southpoint Drive South, Jacksonville, FL 32216.

FAMILY UNIONIDAE

Species of Special Concern

Round Washboard

Megalonaias boykiniana (Lea)

DESCRIPTION: *Megalonaias boykiniana* is the largest mollusk found in
the freshwaters of Florida and reaches lengths of 203 mm (8.0 in). The shell

is thick, moderately inflated, subrhomboidal to somewhat round in outline and dark brown to black. It is heavily sculptured and has corrugated plications, which are best developed posteriorly, and a poorly developed, rounded posterior ridge. The umbos are anterior to the center, elevated and often sculptured with double-looped zigzag ridges. Cavities of the umbos are deep. The hinge plate is broad with two pseudocardinal teeth in each valve. Nacre is iridescent white to bluish white, but may be purplish in larger specimens.

RANGE: *Megalonaias boykiniana* occurs in the larger Gulf Coast drainages of Alabama and Florida from the Escambia River system east to the Ochlockonee River (Clench and Turner 1956). In Florida, it is known from the Escambia, Chipola, Apalachicola, and Ochlockonee rivers and a few of their large tributaries. The only Florida records are from the main channel of the Escambia River near Century, Escambia and Santa Rosa counties. Recent

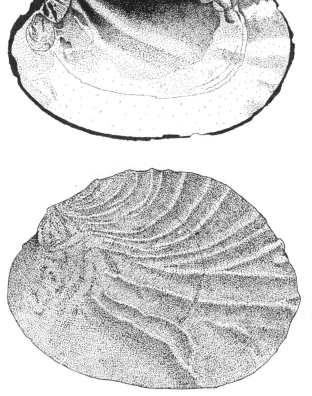

Round Washboard, *Megalonaias boykiniana*, UF 47220, length 105 mm (4.1 in). Florida, Leon County, Ochlockonee River, 17.6 km (11 mi) northwest of Tallahassee (illustration by Tracy Smith).

Distribution of the round
washboard, *Megalonaias
boykiniana.*

Florida records are restricted to a few localities in the main channels of the
Chipola, Apalachicola, and Ochlockonee rivers. It appears to be absent from
the Yellow and Choctawhatchee river systems. Although these rivers have
not been thoroughly sampled, because of its large size *M. boykiniana* is unlikely to be overlooked.

HABITAT: In Florida, *M. boykiniana* has been reported from large creeks,
but usually occurs in the main channels of small to large rivers. The composition of the substrate varies from sand and sandy mud, to gravel and lime-
rock rubble in slow to moderate current.

LIFE HISTORY AND ECOLOGY: Very little information is available on
the biology of *M. boykiniana*. Generic characters include all four demibranchs
marsupial, long term breeders (bradytictic) and glochidia hookless (Heard
and Guckert 1971). Lea (1863a) briefly described the soft anatomy of a non-
gravid female.

SPECIALIZED OR UNIQUE CHARACTERISTICS: *Megalonaias boykin-
iana* is the largest freshwater mussel in Florida. Maximum size of individuals

varies; the population in the Ochlockonee River produces smaller individuals than the Apalachicola River population (Heard 1979).

BASIS FOR STATUS CLASSIFICATION: *Megalonaias boykiniana* is known from limited reaches of four rivers in addition to two collections from large creeks made over 50 years ago. Based on current data, the population in the Escambia River is restricted to the area near the Alabama border. Its distribution in the Chipola River appears presently limited to about 20 km of the main channel of the lower river in the vicinity of Dead Lake. The population in the Apalachicola River is the most extensive, but is also under the greatest threat. Alteration of habitat, both substrate and water quality, from maintenance dredging in the Apalachicola River is a serious threat to all freshwater mussels in that river. In the Ochlockonee River, collections are known from a few localities upstream of Lake Talquin. The primary habitat of this mussel, the main channel of rivers, leaves it vulnerable to all modifications of water quality in the watershed upstream of where it occurs.

RECOMMENDATIONS: A thorough survey to determine the distribution of populations of the round washboard in the four rivers where it occurs is needed before proceeding with conservation measures. The most critical of the four rivers is the Apalachicola River. This river has the largest population and is also the most threatened because of the reoccurring maintenance dredging of the waterway. Future studies to determine the habitat and reproductive requirements will be needed to prepare plans for the protection of Florida's largest freshwater mollusk.

PREPARED BY: James D. Williams, National Biological Survey, 7920 N.W. 71st Street, Gainesville, FL 32653, and Robert S. Butler, U.S. Fish and Wildlife Service, 6620 Southpoint Drive South, Jacksonville, FL 32216.

FAMILY UNIONIDAE

Species of Special Concern

Florida Pigtoe
Pleurobema reclusum (Wright)

DESCRIPTION: *Pleurobema reclusum* is a small to medium-sized mussel that reaches about 55 mm (2.2 in) in length. The shell is ovate or triangular, smooth, somewhat polished dorsally, and moderately inflated. The uniformly curved ventral margin becomes moderately pointed posteriorly. Two slightly raised ridges form the posterior ridge. Color ranges from dark brown to almost black in western populations, whereas eastern populations are tannish brown with distinct growth lines. The umbos are fairly prominent and are characterized by four or five coarse, irregular loops. Internally, the pseudo-cardinal teeth are solid and prominent; two in the left and one in the right valve. The lateral teeth are slightly arcuate; two in the left and two in the right valve. Nacre color is generally bluish white and iridescent, particularly posteriorly.

Pleurobema reclusum has not been recognized as a distinct species since Simpson (1914). Having examined numerous lots from the Ochlockonee and Suwannee river systems, we consider *P. reclusum* distinct from *P. pyriforme*, the species with which most recent authors (e.g., Clench and Turner 1956; Johnson 1970) have synonomized *P. reclusum*. Although some differences are evident between Ochlockonee and Suwannee river populations of *P. reclusum* (see SPECIALIZED OR UNIQUE CHARACTERISTICS section), these two populations are considered a single species at this time.

RANGE: *Pleurobema reclusum* occurs in the Ochlockonee and Suwannee river systems in Georgia and Florida. Florida populations on the Ochlockonee River are known from a few sites in Gadsden and Leon counties. The Suwannee River system population is apparently restricted to Florida and is

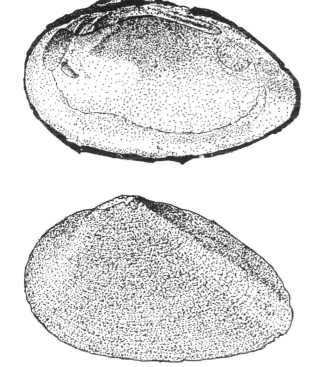

Florida Pigtoe, *Pleurobema reclusum*, UF 134949, length 46.5 mm (1.8 in). Florida, Gadsden County, Ochlockonee River, 9.3 km (5.8 mi) southeast of Havana (illustration by Tracy Smith).

Distribution of the Florida
pigtoe, *Pleurobema
reclusum.*

found predominantly in the upper Santa Fe River drainage above the Santa
Fe Sink in Alachua, Bradford, and Union counties. The lower Suwannee
River at Fanning Springs, Levy County, is the only known occurrence of *P.
reclusum* in the Suwannee system outside the Santa Fe River.

HABITAT: *Pleurobema reclusum* inhabits medium-sized creeks to rivers
with slow current in sand or sand and gravel substrates.

LIFE HISTORY AND ECOLOGY: Unknown.

SPECIALIZED OR UNIQUE CHARACTERISTICS: *Pleurobema reclu-
sum* is the southeasternmost representative of its genus. Specimens from the
Ochlockonee River are dark brown or black and reach greater size than the
tan colored specimens from the Suwannee River system.

BASIS FOR STATUS CLASSIFICATION: The Florida pigtoe is primarily
restricted to the free flowing Ochlockonee River mainstem from Lake Talquin upstream to the Georgia border, where the species is uncommon. Addi-

tionally, a few sites in the upper Santa Fe River drainage are known, including the New River, which has the best remaining population of *P. reclusum*.

RECOMMENDATIONS: Surveys for additional populations and repeated surveys of historical sites in the Suwannee River system should be conducted. Protection of the Ochlockonee River and upper Santa Fe River drainage is critical to the well-being of *P. reclusum*.

PREPARED BY: James D. Williams, National Biological Survey, 7920 N.W. 71st Street, Gainesville, FL 32653, and Robert S. Butler, U.S. Fish and Wildlife Service, 6620 Southpoint Drive South, Jacksonville, FL 32216.

FAMILY UNIONIDAE

Species of Special Concern

Shiny-Rayed Pocketbook

Villosa subangulata (Lea)

DESCRIPTION: *Villosa subangulata* is a medium-sized mussel that reaches approximately 85 mm (3.3 in) in length. The shell is subelliptical, with broad, somewhat inflated umbos and a rounded posterior ridge. The shell is fairly thin but solid. The surface is smooth and shiny, light yellowish brown with fairly wide bright emerald green rays over the entire length of the shell. Older individuals may appear much darker brown with obscure raying. Female specimens are more inflated postbasally, whereas males appear to be more pointed posteriorly. Internally, the pseudocardinal teeth are double and fairly large and erect in the left valve, and one large tooth and one spatulate tooth in the right valve. The nacre is white, with some individuals exhibiting a salmon tint in the vicinity of the umbonal cavity. (See DESCRIPTION section of the *Villosa australis* account and Simpson, 1900, for justification of the generic name of the shiny-rayed pocketbook).

RANGE: *Villosa subangulata* occurs in the Chipola, Apalachicola, and Ochlockonee river systems in Alabama, Georgia, and Florida. Clench and Turner (1956) and Burch (1975) erroneously reported it from the Choctawhatchee River system; these records are based on *V. australis*. In Florida, *V. subangulata* is most common and widespread in the Chipola River system, Jackson and Calhoun counties. Other localities include one site in Mosquito Creek (an Apalachicola River tributary) and three sites in the Ochlockonee River system.

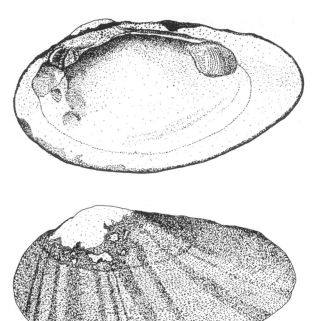

Shiny-Rayed Pocketbook, *Villosa subangulata*, UF 418, length 67.4 mm (2.6 in). Florida, Calhoun County, Chipola River, 3.2 km (2 mi) east of Clarksville (illustration by Tracy Smith).

HABITAT: *Villosa subangulata* inhabits medium-sized creeks to rivers in clean or silty sand substrates in slow to moderate current.

LIFE HISTORY AND ECOLOGY: Unknown.

SPECIALIZED OR UNIQUE CHARACTERISTICS: The yellow shell and brilliant emerald rays make *V. subangulata* one of the most colorful and easily distinguished mussels in Florida streams.

BASIS FOR STATUS CLASSIFICATION: *Villosa subangulata* appears to have relatively healthy populations in the Chipola River, but not elsewhere in Florida. Although some sizable lots representing Ochlockonee River localities are found in museums, the species is now uncommon there. Futhermore, *V. subangulata* may already be extirpated from Mosquito Creek, where it has not been collected in 35 years. Mosquito Creek is the only known Florida locality for *V. subangulata* in the Apalachicola River system outside the Chipola River drainage.

RECOMMENDATIONS: Maintaining water quality in the Chipola River is critical to the shiny-rayed pocketbook. A battery salvage plant that once polluted the system is now an Environmental Protection Agency Superfund site. Such efforts will undoubtedly aid in preserving this unique species.

Distribution of the shiny-
rayed pocketbook, *Villosa
subangulata.*

PREPARED BY: James D. Williams, National Biological Survey, 7920 N.W.
71st Street, Gainesville, FL 32653, and Robert S. Butler, U.S. Fish and Wildlife Service, 6620 Southpoint Drive South, Jacksonville, FL 32216.

FAMILY UNIONIDAE

Status Undetermined

Ochlockonee Arc-Mussel
Alasmidonta wrightiana (Walker)

DESCRIPTION: *Alasmidonta wrightiana* is a subrhomboidal, moderately
inflated, moderately thick-shelled, small to medium-sized species that reaches
a length of 57 mm (2.2 in). The umbos are full and high and extend well

above the dorsal margin. Shell sculpturing is prominent on the broad, slightly concave posterior slope. In some specimens, there are a few poorly developed radial ridges on the anterior portion of the disk. The periostracum is light to dark brown, somewhat cloth-like and, in adults, marked with prominent dark green to black rays of varying widths. Internally, the pseudocardinal teeth are poorly developed, one or two in the left valve, one in the right valve. The lateral teeth are very short and low. The umbonal cavities are broad and deep. Nacre color is bluish white to somewhat pinkish near the umbonal cavities.

Clarke (1981) in his monograph of *Alasmidonta* and related genera found only four individuals in his survey of natural history museums. An additional 11 specimens are in the Florida Museum of Natural History and bring to 15 the total number of specimens available for study. Johnson (1967) corrected Clench and Turner (1956) who considered *A. wrightiana* as a synonym of *A. triangulata*. According to Clarke (1981) *A. triangulata* is a synonym of *A. undulata*.

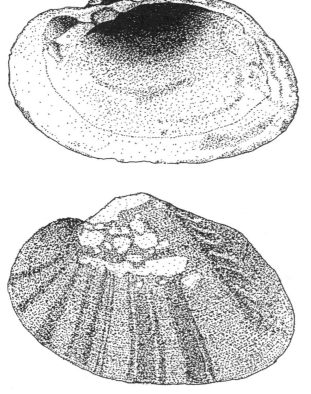

Ochlockonee Arc-mussel, *Alasmidonta wrightiana*, UF 8371, length 54.4 mm (2.1 in). Florida, Leon County, Ochlockonee River, 12.8 km (8 mi) west of Tallahassee (illustration by Tracy Smith).

Distribution of the Ochlockonee arc-mussel, *Alasmidonta
wrightiana.*

RANGE: *Alasmidonta wrightiana* is endemic to the Ochlockonee River in
Florida (Johnson 1967; Burch 1975). It is known from two mainstem sites
upstream of Lake Talquin in Gadsden and Leon counties. Confusion surrounding the collection locality of the type specimen resulted in the species
being reported from the Flint River in Georgia (Walker 1901). This error was
subsequently corrected by Walker (in Simpson 1914).

HABITAT: There is no specific information describing the habitat of the
Ochlockonee arc-mussel. The Ochlockonee River, where the species has been
taken, has a sandy mud substrate, with quiet backwater pools and runs of
slow to moderate current. Much of this species' habitat was probably inundated by Lake Talquin.

LIFE HISTORY AND ECOLOGY: Unknown.

SPECIALIZED OR UNIQUE CHARACTERISTICS: As presently known,
A. wrightiana has one of the most restricted distributions of any North
American unionid mollusks.

BASIS FOR STATUS CLASSIFICATION: The last specimens of the Ochlockonee arc-mussel were collected in the Ochlockonee River, 8 miles west of
Tallahassee, Gadsden and Leon counties, on 13 November 1931. Numerous
collections have been made in the upper Ochlockonee River, which still supports a good unionid assemblage, but no *A. wrightiana* have been found.
The species was reported as possibly extinct by Turgeon et al. (1988). It is
premature to consider this species extinct until a thorough survey of the Ochlockonee River has been undertaken. Undetermined status is based on the
lack of surveys and collections in the lower portion of the Ochlockonee River
(below Jackson Bluff Dam) and the extreme upper portion near the Georgia
state line.

RECOMMENDATIONS: A thorough survey of the entire main channel of
the Ochlockonee River is the highest priority research for the Ochlockonee
arc-mussel. The Florida portion of the river should be examined first and, if
no specimens are found, the search should be expanded to include larger tributaries and the headwaters of the river in Georgia. Pending the results of the
survey, every effort should be made to maintain or improve water quality
and protect riparian habitat in the Ochlockonee River and its tributaries.

PREPARED BY: James D. Williams, National Biological Survey, 7920 N.W.
71st Street, Gainesville, FL 32653, and Robert S. Butler, U.S. Fish and Wildlife Service, 6620 Southpoint Drive South, Jacksonville, FL 32216.

FAMILY UNIONIDAE

Status Undetermined

Roundlake

Amblema perplicata (Conrad)

DESCRIPTION: *Amblema perplicata* is large and reaches 127 mm (5.0 in)
in length. It is heavy shelled, quadrate to subrhomboid, and typically dark
brown to black. It is moderately inflated with five to seven prominent folds
which are almost parallel to the dorsal margin. Many specimens exhibit concentric growth-rest periods which form prominent ridges and grooves that
tend to break the folds where they intersect. The umbos are low and raised
slightly above the hinge line. Internally, the large pseudocardinal teeth, two
in the left valve and two or three in the right valve, are separated from the
lateral teeth by a wide interdentium. The umbonal cavities are moderately
deep. Nacre color is typically white with a purple tint posteriorly. Turgeon et
al. (1988) considered *A. perplicata* a subspecies of the wide ranging species
A. plicata.

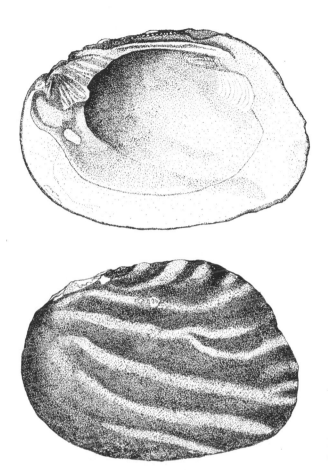

Roundlake, *Amblema perplicata*, UF 1481, length 87.5 mm (3.4 in). Florida, Walton County, Picket Retch Lake (illustration by Gina Collins).

RANGE: Although the range of *A. perplicata* has never been precisely delineated, it is generally considered to be the lower Mississippi River system and Gulf Coast drainages from central Texas east to the Choctawhatchee River system, Florida. Distribution records for *A. perplicata* in Florida are from the Escambia River, Escambia County, and the Choctawhatchee River system in Walton County. Shells collected during the 1930s from Picket Retch Lake, Walton County, were sent to several museums and collectors and appear to be the basis for the report of *A. perplicata* from the Yellow River (Burch 1975). Butler (1989) correctly assigned specimens from this locality to the Choctawhatchee River system. Records exist for the roundlake in the Escambia River in Alabama, but not from the Yellow or Choctawhatchee river systems in Alabama. The records of *A. neislerii* from the Escambia River are based on *A. perplicata* (see RANGE section of the *A. neislerii* account). The range of *A. perplicata* in Florida is apparently confined to the lower portions of the Escambia and Choctawhatchee river systems.

Distribution of the roundlake, *Amblema perplicata.*

HABITAT: *Amblema perplicata* inhabits large creeks to rivers and floodplain lakes in areas with slow or no current. It is found in a variety of substrates including clay, mud, sand, and sand mixed with gravel.

LIFE HISTORY AND ECOLOGY: There are several reports on the anatomy and reproduction of *A. plicata*, but only three (Frierson 1904; Ortmann
1912, 1914) are based on its southern sibling species *A. perplicata.* Frierson
(1904) was the first to report on gravid females of *A. perplicata.* The two
Louisiana specimens, one collected on 7 June 1901 and one on 19 August
1903, had glochidia in all four gills. Ortmann (1912) reported gravid females
discharging glochidia from Bayou Pierre in southwestern Mississippi on 6
August 1910. Subsequently, Ortmann (1914) reported females from Arkansas and Louisiana carrying mature glochidia between 26 June 1911 and 1
August 1912. Measurements for these glochidia were: length 0.20 mm; height
0.21 mm (1/100 in).

SPECIALIZED OR UNIQUE CHARACTERISTICS: The large, heavy,
folded shell of *A. perplicata* makes it one of the most distinctive unionids in
its range.

BASIS FOR STATUS CLASSIFICATION: Habitat degradation from siltation in both the Escambia and Choctawhatchee rivers, much of which comes from upstream areas in Alabama, has likely affected this species in the past. Restriction of *A. perplicata* to short sections of two rivers and the absence of collections of this species during the past 55 years leave its Florida status in question.

RECOMMENDATIONS: A survey to determine the extent of existing populations is needed to determine priorities of conservation actions. There are no museum records from the Choctawhatchee and Escambia river systems since 1934 and 1915, respectively. However, it has been collected in the Escambia River in Alabama during the past 10 years. Once the current Florida range is determined, protection of existing populations is a high priority.

PREPARED BY: James D. Williams, National Biological Survey, 7920 N.W. 71st Street, Gainesville, FL 32653, and Robert S. Butler, U.S. Fish and Wildlife Service, 6620 Southpoint Drive South, Jacksonville, FL 32216.

FAMILY UNIONIDAE

Status Undetermined

Rayed Creekshell

Anodontoides radiatus (Conrad)

DESCRIPTION: *Anodontoides radiatus* is a small to medium-sized species that reaches 75 mm (2.9 in) in length and is moderately inflated, thin, and suboval to elliptical in outline. Anteriorly the shell is rounded but posteriorly it is somewhat pointed. The posterior ridge is broad and rounded; the posterior slope is flat. Umbos of the shell are moderately inflated, slightly raised above the hinge line, and positioned toward the anterior third of the shell. The surface of the shell is smooth, brownish to olive brown with prominent dark green rays of varying widths over the entire shell. Internally, there is a single rudimentary pseudocardinal tooth in the left valve and a long, narrow and low pseudocardinal in the right valve. The hinge plate is thin and the lateral teeth are absent. The umbonal cavities are broad and shallow. Nacre is iridescent, bluish white, and often stained with light yellow spots.

In the absence of basic biological data, this species has been placed in five genera. It is retained in the genus *Anodontoides* until the soft anatomy can be critically examined. The genus *Anodontoides* was described by Simpson (Baker 1898).

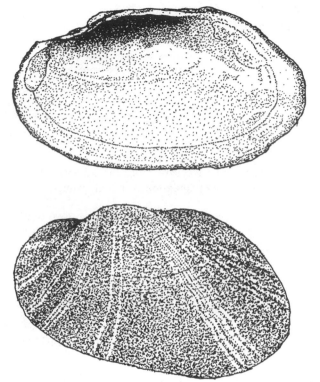

Rayed Creekshell, *Anodontoides radiatus*, UF 64075, length 49.5 mm (1.9 in). Alabama, Russell County, Uchee Creek near Nuckalls (illustration by Tracy Smith).

RANGE: *Anodontoides radiatus* occurs in Gulf Coast drainages from the Tickfaw River system, Louisiana (Vidrine 1985), eastward to the Apalachicola river system (Johnson 1967). In this area, it appears to be absent from the Yellow, Choctawhatchee, and Chipola rivers. In Florida, *A. radiatus* is known only from Mosquito Creek, a tributary of the Apalachicola River, in Gadsden County (Clench and Turner 1956). It has been collected from several localities in the Escambia River system in Alabama but has not been found in this system in Florida. *Anodontoides radiatus* has been confused with *Strophitus subvexus* by some investigators (Clench and Turner 1956). Johnson (1967) reexamined material reported by Clench and Turner (1956) and pointed out that their records from the Chipola River were based on *Strophitus* not *Anodontoides*.

HABITAT: Although the rayed creekshell is known from large rivers (e.g., Chattahoochee River, Muscogee County, Georgia), most collections are from small to medium-sized creeks, presumably its typical habitat, where it occurs in mud, sandy mud, or sand and gravel substrates.

LIFE HISTORY AND ECOLOGY: Information on the life history of the rayed creekshell is limited to a brief description of its soft anatomy (Lea 1863a). This description, under the synonym *Anodonta showalterii*, is based

Distribution of the rayed
creekshell, *Anodontoides*
radiatus.

on specimens from the Coosa River in Alabama. Of the two specimens examined by Lea (1863a), at least one was a gravid female with glochidia in the entire outer gill.

SPECIALIZED OR UNIQUE CHARACTERISTICS: None.

BASIS FOR STATUS CLASSIFICATION: There is only one verifiable record of the rayed creekshell in Florida and it was collected more than three decades ago. The absence of distribution records may indicate rarity but might also reflect the lack of collecting effort in the small headwater woodland streams. Undetermined status is deemed appropriate until additional data are available.

RECOMMENDATIONS: A thorough survey of small headwater streams in the Apalachicola and Escambia river systems is urgently needed. Mosquito Creek should be sampled first in order to determine the status of *A. radiatus* in that tributary system. The Chipola River drainage, an Apalachicola River tributary, has received considerable attention from collectors in recent years and for this reason is a lower priority for survey work.

PREPARED BY: James D. Williams, National Biological Survey, 7920 N.W. 71st Street, Gainesville, FL 32653, and Robert S. Butler, U.S. Fish and Wildlife Service, 6620 Southpoint Drive South, Jacksonville, FL 32216.

FAMILY UNIONIDAE

Status Undetermined

Bankclimber

Plectomerus dombeyanus (Valenciennes)

DESCRIPTION: This large dark brownish to black, heavy-shelled mussel attains a length of 150 mm (5.9 in). It is moderately inflated and quadrate to rhomboid in shape, with a well developed posterior ridge which ends at the base of the shell. The posterior margin of the shell is truncate above and may be biangulate below. On the surface of the shell there are a few oblique folds anterior and posterior to the posterior ridge. Internally, the umbonal cavities are moderately deep. The lateral teeth are long, moderately high, and slightly curved, whereas the pseudocardinal teeth are large and ragged; two in the left valve and one in the right valve. Nacre color varies from purple to purplish white.

RANGE: *Plectomerus dombeyanus* occurs in coastal plain streams of the Gulf drainages from east Texas east to the Mobile basin in Alabama (Burch 1975) and the Escambia River system in Alabama and Florida (Heard 1979). There are two possible records of this species from the state of Florida. One record came from the Escambia River near Century, Escambia and Santa Rosa counties (Heard 1979). According to Heard (1979), this collection consisted of a single shell which he speculated may have washed down from upstream areas in Alabama. The record of *Elliptoideus sloatianus* from the Escambia River near Century is probably based on the conchologically similar *P. dombeyanus*, thus representing the second record of this species from the state.

HABITAT: *Plectomerus dombeyanus* inhabits medium-sized to large rivers and oxbow lakes with slow current. It is typically found in mud, or mud mixed with sand substrates, but occasionally has been found in rivers with moderate current and a sand and gravel substrate.

LIFE HISTORY AND ECOLOGY: The only life history information on *Plectomerus* is a brief description of soft parts by Lea (1863), Frierson (1904), and Ortmann (1912). Frierson (1904) examined "dozens" of gravid

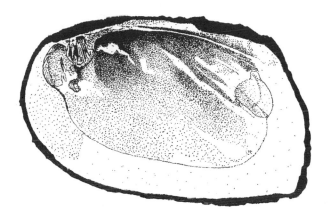

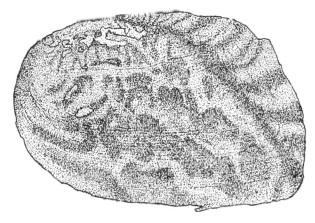

Bankclimber, *Plectomerus dombeyanus*, UF 229777, length 82.2 mm (3.2 in). Alabama, Baldwin County, Tensaw Lake at Upper Bryants (Brants) Landing about 1.6 km (1 mi) northwest of Vaughn (illustration by Tracy Smith).

females and found all four gills being utilized as marsupia for glochidia and reported gravid females from May to September. Heard and Guckert (1971) assigned *Plectomerus* to a group of unionids which exhibit a tachytictic (short term breeders carrying glochidia only during summer months) reproductive strategy.

SPECIALIZED OR UNIQUE CHARACTERISTICS: The genus *Plectomerus* is monotypic and reaches its easternmost distribution along the Gulf Coast in the Escambia River system of Alabama and Florida.

BASIS FOR STATUS CLASSIFICATION: Because only two specimens of *P. dombeyanus* are known from Florida, a status classification of undetermined seems appropriate at this time.

RECOMMENDATIONS: A survey of the main channel of the Escambia River is needed to determine the status of this species. Results of a survey could be used to determine future conservation actions.

Distribution of the bank-
climber, *Plectomerus
dombeyanus.*

PREPARED BY: James D. Williams, National Biological Survey, 7920 N.W.
71st Street, Gainesville, FL 32653, and Robert S. Butler, U.S. Fish and Wildlife Service, 6620 Southpoint Drive South, Jacksonville, FL 32216.

FAMILY UNIONIDAE

Status Undetermined

Southern Kidneyshell
Ptychobranchus jonesi (van der Schalie)

DESCRIPTION: *Ptychobranchus jonesi* is a medium-sized species that
reaches a length of about 65 mm (2.5 in). The shell is inflated and elongate-

elliptical, and the posterior ridge is double with scalloped margins between the ridge extremities. Its epidermis is subshiny, olivaceous green to dark brown with irregular, usually obscure, green rays. A nearly straight to slightly concave ventral margin and a postbasal swelling are characteristic of females, whereas the ventral margin of males is broadly rounded. Internal characteristics include two thin and slightly arcuate lateral teeth and two solid compressed pseudocardinal teeth in the left valve. The right valve has a thin, slightly arcuate lateral tooth and two pseudocardinal teeth; one well developed, the other rudimentary. Nacre color is bluish white with some posterior iridescence.

RANGE: Burch (1975) reported *P. jonesi* from the Choctawhatchee and Escambia river systems in Alabama and Florida. However, Butler (1989) reported the first substantiated Florida records from two localities in the Choctawhatchee River system in Walton County. The species has yet to be discovered in the Yellow River system or the Florida portion of the Escambia River system.

HABITAT: Found in medium-sized creeks to rivers, *P. jonesi* inhabits silty sand substrates with woody debris in slow current.

LIFE HISTORY AND ECOLOGY: Unknown.

SPECIALIZED OR UNIQUE CHARACTERISTICS: Athearn (1964), in correcting Clench and Turner's (1956) assumption that *P. jonesi* was syn-

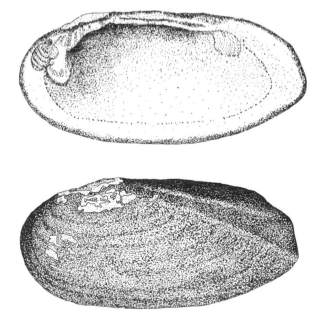

Southern Kidneyshell, *Ptychobranchus jonesi*, UF 65567 (paratype), length 61 mm (2.4 in). Alabama, Covington County, Conecuh River, Rozemans Landing near Crenshaw County line (illustration by Gina Collins).

Distribution of the southern
kidneyshell, *Ptychobranchus
jonesi.*

onymous with *Villosa australis*, noted, among other differences, the characteristic double scalloping of the posterior margin of *P. jonesi. Ptychobranchus*
is the only genus of North American Unionidae known to have folded or
pleated marsupial gills.

BASIS FOR STATUS CLASSIFICATION: *Ptychobranchus jonesi* is known
in Florida from only three specimens collected at two localities, both representing collections made 55 years ago (Butler 1989). Without thoroughly
sampling the Choctawhatchee River system, it cannot be firmly stated that
P. jonesi persists in Florida.

RECOMMENDATIONS: The Choctawhatchee River system needs to be
surveyed to determine the present status of *P. jonesi* in Florida.

PREPARED BY: James D. Williams, National Biological Survey, 7920 N.W.
71st Street, Gainesville, FL 32653, and Robert S. Butler, U.S. Fish and Wildlife Service, 6620 Southpoint Drive South, Jacksonville, FL 32216.

Class Gastropoda
Subclass Pulmonata

Terrestrial Snails

INTRODUCTION: The terrestrial snails of Florida belong to the two major subclasses of the Gastropoda: the Prosobranchiata and the Pulmonata. The Prosobranchiata is characterized by having separate sexes and possessing an operculum, which effectively closes the aperture for protection against desiccation and predation. Members of the Pulmonata are hermaphroditic (male and female sex organs on same individual) and lack an operculum.

One hundred twenty-one native species of terrestrial mollusks have been recorded from Florida. The vast majority of these species are pulmonates; only five species being prosobranchs. Although distributions are poorly known, it appears that about 20 species are endemic to Florida. Three pulmonate families dominate the Florida snail fauna: Pupillidae (23 species), Polygyridae (21 species), and Zonitidae (14 species).

Land snails generally prefer stable habitats that fulfill their sometimes sensitive moisture requirements. They are generally nocturnal or crepuscular due to the usually lower air temperatures and higher relative humidities at these times. Although a few species in Florida are arboreal or semiarboreal, most are encountered among leaf litter around the bases of trees, fallen deadwood, and rocks. Some species are most frequently seen under bark of rotten logs, while others prefer more exposed habitats such as grassy roadsides and ditches. Many species are restricted to areas which have exposed limestone or highly calcareous soils. Very few species occur in sandhill or scrub habitats which are seasonally very dry and susceptible to fire.

Virtually nothing is known about the ecology and life history of the Florida land snail fauna. Only a few arboreal species have been studied, and it is hoped that this lack of knowledge will stimulate future investigations before the habitat destruction caused by urbanization and agricultural pursuits takes its inevitable toll.

PREPARED BY: Kurt Auffenberg, Florida Museum of Natural History, University of Florida, Gainesville, FL 32611.

Endangered

Stock Island Tree Snail
Orthalicus reses reses (Say)

OTHER NAMES: Lazy tree snail, *Oxystyla* tree snail.

DESCRIPTION: *Orthalicus reses reses* is a large snail with a conical shell that is 45–55 mm (1.8–2.2 in) long. The shell is lightweight compared to that of most other species of *Orthalicus*, but shell thickness appears to vary greatly with diet. The external ground color is white to buff overlain by three poorly developed spiral bands and a number of flame-like axial stripes, all purple-brown. The stripes are usually narrower than the whitish interspaces and usually do not fork near the suture. The apical whorls are white. The parietal callus and the columella are white or faintly chestnut. The animal is grayish-tan and unmarked. See Binney (1885) and Pilsbry (1946) for more information.

RANGE: This subspecies is currently known only from Stock Island, Monroe County, Florida, where it is confined to a patch of hammock on the municipal golf course and surrounding properties. Formerly it was also found in Key West but is not represented in museum collections after 1938. A second population may have been introduced into the Goulds area of Dade County, Florida, but this has not yet been verified.

HABITAT: This arboreal snail occurs on a wide variety of native hammock trees and on some introduced exotic ornamentals. It feeds on epiphytic growths such as lichens, fungi, and algae found on leaf and bark surfaces. The northward and inland spread of the species is limited in part by poor cold tolerance.

SPECIALIZED OR UNIQUE CHARACTERISTICS: The Stock Island tree snail is very similar in appearance to the Florida Keys tree snail (*O.r. nesodryas*) but can be distinguished by the white apex and light-colored columellar area. The former subspecies shows narrower, somewhat paler axial stripes than the latter.

BASIS FOR STATUS CLASSIFICATION: This subspecies appears to be limited to one small population (200–800 individuals) in an area that is scheduled to be developed in the near future. Even if the mainland population should prove to be the same subspecies, the area it occupies is subject to cold

Stock Island Tree
Snail, *Orthalicus
reses reses* (courtesy
of Kurt Auffenberg).

Distribution of the
Stock Island tree
snail, *Orthalicus
reses reses.*

weather and insecticide sprays, factors which make its hold in Dade County precarious.

RECOMMENDATIONS: The U.S. Fish and Wildlife Service has proposed a recovery plan that includes protecting the existing snails by reducing predation and enlarging the present habitat by suitable plantings. In addition, there are tentative plans to establish new populations in suitable areas that are not likely to undergo development. See Thompson (1980) for more information.

PREPARED BY: Jane E. Deisler-Seno, Corpus Christi Museum of Science and History, 1900 N. Chaparral, Corpus Christi, TX 78401.

FAMILY BULIMULIDAE

Threatened

Florida Keys Tree Snail
Orthalicus reses nesodryas Pilsbry

OTHER NAMES: *Oxystyla* Tree Snail.

DESCRIPTION: *Orthalicus reses nesodryas* has a large conical shell that is 50–65 mm (2.0–2.6 in) long in mature specimens. The shell is lightweight when compared to other species of *Orthalicus*, but shell weight varies with diet. The external ground color is white to buff overlain by three spiral bands and a number of flame-like axial streaks, all purple-brown. The axial stripes are bold, generally wider than the interspaces, and usually forked near the upper suture. The first 1.5 apical whorls are dark chestnut brown as is the parietal callus. The animal is grayish-tan and unmarked. See Binney (1885) and Pilsbry (1946) for more information.

RANGE: This subspecies has historically been found on the lower Florida Keys, from Grassy Key to Key West. Museum collections also contain specimens from Lower Matecumbe Key and from Flamingo on the mainland, where a colony may have been introduced by man.

HABITAT: This arboreal snail is found on a wide variety of native hammock trees and on a few introduced ornamentals. It feeds on epiphytic growths such as lichens, fungi, and algae found on leaf and bark surfaces. The subspecies is restricted to the southern coast of Florida in part because of poor cold tolerance.

Florida Keys Tree
Snail, *Orthalicus
reses nesodryas*
(courtesy of Kurt
Auffenberg).

Distribution of the
Florida Keys tree
snail, *Orthalicus
reses nesodryas.*

SPECIALIZED OR UNIQUE CHARACTERISTICS: This snail is very similar in appearance to the Stock Island tree snail (*O. reses reses*) but differs primarily in having a dark chestnut brown apex and columellar region. The axial stripes of the Florida Keys tree snail are bolder and wider than those of the Stock Island tree snail and are more likely to fork at the suture.

BASIS FOR STATUS CLASSIFICATION: Because of the intense development of the Florida Keys for recreational purposes, a large proportion of the native hammock habitat has been destroyed or altered. The Florida Keys tree snail has become correspondingly harder to find and has apparently been eliminated from parts of its former range. The populations of this snail are also suffering from increased exposure to mosquito control measures. However, since colonies are found on federally owned keys to which access is restricted, the subspecies is not on the verge of extinction, barring a natural event such as a major hurricane.

RECOMMENDATIONS: The introduction of colonies to widespread suitable habitats will eliminate the possibility of extinction by natural causes. Since the genus appears to be particularly susceptible to cold weather, relocation should be limited to the southernmost parts of the state.

PREPARED BY: Jane E. Deisler-Seno, Corpus Christi Museum of Science and History, 1900 N. Chaparral, Corpus Christi, TX 78401.

FAMILY BULIMULIDAE

Species of Special Concern

Florida Tree Snail
Liguus fasciatus Müller

OTHER NAMES: South Florida tree snail, banded tree snail.

DESCRIPTION: *Liguus fasciatus* is a large snail with an adult shell that is 40–70 mm (1.6–2.7 in) long. The shell is conical and variable in thickness. Its texture ranges from matte to glossy, and it is somewhat porcelain-like, more so than shells of most other Florida snails. The color is extremely variable, ranging from solid white to white with bands and streaks of yellow, brown, pink, and green. The apical whorls and the columellar area are white or pink, unlike any other arboreal snail in the state. The aperture is ovate and oblique, and the columella is truncate to continuous. The animal is grayish-tan and unmarked. See Jones (1977) and Pilsbry (1946) for more information.

Florida Tree Snail,
Liguus fasciatus
(courtesy of Kurt
Auffenberg).

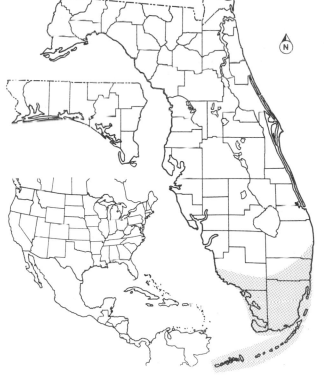

Distribution of the
Florida tree snail,
Liguus fasciatus.

RANGE: This species has been found in Florida throughout most of the keys, from Key West to the mainland. On the west coast *Liguus* has been found as far north as Marco and Goodland Point, Collier County; it has occurred naturally on the east coast as far north as Yamato Hammock, Palm Beach County. Colonies have been introduced by man on Sanibel Island, Lee County, and in Boynton Beach, Palm Beach County. The species is extensively distributed throughout the Everglades National Park and the Big Cypress region. Outside of Florida, *L. fasciatus* occurs on Cuba and the Isle of Pines.

HABITAT: The Florida tree snail is found on a wide variety of native hammock trees and on some introduced ornamentals. It prefers smooth-barked species such as *Lysiloma* and *Ficus*. The snail feeds on epiphytic growths such as lichens, fungi, and algae found on the bark surface. See Davidson (1965) and Voss (1976) for more information.

SPECIALIZED OR UNIQUE CHARACTERISTICS: This species is noted for the beautiful and variable color patterns on the shell. These brilliant markings have led to an intense interest in the systematics and zoogeography of the snail.

BASIS FOR STATUS CLASSIFICATION: There are eight subspecies of *L. fasciatus* found in Florida (Pilsbry 1946): *castaneozonatus, elliottensis, graphicus, lossmanicus, matecumbensis, septentrionalis, solidus,* and *testudineus*. These have been further divided into numerous forms and varieties on the basis of the color patterns on the shell. Neither of the latter categories ordinarily are given systematic validity. The *International Code of Zoological Nomenclature* treats them as legal subspecific names. In the case of *Liguus* such classification is used to express the complicated genetic relationships within the species as evidenced by the shell markings.

Of the subspecies recognized by Pilsbry, only *septentrionalis* is threatened, having been eliminated from its natural habitat. However, many of the varieties included in the other seven subspecies either have been exterminated or are threatened with extinction. The following is a summary of the status and current distribution of the varieties of the Florida tree snail, confirmed Mr. Archie Jones, Miami, Florida (pers. comm.).

Alternatus Simpson (Simpson's tree snail). Formerly found in the now destroyed Black Creek Hammock; presently still in Timm's Hammock (Owaissa Bauer County Park) and introduced into several hammocks in the Everglades National Park.

Aurantius Clench (orange tree snail). Widespread throughout the Everglades area, including the park.

Barbouri Clench (Barbour's tree snail). Widespread throughout the Everglades area, including the park.

Beardi Jones (Beard's tree snail). In two hammocks in the southern Everglades. Endangered.

Capensis Simpson (Cape Sable tree snail). Small colony on Cape Sable; introduced into two or three locations in the Everglades National Park.

Castaneozonatus Pilsbry (brown-banded tree snail). Widely distributed throughout almost the entire range of the species except for the lower keys.

Castaneus Simpson (chestnut tree snail). Widespread throughout the southern Everglades.

Cingulatus Simpson (belted tree snail). Widely distributed but uncommon.

Clenchi Frampton (Clench's tree snail). Common in the Pinecrest area and introduced into the Everglades National Park.

Crassus Simpson (Simpson's thick-shelled tree snail). Big Pine Key, possibly also Ramrod Key and Key West; however, the holotype has been lost, and this may have been only an albino form; dubious designation. Recently extinct.

Deckerti Clench (Deckert's tree snail). Found in several Pinecrest hammocks, Long Pine Key, and Brickell Hammock; reported in the past from Cox's Hammock; transplanted into the Everglades National Park. Rare.

Delicatus Simpson (delicate tree snail). Upper end of Lower Matecumbe Key, Lignumvitae Key, and introduced into the Everglades National Park.

Dohertyi Pfleuger (Doherty's tree snail). Formerly on Lower Matecumbe Key but eliminated by the 1935 hurricane. Recently extinct.

Dryas Pilsbry (wood nymph tree snail). Extinct on No Name Key; a small population remains on Little Pine Key; introduced into the Everglades National Park.

Eburneus Simpson (ivory tree snail). Common in the Redlands area of Dade County and naturally occurring in the Everglades National Park.

Elegans Simpson (elegant tree snail). Found in a large hammock in the southern Everglades National Park and scattered in other sites.

Elliottensis Pilsbry (Elliott's Key tree snail). Appears to be extinct on Elliott's Key but persists on upper Key Largo and perhaps also on Key Vaca. Introduced into the Everglades National Park. Threatened.

Evergladensis Jones (Everglades tree snail). Found in four to five hammocks north of 40-Mile Bend of the Tamiami Trail and introduced into the southern Everglades.

Farnhami Doe. Synonym of variety farnumi Clench.

Farnumi Clench (Farnum's tree snail). Originally found in several Pinecrest hammocks. Never common, now presumed extinct.

Floridanus Clench (Floridian tree snail). Widely distributed throughout the Everglades, including the park.

Framptoni Jones (Frampton's tree snail). Southern Everglades.

Fuscoflamellus Frampton (dusky flamed tree snail). Found in Timm's Hammock (Owaissa Bauer County Park) with one specimen reported from Cox's Hammock. Several pure colonies introduced into the Everglades National Park. Formerly considered very rare.

Gloriasylvaticus Doe (glory of the forest tree snail). Formerly distributed in several hammocks in the Big Cypress area; now restricted to one hammock, which has been largely destroyed; several small colonies introduced into the Everglades National Park. Threatened.

Graphicus Pilsbry (lettered tree snail). Originally widespread in the lower keys, Little Pine Key to Boca Chica; currently two well-established colonies on federally owned Little Pine Key and a remnant colony on No Name Key.

Humesi Jones (Humes' tree snail). Southern Everglades.

Innominatus Pilsbry (No Name Key tree snail). May have been merely a variant of variety graphicus. Formerly on No Name Key. Recently extinct.

Kennethi Jones (Kenneth's tree snail). Southern Everglades. Threatened.

Lignumvitae Pilsbry (Lignumvitae Key tree snail). Found on Lower Matecumbe Key and well-established on Lignumvitae Key. Introduced into the Everglades National Park.

Lineatus Simpson. Synonym of variety simpsoni Pilsbry. Not to be confused with the Cuban lineatus Valenciennes.

Lineolatus Simpson (wide-banded tree snail). Found on small keys off Key Largo and on Key Largo. Two colonies introduced into the Everglades National Park.

Livingstoni Simpson (Livingston's tree snail). Found in various hybrid colonies in the Miami area. Rare.

Lossmanicus Pilsbry (Lossman's Key tree snail). Widely distributed in the central and southern Everglades.

Lucidovarius Doe (Doe's tree snail). Considered by Pilsbry (1946) to be a synonym of variety floridanus Clench. Found in one hammock in the Pinecrest area and introduced into the Everglades National Park. Threatened.

Luteus Simpson (yellow tree snail). Common throughout the southern mainland portion of the range of the species; type locality is Key Vaca.

Margaretae Jones (Margaret's tree snail). Found in limited areas of the Everglades National Park. Threatened.

Marmoratus Pilsbry (marbled tree snail). Found in the past in Key Vaca; currently in Long Pine Key, Brickell Hammock, and the Pinecrest region.

Matecumbensis Pilsbry (Matecumbe tree snail). Almost extinct on Upper and Lower Matecumbe keys but well-established north of Flamingo.

Miamiensis Simpson (Miami tree snail). Several colonies introduced into the Everglades National Park, Long Pine Key, and the Pinecrest area.

Mosieri Simpson (Mosier's tree snail). Widespread but not plentiful in hybrid colonies. Formerly ranged from near Ft. Lauderdale to the Everglades.

Nebulosus Doe (clouded tree snail). Originally found in Bloodhound Hammock as a rare variety. Introduced into the Everglades National Park in two colonies but with uncertain results. Threatened.

Ornatus Simpson (adorned tree snail). Widespread from Key Largo to the mainland and established in the Everglades National Park.

Osmenti Clench (Osment's tree snail). Formerly on the lower keys in the area of Big Pine Key and at one time abundant on federally owned Howe's Key. Introduced into the Everglades National Park.

Pictus (Reeve) (painted tree snail). Extinct in its natural habitat of Big Pine Key. May now occur on Key Largo and has been established in the Everglades National Park. Threatened.

Pseudopictus Simpson (false painted tree snail). Extinct in its natural habitat of Lower Matecumbe Key. Established in the Everglades National Park. Threatened.

Roseatus Pilsbry (roseate tree snail). Widespread throughout southern Florida and the keys.

Septentrionalis Pilsbry (northern tree snail). The only variety in this subspecies. Extinct over its natural range in Broward and Palm Beach counties; two colonies introduced into the Everglades National Park. Threatened.

Simpsoni Pilsbry (Simpson's tree snail). Formerly on Plantation Key. Presently on Lignumvitae Key and Lower Matecumbe Key. Introduced into the Everglades National Park.

Solidulus Pilsbry (Pilsbry's thick-shelled tree snail). Extinct in its native habitat on Stock Island and in the type locality on Big Pine Key. Introduced into the Everglades National Park. Threatened

Solidus Say (Say's thick-shelled tree snail). Formerly inhabited some of the lower keys from Big Pine Key to Key West. Recently extinct.

Solisocassus De Boe (De Boe's thick-shelled tree snail). Considered by Pilsbry (1946) to be a synonym of testudineus Pilsbry. Still found in the Pinecrest area but uncommon. Introduced into the Everglades National Park. Rare.

Splendidus Frampton (splendid tree snail). Extinct in its natural habitat on Lower Matecumbe Key but introduced into the Everglades National Park. Threatened.

Subcrenatus Pilsbry (crenate tree snail). Found on Lignumvitae and Lower Matecumbe keys; introduced into the Everglades National Park.

Testudineus Pilsbry (tortoiseshell tree snail). Remains in Brickell Hammock and in several colonies; introduced into the Everglades National Park.

Vacaensis Simpson (Key Vaca tree snail). Found currently in the area northeast of Flamingo and on Key Largo.

Versicolor Simpson (variegated tree snail). Very common in the type locality of Long Pine Key. Also found in Brickell Hammock.

Violafumosus Doe (smoky tree snail). Considered by Pilsbry (1946) to be a synonym of variety floridanus Clench. Described from the Pinecrest region. Recently extinct.

Vonpaulseni Young (Vonpaulsen's tree snail). Type locality is Middle Torch Key; introduced into the Everglades National Park. Threatened.

Walkeri Clench (Walker's tree snail). Found in several hammocks in the Pinecrest region and introduced into the Everglades National Park in the Long Pine Key area.

Wintei Humes (Winte's tree snail). Found in approximately six hammocks in the Everglades National Park.

RECOMMENDATIONS: During the past two decades several South Florida naturalists have been involved in a project to relocate endangered and threatened varieties of the Florida tree snail to the Everglades National Park. Because of their efforts a number of varieties are no longer in danger of extinction, and the many color patterns of this snail's shell have been preserved. See Craig (1974) for more information.

PREPARED BY: Jane E. Deisler-Seno, Corpus Christi Museum of Science and History, 1900 N. Chaparral, Corpus Christi, TX 78401.

FAMILY BULIMULIDAE

Species of Special Concern

Banded Tree Snail
Orthalicus floridensis Pilsbry

OTHER NAMES: *Oxystyla* Tree Snail.

DESCRIPTION: *Orthalicus floridensis* is a large snail with an inflated conical adult shell that is 50–70 mm (2.0–2.7 in) long. The shell is generally lightweight but can be very heavy in some populations. The external ground color is white to buff. It is overlain by three spiral chestnut brown bands, the topmost of which is often faint. The shell also shows one to four vertical dark brown growth varices. The surface is smooth but with fine vertical striations. The apex and the columellar region are chestnut brown. The external bands and varices show in the aperture, but the ground color is lighter than externally. The animal is grayish-tan to buff and unmarked. See Pilsbry (1946) for more information.

RANGE: This species is the most widespread of the Florida members of the genus, ranging from Big Pine Key northward to the mainland. It is found along the west coast of the state as far north as Chokoloskee Key and, recently, along the east coast as far north as Miami. This species had been introduced by humans as far north as Sanibel Island, Lee County, but it died out due to poor cold tolerance.

HABITAT: This arboreal snail occurs on a wide variety of native and introduced plants and trees. It is naturally a hammock species but has been successfully introduced in suburban settings. The animal feeds on epiphytic growths such as lichens, algae, and fungi found on leaf and bark surfaces. The northward and inland spread of the species is limited to some degree by cold tolerance but not as severely as the other members of the genus. See Craig (1972) for more information.

Banded Tree Snail,
Orthalicus floridensis
(courtesy of Kurt
Auffenberg).

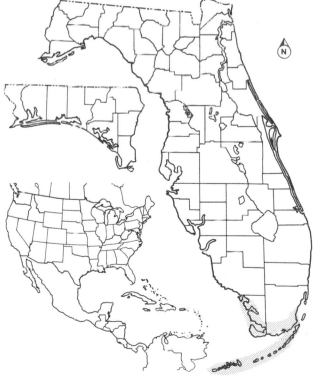

Distribution of the
banded tree snail,
*Orthalicus
floridensis.*

SPECIALIZED OR UNIQUE CHARACTERISTICS: The banded tree snail differs from other Florida *Orthalicus* by its complete lack of flame-like axial stripes. It attains a much larger size than the Florida tree snail and has a more inflated shell. This is the only member of the genus to occur naturally on mainland Florida.

BASIS FOR STATUS CLASSIFICATION: At present, the banded tree snail is the only member of the genus in the state to have expanded its range. This has occurred primarily through the introduction of the snail by interested people onto their property. However, the snail appears to have a somewhat tenuous hold in this area because of lower winter temperatures and increased pesticide exposure, including mosquito sprays. The distribution of this species is affected by real estate development in parts of its natural range, just as the other tree snails of Florida, but it is not in immediate danger of extinction. However, *O. floridensis* is of special concern lest it become threatened.

RECOMMENDATIONS: Because humans are a major threat to the snail in suburban areas to which it has been introduced, it would be beneficial to include this species in public education programs concerning tree snails. In addition, the further introduction of this species to suitable habitats will ensure its survival.

PREPARED BY: Jane E. Deisler-Seno, Corpus Christi Museum of Science and History, 1900 N. Chaparral, Corpus Christi, TX 78401.

Subclass Pulmonata

FAMILY POLYGYRIDAE

Threatened

Ridge Scrubsnail

Praticolella bakeri Vanatta

DESCRIPTION: *Praticolella bakeri* has a medium-sized shell (up to 11 mm [0.5 in]) that is depressed-globose in shape, somewhat thin-shelled, and light brown in color. Embryonic whorls are sculptured with spiral threads. Later whorls are somewhat smooth, axial growth lines are weakly developed. There is a distinct, reddish-brown furrow around the body whorl behind the peristome. The peristome is narrowly expanded, and slightly thickened within. The small umbilicus is sometimes partially covered by the expansion of the peristome at the columella.

Ridge Scrubsnail, *Praticolella bakeri* (courtesy of Kurt Auffenberg).

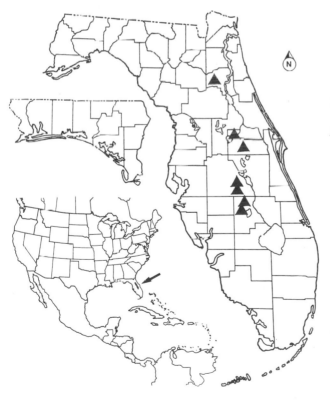

Distribution of the
ridge scrubsnail,
Praticolella bakeri.

RANGE: This snail is known only from sandhill and scrub areas in central Florida in Brevard, Highlands, Orange, Polk, and Putnam counties.

HABITAT: It is apparently restricted to the sandhill and scrub areas of central Florida where it is found in leaf litter around fallen deadwood and the bases of trees.

LIFE HISTORY AND ECOLOGY: Unknown.

BASIS FOR STATUS CLASSIFICATION: The species is ecologically restricted to sandhill and scrub areas in central Florida. These habitats are being destroyed for agricultural and residential uses at an alarming rate.

SPECIALIZED OR UNIQUE CHARACTERISTICS: The unique combination of the characters, size, embryonic whorl sculpture, and the furrow behind the peristome easily distinguishes this species from other *Praticolella* occurring in Florida.

RECOMMENDATIONS: Protection of the remaining unaltered stands of the unique habitats is necessary for the survival of this species.

PREPARED BY: Kurt Auffenberg, Florida Museum of Natural History, University of Florida, Gainesville, FL 32611.

Terrestrial Snail Faunas of Concern

Despite the present lack of adequate collection-based information, there are two very important distributional centers apparent in Florida. First, the Florida panhandle and northeast Florida represent the southern distributional limits of many species of land snails. These species occur in Florida in one or more counties that border Alabama and Georgia, perhaps slightly further south, but rarely below Marion County. Secondly, the fauna of the area south of approximately Palm Beach County on the east coast is unique due to its obvious influence from the Caribbean region. Until future faunal surveys indicate otherwise these two entire faunas should be considered of special concern because of habitat destruction from agriculture, urban and recreational development, and pollution. Surveys are required to determine their present status, and these areas should be monitored in the future.

Faunal lists from these two regions are as follows:
NORTH: *Pomatiopsis lapidaria* (Say), *Gastrocopta armifera* (Say), *G. procera* (Gould), *G. riparia* Hubricht, *G. corticaria* (Say), *Vertigo rugosula* Sterki, *V. teskeyae* Hubricht, *Anguispira strongylodes* (Pfeiffer), *Discus patulus* (De-

shayes), *Helicodiscus notius notius* Hubricht, *Glyphyalinia luticola* Hubricht, *Mesomphix pilsbryi* (Clapp), *Paravitrea conecuhensis* (Clapp), *Ventridens demissus* (Binney), *V. intertextus* (Binney), *Euconulus trochulus* (Reinhardt), *Haplotrema concavum* (Say), *Mesodon perigraptus* (Pilsbry), *Triodopsis palustris* Hubricht, *Stenotrema florida* Pilsbry.

SOUTH: *Lucidella tantilla* (Pilsbry), *Chondropoma dentatum* (Say), *Sterkia eyriesi rhoadsi* (Pilsbry), *Vertigo hebardi, Cerion incanum* (Binney), *Varicella gracillima floridana* Pilsbry, *Lacteoluna seleninu* (Gould), *Hojeda inaguensis* (Weiland), *Thysanophora plagioptycha* (Shuttleworth), *Cochlodinella poeyana* (Orbigny), *Microceramus pontificus* (Gould), *Drymaeus multilineatus* (Say), *Cepolis varians* (Menke).

PREPARED BY: Kurt Auffenberg, Florida Museum of Natural History, University of Florida, Gainesville, FL 32611.

Freshwater Snails

INTRODUCTION: The freshwater snail fauna of Florida includes 83 species and subspecies that belong to 12 families. Most species in freshwater habitats in the state belong to the subclass Prosobranchia. They are characterized by the possession of gills and an operculum that closes across the aperture of the shell. The remainder are in the class Pulmonata and lack these structures. Pulmonates respire using a lung-like cavity in the mantle instead of gills.

Ironically, the smallest freshwater snails (family Hydrobiidae) in the state, some no larger than a grain of sand, are the most species-rich group and have the most restricted geographic ranges and habitat requirements. As you might imagine, these snails are extremely difficult to identify since many have very similar-looking shells. The main features used to distinguish them are found in their reproductive systems and radular teeth.

The largest and most conspicuous freshwater snail native to the state is the apple snail (*Pomacea paludosa*). This snail has the peculiar habit of depositing its pink-shelled eggs out of the water on tree trunks, vegetation, rocks, and other solid objects. Except for the live-bearing snails in the family Viviparidae, most Florida freshwater snails lay gelatinous eggs that are attached to solid objects in the water, particularly aquatic plants, rocks, and other snail shells.

Several snails in the families Pilidae and Thiaridae have been introduced into Florida, possibly originating from releases of aquarium stock. The thiarids are represented by three exotic species in the genera *Tarebia* and *Melanoides* that superficially resemble native species in the family Pleuroceridae. These snails originated in southeast Asia and may compete with native pleurocerids since they inhabit similar habitats. The introduced pilids came from South America. The thiarids are medically important since they can serve as the first intermediate host for the human lung fluke.

The native snail fauna includes both lotic and lentic species. Many of the lotic species occur in springs and spring runs, although several are associated with large rivers that flow southward from Alabama and Georgia. Among the spring forms, a number of species are known from single spring sites, and their total distributions are measured in square meters.

Ecologically, freshwater snails are herbivores or detritivores and play important roles in local food chains. For example, apple snails figure prominently in the diets of snail kites and limpkins. Snails also have been reported from the stomachs of fishes, turtles, and alligators. Unfortunately, we know very little about the ecological roles of the rare or more restricted species. Obviously, even the most minute snails are both ecologically important to many aquatic systems and contribute significantly to the state's overall biotic diversity.

This volume includes nine species of freshwater snails that are considered vulnerable to extinction. Two are listed as endangered. Eight of the nine belong to the family Hydrobiidae and are known from restricted spring sites. The ninth is a pleurocerid snail found only in a short section of the Choctawhatchee River and adjacent tributaries in west Florida.

The current list obviously will be expanded as threats to other Florida taxa are identified. In general, listed species have very restricted ranges and/or habitat requirements and could be significantly threatened by changes in local land use practices and physical disturbance of the habitat that contributes to changes in water quality and/or quantity. For additional information, consult the excellent presentation in *Freshwater Snails of Florida: A Manual for Identification* by Fred G. Thompson.

PREPARED BY: Richard Franz, Florida Museum of Natural History, University of Florida, Gainesville, FL 32611.

Endangered

Freemouth Hydrobe

Aphaostracon chalarogyrus Thompson

OTHER NAMES: Listed as the loose-coiled snail in the 1982 FCREPA volume.

DESCRIPTION: *Aphaostracon chalarogyrus* is a small, slender, brown snail, up to 4 mm (0.16 in) long. The shell is conical, thin, and transparent. There are 4.2–4.5 strongly arched, strongly shouldered whorls (scalariform in large specimens) with a very deeply impressed suture. The aperture is relatively broad (width is 0.80–0.90 times the length) and is widely separated from the preceding whorl. The verge is long and slender and has four to six papillae along the right margin. See Thompson (1968) for more information.

RANGE: This species is restricted to Magnesia Spring, 6 km (3.6 mi) west of Hawthorne, Alachua County, Florida. The spring is in a large circular cement encasement about 7 m (23 ft) in diameter. Adjacent to the cement wall is a small rectangular overflow pool that is 2 m × 3 m (3.3 ft × 10 ft) and only a few centimeters deep. Snails are sparse on the wall and algal mats inside the spring pool but are extremely abundant on algal mats inside the overflow pool.

HABITAT: This snail shows a strong preference for mats of filamentous algae floating in the spring pool and overflow pool at the type locality.

LIFE HISTORY AND ECOLOGY: Unknown.

SPECIALIZED OR UNIQUE CHARACTERISTICS: The species is unique within the genus by having four to six papillae along the right margin of the verge and by having strongly shouldered scalariform whorls with the aperture widely separated from the preceding whorl in mature specimens.

BASIS FOR STATUS CLASSIFICATION: The snail has an extremely restricted range. If the spring is capped to serve as a closed water source, the species will be exterminated. Current developments may cause extinction of this snail.

PREPARED BY: Fred G. Thompson and Kurt Auffenberg, Florida Museum of Natural History, University of Florida, Gainesville, FL 32611.

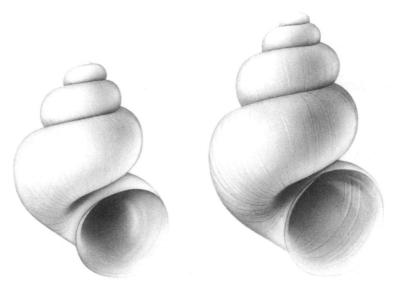

Freemouth Hydrobe, *Aphaostracon chalarogyrus*, front and side (courtesy of Fred G. Thompson).

Distribution of the freemouth hydrobe, *Aphaostracon chalarogyrus*.

Endangered

Enterprise Siltsnail

Cincinnatia monroensis (Dall)

OTHER NAMES: Listed as the Enterprise Spring snail in the 1982 FCREPA volume.

DESCRIPTION: *Cincinnatia monroensis* is a moderately small, brown conical snail with a thick, opaque shell that is about 3.5–4.7 mm (0.14–0.18 in) long. The spire is 1.00–1.35 times the length of the aperture. There are 4.8–5.4 whorls that are separated by a moderately shallow suture. The critical distinguishing features of this species are in the male reproductive system. See Dall (1885) and Thompson (1968) for more information.

RANGE: This species is confined to a small seepage run that originates in a low wooded lot on the south edge of Enterprise, Volusia County, Florida.

Enterprise Siltsnail, *Cincinnatia monroensis* (courtesy of Fred G. Thompson).

Distribution of the Enterprise
siltsnail, *Cincinnatia
monroensis.*

HABITAT: The snail is found on dead leaves along the edge and on the bottom of the seepage run.

LIFE HISTORY AND ECOLOGY: The life history of this species is unknown. Limited ecological data are noted above.

SPECIALIZED OR UNIQUE CHARACTERISTICS: Morphological specialization involves the reproductive structures.

BASIS FOR STATUS CLASSIFICATION: The type locality was the broad stream flowing from Benson's Mineral Spring at Enterprise. Recently the spring was capped as a hydroelectric water source, and all that remains of the original habitat is a small seepage run, originating from a few small seepage springs in a low wooded lot less than three acres in area. The run is less than 175 m (577 ft) long, 0.6 m (2 ft) wide, and 2–12 cm (1–4.7 in) deep. The population density of the snail is very sparse.

RECOMMENDATIONS: The wooded lot serving as a watershed for the seepage run should be maintained in its present state. Efforts should be made to introduce the snail into other springs nearby.

PREPARED BY: Fred G. Thompson and Kurt Auffenberg, Florida Museum of Natural History, University of Florida, Gainesville, FL 32611.

FAMILY HYDROBIIDAE

Threatened

Blue Spring Hydrobe
Aphaostracon asthenes Thompson

OTHER NAMES: Listed as the Blue Spring aphaostracon in the 1982 FCREPA volume.

DESCRIPTION: *Aphaostracon asthenes* is a small, brown snail, up to 2.4 mm (0.1 in) long. The shell is conical, very thin, very fragile, and transparent. There are 4.1–4.5 strongly rounded whorls with a deeply impressed suture. The body whorl is not noticeably enlarged. The aperture is elliptical and is usually attached to the preceding whorl. The verge is long, slender, and devoid of papillae. See Thompson (1968) for more information.

RANGE: This species is confined to the type locality, Blue Spring, 5 km west of Orange City, Volusia County, Florida. It is known from only 15 specimens.

HABITAT: Blue Spring is a large spring that gives rise to a wide, deep spring run that flows west for about 0.4 km (1,320 ft) to the St. Johns River. This snail has been found only in the upper part of the spring run where plants and bottom debris were very sparse.

LIFE HISTORY AND ECOLOGY: Unknown.

SPECIALIZED OR UNIQUE CHARACTERISTICS: The snail is unique among Florida operculate snails because of its very thin, fragile shell.

BASIS FOR STATUS CLASSIFICATION: The Blue Spring hydrobe is known only from the type locality and apparently is very rare.

Blue Spring Hydrobe, *Aphaostracon asthenes*, front and side (courtesy of Fred G. Thompson).

Distribution of the Blue Spring hydrobe, *Aphaostracon asthenes*.

SCALE
0 10 20 30 40 50 Kilometers
0 10 20 30 40 Miles

RECOMMENDATIONS: The type locality should be maintained in as nearly a natural state as possible. Any disturbance is apt to have a severe impact on this already restricted and sparse species.

PREPARED BY: Fred G. Thompson and Kurt Auffenberg, Florida Museum of Natural History, University of Florida, Gainesville, FL 32611.

FAMILY HYDROBIIDAE

Threatened

Wekiwa Hydrobe

Aphaostracon monas (Pilsbry)

OTHER NAMES: Listed as the Wekiwa Springs aphaostracon in the 1982 FCREPA volume.

DESCRIPTION: *Aphaostracon monas* is a small, brown snail, up to 2.5 mm (0.1 in) long. The elongate-conical shell has a deeply impressed suture between the whorls. The whorls are strongly arched but weakly shouldered. The aperture is broadly ovate and is usually free from the preceding whorl. The operculum is nearly multispiral with about six slowly expanding whorls. The verge is elongate and slender and has a single papilla on the right margin near the base. See Thompson (1968) for more information.

RANGE: This species is confined to Wekiwa Springs and spring run from about 1.6 km (1 mi) below the spring, Orange County, Florida.

HABITAT: The snail is found on submerged plants, rocks, and gravel. It is most easily collected by shaking mats of aquatic plants into a pail.

LIFE HISTORY AND ECOLOGY: The life history of this species is unknown. Presumably it is eaten by predaceous arthropods, annelids, and fishes. It feeds primarily on algae.

SPECIALIZED OR UNIQUE CHARACTERISTICS: The multispiral operculum is unique within the genus.

BASIS FOR STATUS CLASSIFICATION: Major alteration of the locality of the snail's restricted distribution could result in extermination of the species.

Distribution of the Wekiwa
hydrobe, *Aphaostracon
monas.*

RECOMMENDATIONS: The spring and run must be left in as nearly a natural state as possible so that no serious environmental disturbance occurs.

PREPARED BY: Fred G. Thompson and Kurt Auffenberg, Florida Museum of Natural History, University of Florida, Gainesville, FL 32611.

FAMILY HYDROBIIDAE

Threatened

Clifton Springs Hydrobe

Aphaostracon theiocrenetus Thompson

OTHER NAMES: Listed as the Sulfur Spring aphaostracon in the 1982 FCREPA volume.

DESCRIPTION: *Aphaostracon theiocrenetus* is a small, brown snail, up to 3 mm (0.12 in) long. The shell is elongate-conical, thin, and subtransparent. There are 4.5–4.9 strongly arched whorls with a deeply impressed suture. The body whorl is inflated. The aperture is elliptical and is loosely attached to or slightly separated from the preceding whorl. The verge is long, slender, and devoid of papillae. See Thompson (1968) for more information.

RANGE: This snail is confined to Clifton Springs Run, about 3 km north of Oviedo, Seminole County, Florida.

HABITAT: The species is found primarily in mats of *Chara* and other vegetation over a clean hard-sand bottom in shallow flowing water.

LIFE HISTORY AND ECOLOGY: Unknown.

SPECIALIZED OR UNIQUE CHARACTERISTICS: The species is unique only by the combination of characters that distinguish it from others of the genus. Nothing is known about the functional adaptations of its morphology or behavior.

Clifton Springs Hydrobe, *Aphaostracon theiocrenetus*, front and side (courtesy of Fred G. Thompson).

Distribution of the Clifton
Springs hydrobe, *Aphaos-*
tracon theiocrenetus.

SCALE

BASIS FOR STATUS CLASSIFICATION: Clifton Springs consists of several small pools that discharge into a common run that enters the south side of Lake Jessup. The spring run is about 175 m (577 ft) long and not more than 7 m (23 ft) wide and 1 m (3.3 ft) deep. The snail is confined to the run and does not occur in the spring pools because of the high concentration of hydrogen sulfide emitted at the boils. Any major alteration, physical or chemical, of the spring run is apt to damage the snail population.

RECOMMENDATIONS: Maintain the spring run in its present condition. Do not permit it to be dredged for a marina.

PREPARED BY: Fred G. Thompson and Kurt Auffenberg, Florida Museum of Natural History, University of Florida, Gainesville, FL 32611.

Species of Special Concern

Dense Hydrobe

Aphaostracon pycnus Thompson

OTHER NAMES: Listed as the thick-shelled aphaostracon in the 1982 FCREPA volume.

DESCRIPTION: *Aphaostracon pycnus* is a small, brown snail, up to 2.8 mm (0.11 in) long. The thick, opaque shell is squat, compact, and cylindric-conical. It has 4.2–4.6 weakly arched whorls with a weakly impressed suture. The body whorl is ponderous. The aperture is auriculate and is tightly appressed against the preceding whorl. The verge is long, slender, and devoid of papillae. See Thompson (1968) for more information.

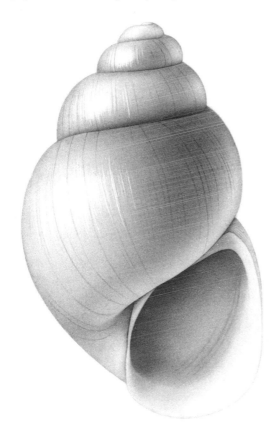

Dense Hydrobe,
Aphaostracon pycnus, front and side
(courtesy of Fred
G. Thompson).

Distribution of the dense hydrobe, *Aphaostracon pycnus.*

RANGE: This species is confined to Alexander Springs Run, Ocala National Forest, Lake County, Florida.

HABITAT: Specimens were found in shallow, quiet pools along the spring run on water lettuce and hyacinths. They occurred over a soft ooze bottom in clean water that contained large, scattered patches of varied aquatic plants.

LIFE HISTORY AND ECOLOGY: The life history is unknown. This snail is a primary consumer, feeding on periphyton; presumably it is eaten by predaceous fishes, arthropods, and annelids.

SPECIALIZED OR UNIQUE CHARACTERISTICS: The thick, compact shell is unique within the genus.

BASIS FOR STATUS CLASSIFICATION: This snail's habitat is protected as part of the Ocala National Forest. However, pollutants from oil drilling operations could eradicate the species if the waterway is contaminated.

RECOMMENDATIONS: The habitat should be maintained in its present nearly natural state.

PREPARED BY: Fred G. Thompson and Kurt Auffenberg, Florida Museum of Natural History, University of Florida, Gainesville, FL 32611.

FAMILY HYDROBIIDAE

Species of Special Concern

Fenney Springs Hydrobe
Aphaostracon xynoelictus Thompson

OTHER NAMES: Listed as the Fenney Springs aphaostracon in the 1982 FCREPA volume.

DESCRIPTION: *Aphaostracon xynoelictus* is a small, slender, brown snail, up to 2.5 mm (0.1 in) long. The shell is conical, thin, and subtransparent. It has 4.0–4.5 strongly rounded whorls that are not shouldered. The suture is deeply impressed. The ovate or elliptical aperture is loosely appressed against or free from the preceding whorl. The verge is long and slender and has three papillae along the right margin. See Thompson (1968) for more information.

RANGE: This snail occurs only at Fenney Springs, 3 km (2 mi) east of Coleman, Sumter County, Florida.

HABITAT: The springs issue from a limestone crevice. During late summer, snails are abundant on the moss-covered limestone boulders at the bottom of the crevice and run.

LIFE HISTORY AND ECOLOGY: This snail is extremely common in August and September. Apparently it is an annual species in which the adults die in the spring and early summer after ovipositing.

SPECIALIZED OR UNIQUE CHARACTERISTICS: The snail is unique only by the combination of characters given above.

BASIS FOR STATUS CLASSIFICATION: The species has an extremely limited distribution. The location of the spring is such that it is not likely to be disturbed by any development. Therefore, even though the snail's range is very restricted, the animal is not in immediate danger.

Distribution of the Fenney
Springs hydrobe, *Aphaos-
tracon xynoelictus.*

RECOMMENDATIONS: The habitat should be maintained in its present
natural state.

PREPARED BY: Fred G. Thompson and Kurt Auffenberg, Florida Museum
of Natural History, University of Florida, Gainesville, FL 32611.

FAMILY HYDROBIIDAE

Species of Special Concern

Ichetucknee Siltsnail

Cincinnatia mica Thompson

OTHER NAMES: Listed as the sand grain snail in the 1982 FCREPA
volume.

DESCRIPTION: *Cincinnatia mica* is a minute, conical, light gray, thin, transparent snail that is up to 2.3 mm (0.1 in) long. The shell has 3.9–4.2 whorls with a deeply impressed suture. The spire is conical and 0.7–1.1 times the length of the aperture. Within its genus the species is characterized primarily by the structure of the male reproductive system. The penis lacks external glandular crests. See Thompson (1968) for more information.

RANGE: This species is confined to a small spring along the west bank of the Ichetucknee River about 1.6 km (1 mi) northeast of U.S. Highway 27, Columbia County, Florida.

HABITAT: The spring issues from two sources beneath a limestone outcropping and forms a small circular pool about 12 m (39 ft) wide and 0.3–0.6 m (1–2 ft) deep. The pool is open and is continuous with the Ichetucknee River. The pool bottom is covered with sand and gravel, and there are moderate deposits of silt along the shore. Snails are found on submerged mosses and on the rootlets throughout the pool. A closely related species, *C. flori dana*, is found immediately adjacent to the pool in the river. The two species do not mix in the river or pool.

LIFE HISTORY AND ECOLOGY: The species has been consistently abundant during the last 13 years at its only known locality.

SPECIALIZED OR UNIQUE CHARACTERISTICS: The extremely small transparent shell is unique within the genus. The lack of a glandular crest on the penis is also unique.

Ichetucknee Siltsnail,
Cincinnatia mica
(courtesy of Fred
G. Thompson).

Distribution of the Ichetucknee siltsnail, *Cincinnatia
mica.*

BASIS FOR STATUS CLASSIFICATION: The species has an extremely
limited distribution. Although its only locality is within the Ichetucknee
State Park, it is confined to an area of less than 110 sq. m and is in danger
of extermination. The shelf on which the spring discharges at this point constitutes a good place to construct a rest station for canoes and swimmers.
Major modifications of this site could eliminate the species.

RECOMMENDATIONS: The particular location of the snail's habitat
should be made inviolate as a natural feature within Ichetucknee State Park.
A permanent sign would focus public notice on the species, and it would also
serve as a marker that would help prevent deliberate modification of the
station.

PREPARED BY: Fred G. Thompson and Kurt Auffenberg, Florida Museum
of Natural History, University of Florida, Gainesville, FL 32611.

Species of Special Concern

Clench's Goniobasis

Elimia clenchi Goodrich

DESCRIPTION: *Elimia clenchi* is an elongated snail that reaches a length of about 28 mm (1.1 in). It has a spire at about 25° angle of expansion and about 9–10 flat-sided whorls. The sculpture consists of 9–12 spiral chords, which bear nodes above the periphery and numerous low arcuate costae or riblets. See Clench and Turner (1956) and Goodrich (1924) for more information.

RANGE: This species is confined to the Choctawhatchee River and its tributaries from the region around Geneva, Alabama, south to Westville, Florida.

Clench's Goniobasis,
Elimia clenchi
(courtesy of Fred
G. Thompson).

Distribution of the Clench's
goniobasis, *Elimia clenchi.*

HABITAT: The snail is found in low-flowing rivers over a sand-silt bottom
and on submerged objects.

LIFE HISTORY AND ECOLOGY: This snail probably feeds on detritus
and periphyton. It is preyed upon by fishes, turtles, and birds.

SPECIALIZED OR UNIQUE CHARACTERISTICS: *Elimia clenchi* is distinguished from all other snails within the Choctawhatchee area by its size,
shape, and sculpture.

BASIS FOR STATUS CLASSIFICATION: The geographic distribution of
this species is extremely restricted.

RECOMMENDATIONS: Maintain the Choctawhatchee River above Westville, Florida, in as nearly a natural state as possible.

PREPARED BY: Fred G. Thompson and Kurt Auffenberg, Florida Museum
of Natural History, University of Florida, Gainesville, FL 32611.

Amphipods

INTRODUCTION: The order Amphipoda contains over 5,500 described species placed in over 100 families. Most amphipod crustaceans are marine, but there are many freshwater species and one family of terrestrial species. The common beach fleas belong to this latter group. These small crustaceans live in burrows in the wet sand or in washed-up sea weed where they scavenge for food. They frequently display the hopping behavior that gives them their name when their seaweed retreats are disturbed. A few groups are parasitic on fish. One group, called whale lice, cling to their mammal hosts and probably feed on diatoms and detritus on the whale's skin.

In Florida, amphipods occur in most freshwater, brackish, marine nearshore, and beach habitats. Two introduced terrestrial species (*Talitrus pacificus, Talitroides alluandi*) have become established in the state. *Hyalella azteca* is probably the most common freshwater amphipod in Florida. It is an extremely important dietary component of many aquatic invertebrates, fishes, and some amphibians and plays a significant role in local aquatic food chains.

Like most marine species, freshwater amphipods generally scavenge plant material, dead animals, and organic detritus. The biology of some common freshwater species is well documented, but little or nothing is known about those that live in groundwater habitats associated with cave or interstitial environments. These are small in size, have unpigmented bodies, and lack eyes. Two groundwater species in the genus *Crangonyx* (family Crangonyctidae) are proposed as species of special concern in the accompanying accounts. Both species are candidates for listing by the U.S. Fish and Wildlife Service. No other species are known to need protection.

PREPARED BY: Richard Franz, Florida Museum of Natural History, University of Florida, Gainesville, FL 32611.

Order Amphipoda
FAMILY CRANGONYCTIDAE

Species of Special Concern

Florida Cave Amphipod
Crangonyx grandimanus Bousfield

DESCRIPTION: *Crangonyx grandimanus* is a 15 mm (0.6 in) long, eyeless species with a translucent, white body that is laterally compressed. The body consists of a short cephalothorax (first thoracic segment fused to the head), series of free thoracic segments, two pairs of antennae, seven pairs of small thoracic legs, several pairs of abdominal swimmerets, and a segmented abdomen. A detailed description of this species is found in Bousfield (1963) and Holsinger (1972, 1977).

RANGE: This species has been collected at 15 sites in Alachua, Dade, Gilchrist, Hernando, Levy, Madison, Marion, Pasco, Suwannee, and Wakulla counties (Franz et al. 1994).

HABITAT: The Florida cave amphipod has been reported from groundwater habitats in caves, wells, and spring caves in Pleistocene, Miocene, Oligocene, and Eocene limestones. It is frequently found in areas of caves where there is little or no visible buildup of organic detritus.

LIFE HISTORY AND ECOLOGY: Sexually mature males are 8–13 mm (0.4–0.6 in) in length; mature females tend to be slightly larger. Females with eggs have been collected in February, March, and December. Breeding is thought to be continuous throughout the year (Holsinger 1972).

SPECIALIZED OR UNIQUE CHARACTERISTICS: This species is one of two obligate cave amphipods known from Florida. It shows the typical reduced eyes and albinistic condition of cave-adapted species.

BASIS FOR STATUS CLASSIFICATION: The species is generally rare but widespread in groundwater habitats. It probably is sensitive to toxic chemicals and other groundwater contaminants.

RECOMMENDATIONS: There are no specific recommendations for this species since it is so widespread, although by protecting caves to conserve other more imperiled cavernicolous crustaceans, this species also will receive protection. Further studies on this biologically unknown amphipod are highly recommended.

PREPARED BY: Richard Franz, Florida Museum of Natural History, University of Florida, Gainesville, FL 32611.

Unidentified amphipod, *Crangonyx* sp. Florida, Jackson County, Florida Caverns State Park, China Cave (courtesy of Barry W. Mansell).

Distribution of the Florida cave amphipod, *Crangonyx grandimanus.*

Species of Special Concern

Hobbs Cave Amphipod

Crangonyx hobbsi Shoemaker

DESCRIPTION: *Crangonyx hobbsi* is a slightly smaller species than *Crangonyx grandimanus*. It is about 11 mm (0.4 in) in total length and eyeless. Its translucent, white body is laterally compressed and consists of a short cephalothorax (first thoracic segment fused to head), series of free thoracic segments, two pairs of antennae, seven pairs of small thoracic legs, a segmented abdomen, and several pairs of abdomenal swimmerets. Specific identification is based on the morphology of the various body segments and appendages. For a detailed description, see Shoemaker (1941) and Holsinger (1972, 1977).

Distribution of the Hobbs cave amphipod, *Crangonyx hobbsi*.

RANGE: *Crangonyx hobbsi* has been reported from 37 sites in Alachua, Citrus, Columbia, Dade, Gilchrist, Hernando, Leon, Levy, Madison, Marion, Pasco, Suwannee, and Wakulla counties (Franz et al. 1994).

HABITAT: This species is confined to groundwater habitats in caves.

LIFE HISTORY AND ECOLOGY: According to Holsinger (1972), breeding takes place all year but ovigerous females are never abundant at any given time. Sexually mature females range in body size from 7.0 to 11.0 mm (0.3–0.4 in); largest males are 9 mm (.36 in).

SPECIALIZED OR UNIQUE CHARACTERISTICS: This amphipod is one of the most specialized species in the genus. Unfortunately, nothing is known concerning the functions of its unusual morphological features.

BASIS FOR STATUS CLASSIFICATION: This crustacean is widespread in groundwater habitats in peninsular Florida. Unlike *Crangonyx grandimanus*, it occasionally can become exceptionally common at some cave sites; the causes of these dramatic population fluctuations are unknown.

RECOMMENDATIONS: Important cave populations, such as those associated with Sweet Gum Cave in Citrus County, and Orange Lake Cave and Sunday Sink in Marion County, should be protected. Since little is known about the natural history, it is desirable to encourage biological studies by qualified persons.

PREPARED BY: Richard Franz, Florida Museum of Natural History, University of Florida, Gainesville, FL 32611.

Isopods

INTRODUCTION: With over 10,000 described species, the order Isopoda is one of the largest groups of crustaceans. In contrast to the laterally compressed bodies of amphipods, the bodies of isopods are flattened dorsoventrally; their heads are usually shield-shaped; and their legs project laterally. Isopods occur in marine, freshwater, and terrestrial habitats. The terrestrial species that occur around Florida homes and lawns commonly are referred to as pill bugs, sow bugs, wood lice, or roly-polies. Terrestrial wood lice have specialized integuments that reduce water loss from their bodies. Most land-dwelling isopods continue to use gills for respiration, although some have developed unique lung-like cavities that assist them in surviving drier conditions.

Most isopods are small (under an inch), but there are at least a few marine species that reach larger sizes, including a group of oceanic species (*Bathynomus*) that can achieve lengths in excess of 1 ft (30 cm). Most species are omnivorous and function as important scavengers in their respective habitats. Certain species are economically important, since they bore into wooden structures, such as pilings, wharfs, and boats, that have been placed in sea or brackish water. Many isopods are parasitic on other crustaceans, cnidarians, sponges, and fish. Wood lice that live in terrestrial settings feed on algae, fungi, moss, bark, and decaying animal and vegetable matter. A few marine and terrestrial isopods are carnivorous.

In freshwater habitats in Florida, aquatic isopods are frequently seen clinging to the undersides of wood, rocks, and other debris in streams, seeps, and springs. Two Florida species, *Caecidotea hobbsi* and *Remasellus parvus*, that occur in groundwater habitats are included in this volume. Certain other species (currently undescribed) recently have been discovered in flooded caves in Orange and Washington counties. However, there is so little known about them at this time that their inclusion in this volume would be premature. Like other crustacean groups, there are probably additional species of marine, freshwater, and terrestrial isopods that will need to be included in future revisions of this volume as threats to them are identified.

PREPARED BY: Richard Franz, Florida Museum of Natural History, University of Florida, Gainesville, FL 32611.

Order Isopoda
FAMILY ASELLIDAE

Rare

Swimming Little Florida Cave Isopod

Remasellus parvus (Steeves)

DESCRIPTION: This cave isopod is superficially similar to *Caecidotea hobbsi* in general appearance but is smaller and has oar-like legs. Specific identification is based on the morphology of the body and appendages. See Bowman and Sket (1985) and Steeves (1964) for detailed descriptions.

RANGE: This species originally was described as *Asellus parva* from specimens taken at Ten Inch Cave in western Alachua County. Additional material was collected by cave divers at Thunder Hole in Madison County, Peacock Springs in Suwannee County, and Split Sink in Wakulla County (Franz et al. 1994).

HABITAT: According to Bowman and Sket (1985), the specimens from Split Sink behaved like the usual asellid isopod while on the walls of this flooded cave, but when they were removed to the water column they swam slowly with what appeared to be metachronal movements of the legs and slight lateral sigmoid movements of the body. Specimens at Peacock Springs were seen in the water about 5 cm (2 in) above the silt.

LIFE HISTORY AND ECOLOGY: Unknown.

SPECIALIZED OR UNIQUE CHARACTERISTICS: Because of its unique morphology and behavior, Bowman and Sket (1985) placed this species of asellid isopod in its own monotypic genus. The species appears to be confined to groundwater habitats in caves in north Florida.

BASIS FOR STATUS CLASSIFICATION: This endemic crustacean is known from only four widely scattered localities in north Florida. Its rarity in collections may be related to this crustacean's small body size, remote habitat, and small population size.

RECOMMENDATIONS: One of the known localities, Peacock Springs, is protected in the Peacock Springs State Preserve. This species, like other Florida cavernicoles, is probably susceptible to groundwater pollution. Cave diving probably does not affect this species. Additional survey efforts for this isopod should be encouraged, and voucher specimens should be taken as new sites are found.

Distribution of the swimming little Florida cave isopod, *Remasellus parvus*.

PREPARED BY: Richard Franz, Florida Museum of Natural History, University of Florida, Gainesville, FL 32611.

FAMILY ASELLIDAE

Species of Special Concern

Florida Cave Isopod
Caecidotea hobbsi (Maloney)

OTHER NAMES: Hobbs cave isopod.

DESCRIPTION: The Florida cave isopod is a small crustacean, about 15 mm (0.6 in) in length, with a translucent, white body that is compressed dorsoventrally. Its head and first body segment are fused into a cephalothorax. The remaining body segments are flattened and extend out over the basal parts of the appendages. The abdominal segments are fused, forming a large shield. Two pairs of antennae and seven pairs of long walking legs are present. Specific identification is based on the morphology of these structures. See Maloney (1939) and Steeves (1964) for detailed descriptions.

RANGE: *Caecidotea hobbsi* is reported from five caves in Alachua, Jackson, and Marion counties, Florida. It also is known from a crayfish burrow in Calhoun County, Florida, and from a spring at Emory University, De Kalb County, Georgia (Franz et al. 1994). Unidentified isopods have been reported from subterranean sites in a number of other Florida counties (Franz et al. 1994).

HABITAT: Specimens are found in small pools in caves with decaying leaves and wood and in wells that intersect caves. The Calhoun County record is based on specimens from a burrow of the crayfish (*Procambarus rogersi*).

Distribution of the Florida
cave isopod, *Caecidotea
hobbsi.*

LIFE HISTORY AND ECOLOGY: Unknown.

SPECIALIZED OR UNIQUE FEATURES: This freshwater isopod is adapted for life in groundwater habitats. It is not totally restricted to caves and may best be considered a phreatobite, a species that lives in the water that is held in interstitial spaces between particles of soil or rock.

BASIS FOR STATUS CLASSIFICATION: Little is known about the distribution and natural history of the Florida cave isopod. It apparently is not common anywhere, although it appears widely distributed. Searches of springs and other groundwater habitats in Florida and Georgia should be encouraged to further define its distribution.

RECOMMENDATIONS: Protection of cave sites within the range of this species should enable the species to survive. It is probably susceptible to groundwater pollution.

PREPARED BY: Richard Franz, Florida Museum of Natural History, University of Florida, Gainesville, FL 32611.

Class Malacostraca
Order Decapoda

Shrimps, Crayfishes, and Crabs

INTRODUCTION: Most of the Florida decapod fauna are marine species. Other than three grapsid crabs intimately tied to mangrove habitats in south Florida, no marine species have been identified as deserving protection.

Seventeen crayfishes and one shrimp are identified in this volume as vulnerable to extinction. Most of these crustaceans are cavernicolous. The remainder live in vulnerable surface environments and have very restricted distributions.

Changes in water quality from increased urban development, some forms of agriculture, siltation, and pollution can have detrimental effects on native freshwater decapods, particularly those associated with specialized habitats.

The Squirrel Chimney cave shrimp, the only shrimp that is included in the present list, is known from one cave site in western Alachua County. It is closely related to the grass shrimp that is abundant in local surface freshwater habitats in peninsular Florida. Because of its restricted range and unique habitat, the Squirrel Chimney cave shrimp is vulnerable to groundwater pollution and can suffer from disruptions in the flow of detrital material into the Squirrel Chimney cave system. Recently, this species was listed as Threatened by the United States Fish and Wildlife Service (Anon. 1990).

Cambarid crayfishes form the largest group of decapods that inhabit freshwater habitats in Florida. This fauna includes 55 taxa (including several subspecies), which belong to six genera: *Cambarellus, Cambarus, Fallicambarus, Faxonella, Procambarus,* and *Troglocambarus* (Franz and Franz 1990). Only Arkansas, Alabama, Georgia, Mississippi, and Tennessee have larger crayfish faunas. A recent key to Florida crayfishes by Hobbs and Hobbs (1991) is extremely helpful in the identification of these species. Crayfishes are unusual among decapod crustaceans in that adult males undergo alternating morphological forms. Breeding males are said to be in the "first form" condition (usually written as Form I). They are distinguished from non-reproductive males in the "second form" condition (Form II) by the presence of corneous processes on the first pleopods. The arrangement of these structures in the Form I male is essential for identification. In the Form II condition, these processes are blunted and never corneous and are less valuable as taxonomic tools. The switching between forms I and II occurs with molting.

Cambarid crayfishes occur in nearly every freshwater habitat in Florida. Ecologically, they have been grouped by their ability to construct burrows. Obligate burrowers (primary burrowers) have complex burrow systems, usually in association with stream banks and floodplain forests. The second group (secondary burrowers) most commonly occurs in flatwoods where soil conditions alternate between wet and dry. The burrows of these species usually consist of simple tubes that penetrate the water table. The third group rarely if ever burrows. They are usually stream species and may excavate only a pallet under debris on the bottom or under the bank, or may be found in aquatic vegetation in the water column. Certain surface crayfish groups in Florida invaded groundwater habitats in the geologic past, giving rise to species that are now restricted to subterranean habitats. These cavernicolous species are not only albinistic with reduced eyes, but also have become physiologically and behaviorally adjusted to dark, low energy environments. Many of these species are known from only one cave system.

The cavernicolous decapods are affected by changes in surface land use practices that disrupt the flow into cave systems of organic detritus that they use as food. Cavernicolous crayfishes have two different life styles, which may be correlated with the vulnerability of populations (Franz and Lee 1982). Members of the *Procambarus lucifugus* complex often select cave habitats that contain large accumulations of organic material in detrital cones under sinkholes or bat roosts. Conversely, *Procambarus pallidus* and possibly *P. orcinus* and *P. horsti* inhabit less enriched cave sites. This apparent difference is thought to be reflected in gill respiration rates (Dickson and Franz 1980), whole metabolic rates (Franz and Lee 1982; DiMarco pers. comm.), and population structures (Franz and Lee 1982). Since crayfishes in the *lucifugus* complex concentrate at sources of organic input, they are more susceptible to local extirpation when cave entrances are destroyed or bat populations are eliminated. Crayfishes in the *pallidus* complex maintain more dispersed populations and are thought to be less vulnerable to these types of perturbations since they are not as dependent on point sources for food. However, some evidence suggests that all of the cavernicolous crustaceans can be affected by the introduction of toxic chemicals, particularly pesticides and herbicides. Several major kills of *P. pallidus* have been reported by divers in caves in the upper Suwannee River basin but the causes were not known (Franz et al. 1993; Streever 1992).

The decapod crustacean fauna in freshwater habitats of Florida is still ecologically unstudied. Since many species are potentially impacted by changes in habitat quality, I encourage more investigations on their life cycles, behavior, and ecology. This information is fundamental in providing sound management to protect these unique invertebrates.

PREPARED BY: Richard Franz, Florida Museum of Natural History, University of Florida, Gainesville, FL 32611.

Endangered

Squirrel Chimney Cave Shrimp
Palaemonetes cummingi Chace

OTHER NAMES: Florida cave shrimp.

DESCRIPTION: The Squirrel Chimney cave shrimp, closely related to the local surface grass shrimp *Palaemonetes paludosus*, is cave-adapted. Its albinistic body is about 1.3 in (30 mm) in total length. Mohr and Poulson (1966) provide an excellent photograph of a similar cave shrimp. Chace (1954) gives a detailed description of the adult.

RANGE: This shrimp apparently is restricted to groundwater habitats in the flooded Squirrel Chimney cave in western Alachua County, Florida.

HABITAT: Squirrel Chimney is a deep sinkhole with vertical walls that lead down to groundwater (see photograph in Mohr and Poulson 1966). Two small holes open in the face of the sink slightly above the water and lead into a wide fissure that is partially filled with water. Shrimps have been sighted at the surface both in the open sink and in this fissure. There are less than a dozen known specimens of this crustacean, but presumably a larger resident population occurs at greater depths. This species has not been observed in other caves and sinks in the surrounding area.

LIFE HISTORY AND ECOLOGY: The life cycle of this species is similar to that reported for the local surface-dwelling grass shrimp, *Palaemonetes pallidosus*, with three larval stages. An ovigerous female collected in July contained 35 embryos. Hatching occurred 29 days later. At hatching the larvae were slightly larger than similar larvae of the surface species. The larvae and first postlarvae have smaller amounts of eye pigment but are otherwise similar to related surface shrimps. See Dobkin (1971) for detailed descriptions of these immature stages. The Squirrel Chimney cave shrimp is associated with *Procambarus lucifugus alachua*, *P. pallidus*, and *Troglocambarus maclanei* at Squirrel Chimney.

SPECIALIZED OR UNIQUE CHARACTERISTICS: *Palaemonetes cummingi* is the only cave shrimp known from Florida.

BASIS FOR STATUS CLASSIFICATION: The entire world population of this shrimp apparently exists in Squirrel Chimney. Efforts to collect this spe-

Distribution of the Squirrel
Chimney cave shrimp,
Palaemonetes cummingi.

cies in other nearby caves have been unsuccessful. Urban development associated with the expansion of the Gainesville metropolitan area could severely alter land use practices in the immediate vicinity of Squirrel Chimney within the near future. These changes could impact groundwater quality and quantity, thus imperiling this rare crustacean.

RECOMMENDATIONS: This shrimp was listed as Threatened on 21 June 1990 by the U.S. Fish and Wildlife Service (Anon. 1990). It is desirable to protect Squirrel Chimney and a buffer zone of native vegetation around the sink. Nothing should impede the natural flow of detrital matter into the cave, and human access should be limited to qualified persons who monitor the status of the shrimp and its environment. Attempts should be made to purchase the sink and its immediate surroundings. The Alachua County Comprehensive Plan and zoning regulations should include restrictions on the type of development and the use of chemical toxins in the immediate area of the sink to protect water quantity and quality.

PREPARED BY: Richard Franz, Florida Museum of Natural History, University of Florida, Gainesville, FL 32611.

Threatened

Orlando Cave Crayfish

Procambarus (*Lonnbergius*) *acherontis* (Lonnberg)

OTHER NAMES: Orange-Seminole cave crayfish

DESCRIPTION: The Orlando cave crayfish has reduced, unpigmented eyes and an albinistic body 55 mm (2.3 in) in total length. Specific identification is based on the features of the first pleopod of the reproductive (Form I) male and other body parts and appendages. For a detailed description of this crayfish, see Hobbs (1942).

RANGE: *Procambarus acherontis* has been reported from a well near Lake Brantley (type locality), Palm Springs, and a well in Altamonte Springs in Seminole County; and from a well at Long Lake, Wekiva Springs, and a cave system near Apopka in Orange County (Franz et al. 1994). These sites lie within a small limestone region along the Wekiva River.

HABITAT: This crayfish is restricted to groundwater sites associated with spring caves and wells. It has been reported from the lighted portions of sinkholes and from the vicinity of spring openings at several sites. At the Apopka site, divers reported finding specimens throughout the cave system, as well as in the lighted "blue hole" portion of the sinkhole entrance. Presumably these white crustaceans are vulnerable to fish predation in the lighted vents of spring caves, such as those at Wekiva and Palm springs.

LIFE HISTORY AND ECOLOGY: Reproductive males (Form I) have been found in March, April, June, and November at the Apopka site (unpublished data) and in November (1938) at Palm Springs. No egg-bearing females have been observed. The Orlando cave crayfish has been found in association with an undescribed species of spider cave crayfish in the genus *Troglocambarus* at the Apopka site.

SPECIALIZED OR UNIQUE CHARACTERISTICS: This cavernicolous crayfish is of particular interest because it represents an aberrant, probably relictual, species with no surviving surface relatives. A closely related species, *Procambarus morrisi* Hobbs and Franz, was recently described from a cave in Putnam County (Hobbs and Franz 1990). Hobbs (1942) suggests that this group of crayfishes was derived from the earliest crayfish stocks that invaded the Florida peninsula.

Orlando Cave Crayfish, *Procambarus acherontis*. Florida, Orange County,
Apopka Blue Sink (courtesy of Barry W. Mansell).

Distribution of the Orlando
cave crayfish, *Procambarus
acherontis*.

SCALE

0 10 20 30 40 50 Kilometers

0 10 20 30 40 Miles

BASIS FOR STATUS CLASSIFICATION: The entire world population of this crayfish is restricted to a small limestone area that lies completely within the Orlando metropolitan area. The extensive urbanization in this area is affecting both water quality and quantity of local groundwater reserves.

RECOMMENDATIONS: Little can be done to conserve this crayfish and its associated fauna, other than protecting known sites of occurrence. Wekiva Springs is protected within the Wekiva Springs State Park; however, Palm Springs and the site near Apopka are still in private ownership. Population trends, particularly at the Apopka site, should be carefully monitored, in order to assess changes in the population and its groundwater environment. Attempts should be made to acquire the site at Apopka. The species is a candidate for listing by the U.S. Fish and Wildlife Service (Wood 1991).

PREPARED BY: Richard Franz, Florida Museum of Natural History, University of Florida, Gainesville, FL 32611.

FAMILY CAMBARIDAE

Threatened

Putnam County Cave Crayfish

Procambarus (Lonnbergius) morrisi Hobbs and Franz

DESCRIPTION: *Procambarus morrisi* has an albinistic body about 50 mm (2 in) in total length and reduced eyes without pigment spots. Specific identification is based on the ornamentation of the first pleopod of reproductive (Form I) males and other body features. A detailed description can be found in Hobbs and Franz (1990).

RANGE: This crayfish is known only from Devil's Sink (type locality), near Interlachen, Putnam County, Florida.

HABITAT: Large numbers of crayfishes were found in a small cave at the bottom of a deep water-filled sinkhole at a water depth in excess of 100 ft.

LIFE HISTORY AND ECOLOGY: Reproductive (Form I) males were found in March. No egg-bearing females are known. No other troglobitic species were encountered at the time these collections were made.

SPECIALIZED OR UNIQUE CHARACTERISTICS: This newly described cave crayfish is a member of the subgenus *Lonnbergius*. Crayfishes in this group appear to represent a relictual distribution associated with the eastern

Distribution of the Putnam
County cave crayfish,
Procambarus morrisi.

slope of the old Northern Highland of the Florida peninsula. Crayfishes in
the subgenus do not share close relationships with any other living crayfish
species.

BASIS OF STATUS CLASSIFICATION: The only known site for this
species is located on private land in the lake district near the town of Interlachen. This area currently is subject to land speculation and development,
particularly around the lakes. The sink is used by locals as a swimming hole
and by SCUBA divers. Divers probably do not pose any threat to these crustaceans, although none of these crayfishes should be collected except in connection with scientific studies. Divers report junk cars and other trash in the
bottom of the sink. There is a real possibility that toxic chemicals could be
dumped into the sink, killing the crayfishes in the cave.

RECOMMENDATIONS: The site should be secured through acquisition or
conservation easement.

PREPARED BY: Richard Franz, Florida Museum of Natural History, University of Florida, Gainesville, FL 32611, and Tom Morris, 2629 NW 12th
Avenue, Gainesville, FL 32605.

Threatened

Panama City Crayfish

Procambarus (Leconticambarus) econfinae Hobbs

DESCRIPTION: The Panama City crayfish is small, up to 48 mm (about 2 in) in total length. Specific identification is based on the ornamentation of the first pleopod of reproductive (Form I) males and other body and append- age features. For a detailed description, see Hobbs (1942).

RANGE: This crayfish is known from a small flatwoods area on the small peninsula on which Panama City (Bay County) is located.

HABITAT: This crayfish is considered a secondary burrower in wet flat- woods soils. It constructs simple burrows that consist of a single passage downward from 1 to 3 ft in depth. The entrance is marked with a crude chimney composed of soil excavated from inside the burrow. Recent speci- mens were netted from flooded roadside ditches that were draining into pine flatwoods (Paul Moler, pers. comm.).

Panama City Crayfish, *Procambarus econfinae*. Florida, Bay County (courtesy of Barry W. Mansell).

Distribution of the Panama
City crayfish, *Procambarus
econfinae.*

LIFE HISTORY AND ECOLOGY: In the original collections, there were
15 Form I males and 8 egg-bearing females caught in April and June (1938).
This species has been collected with the crayfish *Procambarus pycnogono-
podus* (Hobbs 1942).

SPECIALIZATIONS OR UNIQUE CHARACTERISTICS: As a member
of the flatwoods community, this species, like other similar crayfishes, probably plays an important role in local food chains and in the aeration of heavy
clay soils in which it burrows.

BASIS FOR STATUS CLASSIFICATION: Until recently, it was feared
that this species had become extinct as a result of wetland drainage and the
impacts of increased urbanization. However, recent collections in the vicinity
of the type locality (near junction of County Roads 389 and 390) indicate
that the species is still extant, but due to its small range it should be considered extremely vulnerable to extinction because of continued drainage projects and development in the Panama City area.

RECOMMENDATIONS: There is a serious need for an intensive survey to locate additional colonies. As specific sites are identified, they should be protected from human activity. This species has been listed as a Species of Special Concern by the Florida Game and Fresh Water Fish Commission (Wood 1991).

PREPARED BY: Barry Mansell, 2826 Rosselle Street, Jacksonville, FL 32205.

FAMILY CAMBARIDAE

Rare

Miami Cave Crayfish

Procambarus (*Leconticambarus*) *milleri* Hobbs

DESCRIPTION: The Miami cave crayfish has a lightly pigmented and patterned body, up to 30 mm (1.2 in) in total length, with pigmented eyes. Specific identification is based on the ornamentation of the first pleopod in reproductive (Form I) males and other features. A detailed description of this species can be found in Hobbs (1971).

RANGE: This crayfish is known only from shallow wells in Dade County. The type series was taken from a 6.6 m (22 ft) deep well at the Little Bird Nursery and Garden Store (type locality), Miami, in 1968, while a second series was collected in another well near Homestead in 1992 by P. Radice and W. Loftus.

HABITAT: Crayfishes were pumped from solution channels in the Biscayne aquifer.

LIFE HISTORY AND ECOLOGY: Reproductive (Form I) males were found in February, March, and May at the type locality. The original collections from this well also yielded specimens of amphipods *Crangonyx grandimanus*, *C. hobbsi*, and *C. floridensis*. Specimens from the second series are under study, and more information will soon be available (W. Loftus, pers. comm.).

SPECIALIZED OR UNIQUE CHARACTERISTICS: This crayfish possibly represents a Pleistocene relict that evolved from the closely related surface crayfish, *Procambarus alleni*, during a period of lowered sea levels when caves may have been more accessible for colonization. The Miami cave crayfish is the only cavernicolous crayfish known from south Florida.

Miami Cave Crayfish, *Procambarus milleri*. Florida, Dade County, well near Homestead (courtesy of William F. Loftus and P. Radice).

BASIS FOR STATUS CLASSIFICATION: Little is known about this species. It is probably extremely vulnerable to groundwater contamination. Since it is restricted to one of the fastest growing urban areas in the United States, the Miami cave crayfish probably has little chance of survival, particularly in light of the impacts of groundwater pumping, salt water intrusion, and the introduction of other toxins.

RECOMMENDATIONS: Until more is known about the species, there is probably little that can be done to protect it. There should be a continued search for this species at other sites in order to better determine its distribution and status.

PREPARED BY: Richard Franz, Florida Museum of Natural History, University of Florida, Gainesville, FL 32611.

Distribution of the Miami cave crayfish, *Procambarus milleri.*

FAMILY CAMBARIDAE

Rare

Silver Glen Springs Cave Crayfish

Procambarus (Ortmannicus) attiguus Hobbs and Franz

DESCRIPTION: The Silver Glen Springs cave crayfish is a 52 mm (2 in), albinistic species with reduced eyes without facets or pigment. It has a reduced pouch-like protrusion on the anterioventral surface of the branchiostegites which forms the "big-cheek" in the related *Procambarus delicatus.* For more descriptive information, consult Hobbs and Franz (1992).

Distribution of the Silver
Glen Springs cave crayfish,
Procambarus attiguus.

RANGE: This species is known only from Silver Glen Springs cave, Marion County, Florida.

HABITAT: The type series of this crayfish was collected in a large cavern, about 213 m (700 ft) inside the main spring entrance. Specimens have been found in flocculence of reddish organic material, possibly bacterial growth, on a breakdown slope near the floor of the cavern, and floating about 30 m (100 ft) above the floor in the water column, presumably displaced from the ceiling by bubbles of air escaping from the diver's regulator (Hobbs and Franz 1992).

LIFE HISTORY AND ECOLOGY: Nothing is known.

SPECIALIZED OR UNIQUE CHARACTERISTICS: This endemic species in the St. Johns River drainage is an evolutionary link to the unique and highly specialized spider cave crayfish.

BASIS OF STATUS CLASSIFICATION: It is known from only one cave on the west shore of Lake George.

RECOMMENDATIONS: Silver Glen Springs is managed by the U.S. Forest Service. Other than protecting the groundwater and the spring's drainage basin from chemical pollution, little needs to be done to conserve this species. Surveys of other spring sites in the Lake George area should be encouraged in order to determine the geographic range of this species and to resolve its relationship with the big-cheeked cave crayfish.

PREPARED BY: Richard Franz, Florida Museum of Natural History, University of Florida, FL 32611, and Tom Morris, 2629 NW 12th Avenue, Gainesville, FL 32605.

FAMILY CAMBARIDAE

Rare

Big-Cheeked Cave Crayfish
Procambarus (*Ortmannicus*) *delicatus* Hobbs and Franz

OTHER NAMES: Alexander Springs cave crayfish.

DESCRIPTION: This small albinistic crayfish, about 50 mm (2 in) in total length, has reduced eyes without facets or pigment. The combination of enlarged mouth parts, a bulge on the anterioventral branchiostegal region of the carapace, and delicate features suggest a relationship with the cavernicolous crayfishes in the genus *Troglocambarus*. Unfortunately, there are no reproductive (Form I) males available for study at this time, so a determination of the relationships of this species must wait. For a discussion of the unusual features expressed in this crayfish, see Hobbs and Franz (1986). This species is a member of the *seminolae* group (Hobbs and Franz 1986).

RANGE: *Procambarus delicatus* is known only from Alexander Springs in Lake County. Recent specimens collected from Silver Glen Springs along the St. Johns River in Marion County represent the closely related species, *Procambarus attiguus* (see Hobbs and Franz 1992).

HABITAT: The first two specimens reportedly were collected at the mouth of a small vent and in the main spring boil at Alexander Springs (Relyea et al. 1976), while the third specimen was taken in "an algal covered area at a depth of a little less than two meters and about 15 meters from the nearest vent" (Hobbs and Franz 1986).

LIFE HISTORY AND ECOLOGY: Nothing is known concerning the life cycle of this interesting species.

Distribution of the big-
cheeked cave crayfish,
Procambarus delicatus.

SPECIALIZED OR UNIQUE CHARACTERISTICS: This cavernicolous species possibly represents an evolutionary link with the unique spider crayfishes in the genus *Troglocambarus*. Unfortunately, because there are no reproductive males known for this species at this time, its relationships remain unclear.

BASIS FOR STATUS CLASSIFICATION: The species is probably restricted to the limestone area in the vicinity of Lake George in the middle portion of the St. Johns River basin.

RECOMMENDATIONS: It is essential that additional material be collected so that when reproductive males become available a more detailed description can be presented and the affinities of this species to other crayfishes can be determined.

PREPARED BY: Richard Franz, Florida Museum of Natural History, University of Florida, Gainesville, FL 32611 and Tom Morris, 2629 NW 12th Avenue, Gainesville, FL 32605.

Rare

Santa Fe Cave Crayfish

Procambarus (Ortmannicus) erythrops Relyea and Sutton

OTHER NAMES: Red-eyed cave crayfish, Sims Sink cave crayfish.

DESCRIPTION: The Santa Fe cave crayfish reaches 90 mm (3.5 in) in total length. Its body is without pigment, and its eyes are reduced and without facets. Its scientific name refers to the obvious reddish pigment spot found on each eye. Specific identification is based on the ornamentation of the first pleopod of the reproductive (Form I) male and other features. A detailed description is found in Relyea and Sutton (1975). This species is a member of the *lucifugus* complex (Franz and Lee 1982).

RANGE: This crayfish is known from several locations in southern Suwannee County, but only two sites (Sims Sink [type locality] and Azure Blue Sink) contain significant populations. Sims Sink recently was secured by The Nature Conservancy and will be managed to protect this species. The conservation status at most other sites is undocumented, although no crayfishes have been seen at Hildreth Cave after it became a garbage dump in the early 1970s.

HABITAT: *Procambarus erythrops* occupies debris cones under large flooded sinkholes. As yet, no colonies have been found in association with bat colonies. Little or no water flow, other than vertical movements associated with local changes in the water table, has been noted in cave sites where this species occurs. This suggests that this species, like others in *lucifugus* complex, prefers the more stagnant portions of cave systems where detrital material can accumulate without being washed away.

LIFE HISTORY AND ECOLOGY: Reproductive males were caught in January, February, March, May, June, August, September, November, and December. No egg-bearing females are known. In Sims Sink, *P. erythrops* is found in association with *Troglocambarus maclanei* and *Crangonyx hobbsi*.

SPECIALIZED OR UNIQUE CHARACTERISTICS: Like other members of the *lucifugus* complex, this species apparently requires groundwater sites near large accumulations of organic detritus.

BASIS FOR STATUS CLASSIFICATION: This species is limited to the limestone area in southern Suwannee County. Its protection at Sims Sink, through The Nature Conservancy ownership, provides adequate protection

Santa Fe Cave Crayfish, *Procambarus erythrops*. Florida, Suwannee County, Sims Sink (courtesy of Barry W. Mansell).

Distribution of the Santa Fe cave crayfish, *Procambarus erythrops*.

SCALE

0 10 20 30 40 50 Kilometers

0 10 20 30 40 Miles

for this species at this time. However, even the status of this population could change if groundwater becomes contaminated with hazardous chemicals, particularly agricultural pesticides and herbicides.

RECOMMENDATIONS: There should be efforts to secure the population at Azure Blue Sink. Crayfish populations and water quality should be routinely monitored at the two most important localities. This crustacean is listed as a Species of Special Concern by the Florida Game and Fresh Water Fish Commission (Wood 1991).

PREPARED BY: Richard Franz, Florida Museum of Natural History, University of Florida, Gainesville, FL 32611.

FAMILY CAMBARIDAE

Rare

Orange Lake Cave Crayfish
Procambarus (Ortmannicus) franzi Hobbs and Lee

DESCRIPTION: Like other cavernicolous crayfishes, the Orange Lake cave crayfish is albinistic and has reduced eyes with no facets. There is no prominent eye spot in this species. The largest specimens range up to 65 mm (2.5 in) in total body length. Specific identification is based on the first pleopod of the reproductive male (Form I) and other body features. Additional descriptive information can be found in Hobbs and Lee (1976). This species is considered a member of the *lucifugus* complex (Franz and Lee 1982).

RANGE: This cave crayfish is known from only three caves, in the vicinity of Orange Lake in north central Marion County. The most significant site is Orange Lake Cave (type locality).

HABITAT: Two of the three sites are caves that house nursery colonies of the southeastern bat (*Myotis austroriparous*). The third is a flooded cave system that is entered through a big sink that accumulates a large quantity of detritus.

LIFE HISTORY AND ECOLOGY: Reproductive (Form I) males have been found in January, May, and June. No egg-bearing females are known. At Orange Lake Cave, this crayfish was found in association with *Troglocambarus maclanei* and *Crangonyx hobbsi*.

Distribution of the Orange
Lake cave crayfish,
Procambarus franzi.

SPECIALIZED OR UNIQUE CHARACTERISTICS: Like other members
of the *lucifugus* complex, this cavernicolous crayfish focuses its activities at
major sources of detrital input.

BASIS FOR STATUS CLASSIFICATION: Since the species has a very
restricted distribution and is dependent on accumulations of detritus, it is
vulnerable to habitat changes from both within caves and around their entrances. Presumably, changes in groundwater quality and quantity, as well as
disruption of associated bat colonies, could lead to the extirpation of important crayfish colonies. All known localities are in private ownership.

RECOMMENDATIONS: Secure Orange Lake Cave either through purchase
or conservation easement. The crayfish and bats at Orange Lake Cave should
be monitored in order to identify changes in their populations. Attempts also
should be made to monitor water quality at all three sites.

PREPARED BY: Richard Franz, Florida Museum of Natural History, University of Florida, Gainesville, FL 32611.

Rare

Big Blue Spring Cave Crayfish

Procambarus (*Ortmannicus*) *horsti* Hobbs and Means

OTHER NAMES: Horst's cave crayfish.

DESCRIPTION. Like other cavernicolous crayfishes, the body of this species is albinistic; eyes are reduced with no facets or eye spots. The largest crayfishes measure in excess of 83 mm (3 in) in total body length. Specific identification is based on the ornamentation of the first pleopod of the reproductive (Form I) male and other body features. A detailed description is found in Hobbs and Means (1972). This is a member of the *pallidus* complex (Franz and Lee 1982).

RANGE: Specimens of this species are known from Big Blue Spring on the Wacissa River in Jefferson County, a well on the Pichard Farm (4.5 miles east of Tallahassee) in Leon County, and Shepards Spring at the St. Marks Wildlife Refuge in Wakulla County. Reports of this species at Wakulla and Sally Ward Springs in Wakulla County (Morris 1989) need verification. It appears more widely distributed within the Tallahassee area than *Procambarus orcinus*.

HABITAT: The species apparently is associated with spring caves. Crayfishes were seen in the boil area of springs as well as in caves at water depths of 21–26 m (70–80 ft).

LIFE HISTORY AND ECOLOGY: Reproductive males have been collected in October. No egg-bearing females are known.

SPECIALIZED OR UNIQUE CHARACTERISTICS: Like other cavernicolous crayfishes, this species is adapted to a subterranean existence. It appears to be more widely distributed than its close relative *Procambarus orcinus*.

BASIS FOR STATUS CLASSIFICATION: *P. horsti* is confirmed from only three sites, all in the limestone region south of Tallahassee. This crayfish, like other cave species, is dependent on organic detritus from the surface for food. Changes in land use on the surface and presumably groundwater contamination could impact these subterranean crustaceans.

Distribution of the Big Blue
Spring cave crayfish,
Procambarus horsti.

RECOMMENDATION: The upstream drainage basins of the Wacissa River in Jefferson County and Spring Creek in the St. Marks area should be protected. Reports of *P. horsti* from Wakulla and Sally Ward springs should be investigated, and voucher specimens from these sites should be deposited at the Smithsonian Institution, where there is comparative material available for study. There should be an intensive survey of springs and caves in the Tallahassee limestone area to find additional localities where this species exists.

PREPARED BY: Richard Franz, Florida Museum of Natural History, University of Florida, Gainesville, FL 32611.

Rare

Coastal Lowland Cave Crayfish
Procambarus (Ortmannicus) leitheuseri Franz and Hobbs

DESCRIPTION: *Procambarus leitheuseri* is albinistic, and eyes are reduced without facets. Eyes possess dark pigment spots. Identification is based on the ornamentation of the first pleopod of the reproductive (Form I) male and other body features. Descriptive information is available in Franz and Hobbs (1983). This species is a member of the *lucifugus* complex.

RANGE: This crayfish is apparently restricted to freshwater lenses in the limestone area along the Gulf Coast in southwestern Hernando and northwestern Pasco counties. Specimens have been collected from six sites, including one located in a salt marsh area adjacent to the Gulf of Mexico. It also has been sighted at two other sinkhole caves in the area. The type locality is Eagles Nest Sink in Hernando County.

HABITAT: This crustacean has been recovered from vertical sinkholes at water depths in excess of 60 m (200 ft). It has been observed in these caves only in the freshwater layer that lies above salt water zone. Most of the sinks in which this crayfish has been collected show some tidal influences.

LIFE HISTORY AND ECOLOGY: Only one reproductive male has ever been collected. No egg-bearing females are known. At Eagles Nest, troglobitic associates include the northern spider cave crayfish, *Troglocambarus maclanei*, and the amphipods *Crangonyx hobbsi* and *C. grandimanus*.

SPECIALIZED OR UNIQUE CHARACTERISTICS: As a member of the cavernicolous *P. lucifugus* complex, it presumably possesses similar morphological and physiological adaptations for life in high-energy cave environments. This crayfish's presence in deep freshwater sites close to the Gulf of Mexico provides possible clues as to how these crayfishes could have survived past sea level fluctuations.

BASIS OF STATUS CLASSIFICATION: The species is vulnerable to saltwater intrusion and other changes in water quality. As a result of rapid urbanization in Hernando and Pasco counties, the surface area above these deep caves could be affected by changes in land use practices. Alteration of sinkhole ponds that connect with these vertical tubes could change the type, quality, and quantity of detrital matter that enters these caves, thus impacting the crayfish's food supply.

Distribution of the coastal
lowland cave crayfish,
Procambarus leitheuseri.

RECOMMENDATIONS: It is important to protect key sites, such as Eagles
Nest and the Die Polder sinks. Because of the sinks' great depths, it will be
extremely difficult to monitor crayfish populations and water quality; however, checks on the water quality in surface pools may provide an indication
of the conditions in the deep groundwater.

PREPARED BY: Richard Franz, Florida Museum of Natural History, University of Florida, Gainesville, FL 32611.

Rare

Withlacoochee Light-Fleeing Cave Crayfish
Procambarus (*Ortmannicus*) *lucifugus lucifugus* (Hobbs)

DESCRIPTION: *Procambarus lucifugus* is composed of at least four populations, each possibly isolated from one another by surface features that appear to limit contact. Identification of *P. lucifugus* is based on the ornamentation of the first pleopod of reproductive (Form I) males and other body and appendage features. These crayfishes can achieve total body lengths in excess of 3.5 in (90 mm). Morphological differences between various populations are slight, including the presence or absence of a pigmented eye spot. Crayfishes in the Citrus County population lack this spot. Descriptions are available in Hobbs (1942) and Hobbs et al. (1977).

RANGE: *Procambarus l. lucifugus* has been reported from a cave, 14 miles north of Weekiwachee, in Hernando County, and from Sweet Gum Cave (type locality) in Citrus County. The Hernando report is based on two specimens (female and non-reproductive [Form II] male) in the Smithsonian Institution crustacean collection, collected in 1937 (H. H. Hobbs, Jr., pers. comm.), but this cave has not been relocated. This population is restricted to the limestone area between the northern Withlacoochee River and the Gulf Coast. A closely related species, *Procambarus leitheuseri*, is reported from southern Hernando and Pasco counties.

HABITAT: *Procambarus l. lucifugus* is associated with a large nursery colony of southeastern bats (*Myotis austroriparous*) at Sweet Gum Cave. This cave is subject to extreme fluctuations in the local water table. During periods of low water, incredible numbers of this crayfish occur under the traditional bat roost in the rear of the cave. During periods of flooding, crayfishes rarely are seen in the accessible areas near the entrance, even when baited traps are used. This suggests that the residual population remains in deeper portions of the cave where food supplies can be limited during periods when this area is not accessible to bats.

LIFE HISTORY AND ECOLOGY: Reproductive males of this subspecies have been collected in January, March, and May. No egg-bearing females have been found. This crayfish has been found in association with *Troglocambarus maclanei* and *Crangonyx hobbsi* at Sweet Gum Cave.

SPECIALIZED OR UNIQUE CHARACTERISTICS: This crayfish apparently is adapted for life in high energy cave systems. At Sweet Gum Cave the

Withlacoochee Light-Fleeing Cave Crayfish, *Procambarus lucifugus lucifugus*. Florida, Citrus County, Sweet Gum Cave (courtesy of Barry W. Mansell).

Distribution of the Withlacoochee light-fleeing cave crayfish, *Procambarus lucifugus lucifugus*.

population is fueled by guano from a large nursery roost of southeastern bats.

BASIS FOR STATUS CLASSIFICATION: Although reported from two sites, *Procambarus l. lucifugus*, in effect, is known from only a single cave in Citrus County. Its presence at Sweet Gum has been documented with collections that span nearly 100 years. The cave is in private ownership, and the current owner is trying to protect the cave. However, since the crayfish is known only from this site, it remains vulnerable to changes in local land use and encroaching urbanization, and with its dependence on bat guano for food, it could be seriously impacted with changes in the bat population.

RECOMMENDATION: Until other sites are located, Sweet Gum Cave remains the sole locality for this crayfish. This significant site should be secured through acquisition or conservation easement to provide for the crayfish's continued welfare in the future.

PREPARED BY: Richard Franz, Florida Museum of Natural History, University of Florida, Gainesville, FL 32611.

FAMILY CAMBARIDAE

Rare

Alachua Light-Fleeing Cave Crayfish

Procambarus (*Ortmannicus*) *lucifugus alachua* (Hobbs) and intergrade populations in Marion, Gilchrist, and Levy counties.

DESCRIPTION: Like other cavernicolous crayfishes, *Procambarus lucifugus alachua* is albinistic and has reduced eyes without facets. This population has prominent pigmented eye spots, while only portions of the intergrade populations in Marion, Gilchrist, and Levy counties show this feature. This crayfish can achieve body lengths in excess of 90 mm (3.5 in). Specific identifications of each population are based on the ornamentations of the first pleopod of the reproductive male and other body features. Descriptions and a discussion of the intermediate forms are found in Hobbs (1942), Hobbs et al. (1977), and Franz and Lee (1982).

RANGE: *P. l. alachua* is reported from 11 caves in western Alachua County (Franz et al. 1994). The type locality is Hog Sink. Two intergrade populations are known from 14 caves, sinks, and springs in Marion County and in Gilchrist and Levy counties.

Distribution of the Alachua
light-fleeing cave crayfish,
*Procambarus lucifugus
alachua.*

HABITAT: Like *P. l. lucifugus*, these crayfishes apparently require unlighted groundwater habitats associated with caves and sinks that attract large quantities of organic detritus, particularly bat guano, which they use as food.

LIFE HISTORY AND ECOLOGY: Reproductive males of *P. l. alachua* were found in February, March, and October; intergrade Form I males in January, April, May, August, and December. No egg-bearing females have ever been found. Many populations of these crayfishes are found in association with the *Troglocambarus maclanei*. It occurs with *Procambarus pallidus* at only four sites, even though the ranges of the two species broadly overlap in western Alachua County. It also has been found with *Palaemonetes cummingi* at Squirrel Chimney and with cavernicolous amphipods of the genus *Crangonyx* at many localities.

SPECIALIZED OR UNIQUE CHARACTERISTICS: Like other cavernicolous crustaceans, these crayfishes are adapted for a subterranean existence. Specimens of *alachua* retain the dark pigment spot on the eye, while this character is variable in "intergrade" populations. These crayfishes have very restricted ranges, and taxonomic studies are needed to elucidate the taxonomic status of the various populations.

BASIS FOR STATUS CLASSIFICATION: The species' dependence on supplies of concentrated detrital material from the surface and on guano from bats makes these crayfishes vulnerable to changes in aboveground land use. They also are vulnerable to groundwater pollution and other changes in water quality and quantity.

RECOMMENDATIONS: Unfortunately, there are no important populations of *P. lucifugus* protected on public lands. Certain sites, particularly those at Sunday Sink in Marion County and Hog and Goat sinks in Alachua County, are in need of protection.

PREPARED BY: Richard Franz, Florida Museum of Natural History, University of Florida, Gainesville, FL 32611.

FAMILY CAMBARIDAE

Rare

Woodville Cave Crayfish

Procambarus (Ortmannicus) orcinus Hobbs and Means

DESCRIPTION: The Woodville cave crayfish is an albinistic species with reduced eyes, no eye facets, and a small pigmented eye spot. Its body is up to 50 mm (2 in) in length. Specific identification is based on the first pleopod of the reproductive (Form I) male and other morphological features. It is a member of the *pallidus* complex (Franz and Lee 1982). See Hobbs and Means (1972) for specific descriptive information.

RANGE: This species is widespread in cave systems in the Woodville Karst south of Tallahassee (Gopher Sink, type locality). The species is known from 13 sites in Leon and Wakulla counties (Franz et al. 1994). It has been seen in most of the cave systems in the Wakulla-St. Marks drainages south of the Cody Scarp, including the Wakulla Springs and Emerald Sink cave systems.

HABITAT: The Woodville cave crayfish is reported to cling upside down to the ceiling and head down on the vertical walls of flooded caves. Individuals are most numerous along the walls, especially where there are cracks and fissures near the floor. They are seen commonly in both the twilight areas and the dark portions of flooded caves. Caine (1978) provides information on the ecology of this species.

Distribution of the Woodville
cave crayfish, *Procambarus
orcinus.*

LIFE HISTORY AND ECOLOGY: Reproductive males have been collected
in February and April. One copulatory pair was seen in April. No ovigerous
females have been reported. Troglobitic crustacean associates include *Crangonyx grandimanus* and *C. hobbsi.*

SPECIALIZED OR UNIQUE CHARACTERISTICS: This crayfish shows
the reduction in eye structure and body pigmentation that characterizes other
Florida cave crayfishes. It is restricted to flooded caves in the limestone area
south of Tallahassee.

BASIS FOR STATUS CLASSIFICATION: The species probably needs no
special attention at this time. It appears common in the Emerald Sink and
Wakulla Springs cave systems which are largely protected by the United
States Forest Service (Apalachicola National Forest) and Florida Department of Environmental Protection, respectively.

RECOMMENDATIONS: Protection of groundwater from chemical pollutants and safeguarding the natural flow of organic detritus into these systems is essential. Cave diving probably does little harm to this crustacean. Divers should report to appropriate state or federal agencies when they observe any unusual crayfish mortality.

PREPARED BY: Richard Franz, Florida Museum of Natural History, University of Florida, Gainesville, FL 32611.

FAMILY CAMBARIDAE

Rare

Pallid Cave Crayfish
Procambarus (*Ortmannicus*) *pallidus* (Hobbs)

DESCRIPTION: The pallid cave crayfish is albinistic and has reduced eyes with no eye spots. Its body is 80 mm (about 3 in) in length. Specific identification is based on the ornamentation of the first pleopod of the reproductive (Form I) male and other morphological features. A detailed description is found in Hobbs (1942). This species is a member of the *pallidus* complex (Franz and Lee 1982).

RANGE: This crayfish is widely distributed in the upper Suwannee, lower Withlacoochee, and lower Santa Fe river basins and in the limestone plain in western Alachua County. It has been reported from 65 sites in Alachua, Columbia, Gilchrist, Hamilton, Lafayette, Levy, Madison, and Suwannee counties (Franz et al. 1994). A record from Eichelburger's Cave near Ocala in Marion County was questioned by Franz and Lee (1982).

HABITAT: This cavernicolous species is associated with groundwater habitats in caves that are not as heavily enriched with organic debris as those that attract members of the cavernicolous *lucifugus* complex. Divers also report that the species is most strongly associated with caves that have high flow in newly emerging karst area, particularly along the upper Suwannee River area. The crayfish commonly ventures out into the lighted portions of "blue hole" sinks.

LIFE HISTORY AND ECOLOGY: Reproductive males have been found in December, February, March, and July; copulations have been observed at Squirrel Chimney in December. Two females that were maintained in captivity deposited 65 (R. Franz, unpublished data) and 130 eggs (Relyea and Sutton 1973) in October and March, respectively. This species has been collected with a member of the *lucifugus* complex at only four sites. Under these con-

Pallid Cave Crayfish, *Procambarus pallidus* (courtesy of Barry W. Mansell).

Distribution of the pallid
cave crayfish, *Procambarus
pallidus*.

ditions, one or the other species overwhelmingly dominates, and presumably the availability of energy at the site determines this outcome. Associated species include *Palaemonetes cummingi* (at Squirrel Chimney only), *Procambarus lucifugus, Troglocambarus maclanei, Remasellus parvus, Crangonyx hobbsi,* and *C. grandimanus.*

SPECIALIZED OR UNIQUE CHARACTERISTICS: This cavernicolous species is thought to occur in caves in newly emerging limestone areas, particularly along the upper Suwannee River. Its distribution in western Alachua County may align with an old river valley where the species may have evolved (R. Franz, unpublished data).

BASIS FOR STATUS: Although this species is widespread in north central Florida, it occurs in very low densities at most sites. *P. pallidus* may be sensitive to toxic chemicals, which may have been responsible for major crayfish kills reported by divers in spring caves in the upper Suwannee River basin (Streever 1992; Tom Morris, Buford Pruitt, Paul Smith, pers. comm.).

RECOMMENDATIONS: Many cave sites where this species has been collected are currently protected within county and state parks along the Suwannee and Santa Fe rivers. Routine water quality monitoring should be encouraged at protected sites. It is strongly recommended that the cave diving community become involved in reporting crayfish kills or other signs of habitat disintegration to appropriate state or federal agencies.

PREPARED BY: Richard Franz, Florida Museum of Natural History, University of Florida, Gainesville, FL 32611.

FAMILY CAMBARIDAE

Rare

Black Creek Crayfish
Procambarus (Ortmannicus) pictus (Hobbs)

OTHER NAMES: Spotted royal crayfish.

DESCRIPTION: The Black Creek crayfish, when alive, is easily distinguished from other Florida species by its dark brown to black carapace with white to yellowish spots and stripes and rust-colored abdomen. In preservatives, these identifying colors quickly fade, and it is necessary to examine the first pleopod of the reproductive (Form I) male and other morphological features for accurate identification. Hobbs (1942) provides an excellent detailed description of these structures. This crayfish can achieve body lengths of 89 mm (3.5 in) in late summer.

RANGE: Since the publication of the original FCREPA volume on invertebrates, this crayfish has been recorded from a stream near Fort Caroline in Duval County (Franz and Franz 1990) and from Falling Branch and Etonia Creek (at Bardin Road) in the upper portions of Rice Creek in Putnam County (R. Franz, unpublished data). Prior to these discoveries, its distribution was thought to be confined to the Black Creek drainage in Duval and Clay counties (Franz and Franz 1979).

HABITAT: This colorful crayfish inhabits cool, flowing, tannic-stained streams where it hides by day in submerged detritus, tree roots, and vegetation. At night, it is found crawling on the sandy bottoms of streams. Its coloration fits the background colors of the sand and detritus.

LIFE HISTORY AND ECOLOGY: Crayfishes hatching in late summer mature the following spring. Data suggest that they live a maximum of 16 months. Reproductive males, 50-75 mm (2-3 in) in total length, occur in streams from January to September; similar-sized females are found with eggs from June to August. Abdominal eggs number 47-146; hatching begins in July with recruitment of the young into the population in August. This species has been found with the crayfishes *Procambarus fallax* and *P. talpoides*.

SPECIALIZED OR UNIQUE CHARACTERISTICS: The Black Creek crayfish is thought to be closely related to certain species of Florida cave crayfishes (Hobbs 1958). It also is a member of a unique freshwater stream fauna in the lower St. Johns River basin which has relationships with faunas in west Florida and piedmont Georgia (Burgess and Franz 1978).

BASIS FOR STATUS CLASSIFICATION: The species is susceptible to siltation, pollution, and other changes in water quality (Franz and Franz 1979). With the expansion of Orange Park and Middleburg, urbanization is reaching southward along State Route 21. A toll road and an associated high-speed rail system have been proposed to come through the heart of the Black Creek country, which could potentially impact water quality and the long-term rural aspect of this area (Franz and Franz 1990).

RECOMMENDATIONS: Small populations have been located in streams on the Camp Blanding Military Reservation. Protection of the headwater streams would insure the survival of the species, unless water quality is compromised. The species is threatened by expanding urbanization and by chemical spills associated with mining activities. Additional survey work is essential in order to define its range outside of the Black Creek area. This crustacean is listed as a species of special concern by the Florida Game and Fresh Water Fish Commission (Wood 1991).

Black Creek Crayfish, *Procambarus pictus*. Florida, Clay County (courtesy of Ray E. Ashton).

Distribution of the Black Creek crayfish, *Procambarus pictus.*

PREPARED BY: Richard Franz, Florida Museum of Natural History, University of Florida, Gainesville, FL 32611.

FAMILY CAMBARIDAE

Rare

North Florida Spider Cave Crayfish
Troglocambarus maclanei Hobbs

OTHER NAMES: McLane's cave crayfish.

DESCRIPTION: *Troglocambarus maclanei* has a delicate, unpigmented body that is up to 35 mm (1.3 in) in total length. The cephalothorax consists of five pairs of extremely long, spider-like legs, with slightly enlarged pincers on the first pair. Eyes are reduced and unpigmented. The oversized mouth parts include an enlarged pair of maxillipeds equipped with closely interlocking hairs. The abdomen is slender and elongate and possesses feathery swimmerets. A prominent pouch-like protrusion on the anterioventral surface of the branchiostegites contributes to the odd appearance of this species. For more descriptive information, see Hobbs (1942); photographs are found in Hobbs (1942) and Mohr and Poulson (1966).

RANGE: This crayfish is known from cave sites in Alachua, Citrus, Gilchrist, Hernando, Marion, and Suwannee counties. An undescribed member of this genus recently was discovered in a flooded cave system near Apopka, Orange County (R. Franz, unpublished data).

HABITAT: Spider crayfishes have been found in caves, sinks, and spring caves. It has been suggested that the species is attracted to fine detritus that floats near the walls and ceilings of flooded cave passages. The species is cannibalistic in captivity and may be an active predator on small invertebrates in caves. Associates include *Palaemonetes cummingi* (Squirrel Chimney only), *Procambarus erythrops*, *P. franzi*, *P. leitheuseri*, *P. lucifugus* (all populations), *P. pallidus*, *Crangonyx hobbsi*, and *C. grandimanus*. The undescribed species has only been found with *P. acherontis* at one site in Orange County (Franz et al. 1994).

LIFE HISTORY AND ECOLOGY: Reproductive males are reported from March to August. Copulations have been seen between June and August. Enlarged ovarian eggs were observed in one female collected in July (Bruce Sutton, pers. comm.). No egg-bearing females are known.

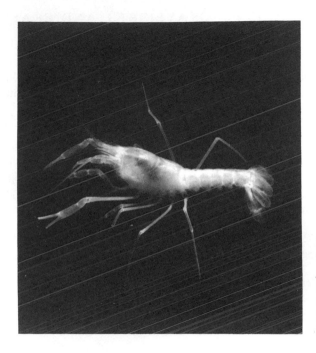

North Florida Spider
Cave Crayfish, *Tro-
glocambarus mac-
lanei*. Florida, Citrus
county, Sweet Gum
Cave (courtesy of
Barry W. Mansell).

Distribution of the north
Florida spider cave crayfish,
Troglocambarus maclanei.

SPECIALIZED OR UNIQUE FEATURES: Spider crayfishes from north Florida and from Orange County are the most specialized crayfishes known. The genus is thought to have affinities with the *seminolae* group in the genus *Procambarus*. The newly described *Procambarus delicatus* from Alexander Springs and *Procambarus attiguus* from Silver Glen Springs appear to be the closest living relatives of the spider crayfishes.

BASIS FOR STATUS CLASSIFICATION: This crayfish is restricted to groundwater habitats in caves, where it maintains small populations, usually in association with fine silt. The species is probably susceptible to groundwater pollution and may be affected by changes in land use.

RECOMMENDATIONS: Little can be done to protect this species other than conserving important cave and spring sites where it is known to occur.

PREPARED BY: Richard Franz, Florida Museum of Natural History, University of Florida, Gainesville FL 32611.

FAMILY CAMBARIDAE

Rare

Apalachicola Cave Crayfish

Cambarus (Jugicambarus) cryptodytes Hobbs

OTHER NAMES: Dougherty Plain cave crayfish, Marianna cave crayfish, Chattahoochee cave crayfish.

DESCRIPTION: *Cambarus cryptodytes* has reduced, unpigmented eyes and a white, translucent body. It can achieve body lengths of 60 mm (about 2.5 in). Specific identification is based on the ornamentation of the first pleopod of the reproductive (Form I) male and other morphological features. See Hobbs (1942, 1981) for detailed descriptions.

RANGE: The crayfish is known from the Apalachicola River basin in Decatur County, Georgia, and Jackson County, Florida. This is the only Florida cave crayfish whose distribution bridges two states. In Georgia the species is known from one cave within the Doughtery Plain (Hobbs 1981), and in Florida, from over a dozen sites in the Marianna Lowlands. The type locality is a well, 2 miles south of Graceville, in Jackson County, Florida. This site has been filled, and is no longer accessible.

Apalachicola Cave Crayfish, *Cambarus cryptodytes*
(courtesy of Barry W. Mansell).

Distribution of the Apalachicola cave crayfish,
Cambarus cryptodytes.

HABITAT: This species has been collected in wells, sinks, shallow caves, and spring caves. The original specimens were taken from a well, 18 m (60 ft) in depth.

LIFE HISTORY AND ECOLOGY: Little information exists concerning its life cycle, although Hobbs (1942) reported reproductive males in November. No egg-bearing females have ever been reported. The species is associated with the cave salamander, *Haideotriton wallacei*, at most sites in Georgia and Florida.

SPECIALIZED OR UNIQUE CHARACTERISTICS: Like other cave crayfishes, this species is adapted to live in dark, low-energy environments. It apparently is restricted to small limestone areas in Jackson County, Florida, and Decatur County, Georgia.

BASIS FOR STATUS CLASSIFICATION: The species has a restricted range and habitat. It is probably susceptible to changes in water quality, particularly associated with toxic chemicals.

RECOMMENDATIONS: The species receives protection at Florida Caverns State Park in Jackson County, Florida. Additional sites, especially those associated with the Merritt Mill Pond area, also should be acquired. As with most cave crayfishes, there is little known concerning its biology, and studies should be encouraged to determine aspects of this species's life cycle and ecology. Voucher specimens should be collected when new sites are identified, particularly in light of a recent collection of a very unusual specimen from Blue Hole in Florida Caverns State Park that may represent a new taxon. Areas between sites in Jackson County (Florida) and Decatur County (Georgia) should be inspected for this species.

PREPARED BY: Richard Franz, Florida Museum of Natural History, University of Florida, Gainesville, FL 32611.

FAMILY CAMBARIDAE

Rare

Red-Back Crayfish

Cambarus (Depressicambarus) pyronotus Bouchard

DESCRIPTION: Hobbs (1942) reported digging "orange-red" crayfishes from complex burrow systems in a ravine along the east side of the Apalachicola River. He stated that "until further specimens have been procured it seems advisable to do nothing more than call attention to its presence in the state." More recently, while reviewing the subgenus *Depressicambarus*, Bouchard (1978) named this population *Cambarus pyronotus*. Besides its startling coloration, this crayfish possesses unique ornamentation on the first pleopod of the reproductive (Form I) male, as well as other morphological features. For detailed information, see Hobbs (1942) and Bouchard (1978).

RANGE: The distribution of this species is unknown. Bouchard's (1978) description of *Cambarus pyronotus* was based on specimens that were obtained by Horton H. Hobbs, Jr. (see Hobbs 1942). Bouchard (1978) suggested that the type locality was possibly Beaver Dam Creek in Liberty County. Although no additional specimens have been collected in the last 50 years, there is no reason to suspect that there has been a decline of this crayfish in the interim.

HABITAT: Hobbs (1942) reported that the red-back crayfish was dug from complex burrow systems which extended downward and beneath the banks of the creek. The burrows were entwined with the masses of roots in the soil, which made them difficult to dig. The species probably occurs in many of

Distribution of the red-back crayfish, *Cambarus pyronotus*.

the small creeks and seeps that flow through shaded ravines from the bluff on the east side of the Apalachicola River.

LIFE HISTORY AND ECOLOGY: Unknown.

SPECIALIZED OR UNIQUE CHARACTERISTICS: Its bright red body coloration readily distinguishes it from other crayfishes in the Apalachicola area. It seems to occupy a very limited area and has very restrictive habitat requirements.

BASIS FOR STATUS CLASSIFICATION: Probably most of the potential habitat for this species has been incorporated into Torreya State Park and The Nature Conservancy's Alum Bluff Preserve.

RECOMMENDATIONS: The habitat of this crayfish receives adequate protection on conservation lands. It is important to maintain the peculiar aspect of these ravines through fire management and protection of the watersheds that control the ravine seeps. It is highly recommended that an intensive survey be made for this species in order to better define its distribution and habitat requirements.

PREPARED BY: Richard Franz, Florida Museum of Natural History, University of Florida, Gainesville, FL 32611.

Order Decapoda
FAMILY GRAPSIDAE

Threatened

Mangrove Crab
Aratus pisonii (H. Milne Edwards)

OTHER NAMES: Mangrove tree crab, soldier crab, shieldback crab.

DESCRIPTION: *Aratus pisonii*, about 22 mm (less than 1 in) in carapace length, is an extremely agile, brightly colored, keystone-shaped crab with orange, purple, or reddish claws bearing a distinct tuft of bristles on their outer surface. Carapace coloration may vary from muddy brown to reddish, speckled with white and blue or with bright green and yellow mottlings, tinged with yellowish-brown on the hind parts.

Distribution of the
mangrove crab,
Aratus pisonii.

RANGE: This species is found from the Indian River region and Tampa throughout southern Florida. It also occurs in the Antilles, in Brazil, and from Nicaragua to Peru on the eastern Pacific Coast (Holthuis 1959).

HABITAT: This crab is found among the roots and especially on the branches of mangrove trees along estuarine to nearly freshwater shorelines.

LIFE HISTORY AND ECOLOGY: Hartnoll (1965) and Warner (1968) both provide descriptions of the larvae and larval development. The species presumably is restricted to mangrove areas and spends its entire life foraging for food among the branches of mangrove trees (Beever et al. 1979), especially the red mangrove (*Rhizophora mangle*). It also may be found occasionally on wharves and pier pilings in estuarine and marine areas, where it apparently feeds on algae, detritus, and perhaps small animals. Egg-bearing females occur in Florida from early spring through summer.

SPECIALIZED OR UNIQUE CHARACTERISTICS: This crustacean is one of the few crabs that actually climb trees to obtain food. In areas where it is abundant, it may be seen up to the topmost branches of the mangrove.

BASIS OF STATUS CLASSIFICATION: The species is widely distributed throughout the Caribbean and along the tropical eastern Pacific coastline. Local populations of this interesting crab, such as those in the keys or in southern and central coastal Florida, are threatened when mangrove areas are destroyed in the process of land development. This crab, being dependent on mangroves, is not found elsewhere in the continental United States.

RECOMMENDATIONS: In order to maintain viable populations it is necessary to curtail further destruction of mangrove areas.

PREPARED BY: Robert H. Gore, Naithloriendun Wildlife Sanctuary, P.O. Box 10053, Naples, FL 33941.

FAMILY GRAPSIDAE

Threatened

Mangrove Crab

Goniopsis cruentata (Latreille)

OTHER NAMES: Tree crab, Devil's crab, quadrangular crab.

DESCRIPTION: *Goniopsis cruentata* is 50 mm (2 in) in carapace length. This extremely agile, brightly colored, square-bodied crab has a golden or yellow carapace fading to red covered with white spots posteriorly. Its red to purple legs are maculated with white or yellow.

RANGE: This crab is found in Appalachee Bay in northwest Florida; in central and southern Florida, near Miami; and from Bermuda and the Antilles to Brazil (Holthuis 1959). It also is found from Bengal to northern Angola and on the western coast of Africa.

HABITAT: The crab occurs in low muddy areas adjacent to estuarine environments, especially mangrove swamps where it may be found in some numbers. It is often found well away from water in the interior of such swamps when the tide has receded. The species is extremely shy and will utilize almost any hole or depression to escape capture.

LIFE HISTORY AND ECOLOGY: Although the species is well known throughout the tropical regions of the West Indies, it has received little study, probably due to the combination of inaccessible or inhospitable habitat and its ability to move extremely rapidly to avoid capture. Presumably the species feeds on detritus and plant material, as do other members of the family

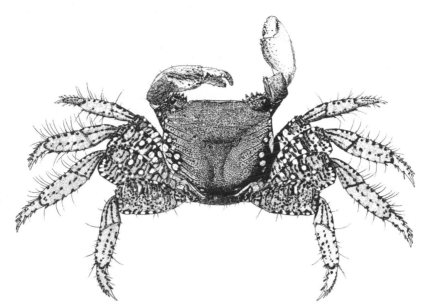

Mangrove Crab, *Goniopsis cruentata* (courtesy of Horton H. Hobbs, Jr.).

Distribution of the mangrove crab, *Goniopsis cruentata.*

Grapsidae in similar habitats. Thus, it probably is an important member in the estuarine food chain.

SPECIALIZED OR UNIQUE CHARACTERISTICS: This species is the most colorful mangrove crab in the western Atlantic. Its bright yellow, gold, and red coloration is a striking contrast to the drab floor of a typical mangrove forest. No one who has seen this brilliantly colored crab against a muddy backdrop of litter in a mangrove forest can fail to appreciate or wonder about the curious contrasts that this species presents, it being so unlike its drab brown and black relatives of the genus *Sesarma*. While found commonly throughout the Caribbean, its occurrence in the continental United States is mostly restricted to mangrove forests in central and southern Florida.

BASIS FOR STATUS CLASSIFICATION: This crab is widely distributed throughout the West Indies and, with the exception of the southern Florida populations, is in little danger yet from human encroachment. Elimination or reduction of mangrove forests will severely restrict the distribution of the species and in some cases probably extirpate it locally.

RECOMMENDATIONS: Present populations presumably could be maintained provided that no further destruction of mangrove forests bordering estuarine areas is allowed, especially in the Florida Keys and on the southern tip of the mainland.

PREPARED BY: Robert H. Gore, Naithloriendun Wildlife Sanctuary, P.O. Box 10053, Naples, FL 33941.

FAMILY GRAPSIDAE

Status Undetermined

Benedict's Wharf Crab
Sesarma (Holometopus) benedicti Rathbun

DESCRIPTION: *Sesarma benedicti* is 25 mm (1 in) in carapace length, dark-colored, and square-bodied, with a relatively wide frontal region, large eyes, and roughly granulated claws. The fingers of the claws in the male are much expanded and flattened when viewed from above, more so than any other species of *Sesarma* in the Americas. When viewed from the front, the fingers show a distinct gape; they are irregularly toothed on the distal half (see Abele 1974).

Distribution of
Benedict's wharf
crab, *Sesarma
benedicti.*

RANGE: In the United States this crab is known only from Key West, Florida. It also has been collected in Guyana, Surinam, and Brazil (Holthuis
1959). The Key West specimens are in the Museum of Comparative Zoology,
Harvard University (Rathbun 1918), and the species apparently has not been
collected from Florida again.

HABITAT: This crab is found under wood or stones along banks bordering
brackish streams or nearly fresh water.

LIFE HISTORY AND ECOLOGY: Unknown.

SPECIALIZED OR UNIQUE CHARACTERISTICS: The species is probably a detrital feeder as are other members of the genus. It would be of some
importance in estuarine food chains.

BASIS FOR STATUS CLASSIFICATION: The species has not been collected in Florida since Rathbun's notation in 1918. In view of the land development in Key West and the lower keys, the habitat may have been eliminated, thus extirpating the species. The Key West record may represent the
northern range limit for this species.

RECOMMENDATIONS: Preservation of mangrove-lined estuarine areas in the lower keys would presumably insure a suitable habitat in which the species could recover should it still be present, asssuming the Key West record is valid.

PREPARED BY: Robert H. Gore, Naithloriendun Wildlife Sanctuary, P.O. Box 10053, Naples, FL 33941.

Class Arachnida

Spiders

INTRODUCTION: There are over 700 species of spiders known from Florida, with many of the smallest species still undescribed. With some exceptions, spiders do not seem to be highly specialized with respect to the species of prey they will accept, and there are no documented cases of spiders that are rare because of a specific host dependence. Spiders are, however, often highly specialized with respect to habitat preference, and there are undoubtedly many species that are restricted to threatened habitats in Florida. Since spiders are wingless, they may become isolated on islands of suitable habitat, which could lead to evolutionary divergence and the appearance of isolated species and subspecies. This seems to have happened in the *Lycosa lenta* species group. The male genitalia of most groups of spiders (carried on enlarged anterior appendages called pedipalps) are highly complex, and, in some cases, appear subject to rapid evolutionary change over relatively short periods of time, increasing the chance of divergence between isolated populations. On the other hand, many spiders disperse widely, carried aloft by long strands of silk that the spiders (usually immature individuals) release into the breeze. As a group, spiders are the first arthropods to colonize new habitats. The distribution of spider species, therefore, is often highly unpredictable, and collection records are often inadequate. With spiders, as with most major groups of arthropods, we are in the frustrating position of recognizing that the group must include many rare and endangered species without being able to recognize many of the species themselves.

There are no general guides to the species of Florida spiders; there is a key to the genera of North American spiders (Roth 1985) which includes references to revisions of families and genera when such revisions exist.

PREPARED BY: Mark Deyrup, Archbold Biological Station, Lake Placid, FL 33852.

Order Araneae
FAMILY GNAPHOSIDAE

INTRODUCTION: Gnaphosids are fast-running, often nocturnal spiders, most of which live on the ground. They often spend the day in an inconspicuous silken retreat, and when disturbed dart away into leaf litter.

PREPARED BY: Mark Deyrup, Archbold Biological Station, Lake Placid, FL 33852.

FAMILY GNAPHOSIDAE

Threatened

Keys Cesonia Spider
Cesonia irvingi (Mello-Leitão)

DESCRIPTION: *Cesonia irvingi* is a light-colored, moderately elongate spider, 5-9 mm (0.2-0.35 in) in length. The abdominal dorsum has an incomplete central stripe and a row of dark spots on each side. The genus *Cesonia* was revised by Platnick and Shadab (1980).

RANGE: This spider is known only from the Florida Keys and South Bimini, Bahamas.

HABITAT: Unknown. Most gnaphosids live on the ground, and species of *Cesonia* have been characterized as agile hunters, found on sandy soils under loose leaf litter.

LIFE HISTORY AND ECOLOGY: Adults have been collected in February and May.

SPECIALIZED OR UNIQUE CHARACTERISTICS: This is the only species of *Cesonia* occurring in the Florida Keys. It differs in both color pattern and genitalia from the common *C. bilineata*, which occurs on the mainland.

BASIS FOR STATUS CLASSIFICATION: This species is apparently greatly restricted in range. Only three specimens are known, one each taken

Distribution of the
Keys cesonia spider,
Cesonia irvingi.

at Key West, Bob Allen Keys, and South Bimini. Development of the keys threatens this and many other species of wildlife.

RECOMMENDATIONS: Remaining natural habitats in the Florida Keys should be strongly protected.

PREPARED BY: G. B. Edwards, Florida State Collection of Arthropods, P.O. Box 147100, Gainesville, FL 32614-7100.

Order Araneae
FAMILY LYCOSIDAE

INTRODUCTION: The Lycosidae, or wolf spiders, are hunting spiders, most of which make burrows or retreats in soil or leaf litter. For this reason, they are often rather sensitive to edaphic conditions, and may be restricted to particular soil or litter types. Most species are nocturnal, but they are relatively large and are vulnerable to pitfall trapping. This family is marginally better known than most large families of Florida spiders, and it is clear that there are a number of species with narrowly restricted distributions.

PREPARED BY: Mark Deyrup, Archbold Biological Station, Lake Placid, FL 33852.

FAMILY LYCOSIDAE

Endangered

Lake Placid Funnel Wolf Spider

Sosippus placidus Brady

DESCRIPTION: *Sosippus placidus* is a large wolf spider, 15–18 mm (0.6 in) in length. Dorsally it is brown with white markings, but its most distinguishing color feature is the striking yellowish-orange to reddish-orange ventral surface. A formal description is provided by Brady (1972).

RANGE: This species is known only from a scrub area 9.6 km (6 mi) south of Lake Placid and from Archbold Biological Station, both in Highlands County; from a scrub area 9.6 km (6 mi) SW of Frostproof, Polk County; and from a scrub area in Arbuckle State Forest in Polk County.

HABITAT: It occurs in open scrub habitat with patches of bare sand.

LIFE HISTORY AND ECOLOGY: This species has been collected in June, October, December, and January. Webs are usually associated with low vegetation (in one case a rotten pine log), which supports the sheet web. Threads above the web may serve to tangle flying insects, which fall into the web. The retreat at the base of the web takes the form of a silken tube which leads to an underground burrow. In captivity a wide variety of large insects are accepted by this species. The young remain with the mother until about half adult size. The female leaves dead prey in the web, and the young emerge from their underground retreat to feed.

SPECIALIZED OR UNIQUE CHARACTERISTICS: The color pattern, three posterior cheliceral teeth, and habitat preference separate this species from the common, sympatric *S. floridanus*.

Distribution of the Lake Placid funnel wolf spider, *Sosippus placidus*.

BASIS FOR STATUS CLASSIFICATION: The locality 9.6 km (6 mi) south of Lake Placid has been destroyed and planted in citrus, but a population occurs on the Archbold Biological Station. A single specimen was collected in a Nature Conservancy preserve southwest of Frostproof. It has also been seen at Arbuckle State Forest. This species is never known to be abundant, and most of its habitat has been eradicated, the remainder disappearing at an increasing rate. Like other species dependent on open scrub habitat, this species requires management of its habitat to prevent formation of a closed canopy of scrub pines and oaks.

RECOMMENDATIONS: Preservation and management of remaining fragments of habitat are necessary for this species.

PREPARED BY: G. B. Edwards, Florida State Collection of Arthropods, P.O. Box 147100, Gainesville, FL 32614-7100.

Rare

McCrone's Burrowing Wolf Spider

Geolycosa xera McCrone

DESCRIPTION: A moderately large wolf spider, 12–15 mm (0.5–0.6 in) long. The carapace is tan or orange, covered with whitish-gray pubescence. The abdomen is beige with a dark median band on the venter. The venters of the first two legs are variable in color but similar within populations. McCrone (1963) described two subspecies based on leg coloration: *G. x. xera*, in which the venters of legs I and II were mostly or completely dark, and *G. x. archboldi*, in which the venters of legs I and II were mostly or completely pale.

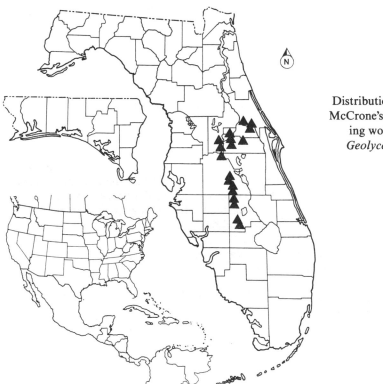

Distribution of the McCrone's burrowing wolf spider, *Geolycosa xera.*

RANGE: The range of this species corresponds to Pleistocene islands of peninsular Florida. *G. x. xera* occurs in southern Volusia County, Seminole County, western Orange County, and Polk County south to the north boundary of Highlands County. *G. x. archboldi* occurs from just south of Avon Park to the south end of the Lake Wales Ridge near Venus, Highlands County.

HABITAT: This spider occurs in open sand in sand hills and sand pine scrub habitats. It is not tolerant of leaf litter.

LIFE HISTORY AND ECOLOGY: Adult females are found from August through April, but males have only been taken in October and November. This species makes vertical burrows about 20 cm (8 in) deep in sandy, well-drained, exposed soils. The burrow entrance has a low lip, but no turret. The burrows are often aggregated, giving the impression of a nesting of bees or wasps.

BASIS FOR STATUS CLASSIFICATION: The dispersal ability of *Geolycosa xera* is apparently poor, and the species is restricted in habitat. It is under constant pressure from residential construction and citrus grove expansion. Populations of *G. x. archboldi* are protected at Archbold Biological Station, Highlands Hammock State Park, and Lake Apthorpe Nature Conservancy Preserve. *G. x. xera* is protected at Bok Tower Gardens, Saddle Blanket Scrub Preserve, and Lake Arbuckle State Forest.

RECOMMENDATIONS: Fossil dunes on the Lake Wales Ridge and elsewhere must be set aside and maintained in their natural state.

PREPARED BY: G. B. Edwards, Florida State Collection of Arthropods, P.O. Box 147100, Gainesville, FL 32614-7100.

FAMILY LYCOSIDAE

Rare

Escambia Burrowing Wolf Spider

Geolycosa escambiensis Wallace

DESCRIPTION: *G. escambiensis* is small for the genus, and is a straw color with dark bands around distal ends of the tibia and metatarsi of the first pair of legs (total length: 9.7-15.2 mm, 0.39-0.61 in; X = 11.7 ± 2.3 mm, 0.47 ± 0.09 in; N = 5).

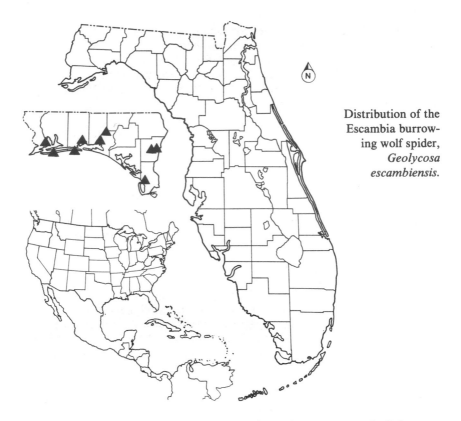

Distribution of the
Escambia burrow-
ing wolf spider,
*Geolycosa
escambiensis.*

RANGE: This species has been reported from the western end of the panhandle east to Walton County and Calhoun and Gulf counties. Its range is
restricted in the east by the Apalachicola River. *G. ornatipes* replaces *G. escambiensis* to the east of the Apalachicola River and is very similar in appearance (Wallace 1942).

HABITAT: *G. escambiensis* is found in coastal and inland scrubs.

LIFE HISTORY AND ECOLOGY: Mature males and females have been
seen in November (Wallace 1942) and adult females and first instar spider-
lings have been collected in May. The species lives its life in association with
a burrow. These burrows lack any turret. *G. escambiensis* is found in open
sandy areas and is probably like *G. xera* in its dependence on open sand. A
population was observed near Port St. Joe in a rosemary scrub in association with *G. micanopy*, a widespread species which builds a turret.

BASIS OF STATUS CLASSIFICATION: *G. escambiensis* is restricted to
threatened habitats. The type locality, the east end of Santa Rosa Island, is
now developed, and the other coastal areas from which it was described are
being rapidly developed for tourism. A brief survey of the western end of

Santa Rosa Island in May 1992 yielded few individuals, and none were found at Saint George Island State Park.

RECOMMENDATIONS: The existence of protected populations of this species needs to be verified. Any sites containing scrub with open sand microhabitats should be surveyed. Habitats lacking open sand will not support this species.

PREPARED BY: Samuel D. Marshall, Dept. of Zoology, University of Tennessee, Knoxville, TN 37996.

FAMILY LYCOSIDAE

Rare

Rosemary Wolf Spider
Lycosa ericeticola Wallace

DESCRIPTION: A buff-colored wolf spider, about 25 mm (1.0 in) long. Dorsal stripe indistinct in front of dorsal groove, narrowing posteriorly; marginal light area indistinct, wider than dorsal stripe; pattern on carapace obscured by dense covering of light hairs (Wallace 1942). Identification is best determined by microscopic examination of the genitalia, illustrated in Wallace (1942).

RANGE: This spider is known only from the northwestern corner of Putnam County (Reiskind 1987).

HABITAT: The rosemary wolf spider occurs in open sites with well-drained, sandy soil somewhat similar to high pine-turkey oak but with a high proportion of rosemary in the plant association.

LIFE HISTORY AND ECOLOGY: Adult males and females have been collected in March, May, and August and adult males in November.

SPECIALIZED OR UNIQUE CHARACTERISTICS: The male palpus is quite distinct from that of any other member of the *lenta* group of wolf spiders; the female is indistinguishable from several species. This unique spider is apparently restricted to a small area with a unique plant association.

BASIS FOR STATUS CLASSIFICATION: This species occurs on 2,000 to 3,000 acres of habitat in northwest Putnam County, and seems to be absent in identical habitat nearby. Much of this area is already scheduled for devel-

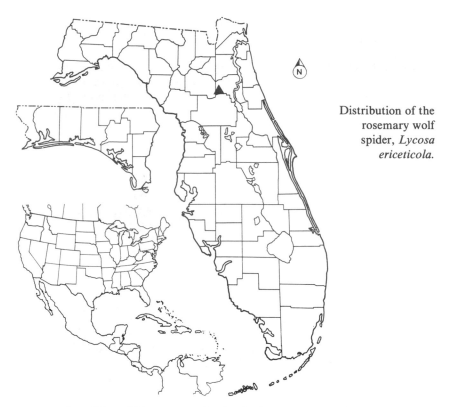

Distribution of the
rosemary wolf
spider, *Lycosa
ericeticola.*

opment, but 200 to 300 acres are in the Ordway Preserve of the University
of Florida, where the species will presumably be protected (Reiskind 1987).

RECOMMENDATIONS: Although this species is protected on a small part
of its range, it would be highly desirable to have more than one protected
site. This is another species that may require some habitat management.

PREPARED BY: H. K. Wallace, Dept. of Zoology, University of Florida,
Gainesville, FL 32611.

Order Araneae

FAMILY ARANEIDAE

INTRODUCTION: The Araneidae, or orb-weavers, seem to show less of a
tendency to produce highly localized species, and many species are remarkably widespread. Long-range wind dispersal of baby spiders clinging to
strands of silk is common in the family.

PREPARED BY: G. B. Edwards, Florida State Collection of Arthropods, P.O. Box 147100, Gainesville, FL 32614-7100.

FAMILY ARANEIDAE

Threatened

Eleuthra Orb Weaver

Eustala eleuthra Levi

DESCRIPTION: *Eustala eleuthra*, unlike other species of the genus in Florida, is a yellow spider with black specks on the abdomen and only an outline of a foliar pattern. The body is 3-6 mm (0.1-0.2 in) long; females are larger than males.

RANGE: This species is found in southwest Florida, at Cape Sable and near Flamingo in Monroe County; also known from the Bahamas and Jamaica.

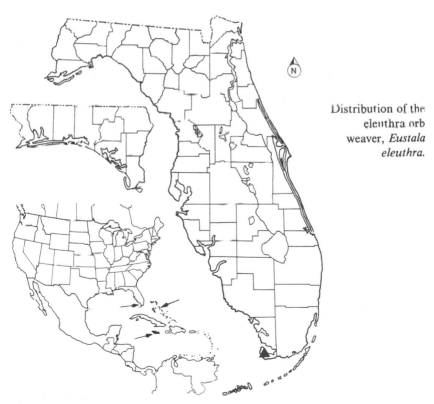

Distribution of the eleuthra orb weaver, *Eustala eleuthra*.

HABITAT: Uncertain, probably tropical hardwood hammocks.

LIFE HISTORY AND ECOLOGY: The holotype male was collected in April. Other records are not accompanied by dates of collection.

BASIS FOR STATUS CLASSIFICATION: Only two records are known from Florida, both from an area noted for the presence of a number of other rare and threatened organisms, particularly plants.

RECOMMENDATIONS: Maintenance and proper management of tropical hammocks is probably the only way to ensure the continued survival of this species in Florida.

PREPARED BY: G. B. Edwards, Florida State Collection of Arthropods, P.O. Box 147100, Gainesville, FL 32614-7100.

Order Araneae
FAMILY SALTICIDAE

INTRODUCTION: The Salticidae, or jumping spiders move about very actively as adults, and many species can disperse more widely on floating silk threads. Many jumping spiders are not only habitat-specific, but also micro-habitat-specific, and may be more vulnerable to habitat change than is presently recognized. A species found on pine trees, for example, may require that the trees be large with hiding places sheltered by many layers of insulating bark, and might further require that the tree be free-standing, not shaded by other trees.

PREPARED BY: Mark Deyrup, Archbold Biological Station, Lake Placid, FL 33852.

FAMILY SALTICIDAE

Rare

Little Mountain Jumping Spider
Habrocestum parvulum (Banks)

DESCRIPTION: Spiders are 2.5–4.0 mm (0.1–0.15 in) long. Females are an inconspicuous brown; males are black, with the thoracic area of the carapace and the femora pale yellow. The dorsum of the male's abdomen has four white spots: two unpaired spots anteriorly and a pair of spots posteriorly.

RANGE: This jumping spider is known from the Appalachian Mountains, with scattered reports from various mideastern locales, and disjunct populations in southern Alabama and the Apalachicola River bluffs. The only known Florida locale is Torreya State Park in Liberty County.

HABITAT: It has been found in leaf litter in deciduous climax forest.

LIFE HISTORY AND ECOLOGY: In Florida, adults of both sexes have been collected in April, May, and September.

SPECIALIZED OR UNIQUE CHARACTERISTICS: Although the color pattern is different from that of related species, the genitalia are more reliable for separating this species from sympatric congeners.

BASIS FOR STATUS CLASSIFICATION: The single known Florida population is within the confines of Torreya State Park and is not at present threatened.

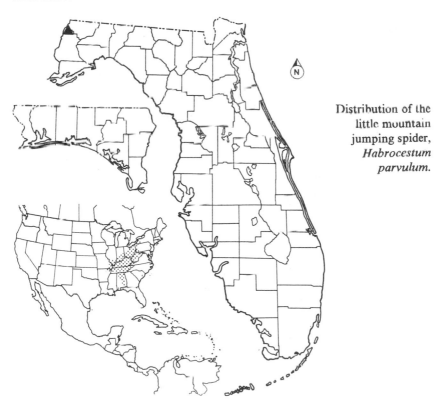

Distribution of the little mountain jumping spider, *Habrocestum parvulum.*

PREPARED BY: G. B. Edwards, Florida State Collection of Arthropods, P.O. Box 147100, Gainesville, FL 32614-7100.

FAMILY SALTICIDAE

Rare

Workman's Jumping Spider

Phidippus workmani G. & E. Peckham

DESCRIPTION: This species is a moderately large jumping spider, 6–12 mm (0.2–0.5 in) long. Females are usually slightly larger than males and have gray or yellow bands on the sides of the carapace and yellow or orange bands and spots on the dorsum of the abdomen. The dorsal white spot in the ocular area of females is unique for Florida species of *Phidippus*. Males are black with white markings and can be distinguished from similar species by the presence of three pairs of white spots on the posterior dorsum of the abdomen. Listed in the FCREPA 1982 edition as *P. xeros*.

RANGE: This spider is known from central peninsular Florida, with one record from the panhandle (Pensacola) (Edwards 1978).

HABITAT: Workman's jumping spider occurs on herbs and shrubs in open

Workman's Jumping Spider, *Phidippus workmani* (courtesy of G. B. Edwards).

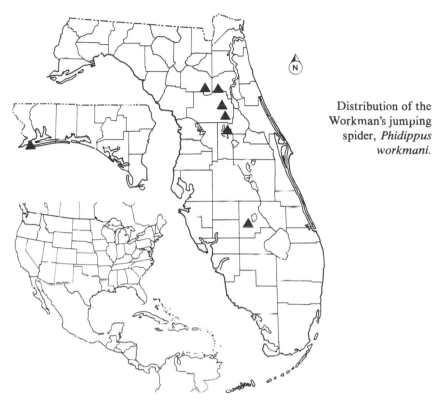

Distribution of the
Workman's jumping
spider, *Phidippus
workmani.*

xeric habitats, especially sand pine scrub. It is most frequently found in localized areas where the canopy trees have been removed.

LIFE HISTORY AND ECOLOGY: Adults are found from late June
through early September.

SPECIALIZED OR UNIQUE CHARACTERISTICS: Color patterns and
distinctive genitalia separate this species from its Florida relatives.

BASIS FOR STATUS CLASSIFICATION: *Phidippus workmani* appears
to be an inhabitant of early plant successional stages of xeric habitats. Habitat is created by fire and activities of man (e.g., maintenance of cleared areas
along power line routes). There are fewer than 30 specimens in all major
arthropod collections combined.

RECOMMENDATIONS: Proper habitat management in areas such as
Ocala National Forest should provide sufficient habitat for the species to
survive.

PREPARED BY: G. B. Edwards, Florida State Collection of Arthropods,
P.O. Box 147100, Gainesville, FL 32614-7100.

Order Araneae
FAMILY CTENIZIDAE

INTRODUCTION: The Ctenizidae, or trap-door spiders, are a group that appears to be morphologically conservative, and that includes a number of genera with unusual relict distribution. Diaxial fang movement and two pairs of book lungs are among the primitive features retained by these spiders. Many species probably require both a special habitat and special soil conditions. All species are normally difficult to find because they live in concealed burrows. Some, however, may be locally abundant: pompilid wasps of the genus *Psorthaspis*, which prey on ctenizids, are very common (males only) in Malaise traps in scrub habitat at the Archbold Biological Station. Some genera show unusual distributions. The genus *Cyclocosmia*, for example, includes two species in the southeastern U.S., one in eastern Mexico, and one in southeast Asia (Gertsch & Platnick 1975).

PREPARED BY: Mark Deyrup, Archbold Biological Station, Lake Placid, FL 33852.

FAMILY CTENIZIDAE

Rare

Torreya Trap-door Spider
Cyclocosmia torreya Gertsch & Platnick

DESCRIPTION: This trap-door spider is about 25 mm (1.0 in) long and dark brown in color. The abdomen of the female is truncate behind. This truncation is circular and quite well sclerotized and is used in an interesting way. Although the spider spins a thin, wafer-type trap-door (usually well camouflaged) at the entrance to the burrow, it does not rely on this for protection. Rather, when disturbed, it runs headfirst into the narrowing burrow until the truncation is in contact with the sides of the burrow, thus presenting to any intruder a facade resembling a manhole cover. The male also has a well-sclerotized truncation, but in the adult, at least, it is rounded off posteriorly and does not appear to be as functional as that of the female.

RANGE: Ravines of west Florida such as those along the Apalachicola River. Known from Columbia, Gadsden, Jackson, and Liberty counties in Florida, and from Clay County, Georgia (Gertsch & Platnick 1975).

Torreya Trap-Door
Spider, *Cyclocosmia
torreya*. Florida, Lib-
erty County, ravine
near Bristol
(courtesy of Barry
W. Mansell).

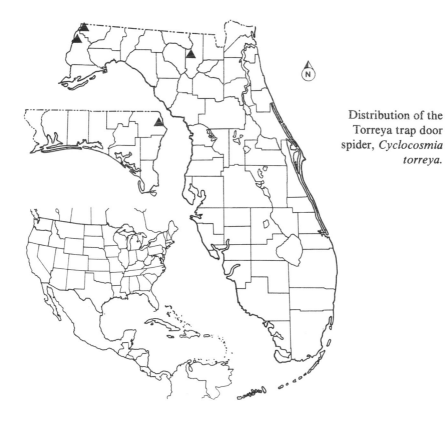

Distribution of the
Torreya trap door
spider, *Cyclocosmia
torreya*.

HABITAT: It occurs in shady mesic habitats such as that afforded by the tree-covered slopes of mesic ravines.

LIFE HISTORY AND ECOLOGY: Little is known about the life history. Specimens of several different sizes, probably including adult females, have been collected in April and May. It probably takes several years for the species to reach maturity, and adult females probably live longer than one year.

SPECIALIZED OR UNIQUE CHARACTERISTICS: *Cyclocosmia*'s truncated abdomen and its function is unique among North American spiders.

BASIS FOR STATUS CLASSIFICATION: This species apparently requires a shady mesic habitat. We have seen it disappear from a ravine due to lumbering and feral hog activities.

RECOMMENDATIONS: This species can probably be saved by maintaining areas like Torreya State Park in an undisturbed condition.

PREPARED BY: H. K. Wallace and G. B. Edwards, Florida State Collection of Arthropods, P.O. Box 147100, Gainesville, FL 32614-7100.

FAMILY CTENIZIDAE

Status Undetermined

Florida Trap-door Spiders

Ummidia species
Myrmekiaphila species

DESCRIPTION: *Ummidia* and *Myrmekiaphila* species are large, black or brown, shiny spiders with an adult female body length of about 30–50 mm (1.2–2.0 in) long. Males are somewhat smaller than females. Identification of species awaits revision of the genera.

RANGE: These species are widely distributed in Florida in appropriate situations, but they are so secretive and rare that little is known about their occurrence except in the northwestern part of the state where they are found with *Cyclocosmia*.

HABITAT: They occur usually in mesophytic environments, although occasional specimens have been encountered in xeric habitats.

Florida Trap-Door
Spider, *Ummidia* sp.
Florida, Liberty
County, Bristol
(courtesy of Barry
W. Mansell).

Florida Trap-Door
Spider, *Myrmekia-*
phila sp. Florida,
Liberty County, Bris-
tol (courtesy of Barry
W. Mansell).

LIFE HISTORY AND ECOLOGY: These species take several years to
reach maturity, and adult females probably live for some years.

SPECIALIZED OR UNIQUE CHARACTERISTICS: *Ummidia* spins a
cork-type trap-door, usually well camouflaged and difficult to find. The

door built by an adult female is 25 mm or more in diameter and 3 mm (0.1 in) thick. The burrow is only about 100–150 mm (4–6 in) deep, and the spider depends upon brute strength for protection. When disturbed, she inserts her fangs into holes in the door and holds on to the sides of the burrow with all eight legs. It is unlikely that any predator except humans or something as strong as a raccoon could pull the door open when the inhabitant is holding it shut. *Mrymekiaphila* trap-doors are much thinner and wafer-like. When disturbed, these spiders run to the bottom of their burrow, sometimes down a side tunnel.

BASIS FOR STATUS CLASSIFICATION: These spiders are so secretive and the nests so well-camouflaged that they are seldom collected, and almost nothing is known about their distribution in peninsular Florida except for a few males found wandering in search of females. There are probably several species. Specialized habitat requirements, sensitivity to disturbance, and inefficient dispersal almost guarantee that Florida species are rare or endangered.

RECOMMENDATIONS: The maintenance of park areas in a natural condition will probably enable most of these spiders to survive.

PREPARED BY: H. K. Wallace and G. B. Edwards, Florida State Collection of Arthropods, P.O. Box 147100, Gainesville, FL 32614-7100.

Order Araneae
FAMILY ATYPIDAE

INTRODUCTION: The Atypidae, or purseweb spiders, is an ancient family whose species are seldom common. Some species are rather widespread, and there is one report of aerial dispersal by the young in one species (Gertsch & Platnick 1980).

PREPARED BY: Mark Deyrup, Archbold Biological Station, Lake Placid, FL 33852.

Rare

Blue Purseweb Spider
Sphodros abboti Walckenaer

Red-Legged Purseweb Spider
Sphodros rufipes (Latreille)

DESCRIPTION: The females of *Sphodros abboti* and *S. rufipes* are very similar in appearance although *rufipes* is larger than *abboti*, the former being about 25 mm (1.0 in) long and the latter only 19 mm (0.7 in). Both are dark brown to black. The males of *abboti* are dark, iridescent gun-metal blue; males of *rufipes* are black with bright red or orange legs. The posterior spinnerets of *abboti* are four-jointed, those of *rufipes* three-jointed.

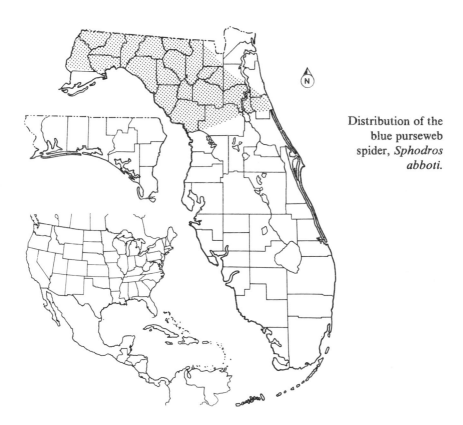

Distribution of the blue purseweb spider, *Sphodros abboti.*

Red-Legged Pur-
seweb Spider, *Spho-
dros rufipes*
(courtesy of Barry
W. Mansell).

RANGE: *Sphodros abboti* occurs in northern Florida from Marion County
north, with one known Georgia locality near the Florida border; *S. rufipes*
occurs from New York to Texas, including extreme north Florida (Gertsch
& Platnick 1980).

HABITAT: Both species inhabit mesic woods, where they build their tubular
webs up the sides of trees and bushes; the bottoms of the tubes extend several inches into the ground to where the soil is damp. *Sphodros abboti*'s
webs are at most 20–25 cm high and 1.9 cm in diameter; *S. rufipes* webs
have been reported to be 60 cm high and more than 2.5 cm in diameter. The
tubes built by the males are somewhat smaller than those of the females.

LIFE HISTORY AND ECOLOGY: Males of both species mature around
the first of June, when they leave the tube to search for females. Females
probably live several years. They keep the young with them for a while, but
the tiny tubes on trees indicate that the young leave while still quite small.
The tough tubes of *Sphodros* serve as both shelters and hunting sites. Insects that crawl over the tube are impaled from within the tube by the long,
thin fangs of the spider, then drawn into the tube through a slit cut for the
purpose (Gertsch & Platnick 1980).

SPECIALIZED OR UNIQUE CHARACTERISTICS: The tube-like web
they spin up the base of trees is unique.

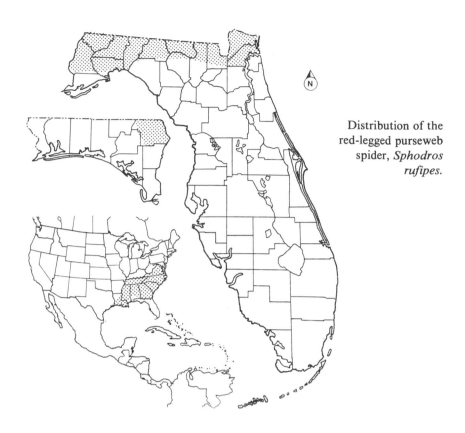

Distribution of the red-legged purseweb spider, *Sphodros rufipes.*

BASIS FOR STATUS CLASSIFICATION: These spiders live in mesic hardwood forests, and if the areas are disturbed badly the species cannot survive.

RECOMMENDATIONS: Representative natural mesic woodlands in the Florida Park System should be preserved to safeguard these spiders. *S. abboti* is known from Devil"s Millhopper, Roess Goldhead Branch, O"Leno, Ichetucknee Springs, Manatee Springs, and Suwannee Springs state parks (Gertsch & Platnick 1980). *S. rufipes* is known from Florida Caverns and Torreya state parks (Gertsch & Platnick 1980).

PREPARED BY: H. K. Wallace and G. B. Edwards, Florida State Collection of Arthropods, P.O. Box 147100, Gainesville, FL 32614-7100.

Order Araneae
FAMILY THERIDIIDAE

Species of Special Concern

Red Widow Spider
Latrodectus bishopi Kaston

DESCRIPTION: A reddish-orange spider with a black abdomen that is frequently marked with red spots dorsally (sometimes each spot is encircled with yellow or white). One or two red spots occur on the abdominal venter but never a complete hourglass marking as in some other widow species. Females are 9–11 mm (0.3–0.4 in) long, males 4–5 mm (0.15 in).

RANGE: Red widow spiders are found in sand pine scrub areas in central and southeastern Florida.

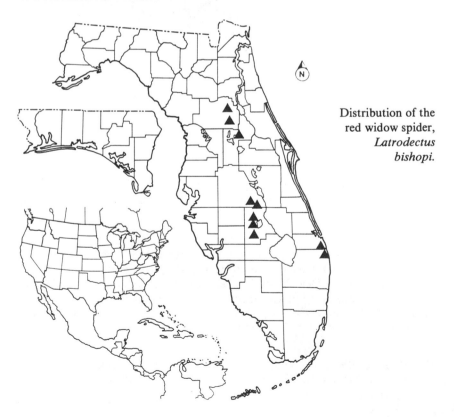

Distribution of the red widow spider, *Latrodectus bishopi.*

HABITAT: The spider almost always makes its large tangled webs in scrub palmettoes (*Sabal etonia and Serenoa repens*) in Florida scrub habitat. The web retreat is made in folded or creased palmetto leaves.

LIFE HISTORY AND ECOLOGY: Adults have been found throughout the year. The egg sacs are hung inside the web retreat.

SPECIALIZED OR UNIQUE CHARACTERISTICS: The unique color pattern enables this species to be recognized easily. With the infrequent exception of *L. mactans*, the southern black widow, which makes its web near the ground, the red widow is the only species of *Latrodectus* that occurs in sand pine scrub habitats.

BASIS FOR STATUS CLASSIFICATION: This species is restricted to sand pine scrub in peninsular Florida. Populations occur in the Ocala National Forest, Jonathan Dickinson State Park, Arbuckle State Forest, and the Archbold Biological Station. With proper habitat management in these areas, the species should not become threatened.

PREPARED BY: G. B. Edwards, Florida State Collection of Arthropods, P.O. Box 147100, Gainesville, FL 32614-7100.

Endangered

Dusky-Handed Tailless Whip Scorpion

Paraphrynus raptator (Pocock)

DESCRIPTION: *Paraphrynus raptator* is a large species (length of holotype, 29 mm [1.1 in]); its color in alcohol is dark reddish-brown. It can be distinguished from all other *Paraphrynus* species in several ways. Counting from the proximal end, on the ventral surface of the pedipalp femur, the difference in length between the first and second spines is conspicuously less than the difference in the length between the second and third. Also on the pedipalp basitarsus ("hand"), the first dorsal spine is longer than the third. In addition, there is no suture subdividing the most distal segment of the pedipalp (the tarsus), and there is a small tooth dorsally on the proximal end of this segment. A detailed description of this species, the only member of the genus in eastern North America, was given by Mullinex (1975). It can be distinguished from other and smaller species of tailless whip scorpion which occur in Florida and from the spotted tailless whip scorpion, *Phrynus marginemaculata* (C. L. Koch), by the presence of two spines between the two longest spines on the dorsal surface of the pedipalp tibia; *P. marginemaculata* has only one spine between the two longest spines.

RANGE: This species is found in northern Honduras; parts of Guatemala; the Yucatan Peninsula to Tabasco, Mexico; and Key West, Monroe County, Florida.

HABITAT: The few Florida records for this species and the more common *Phrynus marginemaculata* indicate that they are found most often in privies and old cisterns and under debris such as old lumber, weathered sheets of plywood and cardboard, and flat rocks on the ground surface. Records for *P. raptator* for the Yucatan Peninsula indicate that it lives mostly in caves.

LIFE HISTORY: Behavior, ecology, and life histories of this and other North American amblypygids are not well known. These organisms are predaceous on insects and other arthropods and are harmless to man.

SPECIALIZED OR UNIQUE CHARACTERISTICS: Specimens from Florida and Honduras most closely resemble the holotype from Teapa, Tabasco, Mexico. The Florida form has shorter spines than the Yucatan form.

252

Distribution of the dusky-handed tail-less whip scorpion, *Paraphrynus raptator.*

BASIS OF STATUS CLASSIFICATION: Most of the records for this species are for Mexico, but even there it does not appear to be abundant. In Florida, it appears to be rare and restricted to the Key West area. Lack of recent collection records may reflect, at least in part, lack of extensive collecting, but gradual elimination of privies and cisterns has reduced the specialized habitats where the species has been found in earlier years.

RECOMMENDATIONS: The present occurrence of this species in Florida is questionable, and probably little can be done to ensure its continuing existence here. The distribution of this species suggests it could be exotic in Florida; it if were possible to demonstrate that the species is not native, it would be possible to remove it from the FCREPA list.

PREPARED BY: Howard V. Weems, Jr., and Carolyn Mullinex Tibbets, Florida Collection of Arthropods, P.O. Box 147100, Gainesville, FL 32614-7100.

INTRODUCTION: Millipedes are an ancient group of arthropods that usually feed on vegetable detritus. Some species are widely distributed, including some species distributed through commerce. Many species, however, are narrowly distributed, due to strict habitat requirements and poor dispersal ability. The southern Appalachian region is a notable center of endemic millipedes, and it would not be surprising to find narrowly distributed species in the Apalachicola River basin. The only well-documented case of a rare Florida species occurs, rather unexpectedly, in scrub habitat, where there are several millipedes that burrow in sand.

PREPARED BY: Mark Deyrup, Archbold Biological Station, Lake Placid, FL 33852.

FAMILY FLORIDOBOLIDAE

Rare

Florida Scrub Millipede
Floridobolus penneri Causey

DESCRIPTION: About 90 mm (3.5 in) long, about 11.5 mm (0.5 in) wide, this millipede appears somewhat thick-bodied, tapering slightly at both ends. This non-cylindrical shape, combined with a uniform lead-grey color, distinguished this species from sympatric species of *Narceus* and *Chicobolus*. In addition, the ventral margin of the mandibular cheeks is rounded, and the end of the telopodite of posterior gonopods is divided into short, irregular lobes. A published description is found in Causey (1957).

RANGE: This millipede occurs on the Lake Wales Ridge in Highlands and Polk counties, north to Lake Wales.

HABITAT: It is found in open sand pine scrub.

LIFE HISTORY AND ECOLOGY: Largely unknown. In the laboratory this species feeds on dead leaves, especially scrub oaks, refusing fresh leaves. It is nocturnally active, remaining buried in sand during the day. Pitfall traps capture adults in the fall, seldom catching immatures any time of year; this suggests that this species may be active on the surface only during reproductive season. The growth rate is likely to be slow, as in other large millipedes, and the adult life span long.

Florida Scrub Milli-
pede, *Floridobolus
penneri* (courtesy of
Mark Deyrup).

Distribution of the
Florida scrub milli-
pede, *Floridobolus
penneri.*

SPECIALIZED OR UNIQUE CHARACTERISTICS: This species resembles the sand skink, *Neoseps reynoldsi*, in that it is an old, isolated scrub-inhabiting lineage with no close relatives anywhere.

BASIS FOR STATUS CLASSIFICATION: The Florida scrub millipede has a very small world distribution, and only one known protected population (Archbold Biological Station). It may well occur at Lake Apthorpe Preserve (Nature Conservancy) and Arbuckle State Forest. Although populations can probably persist in areas as small as a few acres, these patches of habitat must be maintained as open scrub with clumps of scrub oak.

RECOMMENDATIONS: Survey for this millipede on existing scrub refuges on the Lake Wales Ridge. Compare specimens from different sites to see if there has been differentiation into recognizable forms or species. Efforts to set up refuges for rare plants and scrub jays on the Lake Wales Ridge would, if successful, protect this remarkable species as well.

PREPARED BY: Mark A. Deyrup, Archbold Biological Station, Lake Placid, FL 33852.

Mayflies

INTRODUCTION: Ephemeropterans are aquatic insects of great ecological importance as they breed in well-oxygenated, unpolluted water. All species have wings as adults, but most use these wings for courtship acrobatics rather than long-range dispersal, and a short adult lifespan further reduces dispersal ability. These characteristics explain a low mayfly diversity in southern Florida, where water is warm, slow-moving, and frequently polluted. In north Florida there is a much richer mayfly diversity, with many species isolated in one or a few drainage systems. All our highly restricted mayflies are vulnerable because they could be extirpated by even a short-term episode of pollution. Many of these insects should be considered threatened or species of special concern. All these species occur in stream systems that also include rare or endangered mussels, dragonflies, or caddisflies. We have maintained the mayfly accounts as they appeared in the first edition and have included a list of 16 others that probably deserve attention. We refer the readers to the *Mayflies of Florida*, revised edition, by Berner and Pescador (1988) for further information on rare and endangered mayflies.

PREPARED BY: Mark Deyrup, Archbold Biological Station, Lake Placid, FL 33852.

Order Ephemeroptera
FAMILY BEHNINGIIDAE

Threatened

Dolania Mayfly
Dolania americana Edmunds and Traver

DESCRIPTION: The monotypic *Dolania americana* is a medium-sized mayfly with a 35 mm (1.4 in) wingspan. Legs, head, and mouthparts of the nymphs are modified for burrowing deep into the sand. The wings of the adults are modified for swift flight. Adults are whitish and live only one hour. The nymph is illustrated in Berner and Pescador 1988. See Edmunds and Traver (1959) and Peters and Peters (1977) for more information.

RANGE: This species was once probably widespread throughout the Southeast in shifting-sand-bottomed streams. It is reported from the upper Savannah River drainage in Georgia and western South Carolina, from the Shoal, Yellow, and Blackwater rivers in northwest Florida, and from several small streams north of Choctawhatchee Bay in northwest Florida.

HABITAT: The nymphs burrow into clean shifting sand in the fastest portions of the rivers; the sand must be free of silt and must not be compacted. Adults do not leave the river area.

LIFE HISTORY AND ECOLOGY: Adults emerge one hour before sunrise, and mating occurs before full sunlight. Eggs are laid in the rivers and soon hatch into first instar nymphs. Nymphs burrow into shifting sand and take one year to develop. Emergence of adults is keyed to moon phases and occurs only in April and May.

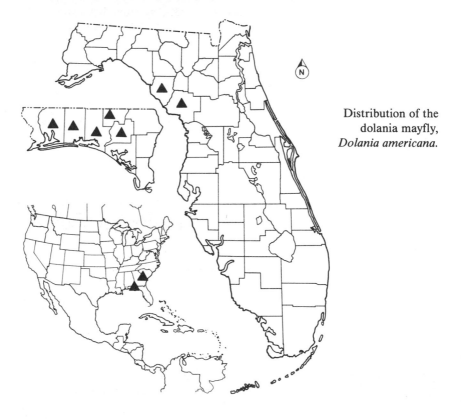

Distribution of the
dolania mayfly,
Dolania americana.

SPECIALIZED OR UNIQUE CHARACTERISTICS: This species is one of only a few mayflies in the world that burrow into sand.

BASIS FOR STATUS CLASSIFICATION: This mayfly is presently confined to several small areas where clean shifting-sand-bottomed rivers are still in their natural state. At one time the species apparently occurred in many sand-bottomed rivers in the Southeast, but it is no longer present due to pollution or siltation. If the remaining few rivers become polluted, *D. americana* will become extinct.

RECOMMENDATIONS: The Blackwater, Shoal, and Yellow river drainages should be fully protected to preserve their natural condition. To prevent siltation, no cutting or farm use should occur within 90 m (300 ft) of these rivers or 23 m (75 ft) of any tributary. Prevention of siltation is most important in preserving the nature of the shifting sand. Further, the rivers must be kept free of urban and industrial pollution. Research into all aspects of the biology of the species should be continued.

PREPARED BY: W. L. Peters, Laboratory of Aquatic Entomology, University P.O. Box 111, Florida A & M University, Tallahassee, FL 32307.

Order Ephemeroptera
FAMILY OLIGONEURIIDAE

Threatened

Blue Sand-River Mayfly

Homoeoneuria dolani Edmunds, Berner, and Traver

DESCRIPTION: *Homoeoneuria dolani* is a medium-sized mayfly with a 22 mm (0.87 in) wingspan. The legs, gills, and mouthparts of the nymphs are modified for burrowing into sand in deep running waters. Adults are bluish and live only one hour. The wings are modified for swift flight. The genus contains one other described species, *H. ammophila*, and one undescribed species from Mississippi and Texas. All species can be determined by the male genitalia and color pattern. See Edmunds et al. (1958) and Pescador and Peters (1980) for more information.

RANGE: This species was once probably widespread throughout the Southeast in shifting-sand-bottomed streams. It is presently reported from the upper Savannah River drainage in Georgia and western South Carolina, and from the Shoal, Yellow, and Blackwater rivers in northwest Florida.

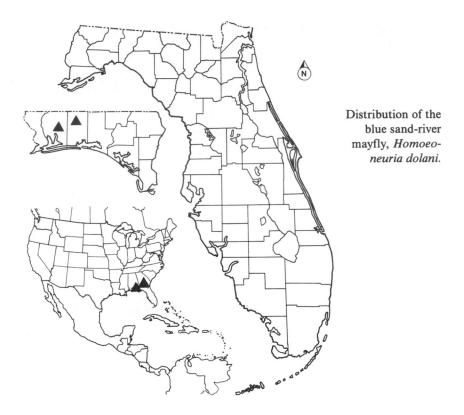

Distribution of the blue sand-river mayfly, *Homoeoneuria dolani.*

HABITAT: The nymphs burrow into clean shifting sand in the deepest and fastest portions of the rivers. The sand must be free of silt and must not be compacted. Adults do not leave the river area.

LIFE HISTORY AND ECOLOGY: Adults emerge in the afternoon and mate in full sunlight. Eggs are laid in the rivers and remain dormant for some months before hatching. The nymphs develop during the summer. Emergence to adults occurs only in August.

SPECIALIZED OR UNIQUE CHARACTERISTICS: This species is one of only a few mayflies in the world that burrow into sand.

BASIS FOR STATUS CLASSIFICATION: *Homoeoneuria dolani* is presently confined to several small areas where clean shifting-sand-bottomed rivers are still in their natural state. At one time the species apparently occurred in many sand-bottomed rivers in the Southeast, but it is no longer present due to pollution or siltation. If the remaining few rivers become polluted, *H. dolani* will become extinct.

RECOMMENDATIONS: The Blackwater, Shoal, and Yellow river drainages should be fully protected to preserve their natural condition. To prevent siltation, no cutting or farm use should occur within 90 m (300 ft) of the rivers or 23 m (75 ft) of any tributary. Avoiding siltation is most important in preserving the nature of the shifting sand. Further, the rivers must be kept free of urban and industrial pollution. Research into all aspects of the biology of the species should be continued.

PREPARED BY: W. L. Peters, Laboratory of Aquatic Entomology, University P.O. Box 111, Florida A & M University, Tallahassee, FL 32307.

Order Ephemeroptera

FAMILY HEPTAGENIIDAE

Threatened

White Sand-River Mayfly

Pseudiron centralis McDunnough

OTHER NAMES: Listed as *Pseudiron meridionalis* in the 1982 FCREPA volume.

DESCRIPTION: *Pseudiron centralis* is a medium-sized mayfly with a 25 mm (1.0 in) wingspan and many nymphal adaptations. The legs, head, and mouthparts of nymphs are modified for burrowing into sand. Adults are whitish and live for about 24 hours. The southeastern form with distinctive pale coloration was originally described as *P. meridionalis* (Pescador 1985). The nymph is illustrated in Berner and Pescador 1988. See Traver (1935) for more information.

RANGE: This species was once probably widespread throughout the Southeast in shifting-sand-bottomed streams. It was originally described from the Chattahoocheee River, near Atlanta, Georgia, but it is no longer there. Today, it occurs in Shoal, Yellow, and Blackwater rivers and in several small streams north of Choctawhatchee Bay, all in northwest Florida.

HABITAT: The nymphs burrow into clean shifting sand in the fastest portions of the rivers. The sand must be free of silt and must not be compacted. The adults do not leave the river area.

LIFE HISTORY AND ECOLOGY: Little is known about this mayfly's life history and ecology. Adults emerge in March and April. The entire life cycle takes one year.

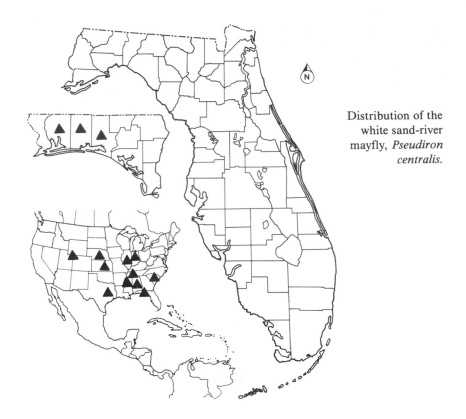

Distribution of the
white sand-river
mayfly, *Pseudiron
centralis.*

SPECIALIZED OR UNIQUE CHARACTERISTICS: This species is one of only a few mayflies in the world that burrow into sand.

BASIS FOR STATUS CLASSIFICATION: This mayfly is presently confined to several small areas where clean shifting-sand-bottomed rivers are still in their natural state. At one time the species apparently occurred in many sand-bottomed rivers in the Southeast, but it is no longer present due to pollution or siltation. If the remaining few rivers become polluted, *P. centralis* will be extirpated in Florida.

RECOMMENDATIONS: The Blackwater, Shoal, and Yellow river drainages should be fully protected to preserve their natural condition. To prevent siltation, no cutting or farm use should occur within 90 m (300 ft) of the rivers or 23 m (75 ft) of any tributary. Avoiding siltation is most important in preserving the nature of the shifting sand. Further, the rivers must be kept free of urban and industrial pollution. Research into all aspects of the biology of the species should be continued.

PREPARED BY: W.L. Peters, Laboratory of Aquatic Entomology, P.O. Box 111, Florida A & M University, Tallahassee, FL 32307.

Mayflies of Concern

The following species of mayflies are likely to be considered for future lists of rare and endangered arthropods:

FAMILY BAETIDAE
  Cleon undescribed species
FAMILY METRETOPODIDAE
  Siphloplecton brunneum Berner
  Siphloplecton fuscum Berner
  Siphloplecton simile Berner
FAMILY OLIGONEURIDAE
  Isonychia berneri Kondratieff and Voshell
  Isonychia sicca (Walsh)
FAMILY HEPTAGENIIDAE
  Macdunnoa brunnea Flowers
  Stenacron floridense (Lewis)
  Stenonema modestum (Banks)
FAMILY LEPTOPHLEBIIDAE
  Leptophlebia collina (Traver)
FAMILY EPHEMERIDAE
  Hexagenia bilineata (Say)
FAMILY EPHEMERELLIDAE
  Attenella attenuata (McDunnough)
  Dannella simplex (McDunnough)
FAMILY TRICORYTHIDAE
  Leptohyphes dolani Allen
FAMILY CAENIDAE
  Brachycercus nasutus Soldán
FAMILY BAETISCIDAE
  Baetisca laurentina McDunnough

PREPARED BY: Mark Deyrup, Archbold Biological Station, Lake Placid, FL 33852.

Dragonflies and Damselflies

INTRODUCTION: Anyone who tarries by the waterside can enjoy the aeronautical skills of the colorful and harmless dragonflies and damselflies. Adult dragonflies and damselflies are most easily distinguished from other insects by the two pairs of membranous wings which cannot be folded roof-like over the abdomen. In addition, the eyes are very large, covering the sides and sometimes also the top of the head, and the antennae are bristle-like and inconspicuous. Dragonflies and damselflies are two separate suborders of the order Odonata. The hindwings of the dragonflies or mosquito-hawks, the suborder Anisoptera, are widened at the base, and the wings are usually held straight out to the sides at rest. The damselflies, the suborder Zygoptera, have the hindwings and forewings shaped alike, and the wings are held pressed together over the back or are only partly spread. Dragonflies are generally larger and more robust than damselflies. Florida dragonflies have a body length of 17–100 mm (0.7–4.0 in); Florida damselflies are 20–60 mm (0.8–2.4 in) long. No single term has come into use to refer to both dragonflies and damselflies, but "odonate" can be used for the Odonata in general.

Odonates are entirely carnivorous and are usually found near water because their larvae (nymphs) are aquatic. The larvae differ from all other animals by having a greatly enlarged lower lip, or labium, which they use for capturing prey. The abdomen of the dragonfly larva is tipped with short pointed appendages, while the abdomen of the damselfly larva is tipped with three leaf-like gills.

The rich Florida fauna contains 112 breeding species of dragonflies and 44 species of damselflies, about a third of all the species in North America. Seven more dragonfly species are vagrants to Florida. Of the 156 resident odonates, 33 (21%) are listed in the accounts here. This list is conservative, for 14 other species are confined to the southern tip of the state, and 10 more species are peripheral in northern Florida but are common farther north. The south Florida species are not listed, except for the Everglades sprite, because they are all pond and canal species. These species can be expected to persist in Florida as long as the construction of new ponds equals the destruction of old ones, or until the introduction of too many super-predatory exotic fish.

Most odonates do not have English names. The names used here are from unpublished works by S. W. Dunkle and D. R. Paulson.

Of the 33 odonates listed here, the larvae of 15 (46%) live in Florida only in panhandle rivers and streams. Six of these occur only in the Apalachicola River and its tributaries, two only in the Blackwater River and its tributaries, and one only in the Yellow River. Obviously, conservation efforts directed at these rivers would be of immediate and lasting benefit. These rivers should not be dammed or dredged, and pollution should be monitored and minimized. As much of their watersheds as is possible should be left in forest to help moderate changes in water level. The watersheds of one or more panhandle streams should be encompassed in a new state park or state forest now. Good candidates are Pond Creek in Santa Rosa County, and Juniper Creek in Calhoun County, each of which has at least six of the listed odonate species (not the same six). All panhandle streams should be protected from excessive pollution, grazing, and deforestation.

Five of the listed dragonflies breed only in sand-bottomed lakes. Three of these are endemic to Florida, the other two nearly so. In fact, several other odonates, not listed here, are far more common in Florida than anywhere else. This is due to the scarcity of this habitat type elsewhere in the Southeast. These odonates are adapted to this environment of low fertility and low competition. Fertilizing such lakes changes the chemical, biological, and bottom characteristics, allowing common species of fertile waters to out-compete the sand lake species. Large numbers of these lakes have already been overfertilized (eutrophicated) by residential development and agriculture such as citrus groves. Probably most owners of sand-bottomed lakes would prefer that the water be clear and the bottom stay sand. They should understand that fertilizer runoff from lawns, septic tanks, or agricultural lands will cause the water to turn green due to algae growth, and the bottom to become mucky as the algae die and settle out. Pesticide runoff or drift also kills the special sand lake odonates and other wildlife.

At least eight of the listed odonates breed in small localized areas such as spring seepages or bogs. Populations of these species could easily be saved at relatively low cost just by purchasing a few acres of habitat.

While the subtropical odonates with restricted ranges in the southern tip of Florida are not included in this list, their populations could be enhanced by vegetating parts of the shores of rockpits and ponds. Establishing emergent grass along the edges of these ponds would create habitat for odonates and other wildlife for conservation and for everyone's enjoyment. Domestic ducks are not compatible with odonates. Not only do the ducks eat the odonate larvae, but the bread and other feeds given to the ducks and processed through them at a rate of $1/3$ lb/duck/day of "fertilizer" quickly turns the water green with algae growth.

PREPARED BY: S. W. Dunkle, Biology Department, Collin County Community College, 2800 East Spring Creek Parkway, Plano, TX 75074.

Order Odonata
Suborder Anisoptera
FAMILY GOMPHIDAE

Threatened

Eastern Ringtail
Erpetogomphus designatus Hagen

DESCRIPTION: This medium-sized (body length 44–52 mm [1.7–2.0 in]) species is very colorful for a clubtail, with a yellow-green thorax and a black-and-white banded abdomen with an orange tip. It can be separated from all other North American clubtails by the domed bulge on the dorsal surface of the occiput. Most recently described in Needham and Westfall (1955).

RANGE: This species is known in Florida only from the Apalachicola River. The range extends north to Maryland, Ohio, and South Dakota; west to Colorado and Nevada; and south into northern Mexico.

HABITAT: This dragonfly occurs on rivers and streams, usually with riffles and rocks.

Eastern Ringtail,
Erpetogomphus
designatus (courtesy
of Sidney
W. Dunkle).

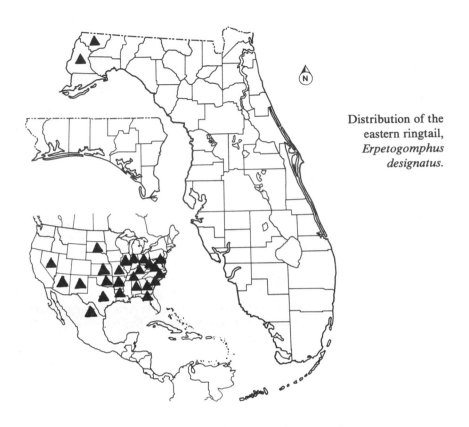

Distribution of the
eastern ringtail,
*Erpetogomphus
designatus.*

LIFE HISTORY AND ECOLOGY: Flight season is from early June to early August in Florida, from mid-April to mid-October elsewhere. Males usually patrol over the water at the heads of riffles while waiting for females, which often lay eggs there. The larvae burrow shallowly in silt deposits.

BASIS FOR STATUS CLASSIFICATION: In Florida this species is found only on the Apalachicola River, which is affected by a dam and dredging for barge traffic. The species was last seen in numbers on the river in 1954, before the Jim Woodruff Dam was closed. Only a few specimens have been seen in Florida since then. This species is common westward, particularly in Texas.

RECOMMENDATIONS: No further dams should be built on the Apalachicola River, and dredging and pollution should be minimized.

PREPARED BY: S. W. Dunkle, Biology Department, Collin County Community College, 2800 East Spring Creek Parkway, Plano, TX 75074.

Threatened

Cocoa Clubtail

Gomphus (Gomphurus) hybridus Williamson

DESCRIPTION: This brown and green dragonfly is smaller (body length 43–55 mm [1.7–2.1 in]) and browner than most other members of the sub-genus *Gomphurus*. The brown stripes of the thorax are somewhat fused together at the shoulders and on the sides, and abdominal segment 8 is brown dorsally with a small pale spot on each side. The occiput of the head is thick and convex, but wedge-like, resembling the blade of an axe. It was most recently described in Needham and Westfall (1955).

RANGE: Known in Florida only from the Apalachicola River. It ranges north to North Carolina, Kentucky, and Illinois, west to eastern Texas.

HABITAT: This dragonfly occurs on mud-bottomed medium to large rivers.

Cocoa Clubtail,
Gomphus hybridus
(courtesy of Sidney
W. Dunkle).

Distribution of the
cocoa clubtail,
Gomphus hybridus.

LIFE HISTORY AND ECOLOGY: Adults were collected in late March and early April in Florida, and to early June elsewhere. Prey includes damselflies, medium-sized dragonflies, and butterflies. Males patrol over the current on the watch for egg-laying females. The larvae burrow shallowly in mud.

BASIS FOR STATUS CLASSIFICATION: The closing of the Jim Woodruff Dam in 1957 may have extirpated this species in Florida. It has not been seen in the state since 1956, despite special searches. It still occurs on the Flint River, a tributary of the Apalachicola, in Georgia.

RECOMMENDATIONS: No further dams should be built on the Apalachicola River, and pollution and dredging of the river should be minimized.

PREPARED BY: S. W. Dunkle, Biology Department, Collin County Community College, 2800 East Spring Creek Parkway, Plano, TX 75074.

Threatened

Gulf Coast Clubtail

Gomphus (Gomphurus) modestus Needham

DESCRIPTION: This clubtail is a rather large (body length 55–64 mm [2.1–2.5 in]) green and black dragonfly with large yellow spots on the sides of abdominal segments 8 and 9, which are widely clubbed. The face has a narrow black cross-line; other *Gomphurus* in Florida have either wide black facial bands or no cross-lines. The female is distinguished from all other *Gomphurus* by the bluntly rounded lobes of the subgenital plate, in combination with the straight occipital crest. The species was most recently described by Westfall (1974).

RANGE: This insect is known in Florida from a few specimens taken on the Yellow River in 1973. It ranges from Florida west to eastern Texas, north into Arkansas.

Gulf Coast Clubtail, *Gomphus modestus* (courtesy of Sidney W. Dunkle).

Distribution of the gulf coast clubtail, *Gomphus modestus.*

HABITAT: This dragonfly occurs on clean rivers and streams with sand or rock bottoms.

LIFE HISTORY AND ECOLOGY: Adults have been recorded in early June in Florida, but are active from late April to late June elsewhere. They apparently spend most of their time in the trees, but males may be seen perching on the bank or on vegetation near riffles, on the watch for ovipositing females. The larvae burrow shallowly in silt deposits.

BASIS FOR STATUS CLASSIFICATION: This species seems rare everywhere, and has been found in Florida only once. It has not been found in the state subsequently, despite searches.

RECOMMENDATIONS: The Yellow River should not be dammed, and development in its watershed should be controlled.

PREPARED BY: S. W. Dunkle, Biology Department, Collin County Community College, 2800 East Spring Creek Parkway, Plano, TX 75074.

Threatened

Cobra Clubtail

Gomphus (Gomphurus) vastus Walsh

DESCRIPTION: This green and black dragonfly has a particularly wide cobra-like expansion near the tip of the abdomen, and the face has wide black cross-bands. Abdominal segments 8 and 9 have bright yellow lateral spots, that of 9 much larger than the spot on 8. The male has a truncate penis hood, while the female has a concave occiput. Body length is 47–58 mm (1.8–2.2 in). This species was most recently described in Walker (1958).

RANGE: This species is known in Florida only from the Apalachicola River. It ranges north to New Hampshire, southern Ontario, and Minnesota, west into Iowa and Texas.

HABITAT: It usually is associated with large rivers, but sometimes occurs in large streams or large lakes.

Cobra Clubtail, *Gomphus vastus* (courtesy of Sidney W. Dunkle).

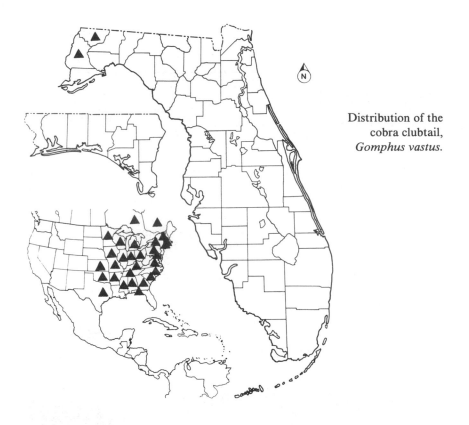

Distribution of the
cobra clubtail,
Gomphus vastus.

LIFE HISTORY AND ECOLOGY: Adults have been recorded in Florida in June, and from early April to mid-September elsewhere. The species preys on other insects, including dragonflies almost as large as itself. Males fly long patrols over the water, but perch occasionally on overhanging leaves at the shoreline. Females may fly far out over the water to oviposit. The larvae burrow shallowly in mud.

BASIS FOR STATUS CLASSIFICATION: Like several other Florida dragonflies, this species has been found only on the Apalachicola River, which is already stressed by a dam and dredging.

RECOMMENDATIONS: No further dams should be built on the Apalachicola River, and pollution and dredging of the river should be minimized.

PREPARED BY: S. W. Dunkle, Biology Department, Collin County Community College, 2800 East Spring Creek Parkway, Plano, TX 75074.

Threatened

Diminutive Clubtail

Gomphus (Phanogomphus) westfalli Carle and May

DESCRIPTION: This is a small (body length 38–44 mm [1.5–1.7 in]) green and black dragonfly. It is distinguished from other *Phanogomphus* by having abdominal segment 9 longer than segment 8 but shorter than segment 7. It is also unusual among *Phanogomphus* species in having a dark facial cross-stripe. The lateral black stripes of the thorax are distinct and well-separated. This species was recently described by Carle and May (1987). This species is closely related to *Gomphus diminutus* Needham, and may be a subspecies of it. *G. diminutus* occurs in the Carolinas and differs from *G. westfalli* in having a brown area between the black lateral thoracic stripes and in details of the sexual structures.

RANGE: This dragonfly is endemic to the western tributaries of the Blackwater River in Santa Rosa County.

Diminutive Clubtail, *Gomphus westfalli* (courtesy of Sidney W. Dunkle).

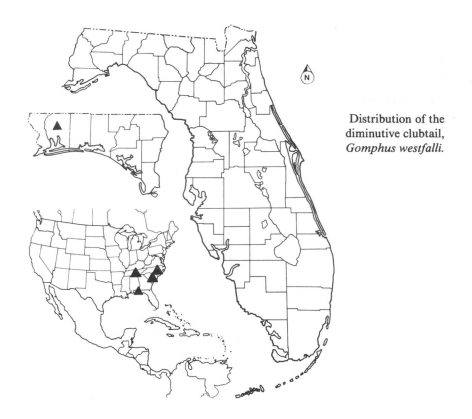

Distribution of the diminutive clubtail, *Gomphus westfalli.*

HABITAT: It is associated with sphagnum-bog trickles and streams.

LIFE HISTORY AND ECOLOGY: The flight season is early and short, from early March to late April. Prey includes damselflies. Males perch on low plants near the shoreline to watch for females. Females oviposit by hovering near marginal plants and dipping to the surface every few seconds to release a group of eggs. The larvae burrow in silt.

BASIS FOR STATUS CLASSIFICATION: The entire known range of this species is only about 25 km in diameter. Most of the range is within the Blackwater River State Forest, where most kinds of development can be controlled.

RECOMMENDATIONS: The watershed of the Blackwater River should be protected against excessive deforestation and pollution. Patchy summer burning should create foraging habitat for the adults the next spring.

PREPARED BY: S. W. Dunkle, Biology Department, Collin County Community College, 2800 East Spring Creek Parkway, Plano, TX 75074.

Threatened

Laura's Clubtail

Stylurus laurae Williamson

DESCRIPTION: This large, elongate (body length 39–45 mm [1.5–1.7 in]) *Stylurus* is green, black, and yellow, with the area between the black lateral thoracic stripes clouded with brown. The face is dark brown and abdominal segments 9–10 are brown dorsally. Most recently described by Needham and Westfall (1955). This species has sometimes been placed in the genus *Gomphus*.

RANGE: It is known in Florida from the eastern tributaries of the Apalachicola River. It ranges north to Maryland, Ohio, and Michigan, west to Arkansas and eastern Texas.

HABITAT: This clubtail occurs on clean streams with sand-mud bottoms, sometimes with rocks.

Laura's Clubtail, *Stylurus laurae* (courtesy of Sidney W. Dunkle).

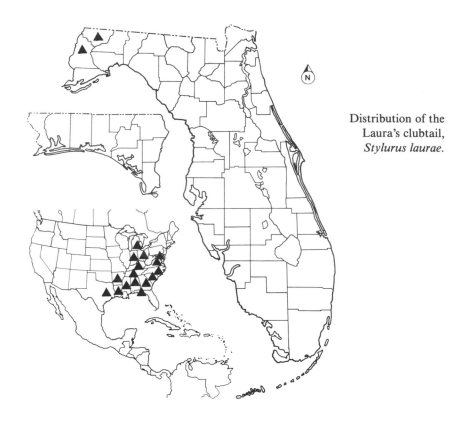

Distribution of the
Laura's clubtail,
Stylurus laurae.

LIFE HISTORY AND ECOLOGY: Adults fly from late May to early August in Florida, and to early October elsewhere. In the evening, males perch on overhanging leaves, usually near riffles while waiting for ovipositing females. Larvae burrow in silty sand.

BASIS FOR STATUS CLASSIFICATION: This species has been collected at only a few adjacent streams in Florida and is uncommon throughout its range.

RECOMMENDATIONS: The watershed of the Apalachicola River should be protected against excessive deforestation and development.

PREPARED BY: S. W. Dunkle, Biology Department, Collin County Community College, 2800 East Spring Creek Parkway, Plano, TX 75074.

Threatened

Yellow-Sided Clubtail
Stylurus potulentus (Needham)

DESCRIPTION: This clubtail is a very slender species, 47–52 mm (1.8–2.0 in) long, mostly black, but with the sides of the thorax yellow. The face is brown, the eyes are dark blue, and the femora of the hind legs are yellow. The female subgenital plate is merely a narrow rim on the underside of abdominal segment 8. It was most recently described in Needham and Westfall (1955). Previously this species has often been placed in the genus *Gomphus*.

RANGE: In Florida this insect occurs in certain panhandle streams; otherwise, it is known only from the coastal plain of Mississippi.

HABITAT: It is associated with clean, sand-bottomed forest streams and rivers.

Yellow-Sided Clubtail, *Stylurus potulentus* (courtesy of Sidney W. Dunkle).

Distribution of the
yellow-sided club-
tail, *Stylurus
potulentus.*

LIFE HISTORY AND ECOLOGY: Adults are active from mid-May to early August. During the day they forage along shady thicket edges. Males patrol over the water in the evening while searching for females. Larvae burrow in silt deposits.

BASIS FOR STATUS CLASSIFICATION: This species is rare even within its small range.

RECOMMENDATIONS: Some of the panhandle streams should be protected in new state or federal parks or forests.

PREPARED BY: S. W. Dunkle, Biology Department, Collin County Community College, 2800 East Spring Creek Parkway, Plano, TX 75074.

Threatened

Townes' Clubtail

Stylurus townesi Gloyd

DESCRIPTION: This medium sized (body length 46-54 mm [1.8-2.1 in]) clubtail is mostly black, marked with green and yellow. The front of the thorax has a pair of narrow green stripes which are widely divergent downward. The face is black, and females have yellow lateral edges on abdominal segments 8 and 9. It was most recently described in Needham and Westfall (1955). This species has sometimes been placed in the genus *Gomphus*.

RANGE: This dragonfly is known in Florida only from the Blackwater River. It ranges in the coastal plain from Mississippi to North Carolina.

HABITAT: This species is found in association with clean sand-bottom forest streams and rivers.

Townes' Clubtail, *Stylurus townesi* (courtesy of Sidney W. Dunkle).

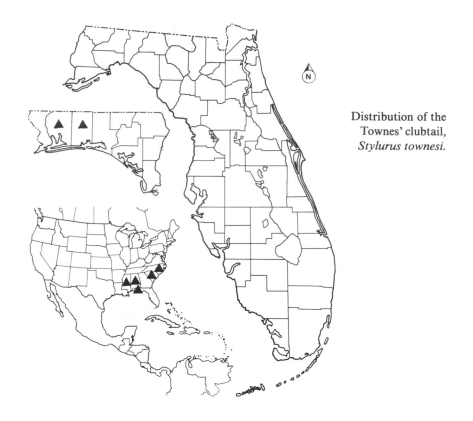

Distribution of the
Townes' clubtail,
Stylurus townesi.

LIFE HISTORY AND ECOLOGY: Adults fly from early June to late September. This species is very unusual among dragonflies in that both females and males spend nearly all of their time on streamside trees and shrubs. Males, which do not patrol over the water, become more active in the evening. Larvae burrow in sand.

BASIS FOR STATUS CLASSIFICATION: This clubtail has been found in Florida on only the Blackwater River, and is uncommon throughout its range.

RECOMMENDATIONS: Protect the watershed of the Blackwater River from excessive deforestation and pollution.

PREPARED BY: S. W. Dunkle, Biology Department, Collin County Community College, 2800 East Spring Creek Parkway, Plano, TX 75074.

Rare

Southeastern Spinyleg
Dromogomphus armatus Selys

DESCRIPTION: The spinylegs are distinguished from all other North American dragonflies by 4-11 long, perpendicular spikes on each femur of the hind legs. The southeastern spinyleg has narrow black and green stripes on the thorax, a brown cross-line on the face, and no pale rings around the abdomen. The clubbed end of the abdomen is bright rusty-orange in males. This is a large species, 63-68 mm (2.5-2.7 in) long. Most recently described by Westfall and Tennessen (1979).

RANGE: This clubtail occurs in Florida south to Orange County. It ranges in the coastal states from Mississippi to North Carolina.

HABITAT: This species usually occurs along forested spring-fed streams with clear water flowing over deep liquid muck, and sometimes in larger

Southeastern Spinyleg, *Dromogomphus armatus*
(courtesy of Sidney W. Dunkle).

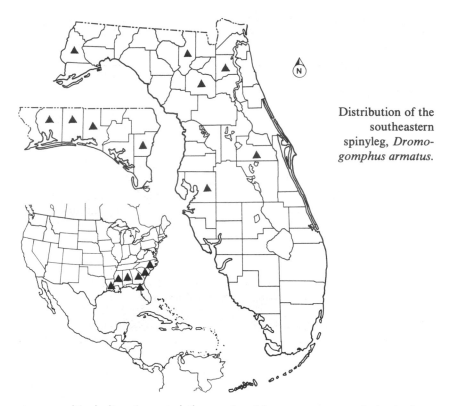

Distribution of the
southeastern
spinyleg, *Dromo-
gomphus armatus.*

streams with similar characteristics produced by sparse emergent plants slow-
ing the current.

LIFE HISTORY AND ECOLOGY: This spinyleg flies in Florida from early
June to late November, beginning in early May elsewhere. This species is
both secretive and wary, often foraging within cover. Males at water are less
wary, and perch on low vegetation or sticks on shore while waiting for females. The larvae burrow in deep muck.

BASIS FOR STATUS CLASSIFICATION: This species is rare throughout
its range, due to the limited larval habitat.

RECOMMENDATIONS: Known habitats, including Pond Creek and other
tributaries of the Blackwater River in Santa Rosa County, should not be
stressed by pollution or excessive deforestation. The larvae of this species, in
their loose muck microhabitat, are easily scoured out of a stream during rain
storms if the watersheds do not absorb the extra load of water.

PREPARED BY: S. W. Dunkle, Biology Department, Collin County Community College, 2800 East Spring Creek Parkway, Plano, TX 75074.

Rare

Hodges' Clubtail

Gomphus (Phanogomphus) hodgesi Needham

DESCRIPTION: This small (body length 39–45 mm [1.5–1.8 in]) green and black dragonfly has a slender body. Abdominal segments 8 and 9 are black dorsally except for a narrow mid-dorsal yellow line. Segment 10 is all black dorsally in males, and the male terminal abdominal appendages in dorsal view are distinctively shaped, like a pair of cow horns. It was most recently described by Westfall (1965).

RANGE: This species ranges throughout the Florida panhandle and west to Louisiana.

HABITAT: It occurs on clean sand-bottomed streams and rivers.

Hodges' Clubtail,
Gomphus hodgesi
(courtesy of Sidney
W. Dunkle).

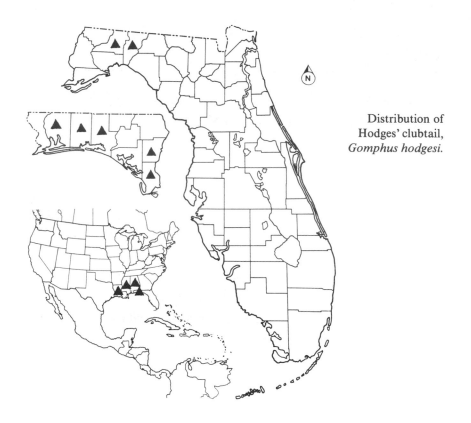

Distribution of
Hodges' clubtail,
Gomphus hodgesi.

LIFE HISTORY AND ECOLOGY: Adults fly from early March to late May, and perch on the ground. Mating in this species apparently occurs mostly away from water, as males do not return to the water until they are quite aged. Larvae burrow in silt deposits.

BASIS FOR STATUS CLASSIFICATION: This species is scarce throughout its small range.

RECOMMENDATIONS: The watersheds of Florida panhandle streams should be protected from excessive deforestation and pollution, and more such streams should be included in future land acquisition proposals. Patchy summer burning would open up the habitats and create foraging areas for adults.

PREPARED BY: S. W. Dunkle, Biology Department, Collin County Community College, 2800 East Spring Creek Parkway, Plano, TX 75074.

Rare

Twin-Striped Clubtail

Gomphus (Gomphus) geminatus Carle

DESCRIPTION: This small (body length 36–43 mm [1.4–1.7 in]), chunky clubtail is mostly black with green stripes on the thorax, a black line across the face, large yellow spots on the sides of abdominal segments 8 and 9, and blue eyes. It is the only member of the subgenus in Florida. This species has sometimes been placed in the subgenus *Hylogomphus*. It was described by Carle (1979).

RANGE: This clubtail occurs in the Florida panhandle and adjacent Alabama, east to central Georgia.

HABITAT: It occurs on clean sand-bottomed streams.

LIFE HISTORY AND ECOLOGY: Adults fly from early March to mid June. They perch on bushes to forage for prey as large as damselflies. Fe-

Twin-Striped Clubtail, *Gomphus geminatus* (courtesy of Sidney W. Dunkle).

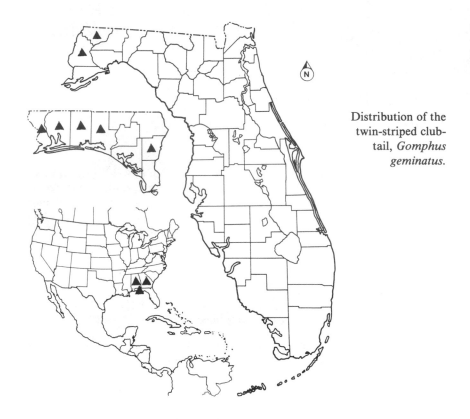

Distribution of the
twin-striped club-
tail, *Gomphus
geminatus.*

males perch on the bank while forming an egg mass which they then tap to
the water in flight. The larvae burrow shallowly in silt deposits.

BASIS FOR STATUS CLASSIFICATION: The species' range is small.
The twin-striped clubtail is very closely related to the Piedmont clubtail, *G.
parvidens*, an uncommon species which is found on the Piedmont from Alabama to Maryland. At present these dragonflies are considered separate species based on details of the female head structure, but more specimens from
central Alabama and central Georgia are needed for study to determine their
specific relationships.

RECOMMENDATIONS: It is necessary to protect the panhandle stream
watersheds from excessive development, deforestation, erosion, and pollution.

PREPARED BY: S. W. Dunkle, Biology Department, Collin County Community College, 2800 East Spring Creek Parkway, Plano, TX 75074.

Rare

Belle's Sanddragon
Progomphus bellei Knopf and Tennessen

DESCRIPTION: This slender brown clubtail has a small brown spot at the base of each wing and two sharply defined squared yellow spots on each side of abdominal segment 8. Body length 53–62 mm (2–2.5 in). A unique feature of the sanddragons among all dragonflies is that the male ventral terminal abdominal appendage is split, with each half movable. A distinctive characteristic of both sexes of North American species of this genus is a finger-like ventral projection on the first abdominal segment. This dragonfly was described by Knopf and Tennessen (1980).

RANGE: This species is known only from the Florida panhandle, and from one specimen taken in south-central North Carolina.

HABITAT: This species uses two habitat types: sand-bottomed lakes, and small sandy spring-fed trickles in the open.

Belle's Sanddragon,
Progomphus bellei
(courtesy of Sidney
W. Dunkle).

Distribution of
Belle's sanddragon,
Progomphus bellei.

LIFE HISTORY AND ECOLOGY: Adults fly from early May to mid August. Males perch on sand near the water, but if no open shores are present they will perch on the tips of weeds overlooking the water. They are remarkably wary. Females oviposit by flying low over the water while tapping clusters of eggs to the surface. The larvae are excellent burrowers in sand, where they leave a distinctive V-shaped track.

BASIS FOR STATUS CLASSIFICATION: The species' range is small.

RECOMMENDATIONS: Some panhandle sand-bottomed lakes should be encompassed in a preserve, and all such lakes should be monitored to see that they are not fertilized and eutrophicated. Some of these lakes are also habitats of the purple skimmer.

PREPARED BY: S. W. Dunkle, Biology Department, Collin County Community College, 2800 East Spring Creek Parkway, Plano TX 75074.

Species of Special Concern

Tawny Sanddragon
Progomphus alachuensis Byers

DESCRIPTION: A slender, brown and yellow dragonfly of medium size (body length 49–57 mm [1.9–2.2 in]). A small brown spot occurs at the base of each wing, and abdominal segment 8 has large diffuse lateral yellow blotches. This species is very similar to Belle's sanddragon; the most obvious difference between them is the color pattern of abdominal segment 8. The third species of sanddragon in Florida, *Progomphus obscurus*, usually has segment 8 all brown. This species was most recently described in Needham and Westfall (1955), with a color photo in Dunkle (1989).

RANGE: This sanddragon is endemic to the Florida peninsula.

HABITAT: It usually occurs in clear sand-bottomed lakes.

Tawny Sanddragon, *Progomphus ala-chuensis* (courtesy of Sidney W. Dunkle).

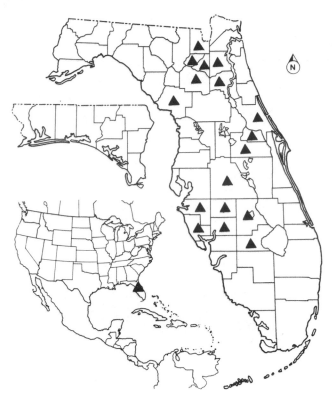

Distribution of the
tawny sanddragon,
*Progomphus
alachuensis.*

LIFE HISTORY AND ECOLOGY: Flight season early April to late August. Away from water this dragonfly perches on weed tips, but at water males perch alertly on a sandy shore, with the abdomen raised. Females lay eggs in open water during a fast, low, erratic flight. The larvae burrow rapidly just under the sand surface of the lake bottom.

BASIS FOR STATUS CLASSIFICATION: The species is restricted to the sand-bottomed lakes of the Florida peninsula, a habitat overwhelmed by development.

RECOMMENDATIONS: Encourage landowner education to prevent eutrophication and other pollution of sand-bottomed lakes.

PREPARED BY: S. W. Dunkle, Biology Department, Collin County Community College, 2800 East Spring Creek Parkway, Plano TX 75074.

Species of Special Concern

Sandhill Clubtail

Gomphus (Phanogomphus) cavillaris Needham

DESCRIPTION: A medium sized (body length 37–45 mm [1.4–1.8 in]) drag-onfly which has a striped pale green thorax, a dark facial cross-stripe, and a mostly dark abdomen with yellow sides on the enlarged segments 7–9. The male cerci each have a large lateral tooth. The crest of the female occiput is straight. The female subgenital plate is very short, 1/10 or less the length of abdominal segment 9. The Florida peninsula subspecies, *G. cavillaris cavillaris*, is marked with brown and dull yellow. The Florida panhandle and North Carolina subspecies, *G. cavillaris brimleyi*, is marked with black and bright yellow. Most recently described by Needham and Westfall (1955), with a color photo of *G. cavillaris cavillaris* in Dunkle (1989).

RANGE: This clubtail occurs in Florida and North Carolina.

Sandhill Clubtail,
Gomphus cavillaris
(courtesy of Sidney
W. Dunkle).

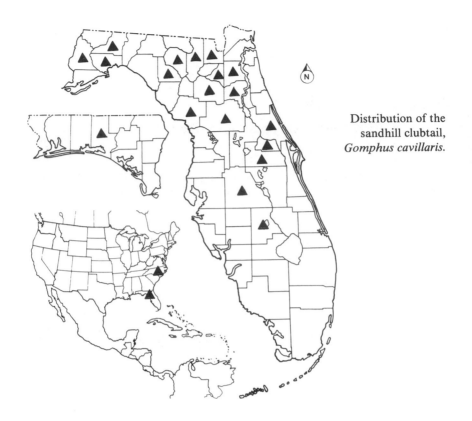

Distribution of the
sandhill clubtail,
Gomphus cavillaris.

HABITAT: It is associated with sand-bottomed lakes.

LIFE HISTORY AND ECOLOGY: Flight season occurs from late January to late May. It usually perches on the ground, from where it makes short sallies for prey such as damselflies and beetles. Males perch on the shore or on floating objects while they wait for females. The female deposits eggs during a fast, low, irregular flight over the water. Larvae burrow in silt deposits.

BASIS FOR STATUS CLASSIFICATION: *G. c. cavillaris* is endemic to the Florida peninsula, and *G. c. brimleyi* also has a restricted distribution. In addition, their sand-bottom lake habitat is being developed very rapidly.

RECOMMENDATIONS: Preserve the water quality of clear sand-bottomed lakes by preventing the input of fertilizers, septic tank leachate, and pesticides.

PREPARED BY: S. W. Dunkle, Biology Department, Collin County Community College, 2800 East Spring Creek Parkway, Plano, TX 75074.

Threatened

Say's Spiketail

Cordulegaster sayi Selys

DESCRIPTION: This beautiful dragonfly has a unique color pattern. The thorax is striped with yellow, magenta, and white, while the abdomen is black with yellow rings, and the eyes are gray-green. The female has a spike-like ovipositor which reaches the end of the abdomen. Body length is 60–69 mm (2.4–2.7 in). The species was most recently described in Needham and Westfall (1955), with a color photo in Dunkle (1989).

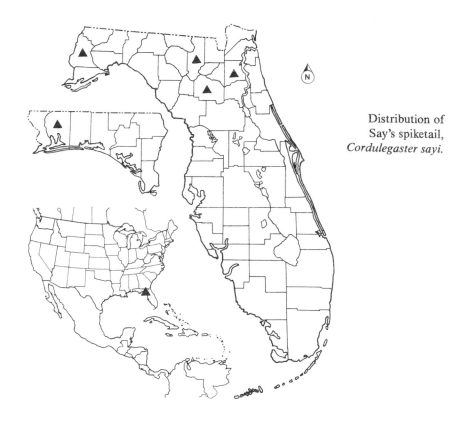

Distribution of
Say's spiketail,
Cordulegaster sayi.

RANGE: It is known from eight localities in northern Florida and one in central Georgia.

HABITAT: The species is associated with silt-bottom spring seepages in hardwood forest, with nearby weedy clearings for foraging.

LIFE HISTORY AND ECOLOGY: The flight season is early and brief, from late February to late April. Adults forage in fields, but males also patrol seepages to wait for females. Females hover to stab eggs into silt under water with a perpendicular sewing-machine-like action. The larvae bury themselves in silt with only the head, front legs, and tip of the abdomen exposed. The life cycle is probably several years.

BASIS FOR STATUS CLASSIFICATION: This species is not common even at its very localized, scattered habitats. Five of the eight known Florida localities are more or less protected in state parks, natural areas, and forests. The remnants of one habitat in Gainesville, Florida, are protected by a neighborhood association. The one definitely known Georgia locality is in a small state park. The breeding habitats at the other two known locales have not been precisely located.

RECOMMENDATIONS: No development should take place near the seepages of known breeding habitats, and some clearings should be maintained nearby. Pesticide use, such as mosquito spraying, near these areas should be eliminated.

PREPARED BY: S. W. Dunkle, Biology Department, Collin County Community College, 2800 East Spring Creek Parkway, Plano, TX 75074.

FAMILY CORDULEGASTRIDAE

Rare

Arrowhead Spiketail

Cordulegaster obliqua fasciata Rambur

DESCRIPTION: This large (body length 78-89 mm [3.0 3.5 inch]) black and yellow dragonfly is easily identified by arrowhead-shaped markings on the abdomen. Other notable bright blue eyes, the triangular occiput, and the long projecting the female. It was most recently described in Needham, with more information on the northern subspecies, *C. o. obliqua* Walker (1932), and a color photo in Dunkle (1989).

Suborder Anisoptera

FAMILY CORDULEGASTRIDAE

Threatened

Say's Spiketail

Cordulegaster sayi Selys

DESCRIPTION: This beautiful dragonfly has a unique color pattern. The thorax is striped with yellow, magenta, and white, while the abdomen is black with yellow rings, and the eyes are gray-green. The female has a spike-like ovipositor which reaches the end of the abdomen. Body length is 60-69 mm (2.4-2.7 in). The species was most recently described in Needham and Westfall (1955), with a color photo in Dunkle (1989).

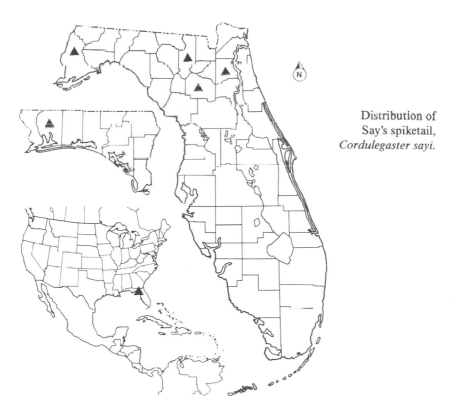

Distribution of
Say's spiketail,
Cordulegaster sayi.

RANGE: It is known from eight localities in northern Florida and one in central Georgia.

HABITAT: The species is associated with silt-bottom spring seepages in hardwood forest, with nearby weedy clearings for foraging.

LIFE HISTORY AND ECOLOGY: The flight season is early and brief, from late February to late April. Adults forage in fields, but males also patrol seepages to wait for females. Females hover to stab eggs into silt under water with a perpendicular sewing-machine-like action. The larvae bury themselves in silt with only the head, front legs, and tip of the abdomen exposed. The life cycle is probably several years.

BASIS FOR STATUS CLASSIFICATION: This species is not common even at its very localized, scattered habitats. Five of the eight known Florida localities are more or less protected in state parks, natural areas, and forests. The remnants of one habitat in Gainesville, Florida, are protected by a neighborhood association. The one definitely known Georgia locality is in a small state park. The breeding habitats at the other two known locales have not been precisely located.

RECOMMENDATIONS: No development should take place near the seepages at known breeding habitats, and some clearings should be maintained nearby. Pesticide use, such as mosquito spraying, near these areas should be eliminated.

PREPARED BY: S. W. Dunkle, Biology Department, Collin County Community College, 2800 East Spring Creek Parkway, Plano, TX 75074.

FAMILY CORDULEGASTRIDAE

Rare

Arrowhead Spiketail

Cordulegaster obliqua fasciata Rambur

DESCRIPTION: This large (body length 78–88 mm [3.0–3.5 in]) and magnificent black and yellow dragonfly is easily identified by the yellow dorsal arrowhead-shaped markings on the abdomen. Other notable features are the bright blue eyes, the conical occiput, and the long projecting ovipositor of the female. It was most recently described in Needham and Westfall (1955), with more information on the northern subspecies *C. obliqua obliqua* in Walker (1958), and a color photo in Dunkle (1989).

Species of Special Concern

Sandhill Clubtail

Gomphus (Phanogomphus) cavillaris Needham

DESCRIPTION: A medium sized (body length 37–45 mm [1.4–1.8 in]) drag-onfly which has a striped pale green thorax, a dark facial cross-stripe, and a mostly dark abdomen with yellow sides on the enlarged segments 7–9. The male cerci each have a large lateral tooth. The crest of the female occiput is straight. The female subgenital plate is very short, 1/10 or less the length of abdominal segment 9. The Florida peninsula subspecies, *G. cavillaris cavilla-ris*, is marked with brown and dull yellow. The Florida panhandle and North Carolina subspecies, *G. cavillaris brimleyi*, is marked with black and bright yellow. Most recently described by Needham and Westfall (1955), with a color photo of *G. cavillaris cavillaris* in Dunkle (1989).

RANGE: This clubtail occurs in Florida and North Carolina.

Sandhill Clubtail,
Gomphus cavillaris
(courtesy of Sidney
W. Dunkle).

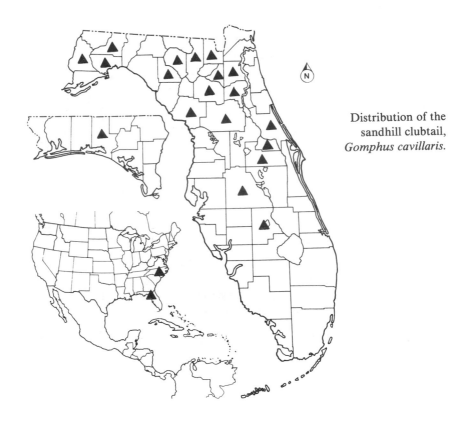

Distribution of the
sandhill clubtail,
Gomphus cavillaris.

HABITAT: It is associated with sand-bottomed lakes.

LIFE HISTORY AND ECOLOGY: Flight season occurs from late January to late May. It usually perches on the ground, from where it makes short sallies for prey such as damselflies and beetles. Males perch on the shore or on floating objects while they wait for females. The female deposits eggs during a fast, low, irregular flight over the water. Larvae burrow in silt deposits.

BASIS FOR STATUS CLASSIFICATION: *G. c. cavillaris* is endemic to the Florida peninsula, and *G. c. brimleyi* also has a restricted distribution. In addition, their sand-bottom lake habitat is being developed very rapidly.

RECOMMENDATIONS: Preserve the water quality of clear sand-bottomed lakes by preventing the input of fertilizers, septic tank leachate, and pesticides.

PREPARED BY: S. W. Dunkle, Biology Department, Collin County Community College, 2800 East Spring Creek Parkway, Plano, TX 75074.

Arrowhead Spiketail, *Cordulegaster obliqua fasciata*
(courtesy of Sidney W. Dunkle).

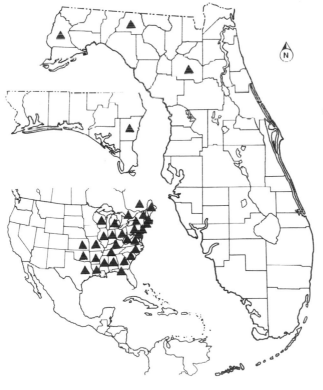

Distribution of the
arrowhead spiketail,
*Cordulegaster
obliqua fasciata*.

RANGE: This species occurs locally in Florida south to Gainesville. It ranges north to Maine, Ontario, and Wisconsin, west to Kansas and eastern Texas. The subspecies *fasciata* ranges from Louisiana to North Carolina.

HABITAT: This dragonfly is associated with small, clear, silt-bottomed spring rivulets in forest.

LIFE HISTORY AND ECOLOGY: This spiketail flies from late May to late July in Florida, from mid April to late August elsewhere. It feeds along forest edges, and perches obliquely on the sides of weed stems and twigs. When alarmed, its flight is almost too fast to follow. Males patrol long distances along the rivulets while searching for females. The females oviposit with an up-and-down sewing-machine motion as they drive eggs into the bottom of shallow water. The larvae hide in muck with only the eyes, antennae, and tip of the abdomen exposed. The life cycle is several years.

BASIS FOR STATUS CLASSIFICATION: This species is seldom encountered because of its localized microhabitat.

RECOMMENDATIONS: Protect the banks of springs and small streams from logging, pesticide use, and livestock grazing and trampling.

PREPARED BY: S. W. Dunkle, Biology Department, Collin County Community College, 2800 East Spring Creek Parkway, Plano, TX 75074.

Suborder Anisoptera
FAMILY MACROMIIDAE

Threatened

Allegheny River Cruiser
Macromia alleghaniensis Williamson

DESCRIPTION: This is a beautiful, large (body length 65–72 mm [2.5–2.8 in]) metallic black and yellow dragonfly with brilliant green eyes. The front of the thorax is all black, and the yellow band on abdominal segment 2 is complete laterally but interrupted dorsally. Males have a yellow ring around the base of abdominal segment 7. It was most recently described in Needham and Westfall (1955).

Allegheny River
Cruiser, *Macromia
allegheniensis*
(courtesy of Sidney
W. Dunkle).

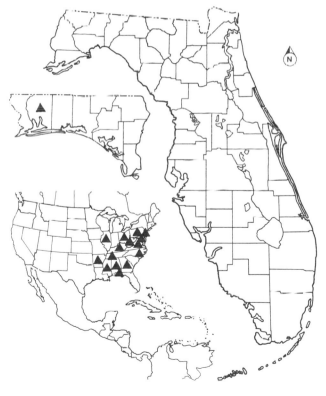

Distribution of the
Allegheny River
cruiser, *Macromia
allegheniensis.*

RANGE: The species is known in Florida only from Pond Creek in Santa Rosa County. It ranges north to New Jersey, and west to Illinois and Arkansas.

HABITAT: It is associated with streams and rivers.

LIFE HISTORY AND ECOLOGY: The flight season in Florida is unknown; it extends from early June to mid-September elsewhere. Adults of this genus forage far and wide until sexual maturity, then the males return to fly long patrols over the water while searching for females. Females fly fast and low over the water, tapping a cluster of their green eggs to the surface every few meters. The long-legged larvae sprawl on the bottom among roots and other obstructions.

BASIS FOR STATUS CLASSIFICATION: It is found in Florida at only one stream, which is unprotected. The species is uncommon throughout its range.

RECOMMENDATIONS: The Pond Creek watershed should be protected in a state park or forest. Several other listed dragonflies also occur at Pond Creek.

PREPARED BY: S. W. Dunkle, Biology Department, Collin County Community College, 2800 East Spring Creek Parkway, Plano, TX 75074.

FAMILY MACROMIIDAE

Species of Special Concern

Maidencane Cruiser
Didymops floridensis Davis

DESCRIPTION: This medium large (body length 61–68 mm [2.4–2.7 in]) gray-brown dragonfly has a single pale yellow band around the thorax, and pale yellow bands around the bases of the middle abdominal segments. The relatively small wings of this swiftly flying insect lack a brown basal spot but have a yellow vein along the front edge. The only other species of the genus, *Didymops transversa*, has brown basal wing spots and a brown vein along the front of each wing. It was most recently described by Needham and Westfall (1955), with color photos of both *Didymops* species in Dunkle (1989).

RANGE: This dragonfly is endemic to Florida.

Maidencane Cruiser, *Didymops floridensis* (courtesy of Sidney W. Dunkle).

Distribution of the maidencane cruiser, *Didymops floridensis.*

HABITAT: The species is associated with sand-bottomed lakes.

LIFE HISTORY AND ECOLOGY: This is a spring species which flies from late January to early May. It feeds by cruising long distances through open woodlands. Males fly fast, long patrols along the edge of maidencane grass or among bald cypress trees. Females lay eggs by tapping the water during a high-speed flight. The long-legged larvae sprawl on the lake bottom.

BASIS FOR STATUS CLASSIFICATION: It is found only on Florida sand-bottomed lakes, prime habitat for development.

RECOMMENDATIONS: Prevent input of fertilizers, septic tank drainage, or insecticides into sand-bottomed lakes.

PREPARED BY: S. W. Dunkle, Biology Department, Collin County Community College, 2800 East Spring Creek Parkway, Plano, TX 75074.

Suborder Anisoptera

FAMILY CORDULIIDAE

Threatened

Robust Baskettail

Epitheca (Tetragoneuria) spinosa Hagen

DESCRIPTION: This medium sized (body length 42–47 mm [1.6–1.8 in]) brown dragonfly has bright green eyes and a yellow stripe along each side of the abdomen. The thorax is covered with white hair, and the body is stouter than in other members of the genus. The male is distinguished from other baskettails in Florida by the cerci, which are bent downward and outward at the tips (cerci not bent in other Florida species). The female is identified by the wide abdomen, 1.6–1.7 mm between the median and lateral ridges on the underside of abdominal segment 6. Like others of the genus, the female has a long, V-shaped subgenital plate under abdominal segment 9. The species was most recently described in Needham and Westfall (1955).

RANGE: The species is known in Florida only from the Dead Lake Swamp on the Chipola River. It ranges on the Coastal Plain from Louisiana to New Jersey. Also found in Arkansas.

HABITAT: The species is associated with river swamps.

Robust Baskettail, *Epitheca spinosa* (courtesy of Sidney W. Dunkle).

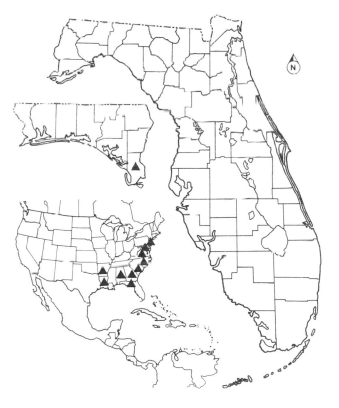

Distribution of the
robust baskettail,
Epitheca spinosa.

LIFE HISTORY AND ECOLOGY: This species flies in early spring, and is the earliest dragonfly to mature within its range. Adults recorded in March in Florida, to early June elsewhere. It forages along forest edges. Males patrol with much hovering in small sunny openings among swamp trees. Females carry an orange ball of eggs with their forked subgenital plate. When deposited in water the ball unrolls into a jelly string containing embedded eggs which is draped over vegetation near the surface, away from bottom predators. Larvae live in the debris on the swamp bottom.

BASIS FOR STATUS CLASSIFICATION: This dragonfly has been found at only one swamp in Florida, and the species is uncommon throughout its range. It has not been seen in Florida since the removal of the Dead Lake Dam in 1987.

RECOMMENDATIONS: The species should be looked for in the Apalachicola River swamps. Pesticide use and development in its habitat should be curtailed.

PREPARED BY: S. W. Dunkle, Department of Biology, Collin County Community College, 2800 East Spring Creek Parkway, Plano, TX 75074.

FAMILY CORDULIIDAE

Threatened

Smoky Shadowfly
Neurocordulia molesta Walsh

DESCRIPTION: This brown dragonfly has olive-green eyes and smoky gray wings. On close examination, a series of brown spots along the front edge of the wing have dark brown edges which look like extra crossveins. Males in most of the species' range have a blunt medial projection on the trochanter near the base of the middle leg. However, this projection is absent in Florida specimens, indicating that they may be a different subspecies. Body length of this species is 42–53 mm (1.6–2.1 in). It was most recently described in Needham and Westfall (1955).

RANGE: This species is known in Florida from the larger panhandle rivers, the Apalachicola, Choctawhatchee, and Escambia. It ranges north to North Carolina, Ohio, and Minnesota, and west to eastern Texas and South Dakota.

HABITAT: The species is associated with large rivers.

Smokey Shadowfly,
*Neurocordulia mo-
lesta* (courtesy of Sid-
ney W. Dunkle).

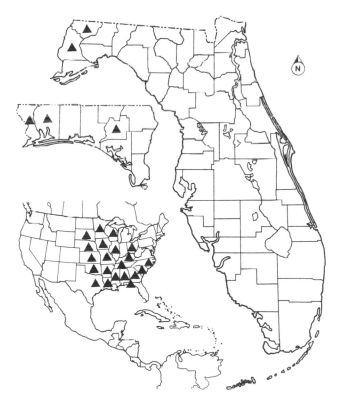

Distribution of the
smokey shadowfly,
*Neurocordulia
molesta.*

LIFE HISTORY AND ECOLOGY: The flight season is from late June to early August in Florida, as early as early April elsewhere. Adults hide in the forest by day, and fly primarily in the last half hour before darkness. Males patrol small areas a few meters from the bank with a rapid bouncy flight. Larvae have a rhinoceros-like horn and cling tightly to logs and other submerged objects.

BASIS FOR STATUS CLASSIFICATION: This dragonfly is uncommon throughout its range.

RECOMMENDATIONS: Protect the large panhandle rivers from pesticides and other pollutants, as well as damming, dredging, and siltation.

PREPARED BY: S. W. Dunkle, Biology Department, Collin County Community College, 2800 East Spring Creek Parkway, Plano, TX 75074.

FAMILY CORDULIIDAE

Threatened

Treetop Emerald
Somatochlora provocans Calvert

DESCRIPTION: This medium-sized (body length 43–58 mm [1.7–2.3 in]), slender metallic brown dragonfly has brilliant green eyes. No wing stripes are present. The abdomen has narrow white rings only between segments 8–9 and 9–10, and segment 10 lacks a pale dorsal spot. The thorax has two white stripes on each side which are nearly equal in width, with the posterior stripes meeting under the thorax. The male cerci are bent downward. It was most recently described in Needham and Westfall (1955).

RANGE: In Florida the species is restricted to a few counties on the east side of the Apalachicola River. It ranges north to New Jersey and Kentucky, west to Louisiana.

HABITAT: It is associated with forest seepages and trickles, especially those with sphagnum moss.

LIFE HISTORY AND ECOLOGY: This species flies from late June to late August, usually at about treetop height. Females lay eggs by hovering low at the edge of a seep and rapidly tapping the tip of the abdomen to very shallow water. The larvae hide in the moss and silt of seepages.

BASIS FOR STATUS CLASSIFICATION: The larvae live in a special microhabitat which is very vulnerable to local disturbance.

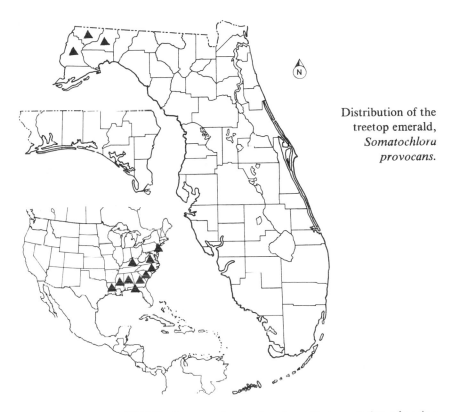

Distribution of the
treetop emerald,
*Somatochlora
provocans.*

RECOMMENDATIONS: Protect the banks of small streams from logging
and from livestock grazing and trampling.

PREPARED BY: S. W. Dunkle, Biology Department, Collin County Community College, 2800 East Spring Creek Parkway, Plano, TX 75074.

FAMILY CORDULIIDAE

Rare

Selys' Sunfly
Helocordulia selysii (Hagen)

DESCRIPTION· This medium sized (body length 37–44 mm [1.4–1.7 in]),
brown dragonfly has a small brown spot at the base of each hindwing. Abdominal segment 3 is nearly encircled by an orange ring, the eyes are pale

green, and the face is yellow. It was most recently described in Needham and Westfall (1955).

HABITAT: It is associated with clear streams and small rivers.

RANGE: In Florida the species occurs west of the Apalachicola River. It ranges in the Coastal Plain from eastern Texas to Virginia.

LIFE HISTORY AND ECOLOGY: This species has one of the earliest flight seasons among our dragonflies, from early March to mid April. It feeds along forest edges, perching obliquely on weed stems near the ground. Males patrol short stretches of stream during the middle part of the day. Females lay eggs in the water near the bank. The larvae hide among debris on the stream bottom.

BASIS FOR STATUS CLASSIFICATION: This species is a clean water indicator that cannot tolerate much pollution. It is not common anywhere.

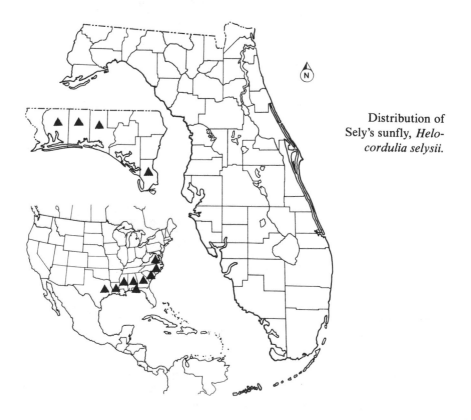

Distribution of Sely's sunfly, *Helocordulia selysii.*

Sely's Sunfly, *He-locordulia selysii* (courtesy of Sidney W. Dunkle).

RECOMMENDATIONS: Protect panhandle streams from pollution, development, and deforestation of their watersheds.

PREPARED BY: S. W. Dunkle, Biology Department, Collin County Community College, 2800 East Spring Creek Parkway, Plano, TX 75074.

FAMILY CORDULIIDAE

Rare

Coppery Emerald

Somatochlora georgiana Walker

DESCRIPTION: This medium-sized (body length 46–49 mm [1.8–1.9 in]) slender dragonfly has two white stripes on each side of the thorax. It differs from other *Somatochlora* in that the body is mostly orange-brown instead of dark brown, and the eyes remain red-brown instead of becoming bright green at maturity. The male cerci are straight with flattened upcurled tips, while the female ovipositor is a vertically projecting spout. It was most recently described in Needham and Westfall (1955).

Coppery Emerald,
*Somatochlora geor-
giana* (courtesy of
Sidney W. Dunkle).

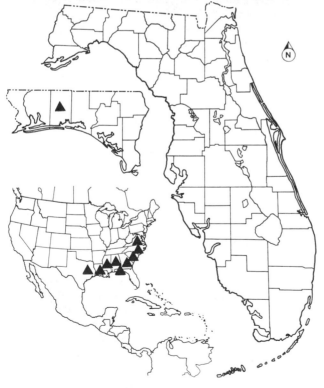

Distribution of the
coppery emerald,
*Somatochlora
georgiana.*

RANGE: This dragonfly is known in Florida only from a few panhandle localities. It ranges in the Coastal Plain from eastern Texas to Massachusetts.

HABITAT: This odonate inhabits small forest streams.

LIFE HISTORY AND ECOLOGY: Adults have been collected in Florida in mid May and early August. It usually is seen feeding over forest roads and in clearings, but males occasionally make short patrols over streams.

BASIS FOR STATUS CLASSIFICATION: This species is uncommon, possibly because of its dependence on small, clean forest streams.

RECOMMENDATIONS: Protect small forest streams in the panhandle from excessive grazing and lumbering. There should be efforts to protect these streams in future conservation land acquisitions.

PREPARED BY: S. W. Dunkle, Biology Department, Collin County Community College, 2800 East Spring Creek Parkway, Plano, TX 75074.

FAMILY CORDULIIDAE

Status Undetermined

Umber Shadowfly

Neurocordulia obsoleta (Say)

DESCRIPTION: This small, dark brown dragonfly has brown spots at the base and middle front edge of each wing. Body length is 41–48 mm (1.6–1.9 in). The eyes are yellowish brown dorsally, pink ventrally. It was most recently described in Needham and Westfall (1955); color photos are found in Dunkle (1989, 1991).

RANGE: In Florida, the species is known only from Santa Fe and Alto lakes in Alachua County. It ranges north to Maine, Ohio, and Illinois.

HABITAT: It is associated with well-oxygenated streams, rivers, and lakes.

LIFE HISTORY AND ECOLOGY: This is a mysterious species in Florida. Only adults emerging from the larval state in early April have been seen, though it flies to late October elsewhere. In the north it hangs in shady undergrowth by day, then flies for a short period at dusk over riffles of rivers and streams. Larvae cling tightly to submerged objects.

Umber Shadowfly, *Neurocordulia obsolete* (courtesy of Sidney W. Dunkle).

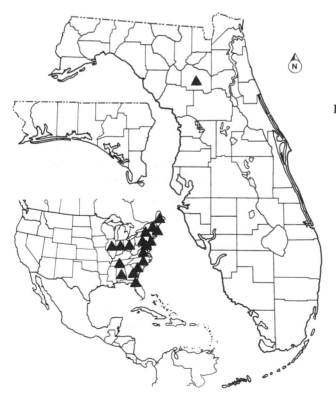

Distribution of the
umber shadowfly,
*Neurocordulia
obsoleta.*

BASIS FOR STATUS CLASSIFICATION: The biology of this rare dragon-fly is unknown.

RECOMMENDATIONS: Protect the known habitats of this species from pesticides and eutrophication.

PREPARED BY: S. W. Dunkle, Biology Department, Collin County Community College, 2800 East Spring Creek Parkway, Plano, TX 75074.

FAMILY CORDULIIDAE

Status Undetermined

Calvert's Emerald

Somatochlora calverti Williamson and Gloyd

DESCRIPTION: This beautiful, metallic brown dragonfly has brilliant green eyes and two white stripes on each side of the thorax. Body length is 47–55 mm (1.8–2.2 in). This species is similar to the treetop emerald, but the males have white rings between abdominal segments 6–10, and nearly always have a white dorsal spot on segment 10. The females, unlike any other *Somatochlora*, have a brown stripe between nodus and stigma in each wing. It was most recently described in Needham and Westfall (1955).

Calvert's Emerald, *Somatochlora calverti* (courtesy of Sidney W. Dunkle).

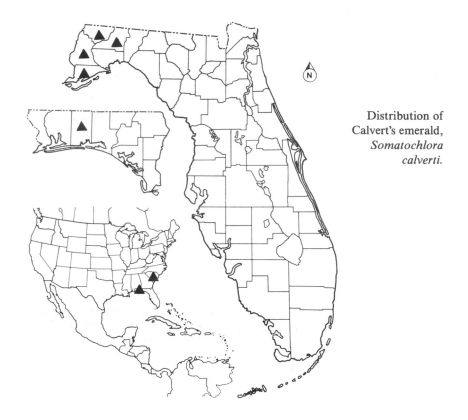

Distribution of
Calvert's emerald,
*Somatochlora
calverti.*

RANGE: This dragonfly has been found only in the Florida panhandle and southeastern South Carolina.

HABITAT: Unknown. By analogy with related species, it probably is associated with small boggy seepage trickles in forest.

LIFE HISTORY AND ECOLOGY: This species is seen from early June to late August feeding over roads and between tree canopies. Mating pairs hang from twigs near the feeding areas. Males have never been seen patrolling water, nor have females been seen ovipositing. The larva has been reared from the egg, but has not been found in the wild.

BASIS FOR STATUS CLASSIFICATION: The biology of this rare odonate is unknown.

RECOMMENDATIONS: The breeding habitat should be found as soon as possible.

PREPARED BY: S. W. Dunkle, Biology Department, Collin County Community College, 2800 East Spring Creek Parkway, Plano, TX 75074.

Suborder Anisoptera
FAMILY LIBELLULIDAE

Threatened

Purple Skimmer

Libellula jesseana Williamson

DESCRIPTION: Body length of this beautiful dragonfly is 48–56 mm (1.9–2.2 in). Males have a diagnostic coloration consisting of a black face, blue body, and deep orange wings. Females have a brown face and a yellow abdomen with a black mid-dorsal stripe. *Libellula jesseana* is identical in structure to the golden-winged skimmer *Libellula auripennis*, in which the males have an orange body. No way is presently known to separate the females of these species except by noting with which male they will mate. The most recent description is the original description of Williamson (1922). A color photo is in Dunkle (1989).

RANGE: This dragonfly is probably endemic to Florida.

Purple Skimmer, *Libellula jesseana* (courtesy of Sidney W. Dunkle).

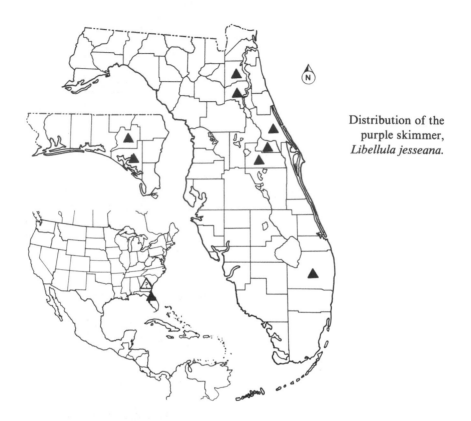

Distribution of the
purple skimmer,
Libellula jesseana.

HABITAT: It inhabits clear-water, sand-bottomed lakes edged with sparse maidencane grass and St. Johns wort bushes.

LIFE HISTORY AND ECOLOGY: Flight season occurs from mid April to mid September. Males defend territories from other males in sparse emergent grass, where the female taps eggs to the water after mating. The purple skimmer is considered a separate species from the golden-winged skimmer due to its shorter flight season, restricted geographical distribution, and the sparser grass selected for male territories. The larvae live in the silt among the grass roots.

BASIS FOR STATUS CLASSIFICATION: This species is very local, occurring only at certain Florida sand-bottomed lakes. Apparently it prefers the least fertile lakes and thus is susceptible to even a little eutrophication.

RECOMMENDATIONS: Lakes where this species occurs should be protected against complete shoreline development, pesticide use, and from eutrophication due to agricultural or residential fertilizers. It is possible that creating patches of sparse grass by pulling out some grass at lakes with dense grass zones would create habitat for the purple skimmer. Such thinning would best be done in the winter to allow silt and nutrients to settle out of the water before the spring algae growing season.

PREPARED BY: S. W. Dunkle, Biology Department, Collin County Community College, 2800 East Spring Creek Parkway, Plano, TX 75074.

FAMILY LIBELLULIDAE

Rare

Elfin Skimmer
Nannothemis bella (Uhler)

DESCRIPTION: This is the smallest North American dragonfly, with a body length of only 17–21 mm (0.7–0.8 in). The face is partly white and the eyes have red-brown vertical stripes. The male is pale blue with a flattened and clubbed abdomen. The female has a black abdomen ringed with yellow, and the basal third of the wings is tinted orange. The female resembles a wasp, and probably thereby gains protection from birds. It was described most recently in Walker and Corbet (1975).

Elfin Skimmer, *Nannothemis bella* (courtesy of Sidney W. Dunkle).

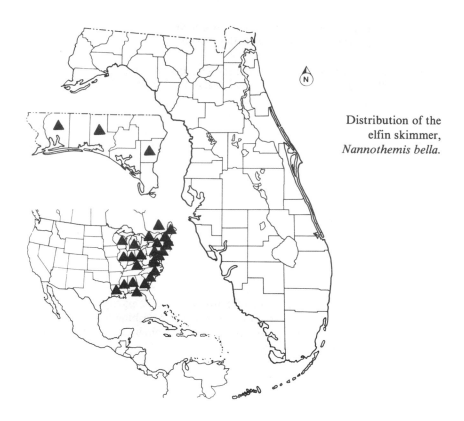

Distribution of the
elfin skimmer,
Nannothemis bella.

RANGE: This dragonfly is known in Florida only west of the Apalachicola River. It ranges north to Maine and west through southern Ontario to Wisconsin, Illinois, and Louisiana.

HABITAT: It is associated with sphagnum bogs, sometimes calcareous fens.

LIFE HISTORY AND ECOLOGY: This species flies from mid-March to late July in Florida, and to early September elsewhere. It is usually seen perching with its wings cocked downward among grasses. It flies below the tops of herbaceous vegetation and seldom leaves cover. Some males defend a territory of about 2 sq. m (18 sq. ft) for their adult life span of approximately three weeks. After mating, the female taps eggs to the water while the male guards her from other males by hovering 15 cm (6 in) above her. The larva lives in debris on the bottom of the bog. The territoriality of the elfin skimmer has been studied by Hilder and Colgan (1985) and by Lee and McGinn (1986).

BASIS FOR STATUS CLASSIFICATION: The elfin skimmer has been found in only five bogs in Florida. Its colonies are incredibly local, sometimes only occupying the space of a small room.

RECOMMENDATIONS: Habitats of the species should be protected against development and pesticides. Three of the five Florida localities are in Blackwater River State Park and Blackwater River State Forest.

PREPARED BY: S. W. Dunkle, Biology Department, Collin County Community College, 2800 East Spring Creek Parkway, Plano, TX 75074.

Suborder Anisoptera

FAMILY PETALURIDAE

Rare

Gray Petaltail

Tachopteryx thoreyi (Hagen)

DESCRIPTION: This large (body length 71–83 mm [2.8–3.3 in]), gray and black dragonfly has its eyes wide apart. The black stigma near each wing tip is long, parallel-sided, and ribbon-like. The female has an ovipositor with blades concealed in a bulge under the tip of her abdomen. These characteristics easily identify this species as the only member of its family in eastern North America. The most recent description is in Needham and Westfall (1955), with a color photo in Dunkle (1989).

RANGE: This dragonfly is known in Florida from eight localities scattered from Gainesville north. It ranges north to the southern edge of the Great Lakes, and west to Illinois and eastern Texas.

HABITAT: This dragonfly occurs near permanent hillside seepages in deciduous forest.

LIFE HISTORY AND ECOLOGY: This species is of particular scientific interest because it is a "living fossil," an example of a family which was widespread at the time of the dinosaurs but which has been reduced to only 9 relict species scattered around the world. The flight season is early March to mid June in Florida, to late September elsewhere. It is one of the few dragonflies that habitually perches on tree trunks. They are usually unwary, and will also perch on a motionless person. Their food includes large insects such as swallowtail butterflies, giant silk moths, and medium-sized dragonflies. Males find females by flying up a succession of tree trunks or by perching near seepage areas. Females oviposit in soil or wet leaves in the seeps. The flat leaf-like larvae hide among wet leaves above or below the water level.

Gray Petaltail, *Tachopteryx thoreyi* (courtesy of Sidney W. Dunkle).

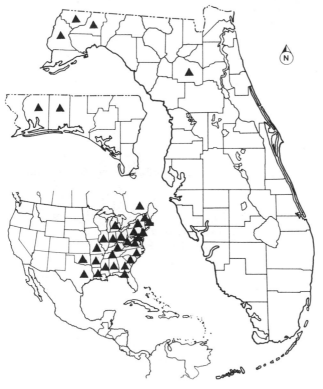

Distribution of the
gray petaltail,
*Tachopteryx
thoreyi.*

The life cycle is several years. The ecology and behavior of this species in Florida was studied by Dunkle (1981).

BASIS FOR STATUS CLASSIFICATION: This species occurs in scattered localized colonies. Five of the eight known Florida colonies are more or less protected in state parks, natural areas, or forests. The remnant of a sixth locality is protected by a neighborhood association in Gainesville, Florida.

RECOMMENDATIONS: No development should take place near the seepage areas of known colonies. Pesticide use, for example spraying against mosquitoes, should be eliminated in such areas. Since this species is usually associated with Say's spiketail in Florida, conserving the habitat of one species also protects the other.

PREPARED BY: S. W. Dunkle, Biology Department, Collin County Community College, 2800 East Spring Creek Parkway, Plano, TX 75074.

Suborder Anisoptera
FAMILY AESHINDAE

Rare

Taper-Tailed Darner
Gomphaeschna antilope (Hagen)

DESCRIPTION: One of the smallest darners (body length 51–60 mm [2.0–2.4 in]). This mostly black species is marked with gray-green abdominal spots. Females may have an orange spot at the middle of the forewing. Males have a tapered abdomen with a forked ventral appendage at the tip. The only other species of the genus, the harlequin darner, *Gomphaeschna furcillata*, is more brightly colored; the male has a cylindrical abdomen, the female has an orange area in the outer half of the forewing. It was most recently described in Needham and Westfall (1955), with a color photo found in Dunkle (1989).

RANGE: This odonate occurs in Florida south to Collier County. Ranges north to New Jersey and Ohio, and west to Louisiana.

HABITAT: So far as known, it inhabits bald cypress swamps with sphagnum moss in the pools.

LIFE HISTORY AND ECOLOGY: This dragonfly flies from late January to early June in Florida, to mid July elsewhere, most commonly in late

Taper-Tailed Darner, *Gomphaeschna antilope*
(courtesy of Sidney W. Dunkle).

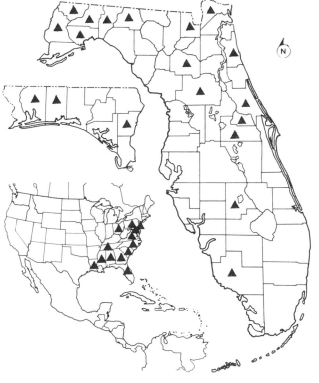

Distribution of the
taper-tailed darner,
Gomphaeschna
antilope.

spring. Adults are usually seen singly, cruising steadily for long distances and feeding along the way, but they can gather to exploit swarming termites. Groups of males are occasionally seen in the lee of trees on windy days feeding on insects blown out of the foliage. This species also occasionally attacks dragonflies larger than itself. Mating behavior has not been observed. Females use their ovipositor blades to insert eggs into wet wood just above the water line. The larvae cling to the undersides of logs.

BASIS FOR STATUS CLASSIFICATION: This species seems to be rare throughout its range.

RECOMMENDATIONS: More data are needed on the breeding habits and habitat of this species. It especially merits such attention because its genus is thought to include the most primitive living members of its family.

PREPARED BY: S. W. Dunkle, Biology Department, Collin County Community College, 2800 East Spring Creek Parkway, Plano, TX 75074.

Suborder Anisoptera

FAMILY LESTIDAE

Rare

Elegant Spreadwing

Lestes inaequalis Walsh

DESCRIPTION: This species is Florida's longest damselfly, with a body length of 46-60 mm (1.8-2.4 in). The body is mostly metallic green, with yellow sides on the thorax. The male is distinguished from all other North American spreadwings by having the ventral apical abdominal appendages longer than the dorsal ones. The female differs from similar spreadwings by lacking a spine on the rectangular plate at the base of the ovipositor, and by lacking black spots on the underside of the thorax. The species was most recently described in Walker (1953), with color photos of both sexes found in Dunkle (1990).

RANGE: This spreadwing is known in Florida only from the northern peninsula. It ranges north to Maine, Ontario, and Minnesota, west to eastern Texas.

HABITAT: This species inhabits marshy or boggy lakes, ponds, and slow streams.

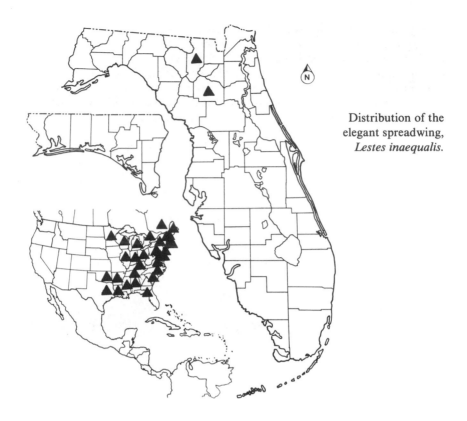

Distribution of the
elegant spreadwing,
Lestes inaequalis.

LIFE HISTORY AND ECOLOGY: The known flight season in Florida is mid-April to early August, extending to mid-September elsewhere. Like other spreadwings, adults perch obliquely on plant stems with the wings partly spread. After mating, the male retains his grip on the female thorax with his abdominal claspers while she lays eggs in plant stems. Sometimes they lay eggs in horizontal water lily leaves, a very unusual habit for a spreadwing. The larva perches on underwater vegetation.

BASIS FOR STATUS CLASSIFICATION: The species is known from only four localities in Florida, two of them in state parks. It is uncommon throughout its range, but the reasons for its particular rarity in Florida are unknown.

RECOMMENDATIONS: The known habitats should be protected from pesticide use or development.

PREPARED BY: S. W. Dunkle, Biology Department, Collin County Community College, 2800 East Spring Creek Parkway, Plano, TX 75074.

Suborder Anisoptera
FAMILY CALOPTERYGIDAE

Species of Special Concern

American Rubyspot

Hetaerina americana (Fabricius)

DESCRIPTION: This large damselfly has a body length of 38–46 mm (1.5–1.8 in). Males are dark metallic red with a large red spot at the base of each wing. The forceps-like male cerci each have two bumps off their inner margin in dorsal view. Females have the front of the thorax all metallic green, and the bases of the wings are amber-tinted. The female abdomen is dark above, tan below, these colors sharply divided. It was most recently described by Walker (1953), with color photos of both sexes in Dunkle (1990).

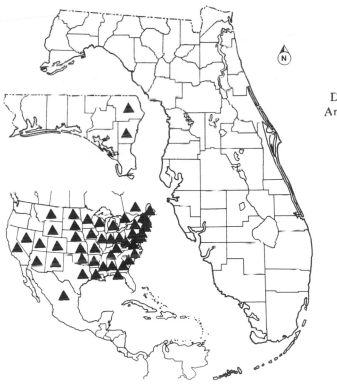

Distribution of the American rubyspot, *Hetaerina americana.*

RANGE: This damselfly is known in Florida only from the Chipola River. It ranges throughout the United States except the Pacific Northwest, north into Ontario and Quebec, and south to Honduras.

HABITAT: This species inhabits the sunny parts of streams and rivers with vegetated edges.

LIFE HISTORY AND ECOLOGY: Adults recorded in Florida from mid April to mid August, from mid March to mid-November elsewhere. Both sexes of this damselfly usually stay near the water, where they perch mostly on overhanging vegetation. Females dive underwater to lay eggs in the underwater parts of plants, logs, or algae-covered rocks. Larvae cling to roots and other vegetation in the current. The behavior of the American rubyspot has been studied by Bick and Sulzbach (1966), Johnson (1961, 1962, 1963), and McCafferty (1979).

BASIS FOR STATUS CLASSIFICATION: Since this species is restricted to one river in Florida, some disaster could eliminate it from the state. It is not known why this widespread and apparently adaptable insect, which is common elsewhere, should have such a restricted range in Florida but the Chipola population seems to be a relict one.

RECOMMENDATIONS: Protect the Chipola River from degradation in water quality due to pollution, excessive development, or deforestation.

PREPARED BY: S. W. Dunkle, Biology Department, Collin County Community College, 2800 East Spring Creek Parkway, Plano, TX 75074.

Suborder Anisoptera
FAMILY COENAGRIONIDAE

Species of Special Concern

Everglades Sprite
Nehalennia pallidula Calvert

DESCRIPTION: This small damselfly, only 24–28 mm (1.0–1.1 in) long, is mostly black dorsally, including abdominal segments 8–9, and mostly blue laterally, including a shoulder stripe and abdominal segments 8–10. The shape of the posterior lobe of the prothorax is unusual in both sexes; rounded and erect in males, horizontal and deeply trilobed in females. This damselfly was previously placed in the genus *Argiallagma*. It was most recently described in DeMarmels (1984); color photos of both sexes are found in Dunkle (1990).

RANGE: It is endemic to the southern Florida peninsula.

HABITAT: This species occurs along marshy ponds and slow streams, particularly the Everglades.

LIFE HISTORY AND ECOLOGY: The flight season is all year, and there may be two generations per year. Adults perch inconspicuously among sedges and bushes near water. It appears that adults survive the winter dry season in a relatively few moist refugia, from which the population expands in the summer wet season. The larvae cling to underwater vegetation.

BASIS FOR STATUS CLASSIFICATION: Only a few specimens of this damselfly have been found in recent years. Invasion by exotic trees and fish, water diversion, and peat fire, even in Everglades National Park, may be stressing populations of this insect.

RECOMMENDATIONS: Locate and protect the dry season refugia from pollutants and air boat traffic. Possibly a number of scattered small dry sea-

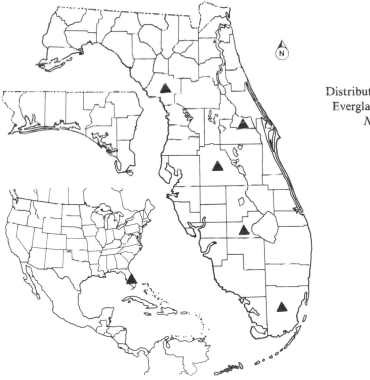

Distribution of the
Everglades sprite,
*Nehalennia
pallidula.*

son refugia could be created by judicious water diversions. Leave some grassy areas near ponds and canals as foraging habitat.

PREPARED BY: S. W. Dunkle, Biology Department, Collin County Community College, 2800 East Spring Creek Parkway, Plano, TX 75074.

Suborder Anisoptera

FAMILY COENAGRIONIDAE

Status Undetermined

Slender Bluet

Enallagma traviatum Selys

DESCRIPTION: This damselfly is about 30 mm (1.2 in) long, with a mostly blue head and thorax. The abdomen is black dorsally except for blue segments 8-9 in the male, 8-10 in the female. The male cerci are forked, the upper branch thin and straight, the lower branch wide and shelf-like. It was most recently described (subspecies *westfalli*) in Donnelly (1964).

RANGE: This bluet was recorded from Leon County in 1927, but no such specimens can be located in museums. It ranges north to Vermont and Michigan, west to Kansas and eastern Texas.

HABITAT: This species requires partially shaded, vegetated ponds and lakes.

LIFE HISTORY AND ECOLOGY: The flight season occurs from mid-April to late September. It usually is found perching on low emergent plants at the edge of the water and stays in the shade more than most related damselflies. Females lay eggs in submerged stems, and larvae cling to such stems.

BASIS FOR STATUS CLASSIFICATION: Little or nothing is known about the species in Florida.

RECOMMENDATIONS: There is a need to search for the species in Florida.

PREPARED BY: S. W. Dunkle, Biology Department, Collin County Community College, 2800 East Spring Creek Parkway, Plano, TX 75074.

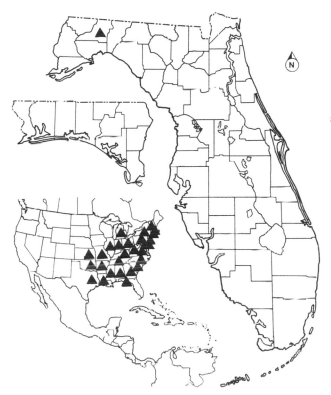

Distribution of the slender bluet, *Enallagma traviatum*.

Grasshoppers and Their Allies

INTRODUCTION: The order Orthoptera has been defined in various ways; here it is defined in a narrow sense to include only the grasshoppers, crickets, and katydids. Most species are large, as insects go, and often advertise their presence with distinctive calls. The number of species known to occur in Florida is not large, probably fewer than 200. Most species are more or less generalist feeders. One might expect that the group would be well known in our region, with only a few candidates for rare and endangered status, but in reality, there are many poorly known species, some unresolved species complexes, and a surprising number of species that are rare. This is because the order Orthoptera characteristically produces large numbers of narrowly distributed endemics. Although few species seem to have highly specialized host requirements, many seem to have highly specific habitat associations. This leads to isolation of populations in patches of a particular habitat. Many species have little need for flight in their daily lives, and this, possibly combined with island effects from living in separate patches of habitat, has repeatedly led to flightless populations. Flightlessness accentuates the isolation of populations. Courtship and mating in the Orthoptera often involve calling songs and elaborate male genitalia. These features seem to evolve relatively rapidly, resulting in numerous reproductively isolated species occupying small geographic areas. The permutations of these processes can be extremely complicated, not to say confusing, as in the case of *Pictonemobius* ground crickets (see Gross et al. 1989). Orthoptera probably reflect the complex fluctuations in Florida's habitats over the last few million years better than any other group of insects. Unfortunately, the taxonomy and distribution of many of the species and incipient species are still poorly understood.

PREPARED BY: Mark Deyrup, Archbold Biological Station, Lake Placid, FL 33852.

Threatened

Big Pine Key Conehead
Belocephalus micanopy Davis

DESCRIPTION: *Belocephalus micanopy* is a green or brown, cylindrical, nearly wingless katydid with a body about 30 mm (1.2 in) long. A short, blunted cone projects forward from between the eyes. The male has a pair of bifurcated, sharp-pointed claspers at the rear; the female has a sword-shaped ovipositor about 20 mm (0.8 in) long. A published description is provided by Davis (1914).

RANGE: This katydid occurs only on Big Pine Key (type locality), Florida.

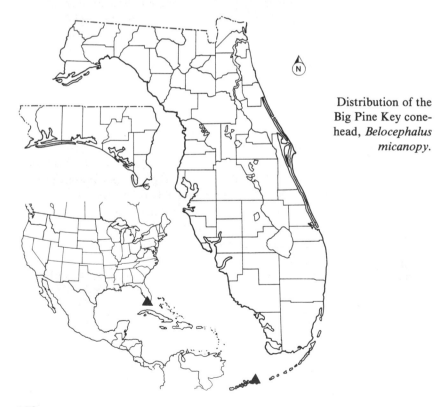

Distribution of the Big Pine Key cone-head, *Belocephalus micanopy.*

HABITAT: It is found in the understory of pine woods.

LIFE HISTORY AND ECOLOGY: Adults are present only in the fall and are most abundant in October (inclusive dates for adults are 5 Sept.–29 Nov.). In the evening, the males sing from understory shrubs such as the silver palm (*Coccothrinax argentata*). Their calling songs are regular sequences of short rattly bursts that can be heard from 35 m (112 ft) away. Nothing else is known of their ecology.

SPECIALIZED OR UNIQUE CHARACTERISTICS: *Belocephalus* is an aberrant genus of coneheads that apparently evolved in Florida. Two of the five species are known only from the Florida Keys, and of these two the Big Pine Key conehead is more restricted in distribution and divergent in morphology and calling song from its mainland counterparts. *Belocephalus* species are flightless and fall into two broadly sympatric species groups. A study of the genus will likely give clues to the events that led to speciation in Florida during the Pleistocene.

BASIS FOR STATUS CLASSIFICATION: The species is threatened by the urbanization of Big Pine Key.

RECOMMENDATIONS: Preservation and proper management (e.g. periodic burning) of a significant amount of pineland on Big Pine Key should make possible the survival of this species. This could be done in conjunction with preserving the key deer.

PREPARED BY: Thomas J. Walker, Department of Entomology and Nematology, University of Florida, Gainesville, FL 32611.

FAMILY TETTIGONIIDAE

Threatened

Keys Short-Winged Conehead

Belocephalus sleighti Davis

DESCRIPTION: *Belocephalus sleighti* adults are grotesque, green or brown, cylindrical, nearly wingless katydids that are about 40 mm (1.6 in) long. A medial thorn-like structure, about 4 mm (0.16 in) long, protrudes from between the eyes. The male's abdomen terminates in a pair of miniature grappling hooks; the female's abdomen terminates in a 1.5 mm (0.6 in) long, sword-shaped ovipositor. A published description is provided by Davis (1914).

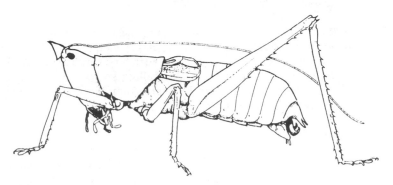

Keys Short-Winged Conehead, *Belocephalus sleighti*
(courtesy of Thomas J. Walker).

RANGE: The Florida Keys from Plantation Key to Sugarloaf Key: Plantation Key, Windleys Key, Upper Matecumbe Key, Lower Matecumbe Key,
Long Key, Grassy Key, Crawl Key, Key Vaca, Big Pine Key (type locality),
Ramrod Key, Summerland Key, Cudjoe Key, and Sugarloaf Key. Hebard
(1926) listed *B. sleighti simplex* as a mainland subspecies of *B. sleighti*; however, his material belonged to *B. sabalis* instead of to *B. sleighti*.

HABITAT: Understory of pine woods on Big Pine Key and in vine-covered,
weedy, open areas and at edges of hammocks on other keys. It is not known
why the Keys Short-Winged Conehead is absent from similar areas on Key
Largo or the keys south of Sugarloaf Key.

LIFE HISTORY AND ECOLOGY: Unlike other species of *Belocephalus* (a
genus endemic to the southeastern United States), the keys short-winged
conehead apparently breeds continuously. Reproductively active adults are
present during all months of the year, although they are most abundant in
July and November and least abundant in March and September. The food
is unknown, but the massive jaws suggest seeds or coarse leaves. No specializations for dispersal are known; adults are flightless.

SPECIALIZED OR UNIQUE CHARACTERISTICS: Adults are striking
in appearance, and males produce a loud, rattling calling song at night that
can be heard 50 m (160 ft) away. The genetic or environmental basis of the
brown-green color dimorphism is not known.

BASIS FOR STATUS CLASSIFICATION: Populations are flourishing in
the two habitats mentioned but in no others. The species is threatened by the
increasingly residential nature of the central Florida Keys. If suitable habitat
is maintained, especially the pineland on Big Pine Key, it should survive.

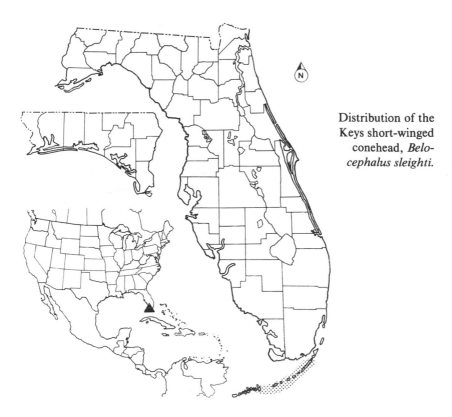

Distribution of the
Keys short-winged
conehead, *Belo-
cephalus sleighti.*

RECOMMENDATIONS: Preserving the habitat for key deer is the most likely salvation for the keys short-winged conehead. Its occurrence elsewhere is likely to end with the "cleaning-up" of roadsides and second-growth areas.

PREPARED BY: Thomas J. Walker, Department of Entomology and Nematology, University of Florida, Gainesville, FL 32611.

Order Orthoptera
FAMILY GRYLLIDAE

Threatened

Keys Scaly Cricket
Cycloptilum irregularis Love and Walker

DESCRIPTION: Small (6–9 mm [0.2–0.3 in]), flat, mottled brown cricket with a lateral white stripe on the head and pronotum. Male forewings are modified for stridulation and are entirely covered by the pronotum. The female is wingless with a 3 mm (0.1 in) ovipositor. The Florida species of *Cycloptilum* are reviewed and discussed by Love and Walker (1979).

RANGE: The species is known from Plantation (type locality), Big Pine, and Sugarloaf keys in the Florida Keys.

HABITAT: All stages live in the litter of tropical hammocks, especially in the grassy, more open parts.

LIFE HISTORY AND ECOLOGY: Adults are present at all seasons with greatest numbers from March to October. Food is unknown, but the species is presumed to be omnivorous. No specializations for dispersal are known; adults are flightless.

SPECIALIZED OR UNIQUE CHARACTERISTICS: This species has no close affinities with other U.S. species of *Cycloptilum*. Its song is a high-pitched (ca. 8 KHz), lilting tinkle lasting about 1 sec. Its unit sounds—a short sound followed by a long one—are unique. The short sound may be made on

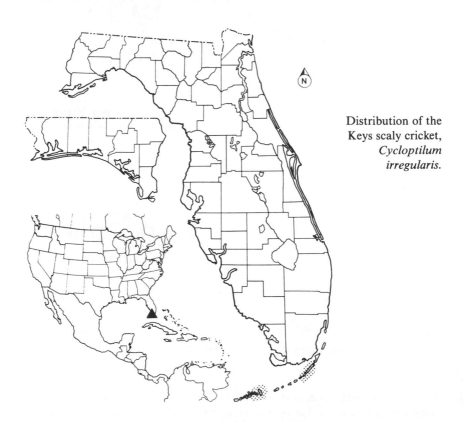

Distribution of the Keys scaly cricket, *Cycloptilum irregularis.*

the opening phase of the wing cycle or is perhaps the first part of a two-movement wing closure.

BASIS FOR STATUS CLASSIFICATION: The Keys scaly cricket is threatened by the continued development of the central Florida Keys and perhaps by aerial spraying and fogging for mosquitos.

RECOMMENDATIONS: Preserving substantial areas of hammocks in the central keys and protecting these areas from mosquito control operations should ensure the survival of this species. If this species occurs on Lignum Vitae Key, it probably has one secure refuge from mosquito control operations.

PREPARED BY: Thomas J. Walker, Department of Entomology and Nematology, University of Florida, Gainesville, FL 32611.

Order Orthoptera
FAMILY ACRIDIDAE

Short-Horned Grasshoppers

INTRODUCTION: The short-horned grasshoppers include about 70 species in Florida. A surprising number of these are apparently confined to areas of natural vegetation and absent from similar-appearing grassy or weedy disturbed areas. For this reason there are many species that are vulnerable as natural habitats become modified. There are also a number of flightless species. As in other families of Orthoptera, there are some confusing species complexes, with allopatric forms that may or may not be valid species. Information on distribution is also difficult to obtain. The most interesting cases may be provided by the genus *Melanoplus*, with a number of poorly known species and subspecies that appear to be restricted to small areas of scrub and sandhill vegetation. This genus of grasshoppers, which includes several undescribed species, is of special value to conservation and ecology because they are indicator species that help us to identify and preserve centers of Florida endemism in the race against habitat destruction.

PREPARED BY: Mark Deyrup, Archbold Biological Station, Lake Placid, FL 33852.

Rare

East Coast Scrub Grasshopper

Melanoplus indicifer Hubbell

DESCRIPTION: Both sexes have their wings reduced to small oval pads. This grayish brown grasshopper has a lateral black stripe on each side of the pronotum and an irregular blackish stripe on the hind legs. The above characters apply to a number of flightless *Melanoplus* of scrub and sandhill areas; genitalic characters are used for species identification. The elaborate male cerci, which are external and easily seen with a 10X hand lens, provide diagnostic characters that can be used on live specimens in the field. Length 14–17 mm (0.5–0.7 in). This grasshopper was described by Hubbell (1932), as *M. insignis*.

RANGE: This species is known from Palm Beach, Martin, Indian River, St. Lucie, and Brevard counties.

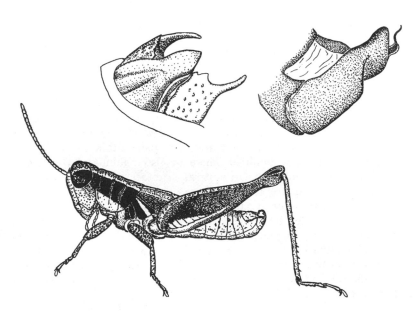

East Coast Scrub Grasshopper, *Melanoplus indicifer*
(courtesy of Mark Deyrup).

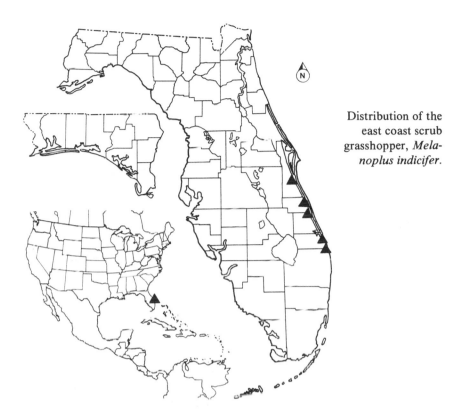

Distribution of the east coast scrub grasshopper, *Melanoplus indicifer.*

HABITAT: It is found in Florida scrub habitats on Atlantic Coastal Ridge, in open areas with low scrub oaks and patches of bare sand.

LIFE HISTORY AND ECOLOGY: Unknown. Adults have been collected from early August through October. Related species feed on a variety of scrub herbs in the laboratory, showing a preference for young leaves of legumes, such as *Galactia* species.

BASIS FOR STATUS CLASSIFICATION: This species is known from a few small remnants of coastal scrub, none of which are protected. It does not seem to occur where exotic grasses have invaded scrub. It will probably become extinct soon unless there are populations in a coastal scrub preserve, specifically Jonathan Dickinson State Park. The species might also occur in the Merritt Island National Wildlife Refuge.

RECOMMENDATIONS: A survey is needed to determine the current range of the species.

PREPARED BY: Mark Deyrup, Archbold Biological Station, Lake Placid, FL 33852.

Rare

Ocala Claw-Cercus Grasshopper
Melanoplus sp. 1

DESCRIPTION: Both sexes have their wings reduced to small oval pads. The length is about 15–20 mm (0.5–0.8 in). This grayish brown grasshopper has a lateral black stripe on each side of the head and thorax, and an irregular blackish stripe bordered below with white or cream on the hind legs. There are similar grasshoppers elsewhere in peninsular Florida, but there are no similar species known from the range of the Ocala claw-cercus grasshopper. The enormous dorsal claw on the male cercus, easily visible in the field with a 10X hand lens, is unique, distinguishing this species from all other North American grasshoppers. The scientific name and description have not yet been published.

RANGE: This species is known only from the Big Scrub area of Ocala National Forest, and from a scrub area east of Alexander Springs Creek, also in Ocala National Forest.

HABITAT: It is found in oak scrub with open patches and occasional areas of bare sand. It is replaced by the common species *M. rotundipennis* in scrub with a dense ground cover of herbs and in sandhill habitat.

LIFE HISTORY AND ECOLOGY: Adults were collected in August and September, and fed on *Galactia* species in captivity. Adults were difficult to find, apparently rare, when the species was studied in 1992.

SPECIALIZED OR UNIQUE CHARACTERISTICS: The remarkable male cercus, which is unique for the genus, is used to clasp the female during mating. The general morphology of the species suggests a close relationship with *M. forcipatus*. It appears that this species evolved from a *forcipatus*-like ancestor on the northern Mount Dora Ridge. The southern Mount Dora Ridge, the Orlando Ridge, and the Lake Wales Ridge are inhabited by *M. forcipatus*.

BASIS FOR STATUS CLASSIFICATION: The geographic range of the species appears extremely limited, and its habitat of oak scrub with bare patches of open sand exists in areas that are managed for sand pine. If the area became too shaded, or if too many herbaceous plants, especially exotic ground covers, appeared after logging, this species could disappear.

RECOMMENDATIONS: Research on the precise habitat requirements of the species may be needed if the species is to persist. Several rare scrub

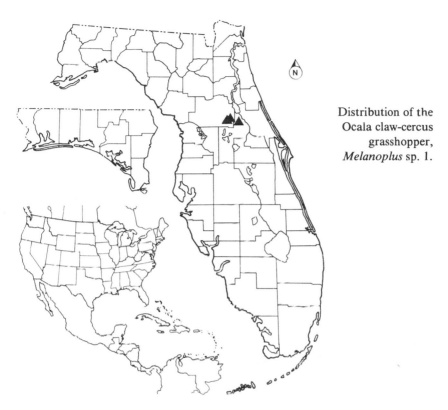

Distribution of the
Ocala claw-cercus
grasshopper,
Melanoplus sp. 1.

plants occur in the same area, so a combined conservation strategy should be possible.

PREPARED BY: Mark Deyrup, Archbold Biological Station, Lake Placid, FL 33852.

FAMILY ACRIDIDAE

Rare

Trail Ridge Scrub Grasshopper
Melanoplus sp. 2

DESCRIPTION: Both sexes have their wings reduced to small oval pads. The length is about 15–18 mm (0.5–0.7 in). This grayish brown grasshopper has a lateral black stripe on each side of the head and thorax, and an irregular blackish stripe bordered below with white or cream on the hind legs. There are no similar grasshoppers known from its range, through it looks almost exactly like *M. tequestae*, found farther south. The male cerci are simple. The internal male genitalia separate this species from *M. tequestae*, but there are no good field characters except for geographic range. The scientific name and description have not yet been published.

RANGE: This species is known from the southern end of Trail Ridge in Clay and Putnam counties. A large population was found in 1992 in a scrub just east of Florahome, and smaller populations were found in 1992 around small lakes in Roess Goldhead Branch State Park and at the Ordway Preserve.

HABITAT: It is found in oak scrub, especially in association with sand live oak (*Quercus geminata*). The habitat includes patches of bare sand and sparse herbs such as *Licania michauxi*, *Panicum* spp., and *Galactia* spp. At Roess Goldhead Branch State Park this species appears to be absent from the sandhill habitat that occupies most of the uplands, and is confined to the oak scrub in the "fire shadow" around sandhill lakes and the broad white sand margins around these lakes.

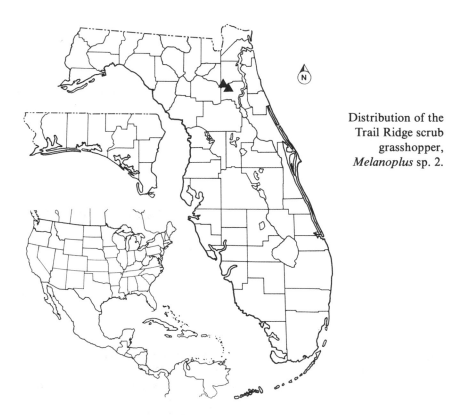

Distribution of the Trail Ridge scrub grasshopper, *Melanoplus* sp. 2.

LIFE HISTORY AND ECOLOGY: Adults were collected in October and November. They probably feed on grasses and legumes.

SPECIALIZED OR UNIQUE CHARACTERISTICS: Like its close relatives *M. forcipatus* and *M. indicifer*, this species appears to be confined to scrub areas in an isolated sand ridge complex. In spite of its close resemblance to *M. tequestae*, which, like the Trail Ridge scrub grasshopper, has simple cerci, the internal genitalic structures link this species with *M. forcipatus*, *M. indicifer*, and the Ocala claw-cercus grasshopper. These four species therefore demonstrate the long-term isolation of the scrubs on the four ridge systems they inhabit. Since the species are differentiated by major genitalic characters, there can be little doubt that they are reproductively isolated. The Trail Ridge scrub grasshopper and its close relatives are ideal indicators of areas of endemism and genetic divergence.

BASIS FOR STATUS CLASSIFICATION: The Trail Ridge uplands are almost completely occupied by sandhill habitat, where natural habitat still exists. Scrub habitat suitable for this species is largely confined to the unprotected Florahome scrub, perhaps a few hundred acres in extent. The populations around sandhill lakes appear to be small, and could easily be eradicated by minor changes in habitat management.

RECOMMENDATIONS: Research on the precise habitat requirements of the species may be needed if the species is to persist. The Florahome scrub, which also harbors a distinctive species of woody mint that is even more endangered than the grasshopper, should be preserved in its natural state.

PREPARED BY: Mark Deyrup, Archbold Biological Station, Lake Placid, FL 33852.

FAMILY ACRIDIDAE

Species of Special Concern

Rosemary Grasshopper
Schistocerca ceratiola Hubbell and Walker

DESCRIPTION: The rosemary grasshopper is unusually small for the genus: length of adult about 25–35 mm (1.0–1.4 in). This species is dark brown, extensively mottled with gray; head and pronotum usually with a dark-bordered pale strip, sometimes with lateral stripes as well. Immatures are usually bright green with yellow markings. The small size and its association with Florida rosemary (*Ceratiola ericoides*) distinguish this grasshopper from other species of *Schistocerca*.

Rosemary Grass-
hopper, *Schistocerca
ceratiola* (courtesy
of Shelley E. Franz).

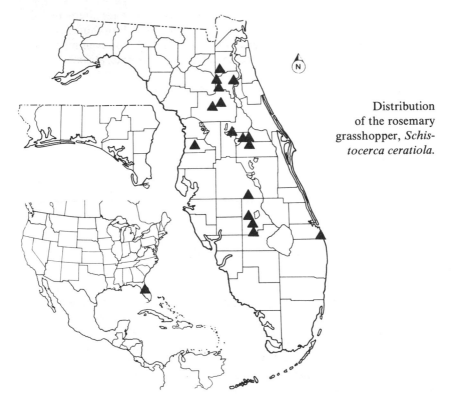

Distribution
of the rosemary
grasshopper, *Schis-
tocerca ceratiola.*

RANGE: Restricted to Florida, found in Orange, Hernando, Polk, Putnam, Seminole, Lake, Clay, Martin, Highlands counties.

HABITAT: It is found only in bushes of *Ceratiola ericoides*, a plant restricted to scrub and sandhill habitats.

LIFE HISTORY AND ECOLOGY: There appears to be one generation per year, with adults occurring July through mid-November. The species appears to be monophagous, which is highly unusual in the Acrididae. At some sites this species is primarily nocturnal, remaining hidden in the interior of the plants by day; at other sites, it is diurnal (Franz and Franz 1989).

BASIS FOR STATUS CLASSIFICATION: This is a Florida endemic completely dependent on a plant that lives only in sandy upland habitats that are threatened over much of the state. It appears to be absent from many rosemary areas within its known range, and is also missing from rosemary scrubs in the panhandle and the western peninsula. The host plant requires open sites, and may disappear in the absence of fire or other factors needed to prevent growth of a dense overstory. A sequence of fires less than 15 years apart can also eliminate *Ceratiola*.

RECOMMENDATIONS: Preserve and manage the remaining large stands of Florida rosemary that support this species.

PREPARED BY: Mark Deyrup, Archbold Biological Station, Lake Placid, FL 33852; and Richard Franz, Florida Museum of Natural History, University of Florida, Gainesville, FL 32611.

FAMILY ACRIDIDAE

Status Undetermined

Tequesta Grasshopper
Melanoplus tequestae Hubbell

DESCRIPTION: Both sexes of this insect have wings reduced to small oval pads. This grayish brown grasshopper has a lateral black stripe on each side of the head and thorax, and an irregular blackish stripe bordered below with white or cream on the hind legs. Length 13–20 mm (0.5–0.8 in). This species is very similar to the sympatric *M. forcipatus*, but can easily be distinguished by the simple (untoothed) male cerci, visible in the field with a 10X hand lens. A published description is found in Hubbell (1932).

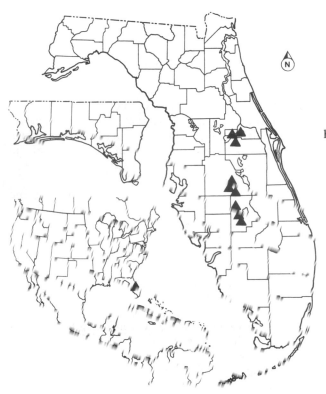

Distribution of the
Tequesta grass-
hopper, *Melanoplus
tequestae.*

RANGE: This grayish brown grasshopper is restricted to Florida and associated with interior scrub ridges from Highlands County north to Orange and Seminole counties.

HABITAT: It occurs in sand pine scrub and sandhill habitats. It appears to be more dependent on open sites than *M. forcipatus*.

LIFE HISTORY AND ECOLOGY: In captivity this species hops primarily on perennial forbs (Bland 1987). Bland (1987) has described courtship and prolonged copulation of this species. Adults are about between August and April.

BASIS FOR STATUS CLASSIFICATION: This is a Florida species restricted to high sand ridges in the interior of the peninsula. Most of this species is scarce and disappearing over much of its range. It appears to be able to persist in small patches of habitat. There are protected populations on the Lake Wales Ridge, at the Archbold Biological Station, at Lake Apthorpe Preserve (Nature Conservancy), at Highlands Hammock State Park, and at Lake Arbuckle State Forest. These are the most populations differ from other populations in features.

RANGE: Restricted to Florida, found in Orange, Hernando, Polk, Putnam, Seminole, Lake, Clay, Martin, Highlands counties.

HABITAT: It is found only in bushes of *Ceratiola ericoides*, a plant restricted to scrub and sandhill habitats.

LIFE HISTORY AND ECOLOGY: There appears to be one generation per year, with adults occurring July through mid-November. The species appears to be monophagous, which is highly unusual in the Acrididae. At some sites this species is primarily nocturnal, remaining hidden in the interior of the plants by day; at other sites, it is diurnal (Franz and Franz 1989).

BASIS FOR STATUS CLASSIFICATION: This is a Florida endemic completely dependent on a plant that lives only in sandy upland habitats that are threatened over much of the state. It appears to be absent from many rosemary areas within its known range, and is also missing from rosemary scrubs in the panhandle and the western peninsula. The host plant requires open sites, and may disappear in the absence of fire or other factors needed to prevent growth of a dense overstory. A sequence of fires less than 15 years apart can also eliminate *Ceratiola*.

RECOMMENDATIONS: Preserve and manage the remaining large stands of Florida rosemary that support this species.

PREPARED BY: Mark Deyrup, Archbold Biological Station, Lake Placid, FL 33852; and Richard Franz, Florida Museum of Natural History, University of Florida, Gainesville, FL 32611.

FAMILY ACRIDIDAE

Status Undetermined

Tequesta Grasshopper
Melanoplus tequestae Hubbell

DESCRIPTION: Both sexes of this insect have wings reduced to small oval pads. This grayish brown grasshopper has a lateral black stripe on each side of the head and thorax, and an irregular blackish stripe bordered below with white or cream on the hind legs. Length 13–20 mm (0.5–0.8 in). This species is very similar to the sympatric *M. forcipatus*, but can easily be distinguished by the simple (untoothed) male cerci, visible in the field with a 10X hand lens. A published description is found in Hubbell (1932).

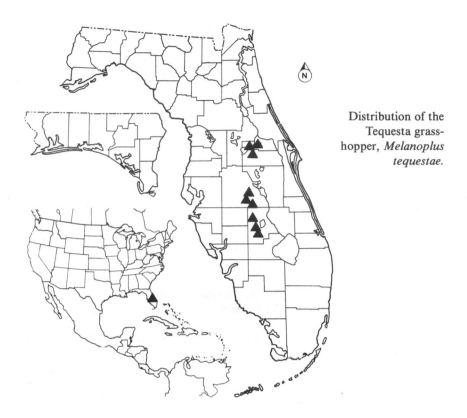

Distribution of the
Tequesta grass-
hopper, *Melanoplus
tequestae.*

RANGE: This grayish brown grasshopper is restricted to Florida and associated with interior scrub ridges from Highlands County north to Orange
and Seminole counties.

HABITAT: It occurs in sand pine scrub and sandhill habitats. It appears to
be more dependent on open sites than *M. forcipatus.*

LIFE HISTORY AND ECOLOGY: In captivity this species appears to feed
primarily on perennial forbs (Bland 1987). Bland (1987) has described the
courtship and prolonged copulation of this species. Adults are most abundant between August and April.

BASIS FOR STATUS CLASSIFICATION: This is a Florida endemic that
is restricted to high sand ridges in the interior of the peninsula. The habitat
of this species is scarce and disappearing over much of its range. Populations
appear to be able to subsist in small patches of habitat. There are four large
protected populations on the Lake Wales Ridge: at the Archbold Biological
Station, at Lake Apthorpe Preserve (Nature Conservancy), at Highlands
Hammock State Park, and at Lake Arbuckle State Forest. The southernmost populations differ from other populations in some minor genitalic
features.

RECOMMENDATIONS: There is a need for further study of distribution and ecological requirements of this species.

PREPARED BY: Mark Deyrup, Archbold Biological Station, Lake Placid, FL 33852.

FAMILY ACRIDIDAE

Status Undetermined

Larger Sandhill Grasshopper
Melanoplus querneus Rehn and Hebbard

DESCRIPTION: The male has a black lateral stripe on the thorax, and hind femurs are mostly black. Both sexes are grayish brown and have wings that are reduced to small oval pads. Male genitalic characters used for species identification. Length 22-33 mm (0.9-1.3 in). A published description is found in Blatchley (1920).

Distribution of the larger sandhill grass-hopper, *Melanoplus querneus.*

RANGE: This species is known from a small area in southwest Georgia (Thomas and Decatur counties) and nearby Florida (Liberty County).

HABITAT: It occurs in sandhill habitats.

LIFE HISTORY AND ECOLOGY: Adults have been found in August, November, and December. They are reported to be sluggish (though they might have been chilled, as the observation is from November or December), and found together in colonies associated with scrub oaks (Blatchley 1920).

BASIS FOR STATUS CLASSIFICATION: This appears to be one of a number of species that has a narrow geographic range in sandhill habitat east of the Apalachicola River. This species was collected in Torreya State Park many years ago, so it is possible that there is a protected population. It probably occurs, or used to occur, in other nearby sandhill areas.

RECOMMENDATIONS: There is need for further study of distribution and ecological requirements of this species.

PREPARED BY: Mark Deyrup, Archbold Biological Station, Lake Placid, FL 33852.

FAMILY ACRIDIDAE

Status Undetermined

Pygmy Sandhill Grasshopper

Melanoplus pygmaeus Davis

DESCRIPTION: Males have a black lateral stripe on the thorax. Both sexes have their wings reduced to small oval pads. Male genitalic characters are used for species identification. Length: 14–23 mm. A published description is found in Blatchley (1920).

RANGE: The reddish brown grasshopper is restricted to Florida, known from Walton, Okaloosa, and Santa Rosa counties.

HABITAT: It occurs in sandhill habitats.

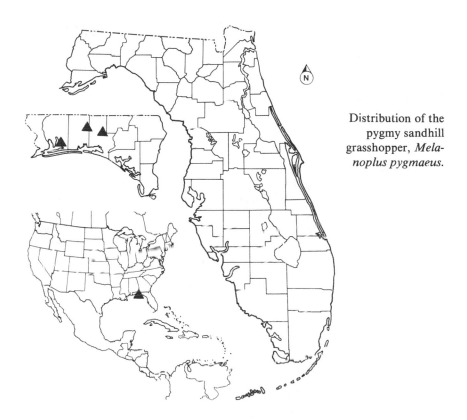

Distribution of the pygmy sandhill grasshopper, *Melanoplus pygmaeus.*

LIFE HISTORY AND ECOLOGY: Adults have been collected between August and February, but otherwise the biology of the species is unknown.

BASIS FOR STATUS CLASSIFICATION: This species appears to be a highly localized species restricted to an areas of uplands in the western panhandle. Like most small flightless *Melanoplus* species, the pygmy sandhill grasshopper is so poorly known that its status cannot be determined. It has not been found in any protected areas.

RECOMMENDATIONS: There is a need for further study of distribution and ecological requirements of this insect.

PREPARED BY: Mark Deyrup, Archbold Biological Station, Lake Placid, FL 33852.

Status Undetermined

Broad Cercus Scrub Grasshopper
Melanoplus forcipatus Hubbell

DESCRIPTION: Both sexes of this grasshopper have their wings reduced to small oval pads. It is grayish brown, usually with a dark lateral stripe on the head and thorax. Occasional specimens are heavily mottled. The hind femur has an irregular blackish stripe bordered below with white or cream. The cerci of the male are greatly expanded, the basal part almost rectangular; this character can be seen in the field with a 10X hand lens. Length: 12–20 mm (0.5–0.8 in). A published description is found in Hubbell (1932).

RANGE: This grasshopper is restricted to Florida, including interior scrub ridges from Highlands County north to Orange County.

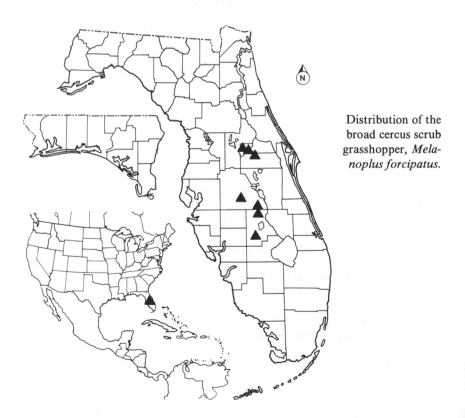

Distribution of the broad cercus scrub grasshopper, *Melanoplus forcipatus.*

HABITAT: It inhabits sand pine scrub with scrub oaks, including areas with a rather dense canopy of pine and oak.

LIFE HISTORY AND ECOLOGY: The biology of this species is almost unknown. Adults have been collected from July to December. Copulating pairs are often seen in the field, which suggests that the species has prolonged bouts of copulation.

BASIS FOR STATUS CLASSIFICATION: This is a Florida endemic that is restricted to sand pine scrub areas in the interior of the peninsula. The habitat of this species is disappearing or has disappeared over much of its range. It is more widespread than some other short-winged *Melanoplus* species, but may not occur on all the sites where there are remnants of habitat. There are recent collections from only five sites, two of which are protected.

RECOMMENDATIONS: There is a need for further study of distribution and ecological requirements of this species.

PREPARED BY: Mark Deyrup, Archbold Biological Station, Lake Placid, FL 33852.

FAMILY ACRIDIDAE

Status Undetermined

Volusia Grasshopper
Menaloplus adelogyrus Hubbell

DESCRIPTION: Both sexes of this grasshopper have their wings reduced to small oval pads. This insect is reddish to grayish brown, yellow underneath; dark stripe on side of pronotum and on side of body below wings; more or less distinct black femoral bands. These characters apply to several species of flightless *Melanoplus* in scrub and sandhill habitats; genitalic characters are used for species identification. Length about 14–17 mm. A published description is found in Hubbell (1932).

RANGE: This grasshopper is known only from Volusia and Putnam counties, Florida, where this species is apparently restricted to Crescent City and the Deland Ridges.

Distribution of the
Volusia grass-
hopper, *Melanoplus
adelogyrus.*

HABITAT: It inhabits scrub, xeric hammock, and longleaf pine flatwoods
with wire grass (Friauf 1953).

LIFE HISTORY AND ECOLOGY: Unknown. Adults were collected in
May, August, September, and October (Hubbell 1932).

BASIS FOR STATUS CLASSIFICATION: This is a Florida endemic that
is restricted to upland areas along the east side of the St. Johns River. It
could be somewhat more widespread, as the upland ridge system on which it
occurs extends up into Putnam County. It occurs on the Welaka Reserve
(Friauf 1953).

RECOMMENDATIONS: There is need for further study of distribution
and ecological requirements of this insect.

PREPARED BY: Mark Deyrup, Archbold Biological Station, Lake Placid,
FL 33852.

Status Undetermined

Apalachicola Grasshopper
Melanoplus apalachicolae Hubbell

DESCRIPTION: Both sexes of this grasshopper have their wings reduced to small oval pads. Grayish brown, it may have black lateral stripe on pronotum. Best distinguished from other small flightless *Melanoplus* species by male genitalic characters. Length 14–17 mm (0.6–0.7 in). It was described and illustrated by Hubbell (1932).

RANGE: It is known only from Liberty County, east of the Apalachicola River.

Distribution of the Apalachicola grasshopper, *Melanoplus apalachicolae.*

HABITAT: The grasshopper occurs in open sandhills with *Quercus laevis* (Hubbell 1932).

LIFE HISTORY AND ECOLOGY: Adults were collected in late July (Hubbell 1932).

BASIS FOR STATUS CLASSIFICATION: This appears to be a Florida endemic restricted to a small area within the state. Not only is its range probably limited, but also the habitat may require management to maintain it in a suitable state. This species seems to have received no attention since its description, and might have a wider distribution.

RECOMMENDATIONS: Surveys are needed to determine whether this species continues to survive. It might occur on state lands, where it could be maintained by proper management of the habitat.

PREPARED BY: Mark Deyrup, Archbold Biological Station, Lake Placid, FL 33852.

Roaches

INTRODUCTION: The cockroaches are represented by only 38 species in Florida (Atkinson et al. 1990), but manage to display the principal biogeographic patterns of Florida arthropods. There are a few widespread southeastern species, a few tropical species restricted to extreme south Florida, a few northern species in extreme north Florida, an endemic species of sandy uplands, and a number of synanthropic exotics. The usual problems of selection and documentation of rare and endangered species also prevail in the cockroaches. There are northern species, such as *Parcoblatta divisa*, *P. uhleriana*, and *P. virginica*, whose populations may be highly localized in Florida, but their distribution remains very poorly known. Some tropical species confined to a small area of south Florida are better known, but all these species have populations elsewhere in the tropics, and any or all species could have been introduced by man. The Florida beetle cockroach, *Plectoptera poeyi*, is one of the tropical species most likely to be native, but even that species might have been introduced from Cuba; some evidence of divergence between the Florida and Cuban populations would be helpful. At present, only the upland endemic Florida sand cockroach fits the criteria of a rare or endangered species.

Native Florida cockroaches almost never breed in buildings, though some species are attracted to lights.

PREPARED BY: Mark Deyrup, Archbold Biological Station, Lake Placid, FL 33852.

Order Blattaria
FAMILY POLYPHAGIDAE

Rare

Florida Sand Cockroach
Arenivaga floridensis Caudell

DESCRIPTION: Females of this cockroach are completely wingless, almost circular in outline, dark brown with pale margins on pronotum, or pale with more or less extensive dark brown markings. Males are winged, pronotum dark brown with pale margins, wings pale to dark brown. Middle and hind femora have a long apical spine. Length 16–21 mm (0.6–0.8 in).

RANGE: This roach is restricted to Florida, known from Alachua, Citrus, Clay, Highlands, Lake, Levy, Marion, Polk, Pinellas, Putnam, and Volusia counties (Atkinson et al. 1990).

HABITAT: It is found in sandy upland habitats, especially scrub, but also sandhill. Open sandy areas seem to be required, as no specimens have been found in areas of closed canopy and deep leaf litter.

LIFE HISTORY AND ECOLOGY: Immatures and females of this species spend their lives burrowing through the sand; mature males emerge to fly low over the sand at dusk, presumably seeking females. In the laboratory this species appears to be a general feeder. Individuals have been found in burrows of oldfield mouse (*Peromyscus polionotus*) (Young 1949) and in nest mounds of southeastern harvester ant (*Pogonomyrmex badius*), where they probably feed on vegetable matter, especially seeds.

SPECIALIZED OR UNIQUE CHARACTERISTICS: The Florida sand cockroach is highly specialized for a life of burrowing in sand. The legs are

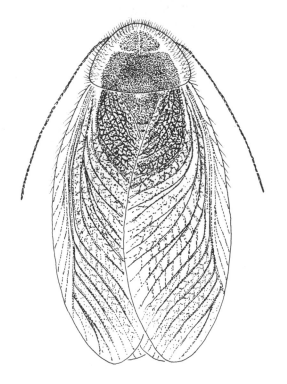

Florida Sand Cock-roach, *Arenivaga flo-ridensis* (courtesy of Mark Deyrup).

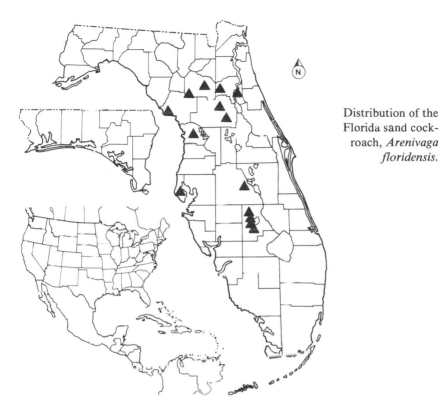

Distribution of the
Florida sand cock-
roach, *Arenivaga
floridensis.*

broad and flattened for digging, and equipped with short, stiff setae. The
female is completely wingless. The short, almost round, dorsally convex, ventrally flattened body is reminiscent of certain wingless, sand-dwelling beetles.
This body-form allows the insect to bury itself quickly by raising the posterior of the body slightly and pushing with the powerful rear legs.

BASIS FOR STATUS CLASSIFICATION: This is a Florida endemic of
scrub and sandhill, with close relatives in southwestern deserts. It occurs in
habitats which are rapidly dwindling. It lives only in areas that are managed
or allowed to burn periodically to provide patches of open sand. It has not
been found in some apparently suitable habitats, especially in east coast and
panhandle scrubs. There are striking differences in color in different parts of
its range, suggesting that there are distinctive geographic races on isolated
ridge systems.

RECOMMENDATIONS: Preserve and manage open scrub and sandhill
habitats. Further research is needed on the distribution and taxonomic status
of the different forms of the species.

PREPARED BY: Mark Deyrup, Archbold Biological Station, Lake Placid,
FL 33852.

Lice

INTRODUCTION: Mallophaga, or chewing lice, live as ectoparasites on most species of birds and many mammals, but not on humans. They are grouped in two suborders (Amblycera and Ischnocera) and six families (Philopteridae on birds, Trichodectidae on mammals, Gyropidae on certain South American mammals, Menopomidae on birds, Laemobthriidae on water birds and birds of prey, Ricinidae on birds, particularly sparrows and hummingbirds). One of the main characters that separate the two suborders is whether the antennae are concealed in a groove (Amblycera) or not concealed in a groove (Ischnocera). There are approximately 2,700 species in the world, with more than 300 reported from North America (Emerson 1972, Emerson and Price 1981).

PREPARED BY: Richard Franz, Florida Museum of Natural History, University of Florida, Gainsville, FL 32611.

Endangered and Threatened

Endangered Mammal Lice
Florida Panther Louse: *Felicola* sp.
Endangered Bird Lice
Wood Stork Lice:
   Ardeicola loculator (Giebel)
   Ciconiphilus quadripustulatus (Burmeister)
   Colpocephalum mycteriae Price and Beer
   Colpocephalum scalariforme Rudow
   Neophilopterus heteropygus (Nitzsch).

Everglade Kite Lice:
   Craspedorrhynchus obscurus (Giebel)
   Falcolipeurus quadriguttatus (Giebel).

Threatened Mammal Lice

Florida Black Bear Louse:
   Trichodectes pinguis euarctidos Hopkins.

Threatened Bird Lice

Eastern Brown Pelican Lice:
   Colpocephalum occidentalis Price
   Pectinopygus occidentalis Thompson
   Piagetiella bursaepelecani (Perry).

Rothschild's Magnificent Frigatebird Lice:
   Colpocephalum spineum Kellogg
   Fregatiella aurifasciata (Kellogg)
   Pectinopygus fregatiphagus (Eichler).

Southern Bald Eagle Lice:
   Colpocephalum flavescens (de Haan)
   Craspedorrhynchus halieti (Osborn)
   Degeeriella discocephalus (Burmeister).

Osprey Louse:
   Kurodaia haliaeeti (Denny).

Southeastern American Kestrel Louse:
   Degeeriella rufa carruthi Emerson.

Audubon's Caracara Lice:
   Acutifrons mexicanus Emerson
   Colpocephalum polybori Rudow
   Falcolipeurus josephi Tandan and Dhanda.

Florida Sandhill Crane Lice:
   Esthiopterum brevicephalum (McGregor)
   Gruimenopon canadense Edwards
   Heleonomus assimilis (Piaget).

American Oystercatcher Lice:
  Actornithophilus grandiceps (Piaget)
  Austromenopon haematopi Timmermann
  Quadraceps auratus (de Haan)
  Saemundssonia haematopi (Linnaeus).

Roseate Tern Louse:
  Quadraceps giebeli (Eichler).

Least Tern Lice:
  Quadraceps nychthemerus (Burmeister)
  Saemundssonia melanocephalus (Burmeister).

Florida Scrub Jay Louse:
  Brueelia deficiens (Piaget).

DESCRIPTION: Chewing lice are flattened, usually elongated, wingless insects. Adults, depending on species, vary from 1 to 11 mm (0.5 in) in length and from milky white to dark brown in color.

RANGE: Lice spend their entire life cycle on the host; therefore, their geographical range is that of the host or hosts.

HABITAT: Adults and nymphs, depending on species, feed on feathers, fur, hair, serum, and secretions of sebaceous glands. Those living on mammals are found on the host's hair or fur. Those living on birds, depending on species, are found on the feathers, inside the primary quills, inside the pouch (of pelicans or cormorants), and running freely over the body. Most populations of Mallophaga on birds are found on the head or wings where their host cannot preen.

LIFE HISTORY AND ECOLOGY: Eggs are attached to the hair, fur, or feathers of the host. There are three nymphal stages, which resemble adults with shrunken or reduced abdomens. The life cycle from egg to adult is about four weeks. Populations are usually small on healthy hosts but may become very large (2,000 +) on hosts that are stressed for prolonged periods of time by injury or disease. Most species of Mallophaga cannot tolerate temperatures much higher than that of their normal host; they are more tolerant of lower temperatures. The microclimate and other ecological conditions found near the host's skin are apparently the greatest influences in determining host specificity. Some species of Mallophaga will live only on one species of host; others will live on several species (or genera) of hosts.

BASIS FOR STATUS CLASSIFICATION: The above species are endangered or threatened in Florida because their hosts are so classified, and they are not found on other species of hosts.

PREPARED BY: K. C. Emerson, 560 Boulder Drive, Sanibel, FL 32957.

Beetles

INTRODUCTION: The Order Coleoptera includes more described species than any other order of animals; the number now approaches 300,000 species, with every indication that great numbers of species remain to be described. On a local scale the diversity is also overwhelming. Any reasonably heterogeneous state park in Florida is likely to harbor at least 1,000 species of beetles, perhaps as many as 1,500 or 2,000. With thousands of species of beetles occurring in Florida, including many species with narrow habitat requirements, one would expect that there would be large numbers of rare and endangered species. There are, for example, several species found only in burrows of gopher tortoises (Woodruff 1982a), another that occupies the nests of caracaras. Whole families of beetles are phytophagous, and a good proportion are host-specific, some of which may well be associated with scarce plants. Many species have relatively poor powers of dispersal, increasing the chance that populations have become isolated and evolved into distinct species. The majority of species spend at least part of their lives in soil or leaf litter; this results in considerable sensitivity to edaphic conditions and increases the likelihood that species will be narrowly habitat-specific, or isolated on disjunct uplands.

Many coleopterists have worked in Florida, but the number of beetles is very large, and many species remain poorly known. The hard wing-covers of beetles allow them to burrow in soil and crawl into concealing places even as adults, so the apparency of many species is minimal. As with other large orders of arthropods, our ignorance of biological requirements and geographic distribution keeps coverage to a token selection of species.

PREPARED BY: Mark Deyrup, Archbold Biological Station, Lake Placid, FL 33852.

Order Coleoptera
FAMILY CICINDELIDAE

Tiger Beetles

INTRODUCTION: Tiger beetles are fiercely predatory insects that usually inhabit open sandy habitats. Adults run rapidly over the ground, taking flight at the least alarm. The larvae live in burrows and ambush passing arthropods. Tiger beetles have specialized habitats both as larvae and as adults, and the dispersal ability of most species seems relatively limited. Many species are restricted to small geographic areas. This group has great appeal to entomologists, and the abundance and distribution of most tiger beetles is relatively well-documented. A number of species have been recognized as rare and endangered in various regions.

Several species are recognized by experts as rare or endangered in Florida, including *Cicindela olivacea*, *C. hirticollis*, *C. dorsalis media*, *C. nigrior*, and *C. striga*, but we have species accounts for only two species.

PREPARED BY: Mark Deyrup, Archbold Biological Station, Lake Placid, FL 33852.

FAMILY CICINDELIDAE

Threatened

Highlands Tiger Beetle
Cicindela highlandensis Choate

DESCRIPTION: The highlands tiger beetle is small for the genus (10.5–12 mm long [0.4–0.5 in]); the labrum is cream-colored; the head, legs, and elytra are black with green, blue, and purple reflections; the abdomen is reddish underneath and has a conspicuous red spot above revealed in flight. It is distinguished from the rather similar *Cicindela abdominalis* and *Cicindela scabrosa* by an absence of conspicuous white flattened hairs on both sides of the thorax and the underside of the abdomen. *C. highlandensis* also lacks the coarse punctures that cover the elytra of the sympatric *C. scabrosa*. Published description, illustrations, and key are found in Choate (1984).

RANGE: This tiger beetle occurs in a few scrub areas in Highlands and southern Polk counties.

HABITAT: It is found in open sandy areas in high well-drained dunes.

LIFE HISTORY AND ECOLOGY: Adults have been found in June and July. The larva is unknown.

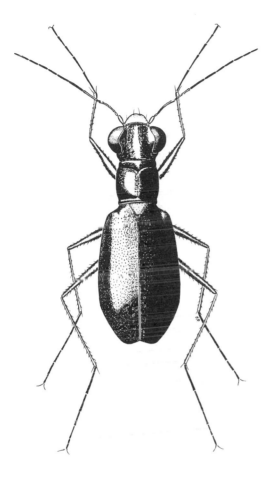

Highlands Tiger Bee-
tle, *Cicindela high-
landensis* (courtesy of
Mark Deyrup).

BASIS FOR STATUS CLASSIFICATION: The entire geographic range of
this species is extremely small, and exhaustive surveys by James M. Hill and
C. Barry Knisley (1991, 1992 unpublished) revealed a small number of surviving populations. No specimens have been seen at the type locality for several years. There is a population at Arbuckle State Forest, but all other
populations are unprotected.

RECOMMENDATIONS: Populations need to be monitored. Two populations occur on sites that are under consideration for purchase as conservation
areas; such purchase is probably the only hope for the species. This tiger beetle is conspicuous and easy to catch, and the populations are likely to be

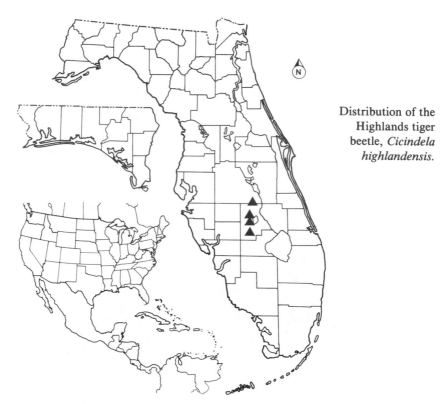

Distribution of the
Highlands tiger
beetle, *Cicindela
highlandensis.*

concentrated in small patches of suitable habitat. Irresponsible collecting easily could affect the remaining populations.

PREPARED BY: Mark Deyrup, Archbold Biological Station, Lake Placid, FL 33852.

FAMILY CICINDELIDAE

Rare

Florida Scrub Tiger Beetle
Cicindela scabrosa Schaupp

DESCRIPTION: This tiger beetle is small for the genus (10–11.5 mm long [0.4 in]); the labrum is cream-colored; the head, legs, and elytra are black, often with green reflections; the abdomen is reddish underneath; the elytra has a white apical mark and usually a few small medial white marks. It can be distinguished from the similar *Cicindela abdominalis* by the heavy punctures on the elytra (illustrated in Choate 1984) and from *Cicindela highlandensis* by the depth and coarseness of the elytral punctures, the presence of white elytral markings, and white flattened hairs on the sides of the thorax and underside of the abdomen. Published description, illustrations, and key are found in Choate (1984).

RANGE: This beetle is confined to peninsular Florida and is widely distributed in isolated scrub habitats.

LIFE HISTORY AND ECOLOGY: Adults are active from early May through mid-September. This species occurs in open patches of sand, almost always in sand pine scrub habitat.

BASIS FOR STATUS CLASSIFICATION: Although this species is widely distributed, many, perhaps most, populations appear to be small and in dwindling patches of habitat. Known populations on protected land are at Archbold Biological Station, Highlands Hammock State Park, and Koreshan State Park.

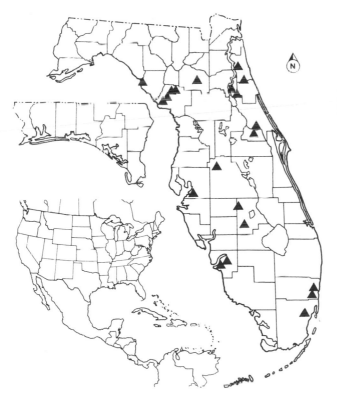

Distribution of the Florida scrub tiger beetle, *Cicindela scabrosa.*

RECOMMENDATIONS: This species is in no immediate danger of extinction, but it is likely to disappear from most of its range without further protection of scrub habitat.

PREPARED BY: Mark Deyrup, Archbold Biological Station, Lake Placid, FL 33852.

Order Coleoptera

FAMILY SCARABAEIDAE

Scarab Beetles

INTRODUCTION: The Scarabaeidae is a large family of beetles that is relatively well-represented in this volume. Some scarabs are specialized scavengers associated with vertebrates, some of which are rare and endangered. There are, for example, species found only in the burrows of gopher tortoises or pocket gophers, and a species apparently restricted to the nests of fox squirrels. Some scarabs are flightless, resulting in examples of species occurring only in small, isolated, and vulnerable populations. Many species are highly dependent on special soil types, with a disproportionate number in modern or ancient dunes, habitats that are rapidly disappearing or undergoing extreme modification.

The scarabs are a relatively well-known group in Florida, rather popular with collectors and often readily collected in various types of traps. For this reason, a species that has only been collected a few times cannot be easily dismissed as a species that is abundant but secretive or difficult to recognize. We list such species as "status undetermined" except when there is reason to believe that they are restricted to a small area of the state, a condition that would place them in the "rare" category. Two volumes have been published on the "Scarabs of Florida" (Woodruff 1973, Woodruff and Beck 1989) and a third volume is in preparation. It was the only family of beetles treated in the original FCREPA volume (Woodruff 1982b). The recent publication on the genus *Phyllophaga* in Florida (Woodruff and Beck 1989) is a particularly important advance in knowledge of Florida scarabs, and requires addition or status change of a dozen species on the previous FCREPA list.

Scarabs are unequalled among beetles in their demonstration of biogeographically significant areas in Florida. The ancient dune systems with scrub or sandhill habitats harbor endemic scarabs. Examples include endemic species on particular ridge systems, of allopatric sibling species that appear to have diverged on isolated ridge systems, and species that show consistent intraspecific variation from one sandy upland to another. Scarabs also are included in the enclaves of northern organisms in the Apalachicola River basin, and there appears to be a separate incursion of northern species into the western-most Florida panhandle counties. More than any other group, scarabs provide striking evidence of a complex pattern of endemism and isolation in patches of sandy uplands throughout the panhandle. It appears that scarabs will be indispensable for locating "hot spots" of endemism that should receive intensive study and protection.

PREPARED BY: Mark Deyrup, Archbold Biological Station, Lake Placid, FL 33852.

FAMILY SCARABAEIDAE

Threatened

Fox Squirrel Scarab

Ataenius sciurus Cartwright

DESCRIPTION: This scarab beetle is large for the genus (length 5-6 mm [0.2 in]). The pronotum is short, hardly more than one third the length of elytra and without marginal setae. Pronotal punctures are close and dense, extending to and including the lateral margin. The posterior femur is slender, subparallel, and the posterior marginal groove is entire. Published descriptions are found in Woodruff (1973) (under the name *brevinotus* Chapin) and Cartwright (1974).

RANGE: The fox squirrel scarab is known from Alachua, Dade, Hillsborough, Putnam, Manatee, Pinellas, and Highlands counties.

HABITAT: It occurs in open areas with large trees where fox squirrels (*Sciurus niger*) occur.

LIFE HISTORY AND ECOLOGY: The beetle is found in fox squirrel nests (Moore 1953), apparently an obligate dung-feeding commensal. Most light-trap collections were taken in May.

BASIS FOR STATUS CLASSIFICATION: As an obligate associate, this beetle shares the threatened status of its fox squirrel host. It was listed as endangered in the FCREPA 1982 edition.

RECOMMENDATIONS: The protection of the host and the host's habitat is necessary to insure the survival of this beetle.

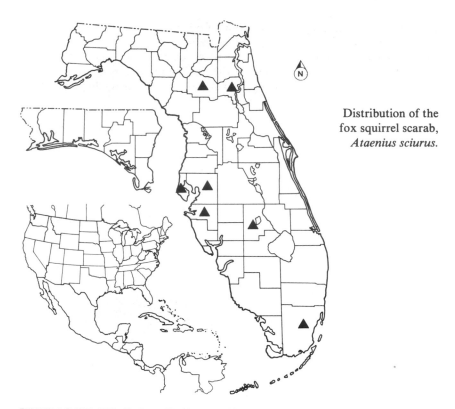

Distribution of the fox squirrel scarab, *Ataenius sciurus.*

PREPARED BY: Robert E. Woodruff, Florida State Collection of Arthropods, P.O. Box 147100, Gainesville, FL 32614–7100, and Mark Deyrup, Archbold Biological Station, Lake Placid, FL 33852.

FAMILY SCARABAEIDAE

Threatened

Southwest Florida Mycotrupes
Mycotrupes pedester Howden

DESCRIPTION: The body of this beetle is oval, convex, and not shining. Elytra are fused, and hind wings are absent. The pronotum is without a median anterior tubercle, or if a tubercle is present it is low and transverse, not conical. A published description is found in Woodruff (1973). The round shape and fused elytra are distinctive characters of the genus. The three species of *Mycotrupes* in Florida seem to have separate geographic ranges.

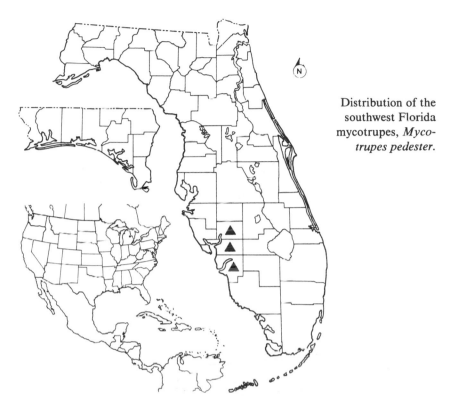

Distribution of the
southwest Florida
mycotrupes, *Myco-*
trupes pedester.

RANGE: This beetle is known from Charlotte, Lee, and DeSoto counties in Florida.

HABITAT: It occurs on deep sand ridges.

LIFE HISTORY AND ECOLOGY: Adults construct burrows, to a depth of 3 m (10.2 ft), in deep sand. Larval food is unknown. Adults have been collected in malt traps.

BASIS FOR STATUS CLASSIFICATION: This flightless beetle appears to have a narrowly restricted distribution and has limited mobility. It occurs in sandy uplands, a habitat never extensive in southwest Florida and now disappearing rapidly.

RECOMMENDATIONS: This species indicates that the remaining fragments of sand ridges in southwest Florida should be examined carefully for additional endemics. Habitat preservation is the only way to preserve this species.

PREPARED BY: Robert E. Woodruff, Florida State Collection of Arthropods, P.O. Box 147100, Gainesville, FL 32614-7100, and Mark Deyrup, Archbold Biological Station, Lake Placid, FL 33852.

Threatened

Gopher Tortoise Copris
Copris gopheri Hubbard

DESCRIPTION: This medium-sized beetle (7.5-10 mm [0.3-0.4 in]) has a very broad, explanate clypeus, notched medially. There are eight elytral striae; coarse punctures are absent on the head, confined to anterior angles on the pronotum. A published description is found in Woodruff (1973).

RANGE: This beetle is known from Alachua, Highlands, Pinellas, Seminole, Flagler, Lake, Volusia, and Palm Beach counties in Florida.

HABITAT: It occurs on sandy uplands inhabited by gopher tortoises (*Gopherus polyphemus*).

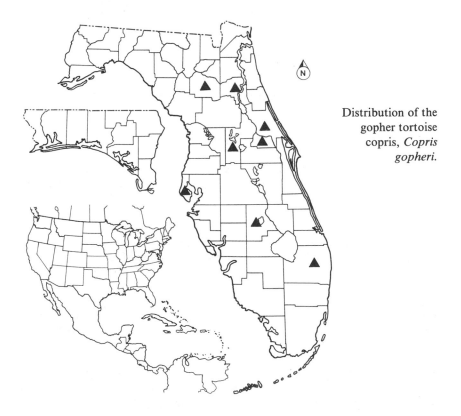

Distribution of the gopher tortoise copris, *Copris gopheri.*

LIFE HISTORY AND ECOLOGY: This beetle lives only in gopher tortoise burrows, where it has been rarely collected during extensive surveys. The female makes balls of gopher dung, burying them 10–12 cm (4 or 5 in) below the floor of the burrow (Hubbard 1894). Adults are occasionally attracted to lights.

BASIS FOR STATUS CLASSIFICATION: This species shares the status of its obligate host. The distribution may be more limited than that of the gopher tortoise, which would increase the vulnerability of the beetles. It was listed as endangered in FCREPA 1982.

RECOMMENDATIONS: The future of this species depends completely upon efforts to save its host. Gopher tortoises relocated to areas lacking previous occupants will probably fail to obtain their community of obligate commensals.

PREPARED BY: Robert E. Woodruff, Florida State Collection of Arthropods, P.O. Box 147100, Gainesville, FL 32614-7100, and Mark Deyrup, Archbold Biological Station, Lake Placid, FL 33852.

FAMILY SCARABAEIDAE

Threatened

Gopher Tortoise Onthophagus
Onthophagus polyphemi Hubbard

DESCRIPTION: This beetle achieves lengths of 4.7–6.9 mm (0.2 in). The body is dark reddish brown (teneral) to black and shining. The central part of the pronotum is virtually impunctate. Males are without horns or protuberances on the head or pronotum, but have two transverse ridges on the head and one on the pronotum. There are two Florida subspecies, *O. polyphemi polyphemi* in peninsular Florida east to the Apalachicola River, and *O. polyphemi sparsisetosus*, found west of the Apalachicola. A published description is found in Woodruff (1973).

RANGE: This beetle's range coincides with that of the gopher tortoise, from southeastern South Carolina, south to Florida, and west to southern Alabama and Mississippi.

HABITAT: It occurs in sandy uplands where gopher tortoises occur.

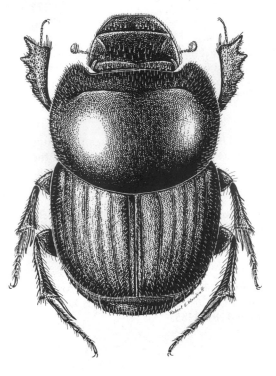

Gopher Tortoise On-
thophagus, *Ontho-
phagus polyphemi*
(courtesy of Robert
E. Woodruff).

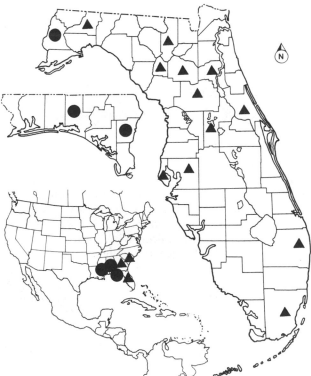

Distribution of the
gopher tortoise on-
thophagus, *Ontho-
phagus polyphemi*
(triangles), *O. p.
sparsiseosus*
(circles).

LIFE HISTORY AND ECOLOGY: An obligate commensal of gopher tortoises, it feeds on dung in the burrow (Hubbard 1894). Adults can sometimes be found at the burrow entrance.

BASIS FOR STATUS CLASSIFICATION: This species shares the status of its host.

RECOMMENDATIONS: The future of this species depends completely upon efforts to save its host. Gopher tortoises relocated to areas lacking previous occupants will probably fail to obtain their community of obligate commensals.

PREPARED BY: Robert E. Woodruff, Florida State Collection of Arthropods, P.O. Box 147100, Gainesville, FL 32614-7100, and Mark Deyrup, Archbold Biological Station, Lake Placid, FL 33852.

FAMILY SCARABAEIDAE

Threatened

Gopher Tortoise Aphodius

Aphodius troglodytes Hubbard

DESCRIPTION: This small beetle (length 3-4 mm [0.1 in]) has a shiny, pale yellow-brown body. Its head is without tubercles; the head and pronotum have scattered minute punctures, without coarse punctures; the first segment of posterior tarsi is longer than the long tibial spur. Published descriptions are found in Woodruff (1973) and Jerath (1960) (larval description).

RANGE: This gopher tortoise commensal is known from Florida, South Carolina, and Mississippi (Lago 1991).

HABITAT: It occurs in sandy uplands where gopher tortoises occur.

LIFE HISTORY AND ECOLOGY: An obligate commensal of gopher tortoises, it feeds on dung in the burrow (Hubbard 1894).

SPECIALIZED OR UNIQUE CHARACTERISTICS: This beetle shows adaptations for cave life, including reduced eyes, pale, translucent integument, elongate tarsi, and long tactile setae.

BASIS FOR STATUS CLASSIFICATION: This species shares the status of its host.

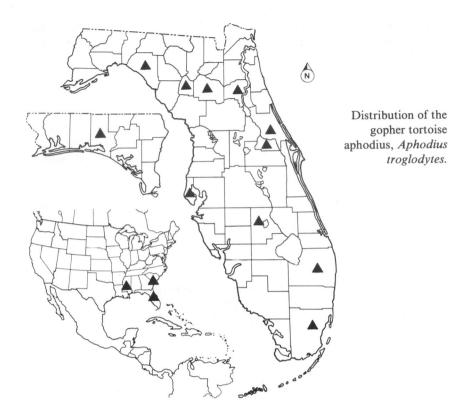

Distribution of the
gopher tortoise
aphodius, *Aphodius
troglodytes.*

RECOMMENDATIONS: The future of this species depends completely upon efforts to save its host. Gopher tortoises relocated to areas lacking previous occupants will probably fail to obtain their community of obligate commensals.

PREPARED BY: Robert E. Woodruff, Florida State Collection of Arthropods, P.O. Box 147100, Gainesville, FL 32614–7100, and Mark Deyrup, Archbold Biological Station, Lake Placid, FL 33852.

FAMILY SCARABAEIDAE

Threatened

Caracara Trox

Trox howelli Howden and Vaurie

DESCRIPTION: The caracara trox is a grayish black species with rows of elongate tubercles on the elytra. The legs, head, and antennae can be re-

Distribution of the
caracara trox,
Trox howelli.

tracted and folded against the body. Published description: Howden and Vaurie 1957. The antennae are short with a rounded club. Genitalic features are the most reliable features for identification of most small species of *Trox*.

RANGE: This beetle is known from Florida and Texas (one from each).

HABITAT: It is found in prairies with scattered pines and cabbage palmettoes.

LIFE HISTORY AND ECOLOGY: In Florida, this species is known only from a nest of Audubon's caracara (*Caracara cheriway auduboni*). There is a possibility that this species also might live in nests of some other large raptor. *Trox* beetles are among the last insects found in the successional stages of carrion on which the birds feed. The elytra and pronotum of these beetles are irregularly roughened and often encrusted with dirt. When they are alarmed they feign death and are likely to go unobserved. This may explain why only a few specimens of the caracara scarab have been found.

BASIS FOR STATUS CLASSIFICATION: Since the caracara is threatened in Florida, its associated beetle should share this status. Even if the beetle is eventually found in the nests of other large raptors, it is a rare species and should be protected.

RECOMMENDATIONS: It is necessary to preserve the host bird to protect this beetle.

PREPARED BY: Robert E. Woodruff, Florida State Collection of Arthropods, P.O. Box 147100, Gainesville, FL 32614–7100, and Mark Deyrup, Archbold Biological Station, Lake Placid, FL 33852.

FAMILY SCARABAEIDAE

Rare

Havana Ataenius

Ataenius havanensis Balthasar

DESCRIPTION: The head, pronotum, and elytra of this beetle are completely covered with an opaque grayish coating. The elytral intervals are weakly carinate; the elytral setae are short, golden, straight, truncate, not enlarged at tip; the pronotal punctures are very coarse, coalescing in places, never with bare areas between punctures. Published descriptions are found in Woodruff (1973) and Cartwright (1974).

RANGE: This beetle is known from the West Indies, Florida Keys (Stock Island), and Dry Tortugas (Garden Key).

HABITAT: Specimens were taken from debris on the beach and at lights.

LIFE HISTORY AND ECOLOGY: Unknown.

BASIS FOR STATUS CLASSIFICATION: The distribution of this beetle suggests that it is a West Indian species associated with beach debris, with an outlier population in the Dry Tortugas and southern keys. Peck and Howden (1985) believe this species dispersed naturally to Florida. It was listed as threatened in the 1982 edition of this book.

RECOMMENDATIONS: Preserve natural beach areas in the Dry Tortugas and southern keys.

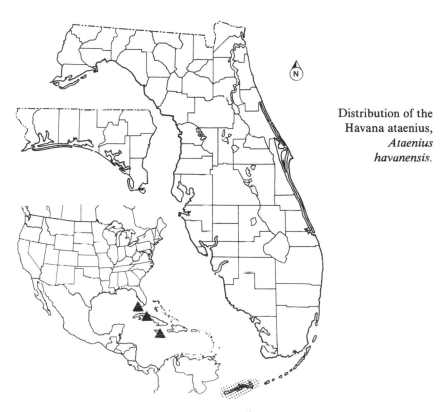

Distribution of the
Havana ataenius,
*Ataenius
havanensis.*

PREPARED BY: Robert E. Woodruff, Florida State Collection of Arthropods, P.O. Box 147100, Gainesville, FL 32614-7100, and Mark Deyrup, Archbold Biological Station, Lake Placid, FL 33852.

FAMILY SCARABAEIDAE

Rare

Panhandle Beach Scarab

Polylamina pubescens (Cartwright)

DESCRIPTION: This species is about 19 mm (0.7 in) long. The background color is brown, obscured by a dense covering of long yellowish brown hair. This species might be mistaken for an unusually small, very hairy *Phyllophaga*, but it (along with *Polyphylla* spp.) has a distinctive antennal club with seven elongate plates, a feature that should be easily visible in the field with a 10X hand lens. (*Phyllophaga* have only three plates in the antennal club.) There is no similar scarab known from its range.

RANGE: It is known from St. Andrews State Park and Sunnyside (Bay County) and from Niceville and Fort Walton Beach (Okaloosa County).

HABITAT: This beetle occurs in dune areas of beaches.

LIFE HISTORY AND ECOLOGY: Adults are diurnal; nothing else is known about this species.

SPECIALIZED OR UNIQUE CHARACTERISTICS: The dense hair is characteristic of scarabs that burrow extensively in loose sand.

BASIS FOR STATUS CLASSIFICATION: There is every reason to believe that this species is restricted to a habitat that occurs in a relatively small area. This beetle was listed as threatened in the FCREPA 1982 edition. There is one known protected population at St. Andrews State Park.

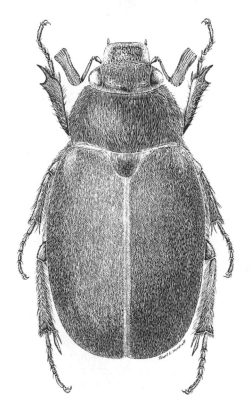

Panhandle Beach Scarab, *Polylamina pubescens* (courtesy of Robert E. Woodruff).

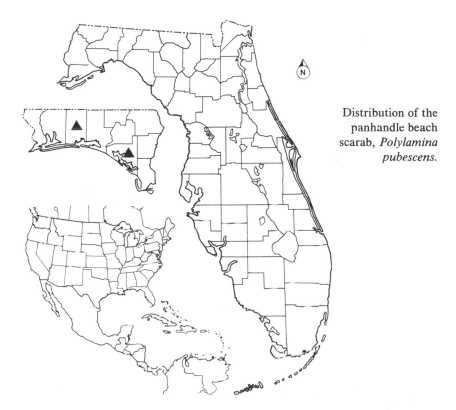

Distribution of the
panhandle beach
scarab, *Polylamina
pubescens.*

RECOMMENDATIONS: Preserve sand dune areas along the central panhandle coast. Research is needed to identify more specific ecological requirements of this beetle.

PREPARED BY: Robert E. Woodruff, Florida State Collection of Arthropods, P.O. Box 147100, Gainesville, FL 32614–7100, and Mark Deyrup,
Archbold Biological Station, Lake Placid, FL 33852.

FAMILY SCARABAEIDAE

Rare

Keys Green June Beetle

Cotinis new sp.

DESCRIPTION: Length about 20 mm, this beetle has elytra somewhat flattened; the clypeus has a horn-like process on the apical margin; it is brilliant

metallic green, with red reflections. There are no similar species within its range. This species remains undescribed.

RANGE: This June beetle is known from Islamorada in the Florida Keys.

HABITAT: It occurs in open areas near hardwood hammocks.

LIFE HISTORY AND ECOLOGY: Larvae feed on grass roots and organic matter in the soil, while adults feed on flowers and fermenting fruits.

BASIS FOR STATUS CLASSIFICATION: This conspicuous species is apparently endemic to Islamorada in the Florida Keys and is likely to be adversely affected by continuing development. It may now be extinct, since none have been collected in several years. It was listed as threatened in the first edition of this book.

RECOMMENDATIONS: Preserve natural habitats on Islamorada.

PREPARED BY: Robert E. Woodruff, Florida State Collection of Arthropods, P.O. Box 147100, Gainesville, FL 32614–7100, and Mark Deyrup, Archbold Biological Station, Lake Placid, FL 33852.

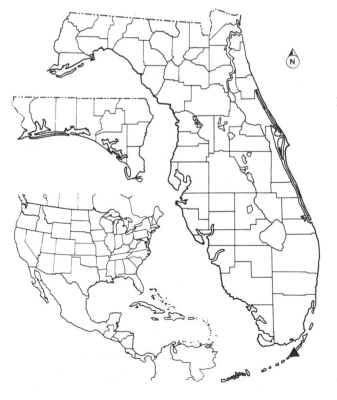

Distribution of the Keys green June beetle, *Cotinis* sp.

Rare

Ocala Deep-Digger Scarab

Peltotrupes youngi Howden

DESCRIPTION: Length 15–23 mm (0.6–0.9 in), this oval beetle is black with a green sheen. It has functional wings; sutural striae near the scutellum are vaguely indicated, the other striae weakly impressed; the anterior tibia of the male has outer apex elongate and is turned inward nearly at a right angle. The large size, evenly oval outline, and shiny black coloration with a green sheen are good characters for identifying this species in the field. The very similar species *P. profundus*, discussed here, has a blue elytral sheen and does not occur in the same area as *P. youngi*. Published descriptions are found in Woodruff (1973) and Howden (1952) (larva).

Distribution of the Ocala deepdigger scarab, *Peltotrupes youngi.*

RANGE: This beetle is found in southern Putnam and eastern Marion counties.

HABITAT: It occurs in scrub and sandhill habitats with deep, well-drained sand.

LIFE HISTORY AND ECOLOGY: This species makes vertical burrows, averaging about 2 m (6.8 ft) deep, creating an impressive mound of sand in the process. At the bottom of this shaft, there is a lateral passage about 12 cm (5 in) long loosely packed with surface litter. The larvae presumably consume this material. Adults may be collected in traps baited with fermenting syrups such as molasses and malt.

SPECIALIZED OR UNIQUE CHARACTERISTICS: The remarkable burrows of this species are often abundant in scrub and sandhill habitats and may be of considerable ecological importance in mixing soil layers and introducing organic matter deep in the sand (Kalisz and Stone 1984).

BASIS FOR STATUS CLASSIFICATION: This species has a restricted distribution. It is dependent on deep sand uplands with natural vegetation; such habitats are being rapidly degraded throughout the state. Some of this species' habitat is in the Ocala National Forest, and is therefore protected where sandhill and scrub habitats are preserved.

RECOMMENDATIONS: Preserve in their natural state scrub and sandhill habitats in the area where this species occurs.

PREPARED BY: Robert E. Woodruff, Florida State Collection of Arthropods, P.O. Box 147100, Gainesville, FL 32614-7100, and Mark Deyrup, Archbold Biological Station, Lake Placid, FL 33852.

FAMILY SCARABAEIDAE

Rare

Cartwright's Mycotrupes
Mycotrupes cartwrighti Olson and Hubbell

DESCRIPTION: About 15 mm (0.6 in) long, this scarab is oval, convex, and not shiny; wing covers are fused, the hind wings are absent; the pronotum has an anterior median tubercle; the elytral striae are almost absent; almost all granules of the elytral disc are distinct, rarely confluent. The round shape and fused wing covers are distinctive characters of the genus. The three species of *Mycotrupes* in Florida have separate geographic ranges. A published description is found in Woodruff (1973).

RANGE: It occurs in southern Georgia and in Leon, Jefferson, and Duval counties in Florida.

HABITAT: This beetle is known from sandhill and mixed hardwood-pine areas on sandy soil.

LIFE HISTORY AND ECOLOGY: The flightless adult constructs burrows more than a meter deep; the larval foods are unknown. Adults have been collected in large numbers in malt traps.

BASIS FOR STATUS CLASSIFICATION: In Florida, this species appears to be restricted to uplands in two areas along the northern border. It requires natural habitat on sandy uplands. There is a protected population at Tall Timbers Research Station in Leon County.

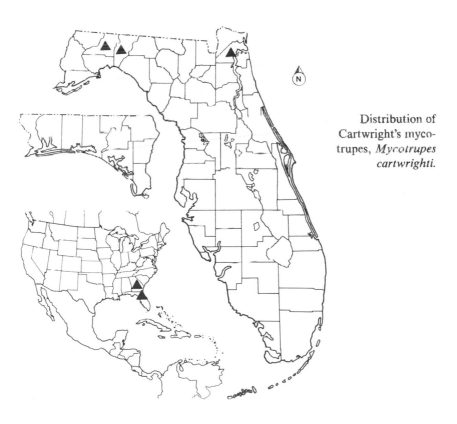

Distribution of Cartwright's mycotrupes, *Mycotrupes cartwrighti.*

RECOMMENDATIONS: Preserve upland habitats where this species occurs. Like other wingless scarabs, this species occurs in populations that may have been isolated for a long time and may show considerable divergence.

PREPARED BY: Robert E. Woodruff, Florida State Collection of Arthropods, P.O. Box 147100, Gainesville, FL 32614-7100, and Mark Deyrup, Archbold Biological Station, Lake Placid, FL 33852.

FAMILY SCARABAEIDAE

Rare

North Peninsular Mycotrupes

Mycotrupes gaigei Olson and Hubbell

DESCRIPTION: About 11 mm (0.5 in) long, this beetle is oval, convex, and not shiny. Its wing covers are fused, and hind wings absent; the elytra each have two double striae faintly indicated; the pronotum has an anterior median tubercle; the granules of elytral disc are mostly confluent. The round shape and fused wing covers are distinctive characters of the genus. The three species of *Mycotrupes* in Florida have separate geographic ranges. Published descriptions are found in Woodruff (1973) and Howden (1954) (larva).

RANGE: This beetle is found in north-central Florida in Alachua, Gilchrist, Dixie, Levy, Marion, Columbia, Lafayette, Suwannee, and Seminole counties.

HABITAT: It occurs in sandhill and scrub areas.

LIFE HISTORY AND ECOLOGY: Adults construct burrows more than a meter deep, marked by conspicuous "push-ups" of sand. The burrow appears to have several branches at different depths. Adults stridulate when handled and are attracted to fermenting molasses and malt traps. The larval food is unknown.

BASIS FOR STATUS CLASSIFICATION: This species is restricted to uplands and occurs only in Florida, where it is restricted to a relatively small area. Within this area, populations may have been isolated for a long time, as there are noticeable differences between populations. Further research may show that there is more than one species included under the name *M. gaigei*.

RECOMMENDATIONS: Further research is needed to determine whether there is one rare species or more than one, as well as to determine more spe-

North Peninsula
Mycotrupes, *Myco-
trupes gaigei* (cour-
tesy of Robert E.
Woodruff).

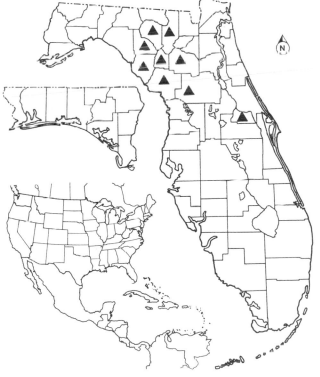

Distribution of the
north peninsular
mycotrupes, *Myco-
trupes gaigei.*

cific habitat requirement. Preservation of natural upland habitat in the range of *M. gaigei* with special reference to isolated and peripheral populations is essential for its preservation.

PREPARED BY: Robert E. Woodruff, Florida State Collection of Arthropods, P.O. Box 147100, Gainesville, FL 32614-7100, and Mark Deyrup, Archbold Biological Station, Lake Placid, FL 33852.

FAMILY SCARABAEIDAE

Rare

Uneasy June Beetle
Phyllophaga anxia (LeConte)

DESCRIPTION: This June beetle is dark brown and hairless. Similar to several other Florida species of *Phyllophaga*, it can be distinguished by genitalic characters. Published descriptions of adult and larva and identification keys to Florida *Phyllophaga* are provided by Woodruff and Beck (1989).

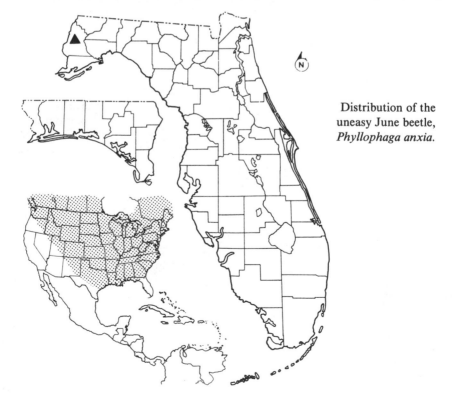

Distribution of the uneasy June beetle, *Phyllophaga anxia.*

RANGE: This beetle occurs in almost every state in the U.S. and the southern provinces of Canada. In Florida, it is known only from Liberty County.

HABITAT: It is found usually in lowland forests.

LIFE HISTORY AND ECOLOGY: Larvae feed on roots in the ground; adults consume leaves of a great variety of plants and may cause some economic damage. This species has been extensively studied in the northern United States, but has not been studied in Florida, where it was only recently discovered.

BASIS FOR STATUS CLASSIFICATION: This northern species has a small range extension into the Apalachicola River area, where many other northern species of plants and animals also occur. There is a protected population at Torreya State Park.

RECOMMENDATIONS: Preserve enclaves of northern habitats along the Apalachicola River.

PREPARED BY: Robert E. Woodruff, Florida State Collection of Arthropods, P.O. Box 147100, Gainesville, FL 32614-7100, and Mark Deyrup, Archbold Biological Station, Lake Placid, FL 33852.

FAMILY SCARABAEIDAE

Rare

Elizoria June Beetle

Phyllophaga elizoria Saylor

DESCRIPTION: This brown beetle (14.4–17.3 mm [0.6–0.7 in]) is densely covered with long fine hairs. It is distinguished from the similar species *P. okeechobea* and *P. skelleyi* by genitalic characters. They are the only known densely hairy June beetles that are sympatric in Florida scrub. All are considered rare. A published description of this species, and keys for identification of Florida *Phyllophaga*, are provided by Woodruff and Beck (1989).

RANGE: This June beetle is confined to Highlands, Polk, Okeechobee, Palm Beach, and Brevard counties.

HABITAT: It occurs in sand pine scrub.

LIFE HISTORY AND ECOLOGY: Adults emerge from February through early April and, unlike the similar *P. okeechobea*, are attracted to lights.

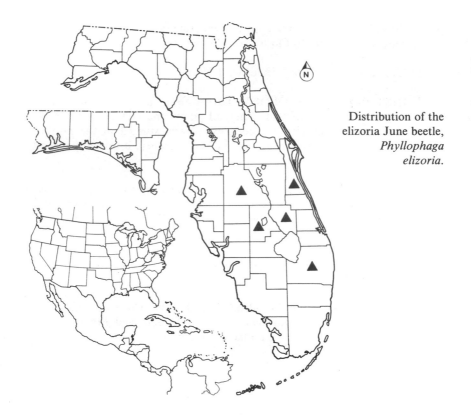

Distribution of the
elizoria June beetle,
Phyllophaga
elizoria.

Larval host and habits are unknown, but like other *Phyllophaga*, the larva probably feeds on roots.

SPECIALIZED OR UNIQUE CHARACTERISTICS: The dense covering of long hair is a characteristic of a number of scarabs of sand pine scrub and might assist the beetles in moving through loose sand.

BASIS FOR STATUS CLASSIFICATION: This species is an endemic of Florida's deep sand ridges in the southern half of the state. These ridges are highly localized and their native fauna and flora mostly destroyed by agricultural and residential development. A large population seems to be thriving at the Archbold Biological Station, and there may be other protected populations in Highlands and Polk counties.

RECOMMENDATIONS: Preserve scrub habitats in southern Florida; survey for remaining populations.

PREPARED BY: Robert E. Woodruff, Florida State Collection of Arthropods, P.O. Box 147100, Gainesville, FL 32614-7100, and Mark Deyrup, Archbold Biological Station, Lake Placid, FL 33852.

Rare

Elongate June Beetle

Phyllophaga elongata (Linell)

DESCRIPTION: About 14 mm (0.6 in) long, this pale brown beetle is covered with brown, fine pubescence. The antennae are 10-segmented, and there is a feeble sub-basal tooth of the tarsal claw. It is distinguished from the similar *Phyllophaga panorpa*, also a rare species, by genitalic characters. A published description of this species, and keys for identification of Florida *Phyllophaga*, are provided by Woodruff and Beck (1989).

RANGE: This beetle is confined to Florida and is widely distributed in the appropriate habitat.

HABITAT: Almost all specimens have been collected in sand pine scrub.

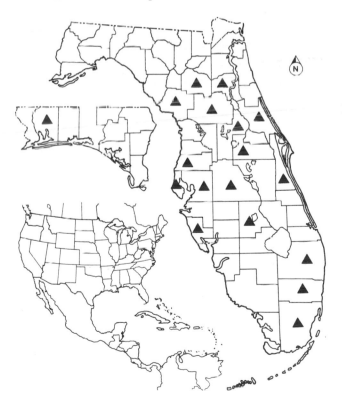

Distribution of the elongate June beetle, *Phyllophaga elongata*.

LIFE HISTORY AND ECOLOGY: Adults are collected in flight traps and light traps from April to September. Larval host and habits are unknown, but the larvae undoubtedly feed on roots.

BASIS FOR STATUS CLASSIFICATION: Although this species appears to be widely distributed, it is restricted to a rare and vanishing habitat; a number of the older collection records are probably from sites where this species no longer exists. There is a protected population at Archbold Biological Station, and the Ocala National Forest population might also be considered protected.

RECOMMENDATIONS: Preserve Florida scrub habitats.

PREPARED BY: Robert E. Woodruff, Florida State Collection of Arthropods, P.O. Box 147100, Gainesville, FL 32614-7100, and Mark Deyrup, Archbold Biological Station, Lake Placid, FL 33852.

FAMILY SCARABAEIDAE

Rare

Forbes' June Beetle

Phyllophaga forbesi Glasgow

DESCRIPTION: This dorsally hairless beetle, 14.3–17.9 mm (0.6–0.7 in) in length, is pale reddish brown. Its clypeus is broadly emarginate. It is distinguished from similar species by genitalic characters. A published description of this species, and keys for identification of Florida *Phyllophaga*, are provided by Woodruff and Beck (1989).

RANGE: This June beetle is known from the midwestern United States. In Florida, it is found in Escambia and Santa Rosa counties.

HABITAT: It is found in mesic woodlands.

LIFE HISTORY AND ECOLOGY: Adults emerge from April through September (latter record from Florida) and feed on a wide variety of broadleaf plants. Larval host and habits are unknown.

BASIS FOR STATUS CLASSIFICATION: In Florida this species appears to be at the southernmost extreme of its range. Only two specimens have been collected in the state, and populations are probably small and localized. No protected populations are known in Florida.

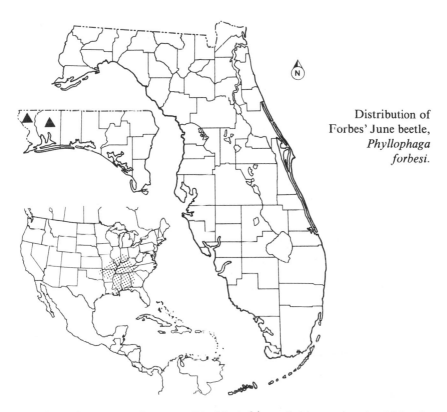

Distribution of
Forbes' June beetle,
*Phyllophaga
forbesi.*

RECOMMENDATIONS: The Florida habitat of this species should be determined before consideration of conservation measures.

PREPARED BY: Robert E. Woodruff, Florida State Collection of Arthropods, P.O. Box 147100, Gainesville, FL 32614–7100, and Mark Deyrup, Archbold Biological Station, Lake Placid, FL 33852.

FAMILY SCARABAEIDAE

Rare

Horn's June Beetle
Phyllophaga hornii Smith

DESCRIPTION: This dark brown beetle, 19–23 mm (0.7–0.9 in), is dorsally hairless. Its large size, dark color, and hairlessness make it similar to two other species, *P. perlonga* and *P. profunda*, both of which are discussed in this volume. Specific identification is based on the male genitalia. A published description of this species, and keys for identification of Florida *Phyllophaga*, are provided by Woodruff and Beck (1989).

RANGE: This June beetle is widely distributed in the Northeast and Midwest and absent from most of the Southeast. There is a southern range extension into the central Florida panhandle in Liberty, Gadsden, and Leon counties.

HABITAT: It inhabits hardwood forests.

LIFE HISTORY AND ECOLOGY: Adults appear from mid-March to late June. Larval host and habits are unknown.

BASIS FOR STATUS CLASSIFICATION: This species reaches the southern extreme of its range in extreme north Florida, where it joins a large number of other northern relicts in the Apalachicola River drainage. A protected population occurs at Torreya State Park.

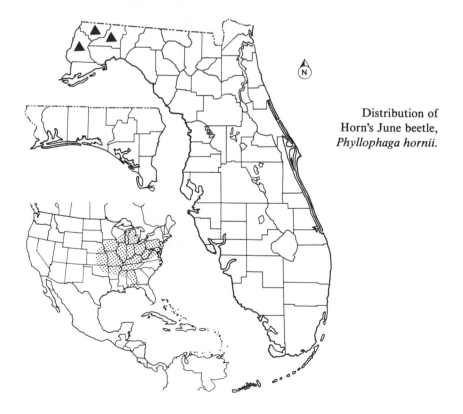

Distribution of Horn's June beetle, *Phyllophaga hornii.*

RECOMMENDATIONS: Preserve remnant northern forest refuges in the Apalachicola drainage.

PREPARED BY: Robert E. Woodruff, Florida State Collection of Arthropods, P.O. Box 147100, Gainesville, FL 32614-7100, and Mark Deyrup, Archbold Biological Station, Lake Placid, FL 33852.

FAMILY SCARABAEIDAE

Rare

Diurnal Scrub June Beetle
Phyllophaga okeechobea Robinson

DESCRIPTION: This beetle, 13-16 mm (0.5-0.6 in), is densely pubescent. Its clypeus is deeply emarginate and densely punctate. It is best distinguished from the two other hairy Florida species, *P. elizoria* and *P. skellyi* by genitalic characters, though its distribution does not overlap with the latter species. All three species are considered rare. A published description of this species, and keys for identification of Florida *Phyllophaga*, are provided by Woodruff and Beck (1989).

RANGE: This beetle is confined to Florida. The type specimen is from Okeechobee; all other specimens are from the Lake Wales Ridge in Highlands, Polk, and Lake counties.

HABITAT: It inhabits sand pine scrub.

LIFE HISTORY AND ECOLOGY: Adults are active in March and April and are most commonly collected on citrus. Larval host and habits are unknown.

SPECIALIZED OR UNIQUE CHARACTERISTICS: Unlike other *Phyllophaga*, this species appears to be active during the day. The dense covering of hair is characteristic of a number of scarabs living in sand pine scrub and might be an adaptation associated with burrowing through loose sand.

BASIS FOR STATUS CLASSIFICATION: This species is probably confined to the Lake Wales Ridge (there is virtually no remaining scrub in the Okeechobee area), a rapidly changing area with a large number of endemic species. There is a protected population on the Archbold Biological Station, and it may occur in the Lake Arbuckle State Forest, as there are old records from Avon Park.

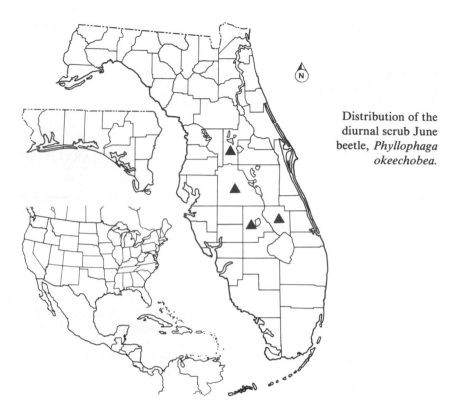

Distribution of the
diurnal scrub June
beetle, *Phyllophaga
okeechobea.*

RECOMMENDATIONS: Preserve remaining scrub habitats on the Lake
Wales Ridge.

PREPARED BY: Robert E. Woodruff, Florida State Collection of Arthropods, P.O. Box 147100, Gainesville, FL 32614–7100, and Mark Deyrup,
Archbold Biological Station, Lake Placid, FL 33852.

FAMILY SCARABAEIDAE

Rare

Oval June Beetle
Phyllophaga ovalis Cartwright

DESCRIPTION: This beetle (length 18.4–21.6 mm [0.6–0.8 in]) is oblong
(the elytra are not at all parallel-sided in dorsal view as in many other spe-

cies); it is highly convex, hairless, and shiny. It is distinguished from similar species by genitalic characters. A published description of this species, and keys for identification of Florida *Phyllophaga*, are provided by Woodruff and Beck (1989).

RANGE: This beetle is confined to Florida, in Santa Rosa, Okaloosa, and Walton counties.

HABITAT: It occurs in sandhill habitats.

LIFE HISTORY AND ECOLOGY: Adults emerge in April and feed on young oak leaves, especially *Quercus laevis*. Larval host and habits are unknown.

BASIS FOR STATUS CLASSIFICATION: This species, like several other insects, appears to be restricted to uplands in a small area of the western panhandle. There are no known protected populations. It probably occurs on the Eglin Air Force Base, and should benefit from the program of restoration of natural areas.

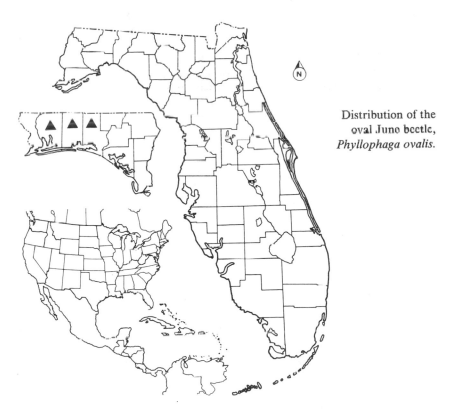

Distribution of the oval Juno beetle, *Phyllophaga ovalis*.

RECOMMENDATIONS: The habits and distribution of this species need further study. Sandhill areas in the western panhandle should be preserved in their natural state.

PREPARED BY: Robert E. Woodruff, Florida State Collection of Arthropods, P.O. Box 147100, Gainesville, FL 32614–7100, and Mark Deyrup, Archbold Biological Station, Lake Placid, FL 33852.

FAMILY SCARABAEIDAE

Rare

Southern Lake Wales Ridge June Beetle

Phyllophaga panorpa Sanderson

DESCRIPTION: About 16–19 mm (0.6–0.7 in) in length, this beetle is elongate and cylindrical, covered with short, closely spaced, semi-erect yellowish hairs; it is light reddish brown. This species is very similar to *Phyllophaga elongata*, also a rare species, and genitalic characters are used for positive identification. A published description of this species, and keys for identification of Florida *Phyllophaga*, are provided by Woodruff and Beck (1989).

RANGE: This species is confined to Florida where it occurs on the Lake Wales Ridge in Highlands and southern Polk counties.

HABITAT: It occurs probably in sand pine scrub.

LIFE HISTORY AND ECOLOGY: Adults have been collected at blacklights from early May to early October. Larval host and habits are unknown, but the larvae undoubtedly feed on roots.

BASIS FOR STATUS CLASSIFICATION: This species appears to be restricted to the dwindling natural habitats of the Lake Wales Ridge, a geographic feature rich in endemics. There is a protected population at the Archbold Biological Station.

RECOMMENDATIONS: Preserve the remaining sand pine scrub on the Lake Wales Ridge.

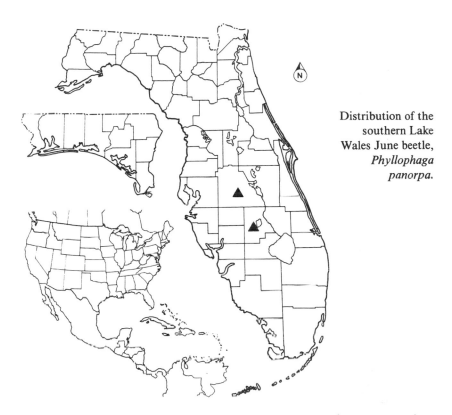

Distribution of the southern Lake Wales June beetle, *Phyllophaga panorpa.*

PREPARED BY: Robert E. Woodruff, Florida State Collection of Arthropods, P.O. Box 147100, Gainesville, FL 32614-7100, and Mark Deyrup, Archbold Biological Station, Lake Placid, FL 33852.

FAMILY SCARABAEIDAE

Rare

Long June Beetle
Phyllophaga perlonga Davis

DESCRIPTION: Unusually large for Florida species (20.8–24.7 mm long [0.8–1.0 in]), this June beetle has an elongate and parallel body. The dorsum is not noticeably convex and is hairless. The pronotum is notably more shining than the elytra; the pygidium is highly convex. It is similar to *P. pro-*

funda and *P. hornii*, both of which are discussed in this volume. The genitalic characters are diagnostic. A published description of this species, and keys for identification of Florida *Phyllophaga*, are provided by Woodruff and Beck (1989).

RANGE: This beetle is known from Alabama, Arkansas, Georgia, Kentucky, Mississippi, Louisiana, Missouri, Tennessee. In Florida, it is known only from Gadsden and Liberty counties near the Apalachicola River.

HABITAT: It inhabits hardwood bottomlands.

LIFE HISTORY AND ECOLOGY: Adults are active in spring and feed on a variety of broadleaf trees. Larval host and habits are unknown.

BASIS FOR STATUS CLASSIFICATION: It is highly probable that this is another species whose southernmost range extension is a small area along the Apalachicola River. There is a protected population at Torreya State Park.

RECOMMENDATIONS: Preserve the remnant northern forest refuges along the Apalachicola River.

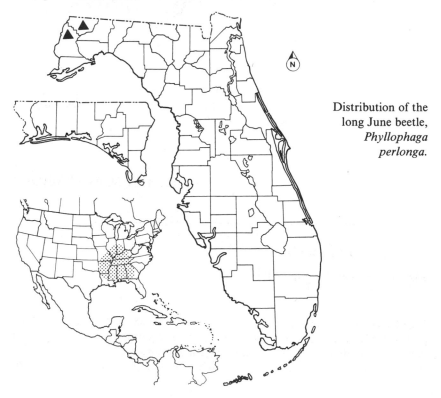

Distribution of the long June beetle, *Phyllophaga perlonga.*

PREPARED BY: Robert E. Woodruff, Florida State Collection of Arthropods, P.O. Box 147100, Gainesville, FL 32614-7100, and Mark Deyrup, Archbold Biological Station, Lake Placid, FL 33852.

FAMILY SCARABAEIDAE

Rare

Skelley's June Beetle
Phyllophaga skelleyi Woodruff and Beck

DESCRIPTION: This brown beetle is densely covered with long fine hairs; length 15-19.4 mm (0.6-0.7 in). It is distinguished from a similar species, the sympatric *P. elizoria*, by genitalic characters. A published description of this species, and keys for identification of Florida *Phyllophaga*, are provided by Woodruff and Beck (1989).

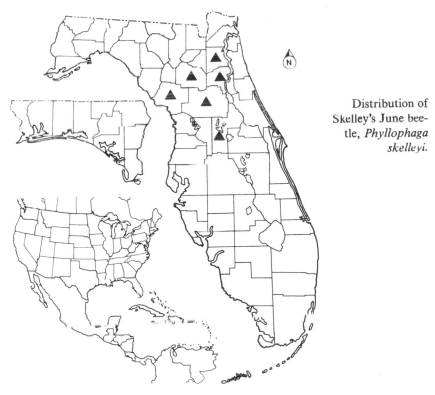

Distribution of Skelley's June beetle, *Phyllophaga skelleyi*.

RANGE: This beetle is confined to Florida, in Putnam, Alachua, Clay, Lake, Levy, and Marion counties.

HABITAT: It occurs in sandhills with *Quercus laevis*.

LIFE HISTORY AND ECOLOGY: Adults appear from March to May and may be found on *Quercus laevis*. Larval host and habits are unknown.

SPECIALIZED OR UNIQUE CHARACTERISTICS: The dense covering of long hair is a characteristic of a number of scarabs of sandhill and sand pine scrub, and might assist the beetles in moving through loose sand.

BASIS FOR STATUS CLASSIFICATION: This Florida endemic occurs in a relatively small area of the state in upland sites that are easily developed and require management to be kept in a natural state. It is protected in the Ocala National Forest. It also probably occurs on the Ordway Preserve managed by the University of Florida.

RECOMMENDATIONS: It is necessary to preserve and manage turkey oak sandhill sites.

PREPARED BY: Robert E. Woodruff, Florida State Collection of Arthropods, P.O. Box 147100, Gainesville, FL 32614-7100, and Mark Deyrup, Archbold Biological Station, Lake Placid, FL 33852.

FAMILY SCARABAEIDAE

Rare

Spiny Burrowing June Beetle

Gronocarus multispinosus Howden

DESCRIPTION: This beetle has the clypeus semicircular, almost two-thirds as long as wide, the edges reflexed, otherwise flat with scattered punctures. The apex of the hind tibia is greatly expanded, with two large spurs and a series of about 20 stout acute spines. The length of the body is 12.5 mm (0.5 in). Females are flightless. A published description is found in Howden (1961).

RANGE: This burrowing June beetle is confined to Florida, in Walton and Calhoun counties, with a distinctive population (solid circle), possibly a new species, in Bay County.

Distribution of the
spiny burrowing
June beetle, *Grono-
carus multispinosus.*

HABITAT: It is found in sandhills with *Quercus laevis.*

LIFE HISTORY AND ECOLOGY: Adults have been collected from November through March. Larval host and habits are unknown.

SPECIALIZED OR UNIQUE CHARACTERISTICS: The lack of wings in the female is probably associated with extensive burrowing in sandy soil.

BASIS FOR STATUS CLASSIFICATION: The apparently narrow range of this species, its restriction to a specific habitat, and its limited mobility support its status as a rare species.

RECOMMENDATIONS: Further studies on its ecology and preservation of remnant habitat within its range are needed.

PREPARED BY: Robert E. Woodruff, Florida State Collection of Arthropods, P.O. Box 147100, Gainesville, FL 32614-7100, and Mark Deyrup, Archbold Biological Station, Lake Placid, FL 33852.

Rare

Panhandle Beach Anomala

Anomala flavipennis okaloosensis Potts

DESCRIPTION: This beetle has a brownish-black pronotum and yellowish-brown elytra. The elytral punctures are not colored or are very lightly colored; the clypeus is thickened apically, and not strongly reflexed; the pronotum is clearly longer than broad, widest near middle or apically. The length is 9–11 mm (0.4–0.5 in). A published description is found in Potts (1977a).

RANGE: It is confined to Florida, known only from Santa Rosa and Okaloosa counties.

HABITAT: This beetle is associated with coastal dunes.

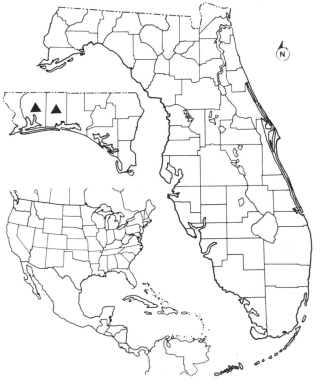

Distribution of the panhandle beach anomala, *Anomala flavipennis okaloosensis.*

LIFE HISTORY AND ECOLOGY: Adults were collected in May. Larval host and habits are unknown.

BASIS FOR STATUS CLASSIFICATION: This subspecies, which is defined primarily by color, appears to be isolated in the same habitat and region as the scarab *Polylamina pubescens*. Development along panhandle beaches could threaten this species. A population could easily occur in John Heasley State Park, as the type locality is in Destin.

RECOMMENDATIONS: Preserve sand dune areas on the central panhandle coast.

PREPARED BY: Robert E. Woodruff, Florida State Collection of Arthropods, P.O. Box 147100, Gainesville, FL 32614-7100, and Mark Deyrup, Archbold Biological Station, Lake Placid, FL 33852.

FAMILY SCARABAEIDAE

Rare

Scrub Anomala
Anomala eximia Potts

DESCRIPTION: This beetle has the pronotum blackish brown and the elytra yellowish with variable dark brown markings that may coalesce to cover most of the elytra; the clypeus is thickened apically, strongly reflexed; the protibiae lack an external tooth; length 6.5–7.5 mm (0.2–0.3 in). A published description is found in Potts 1976, and a key to species of the genus is found in Potts 1977b.

RANGE: This beetle is confined to Florida, known only from Highlands County.

HABITAT: It occurs in sand pine scrub.

LIFE HISTORY AND ECOLOGY: Adults fly in May and June. They are apparently diurnal and not attracted to lights, but are easily collected in Malaise traps. Larval host and habits are unknown.

BASIS FOR STATUS CLASSIFICATION: This species, like a number of other organisms, appears to be confined to scrub areas at the southern end of the Lake Wales Ridge. The scrubs of this region are rapidly vanishing. There is a protected population at the Archbold Biological Station.

Distribution of the
scrub anomala,
Anomala eximia.

RECOMMENDATIONS: Preserve remaining fragments of habitat on the
southern Lake Wales Ridge. There should be surveys for this species in scrub
areas north of Lake Placid.

PREPARED BY: Robert E. Woodruff, Florida State Collection of Arthropods, P.O. Box 147100, Gainesville, FL 32614-7100, and Mark Deyrup,
Archbold Biological Station, Lake Placid, FL 33852.

FAMILY SCARABAEIDAE

Rare

Pygmy Anomala
Anomala exigua (Schwarz)

DESCRIPTION: This beetle is very small for the genus (length 3.9-4.5 mm
[0.1-0.2 in]). The pronotum is pale brown or a central spot; the protibia is

lacking an external tooth. A published description is found in Schwarz (1878), and a key to species of *Anomala* is in Potts (1977b).

RANGE: This beetle is confined to Florida, known from Polk and Sumter counties.

HABITAT: Unknown.

LIFE HISTORY AND ECOLOGY: Unknown; one specimen was collected in late April.

BASIS FOR STATUS CLASSIFICATION: This distinctive species is known from only a few specimens, with only one specimen found in this century. Potts, the principal student of the genus *Anomala*, stated (1977a) that the species is "probably extinct." As nothing is known about the habits, habitat, or any method of finding this species, it seems premature to consider it extinct.

RECOMMENDATIONS: There should be an attempt to survey areas near known historical sites for this species in late April. If it is diurnally active, Malaise traps would increase the chance of survey success.

Distribution of the pygmy anomala, *Anomala exigua*.

PREPARED BY: Robert E. Woodruff, Florida State Collection of Arthropods, P.O. Box 147100, Gainesville, FL 32614-7100, and Mark Deyrup, Archbold Biological Station, Lake Placid, FL 33852.

FAMILY SCARABAEIDAE

Rare

Scrub Palmetto Scarab

Trigonopeltastes floridana (Casey)

DESCRIPTION: About 7 to 8 mm (0.3 in) in length, this beetle has its pronotum black with cream-colored edges and V-shaped central marking; the head is black; the elytra are usually chestnut with variable black patches and cream spots and dashes, the chestnut occasionally eclipsed by black; legs are red, long, and the hind femur almost reaches the apex of the abdomen; the hind tarsi are as long as the elytra. A published description is found in Woodruff (1960).

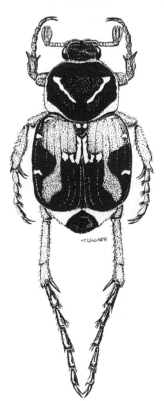

Scrub Palmetto Scarab, *Trigonopeltastes floridana* (illustration by James Wagner, courtesy of Robert E. Woodruff).

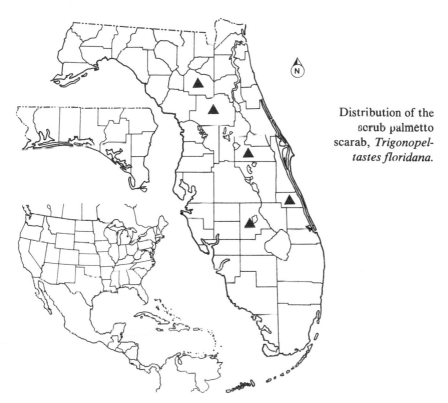

Distribution of the
scrub palmetto
scarab, *Trigonopel-
tastes floridana.*

RANGE: This scarab is confined to Florida, it is known from Highlands, Marion, Alachua, Orange, and Indian River counties.

HABITAT: It inhabits sand pine scrub, occasionally sandhill.

LIFE HISTORY AND ECOLOGY: Adults are usually found on flowers of scrub palmetto (*Sabal etonia*), less frequently on other flowers. The adult flight period is May and June. Larval host and habits are unknown.

BASIS FOR STATUS CLASSIFICATION: This species is almost entirely restricted to scrub habitats, and appears to be absent from some scrubs. Its habitat has been destroyed or reduced to remnants through much of its range. There are protected populations at the Archbold Biological Station, Ocala National Forest, and Tiger Creek Preserve (Nature Conservancy); it is also highly probable that there is a population at Arbuckle State Forest.

RECOMMENDATIONS: Preserve remaining scrub ridges in central and east coast areas of Florida.

PREPARED BY: Robert E. Woodruff, Florida State Collection of Arthropods, P.O. Box 147100, Gainesville, FL 32614-7100, and Mark Deyrup, Archbold Biological Station, Lake Placid, FL 33852.

Rare

Frost's Silky June Beetle

Serica frosti Dawson

DESCRIPTION: Frost's silky June beetle is light brown with an opalescent sheen. *Serica* species are small (about 8 mm), brown, long-legged scarabs that look much like miniature June beetles of the genus *Phyllophaga*. Unlike *Phyllophaga* and the small June beetles of the genus *Diplotaxis*, the elytra of *Serica* are evenly striate, usually dull with an opalescent sheen. Determination of species usually requires examination of the internal male genitalia. Length: 6.5–7 mm (0.2–0.3 in). A published description is found in Dawson (1967).

Distribution of Frost's silky June beetle, *Serica frosti.*

RANGE: This beetle is restricted to Florida, known only from the southern Lake Wales Ridge, Highlands County.

HABITAT: It probably occurs in sand pine scrub, where specimens have been collected in Malaise traps and at lights.

LIFE HISTORY AND ECOLOGY: Unknown. Adults fly from February through April.

BASIS FOR STATUS CLASSIFICATION: This species fits the pattern of a highly localized endemic, as it is abundant every year in one area, unknown from any other area. It is probably dependent on sand pine scrub, a habitat that supports a number of plants and animals restricted to the southern Lake Wales Ridge. There appears to be a large population on the Archbold Biological Station.

RECOMMENDATIONS: Conduct surveys for this species on the Lake Wales Ridge; preserve and manage the southern Lake Wales Ridge scrub areas.

PREPARED BY: Robert E. Woodruff, Florida State Collection of Arthropods, P.O. Box 147100, Gainesville, FL 32614-7100, and Mark Deyrup, Archbold Biological Station, Lake Placid, FL 33852.

FAMILY SCARABAEIDAE

Rare

Howden's Copris
Copris howdeni Matthews and Halffter

DESCRIPTION: The clypeus of this beetle has a median notch; the head is without a horn in either sex. The body is covered with coarse punctures. Body length is 13–15 mm (0.5–0.6 in). A published description of this species and a key to Florida *Copris* is provided by Woodruff (1973).

RANGE: This beetle is confined to Florida, known from Highlands, Osceola, Manatee, and Monroe (Big Pine Key) counties.

HABITAT: Unknown.

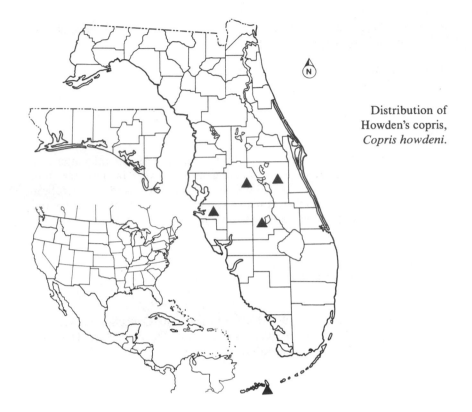

Distribution of
Howden's copris,
Copris howdeni.

LIFE HISTORY AND ECOLOGY: Like other members of its genus, this species must feed on dung, but its host animals are completely unknown.

BASIS FOR STATUS CLASSIFICATION: This is a particularly mysterious beetle, as it is widely distributed in the southern half of the peninsula, but almost never seen. There is nothing about the distribution to suggest a particular vertebrate host. There have been repeated unsuccessful attempts at all the collecting sites to obtain more specimens. The largest series of specimens by far is from Big Pine Key, as if that population had been in some way protected by its isolation.

RECOMMENDATIONS: Studies of the distribution and biology of this species are required before consideration of conservation methods.

PREPARED BY: Robert E. Woodruff, Florida State Collection of Arthropods, P.O. Box 147100, Gainesville, FL 32614-7100, and Mark Deyrup, Archbold Biological Station, Lake Placid, FL 33852.

FAMILY SCARABAEIDAE

Species of Special Concern

Small Pocket Gopher Scarab

Aphodius aegrotus Horn

DESCRIPTION: The dorsal surface of this beetle is shiny, hairless, and deep red-brown; the head is without tubercles, lightly punctate with fine punctures; the pronotum is finely punctate, with a group of coarse punctures on lateral third; the pronotum is without lateral marginal setae, the basal marginal line complete; the tarsal claws are narrow and extremely elongate for genus; the length of the body is about 4.4 mm (0.2 in). A published description of this species, and a key to Florida *Aphodius*, is provided by Woodruff (1973).

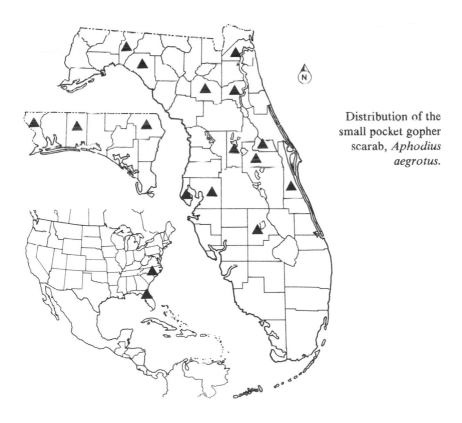

Distribution of the small pocket gopher scarab, *Aphodius aegrotus*.

RANGE: Type specimens are labelled North Carolina, although all other specimens are from northern and central Florida.

HABITAT: It occurs in sandy uplands, primarily sandhill, where its host occurs.

LIFE HISTORY AND ECOLOGY: This beetle occurs in burrow systems of pocket gophers (*Geomys pinetis*), where it feeds on dung. Adults are attracted to light.

SPECIALIZED OR UNIQUE CHARACTERISTICS: The unusually elongate claws are probably an adaptation associated with the peculiar habitat of this species.

BASIS FOR STATUS CLASSIFICATION: The decline of the host species through much of its range, including the extinction of one host subspecies (*G. pinetis goffi*), is a cause for concern. It is also possible that populations associated with different pocket gopher subspecies are themselves distinctive.

RECOMMENDATIONS: Monitor populations of the host, with particular attention to its local extirpation.

PREPARED BY: Robert E. Woodruff, Florida State Collection of Arthropods, P.O. Box 147100, Gainesville, FL 32614-7100, and Mark Deyrup, Archbold Biological Station, Lake Placid, FL 33852.

FAMILY SCARABAEIDAE

Species of Special Concern

Large Pocket Gopher Scarab
Aphodius laevigatus Haldemann

DESCRIPTION: One of largest (length 6.5-8 mm [0.2-0.3 in]) of Florida *Aphodius*, this species has its dorsal surface shiny, dark brown, and hairless; the head is transversely carinate, not tuberculate; most of the dorsal surface is impunctate or with minute punctures except for a few larger ones near anterior pronotal angles. A published description of this species, and a key to Florida *Aphodius*, is provided by Woodruff (1973).

RANGE: This scarab is known only from Florida, in the central part of the state.

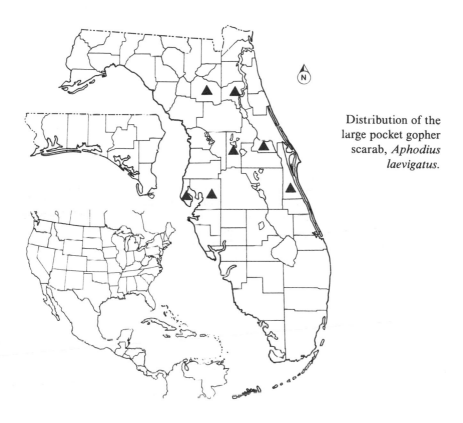

Distribution of the large pocket gopher scarab, *Aphodius laevigatus.*

HABITAT: It inhabits sandy uplands, primarily sandhill, where its host occurs.

LIFE HISTORY AND ECOLOGY: The species occurs in burrow systems of pocket gophers (*Geomys pinetis*) where it feeds on dung. Adults are attracted to light.

BASIS FOR STATUS CLASSIFICATION: A decline of this beetle would coincide with the loss of the host species through much of its range, including the extinction of one host subspecies (*G. pinetis goffi*). It is also possible that populations associated with different pocket gopher subspecies are themselves distinctive.

RECOMMENDATIONS: Monitor populations of the host, with particular attention to local extirpation.

PREPARED BY: Robert E. Woodruff, Florida State Collection of Arthropods, P.O. Box 147100, Gainesville, FL 32614-7100, and Mark Deyrup, Archbold Biological Station, Lake Placid, FL 33852.

Species of Special Concern

Broadspurred Pocket Gopher Scarab

Aphodius hubbelli Skelley and Woodruff.

DESCRIPTION: This species is similar to *A. haldemani*. Dorsal surface of this beetle is shiny, dark brown, and hairless; the pronotal sides are explanate; the anterior tibial spur of male is greatly expanded, several times as wide as the tarsi and longer than the first four tarsal segments combined; length 8 mm (0.3 in). See Skelley and Woodruff (1991) for published description of this species. A key to Florida *Aphodius* is provided by Woodruff (1973), in which *A. hubbelli* will key to *A. haldemani*.

RANGE: It is known from Alachua and Okaloosa counties, Florida, and southern Alabama.

Distribution of the broadspurred pocket gopher scarab, *Aphodius hubbelli.*

HABITAT: This species inhabits sandy uplands where its host occurs.

LIFE HISTORY AND ECOLOGY: This species lives in burrow systems of pocket gophers (*Geomys pinetis*), like the closely related *A. haldemani*.

BASIS FOR STATUS CLASSIFICATION: A decline of this beetle would coincide with the loss of the host species through much of its range, including the extinction of one host subspecies (*G. pinetis goffi*). It is also possible that populations associated with different pocket gopher subspecies are themselves distinctive.

RECOMMENDATIONS: Monitor populations of the host, with particular attention to local extirpation.

PREPARED BY: Robert E. Woodruff, Florida State Collection of Arthropods, P.O. Box 147100, Gainesville, FL 32614-7100, and Mark Deyrup, Archbold Biological Station, Lake Placid, FL 33852.

FAMILY SCARABAEIDAE

Species of Special Concern

Florida Deepdigger Scarab
Peltotrupes profundus Howden

DESCRIPTION: This beetle has an oval, black body with a purple or blue sheen; functional wings are present; sutural striae near scutellum are definitely impressed; the anterior tibia of the male has its outer apex elongate and turned inward nearly at a right angle. The length is 15-23 mm (0.6-0.9 in). The large size of this species, combined with its shiny black appearance and blue or purple sheen, distinguishes it from the other Florida species. A published description is found in Woodruff (1973).

RANGE: This scarab is restricted to peninsular Florida, from Martin and Highlands counties north to Columbia County.

HABITAT: It occurs in scrub and sandhill habitats with deep, well-drained sand.

LIFE HISTORY AND ECOLOGY: This species makes deep (to 10 ft) vertical burrows, which are marked by a large mound of sand. Larvae apparently feed on dead bits of vegetation packed into a lateral passage at the bottom of

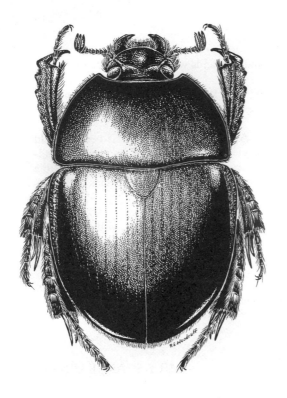

Florida Deep-Digger
Scarab, *Peltotrupes
profundus* (courtesy
of Robert E.
Woodruff).

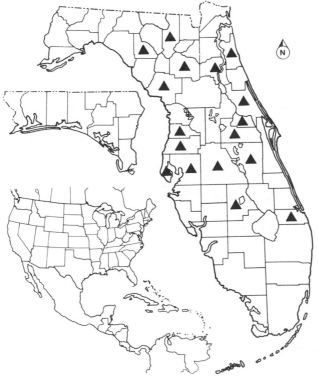

Distribution of the
Florida deepdigger
scarab, *Peltotrupes
profundus.*

the shaft. Adults emerge at dusk and may fly about; they may be attracted to light or to fermenting malt traps. During copulation, the unique tibial extension of the male fits into a flange on the anteriolateral rim of the female elytra.

SPECIALIZED OR UNIQUE CHARACTERISTICS: The remarkable burrows of this species, like those of *P. youngi*, are often abundant in scrub and sandhill habitats, and may be of considerable ecological importance in mixing soil layers and introducing organic matter deep into the sand (Kalisz and Stone 1984).

BASIS FOR STATUS CLASSIFICATION: This species is a Florida peninsular endemic, and a characteristic species of sandhill, a habitat that is reduced or vanishing over much of the peninsula. Populations from place to place show consistent variations, suggesting that populations have been cut off from each other on isolated sand ridge systems for a very long time. This scarab may be important in providing information on the biogeography of Florida, if isolated populations can survive long enough to be studied. Judging by the number of mounds, the Florida deep-digger scarab seems rather abundant in some areas. Populations may be less secure than they seem however, as the adults are large, rather clumsy insects that are likely to be favorite prey of vertebrates. The reproductive rate cannot be very great, considering that digging and stocking each burrow (which is usually occupied by a single larva) requires a tremendous effort. Most state parks and other preserves within the range of this species are likely to have a population if there is sufficient upland habitat.

RECOMMENDATIONS: Preserve sandhill and scrub habitats in areas where this species occurs. A study of the population dynamics of this species and its intraspecific variation would be appropriate.

PREPARED BY: Robert E. Woodruff, Florida State Collection of Arthropods, P.O. Box 147100, Gainesville, FL 32614-7100, and Mark Deyrup, Archbold Biological Station, Lake Placid, FL 33852.

FAMILY SCARABAEIDAE

Species of Special Concern

Florida Hypotrichia

Hypotrichia spissipes LeConte

DESCRIPTION: Males of this scarab are not shiny and are densely punctate. The thorax, scutellum, and head except for clypeus are covered with long pubescence, the elytra have short pubescence, the underside of the body is covered with long silky hairs. The female thorax is shining, almost impunctate, the elytra shining, with a few hairs and punctures; the underside of the body has dense fine hairs that are shorter than those of the male. Males are excellent fliers, while females are flightless. Length is about 12 mm (0.5 in).

RANGE: This beetle is restricted to Florida, occurring from southern Highlands County to southern Columbia County.

HABITAT: It inhabits sand pine scrub and sandhill habitats.

LIFE HISTORY AND ECOLOGY: Largely unknown. Males are diurnal and fly from May through October. Females probably spend their entire life burrowing in the sand. On two occasions males were found digging out females close to the surface of the sand.

SPECIALIZED OR UNIQUE CHARACTERISTICS: A number of scrub and sandhill scarabs are unusually hairy. The remarkable sexual dimorphism including flightlessness in the female, is usual in several groups of Melolon-

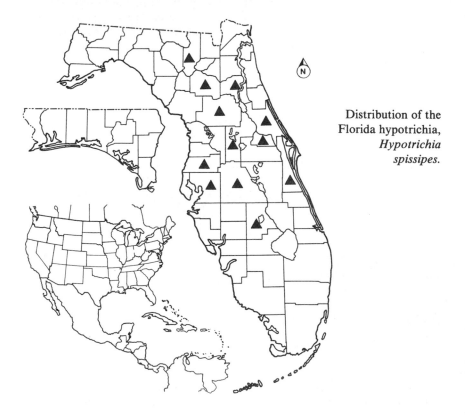

Distribution of the
Florida hypotrichia,
*Hypotrichia
spissipes.*

thinae occupying relictual habitats, and is probably associated with extensive burrowing by the female.

BASIS FOR STATUS CLASSIFICATION: This species is a Florida endemic restricted to the central part of the state, where it lives only in sandy uplands. Within its habitat it is often abundant, but seldom seen because males do not come to light traps, and their flight is fast and evasive. In spite of its abundance, this species merits special concern, because it is a peninsular endemic, occurs in habitats that are rapidly disappearing on the peninsula, and appears to vary from site to site, suggesting that populations may be distinct. Populations are known from Archbold Biological Station, and Ocala National Forest; it probably occurs at a number of other protected sites.

RECOMMENDATIONS: Little is known of the biology of this scarab, and an informed effort to preserve the species would require a study of its ecological requirements. As in many similar instances, however, the species probably can be maintained indefinitely on many sites by preserving tracts of upland habitat in a natural state.

PREPARED BY: Robert E. Woodruff, Florida State Collection of Arthropods, P.O. Box 147100, Gainesville, FL 32614-7100, and Mark Deyrup, Archbold Biological Station, Lake Placid, FL 33852.

FAMILY SCARABAEIDAE

Status Undetermined

Clemens' June Beetle
Phyllophaga clemens Horn

DESCRIPTION: Small for the genus (length 9.5-11 mm [0.4-0.5 in]), this beetle is pale yellow and dorsally hairless. It is distinguished from similar species by genitalic characters. A published description of this species, and identification keys to Florida *Phyllophaga*, are provided by Woodruff and Beck (1989).

RANGE: It occurs in South Carolina, Georgia, and Florida. In Florida, it is recorded from Leon and Alachua counties.

HABITAT: Unknown.

Distribution of
Clemens' June bee-
tle, *Phyllophaga
clemens.*

LIFE HISTORY AND ECOLOGY: Specimens have been taken at lights. Larval host and habits are unknown.

BASIS FOR STATUS CLASSIFICATION: This species appears to be rare and narrowly distributed; it may well have special habitat or host require- ments. Clemens' June beetle occurs at Tall Timbers Research Station; there are no other records from protected habitats.

RECOMMENDATIONS: No recommendations are possible until more is known about habitat requirements.

PREPARED BY: Robert E. Woodruff, Florida State Collection of Arthro- pods, P.O. Box 147100, Gainesville, FL 32614-7100, and Mark Deyrup, Archbold Biological Station, Lake Placid, FL 33852.

Status Undetermined

Profound June Beetle

Phyllophaga profunda (Blanchard)

DESCRIPTION: This June beetle is oblong, slightly broader behind, dark reddish-brown, and dorsally hairless. Male genitalia are asymmetrical (like a number of other species) with a unique carina on the outside of the left clasper. Length 18.7–25.2 mm (0.7–1.0 in). A published description (adult and larva) of this species and keys to Florida *Phyllophaga* are provided by Woodruff and Beck (1989).

RANGE: This June beetle is distributed from lower Midwest through east Texas. In Florida, it is known only from Jackson County.

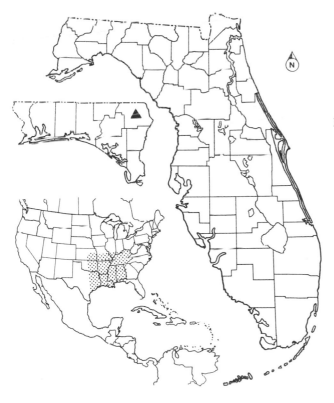

Distribution of the profound June beetle, *Phyllophaga profunda*.

HABITAT: It inhabits hardwood forests.

LIFE HISTORY AND ECOLOGY: Adults are active from mid-March to mid-July, feeding on a wide variety of broadleaf trees. Larval host and habits are unknown.

BASIS FOR STATUS CLASSIFICATION: This species could easily be another species whose Florida distribution is confined to a small area in the Apalachicola River basin. Since it also occurs in a broad area west and south of Florida, it may be more widely distributed in the panhandle. The only Florida specimens are from Florida Caverns State Park.

RECOMMENDATIONS: Further study is needed to establish the range of this species in Florida.

PREPARED BY: Robert E. Woodruff, Florida State Collection of Arthropods, P.O. Box 147100, Gainesville, FL 32614-7100, and Mark Deyrup, Archbold Biological Station, Lake Placid, FL 33852.

FAMILY SCARABAEIDAE

Status Undetermined

Yemassee June Beetle
Phyllophaga yemasseei Cartwright

DESCRIPTION: This June beetle is pale yellow and dorsally hairless. It is similar to several other Florida species, some of which are also rare, and is distinguished by genitalic characters. Length 10.0–10.9 mm (0.4 in). A published description of this species and keys for the identification of Florida *Phyllophaga* are provided by Woodruff and Beck (1989).

RANGE: It occurs in South Carolina, Georgia, and Florida. The Florida record is based on one Escambia County collection.

HABITAT: Unknown.

LIFE HISTORY AND ECOLOGY: Adults have been collected at lights in June. Larva and host are unknown.

Distribution of the
Yemassee June bee-
tle, *Phyllophaga
yemasseei.*

BASIS FOR STATUS CLASSIFICATION: This species is known from only a few specimens and appears to be rare throughout its range. With so few known sites, it does not fit any geographic pattern of species with a highly restricted Florida distribution, nor has it been associated with a rare host or habitat. Further research, however, would probably show that this is a rare species, at least in Florida.

RECOMMENDATIONS: Information on distribution and biology is needed for any evaluation of the status of this species.

PREPARED BY: Robert E. Woodruff, Florida State Collection of Arthropods, P.O. Box 147100, Gainesville, FL 32614-7100, and Mark Deyrup, Archbold Biological Station, Lake Placid, FL 33852.

Status Undetermined

Robinson's Anomala

Anomala robinsoni Potts

DESCRIPTION: This beetle is entirely black, often with a greenish metallic luster; the labrum is not visible in front of the clypeus; the elytra have four prominent lateral interstriae. A key to *Anomala* species is found in Potts (1977b).

RANGE: It is confined to Florida and known only from Dade County.

HABITAT: Unknown.

LIFE HISTORY AND ECOLOGY: Unknown.

Distribution of Robinson's anomala, *Anomala robinsoni.*

BASIS FOR STATUS CLASSIFICATION: This species is known from a few specimens from Florida City, Coral Gables, and Miami. There are certainly local natural habitats, such as the Miami Rocklands, whose near-disappearance could explain the rarity of this species. On the other hand, the area is the new home of a great variety of exotic insects from the West Indies and elsewhere, and some of these exotics are rare or have had only ephemeral populations.

RECOMMENDATIONS: There is a need to find the habitat of this species and to discover its relationship to other *Anomala* species before assigning a status.

PREPARED BY: Robert E. Woodruff, Florida State Collection of Arthropods, P.O. Box 147100, Gainesville, FL 32614-7100, and Mark Deyrup, Archbold Biological Station, Lake Placid, FL 33852.

FAMILY SCARABAEIDAE

Status Undetermined

Woodruff's Ataenius

Ataenius woodruffi Cartwright

DESCRIPTION: Very large (length 6.4 mm [0.25 in]) for its genus, this beetle is shiny and black faintly tinged with red. The clypeus is broadly rounded on each side of the median emargination, the clypeal sides nearly straight to the wide-angled genae. The pronotum has mixed fine and coarse punctures, coarse punctures more crowded laterally; the elytral striae are wide, deep, shining; the interstriae on the central area of elytra are evenly, strongly convex. A published description is found in Cartwright (1974).

RANGE: The beetle is known from a single specimen collected in a light trap at Flagler Beach, Flagler County.

HABITAT: Unknown.

LIFE HISTORY AND ECOLOGY: Unknown.

BASIS FOR STATUS CLASSIFICATION: This could be a rare species confined to beach dune areas on the Atlantic Coast of Florida, or it could be a rare widespread species, or even an exotic.

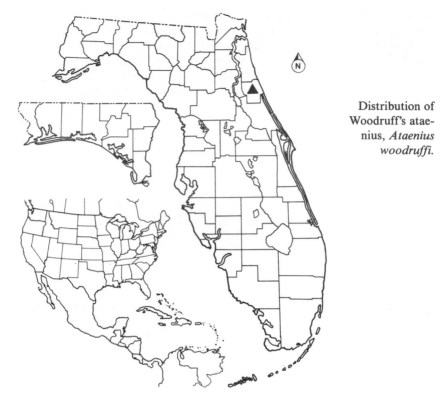

Distribution of
Woodruff's atae-
nius, *Ataenius
woodruffi.*

RECOMMENDATIONS: No recommendations are possible until more is
known about this species.

PREPARED BY: Robert E. Woodruff, Florida State Collection of Arthropods, P.O. Box 147100, Gainesville, FL 32614–7100, and Mark Deyrup,
Archbold Biological Station, Lake Placid, FL 33852.

FAMILY SCARABAEIDAE

Status Undetermined

Big Pine Key Ataenius
Ataenius superficialis Cartwright

DESCRIPTION: The body of this beetle is covered with an opaque gray
film, giving a gray cast; the elytral intervals are weakly convex, the striae are

usually in part quite wide and shiny; the elytra are short, less than twice the width, the setae inconspicuous. Length 3.6 mm (0.14 in). A published description is found in Cartwright (1974).

RANGE: This beetle is known only from a few specimens taken on Big Pine Key (Monroe County).

HABITAT: Unknown, probably from the pine rocklands that cover most of the island.

LIFE HISTORY AND ECOLOGY: Type series was collected in May "under animal dropping (possibly from a raccoon)" (Cartwright 1974).

BASIS FOR STATUS CLASSIFICATION: This species has been considered an endemic of the Florida Keys (Woodruff 1973, Peck and Howden 1985), and it is easy to imagine that it is a recently diverged species (perhaps from an isolated population of the similar *A. imbricatus*) analogous to a number of Big Pine Key species or subspecies. On the other hand, the Florida Keys also harbor many exotic species, some of which were actually first described from specimens taken in southern Florida, and some of which

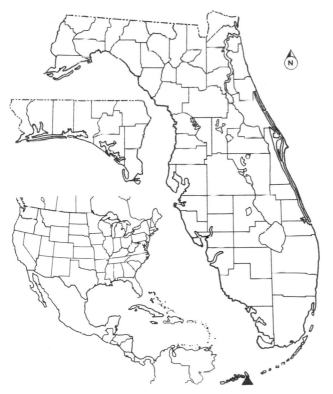

Distribution of the Big Pine Key ataenius, *Ataenius superficialis*.

seem to have had only a temporary occupancy in Florida. Until this species is better known, its relationships, vertebrate hosts, and mobility assessed, it is left in an undetermined status.

RECOMMENDATIONS: Further research is necessary on the biology and taxonomy of this species.

PREPARED BY: Robert E. Woodruff, Florida State Collection of Arthropods, P.O. Box 147100, Gainesville, FL 32614-7100, and Mark Deyrup, Archbold Biological Station, Lake Placid, FL 33852.

FAMILY SCARABAEIDAE

Status Undetermined

Sandyland Onthophagus

Onthophagus aciculatulus Blatchley

DESCRIPTION: This beetle is black and shiny. The clypeus has two weak marginal teeth; the head has two basal and one median tubercle; the pronotum has a weak anteriomedian convex projection; the pronotal punctures are shallow, each with a minute tubercle on the anterior margin; the length is 3.8–4.5 mm (0.15–0.2 in). A published description of this species and a key to the Florida species of *Onthophagus* are provided by Woodruff 1973.

RANGE: This beetle is confined to Florida, known from Highlands, Polk, Pinellas and Pasco counties.

HABITAT: It is common in sand pine scrub at the Archbold Biological Station in Highlands County. It also was collected in scrub in Polk County. The Pinellas County (Dunedin) record is probably from scrub, but the Pasco record (locality unknown) is more likely to be from sandhill.

LIFE HISTORY AND ECOLOGY: A few specimens were taken under raccoon dung (Brach 1976), but it cannot usually be attracted to dung. Adults do not seem to fly to light, but can be captured in numbers in Malaise traps with pans of water at the base of the net. Most records are from winter and spring.

BASIS FOR STATUS CLASSIFICATION: This species may well be a narrowly restricted sand pine scrub endemic which should be considered rare because its habitat is rapidly vanishing. It is possible, however, that it is a more widely distributed species of sandy uplands, and is rare in collections because it is not attracted to baits or light.

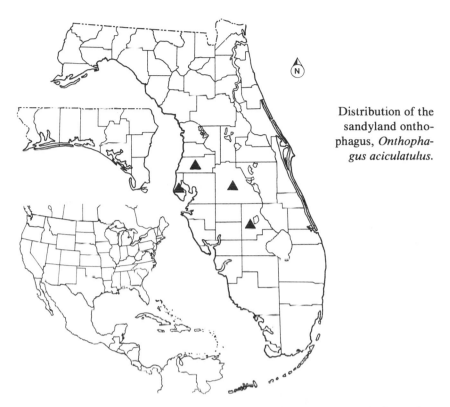

Distribution of the
sandyland ontho-
phagus, *Onthopha-
gus aciculatulus.*

RECOMMENDATIONS: Information is needed on the ecological requirements of this species before consideration of conservation measures.

PREPARED BY: Robert E. Woodruff, Florida State Collection of Arthropods, P.O. Box 147100, Gainesville, FL 32614-7100, and Mark Deyrup,
Archbold Biological Station, Lake Placid, FL 33852.

FAMILY SCARABAEIDAE

Status Undetermined

Strohecker's Ataenius
Ataenius stroheckeri Cartwright

DESCRIPTION: This beetle is elongate, parallel-sided, narrow, shiny, and
black. The lateral interstriae of the elytra are roughly punctate; the clypeal
margin is sharply bidentate; the punctures on the front are coarser than

those on clypeus. Length is 3.2 mm (0.15 in). A published description is found in Cartwright (1974).

RANGE: This species is known only from Florida, in Dade and Manatee counties.

HABITAT: Unknown.

LIFE HISTORY AND ECOLOGY: Adults have been collected in May, June, and September.

BASIS FOR STATUS CLASSIFICATION: The position of this species on the FCREPA list is questionable. It is known from only a few specimens but is a species that could easily be confused with the common species *A. exiguus* and *A. gracilis* until examined under the microscope. The latter species, in particular, often appears in light trap samples in very large numbers. It is also somewhat suspicious when most specimens of a species originate from the Miami area, a notorious point of entry for exotic insects. The Manatee County specimen only serves to dispel the notion that *A. stroheckeri* might be restricted to some endangered Dade County habitat. On the other hand, it is still possible that this is a rare species with specialized habits.

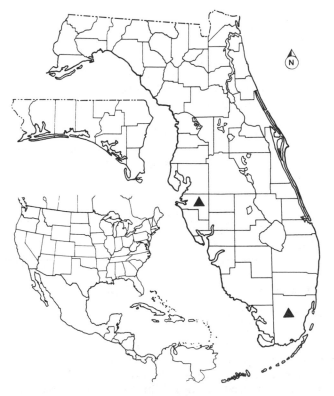

Distribution of Strohecker's ataenius, *Ataenius stroheckeri.*

RECOMMENDATIONS: More information is needed on the distribution and ecology of this species before any consideration of conservation.

PREPARED BY: Mark Deyrup, Archbold Biological Station, Lake Placid, FL 33852.

FAMILY SCARABAEIDAE

Status Undetermined

Sand Pine Scrub Ataenius
Ataenius saramari Cartwright

DESCRIPTION: This beetle is oval and shiny. The clypeus is deeply emarginate; the elytra, as well as pronotum, have a marginal fringe of short broad setae; the fifth sternum has a transverse row of stiff setae; hind wings are unusually short for the genus. Length 3.0 to 3.2 mm (0.1 in). Published descriptions are found in Woodruff (1973) and Cartwright (1974).

RANGE: This beetle is confined to Florida, known from Martin, St. Lucie, Highlands, Hillsborough, Osceola, and Marion counties.

HABITAT: It occurs in sand pine scrub.

LIFE HISTORY AND ECOLOGY: This species appears to be a rather widespread endemic of sand pine scrub. It appears to aggregate around concentrations of leaf litter in open scrub, such as the ruts at the edges of firelanes. At the Archbold Biological Station it is not unusual to find 10 individuals in an area of 2 sq. m, and this may actually be one of the commonest scarabs in scrub habitat. Its rarity in collections is due to its restricted habitat, and its failure to appear at light traps or in baited pitfalls.

SPECIALIZED OR UNIQUE CHARACTERISTICS: The wings of specimens examined appear to be unusually short for the genus, and it is likely that at least some individuals or whole populations are flightless. This could be an adaptation to a life spent entirely under the sand combined with generalist feeding habits that seldom require long-distance dispersal.

BASIS FOR STATUS CLASSIFICATION: Although this species is much commoner than it was once considered, it is apparently confined to scrub habitat, which has declined greatly from its former extent. *A. saramari* may also be absent from some scrub areas. There are protected populations at

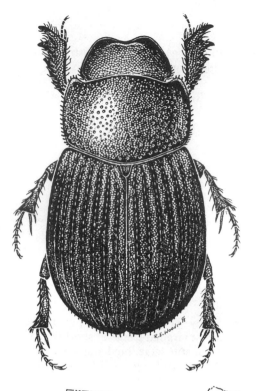

Sand Pine Scrub
Ataenius, *Ataenius
saramari* (courtesy of
Robert E. Woodruff).

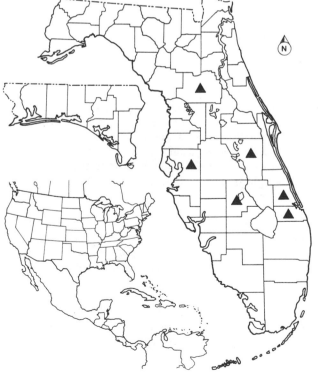

Distribution of the
sand pine scrub
ataenius, *Ataenius
saramari*.

Archbold Biological Station, Johnathan Dickinson State Park, and Ocala National Forest.

RECOMMENDATIONS: This species probably has undemanding dietary requirements and is unlikely to disperse on a large scale from suitable patches of habitat. It should be easy to maintain populations through preservation of sand pine scrub habitat.

PREPARED BY: Robert F. Woodruff, Florida State Collection of Arthropods, P.O. Box 147100, Gainesville, FL 32614-7100, and Mark Deyrup, Archbold Biological Station, Lake Placid, FL 33852.

FAMILY SCARABAEIDAE

Status Undetermined

Florida Coast Scarab

Atuenius rudellus Fall

DESCRIPTION: This scarab is feebly shiny and black. The pronotum has almost uniformly distributed coarse punctures; the sides of clypeus are feebly transversely wrinkled, and closely punctate, and there is a band of coarse punctures at base of head; the elytra have the interstriae feebly convex, noticeably punctate. Length 3.9-4.5 mm (0.15-0.2 in). Published descriptions are found in Woodruff (1973) and Cartwright (1974).

RANGE: This species is known from coastal Florida, with records from Duval, Dade, Monroe, Lee, Charlotte, and Pinellas counties.

HABITAT: It probably is found in coastal hammocks rather than dunes, as specimens have been taken on No Name Key, where there are no dune areas.

LIFE HISTORY AND ECOLOGY: Unknown. Adults have been collected at lights throughout the year.

BASIS FOR STATUS CLASSIFICATION: This species is not frequently collected, and some Florida coastal habitats are undergoing rapid change. There are apparently protected populations at Bahia Honda State Park, No Name Key, and in Everglades National Park.

RECOMMENDATIONS: Surveys are needed to determine the distribution and ecology of this species.

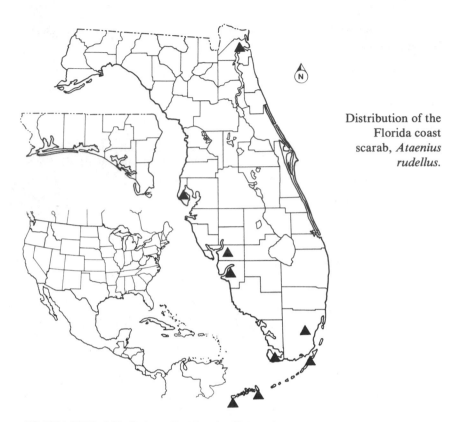

Distribution of the
Florida coast
scarab, *Ataenius
rudellus*.

PREPARED BY: Robert E. Woodruff, Florida State Collection of Arthropods, P.O. Box 147100, Gainesville, FL 32614-7100, and Mark Deyrup,
Archbold Biological Station, Lake Placid, FL 33852.

FAMILY SCARABAEIDAE

Status Undetermined

Carolina Forest Scarab

Aphotaenius carolinus (Van Dyke)

DESCRIPTION: This scarab is blackish and shiny; the legs and the front of
head are reddish; there is no apical fringe of setae on the hind tibia, the apex
of hind tibia has two small teeth; the clypeus has a pair of conspicuous teeth;
the anterior part of the head is impunctate. Length 2.5-3.1 mm (0.1 in). Published descriptions are found in Woodruff (1973) and Cartwright (1974); a
larval description in Jerath (1960).

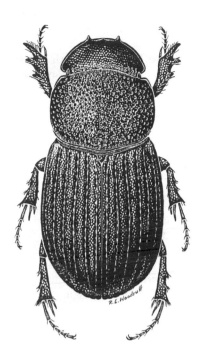

Carolina Forest
Scarab, *Aphotaenius
carolinus* (courtesy of
Robert E. Woodruff).

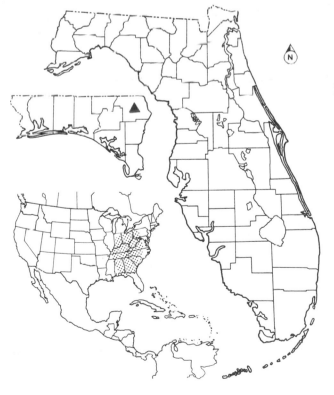

Distribution of the
Carolina forest
scarab, *Aphotae-
nius carolinus.*

RANGE: This beetle is found from Indiana to Maryland, south to Florida. In Florida, the only authenticated record is from Florida Caverns State Park, Jackson County.

HABITAT: It is usually found in deciduous forests.

LIFE HISTORY AND ECOLOGY: It breeds in dung, especially that of deer; the Florida specimens were in pack rat dung. Adults have been collected from late April through mid-September (Cartwright 1974).

BASIS FOR STATUS CLASSIFICATION: The distribution of this species is poorly known, perhaps because it is a small species usually found in deep woods. Cartwright (1974) does not record that any specimens were captured at lights; a failure to respond to lights would do much to explain the rarity of the species. Based on the highly fragmentary distribution data, it seems possible that this species fits the familiar pattern of a northern insect whose range extends into Florida only in the area of the Apalachicola drainage.

RECOMMENDATIONS: More distributional information is needed before considering conservation of this species.

PREPARED BY: Robert E. Woodruff, Florida State Collection of Arthropods, P.O. Box 147100, Gainesville, FL 32614-7100, and Mark Deyrup, Archbold Biological Station, Lake Placid, FL 33852.

FAMILY SCARABAEIDAE

Status Undetermined

Bicolored Burrowing Scarab

Bolbocerasoma hamatum Brown

DESCRIPTION: This beetle is highly convex, shiny, and bi-colored orange and black. The body outline is almost circular; the head medially is emarginate; the pronotum is orange with a black basal marking; the apical two-thirds of the elytra are black, the bases orange; elytral striae are strong and conspicuous. Length 8-10 mm (0.3-0.4 in). The orange-brown and black markings make this species easy to distinguish from all other Florida species. A published description is found in Woodruff (1973).

RANGE: This scarab is restricted to southern Georgia, southern Alabama, and Florida. It is widespread in Florida except for the southwest part of the peninsula.

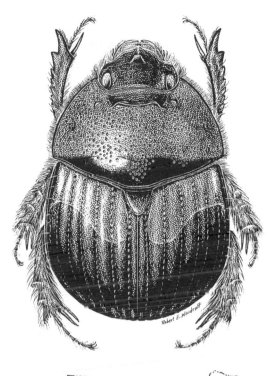

Bicolored Burrowing
Scarab, *Bolbocero-
soma hamatum*
(courtesy of Robert
E. Woodruff).

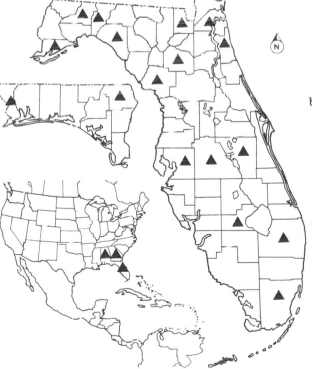

Distribution of the
bicolored burrowing
scarab, *Bolbocero-
soma hamatum.*

HABITAT: Unknown, as almost all specimens were taken at lights after dark.

LIFE HISTORY AND ECOLOGY: Adults fly through most of the year; larval food and habits are unknown.

BASIS FOR STATUS CLASSIFICATION: This is a conspicuous species that is attracted to lights and is also attractive to beetle collectors, but relatively few specimens have been collected. This species cannot be categorized as rare, however, until enough is known of its habits to ensure that it is not a common but secretive species. It does not appear to be common on any ecological preserve, though a few specimens are known from Tall Timbers Research Station and from Archbold Biological Station.

RECOMMENDATIONS: There is need for research on the ecology of the species.

PREPARED BY: Robert E. Woodruff, Florida State Collection of Arthropods, P.O. Box 147100, Gainesville, FL 32614-7100, and Mark Deyrup, Archbold Biological Station, Lake Placid, FL 33852.

FAMILY SCARABAEIDAE

Status Undetermined

Mat Red Globe Scarab
Eucanthus alutaceus Cartwright

DESCRIPTION: This beetle is highly convex, dark red-brown, and not shiny. The body is very broadly oval in outline and the clypeus and vertex each have a transverse ridge, produced into a horn in the male; the eyes are partly divided by a ridge; the pronotum has broad punctate impressions and a transverse anterior ridge. Length 10–14 mm (0.4–0.6 in). A published description is found in Woodruff (1973).

RANGE: This scarab occurs in northern Florida, southern Alabama, Mississippi, and Georgia. In Florida, it is known from Baker, Leon, Alachua, and Manatee counties.

HABITAT: Unknown, but probably sandy uplands, as members of the genus *Eucanthus* are known to dig deep burrows.

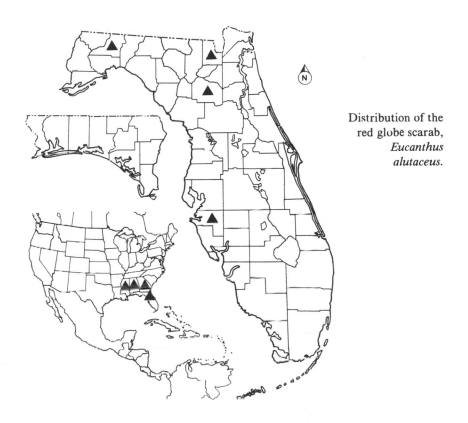

Distribution of the
red globe scarab,
*Eucanthus
alutaceus.*

LIFE HISTORY AND ECOLOGY: Almost all specimens were collected at lights. Larval food and habits are unknown for any species in the genus.

BASIS FOR STATUS CLASSIFICATION: This species is known from four states, but almost all specimens are from a small area including parts of the southern borders of three states and the northern border of Florida. The habitat is likely to be sandhill, of which only remnants occur in much of the range. The species is rare in collections, even though adults are attracted to light. The only known protected population is at Tall Timbers Research Station.

RECOMMENDATIONS: More information is needed on distribution and ecology before its status can be established.

PREPARED BY: Robert E. Woodruff, Florida State Collection of Arthropods, P.O. Box 147100, Gainesville, FL 32614-7100, and Mark Deyrup, Archbold Biological Station, Lake Placid, FL 33852.

Status Undetermined

Shining Ball Scarab

Ceratocanthus aeneus (MacLeay)

DESCRIPTION: This beetle is 7 mm (0.27 in) long when it is extended. It is black and shiny, with a green sheen; the clypeus is bluntly triangular; the middle and hind tibiae are greatly expanded and flattened, as wide as the length of tarsi; the body is completely contractile (capable of rolling into a ball). It is our only contractile scarab that is very shiny with a green sheen. A published description is found in Woodruff (1973).

RANGE: This scarab occurs from North Carolina and Tennessee through Florida. In Florida, it is known from Alachua, Putnam, Volusia, Highlands, Liberty, and Monroe counties.

HABITAT: Most specimens are from forested areas.

Shining Ball Scarab, *Ceratocanthus aeneus* (courtesy of Robert E. Woodruff).

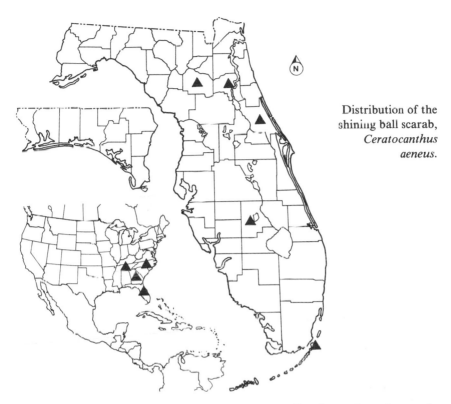

Distribution of the shining ball scarab, *Ceratocanthus aeneus.*

LIFE HISTORY AND ECOLOGY: Unknown. Specimens have been collected by beating dead vines and in moist tree holes. Larvae and pupae were described by Choate (1987).

BASIS FOR STATUS CLASSIFICATION: In the 162 years since its description, about 15 specimens have been seen, except for those recently collected at Torreya State Park in tree holes. This beetle appears to be inconspicuous and secretive, and is probably not attracted to light. It is not listed as rare because it could be more abundant than it appears to be. There is no reason to believe that it lives in a threatened or vulnerable habitat, or that it is dependent on some rare host organism. A specimen was collected from Highlands Hammock State Park, and many at Torreya State Park. A single aberrant specimen, which may represent a new species, was collected from Key Largo; there is now a large state preserve on Key Largo.

RECOMMENDATIONS: More distributional and habitat information is a prerequisite for considering conservation.

PREPARED BY: Robert E. Woodruff, Florida State Collection of Arthropods, P.O. Box 147100, Gainesville, FL 32614-7100, and Mark Deyrup, Archbold Biological Station, Lake Placid, FL 33852.

Status Undetermined

Red Diplotaxis
Diplotaxis rufa Linell

DESCRIPTION: Members of this genus are about 8 mm long, elongate oval, with long, non-retractile legs. The elytra are shining, roughened between the striae. The antennal club has three segments. The male genitalia provide definitive diagnostic characters. Published descriptions: Linell 1895, Vaurie 1956.

RANGE: This species is known only from Brevard, Lake, Marion, Orange, and Volusia counties.

HABITAT: Unknown.

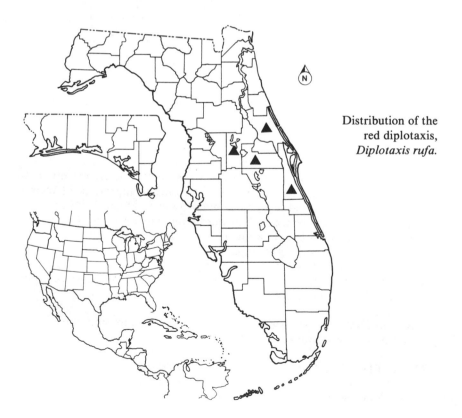

Distribution of the red diplotaxis, *Diplotaxis rufa.*

LIFE HISTORY AND ECOLOGY: Unknown. Adults were collected at lights after dark.

BASIS FOR STATUS CLASSIFICATION: Only a small number of specimens have been collected. All specimens are from a series of localities in the east-central part of the state, suggesting that this is a local endemic species. Without more distributional data and some clue as to habitat requirements, this species cannot be assigned a status.

RECOMMENDATIONS: More information should be collected to clarify the status of this species.

PREPARED BY: Robert E. Woodruff, Florida State Collection of Arthropods, P.O. Box 147100, Gainesville, FL 32614-7100, and Mark Deyrup, Archbold Biological Station, Lake Placid, FL 33852.

FAMILY SCARABAEIDAE

Status Undetermined

Delicate Silky June Beetle

Serica delicatula Dawson

DESCRIPTION: *Serica* species are small (about 8 mm [0.3 in]), brown, long-legged scarabs that look much like miniature June beetles of the genus *Phyllophaga*. Unlike *Phyllophaga* and the small June beetles of the genus *Diplotaxis*, the elytra of *Serica* are evenly striate, usually dull with an opalescent sheen. Determination of species usually requires examination of the internal male genitalia. Published description: Dawson 1922.

RANGE: This species is restricted to Florida, known from a band of interior counties extending from Highlands north to Clay and Bradford counties.

HABITAT: Unknown.

LIFE HISTORY AND ECOLOGY: Unknown. Adults have been collected at lights in February.

BASIS FOR STATUS CLASSIFICATION: This beetle is a Florida endemic that is known from only a small series of specimens. It belongs to a genus that seems to have speciated rapidly, resulting in numerous localized species. It could, however, be more widely distributed or more common than it appears at present.

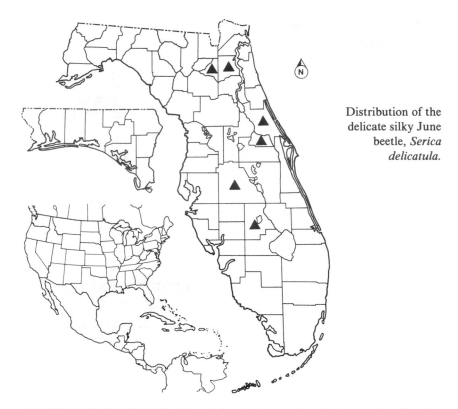

Distribution of the
delicate silky June
beetle, *Serica
delicatula.*

RECOMMENDATIONS: More information on distribution and habitat is a
prerequisite for conservation considerations.

PREPARED BY: Robert E. Woodruff, Florida State Collection of Arthropods, P.O. Box 147100, Gainesville, FL 32614–7100, and Mark Deyrup,
Archbold Biological Station, Lake Placid, FL 33852.

FAMILY SCARABAEIDAE

Status Undetermined

Pygmy Silky June Beetle
Serica pusilla Dawson

DESCRIPTION: *Serica* species are small (about 8 mm [0.3 in]), brown,
long-legged scarabs that look much like miniature June beetles of the genus

Phyllophaga. Unlike *Phyllophaga* and the small June beetles of the genus *Diplotaxis*, the elytra of *Serica* are evenly striate, usually dull with an opalescent sheen. Determination of species usually requires examination of the internal male genitalia. Published description: Dawson 1922.

RANGE: This beetle is restricted to Florida, known from Marion, Pinellas, Alachua, Hernando, Lake, and Seminole counties.

HABITAT: Unknown. Most of the collection sites are scrub or sandhill habitats.

LIFE HISTORY AND ECOLOGY: Unknown.

BASIS FOR STATUS CLASSIFICATION: This beetle is a Florida endemic that is known from only a small series of specimens. The collection sites are loosely grouped in the middle of the state. It would not be surprising if this were another species confined to sandy uplands in the central peninsula, but there is no good evidence at present.

RECOMMENDATIONS: More information on distribution and habitat is a prerequisite for conservation considerations.

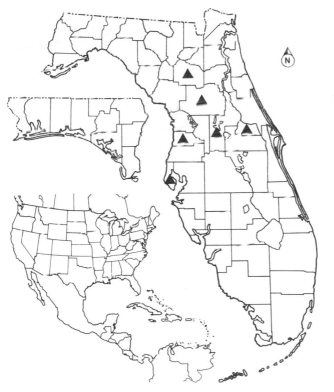

Distribution of the pygmy silky June beetle, *Serica pusilla*.

PREPARED BY: Robert E. Woodruff, Florida State Collection of Arthropods, P.O. Box 147100, Gainesville, FL 32614–7100, and Mark Deyrup, Archbold Biological Station, Lake Placid, FL 33852.

FAMILY SCARABAEIDAE

Status Undetermined

Crooked Silky June Beetle
Serica rhypha Dawson

DESCRIPTION: *Serica* species are small (about 8 mm [0.3 in]), brown, long-legged scarabs that look much like miniature June beetles of the genus *Phyllophaga*. Unlike *Phyllophaga* and the small June beetles of the genus *Diplotaxis*, the elytra of *Serica* are evenly striate, usually dull with an opalescent sheen. Determination of species usually requires examination of the internal male genitalia. Published description: Dawson 1922.

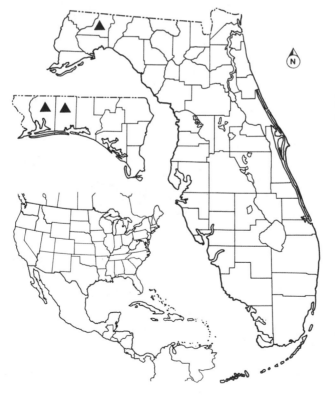

Distribution of the crooked silky June beetle, *Serica rhypha.*

RANGE: This beetle is known only from Florida, in Leon, Santa Rosa, and Okaloosa counties.

HABITAT: Unknown.

LIFE HISTORY AND ECOLOGY: Unknown. Adults were collected at lights in April and May.

BASIS FOR STATUS CLASSIFICATION: This species, which is known from only a small number of specimens, is probably a Florida endemic. Two of the collecting sites have produced other scarabs that are confined to sandy uplands in the panhandle, and this species may share the same habitats. The genus *Serica* as a whole seems to have produced many localized endemic species, and this may well be another example.

RECOMMENDATIONS: More information on distribution and habitat is a prerequisite for conservation considerations.

PREPARED BY: Robert E. Woodruff, Florida State Collection of Arthropods, P.O. Box 147100, Gainesville, FL 32614-7100, and Mark Deyrup, Archbold Biological Station, Lake Placid, FL 33852

FAMILY SCARABAEIDAE

Status Undetermined

Little Silky June Beetle
Serica tantula Dawson

DESCRIPTION: *Serica* species are small (about 8 mm [0.3 in]), brown, long-legged scarabs that look much like miniature June beetles of the genus *Phyllophaga*. Unlike *Phyllophaga* and the small June beetles of the genus *Diplotaxis*, the elytra of *Serica* are evenly striate, usually dull with an opalescent sheen. Determination of species usually requires examination of the internal male genitalia. Published description: Dawson 1922.

RANGE: This beetle is known only from Palm Beach County.

HABITAT: Unknown.

Distribution of the little silky June beetle, *Serica tantula.*

LIFE HISTORY AND ECOLOGY: Unknown.

BASIS FOR STATUS CLASSIFICATION: This species is known from a single specimen taken in 1889 at Lake Worth. Intensive development of the coastal areas may have eliminated this species, but it is also possible that it is unusually elusive and still persists somewhere on the Atlantic Coast. Johnathan Dickinson State Park might be a good site to look for this species. There is no reason to believe that the species might be exotic.

RECOMMENDATIONS: There should be an attempt to rediscover the species in Palm Beach or adjacent counties.

PREPARED BY: Robert E. Woodruff, Florida State Collection of Arthropods, P.O. Box 147100, Gainesville, FL 32614–7100, and Mark Deyrup, Archbold Biological Station, Lake Placid, FL 33852.

Status Undetermined

Handsome Flower Scarab
Rutela formosa Burmeister

DESCRIPTION: The flower scarab is golden with irregular green stripes on the elytra, with a large green angular spot on the pronotum; the head is green with a median stripe; the head, pronotum, and elytra are smooth and shiny. Length 14–15 mm (0.55 in).

RANGE: This beetle is known from the Bahamas, Florida Keys, and the adjacent mainland in Dade and Monroe counties.

HABITAT: This species is found in tropical hardwood hammocks.

Distribution of the handsome flower scarab, *Rutela formosa.*

LIFE HISTORY AND ECOLOGY: Adults feed on pollen of the royal poinciana, Jamaica dogwood, and probably other tropical trees. Larvae and larval habits are unknown.

BASIS FOR STATUS CLASSIFICATION: This tropical species is an excellent flier and almost certainly arrived in Florida without human assistance. In Florida it appears to be confined to tropical hardwood hammocks, à rare habitat which harbors many species that occur nowhere else in the U.S. Even in its habitat, this species appears to be uncommon, but it may spend much of its adult life in the canopy. Further research may prove that this is a rare insect, but it is also possible that it is no rarer than hundreds of other West Indian species that have native populations on the Florida Keys.

RECOMMENDATIONS: Further research on the habits, distribution, and population levels of this species are needed before it can be assigned a status.

PREPARED BY: Robert E. Woodruff, Florida State Collection of Arthropods, P.O. Box 147100, Gainesville, FL 32614–7100, and Mark Deyrup, Archbold Biological Station, Lake Placid, FL 33852.

FAMILY SCARABAEIDAE

Status Undetermined

Miami Chafer

Cyclocephala miamiensis Howden and Endrodi

DESCRIPTION: The Miami chafer is a shining reddish-brown scarab with the top of the head and the margins of the legs black. The body is elongate oval, 13–14 mm (.56 in) in length. This species is distinguished from similar-appearing species by the non-shining last visible dorsal segment and distinctive genitalia of the male and the heavily punctured pronotum of the female. Published description: Howden and Endrodi 1966.

RANGE: This beetle is known only from Florida, recorded from Miami (Dade County) and the southernmost keys (Monroe County).

HABITAT: Unknown.

LIFE HISTORY AND ECOLOGY: Unknown. Adults are attracted to lights.

BASIS FOR STATUS CLASSIFICATION: This species was described from a series of 500 specimens collected from Coral Gables to Key West, but there

Distribution of the
Miami chafer,
*Cyclocephala
miamiensis.*

have been no recent records of specimens, and it appears that populations may have diminished. True endemics in tropical Florida are unusual; most species confined to tropical Florida in the U.S. also occur in the West Indies. Tropical exotics are also common in tropical Florida, and a few of these seem to go through brief population explosions soon after arrival. On the other hand, there are many endemic subspecies and a few endemic species in tropical Florida, and the Miami chafer could be one of these which is becoming scarce because of changes in its habitat.

RECOMMENDATIONS: It is not advisable to declare a status for this species until more is known about its distribution, habitat, and its closest relatives.

PREPARED BY: Robert E. Woodruff, Florida State Collection of Arthropods, P.O. Box 147100, Gainesville, FL 32614-7100, and Mark Deyrup, Archbold Biological Station, Lake Placid, FL 33852.

Status Undetermined

Scaly Anteater Scarab
Cremastocheilus squamulosus LeConte

DESCRIPTION: Published key to species: Potts 1945.

RANGE: This scarab is known from North Carolina to Florida. In Florida, it has been found in Lake, Seminole, and Palm Beach counties.

HABITAT: Unknown.

LIFE HISTORY AND ECOLOGY: Larvae of all species of the genus feed on dead vegetable matter in ant nests, while the adults feed on ant larvae. Ant hosts for this species are unknown.

BASIS FOR STATUS CLASSIFICATION: This species is known from only a few specimens, taken in widely dispersed sites. If we knew the host

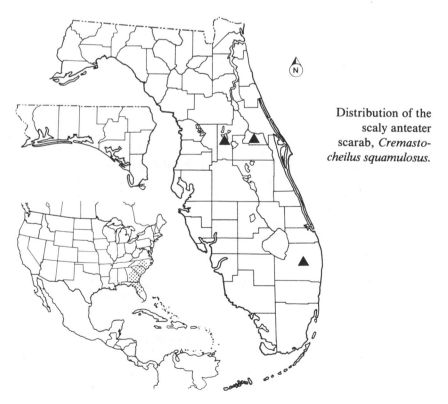

Distribution of the scaly anteater scarab, *Cremasto-cheilus squamulosus.*

ant, it would be easier to estimate the potential distribution and abundance of the anteater scarab. It might be relatively easy to find specimens if we knew the host, though members of the genus feign death and are difficult to see, especially when surrounded by hordes of frantic ants in a recently opened nest. Even if the host were common, its predator might be rare; there are a number of ant associates that may be genuinely rare.

RECOMMENDATIONS: This species cannot be given a status until more is known about its distribution and hosts.

PREPARED BY: Robert E. Woodruff, Florida State Collection of Arthropods, P.O. Box 147100, Gainesville, FL 32614–7100, and Mark Deyrup, Archbold Biological Station, Lake Placid, FL 33852.

Order Coleoptera
FAMILY CERAMBYCIDAE

INTRODUCTION: Compared with the continental fauna of some states (for example, Knull [1946] estimated 267 species in Ohio), Florida's fauna of about 200 cerambycid species is somewhat depauperate and, despite extensive collecting in the last two decades, is still incompletely known. This fact is emphasized by the very recent discovery of an unknown species in the scrub near Sebring.

In effect, Florida has three distinctive longhorn faunas, although there is so much overlap in both directions that it is impossible to draw hard and fast lines delineating the boundaries of the faunas. There is a northern component, composed of widespread eastern or southeastern coastal plain species and Appalachian species. Some of this northern fauna filters down to the Keys (e.g., *Elaphidion mucronatum*), and some is found only in extreme northern Florida, primarily in the Apalachicola River drainage system (e.g., *Analeptura lineola, Trigonarthris minnesotana, Brachyleptura* spp.). There is a distinctive precinctive fauna in the central part of the state, often associated with scrub areas (e.g., *Strangalia strigosa, Typocerus flavocinctus, Aethecerinus hornii*). Finally, there is a tropical fauna restricted to the Florida Keys and southern coastal areas. This fauna, as presently known, is often specifically or subspecifically distinct from, but clearly related to, a much richer Antillean fauna. This fauna is probably in the most precarious situation of all, as development is rapidly destroying the few remaining unprotected tropical hardwood forests in south Florida. The recent protection of much of Upper Key Largo by the state goes a long way toward preserving the fauna associated with the tropical hardwoods, but even there pressure continues in the form of "tree rustling" (the theft of trees or dead wood for resale), and destructive hurricanes.

PREPARED BY: Michael C. Thomas, Florida State Collection of Arthropods, P.O. Box 147100, Gainesville, FL 32614–7100.

Endangered

___

Florida Forestiera Borer

Nesostizocera floridana (Linsley)

DESCRIPTION: This beetle is elongate, subcylindrical, shining, pale reddish brown; the pronotum is laterally and dorsally tuberculate; the elytral apices are emarginate, bispinose. Length, 13 mm (0.5 in).

RANGE: Known only from two localities on Florida's southwest coast, Marco Island in Collier County and Sanibel Island in Lee County.

HABITAT: It is known from coastal thickets where its host, *Forestiera segregata* var. *segregata*, occurs.

Florida Forestiera,
Nesostizocera flori-dana (courtesy of
Michael C. Thomas).

Distribution of the
Florida foresticra
borer, *Nesosti-
zocera floridana.*

LIFE HISTORY AND ECOLOGY: This Florida precinctive was described from only two specimens collected at Marco Island, Collier County, and until recently nothing else was known of its distribution or habitats. Hovore ct al. (1978) reported on individuals of a population on Sanibel Island: "walking, mating and ovipositing at night on dead limbs of Florida privet (*Forestiera segregata* var. *segregata* [Jacq.] Klug & Urban) in a thickct at the south end of the island. Numcrous adults have subsequently been reared from this host."

BASIS FOR STATUS CLASSIFICATION: This beetle is known from two localities, comprising only a few acres, on Florida's southwest coast.

RECOMMENDATIONS: Protect the remaining coastal thickets where its plant host occurs in southwest Florida.

PREPARED BY: Michael C. Thomas, Florida State Collection of Arthropods, P.O. Box 147100, Gainesville, FL 32614-7100.

Endangered

Round-Necked Romulus

Romulus globosus Knull

DESCRIPTION: This robust beetle is dark reddish brown, with its head and pronotum darker. It is similar to *Enaphalodes hispicornis*, but the pronotum is smooth and the antennae and elytral apices are not spinose. Length, 29 mm-35 mm (1.1–1.4 in).

RANGE: This large beetle is known in peninsular Florida, from Marion County south to Dade County.

HABITAT: Unknown, presumably scrub areas.

LIFE HISTORY AND ECOLOGY: Unknown.

Round-Necked Romulus, *Romulus globosus* (courtesy of Michael C. Thomas).

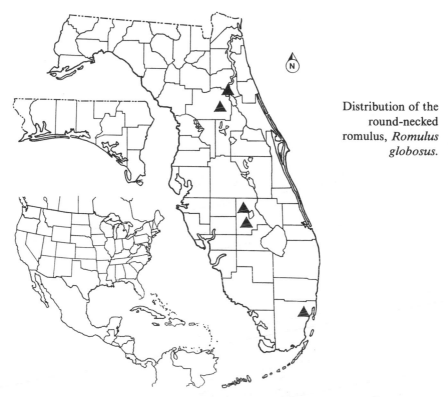

Distribution of the
round-necked
romulus, *Romulus
globosus.*

BASIS FOR STATUS CLASSIFICATION: This beetle was described in 1948 by Knull from a total of four specimens. The holotype and one paratype were collected in Coral Gables in Dade County. The other two paratypes were collected in the Ocala National Forest, which is in Marion, Lake, and Putnam counties, and at Crescent City in Putnam County. The earliest collection date was 10 May; the latest was 27 July. Linsley (1963) merely repeated the original description and gave the distribution as "South Florida." There are two specimens in the Carnegie Museum collected in Miami in May of 1927 and June of 1931, and there is one specimen in the Florida State Collection of Arthropods, collected at the University of Miami campus in 1949. Until recently, the 1949 specimen was the last known specimen collected of this species. In 1991, two specimens were collected in Highlands County (Thomas 1991): one at the Archbold Biological Station at Lake Placid on June 20 and one near Highlands Hammock State Park on June 15. Both were collected at electric lights. Why there was a more than 40-year gap in collections of this beetle is unknown, and it remains one of the rarest insects in Florida.

RECOMMENDATIONS: Since virtually nothing is known about the habits of this species it is premature to consider conservation strategies. The biology of this beetle should be studied if enough individuals are ever found to make such a study possible.

PREPARED BY: Michael C. Thomas, Florida State Collection of Arthropods, P.O. Box 147100, Gainesville, FL 32614–7100.

FAMILY CERAMBYCIDAE

Threatened

Chevrolat's Stenodontes

Stenodontes (Stenodontes) chevrolati Gahan

DESCRIPTION: This large, flattened, black prionine beetle ranges in length to more than 70 mm (2.7 in), making it one of the largest beetles in the United States. Major males have elongate mandibles that are longer than the head.

Chevrolat's Stenodontes, *Stenodontes chevrolati* (courtesy of Michael Thomas).

Distribution of
Chevrolat's steno-
dontes, *Stenodontes
chevrolati.*

RANGE: It has been reported in Florida only from the keys (Linsley 1962a), although specimens in the Florida State Collection of Arthropods indicate it also ranges into southern Dade County. Outside of Florida, it occurs in Cuba and the Bahamas (Linsley 1962a).

HABITAT: This beetle occurs in tropical hardwood hammocks in extreme south Florida.

LIFE HISTORY AND ECOLOGY: Like other members of this genus, larvae are heartwood borers in a variety of decaying hardwoods. Specific hosts for this species include hog plum (*Spondias purpurea*) (Linsley 1962a), and gumbo limbo (*Bursera semirubra*) (M. Thomas, pers. obscrv.). Adults are nocturnal and sometimes attracted to light.

BASIS FOR STATUS CLASSIFICATION: It is restricted to tropical hardwood hammocks in extreme south Florida. Although a conspicuous member of the tropical insect fauna of southern Florida, examples of this species are uncommon in collections.

RECOMMENDATIONS: Protection of tropical hardwood hammocks is the only way to protect this species.

PREPARED BY: Michael C. Thomas, Florida State Collection of Arthropods, P.O. Box 147100, Gainesville, FL 32614-7100.

FAMILY CERAMBYCIDAE

Threatened

Strohecker's Eburia

Eburia stroheckeri Knull

DESCRIPTION: This beetle (12–21 mm [0.5–0.8 in]) is light-brown with four ivory-colored spots on each elytron. Large males have antennae as much as twice as long as their body, with the last antennal segment as long as the body.

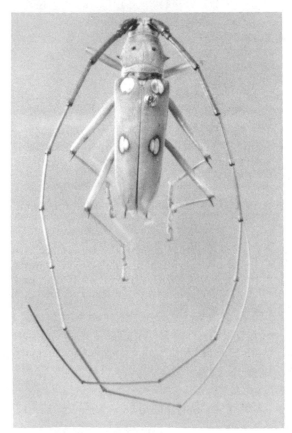

Strohecker's Eburia,
Eburia stroheckeri
(courtesy of Michael
C. Thomas).

Distribution of
Strohecker's eburia,
Eburia stroheckeri.

RANGE: This species is known from Dade and Monroe counties.

HABITAT: It is found in tropical hardwood hammocks.

LIFE HISTORY AND ECOLOGY: Unknown.

BASIS FOR STATUS CLASSIFICATION: This species was described
(Knull 1949) from a single specimen from Matheson Hammock in Dade
County, and has been taken rarely since in tropical hardwood hammocks of
southern Dade County and the Upper Keys, usually by beating or at light. It
is known only from Florida and, according to the original description, is
most closely related to a Jamaican species, *E. jamaicae.*

RECOMMENDATIONS: Research to find the host of this species might
lead to more specific protection. In the meantime, protection of tropical
hardwood hammocks is the best general conservation measure.

PREPARED BY: Michael C. Thomas, Florida State Collection of Arthropods, P.O. Box 147100, Gainesville, FL 32614-7100.

Threatened

Delong's Aneflomorpha

Aneflomorpha delongi (Champlain & Knull)

DESCRIPTION: This beetle (13 mm [0.5 in]) is elongate, parallel-sided, and pale brownish. Its antennae surpass the elytra by about one-third in males and by about one segment in females, with a very long spine on the third segment.

DeLong's Aneflo-
morpha, *Aneflomor-
pha delongi* (courtesy
of Michael C.
Thomas).

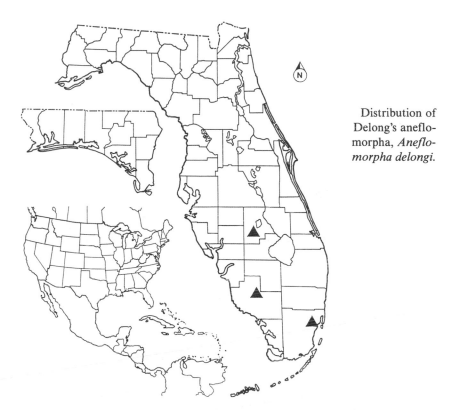

Distribution of Delong's aneflomorpha, *Aneflomorpha delongi.*

RANGE: This beetle is known only from Florida in Dade, Collier, and Highlands counties.

HABITAT: Unknown. This beetle has only been collected at lights after dark.

LIFE HISTORY AND ECOLOGY: Unknown.

BASIS FOR STATUS CLASSIFICATION: Linsley (1963) did not see any specimens of this Florida precinctive, described from a single specimen collected in April in Miami. No other specimens are known from Dade County. Recently, Lampert (1977) reported a population of this species at the Archbold Biological Station in Highlands County. Adults of that population are active in September. There is a single specimen, collected at Bear Island in the Big Cypress National Wildlife Refuge in Collier County on 10 June 1988. No other populations are known to exist and the larval host is unknown.

RECOMMENDATIONS: There can be no recommendations for the conservation of Delong's aneflomorpha as long as its biology is completely unknown. Two of the sites where it occurs are being maintained as natural habitats.

PREPARED BY: Michael C. Thomas, Florida State Collection of Arthropods, P.O. Box 147100, Gainesville, FL 32614-7100.

FAMILY CERAMBYCIDAE

Threatened

White-Spotted Longhorn

Linsleyonides albomaculatus (Champlain & Knull)

DESCRIPTION: This longhorn beetle is elongate, slender, and reddish-brown with conspicuous snow-white patches of appressed pubescence on pronotum and elytra. Length, 11–13 mm (0.5 in).

RANGE: This species is known from Dade and Monroe counties in Florida, and from Cuba.

White-Spotted Longhorn, *Linsleyonides albomaculatus* (courtesy of Michael C. Thomas).

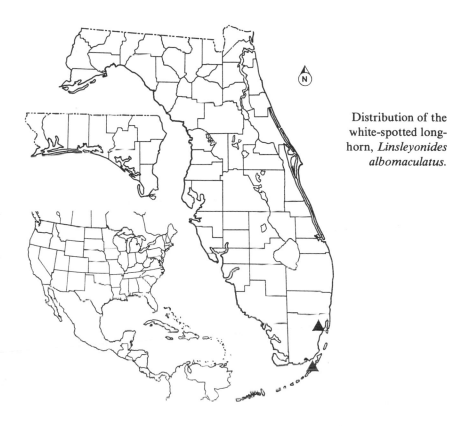

Distribution of the
white-spotted long-
horn, *Linsleyonides
albomaculatus.*

HABITAT: It occurs in tropical hardwood hammocks.

LIFE HISTORY AND ECOLOGY: Unknown.

BASIS FOR STATUS CLASSIFICATION: This small longhorn was described from Miami. Only a few specimens have been collected, mostly at
electric lights on Upper Key Largo, and nothing is known of its biology.

RECOMMENDATIONS: The acquisition by the state of large areas of
tropical hammock on North Key Largo should help protect this species. No
more specific conservation measures can be considered until more is known
about the biology of the insect.

PREPARED BY: Michael C. Thomas, Florida State Collection of Arthropods, P.O. Box 147100, Gainesville, FL 32614–7100.

Threatened

Cape Sable Longhorn

Heterachthes sablensis Blatchley

DESCRIPTION: This beetle is elongate (9–13 mm [0.4–0.5 in]) and slender. It is brown, with yellow subapical spots on the elytra. Elytral apices are obliquely truncate and slightly emarginate.

RANGE: This longhorn beetle is known only from Florida in Monroe and Dade counties.

HABITAT: It has been found in coastal mangrove forests.

Cape Sable Long-horn, *Heterachthes sablensis* (courtesy of Michael C. Thomas).

Distribution of the
Cape Sable long-
horn, *Heterachthes
sablensis.*

LIFE HISTORY AND ECOLOGY: Unknown, "swept from low herbs just back of the beach" at Cape Sable, Monroe County, in February (Blatchley 1920). There are only two specimens of this species in the Florida State Collection of Arthropods, collected at Virginia Key, Dade County, in May and June in the early 1960s and associated with black mangrove. Two additional specimens were collected recently by R. H. Turnbow, Jr., beating in a mixed mangrove thicket on Virginia Key.

BASIS FOR STATUS CLASSIFICATION: Linsley (1963) apparently saw no specimens of this Florida precinctive, and it is very rare in collections.

RECOMMENDATION: The type locality is protected by Everglades National Park. No specific conservation measures can be suggested until we know more about the biology of this species.

PREPARED BY: Michael C. Thomas, Florida State Collection of Arthropods, P.O. Box 147100, Gainesville, FL 32614-7100.

Status Undetermined

Horn's Aethecerinus

Aethecerinus hornii (Lacordaire)

DESCRIPTION: This beetle is elongate (10–17 mm [0.4–0.7 in]), parallel-sided, and somewhat wasp-like. It is reddish-brown, with a transverse yellow band at the base of the elytra and an oblique yellow band at about midpoint; the oblique band has a darker border and the apical half of the elytra is more or less infuscate.

RANGE: It occurs only in Florida. Specimens in the Florida State Collection of Arthropods were collected in Dixie, Highlands, Lee, Polk, and Martin counties.

Horn's Aethecerinus,
Aethecerinus hornii
(courtesy of Michael
C. Thomas).

Distribution of
Horn's Aethec-
erinus, *Aethecerinus
hornii.*

HABITAT: Although apparently not restricted to true scrub areas, this species does seem to prefer fairly xeric habitats.

LIFE HISTORY AND ECOLOGY: Little is known of the biology of this
species except that the adults are diurnal, active usually late in the afternoon
during April and May, feeding at fermenting exudates of decaying hardwood
logs and stumps, and forming large mating aggregations of as many as 13
individuals on oak stumps (Turnbow & Hovore 1979; M. Thomas, pers.
observ.).

BASIS FOR STATUS CLASSIFICATION: This enigmatic Florida precinctive was so rare that in his recent family monograph, Linsley (1962b)
merely repeated Lacordaire's Latin description. Woodruff (1972) recorded
the capture of six specimens, probably the largest series captured up to that
time, in pitfall traps baited with fermenting malt solution in a scrub area of
Lee County. A large population was discovered in the late 1970s near Old
Town in Dixie County (Turnbow & Hovore 1979). Much slash had accumulated over several years from logging operations in the area and many otherwise uncommon or rare woodboring beetles also had built up large populations. Populations seem to be highly localized. The factors limiting the
distribution of this species are unknown.

RECOMMENDATION: No recommendations are possible until we know more about the biological requirements of the species.

PREPARED BY: Michael C. Thomas, Florida State Collection of Arthropods, P.O. Box 147100, Gainesville, FL 32614–7100.

FAMILY CERAMBYCIDAE

Status Undetermined

Cabbage Palm Longhorn

Osmopleura chamaeropis (Horn)

DESCRIPTION: "This species may be readily recognized by the elongate, attenuate form, the longitudinal lines of white pubescence on the pronotum, and the uniformly reddish brown, coarsely pubescent elytra without integumental bands or spots" (Linsley 1964).

Cabbage Palm Longhorn, *Osmopleura chamaeropis* (courtesy of Michael C. Thomas).

Distribution of the cabbage palm longhorn, *Osmopleura chamaeropis.*

RANGE: This beetle is known from Florida and Georgia.

HABITAT: It occurs in pine-palmetto woodlands.

LIFE HISTORY AND ECOLOGY: Adults can be found on cabbage palms, *Sabal palmetto*, in which the larvae breed. This species is rarely collected but can be locally abundant, according to Turnbow & Hovore (1979), who reported on its habits at Long Pine Key and Pinelands Trail at Everglades National Park: "Occasional individuals were collected from blossoms or resting on foliage of *S. palmetto*, but the majority were found in the deep interspaces between living stems in the basal rosettes of the palmettos. The cuneate elytra allowed for deep retreat upon disturbance, and the striped head and prothorax blended well with the decomposing litter accumulated in the rosette. Feeding larvae, pupae, and teneral adults were collected from dead, dry inflorescences, and from dead leaf bases persisting on the trees. The eggs are apparently laid on green inflorescences or at the bases of the outermost living leaves, as feeding larvae were always found in the most recent, completely dead portions of the plant."

BASIS FOR STATUS CLASSIFICATION: Individuals of this species are uncommon in collections. Populations seem to be highly localized. The factors limiting the distribution of this species are unknown.

RECOMMENDATION: The host plant is very abundant. No recommendations are possible until we know what factors are responsible for the apparent rarity of the species. There are "naturally rare" species whose populations have always been kept low by natural factors that have nothing to do with human activities. Such species do not require our intervention for their protection as long as there is an adequate area of habitat.

PREPARED BY: Michael C. Thomas, Florida State Collection of Arthropods, P.O. Box 147100, Gainesville, FL 32614–7100.

Status Undetermined

Yellow-Banded Typocerus
Typocerus flavocinctus Knull

DESCRIPTION: This beetle (10–12 mm [0.5 in]) is entirely black except for a transverse yellow band just before the middle of the elytra; two small yellow spots may be present behind the band.

RANGE: It is known from central Florida.

HABITAT: This beetle occurs in pine flatwoods.

LIFE HISTORY AND ECOLOGY: Adults have been collected at flowers of *Ilex glabra* and *Serenoa repens*. Adults are active for only a few hours in the morning. Larval hosts are unknown.

BASIS FOR STATUS CLASSIFICATION: Only described in 1956 by Knull, this species was until recently known only from Sebring and Highlands Hammock State Park, Highlands County. In the past few years additional populations have been discovered at North Port, Sarasota County (Jeffrey P. Huether, pers. comm.), and in the Withlacoochee State Forest,

Yellow-banded Typocerus, *Typocerus flavocinctus* (courtesy of Michael C. Thomas).

Hernando County (Roy Morris, pers. comm.). Populations seem to be highly localized. The factors limiting the distribution of this species are unknown.

RECOMMENDATION: There are populations in protected natural habitat at Archbold Biological Station and Highlands Hammock State Park. No specific recommendations are possible until more is known about the biology of this species.

PREPARED BY: Michael C. Thomas, Florida State Collection of Arthropods, P.O. Box 147100, Gainesville, FL 32614–7100.

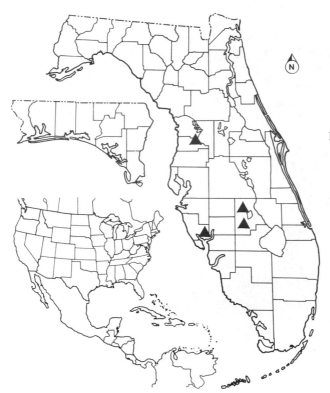

Distribution of the
yellow-banded ty-
pocerus, *Typocerus
flavocinctus.*

Cerambycid Beetles of Concern

The following beetles are rarely collected south Florida species and probably should be listed, although there is justification for listing all species with Florida distributions that are restricted to the Florida Keys.

Heterops dimidiata
Elaphidion clavis
Elaphidion tectum
Neoclytus longipes
Curtomerus fasciatus
Parmenonta thomasi.

PREPARED BY: Michael C. Thomas, Florida State Collection of Arthropods, P.O. Box 147100, Gainesville, FL 32614-7100.

Order Coleoptera
FAMILY HISTERIDAE

INTRODUCTION: Hister beetles are small, usually shiny black insects whose appendages can be withdrawn into various slots and grooves so that the insect resembles a hard black seed. Both larvae and adults are predaceous, usually feeding on larvae of flies or beetles. Many species are highly specific in their habitat requirement, and there are species specialized for life in the nests of certain species of ants, termites, and vertebrates.

PREPARED BY: Mark A. Deyrup, Archbold Biological Station, Lake Placid, FL 33852.

FAMILY HISTERIDAE

Threatened

Gopher Tortoise Hister Beetle
Chelyoxenus xerobatis Hubbard

DESCRIPTION: This small beetle (3–4 mm long [0.2 in]) is oval and shiny black, with eight fine elytral striae, including a marginal stria and a short humeral stria. It can be distinguished from all similar species by the claws of the middle and hind tarsi: the outer claw is minute, the inner claw much enlarged, so that at first glance there appears to be a single claw. *C. xerobatis* is the only member of its genus. Published description and illustrations are found in Hubbard (1894).

RANGE: This hister beetle probably occurs throughout the range of the gopher tortoise (Woodruff 1982a). It is known from scattered localities in Florida, Georgia, and Mississippi.

LIFE HISTORY AND ECOLOGY: It probably is a predator of fly larvae or other insect larvae in gopher tortoise burrows, but the exact diet is unknown.

BASIS FOR STATUS CLASSIFICATION: This species shares the status of its obligate host.

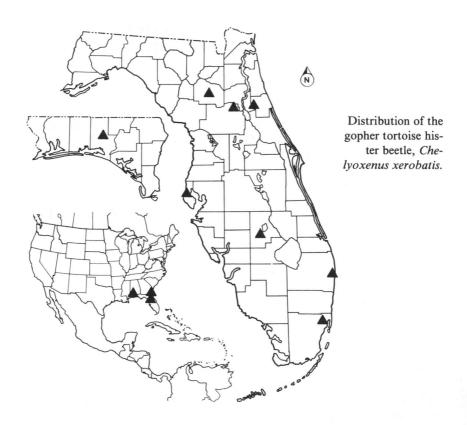

Distribution of the gopher tortoise hister beetle, *Chelyoxenus xerobatis*.

RECOMMENDATIONS: The future of this species depends completely upon efforts to save its host. It may not be able to colonize burrows of tortoises that have been relocated to areas from which tortoises had been extirpated.

PREPARED BY: Mark A. Deyrup, Archbold Biological Station, Lake Placid, FL 33852.

Order Coleoptera
FAMILY CEBRIONIDAE

INTRODUCTION: Cebrionid beetles are a small group whose wireworm-like larvae, which live in the soil, are presumed to feed on roots. Both edaphic requirements and host specificity might serve to isolate populations in patches of suitable habitat. More important, females are flightless, greatly increasing the chance of isolation, hence evolutionary divergence, of populations. Adult cebrionids remain underground until they emerge to mate, often in large numbers, during heavy summer rainshowers. Males are readily captured in flight traps or light traps, and there has been a recent survey of North American material in museums (Galley 1990), so our knowledge of the distribution of species is better than might be expected for such an obscure group of beetles. Because of their sedentary habits, females are seldom collected, and few are known. Galley (1990) has provided keys to species of *Selonodon*, the only cebrionid genus known to occur in Florida. Five species discussed below have manuscript (thesis) names which should not be used until formally published.

Cebrionid larvae can be distinguished from most other wireworm-like larvae by the elongate prothorax, which covers the posterior part of the head, and the cervical membrane, which can be everted when the head is thrown back (Böving & Craighead 1931). *Selonodon* adults somewhat resemble brown click beetles (Elateridae), ranging from 12mm to 16 mm (0.5 to 0.6 in) long, but with a short prosternum, a long and narrow prosternal process, and prominent, crescent-shaped mandibles. Females are larger and stouter than males, with shortened antennae and tarsi. Currently, females must be associated with males for accurate identification.

PREPARED BY: Krista E. M. Galley, Department of Entomology, Cornell University, Ithaca, NY 14853, and Mark A. Deyrup, Archbold Biological Station, Lake Placid, FL 33852.

Rare

Simple Cebrionid

Selonodon simplex (LeConte)

DESCRIPTION: Males are relatively large (mean elytra length 12.7 mm [0.5 in]). The antenna is relatively short, exceeding the apex of the hind angle of the pronotum by one segment; the clypeolabral suture is strongly curved; the median lobe of aedeagus is slender throughout; the pronotum and elytra are gray brown to dark brown. The female is unknown.

RANGE: This beetle is known from northernmost Florida (Suwanee County) and southernmost Georgia (Lowndes County). This species might be associated in some way with the Suwanee River drainage.

HABITAT: Unknown.

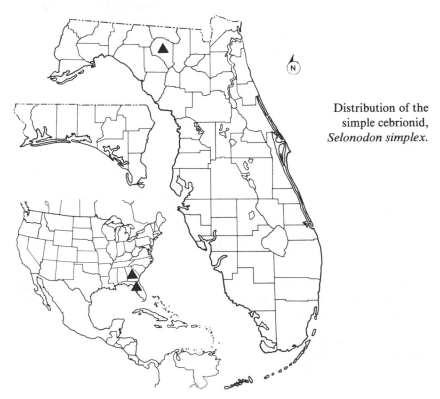

Distribution of the
simple cebrionid,
Selonodon simplex.

LIFE HISTORY AND ECOLOGY: Adults are active June-July. Like other members of the genus, this species probably flies during rains.

BASIS FOR STATUS CLASSIFICATION: This species belongs to a group of three related species in Florida that appear to be geographically isolated from each other (Galley 1990). A highly restricted distribution is typical of the majority of species in *Selonodon*.

RECOMMENDATIONS: The habitat requirements of this species must be discovered if this beetle is to be protected.

PREPARED BY: Krista E. M. Galley, Department of Entomology, Cornell University, Ithaca, NY 14853, and Mark A. Deyrup, Archbold Biological Station, Lake Placid, FL 33852.

FAMILY CEBRIONIDAE

Rare

Archbold Cebrionid
Selonodon sp. 1

DESCRIPTION: Males have a slender mandible, bent at right angle. The antenna is relatively long, exceeding the apex of the hind angle of the pronotum by at least three segments; the clypeolabral suture is slightly curved; the median lobe of the aedeagus is expanded medially; the pronotum and elytra are very dark, almost black. Females are unknown.

RANGE: This undescribed species is known from Highlands County.

HABITAT: It has been taken in sand pine scrub.

LIFE HISTORY AND ECOLOGY: Adults are active late May to early June. Like other members of the genus, this species' adult emergence is associated with heavy rains (Galley 1990).

BASIS FOR STATUS CLASSIFICATION: It is known from only two scrub sites on the southern Lake Wales Ridge, an area showing a high degree of endemism in scrub species. This species occurs in an area of natural habitat protected by the Archbold Biological Station.

RECOMMENDATIONS: Preserve scrub habitat on the southern Lake Wales Ridge.

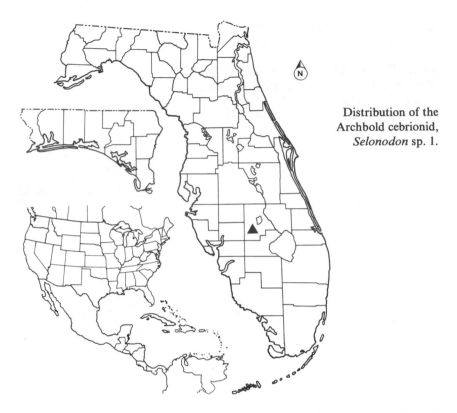

Distribution of the
Archbold cebrionid,
Selonodon sp. 1.

PREPARED BY: Krista E. M. Galley, Department of Entomology, Cornell University, Ithaca, NY 14853, and Mark A. Deyrup, Archbold Biological Station, Lake Placid, FL 33852.

FAMILY CEBRIONIDAE

Rare

Santa Rosa Cebrionid

Selonodon sp. 2

DESCRIPTION: Males have an antenna that exceeds the apex of hind angle of pronotum by two segments; the clypeolabral suture is strongly curved; the basal fused areas of aedeagus are relatively long, more than one third the length of the aedeagus; the pronotum and elytra are light brown to rust brown. Females are unknown.

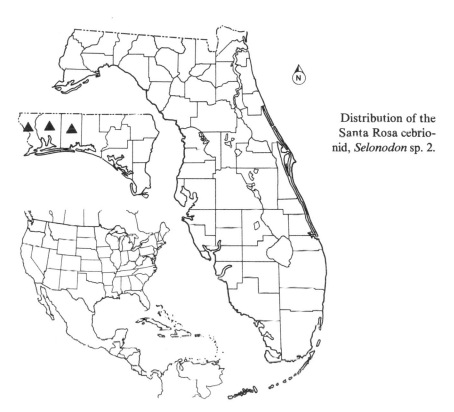

Distribution of the
Santa Rosa cebrio-
nid, *Selonodon* sp. 2.

RANGE: This undescribed beetle is known from Escambia, Okaloosa, and Santa Rosa counties.

HABITAT: Unknown.

LIFE HISTORY AND ECOLOGY: Adults are active mid-June to mid-July. Like other members of the genus, this species probably flies during rains.

BASIS FOR STATUS CLASSIFICATION: It is known from a small area of Florida where there are a number of upland species whose ranges (at least in Florida) are small. This species belongs to a group of three related species in Florida that appear to be geographically isolated from each other (Galley 1990). This species has been taken in the Blackwater State Forest, and it probably also occurs in natural areas of the Eglin Air Force Base.

RECOMMENDATIONS: Research on distribution and habitat requirements is necessary in order to determine the best measures to protect this beetle.

PREPARED BY: Krista E. M. Galley, Department of Entomology, Cornell University, Ithaca, NY 14853, and Mark A. Deyrup, Archbold Biological Station, Lake Placid, FL 33852.

Rare

Similar Cebrionid
Selonodon sp. 3

DESCRIPTION: Males are relatively large (mean length of elytra 13.6 mm [0.5 in]). The antenna exceeds the apex of the hind angle of the pronotum by 1–2 segments; the clypeolabral suture is moderately curved; the median lobe of the aedeagus is long and slender; the pronotum and elytra are brownish grey. Females are unknown.

RANGE: It is known from Leon County.

HABITAT: Unknown. This is probably an upland species associated with the "red hills" region.

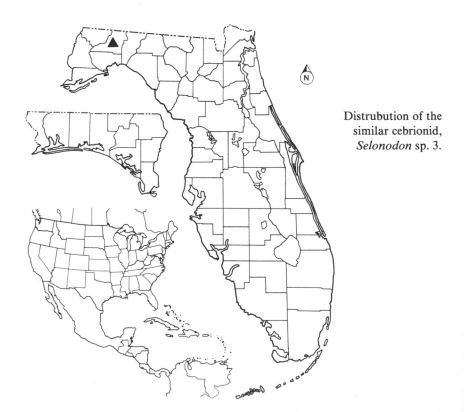

Distrubution of the similar cebrionid, *Selonodon* sp. 3.

LIFE HISTORY AND ECOLOGY: Adults are active late June through July. Like other members of the genus, this species probably flies during rains.

BASIS FOR STATUS CLASSIFICATION: It is known from a small edaphically distinctive area of Florida. It occurs in protected natural habitat at Tall Timbers Research Station.

RECOMMENDATIONS: There is a need for research on distribution and habitat requirements of this undescribed beetle.

PREPARED BY: Krista E. M. Galley, Department of Entomology, Cornell University, Ithaca, NY 14853, and Mark A. Deyrup, Archbold Biological Station, Lake Placid, FL 33852.

FAMILY CEBRIONIDAE

Rare

Rusty Cebrionid
Selonodon sp. 4

DESCRIPTION: Males are relatively large (mean length of elytra 13.5 mm [0.5 in]). The antenna is relatively short, exceeding the apex of the hind angle of the pronotum by one segment or less; the clypeolabral suture is moderately curved; the median lobe of the aedeagus is widened medially The apical two thirds of the pronotum are medium brown, the posterior third is light brown, and the elytra is rusty brown. Females are similar to males in coloration, but they should be associated with males for accurate identification.

RANGE: It is known from Liberty, Jackson, and Gadsden counties in Florida and Baker and Decatur counties in Georgia.

HABITAT: Unknown.

LIFE HISTORY AND ECOLOGY: Adults are active from mid-June to mid-July. Like other members of the genus, this species probably flies during rains.

BASIS FOR STATUS CLASSIFICATION: This undescribed beetle is known from several sites in Florida and Georgia, centering around the Apalachicola drainage, a notable area of endemism. It occurs in protected habitats of Torreya State Park and Florida Caverns State Park.

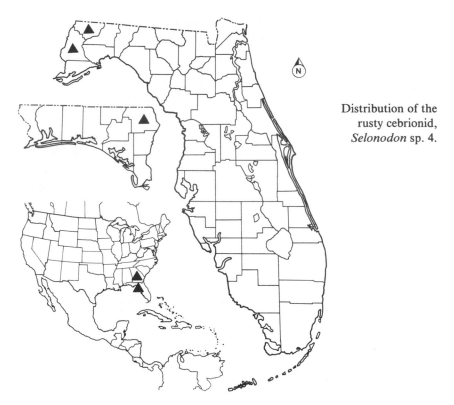

Distribution of the
rusty cebrionid,
Selonodon sp. 4.

RECOMMENDATIONS: There is a need for research on distribution and habitat requirements for this beetle.

PREPARED BY: Krista E. M. Galley, Department of Entomology, Cornell University, Ithaca, NY 14853, and Mark A. Deyrup, Archbold Biological Station, Lake Placid, FL 33852.

FAMILY CEBRIONIDAE

Status Undetermined

Large-Jawed Cebrionid

Selonodon mandibularis (LeConte)

DESCRIPTION: Males have very long mandibles that are curved and very slender. The clypeolabral suture is straight, often faint or absent; the antenna exceeds the apex of the hind angle of the pronotum by four segments; the pronotum and the elytra are light brown and rust brown; the prosternal process is very narrow along its length. The female can only be identified when with the male.

RANGE: This cebrionid beetle is known from central and southern Florida, north to Alachua County (one record from Leon County), south to Highlands County.

HABITAT: Unknown, probably sandy uplands.

LIFE HISTORY AND ECOLOGY: Adults are active from late June (Highlands County) to early August (Alachua County); like other members of the genus, this species' adult emergence is associated with heavy rains (Galley 1990).

BASIS FOR STATUS CLASSIFICATION: This Florida endemic beetle belongs to a group of four related species occurring in Alabama, Louisiana, Mississippi, and eastern Oklahoma (Galley 1990). It is probably restricted to

Distribution of the large-jawed cebrionid, *Selonodon mandibularis.*

patches of sandy uplands. This species occurs on protected habitat at the Archbold Biological Station.

RECOMMENDATIONS: Research on distribution and habitat requirements is needed before protective measures can be considered.

PREPARED BY: Krista E. M. Galley, Department of Entomology, Cornell University, Ithaca, NY 14853, and Mark A. Deyrup, Archbold Biological Station, Lake Placid, FL 33852.

FAMILY CEBRIONIDAE

Status Undetermined

Florida Cebrionid

Selonodon sp. 5

DESCRIPTION: The male is moderately large (mean length of elytra 12.2 mm); the clypeolabral suture is strongly curved; the antenna exceeds the apex of the hind angle of the pronotum by one or two segments; the median lobe of the aedeagus is variable, but usually slightly broadened medially, tapered to the apex; the pronotum and elytra are dark brown. The female must be associated with the male for accurate identification.

RANGE: Central Florida, north to Alachua County, south to Manatee County.

HABITAT: Unknown, probably sandy uplands.

LIFE HISTORY AND ECOLOGY: Adults are active late May to late July; like other members of the genus, this species probably flies during rains.

BASIS FOR STATUS CLASSIFICATION: This Florida endemic belongs to a group of three related species in Florida that appear to be geographically isolated from each other (Galley 1990). This species is probably restricted to patches of sandy upland. It probably occurs in protected natural habitat in Ocala National Forest.

RECOMMENDATIONS: Research is needed on the distribution and habitat requirements of this species.

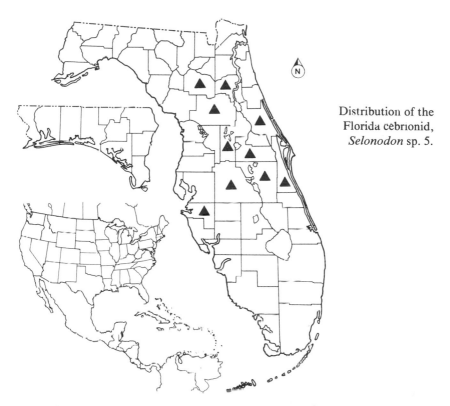

Distribution of the
Florida cebrionid,
Selonodon sp. 5.

PREPARED BY: Krista E. M. Galley, Department of Entomology, Cornell University, Ithaca, NY 14853, and Mark A. Deyrup, Archbold Biological Station, Lake Placid, FL 33852.

Order Coleoptera
FAMILY EROTYLIDAE

INTRODUCTION: The Erotylidae, or pleasing fungus beetles, are almost always associated with fungi. Many members of the family appear to be generally uncommon; these species may feed on only a few species of fungi in a particular habitat. The fruiting bodies of fungi constitute a rich, rather ephemeral resource, which are often exploited by specialized insects that may have a highly developed ability to find fungi. Such resources, which themselves tend to be relatively rare, patchy, or sporadic, seem able to support populations of rare insects. As with many insects, erotylid life histories remain a mystery for most species. Of those covered here, three are known only from peninsular Florida, three are northern species with peripheral populations in

Florida, and one is so rarely collected that little can be discussed about it. Because so little is known about them there is need for further surveys, life history studies, and protection of their habitats in Florida. Keys to Florida species are in Skelley (1988); the North American fauna was revised by Boyle (1956).

PREPARED BY: Mark A. Deyrup, Archbold Biological Station, Lake Placid, FL 33852.

FAMILY EROTYLIDAE

Rare

Scrub Ischyrus

Ischyrus dunedinensis Blatchley

DESCRIPTION: This beetle is elongate-oval in shape, orange with black markings, and has three distinctive pronotal spots. Length 5.0–7.2 mm (0.2–0.3 in). A published description is found in Skelley and Goodrich (1989).

Scrub Ischyrus, *Ischyrus dunedinensis* (courtesy of Paul E. Skelley).

Distribution of the
scrub ischyrus,
*Ischyrus
dunedinensis.*

RANGE: This beetle is known only from peninsular Florida and Carlton County, Georgia.

HABITAT: *Ischyrus dunedinensis* appears to be a scrub species, with most known specimens from the Archbold Biological Station.

LIFE HISTORY AND ECOLOGY: Unknown. Specimens have been taken in flight traps from May to September.

BASIS FOR STATUS CLASSIFICATION: This is a conspicuous species that is rare in collections. It also appears to be associated with Florida scrub, a habitat that has been rapidly disappearing. It occurs in protected habitat at the Archbold Biological Station and Ocala National Forest.

RECOMMENDATIONS: Preservation of natural habitats where this species lives; more specific protection requires research on the biology of the species.

PREPARED BY: Paul E. Skelley, Florida State Collection of Arthropods, P.O. Box 147100, Gainesville, FL 32614-7100.

Rare

Alachua Triplax

Triplax alachuae Boyle

DESCRIPTION: The shape of this beetle is elongate-oval. The maxillary palps have an apical brush of setae; the color is orange except for the black head, antennae, and elytra; the elytra have impressed strial punctures and their surface is covered with microsculpture, giving them a dull appearance. Length is 4.83–6.07 mm (0.2 in).

RANGE: The Alachua triplax occurs in peninsular Florida.

HABITAT: This beetle inhabits scrub and sandhill habitats.

Distribution of the
Alachua triplax,
Triplax alachuae.

LIFE HISTORY AND ECOLOGY: Larvae and adults are found under bark of dead *Quercus laevis* (turkey oak) infested with the fungus *Inonotus andersonii*. Larvae feed on hyphae-filled wood under the loose bark and make pupal chambers in the wood.

BASIS FOR STATUS CLASSIFICATION: This species is very rare in collections, appears to have a specialized diet, and is restricted to upland habitats that are rapidly becoming scarce. This species is known from areas of protected natural habitat at San Felasco Hammock, Roess Goldhead Branch State Park, and Archbold Biological Station.

RECOMMENDATIONS: Large stands of *Quercus laevis* may be necessary to maintain populations of this species.

PREPARED BY: Paul E. Skelley, Florida State Collection of Arthropods, P.O. Box 147100, Gainesville, FL 32614-7100.

FAMILY EROTYLIDAE

Status Undetermined

Handsome Tritoma

Tritoma pulchra Say

DESCRIPTION: This beetle is ovoid in shape. Its color is black, except for a broad orange band on the basal half of the elytra. Length is 2.62-4.00 mm (0.1-0.2 in). A published illustration is found in Dillon and Dillon (1961).

RANGE: This species occurs in northeastern U.S., extending down the Appalachian Mountains. In Florida, it is known only from Torreya State Park in Liberty County.

HABITAT: This species inhabits mesic forests.

LIFE HISTORY AND ECOLOGY: Known to feed on the fungus *Tyromyces chioneus*.

BASIS FOR STATUS CLASSIFICATION: In Florida this conspicuous species may be restricted to be Apalachicola River area, where there are a number of northern plants and animals absent from the rest of Florida. A protected population occurs at Torreya State Park.

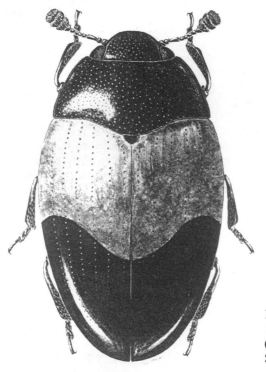

Handsome tritoma,
Tritoma pulchra
(courtesy of Paul E.
Skelley).

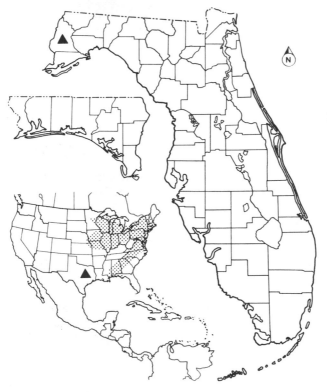

Distribution of the
handsome tritoma,
Tritoma pulchra.

RECOMMENDATIONS: Maintain and expand refuges for northern species in the Apalachicola River drainage.

PREPARED BY: Paul E. Skelley, Florida State Collection of Arthropods, P.O. Box 147100, Gainesville, FL 32614-7100.

FAMILY EROTYLIDAE

Status Undetermined

Red-Winged Tritoma

Tritoma sanguinipennis (Say)

DESCRIPTION: The shape of this beetle is ovoid. Its color is black, except for the entirely orange elytra and the clypeus which has a shallow V-shaped apical notch. Length is 3.17-5.0 mm (0.15-0.2 in). Dillon and Dillon (1961) and Froeschner and Meiner (1953) illustrate this species.

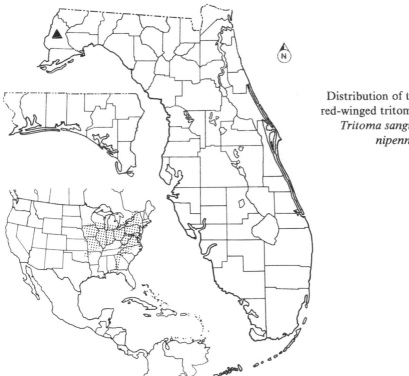

Distribution of the red-winged tritoma, *Tritoma sanguinipennis*.

RANGE: This beetle occurs in the northeastern U.S., extending down the Appalachian Mountains. In Florida, it is known only from Torreya State Park in Liberty County.

HABITAT: This species occurs in mesic forest.

LIFE HISTORY AND ECOLOGY: It was collected from the fungi, *Polyporus alveolaris* and *P. arcularius*.

BASIS FOR STATUS CLASSIFICATION: In Florida this conspicuous species may be restricted to the Apalachicola River area, where there are a number of northern plants and animals absent from the rest of Florida. A protected population occurs at Torreya State Park.

RECOMMENDATIONS: Maintain and expand refuges for northern species in the Apalachicola River drainage.

PREPARED BY: Paul E. Skelley, Florida State Collection of Arthropods, P.O. Box 147100, Gainesville, FL 32614-7100.

FAMILY EROTYLIDAE

Status Undetermined

Darkling Tritoma

Tritoma tenebrosa Fall

DESCRIPTION: This ovoid beetle is dark-brown to black in color and unpatterned; the eyes are finely faceted; the tibia is strongly angularly dilated. It superficially resembles *Pseudischyrus nigrans*, but is larger and has finely faceted eyes. Length is 3.80-5.66 mm (0.1-0.2 in).

RANGE: This species occurs throughout the eastern U.S., including the northern three fourths of peninsular Florida.

HABITAT: Unknown.

LIFE HISTORY AND ECOLOGY: Unknown. The angularly dilated tibiae might indicate that this species is fossorial.

BASIS FOR STATUS CLASSIFICATION: Even though this species is apparently widespread, occurring within the collecting range of many coleopterists, it is known from very few specimens.

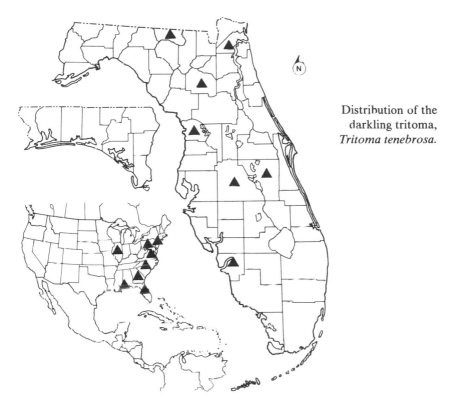

Distribution of the darkling tritoma, *Tritoma tenebrosa.*

RECOMMENDATIONS: Research on the biology and distribution of this species should precede any recommendations for its protection.

PREPARED BY: Paul E. Skelley, Florida State Collection of Arthropods, P.O. Box 147100, Gainesville, Fl. 32614-7100.

FAMILY EROTYLIDAE

Status Undetermined

Black-Headed Triplax

Triplax frontalis Horn

DESCRIPTION: This elongate-oval beetle is orange in color except for the black head, antennae, and elytra; the elytra are smooth and shiny; maxillary palps have an apical brush of setae. Length is 3.93–5.87 mm (0.15–0.2 in).

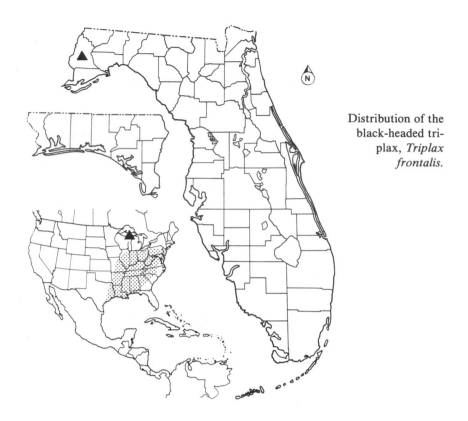

Distribution of the
black-headed tri-
plax, *Triplax
frontalis.*

RANGE: It occurs in the eastern U.S. In Florida, it is known only from Torreya State Park in Liberty County.

HABITAT: Unknown.

LIFE HISTORY AND ECOLOGY: This species has been collected on the
wood-rotting fungi *Inonotus andersonii* and *I. cuticularis.*

BASIS FOR STATUS CLASSIFICATION: In Florida this species may be
restricted to the Apalachicola River area, where there are a number of northern plants and animals absent from the rest of Florida. A protected population occurs at Torreya State Park.

RECOMMENDATIONS: Maintain and expand refuges for northern species in the Apalachicola River drainage.

PREPARED BY: Paul E. Skelley, Florida State Collection of Arthropods,
P.O. Box 147100, Gainesville, FL 32614-7100.

Status Undetermined

Florida Pseudischyrus

Pseudischyrus nigrans (Crotch)

DESCRIPTION: This ovoid beetle is dark-brown to black in color and un-patterned; the eyes are coarsely faceted; the tibia is strongly dilated; the pros-ternal lines are convergent anteriorly. It is similar in appearance to *Tritoma tenebrosa*, except for its coarsely faceted eyes and smaller size. Length 3.04–4.83 mm (0.1–0.2 in).

RANGE: The species occurs in Florida and extreme southern Georgia.

HABITAT: It inhabits sandy uplands, especially Florida scrub.

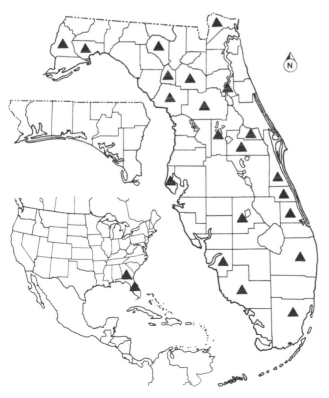

Distribution of the Florida pseudischy-rus, *Pseudischyrus nigrans.*

LIFE HISTORY AND ECOLOGY: *Pseudischyrus nigrans* seems common in scrub on mushrooms of the genera *Russula* and *Amanita* (Skelley 1988).

BASIS FOR STATUS CLASSIFICATION: This species seems restricted to natural sandy upland habitats, which are rapidly disappearing. This species is known from protected natural habitats at the University of Florida Welaka Conservation Reserve, Suwannee River State Park, San Felasco State Park, Torreya State Park, Archbold Biological Station, and Ocala National Forest.

RECOMMENDATIONS: Further surveys of the distribution of this species, especially in newly acquired upland preserves, might show that it needs no additional protection.

PREPARED BY: Paul E. Skelley, Florida State Collection of Arthropods, P.O. Box 147100, Gainesville, FL 32614-7100.

Caddisflies

INTRODUCTION: The caddisflies are aquatic insects that resemble moths, to which they are quite closely related. Adults have two pair of wings, at rest folded rooflike over the body. The antennae are usually long. The wings are more or less hairy and have subdued colors that help conceal the resting insect. Larvae are aquatic and often live in cases constructed from sand or vegetable matter held together with silk. Caddisfly larvae may be fantastically abundant and are of great ecological importance as decomposers, predators, and food for other organisms, especially fish. Like some other groups of aquatic insects, caddisflies provide many species that indicate water quality or pinpoint the location of rare aquatic habitats and interesting biogeographic disjunctions.

Since the appearance of the first edition of FCREPA series, 9 of the 21 species of Trichoptera included have not changed their status categories. Further information on the other 12 suggests a need for change in their status or deletion from the list. Eighteen species were either overlooked in the 1982 report or were described for the first time since then. Presently, 15 Trichoptera species are threatened in Florida; 14 are rare; and 5 are of undetermined status. Five species from the previous FCREPA report are removed from immediate conservation concern.

PREPARED BY: Mark Deyrup, Archbold Biological Station, Lake Placid, FL 33852.

Order Trichoptera
FAMILY SERICOSTOMATIDAE

Threatened

Zigzag Blackwater River Caddisfly
Agarodes (Agarodes) ziczac Ross and Scott

DESCRIPTION: *Agarodes ziczac* is a medium-sized (11 mm [0.5 in] long) caddisfly, various shades of brown in color. The male is distinguishable from that of other *Agarodes* species by the sharply double-angled zigzag of the tip of tenth tergum, best seen in lateral view. The female and the immature stages of the species are unknown. Females of related species were described by Ross and Scott (1974). Larvae of related species were described by Ross and Wallace (1974) and by Wiggins (1977).

RANGE: This species is known only from the holotype specimen collected in Okaloosa County beside the Blackwater River, 4 km (2.4 mi) west of Holt, Florida.

HABITAT: Since the larva of *A. ziczac* is unknown, a specific description of its microhabitat is not possible. However, presumably this species is, like the others in the genus, restricted to small streams with medium currents and sandy bottoms. Most of these streams are fed by artesian springs, which keep summer water temperatures well below those of streams fed only by surface drainage (Ross and Scott 1974).

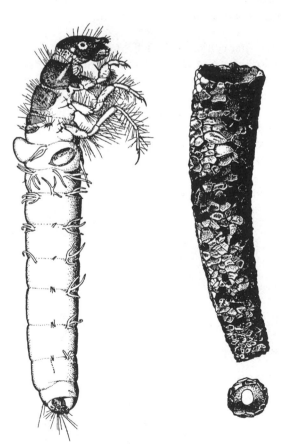

Caddisfly larva and case, *Agarodes* sp. (courtesy of the Department of Entomology, Royal Ontario Museum, Toronto).

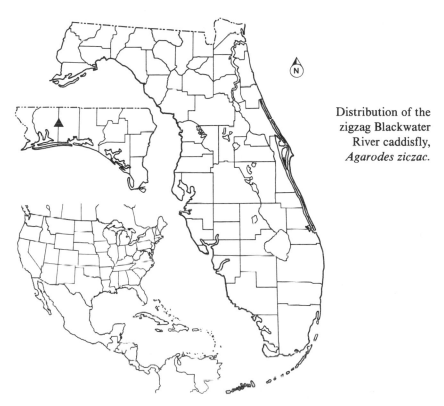

Distribution of the zigzag Blackwater River caddisfly, *Agarodes ziczac.*

LIFE HISTORY AND ECOLOGY: Observations of *A. ziczac* life history and ecology have not been made; its larva probably builds a stone case. Wiggins (1977) noted, "Since *Agarodes* larvae are rarely seen [collected] other than by sifting sand and gravel, I presume they are chiefly burrowing detritivores in these materials; guts of larvae (3) we examined contained pieces of vascular plants and fine organic particles for the most part." The single known locality for *A. ziczac* is also one of the few known localities for the threatened mayfly, *Dolania americana* Edmunds et al. Their very strict ecological requirements are apparently very similar.

SPECIALIZED OR UNIQUE CHARACTERISTICS: Like *D. americana*, and other Sericostomatidae species, this aquatic species seems to be one of only a few in the world that burrow into shifting sand.

BASIS FOR STATUS CLASSIFICATION: This species is known from only the single natural stream with clean shifting-sand bottom. If this stream becomes polluted, *A. ziczac* might become extinct.

RECOMMENDATIONS: The Blackwater River should be fully protected to preserve its natural condition. This species is one of several rare or threatened species found in this river.

PREPARED BY: John C. Morse, Department of Entomology, Clemson University, Clemson, SC 29634.

Order Tricoptera
FAMILY HYDROPSYCHIDAE

Threatened

Gordon's Little Sister Sedge

Cheumatopsyche gordonae Lago and Harris

DESCRIPTION: *Cheumatopsyche gordonae* belongs to the *C. campyla* group as defined by Gordon (1974), in which it most closely resembles *C. campyla*, differing in the smaller size (adult length 5.3 mm [0.2 in]), the more uniformly colored wings without a large light area on the anal margin near the apex, the shorter and more acutely shouldered apical lobes of the 10th tergum (resembling those of *C. logan*), and the presence of a median dorsal hump on the 10th tergum (Lago and Harris 1983). The immature stages are unknown. Larvae of related species were discussed by Ross (1944) and Wiggins (1977). Illustrations of a larva of *Cheumatopsyche* sp. and an adult of closely related *Hydropsyche simulans* are provided.

RANGE: This species is known only from the type localities in Walton County (headwaters of Rocky Creek, Eglin Air Force Base, 6.4 km southwest of Mossy Head) and Okaloosa County (Bull Creek, 16 km east-southeast of Crestview), Florida (Harris et al. 1982; Lago and Harris 1983; Gordon 1984).

HABITAT: Adults of the species were taken beside small clear streams with moderate streamflow in wooded areas or below a small impoundment (Harris et al. 1982; Lago and Harris 1983; Scheiring 1985). The specific habitat of the immature stages is unknown.

LIFE HISTORY AND ECOLOGY: Presumably *C. gordonae* larvae, like those of other species in the genus, spin nets through which suspended food particles are filtered from the water column. *Cheumatopsyche* species usually have short egg, pupal, and adult phases and a long larval phase. *C. gordonae* adults have been captured from 20 April through 19 September (Harris et al. 1982; Lago and Harris 1983).

SPECIALIZED OR UNIQUE CHARACTERISTICS: This species is presumably specialized as a filter-feeder in lotic habitats as are most other species of Hydropsychidae.

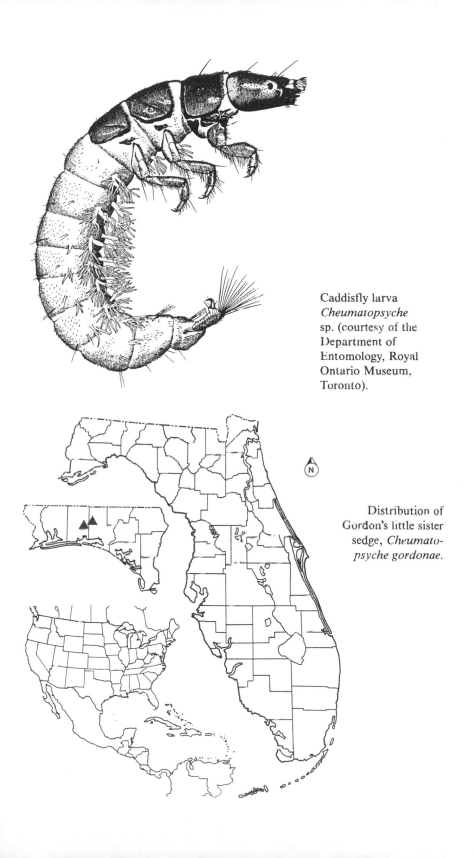

Caddisfly larva
Cheumatopsyche
sp. (courtesy of the
Department of
Entomology, Royal
Ontario Museum,
Toronto).

Distribution of
Gordon's little sister
sedge, *Cheumato-
psyche gordonae.*

BASIS FOR STATUS CLASSIFICATION: The species is known only from two neighboring catchments in a very small area of Florida. This species could become extinct if its habitat on the U.S. Air Force Base is severely damaged and there are no remaining populations elsewhere.

RECOMMENDATIONS: The type localities should be protected to preserve their natural condition.

PREPARED BY: John C. Morse, Department of Entomology, Clemson University, Clemson, SC 29634.

FAMILY HYDROPSYCHIDAE

Rare

Peters' Little Sister Sedge

Cheumatopsyche petersi Ross, Morse, and Gordon

DESCRIPTION: *Cheumatopsyche petersi* is a medium-sized (7 mm [0.3 in] long) net-spinning caddisfly. Its body, wings, and appendages are dark brown, and the antennae and mouthparts are paler at the base. The forewings have a few light spots. The male of *C. petersi* closely resembles that of *Cheumatopsyche pettiti* and *Cheumatopsyche helma*, but differs from both in the wide-shouldered apical lobes of the 10th tergum and in the shape of the clasper, which is very narrow at the apex of the basal segment and which has a very wide apical segment, particularly at the base (Gordon 1974). *Cheumatopsyche petersi* can be further distinguished from *Cheumatopsyche pettiti* by the short basal segment of the clasper. The *C. petersi* female differs from that of *pettiti* in the simple median plate on the venter of the 11th segment and in the shape of the clasper receptacle, which is more perpendicular and has an angular ventral margin (Gordon 1974). The immature stages are unknown. Larvae of related species were described by Ross (1944) and Wiggins (1977).

RANGE: At the time of the previous FCREPA report, this species was known only from a few localities on the Blackwater River in Okaloosa and Santa Rosa counties, Florida. Since then, it has been reported from Eglin Air Force Base (Rocky Creek, Walton County, and Bull Creek, Okaloosa County) in Florida (Harris et al. 1982) and from the states of Alabama (Baldwin, Conecuh, Mobile, Monroe, and Washington counties; Lago and Harris 1987) and Mississippi (Harrison County; Lago et al. 1982). Listed as "Peters' Cheumatopsyche Caddisfly" in 1982 FCREPA edition.

Distribution of Peter's little sister sedge, *Cheumatopsyche petersi.*

HABITAT: It is associated with small, clear lower Coastal Plain streams with moderate flow (Harris et al. 1982; Lago and Harris 1987b).

BASIS FOR STATUS CLASSIFICATION: This species apparently is endemic to the lower Coastal Plain streams of the Florida panhandle and westward, reportedly "common" in such streams in Alabama (Lago and Harris 1987b), but apparently more sporadic in those of Florida and Mississippi. It was listed as threatened in the 1982 FCREPA edition.

RECOMMENDATIONS: The few Florida populations should be monitored to assure their continuation.

PREPARED BY: John C. Morse, Department of Entomology, Clemson University, Clemson, SC 29634.

Order Trichoptera
FAMILY HYDROPTILIDAE

Threatened

Wakulla Springs Vari-Colored Microcaddisfly

Hydroptila wakulla Denning

DESCRIPTION: *Hydroptila wakulla* is a very small caddisfly (male 2.3 mm [0.1 in] long, female 2.7–4.1 mm [0.1–0.16 in] long), whose adults probably have patches of black and white hairs on the head and wings in a variegated pattern characteristic of this large genus. The species belongs to the *Hydroptila salmo, waubesiana*, and *acadia* section of the genus. It can be distinguished from those species by the very slender inferior appendages and the upturned hooks of the 10th tergum (Denning 1947; Blickle 1979). Immature stages and the female are unknown. Illustrations of the adult of *Hydroptila hamata*, and of the larva of *Hydroptila* species are provided.

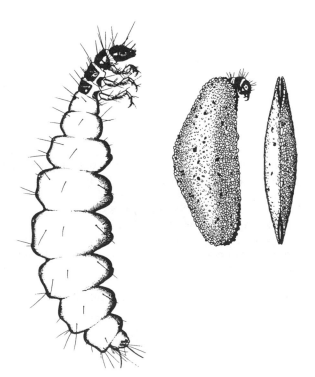

Caddisfly larva and case, *Hydroptila* sp. (courtesy of the Department of Entomology, Royal Ontario Museum, Toronto).

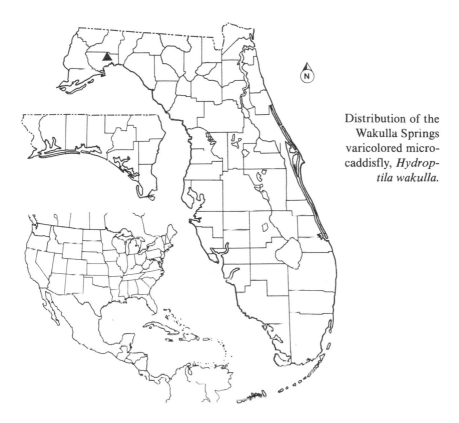

Distribution of the Wakulla Springs varicolored micro-caddisfly, *Hydrop-tila wakulla.*

RANGE: The species is known only from the 11 adult specimens of the type series taken at Wakulla Springs, Wakulla County, Florida (Denning 1947).

HABITAT: Since the immature stages of this species have not been recognized, its particular microhabitat is unknown.

LIFE HISTORY AND ECOLOGY: Although the immature stages have not been seen, it is assumed that the larva of this species feeds on pierced filamentous algae, or scrapes algae and associated material from stones and other large pieces of substrate (Wiggins 1984). Like other members of the genus, the larva probably undergoes hypermetamorphosis and constructs a purse-shaped case of silk and other materials only in the last (fifth) instar. The subsequent pupal, adult, and egg stages typically are relatively brief in an annual or twice-annual life cycle. The adults of this species were captured on 23 October (Denning 1947).

SPECIALIZED OR UNIQUE CHARACTERISTICS: The living requirements of the species are unknown. However, the apparently extremely localized distribution of this species suggests that its ecological requirements probably are very restricted.

BASIS FOR STATUS CLASSIFICATION: Wakulla Springs, the only known locality for this species, is a popular tourist attraction whose environmental parameters are subject to human-caused changes. The species was last seen here in 1945.

RECOMMENDATIONS: The existence and density of this population should be confirmed and monitored and the Wakulla Springs management program for its environmental protection reviewed periodically.

PREPARED BY: John C. Morse, Department of Entomology, Clemson University, Clemson, SC 29634.

FAMILY HYDROPTILIDAE

Threatened

Okaloosa Somber Microcaddisfly
Ochrotrichia okaloosa Harris

DESCRIPTION: Adults of species of *Ochrotrichia* may be distinguished by the presence of two, three, and four spurs on each of their fore-, meso-, and metatibiae, respectively, and of a slightly arcuate, line-like fracture running from one lateral angle of the mesoscutellum to the other (Ross 1944). Last (fifth) instar larvae of species of *Ochrotrichia* may be distinguished from those of other genera of Hydroptilidae by the following combination of characters: (1) thoracic nota each with a mid-dorsal ecdysial line; (2) metatarsi each about as long as its claw; (3) abdomen laterally compressed; (4) tarsal claws slender, smoothly curved, each with a thick pointed spur at base; (5) meso- and metathoracic legs not more than 1.5 times as long as prothoracic legs; (6) posterior end of abdomen without filamentous gills; (7) intersegmental grooves on venter of abdomen not much deeper than those on dorsum; and (8) transverse sulcus often present on second through fifth abdominal sterna, but not on sixth or seventh (Wiggins 1977). Adults of *Ochrotrichia okaloosa* are very small (male 2.7 mm [0.16 in] long); immature stages and the female are unknown. The male of this species appears most similar to that of *Ochrotrichia tenuata*. Although the configuration of the male 10th abdominal segment is similar to *O. tenuata*, a western species, *O. okaloosa* is easily recognized by the large ventromesal lobes of the inferior appendages (Harris and Armitage 1987). Ross (1944) has described females and larvae, and Wiggins (1977) a larva, of closely related species. An illustration of the larva of an unknown species of *Ochrotrichia* (Wiggins 1977) is provided.

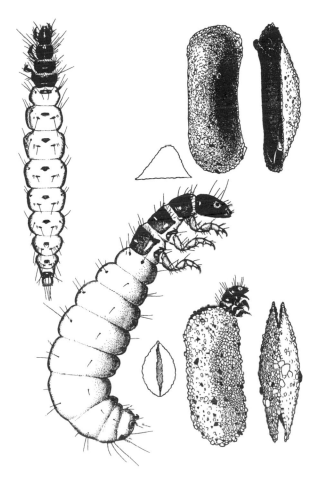

Caddisfly larva and case, *Ochrotrichia* sp. (courtesy of the Department of Entomology, Royal Ontario Museum, Toronto).

RANGE: It is known only from the type locality in Okaloosa County, Florida (Eglin Air Force Base, Turkey Creek at Base Road 233, 8 km northwest of Niceville; Harris and Armitage 1987).

HABITAT: Since the immature stages of this species have not been discovered, the particular habitat is unknown. According to Wiggins (1977), *Ochrotrichia* larvae live in running waters of wide diversity, from rivers and warm springs to cold spring runs and evidently in temporary streams as well (Ross 1944). They are also sometimes found in hygropetric situations, where a thin film of water is flowing over rocks (Vaillant 1965).

LIFE HISTORY AND ECOLOGY: Virtually unknown for this species. *Ochrotrichia* larvae are said to be collecting-gatherers of fine bottom detritus, piercing herbivores of filamentous algae (Wiggins 1984), and scrapers (Vaillant 1965). Last (fifth) instar larvae make laterally compressed cases of

Distribution of the
Okaloosa somber
microcaddisfly,
*Ochrotrichia
okaloosa.*

two silken valves covered with sand grains (Wiggins 1977). The single male specimen was captured on 14 August (Harris and Armitage 1987).

SPECIALIZED OR UNIQUE CHARACTERISTICS: Unknown.

BASIS FOR STATUS CLASSIFICATION: Despite several collections in this area in recent years, the species is known from only one male specimen captured in 1985.

RECOMMENDATIONS: Additional collecting at the type locality should be conducted to find and associate the immature stages and female with the male in order to ascertain the biology of the species. Then, other likely sites should be investigated for other populations. The type locality and any other sites discovered should be protected from pollution and disturbance.

PREPARED BY: John C. Morse, Department of Entomology, Clemson University, Clemson, SC 29634.

FAMILY HYDROPTILIDAE

Threatened

Provost's Somber Microcaddisfly
Ochrotrichia provosti Blickle

OTHER NAMES: Listed as "Provost's Microcaddisfly" in 1982 FCREPA edition.

DESCRIPTION: *Ochrotrichia provosti* is a very small caddisfly, about 3 mm long. Its body and appendages are dark brown to black with spots of white on the body and legs, and a narrow white band on the front wings. The male differs from others in the genus in that it possesses two sclerotized rods, or processes, on the tenth tergite (Blickle 1961). The female and immature stages of the species are unknown. Ross (1944) has described females and larvae, and Wiggins (1977) a larva, of closely related species.

Distribution of Provost's somber microcaddisfly, *Ochrotrichia provosti*.

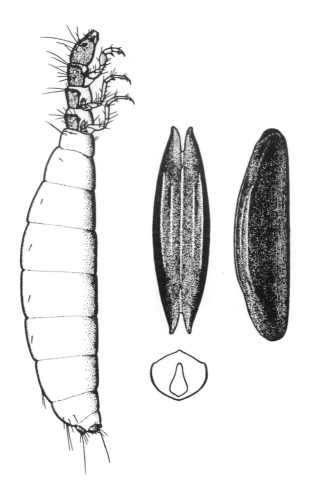

Caddisfly larva and
case, *Orthotrichia* sp.
(courtesy of the De-
partment of Ento-
mology, Royal
Ontario Museum,
Toronto).

RANGE: This species is known only from a single male specimen captured
at Temple Terrace, Hillsborough County, Florida, on 12 July 1957.

HABITAT: Since the immature stages of this species have not been collected, its particular microhabitat is unknown. Ross (1944) indicated that "all
the species [of *Ochrotrichia*] frequent clea₁ ₁nd rapid streams, including
some which dry in summer." Wiggins (1977) added: "*Ochrotrichia* larvae live
in running waters of wide diversity from rivers and warm streams to cold
spring runs."

LIFE HISTORY AND ECOLOGY: Unknown. This species probably constructs a purse-shaped sand case. Larvae of this genus feed by scraping diatoms from rock surfaces (Vaillant 1965).

BASIS FOR STATUS CLASSIFICATION: *Ochrotrichia provosti* is known only from a single locality near Tampa, Florida. If its aquatic habitat is not fully protected from pollution, the species could become extinct.

RECOMMENDATIONS: The microhabitat of the population at Temple Terrace must be determined and every precaution taken to protect it. Attempts should be made to locate populations in similar microhabitats away from the rapidly developing Tampa area.

PREPARED BY: John C. Morse, Department of Entomology, Clemson University, Clemson, SC 29634.

FAMILY HYDROPTILIDAE

Threatened

Dentate Orthotrichian Microcaddisfly

Orthotrichia dentata Kingsolver and Ross

DESCRIPTION: *Orthotrichia dentata* is a very small (3.0–3.5 mm [0.1 in] long) caddisfly with uniformly grayish-brown wings and black eyes. According to Kingsolver and Ross (1961), "The mesal lobe of the clasper [in the male] is similar to that of *cristata*, but the lateral lobe is shorter and less conspicuous. The sclerotized area and sickle-shaped spine of the tenth tergite places this species close to *instabilis* and *baldufi*, but the claspers are of a different shape." The female and immature stages of this species are unknown. Ross (1944) described the female genitalia of *O. cristata* and the larva of an *Orthotrichia* species. Wiggins (1977) described the larva of an *Orthotrichia* species.

RANGE: In the previous report, *Orthotrichia dentata* was cited from only two locations in Florida (Hillsborough County) and South Carolina (Berkeley-Dorchester counties). Since then, it has been noted in an additional South Carolina location (Aiken County; Morse et al. 1980) and from the state of Mississippi (a single specimen in Hancock County; Harris et al. 1982).

HABITAT: Adults were collected beside medium to large, slowly to swiftly flowing blackwater streams of the southeastern sandhills and coastal plain in South Carolina and Mississippi (Morse et al. 1980; Harris et al. 1982).

Distribution of the
dentate orthotrichian
microcaddisfly,
Orthotrichia dentata.

LIFE HISTORY AND ECOLOGY: Adults have been taken during April through mid-October (Kingsolver and Ross 1961; Harris et al. 1982; Unzicker et al. 1982). No additional information has been published.

BASIS FOR STATUS CLASSIFICATION: No collections of Florida populations have been taken since 1958. Even in the few widely scattered locations where it has been found, few specimens have been seen.

RECOMMENDATIONS: Attempts to locate the original and other populations in Florida should continue and, if found, they should be protected from pollution and disturbance.

PREPARED BY: John C. Morse, Department of Entomology, Clemson University, Clemson, SC 29634.

Threatened

Changeable Orthotrichian Microcaddisfly

Orthotrichia instabilis Denning

DESCRIPTION: The female of *Orthotrichia instabilis* differs from that of *O. aegerfasciella* by having the median process of the eighth sternum three-lobed and from that of *O. cristata* in having the median process flared and the mesal portion of the eighth sternum membranous, in addition to the above trilobed mesal process (Blickle and Morse 1957).

RANGE: This species has a broad range but only occurs in very localized populations, a situation indicative of rapid disappearance of what was once a

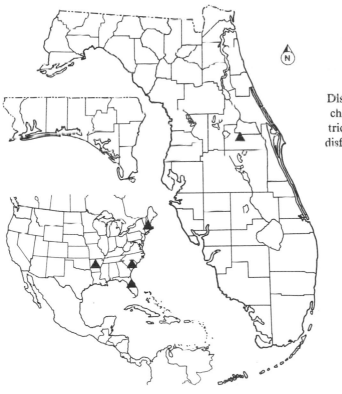

Distribution of the changeable ortho-trichian microcad-disfly, *Orthotrichia instabilis.*

common eastern species. Today it is known only from Durham and Lee, Stafford County, New Hampshire; Francis Beidler Forest, Dorchester County, South Carolina; and Winter Park, Orange County, Florida.

HABITAT: The habitat of this species has been reported variously as a river (Bowles and Mathis 1989), a "small blackwater stream" (Harris 1986a), and streams and marshes (Harris 1990).

LIFE HISTORY AND ECOLOGY: Adults have been collected during May, July, and August (Denning 1948; Kingsolver and Ross 1961; Unzicker et al. 1982; Harris 1986a; Bowles and Mathis 1989). No additional information has been published.

BASIS FOR STATUS CLASSIFICATION: Despite the discovery of more southeastern populations, the species is still considered rare by all recent authors (Bowles and Mathis 1989; Harris 1990). The type series (from Winter Park, Orange County, Florida), representing the only recorded population in Florida, was collected in 1940.

RECOMMENDATIONS: The type habitat and population of this species should be sought and reconfirmed; other populations should continue to be sought; at least some of these populations should be protected from pollution and disturbance.

PREPARED BY: John C. Morse, Department of Entomology, Clemson University, Clemson, SC 29634.

FAMILY HYDROPTILIDAE

Threatened

Florida Cream and Brown Mottled Microcaddisfly
Oxyethira (Dampfitrichia) florida Denning

OTHER NAMES: Listed as "Denning's Florida Oxyethiran Microcaddisfly" in the 1982 FCREPA edition.

DESCRIPTION: Kelley (1984) placed *Oxyethira florida* in the *Oxyethira (Dampfitrichia) ulmeri* group along with *O. aculea*, from the southeastern United States and Mexico, two species from southeastern Asia and Australia, and two species from South America, providing phylogenetic homologues (= synapomorphies) as evidence for his conclusions. Distinguishing characters for adults of *Dampfitrichia* include the fused condition of veins R_4 and R_4 in each forewing and, in some species, the presence of a small preapical spur on each mesothoracic tibia (Kelley 1984). The female of *O. florida* has its 10th tergum more deeply excised distally in dorsal view than does *O. aculea* (Kelley and Morse 1982). Immature stages of *O. florida* still are unknown.

RANGE: In addition to the type localities in Florida (Temple Terrace near Tampa [Hillsborough County] and Miami [Dade County]) mentioned in the previous FCREPA report, the species has been cited from Texas (Edwards and Arnold 1961). No additional information has been published.

HABITAT: Unknown; adults were taken at an electric light.

BASIS FOR STATUS CLASSIFICATION: The record from Texas does not alter the situation for the species in Florida, if indeed the Texas specimens were correctly identified. The species remains threatened in Florida.

RECOMMENDATIONS: The specific microhabitat should be determined and protected insofar as possible. Such microhabitats outside these metropolitan areas should be explored to discover and protect any other populations.

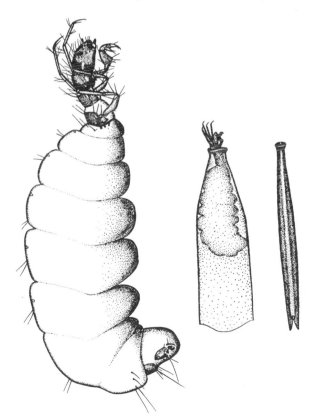

Caddisfly larva and case, *Oxyethira* sp. (courtesy of the Department of Entomology, Royal Ontario Museum, Toronto).

Distribution of the
Florida cream and
brown mottled
microcaddisfly,
Oxyethira florida.

PREPARED BY: John C. Morse, Department of Entomology, Clemson University, Clemson, SC 29634.

FAMILY HYDROPTILIDAE

Threatened

Kelley's Cream and Brown Mottled Microcaddisfly
Oxyethira kelleyi Harris

DESCRIPTION: Adults of *Oxyethira* species may be distinguished from those of other Hydroptilidae genera by the following combination of characters: (1) ocelli present; (2) spurs 0, 3, and 4 on each of the pro-, meso-, and metathoracic tibia, respectively; (3) mesoscutellum broadly triangular, its dorsal posterior corner touching the posterior edge of the scutellum; (4) metascutellum triangular; and (5) forewings very narrow and lanceolate and having only two veins distally (Ross 1944; Schmid 1980). Larvae of *Oxyethira* species are distinguished from those of other Hydroptilidae genera primarily by the unusually long and slender meso- and metathoracic legs, each about 2.5 times as long as a prothoracic leg and very different from it in structure; also, the long distoventral lobe of each prothoracic tibia is distinctive (Wiggins 1977). The male of *Oxyethira kelleyi* is very small (1.8–2.2 mm [0.1 in] long); it differs strikingly from those of all other species of the genus in the elaborate feathering at the apex of the phallus (Harris and Armitage 1987). The female and immature stages are unknown. An illustration of the larva and its case of an unknown species of *Oxyethira* is provided.

RANGE: This caddisfly is known only from Eglin Air Force Base, Okaloosa County, Florida (Turkey Creek at Base Road 233, 8 km [4.8 mi] northwest of Niceville; Rouge Creek at Base Road 233, 5.3 km [3.2 mi] northwest of Niceville; and unnamed tributary to Turkey Creek at Base Road 619, 7.4 km [4.4 mi] northwest of Niceville) (Harris and Armitage 1987).

Distribution of Kelley's cream and brown mottled microcaddisfly, *Oxyethira kelleyi.*

HABITAT: Harris and Armitage (1987) did not provide a general description of the streams beside which the adults of this species were captured. Also, lack of knowledge of the immature stages precludes an understanding of the details of the microhabitat of the species. According to Wiggins (1977, 1984), *Oxyethira* species larvae frequent submerged beds of aquatic plants.

LIFE HISTORY AND ECOLOGY: Since the immature stages of this species are unknown, little can be said about its particular life history and ecology. Larvae of other species of *Oxyethira* primarily are piercing herbivores of filamentous algae; they may also gather fine detritus and scrape attached algae and associated material from the surfaces of plants and other larger substrates (Wiggins 1977, 1984). Adults of this species were captured on 14 August (Harris and Armitage 1987).

SPECIALIZED OR UNIQUE CHARACTERISTICS: This species does not fit well into any of the species groups proposed by Kelley (1984), although it has some similarity to *O. elerobi* (Blickle 1961) and members of the subgenus *Holarctotrichia* (Harris and Armitage 1987).

BASIS FOR STATUS CLASSIFICATION: This species is known from only three sites very close together on Eglin Air Force Base. Perturbations on the watershed could eliminate all known populations.

RECOMMENDATIONS: Additional populations and the female and immature stages of the species should be sought. Once a more general understanding of the range and habitat requirements of the species are known, a more informed protection program can be instituted. In the meantime, the type streams should be protected from pollution and riparian disturbance.

PREPARED BY: John C. Morse, Department of Entomology, Clemson University, Clemson, SC 29634.

FAMILY HYDROPTILIDAE

Threatened

King's Cream and Brown Mottled Microcaddisfly
Oxyethira (*Dactylotrichia*) *kingi* Holzenthal and Kelley

DESCRIPTION: Characters for distinguishing species of *Oxyethira* from those of other genera of Hydroptilidae are discussed for *Oxyethira kelleyi* in this volume. *Oxyethira kingi* is a member of the *Oxyethira* subgenus *Dactylotrichia* (Holzenthal and Kelley 1983; Kelley 1984), whose males have an elongate finger-like process of the ninth sternum (Kelley, 1984). The male of this species is very small (2.6 mm long [0.1 in]) and, unlike that of other members of the subgenus, has short ventrolateral processes on the ninth sternum (Holzenthal and Kelley 1983). The female and immature stages are unknown. An illustration of the larva and case of an unknown species of *Oxyethira* is provided.

RANGE: The species is known only from a single male taken at an ultraviolet light at the Plant Inspection Station in Miami (Dade County), Florida.

HABITAT: Since the immature stages are unknown, the habitat of the species likewise is unknown. According to Wiggins (1977, 1984), larvae of species of *Oxyethira* live in lakes and other standing waters or in areas of slow current in rivers, where they inhabit submerged beds of aquatic plants.

LIFE HISTORY AND ECOLOGY: Since the immature stages of this species are unknown, little can be said about its particular life history and ecology. Larvae of other species of *Oxyethira* are primarily piercing herbivores of filamentous algae; they may also gather fine detritus and scrape attached algae and associated material from the surfaces of plants and other larger

Distribution of King's cream and brown mottled microcaddisfly, *Oxyethira kingi.*

substrates (Wiggins 1977, 1984). The single male adult was captured on 21 December (Holzenthal and Kelley 1983).

SPECIALIZED OR UNIQUE CHARACTERISTICS: The ability of this species to thrive in heavily populated Miami is surprising if, in fact, it still is doing so.

BASIS FOR STATUS CLASSIFICATION: The single specimen was taken in 1964 in Miami, a heavily populated and ecologically highly disturbed region. If its particular habitat, whatever it may be, is further disturbed, the species may become extinct.

RECOMMENDATIONS: The locality and habitat of this species should be investigated, population levels confirmed and monitored, and the waterway protected from pollution and human disturbance.

PREPARED BY: John C. Morse, Department of Entomology, Clemson University, Clemson, SC 29634.

FAMILY HYDROPTILIDAE

Rare

Broad Varicolored Microcaddisfly
Hydroptila latosa Ross

DESCRIPTION: *Hydroptila latosa* is a very small caddisfly (male 2.5 mm long [0.1 in]), whose adults are gray brown with underparts and appendages lighter. The male of the species most closely resembles that of *Hydroptila quinola*, but differs from it in the elongate lateral process of each inferior appendage, the convergence of these appendages apically, and the broad, round ventral plate of *H. latosa* (Ross 1947; Blickle 1979). Immature stages and the female are unknown. Illustrations of the adult of *Hydroptila hamata*, and of the larva of *Hydroptila* species are provided.

RANGE: This species is reported from Walton County, Florida (Eglin Air Force Base, Rocky Creek; Harris et al. 1982), and from the states of Alabama (Washington, Escambia, Baldwin, and Mobile counties; Harris 1986a) and Georgia (Houston County; Ross 1947; Blickle 1979).

HABITAT: It is associated with small, clear blackwater streams with sandy or sand and gravel substrate in the lower coastal plain (Harris et al. 1982; Harris 1986a).

Distribution of the
broad varicolored
microcaddisfly,
Hydroptila latosa.

LIFE HISTORY AND ECOLOGY: Although the immature stages have not been seen, it is assumed that the larva of this species feeds on pierced filamentous algae or scrapes algae and associated material from stones and other large pieces of substrate (Wiggins 1977, 1984). Like other members of the genus, the larva probably undergoes hypermetamorphosis and constructs a purse-shaped case of silk and other materials only in the last (fifth) instar. The subsequent pupal, adult, and egg stages typically are relatively brief in an annual or twice-annual life cycle. The adults of this species were captured from March to October (Ross 1947; Harris 1986a).

SPECIAL OR UNIQUE CHARACTERISTICS: The fact that the species is known from only a single stream in Florida suggests that it may have ecological requirements that are met only rarely in the state.

BASIS FOR STATUS CLASSIFICATION: The restricted Florida distribution indicates a need to continue to monitor the species in the state to prevent its loss here.

RECOMMENDATIONS: The immature stages especially need to be found in order to discover what particular habitat requirements cause its range to be so restricted in Florida. Other populations should continue to be sought.

PREPARED BY: John C. Morse, Department of Entomology, Clemson University, Clemson, SC 29634.

FAMILY HYDROPTILIDAE

Rare

Llogan's Varicolored Microcaddisfly
Hydroptila lloganae Blickle

DESCRIPTION: *Hydroptila lloganae* is a very small caddisfly (adult 2.5 mm [<0.1 in] long), probably with patches of black and white hairs on the head and wings in a variegated pattern characteristic of this large genus. In the ventral view of its male genitalia, this species resembles *Hydroptila latosa*, except that the internal process of the ninth segment is shorter and the inferior appendages do not have lateral processes on the base (Blickle 1961, 1979). Immature stages and the female are unknown. Illustrations of the adult of *Hydroptila hamata*, and of the larva of *Hydroptila* species are provided.

RANGE: This species is known only from the Florida type localities in Gadsden County (Chattahoochee), Highlands County (Highlands Hammock State Park), Hillsborough County (Temple Terrace), and Jefferson County ("Goose Prairie" = Goose Pasture) (Blickle 1961, 1962; Deyrup, pers. comm.).

HABITAT: Since the immature stages of this species have not been collected, its particular microhabitat is unknown. Species of the genus are known to thrive in a wide range of running water habitats, both erosional and depositional, including seeps (Wiggins 1984).

LIFE HISTORY AND ECOLOGY: Very little is known about the life history and ecology of this particular species. According to Wiggins (1977), *Hydroptila* species produce one or two generations per year and larvae feed on diatoms and filamentous and unicellular algae. The aquatic egg and pupal phases and the aerial adult phase are of relatively short duration; the larval phase lasts much longer. *Hydroptila* larvae undergo hypermetamorphosis, such that only the last (fifth instar) larva builds a case. The larva of this species probably constructs a purse-shaped silk case similar to that of other spe-

Distribution of Llo-
gan's varicolored
microcaddisfly,
*Hydroptila
lloganae.*

cies of the genus. Adults have been captured from 15 March through 27
December.

SPECIALIZED OR UNIQUE CHARACTERISTICS: Known larvae of
this genus either pierce the walls of filamentous algal cells to suck their proto-
plasmal contents or scrape algae and associated material from large bottom
substrates.

BASIS FOR STATUS CLASSIFICATION: *Hydroptila lloganae* is known
only from a few localities and has not been collected since the late 1950s. If
its aquatic habitat at these sites becomes polluted, the species could become
extinct.

RECOMMENDATIONS: The specific microhabitat of the species should
be ascertained and fully protected in at least some of the breeding sites.

PREPARED BY: John C. Morse, Department of Entomology, Clemson University, Clemson, SC 29634.

Rare

Molson's Varicolored Microcaddisfly
Hydroptila molsonae Blickle

DESCRIPTION: *Hydroptila molsonae* is a very small (3 mm [<0.1 in] long) caddisfly with patches of black and white hairs on the head and wings in a "salt and pepper" pattern characteristic of this large genus. According to Blickle (1961), "This is a striking and easily recognized species due to the long spines on the eighth tergite. *Hydroptila lonchera* Blickle and Morse also has similar spines on the apicolateral margin of the eighth tergite. The long upcurved arms, corresponding to the parameres of A. Nielsen, are also distinctive." The female and the immature stages of this species are unknown. The females and a larva of related species have been described by Ross (1944) and Wiggins (1977), respectively.

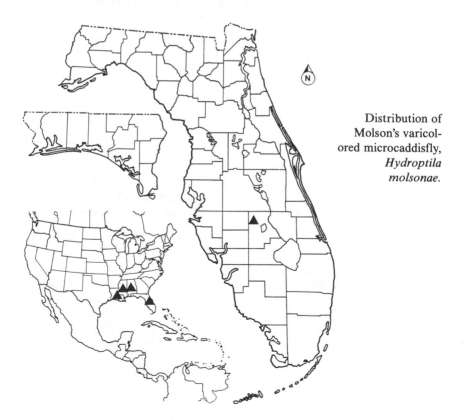

Distribution of
Molson's varicol-
ored microcaddisfly,
Hydroptila
molsonae.

RANGE: At the time of the previous FCREPA report, this species was known only from the type locality in Highlands County (Highlands Hammock State Park), Florida. Since then, it has been cited from Alabama (Baldwin, Mobile, Monroe, and Washington counties; Harris 1986a), Louisiana (St. Tammany Parish; Harris et al. 1982), and Mississippi (Stone County; Harris et al. 1982).

HABITAT: It is associated with small blackwater streams with abundant vegetation (Harris 1986a).

LIFE HISTORY AND ECOLOGY: The adults of this species have been taken during March through September. No additional information has been published.

BASIS FOR STATUS CLASSIFICATION: Although the species now is known to have a wider range, it still is known from only a single site in central Florida, despite extensive collecting on the Florida panhandle, closer to other known populations in Alabama and westward. In Florida, the species has not been collected since 1958. This species was listed as threatened in the 1982 FCREPA edition.

RECOMMENDATIONS: The search for additional populations of this species should continue in Florida, and the single known habitat should continue to receive protection.

PREPARED BY: John C. Morse, Department of Entomology, Clemson University, Clemson, SC 29634.

FAMILY HYDROPTILIDAE

Rare

Short Orthotrichian Microcaddisfly
Orthotrichia curta Kingsolver and Ross

DESCRIPTION: *Orthotrichia curta* is a very small (2.0–2.5 mm [<0.1 in] long) caddisfly with grayish-brown wings and black eyes. The male differs from that of all other Nearctic *Orthotrichia* species in the apex of its tenth tergite, which is rounded, simple, and entirely membranous, without a long sclerotized process arising from its left margin. The female and immature stages are unknown. Ross (1944) described females and larvae, and Wiggins (1977) a larva of closely related species.

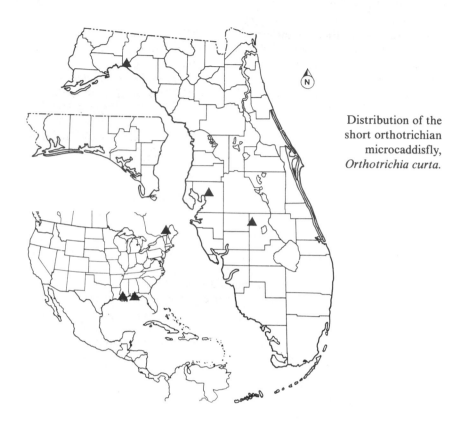

Distribution of the
short orthotrichian
microcaddisfly,
Orthotrichia curta.

RANGE: In the previous report, this species was cited from three localities in Florida (Highlands, Hillsborough, and Jefferson counties). Since that time additional records have been noted from Alabama (Baldwin, Choctaw, Clarke, Covington, Escambia, Houston, Lee, Marengo, Mobile, Tuscaloosa, and Washington counties; Harris et al. 1983; Harris 1986a), Louisiana (St. Tammany Parish; Harris et al. 1982), and Quebec (near St. Lawrence River; Roy and Harper 1979). This is primarily a species of the southeastern Coastal Plain.

HABITAT: An adult of the species was collected near a small, spring-fed blackwater stream in Louisiana (Harris et al. 1982).

LIFE HISTORY AND ECOLOGY: Adults have been collected during April through October (Harris 1986a). No additional information has been published.

BASIS FOR STATUS CLASSIFICATION: No Florida populations have been collected since 1958. The species is considered rare in Louisiana (Harris et al. 1982) and, although found at several locations in Alabama, "never in large numbers" (Harris 1986a).

RECOMMENDATIONS: The old records for Florida should be confirmed and additional Florida populations sought, at least a few of which should be protected against pollution and disturbance.

PREPARED BY: John C. Morse, Department of Entomology, Clemson University, Clemson, SC 29634.

FAMILY HYDROPTILIDAE

Rare

Elerob's Cream and Brown Mottled Microcaddisfly

Oxyethira (Holarctotrichia) elerobi (Blickle)

OTHER NAMES: Listed as "Elerob's Microcaddisfly" in the 1982 FCREPA edition, under the scientific name *Neotrichia elerobi.*

DESCRIPTION: After the previous report, Kelley (1981) redescribed the male, described the female, and transferred this species to the genus *Oxyethira*. He later (1984) included it in his *Oxyethira (Holarctotrichia) archaica* group, the other two species of which occur in Portugal. Males of species of the subgenus *Holarctotrichia* are distinctive in their possession of spines and teeth on the elongated dorsolateral processes of the eighth segment (Kelley 1984). Among North American species, *Oxyethira elerobi* most closely resembles *O. serrata*, but is distinctive in the flattened subgenital plate, the twisted and free distal end of its phallic sclerotization, the infolded processes of the eighth segment, and the lack of an apicomesal spur on the 7th sternite (Kelley 1981). The female is distinctive in having on the 8th sternum a pair of sclerites that are congruent anteriorly and diverging posteriorly; an apicomesal process is absent from the sixth sternum (Kelley and Morse 1982).

RANGE: Since the time of the previous report, this species has been cited from an additional location in Florida (one specimen from Eglin Air Force Base, Walton County, Rocky Creek; Harris, Lago, and Scheiring 1982) and others from Alabama ("locally common" in Baldwin, Choctaw, Covington, Escambia, Lauderdale, Marengo, Mobile, Monroe, Tuscaloosa, and Washington counties; Harris 1986a) and South Carolina (location unspecified; Kelley and Morse 1982). This species is primarily an inhabitant of the southeastern coastal plain.

HABITAT: The Walton County, Florida, location is a small, clear second order stream with moderate streamflow under fairly heavy canopy (Harris et al. 1982).

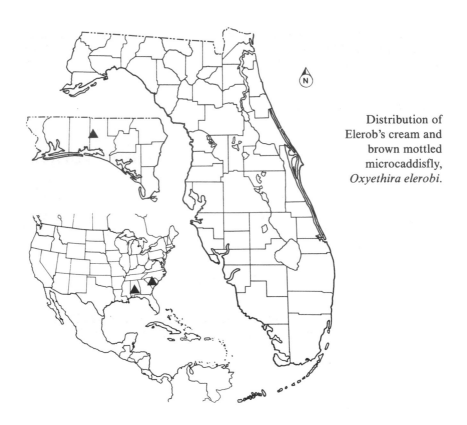

Distribution of
Elerob's cream and
brown mottled
microcaddisfly,
Oxyethira elerobi.

LIFE HISTORY AND ECOLOGY: Adults have been seen during March through October (Harris 1986a). No additional information has been published.

BASIS FOR STATUS CLASSIFICATION: Despite considerable collecting, especially in the Florida panhandle, this species still is known from only two specimens in Florida, although it is "locally common" further north. The Laurel Hill, Florida, population was sampled in 1957, but no specific waterway was identified. This species was listed as threatened in the 1982 FCREPA edition.

RECOMMENDATIONS: The particular stream habitat of the population at Laurel Hill, Florida, should be determined; other Florida habitats should be searched; and at least some of the streams should be protected from pollution and disturbance.

PREPARED BY: John C. Morse, Department of Entomology, Clemson University, Clemson, SC 29634.

Rare

Setose Cream and Brown Mottled Microcaddisfly

Oxyethira (Holarctotrichia) setosa Denning

DESCRIPTION: Distinguishing characteristics for adults and larvae of species of *Oxyethira* are provided in the foregoing discussion for *O. kelleyi*, and distinguishing characters for males of the subgenus *Holarctotrichia* are provided in the discussion for *O. elerobi*. *Oxyethira setosa* is a very small caddisfly (male 2.9 mm [<0.1 in] long) whose male may be distinguished (1) by the presence of a pair of apicolateral processes on the eighth abdominal segment, each tapering to a long, slender, quadrate process, bearing a set of three flat "leaflets," and (2) by the division of the apex of the phallus into one short and two long sclerotized projections (Denning 1947; Blickle 1979). The female and immature stages of this species remain unknown. An illustration of the larva and case of an unknown species of *Oxyethira* is provided.

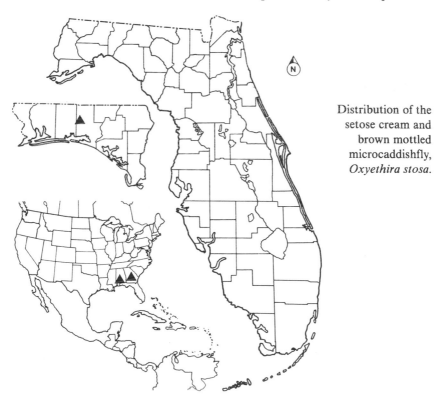

Distribution of the setose cream and brown mottled microcaddishfly, *Oxyethira stosa.*

RANGE: Originally described from Macon, Georgia (Denning 1947), this species was reported from an unspecified location in Florida by Blickle (1979) and later from Eglin Air Force Base (a single specimen from Walton County, Rocky Creek), Florida, by Harris et al. (1982). Harris (1986a) reported it as uncommon in Alabama (Autauga, Covington, Lauderdale, Lowndes, Marion, Mobile, Monroe, and Tuscaloosa counties).

HABITAT: The Walton County, Florida, habitat is a small, clear stream with moderate streamflow in an open area immediately below a small impoundment (Harris et al. 1982).

LIFE HISTORY AND ECOLOGY: Since the immature stages of this species are unknown, little can be said about its particular life history and ecology. Larvae of other species of *Oxyethira* primarily are piercing herbivores of filamentous algae; they may also gather fine detritus and scrape attached algae and associated material from the surfaces of plants and other larger substrates (Wiggins 1977, 1984). Adults of this species were captured during May through August (Harris 1986a).

SPECIALIZED OR UNIQUE CHARACTERISTICS: The apparently very limited distribution of this species in Florida suggests that its environmental requirements may be very restricted.

BASIS FOR STATUS CLASSIFICATION: The species is known from only one specified locality in Florida and is uncommon or very rare elsewhere.

RECOMMENDATIONS: Additional populations of this species should be sought in Florida; any discovered, along with the Walton County site, should be protected from pollution and disturbance.

PREPARED BY: John C. Morse, Department of Entomology, Clemson University, Clemson, SC 29634.

Order Trichoptera

FAMILY LEPIDOSTOMATIDAE

Threatened

Morse's Little Plain Brown Sedge

Lepidostoma (*Mormomyia*) *morsei* Weaver

DESCRIPTION: This medium-sized caddisfly species belongs with *L. griseum* in Weaver's (1988) *Lepidostoma* (*Mormomyia*) *griseum* group, in which the male maxillary palps are angled in front of the face and its setal warts on the ninth abdominal tergum are oval and aligned transversely. Only adults of the species of the *Lepidostoma* subgenus *Mormomyia* have a dorsal pair of setose warts on the ninth tergum. The male of the species is distinguishable from that of *Lepidostoma griseum* in that the setae of the mesonotum are not stout and scaly and in that the ventrolateral processes of the 10th abdominal segment are longer in lateral view in this species (Weaver 1988).

RANGE: This caddisfly has been reported only from Mississippi (Stone County) and Florida (Walton County, Portland, Little Alaqua Creek, although some of this locality information is questioned by Weaver 1988). Presently this is the only species of Lepidostomatidae known from Florida (Weaver 1988).

HABITAT: Unknown. The immatures of species of this large genus occur in a wide range of erosional and depositional running water habitats, including headwater streams and springs, usually among dead plant detritus (Wiggins 1984). Immatures of species of the *Lepidostoma* subgenus *Mormomyia* are endemic to springs or occur in small streams (Weaver 1988).

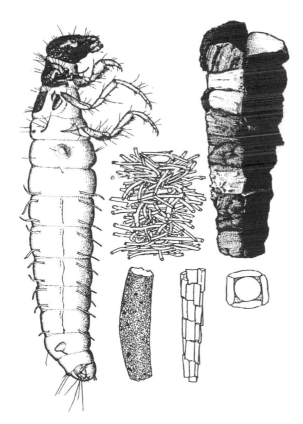

Caddisfly larva and case, *Lepidostoma* sp. (courtesy of the Department of Entomology, Royal Ontario Museum, Toronto).

Distribution of
Morse's little plain
brown sedge, *Lepi-
dostoma morsei.*

LIFE HISTORY AND ECOLOGY: The immature stages and female of this
species are unknown. Larvae of other species of the genus are climbers,
sprawlers, and clingers, feeding as shredding detritivores on dead plant material and occasionally on dead animals (Wiggins 1984). The larvae of species
of *Lepidostoma* subgenus *Mormomyia* each make cylindrical sand cases in
early instars and, in the final instar, a four-sided case of dead leaf panels
(Weaver 1988). Pupal, adult, and egg stages typically are relatively short, the
larval stage much longer, generally with an annual life cycle. Adults of this
species were captured on 18 and 19 October (Weaver 1988).

SPECIALIZED OR UNIQUE CHARACTERISTICS: Because of their
probable habitat, feeding, and case-making requirements, the larvae of this
species likely need streamside (riparian) deciduous trees and other deciduous
vegetation.

BASIS FOR STATUS CLASSIFICATION: The species is known from
only two localities whose environmental status has not been investigated. It
occurs at the southeastern limit of the distribution of the genus and thus may
experience especially stressful ecological pressures.

RECOMMENDATIONS: The localities should be confirmed, the habitat and environmental requirements discovered, and other potential localities searched. Need for protection is indicated, but specific recommendations for protection should be based on the findings of these studies.

PREPARED BY: John C. Morse, Department of Entomology, Clemson University, Clemson, SC 29634.

Order Trichoptera

FAMILY LEPTOCERIDAE

Threatened

Porter's Long-Horn Sedge

Oecetis porteri Ross

DESCRIPTION: *Oecetis* adults can be segregated from those of other genera by the apparently unbranched M vein in each forewing, complete to the base; the larvae are recognizable by their long mouthparts and knife-like mandibles (Ross 1944; Wiggins 1977). *Oecetis porteri* is a small species (adult length 5.5 mm) and a close relative of *Oecetis inconspicua*, from which it differs in the uniformly dark color of the forewing (without any trace of the darker mark across the cord which is characteristic of *O. inconspicua*), in the longer and cylindrical male aedeagus, and the much more sharply sinuate male inferior appendages (Ross 1947). The immature stages are unknown. An illustration of the larva and case of an unknown species of *Oecetis* is provided.

RANGE: This caddisfly is known from along the Atlantic coast of Florida, including Miami (Dade County), Daytona Beach, and New Smyrna (Volusia County) (Ross 1947; Gordon 1984).

HABITAT: Because the immature stages are unknown, the habitat requirements of the species also are unknown. Larvae of other species of *Oecetis* are bottom dwellers, living in both lentic and lotic waters (Wiggins 1977, 1984).

LIFE HISTORY AND ECOLOGY: Because the immature stages have not been described, few details of the life history and ecology are known for the species. According to Wiggins (1977), early instars of at least some species of *Oecetis* can swim, but later instars have not been observed doing this. Spe-

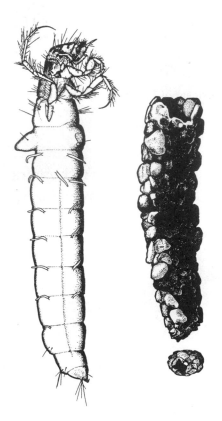

Caddisfly larva and
case, *Oecetis* sp.
(courtesy of the De-
partment of Ento-
mology, Royal
Ontario Museum,
Toronto).

cies of the genus apparently are usually predators (Wiggins 1977, 1984). Larval cases of *Oecetis* species are varied in both form and materials: small
fragments of rock, often combined with bark or leaves; and short lengths of
stems and twigs placed transversely, with a length up to 15 mm (0.6 in)
(Wiggins 1977). Adults were captured at Miami during mid-November and
at Daytona Beach and New Smyrna during late July and early August (Ross
1947).

SPECIALIZED OR UNIQUE CHARACTERISTICS: The predatory larval feeding habits of species of the genus are unusual for Leptoceridae.

BASIS FOR STATUS CLASSIFICATION: Several additional specimens of
this species have been captured since 1943 and 1945. The type localities are in
highly developed areas subject to pollution and disturbance.

RECOMMENDATIONS: A concerted effort should be made to discover
populations of this species and provide protection for them from pollution
and drainage of their habitat.

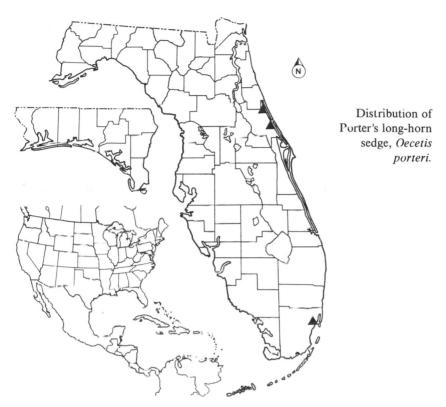

Distribution of
Porter's long-horn
sedge, *Oecetis
porteri.*

PREPARED BY: John C. Morse, Department of Entomology, Clemson University, Clemson, SC 29634.

FAMILY LEPTOCERIDAE

Threatened

Little Meadow Long-Horn Sedge

Oecetis pratelia Denning

OTHER NAMES: Listed as the "Little Meadow Long-horned Caddisfly" in the 1982 FCREPA edition.

DESCRIPTION: *Oecetis pratelia* is a medium-sized (8.5 mm [0.3 in] long), long-horned caddisfly, uniformly light brown except the appendages, which are slightly lighter. The species is closely related to *O. inconspicua* from which

the male can be readily distinguished by the elongate, prominent tenth tergites, the lateral aspect of the ninth segment, and minor differences in the
cerci and claspers (Denning 1948). The female and immature stages are unknown. Ross (1944) described the females and larvae, and Wiggins (1977) a
larva, of closely related species.

RANGE: The species is known only from the single male holotype collected
at LaBelle, Hendry County, Florida, on 16 July 1939.

HABITAT: Unknown, but possibly some microhabitat in the Caloosahatchee River. Other species of this genus are bottom dwellers and live in both
lentic and lotic waters; some Palearctic species are reported from brackish
water (Wiggins 1977).

LIFE HISTORY AND ECOLOGY: Unknown. The species probably constructs a cylindrical case. Wiggins (1977) noted that "early instar larvae of at
least some species [of *Oecetis*] can swim, but we have not observed later instars doing so. The long mandibles identify *Oecetis* larvae as predators."

Distribution of the
little meadow long-
horn sedge, *Oecetis
pratelia.*

SPECIALIZED OR UNIQUE CHARACTERISTICS: *Oecetis pratelia* has very particular ecological requirements as indicated by its very restricted distribution.

BASIS FOR STATUS CLASSIFICATION: The species is known only from a single locality, possibly a short segment of the Caloosahatchee River. If its habitat is further altered or otherwise polluted, the species could become extinct.

RECOMMENDATIONS: The single known population, and any other possible populations, should be monitored to ascertain present numbers. Immatures should be collected and associated with identifiable adults as soon as possible. Every effort should be made to prevent deterioration of the water quality of the Caloosahatchee River.

PREPARED BY: John C. Morse, Department of Entomology, Clemson University, Clemson, SC 29634.

FAMILY LEPTOCERIDAE

Threatened

Little-Fork Triaenode Caddisfly
Triaenodes furcella Ross

DESCRIPTION: *Triaenodes furcella* is a medium-sized (12 mm [0.5 in] long) long-horned caddisfly. It is tawny with a cream and brown pattern on the front wings. According to Ross (1959), this species is readily separated from its closest relative *T. injusta* by the truncate arms of the [male] tenth tergite (pointed in *T. injusta*), and the female has a short sclerotized internal pouch which is larger in *T. injusta*. The immature stages of this species are unknown, but Ross (1944) described the larva of *T. injusta* and four other species of *Triaenodes*, and Wiggins (1977) illustrated that of another.

RANGE: This species is known from only three populations: one at Georgetown, Putnam County, Florida, at the outlet of Lake George on the St. Johns River; another at Orlando, Orange County, Florida; and one record from Hillsborough County.

HABITAT: Since the larvae of this species have never been observed, its particular microhabitat is unknown. Other species of *Triaenodes* inhabit both lentic and lotic waterways.

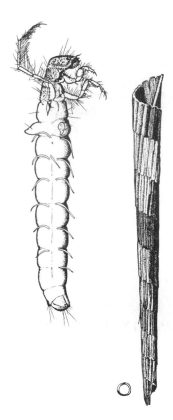

Caddisfly larva and case, *Triaenodes* sp. (courtesy of the Department of Entomology, Royal Ontario Museum, Toronto).

LIFE HISTORY AND ECOLOGY: Unknown. The larva probably makes a slender, tapered case of pieces of green plants arranged spirally. Wiggins (1977) noted that larvae of the genus swim among dense beds of submerged aquatic plants, ingesting green plant tissue and incorporating it in their cases. Adults of the species were captured in April and May.

SPECIALIZED OR UNIQUE CHARACTERISTICS: The ability of late instar larvae of *Triaenodes* species to swim is very unusual for Trichoptera. The limited distribution of *T. furcella* indicates that its ecological requirements are very strict.

BASIS FOR STATUS CLASSIFICATION: *Triaenodes furcella* is known from only three localities. Two are rapidly expanding metropolitan areas; the other is on a large river subject to considerable perturbation from cities and towns upstream. The species was collected 30 years ago but has not been seen since then. If the particular microhabitat is not protected, this caddisfly may become extinct, if in fact it still exists.

RECOMMENDATIONS: Attempts should be made to rediscover this interesting species, to determine its microhabitat, and to protect it. Exploration

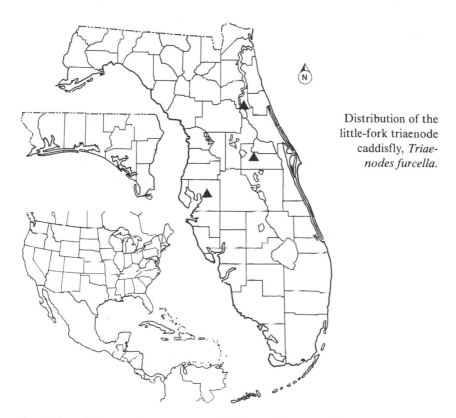

Distribution of the little-fork triaenode caddisfly, *Triaenodes furcella.*

for *T. furcella* in nearby waterways which may have experienced less environmental alteration is especially warranted.

PREPARED BY: John C. Morse, Department of Entomology, Clemson University, Clemson, SC 29634.

FAMILY LEPTOCERIDAE

Rare

Tavares White Miller

Nectopsyche tavara Ross

DESCRIPTION: Adults of species of *Nectopsyche* may be distinguished from those of other genera of Leptoceridae by the truncate dorsal apex of the mesothoracic katepisternum, the nearly completely membranous mesothoracic epimeron, and the absence of the bases of veins RS and M in each hind wing (Ross 1944; Schmid 1980). The larvae of the genus are recognizable by their slender shape, and the presence of only a ventral band of small spines on each side of the anal opening or no spines at all (Wiggins 1977). The pretty white adult of *Nectopsyche tavara* is a medium-sized caddisfly (male 12 mm [0.5 in] long), recognizable by the absence of distinct patches of dark hair on the fringe of the forewing, the quadrate apex of the male inferior appendage, and the medium development of the base of that appendage (Ross 1944; Haddock 1977). Distinctions separating the larva from those of other species of the genus include the following: (1) lack of a ventral band of tiny spines laterad of the anal opening; (2) the presence of a medial, longitudinal, brown stripe dividing four oval, luteous spots that appear as "figure 8s" on the anterior half of the fronto-clypeus; (3) the presence of an inconspicuous gill on the posterolateral region of the metanotum; (4) the presence of a well-developed swimming brush on each metathoracic leg; and (5) the absence of gills on the first abdominal segment (Daigle and Haddock 1981). The larval case is elongate-linear, gradually tapering from anterior to posterior end, about 18 mm [0.7 in] long, composed primarily of sand grains and typically with a plant stem attached to the anterodorsal side. Prior to pupation, the larva removes part of the posterior end of the case and any inherent plant matter and affixes the modified case to plant leaves and stems with a holdfast at each end (Daigle and Haddock 1981).

RANGE: This species has been reported from Tavares (Lake County); Winter Park, Lake Conway, and Lake Fredricka (Orange County); Chiefland (Levy County); Lake Placid (Highlands County); and Prairie Lake (Seminole County) (Ross 1944; Daigle and Haddock 1981).

HABITAT: It is associated with unpolluted mesotrophic lakes of the central Florida highlands region. In these locations, larvae and pupae are found on submerged aquatic vascular plants (Daigle and Haddock 1981).

LIFE HISTORY AND ECOLOGY: The species appears to be multivoltine, since many size classes of larvae can be collected. Pupation duration averages about 20 days except for the overwintering generation. An adult emergence period occurs in late March followed by the peak summer emergence in early July. A smaller fall emergence follows in late September. The larva is phytophagous, feeding on submerged plants such as southern naiad (*Najas guadalupensis*), fanwort (*Cabomba caroliniana*), Illinois pondweed (*Potamogeton illinoensis*), stonewort (*Nitella megacarpa*), and hydrilla (*Hydrilla verticillata*). Both early and late instar larvae swim, using the swimming brush on the metathoracic leg (Daigle and Haddock 1981).

SPECIALIZED OR UNIQUE CHARACTERISTICS: The distribution of this species suggests that it may be part of the biological evidence for an ancient Florida island refugium that persisted during the Pliocene and Pleistocene epochs (Daigle and Haddock 1981; Deyrup 1990).

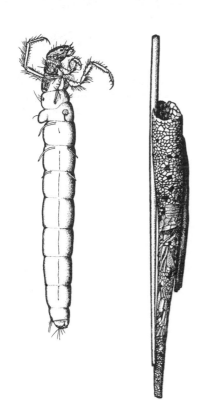

Caddisfly larva and case, *Nectopsyche* sp. (courtesy of the Department of Entomology, Royal Ontario Museum, Toronto).

Distribution of the Tavares white miller, *Nectopsyche tavara*.

BASIS FOR STATUS CLASSIFICATION: This species, with its restricted distribution, remained poorly known until 1981. Continued human population growth and development in central Florida may cause pollution that reduces or eliminates some of the populations of this species.

RECOMMENDATIONS: The known populations of this species should be confirmed and additional likely locations should be investigated. These populations should be checked periodically to assure their continuing survival and densities.

PREPARED BY: John C. Morse, Department of Entomology, Clemson University, Clemson, SC 29634.

FAMILY LEPTOCERIDAE

Rare

Floridian Triaenode Caddisfly

Triaenodes florida Ross

DESCRIPTION: *Triaenodes florida* is a medium-sized (9.5 mm [0.4 in] long-horned caddisfly, light brown except for dark annulations at each antennal joint, and black tufts of hair on the maxillary palps and legs. Each front wing has a longitudinal area down the center which is lighter than the rest. This species resembles *T. taenia*, but each male clasper has a double mesal lobe and a short filiform basal appendage. The female and the immature stages are unknown. Ross (1941, 1944) has described females and larvae, and Wiggins (1977) a larva, of related species. Unzicker (1968) described the female genitalia as an example of the family, but did not give diagnostic characters.

RANGE: In the 1982 FCREPA edition, this caddisfly was reported from Gainesville, Alachua County, and Ebro, Washington County, near the Choctawhatchee River. Gordon (1984) has indicated new records for this species from Levy and Putnam counties, Florida (but without detailed localities), and Harris and Lago (1990) and Harris (1990) have cited it from Alabama (Covington County). No additional information has been published.

BASIS FOR STATUS CLASSIFICATION: The additional records, although sparse, suggest that the species is in less immediate danger of extirpation than previously thought. It was listed as threatened in the 1982 FCREPA edition.

LIFE HISTORY AND ECOLOGY: Unknown. The larva probably makes a slender, tapered case of pieces of green plants arranged spirally. Wiggins

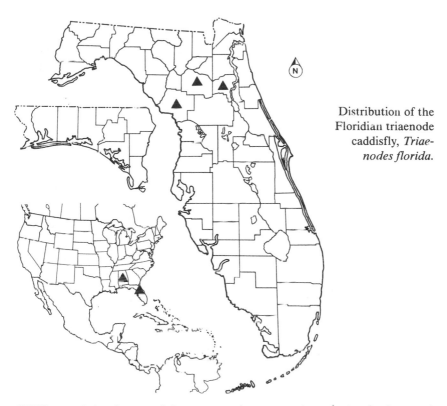

Distribution of the Floridian triaenode caddisfly, *Triaenodes florida.*

(1977) noted that larvae of the genus swim among dense beds of submerged aquatic plants, ingesting green plant tissue and incorporating it in their cases. Adults were captured in April and May.

RECOMMENDATIONS: The particular microhabitat of *T. florida* should be identified.

PREPARED BY: John C. Morse, Department of Entomology, Clemson University, Clemson, SC 29634.

FAMILY LEPTOCERIDAE

Rare

Marsh Triaenode Caddisfly
Triaenodes helo Milne

DESCRIPTION: Adults of species of *Triaenodes* may be distinguished from those of other genera of Leptoceridae by the apparent absence of the stem of

the M vein in each forewing (Ross 1944). Larvae of the genus may be distinguished by the rectangular ventral apotome of the head, the constriction near
the middle of each hind tibia, the close-set fringe of long swimming hairs on
the hind legs, and the distinctive long spiral case made of plant pieces (Wiggins 1977). *Triaenodes helo* is a medium-sized caddisfly (male forewing 7 mm
[0.3 in] long), yellow with a fringe on the forewing darkest at the anal angle
(Milne 1934). The male of the species most closely resembles *Triaenodes
abus*, but the process from the base of each inferior appendage is longer and
apically foliaceous and the apex of the 10th tergum is well-developed. It also
resembles *T. pernus*, but the right inferior appendage process in *T. helo* is not
as broad apically. The female and immature stages are unknown. An illustration of the larva and case of an unknown species of *Triaenodes* is provided.

RANGE: This caddisfly was originally described from North Carolina (Milne
1934) and later noted from North and South Carolina (without specified locality; Unzicker et al. 1982). This species was discovered in Florida by Harris
et al. (1982, Eglin Air Force Base, Rocky Creek in Walton County, Bull
Creek and Ramer Branch in Okaloosa County; Gordon 1984) and in Alabama by Harris and Lago (1990, Baldwin, Houston, and Mobile counties;

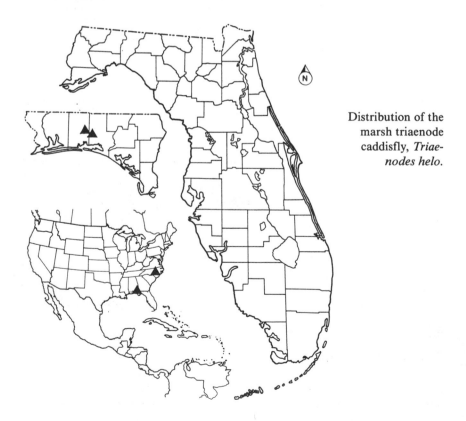

Distribution of the
marsh triaenode
caddisfly, *Triae-
nodes helo.*

Harris 1990). Apparently the species is restricted to the southeastern coastal plain (Harris and Lago 1990).

HABITAT: Sandy-bottomed, small, clear streams with moderate streamflow under fairly heavy riparian canopy (Harris et al. 1982; Harris 1990).

LIFE HISTORY AND ECOLOGY: Because the immature stages of this species are unknown, little can be said about its particular life history and ecology. "*Triaenodes* larvae occur in plant beds in both lotic and lentic waters where they swim with their cases [slender, tapered, composed of pieces of green plants arranged longitudinally in a dextral or a sinistral spiral], propelled by their hind legs" (Wiggins 1977). They are shredding herbivores of vascular plants (Wiggins 1977, 1984). Adults have been collected during April-June, August, and September (Harris et al. 1982; Harris and Lago 1990).

SPECIALIZED OR UNIQUE CHARACTERISTICS: Shredding herbivory occurs in a few other Leptoceridae genera but is not common among aquatic insects. The peculiar case of the larva is very distinctive.

BASIS FOR STATUS CLASSIFICATION: The species is known in Florida only from three neighboring streams. The species is "rare in collections" (Harris and Lago 1990).

RECOMMENDATIONS: The three neighboring stream habitats for this species in Florida should be protected from pollution and disturbance. Other likely Florida habitats should be searched for additional populations.

PREPARED BY: John C. Morse, Department of Entomology, Clemson University, Clemson, SC 29634.

FAMILY LEPTOCERIDAE

Rare

Daytona Long-Horn Sedge
Oecetis daytona Ross

OTHER NAMES: Listed as "Daytona Long-horned Caddisfly" in the 1982 edition.

DESCRIPTION: *Oecetis daytona* is a small (5.5 mm [0.2 in] long, excluding antennae), long-horned caddisfly. It is light brown except for a few darker markings on the forewings, especially at the forks of veins. The species most closely approaches *O. immobilis*, but the male differs from it radically in the shape of the aedeagus and clasper (Ross 1947). The female is similar to the male in size and general structure. Its genitalia are very simple, "differing from those of *immobilis* chiefly in lacking the diamond-shaped sclerotized mark on the eighth sternite" (Ross 1947). The immature stages are unknown; those of closely related species were illustrated by Ross (1944) and Wiggins (1977).

RANGE: At the time of the previous report, this species was known only from two localities in metropolitan areas (Jacksonville and Daytona Beach) on the Atlantic coast of Florida. Gordon (1984) added a citation for Baker County (unspecified location) in Florida. The species now has also been reported from Alabama (Baldwin, Escambia, Mobile, and Washington counties; Harris and Lago 1990; Harris 1990), Mississippi (George and Perry counties; Holzenthal et al. 1982), and North and South Carolina (without specific locality, Unzicker et al. 1982). It is endemic to the southeastern coastal plain.

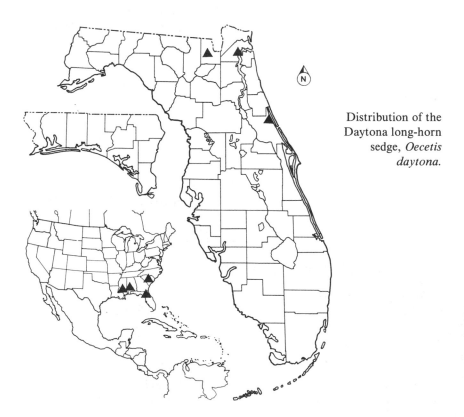

Distribution of the Daytona long-horn sedge, *Oecetis daytona*.

HABITAT: Small coastal plain streams (Unzicker et al. 1982; Harris and Lago 1990; Harris 1990).

LIFE HISTORY AND ECOLOGY: Adults have been captured during April through August (Unzicker et al. 1982; Holzenthal et al. 1982; Harris and Lago 1990). No additional information has been published.

BASIS FOR STATUS CLASSIFICATION: The two original collections were made in 1945. Gordon's unspecified locality is the only other record for Florida. The species is considered "rare" in Alabama (Harris and Lago 1990; Harris 1990). It was listed as "threatened" in the 1982 FCREPA edition.

RECOMMENDATIONS: Continued search should be made for Florida populations of this species and efforts made to protect their habitats from pollution and disturbance.

PREPARED BY: John C. Morse, Department of Entomology, Clemson University, Clemson, SC 29634.

FAMILY LEPTOCERIDAE

Rare

Morse's Long-Horn Sedge

Oecetis morsei Bueno-Soria

DESCRIPTION: *Oecetis* adults can be segregated from those of other genera by the apparently unbranched M vein in each forewing, complete to the base; the larvae are recognizable by their long mouthparts and knife-like mandibles (Ross 1944; Wiggins 1977). *Oecetis morsei* is a small caddisfly (male 6.5 mm [0.2 in] long) closely related to *Oecetis scala* and *Oecetis sphyra*. Unlike *O. sphyra*, the lobes of the male 10th segment each have a subapical spine in addition to the apical spine seen in both species; also, the superior appendages are shorter and thicker in *O. morsei*. The inferior appendages are broader basally in *O. morsei* than in *O. sphyra*. The immature stages are unknown. An illustration of the larva and case of an unknown species of *Oecetis* is provided.

RANGE: The species was reported from Eglin Air Force Base (Okaloosa County, Ramer Branch) in Florida (Harris, Lago, and Scheiring 1982). It also is known from Alabama (Bibb and Perry counties; Harris et al. 1984; Harris and Lago 1990; Harris 1990) and South Carolina (Aiken County, Bueno-Soria 1981).

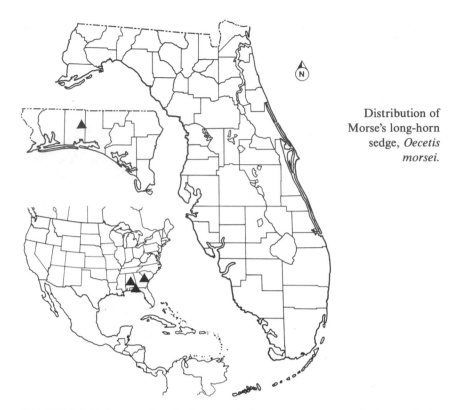

Distribution of
Morse's long-horn
sedge, *Oecetis
morsei.*

HABITAT: It is associated with sandy bottom streams and rivers of the southeastern sandhills and coastal plain (Morse et al. 1980; Harris et al. 1982; Harris et al. 1984; Harris and Lago 1990; Harris 1990).

LIFE HISTORY AND ECOLOGY: Because the immature stages have not been described, few details of the life history and ecology are known for the species. According to Wiggins (1977), early instars of at least some species of *Oecetis* can swim, but later instars have not been observed doing this. Species of the genus apparently are usually predators (Wiggins 1977, 1984). Larval cases of *Oecetis* species are varied in both form and materials: small fragments of rock, often combined with bark or leaves; and short lengths of stems and twigs placed transversely, with a length up to 15 mm (0.6 in) (Wiggins 1977).

SPECIALIZED OR UNIQUE CHARACTERISTICS: The predatory larval feeding habits of species of the genus are unusual for Leptoceridae.

BASIS FOR STATUS CLASSIFICATION: The species is known from only three widely separated streams of differing sizes in the southeastern sandhills and coastal plain. Only a single population is known in Florida.

RECOMMENDATIONS: Additional populations of this species should be sought in Florida and the one known Florida locality protected from pollution and disturbance.

PREPARED BY: John C. Morse, Department of Entomology, Clemson University, Clemson, SC 29634.

FAMILY LEPTOCERIDAE

Status Undetermined

Florida Scaly Wing Sedge
Ceraclea (C.) *floridana* (Banks)

OTHER NAMES: Listed as "Banks' Florida Ceraclean Caddisfly" in the 1982 FCREPA edition.

DESCRIPTION: *Ceraclea floridana* is a medium-sized (10 mm [0.4 in] long) long-horned caddisfly. The head is yellowish, clothed with long white hair. The pronotum has long white hair; the rest of the thorax is yellowish with shorter and sparser hair. The antennae are white, narrowly annulate with dark brown. The legs are yellow with short white hair, their tarsi banded on the tips with brown. The forewings are pale brown, rather densely clothed with white hair, mostly in small patches, giving the wings a marmorate appearance, with the apical fringe alternately brown and white. The apical part of the hindwings is slightly infuscated. The female abdomen is broken off and missing from the only known specimen of this species. The male and the immature stages are unknown.

RANGE: This species is known only from the holotype specimen collected beside Biscayne Bay, Florida, some time before 1903.

HABITAT: This caddisfly is probably a freshwater inhabitant. No other information is known.

LIFE HISTORY AND ECOLOGY: Unknown. The species is probably a case maker.

SPECIALIZED OR UNIQUE CHARACTERISTICS: *Ceraclea floridana* probably has (or had) very particular ecological requirements as indicated by its very restricted distribution.

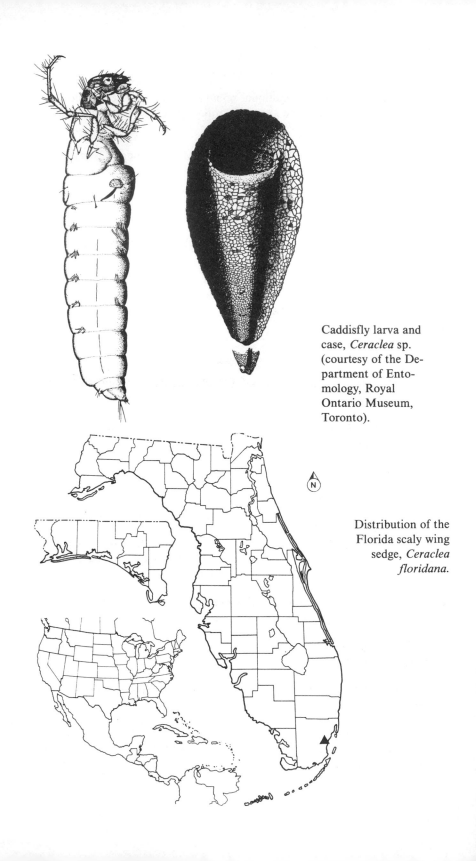

Caddisfly larva and case, *Ceraclea* sp. (courtesy of the Department of Entomology, Royal Ontario Museum, Toronto).

Distribution of the Florida scaly wing sedge, *Ceraclea floridana.*

BASIS FOR STATUS CLASSIFICATION: The species may now be extinct. It has not been seen since 1903, and the Biscayne Bay (Coral Gables, Miami, etc.) area is now heavily populated.

RECOMMENDATIONS: The Biscayne Bay area should be explored in an attempt to find and study the species.

PREPARED BY: John C. Morse, Department of Entomology, Clemson University, Clemson, SC 29634.

FAMILY LEPTOCERIDAE

Status Undetermined

Marsh-Dwelling White Miller

Nectopsyche paludicola Harris

DESCRIPTION: Adults of species of *Nectopsyche* may be distinguished from those of other genera of Leptoceridae by the truncate dorsal apex of the mesothoracic katepisternum, the nearly completely membranous mesothoracic epimeron, and the absence of veins RS and M in each hind wing (Ross 1944; Schmid 1980). The larvae of the genus are recognizable by their slender shape, and the presence of only a ventral band of small spines on each side of the anal opening, or no spines at all (Wiggins 1977). Like *Nectopsyche exquisita* and *Nectopsyche candida*, the base of each male inferior appendage is narrow; however, the overall appearance of this appendage in *N. paludicola* is more stout than in either of these other species and the adult forewings, rather than having a white background, are gray to tawny with indistinct brown spots along the veins and near the apex (Harris 1986b). The species name *Nectopsyche texana* is a *nomen dubium* whose unique type specimen lacks a metathorax, abdomen, and one antenna; its forewings, however, have a color pattern very similar to that described for *N. paludicola* (Haddock 1977). The immature stages of *N. paludicola* are unknown.

RANGE: This species was described from Alabama (Baldwin, Mobile, and Washington counties; Harris 1986b). Gordon (1984) mentioned "*N.* n. sp." for Marion County, Florida, which she and Harris believe may be *N. paludicola* (Harris, pers. comm.). The unique type of *N. texana* was collected at San Antonio, Texas (Banks 1905; Haddock 1977).

HABITAT: Small streams of the coastal plain (Harris and Lago 1990). The etymology for the species name (*paludicola* means "marsh-dweller") refers to the habitat of the species according to Harris (1986b).

Distribution of the marsh-dwelling white miller, *Necto-psyche paludicola.*

LIFE HISTORY AND ECOLOGY: Because the immature stages still are unknown, little is known about the life history and ecology of this species. Larvae of other species of *Nectopsyche* construct cases that usually are long and slender (up to 31 mm [1.2 in] long), composed of plant and mineral fragments with one or two twigs or conifer needles extending beyond one end. *Nectopsyche* larvae inhabit lakes and slower rivers, living either on the bottom or on plants, and feeding primarily on plants or fine bottom detritus (Wiggins 1977, 1984). Adults have been captured during May through August (Harris and Lago 1990).

SPECIALIZED OR UNIQUE CHARACTERISTICS: The brown forewings of the adult and the marsh-dwelling habit of the immature stages are unusual for species of the genus *Nectopsyche.*

BASIS FOR STATUS CLASSIFICATION: The existence of the species in Florida has not yet been confirmed and the possible synonymy with *N. texana* has not been investigated.

RECOMMENDATIONS: The Marion County, Florida, specimens examined by Gordon (1984) and the unique holotype of *N. texana* should be compared with those of the type series of this species. Additional populations should be sought in small, marshy streams, especially in central and western Florida.

PREPARED BY: John C. Morse, Department of Entomology, Clemson University, Clemson, SC 29634.

FAMILY LEPTOCERIDAE

Status Undetermined

Florida Long-Horn Sedge
Oecetis floridana (Banks)

DESCRIPTION: *Oecetis* adults can be segregated from those of other genera by the apparently unbranched M vein in each forewing, complete to the base (Ross 1944; Schmid 1980); the larvae are recognizable by their long mouthparts and knife-like mandibles (Ross 1944; Wiggins 1977). Banks (1905) described the species as follows: "Head yellowish, clothed with golden hair; palpi clothed with gray hair; antennae pale, narrowly annulate with brown; thorax pale, with golden hair; legs pale yellowish; abdomen yellowish. Wings gray, clothed with short golden hair and some black hair intermixed, the anastomosis and extreme tip darker, fringe black at tip, elsewhere gray; hindwings dusky hyaline, scarcely darker at tip, fringe very long, gray. Both pairs of wings very long, slender and acute. Expanse 13 mm (0.5 in)." The unique type specimen is a female (Holzenthal 1982). The male and immature stages are unknown. *Oecetis floridana* originally was described as a species of the genus *Setodes*, but was transferred to *Oecetis* by Holzenthal (1982). The transfer apparently makes the name a secondary junior homonym of *Oecetis floridana*, originally described as *Oecetina floridana*, which is itself a synonym of *Oecetis cinerascens*. No replacement name has been proposed for *Oecetis floridana* nor has any possible synonymy with currently recognized species been investigated. An illustration of the larva and case of an unknown species of *Oecetis* is provided.

RANGE: The unique type specimen was collected at Biscayne Bay, Florida.

HABITAT: The habitat of this species is unknown. Other species of *Oecetis* are bottom dwellers in both lentic and lotic habitats.

Distribution of the
Florida long-horn
sedge, *Oecetis
floridana.*

LIFE HISTORY AND ECOLOGY: The life history and ecology of this species are unknown. Larvae of other species of *Oecetis* are mostly predators or occasionally shredding herbivores, living in tube cases that are usually tapered, composed of coarse mineral and plant fragments (Wiggins 1977, 1984).

SPECIALIZED OR UNIQUE CHARACTERISTICS: The predatory behavior of *Oecetis* larvae is unusual for Leptoceridae.

BASIS FOR STATUS CLASSIFICATION: The identity, the male and immature stages, the range, the habitat, and the life history and ecology of this species all are uncertain or unknown.

RECOMMENDATIONS: The important unknown aspects of this species cited in the "Basis for Status Classification" should be investigated before any recommendations for species protection can be made.

PREPARED BY: John C. Morse, Department of Entomology, Clemson University, Clemson, SC 29634.

FAMILY LEPTOCERIDAE

Status Undetermined

Little Long-Horn Sedge

Oecetis (Setodina) parva (Banks)

OTHER NAMES: Listed as "Banks' Little Setodine Caddisfly" in the 1982 FCREPA edition.

DESCRIPTION: *Oecetis parva* is a small (5.5 mm [0.2 in] long, excluding antennae) long-horned caddisfly. It is dull pale gray, and the wings are clothed with gray hairs, but the legs and antennae are yellowish. The male genitalia are extremely similar to those of *O. avara* except for the claspers, wherein they differ by lacking the large setose dorsal lobe (Ross 1938). The female and the immature stages are unknown. Ross (1944) described the female and the larva of *O. avara* and other closely related species of *Oecetis*, and Wiggins (1977) described a larva of an *Oecetis* species.

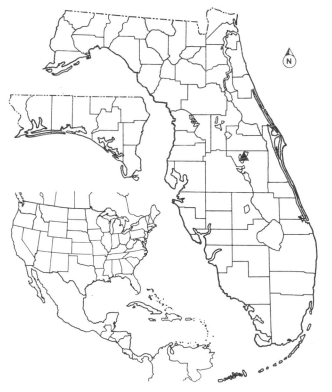

Distribution of the little long-horn sedge, *Oecetis parva.*

RANGE: This species is known only from three specimens captured at Kissimmee, Osceola County, Florida, in November, some time before 1907.

HABITAT: Unknown; possibly Tohopekaliga Lake. Other species of this genus are bottom dwellers and live in both lentic and lotic waters; some Palearctic species are reported from brackish water (Wiggins 1977).

LIFE HISTORY AND ECOLOGY: Unknown. The species probably constructs a cylindrical case. Wiggins (1977) noted that "early larvae of at least some species [of *Oecetis*] can swim, but we have not observed later instars doing so. The long mandibles identify *Oecetis* larvae as predators."

SPECIALIZED OR UNIQUE CHARACTERISTICS: *Oecetis parva* probably has (or had) very particular ecological requirements as indicated by its very restricted distribution.

BASIS FOR STATUS CLASSIFICATION: The species may now be extinct. It has not been seen for 70 years, and the urban type locality undoubtedly has been altered during that time.

RECOMMENDATIONS: Tohopekaliga Lake and associated waterways should be explored to determine if the species still exists.

PREPARED BY: John C. Morse, Department of Entomology, Clemson University, Clemson, SC 29634.

Order Trichoptera
FAMILY POLYCENTROPIDAE

Threatened

Florida Brown Checkered Summer Sedge
Polycentropus floridensis Lago and Harris

DESCRIPTION: Adults of *Polycentropus sensu lato* may be distinguished from those of other genera of Polycentropidae by the presence of a preapical spur on each of the fore tibiae, by the presence of only two median veins in each posterior wing, and by the branching of R_2 and R_3 near the apex of the front and/or hind wings (Ross 1944; Schmid 1980). Larvae of this genus are distinguishable by (1) the two, touching dark bands in the dorsal region between the anal claw and sclerite of the distal segment of each anal proleg and either (2a) each fore tarsus being broad and only 1/2 as long as its fore tibia or (2b) each anal claw obtusely curved or (2c) each anal claw with two or three dorsal accessory spines (Morse and Holzenthal 1984).

Polycentropus floridensis belongs to the *P. maculatus* Group (Hamilton 1986). In the male, the ninth sternite is wide and its cerci are shaped similar to those of *Polycentropus confusus*, although these latter structures are somewhat larger basally in *P. floridensis*; the apicodorsal process of each cercus has a rounded lobe basally as in *Polycentropus neiswanderi*, and the phallus resembles that of *Polycentropus pentus*, although the ventral hump of the phallus is larger and its apex is more sinuous in *P. floridensis* (Lago and Harris 1983). The female and immature stages of the species are unknown.

RANGE: *Polycentropus floridensis* is known only from its type localities in Alabama (Baldwin County) and Florida (Walton County, headwaters of Rocky Creek 6.4 km [3.8 mi] southwest of Mossy Head) (Harris et al. 1982;

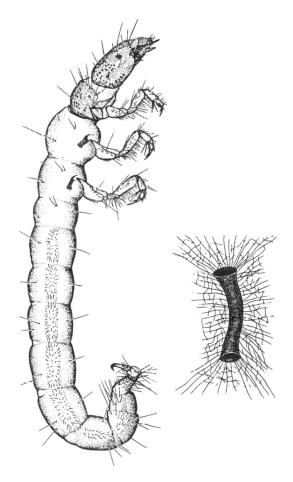

Caddisfly larva and case, *Polycentropus* sp. (courtesy of the Department of Entomology, Royal Ontario Museum, Toronto).

Distribution of the
Florida brown
checkered summer
sedge, *Polycentro-
pus floridensis.*

Lago and Harris 1983, 1987; Scheiring 1985). Gordon (1984) listed it from Hamilton County, Florida, but not from its type locality in Walton County, suggesting that she may have made an error.

HABITAT: The habitat for the Florida population was described as a small, clear stream with moderate flow in sandhills with a fairly heavy canopy of pine-oak association (Harris et al. 1982; Scheiring 1985).

LIFE HISTORY AND ECOLOGY: Because the immature stages of the species are unknown, details about its life history and ecology are generally not available. Larvae of other species in the genus are clingers in silk re-treats, either a tube open and flared at both ends and with an irregular maze of trip lines for signalling the presence of prey, or a bag-like structure expanded by the current (Wiggins 1977, 1984). They are primarily predacious, but also are reported as filtering collectors and as shredding herbivores (Wiggins 1977, 1984). The four adult males of the type series, the only adults collected, were all captured on 11 May.

SPECIALIZED OR UNIQUE CHARACTERISTICS: Unlike so many other caddisflies, adults of this genus are not usually collected in large numbers at light traps. Therefore, it is possible that other populations exist but have not been discovered.

BASIS FOR STATUS CLASSIFICATION: The species is known only from four specimens taken at two localities. It is listed as "rare or restricted in occurrence" in Alabama (Harris 1990), a general phrase for all species that are of concern in that state. Unless other populations can be found, it is reasonable to suspect that it has a restricted habitat which, because of its limited occurrence, should be protected.

RECOMMENDATIONS: Additional populations and the unknown stages of this species should be sought in order to obtain a better understanding of its range and habitat requirements. The two known stream localities should be protected from pollution and disturbance.

PREPARED BY: John C. Morse, Department of Entomology, Clemson University, Clemson, SC 29634.

FAMILY POLYCENTROPIDAE

Rare

Florida Cernotinan Caddisfly

Cernotina truncona Ross

DESCRIPTION: *Cernotina truncona* is a small (5 mm [0.2 in] long) caddisfly with prominent black eyes, a light yellowish-brown body and wings, and paler antennae and legs. The male is distinguishable from that of closely related species by the apical position of the dorsal arm of each clasper and by the more generalized condition of the cerci. The female and the immature stages are unknown. Ross (1944) illustrated the female genitalia, and Flint (1968, 1971) described the probable larva, of closely related species.

RANGE: In addition to the original record at Daytona Beach (Volusia County), Florida, the species was cited for Alachua, Baker, Pasco, and Putnam counties (but without further collection details) in Florida by Gordon (1984); in Alabama (Barbour, Covington, Escambia, and Mobile counties) by Lago and Harris (1987) and Harris (1990); in North and South Carolina (but without specific locality) by Unzicker et al. (1982); and in Virginia (but without specific locality) by Parker and Voshell (1981).

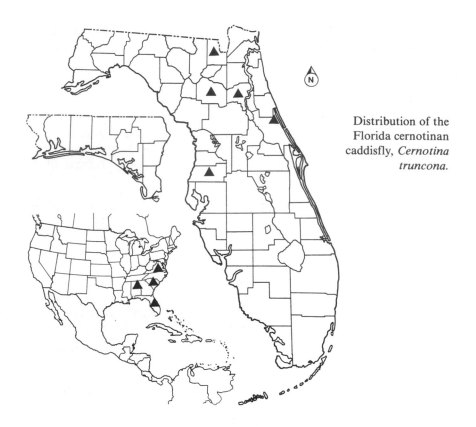

Distribution of the
Florida cernotinan
caddisfly, *Cernotina
truncona.*

HABITAT: This caddisfly is associated with coastal plain ponds and lakes (Lago and Harris 1987) and streams (Harris 1990).

LIFE HISTORY AND ECOLOGY: Adults were captured during April through June (Lago and Harris 1987).

BASIS FOR STATUS CLASSIFICATION: Although widely distributed, the collections are always sparse, suggesting small populations. Harris (1990) considered it "rare or restricted in occurrence" in Alabama. It was listed as "status undetermined" in the 1982 FCREPA edition.

RECOMMENDATIONS: The few Florida populations should continue to be monitored to assure that they do not decline.

PREPARED BY: John C. Morse, Department of Entomology, Clemson University, Clemson, SC 29634.

Rare

Morse's Dinky Light Summer Sedge

Nyctiophylax morsei Lago and Harris

DESCRIPTION: Adults of the genus *Nyctiophylax* lack not only preapical spurs on the foretibiae, but also the first fork of the radial sector in the wings; the second segment of each maxillary palp is only 1/3 as long as the third segment (Ross 1944). Larvae of the genus have tarsi all nearly cylindrical and narrower than their tibiae; the anal claw has short conspicuous ventral teeth and a dorsal accessory spine; and the pronotum has a short, stout bristle near each lateral margin (Morse and Holzenthal 1984). The male of this small species (5.2 mm [0.2 in] long) may be distinguished from those of other species of *Nyctiophylax* by the combination of the presence of a pair of phallic parameres, the blunt lateral appearance of the 10th tergum only slightly longer than the superior appendages, and the thick and truncate periproctal processes (Lago and Harris 1983, Morse 1990). The immature stages and female of this species are unknown. Ross (1944), Schmid (1980), and Morse (1990) have described females of related species; Wiggins (1977) provided a description for the larva of an unknown *Nyctiophylax* species.

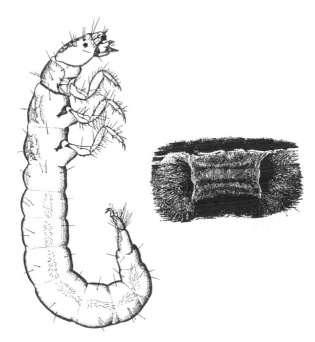

Larva and case, *Nyctiophylax* sp. (courtesy of the Department of Entomology, Royal Ontario Museum, Toronto).

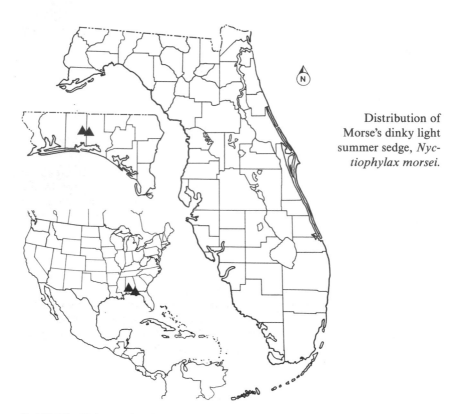

Distribution of
Morse's dinky light
summer sedge, *Nyc-
tiophylax morsei.*

RANGE: This species is known only from Alabama (Baldwin and Mobile counties) and, in Florida, Eglin Air Force Base sites in Walton County (headwaters of Rocky Creek 6.4 km [3.8 mi] southwest of Mossy Head) and Okaloosa County (Bull Creek 16 km [9.6 mi] east-southeast of Crestview) (Lago and Harris 1983, 1987; Gordon 1984; Harris 1990).

HABITAT: The Florida collection sites were small clear streams with moderate streamflow; the stream substrate was usually primarily sand. Water quality was good, although pH and mineral content were low (Harris et al. 1982; Scheiring 1985).

LIFE HISTORY AND ECOLOGY: Since the immature stages of this species are unknown, its specific ecological requirements are unknown. Larvae of other species of *Nyctiophylax* are usually predators, rarely filtering collectors or shredding herbivores, living in silk tube retreats (Wiggins 1977, 1984). Usually, the pupal, adult, and egg stages are relatively much shorter than the larval stage. Males of the species were taken on 2 and 25 April, 11 and 12 May, and 19 September.

SPECIALIZED OR UNIQUE CHARACTERISTICS: The larvae of species of *Nyctiophylax* lie in wait for their prey in their silk tube retreats, open at both ends, darting out from the retreat to capture any small creature causing threshold silk threads of the retreat to move (Noyes 1914).

BASIS FOR STATUS CLASSIFICATION: The known range of *Nyctiophylax morsei* is limited to four streams in two pairs of contiguous coastal counties. The species is considered "rare or restricted in occurrence" in Alabama (Harris 1990).

RECOMMENDATIONS: Other likely small, sandy stream habitats should be investigated in the Florida panhandle. The few known locations should be monitored periodically for any changes in the current population levels.

PREPARED BY: John C. Morse, Department of Entomology, Clemson University, Clemson, SC 29634.

Order Trichoptera
FAMILY PHILOPOTAMIDAE

Status Undetermined

Silvery Little Black Sedge
Chimarra argentella (Ulmer)

DESCRIPTION: Adults of the genus *Chimarra* may be distinguished from those of other genera of Philopotamidae by the presence of only one foretibial spur, rather than two as in other genera (Schmid 1980). Larval forecoxae are without a long subapical process and the pair of ventral head setae arise near the midlength of the head (Weaver et al. 1981).

Chimarra argentella is a medium-sized caddisfly (adult 6-8 mm [0.24-0.36 in] long) with an orange body and brownish-gray or black wings having five patches of silvery hair. It is related to *C. braconoides*, but is easily recognized in the male sex by the very long dorsomesal process of the 10th tergum (Ulmer 1906; Flint 1968). The female 8th segment is terete, with two blackened spots bearing many long setae; the 9th tergum is declivious, with basoventral angles produced into processes; the 10th tergum is rounded, with apical papillae (Flint 1968). The mature larva presumed to be of this species is 18 mm (0.7 in) long, having an orange body with reddish-brown sclerites; the pronotum has a black posterior margin; the anterior margin of the frontoclypeus is markedly asymmetrical; the left mandible has a distinct molar tooth basally. The pupa and egg stages are unknown. An illustration of the larva of an unknown species of *Chimarra* was provided in the previous FCREPA report.

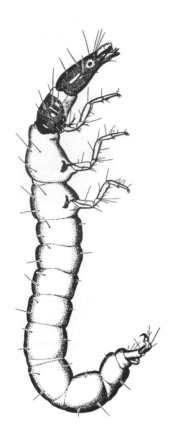

Caddisfly larva,
Chimarra sp. (cour-
tesy of the Depart-
ment of Entomol-
ogy, Royal Ontario
Museum, Toronto).

RANGE: This species was described from Jamaica by Ulmer (1906). According to Flint (1968), the species is found over most of the island at all elevations. Milne (1936) reported it from Florida, but without specific locality.

HABITAT: According to Flint (1968), the larval records are from the larger
streams at low and intermediate elevations, but the species probably occurs
in small highland streams as well.

LIFE HISTORY AND ECOLOGY: Details of the ecology of this species
have not been studied. Larvae of other species of *Chimarra* live in fast-
flowing, usually warmer rivers where they are filtering collectors, construct-
ing silk nets in rows of about five or six nets per row, each about 25 mm (1.0
in) long and 3 mm (0.1 in) in diameter, with which to catch detritus, algae,
and rarely smaller animals (Noyes 1914; Wiggins 1977, 1984). On Jamaica,
adults were captured during May, July, and November (Flint 1968).

SPECIALIZED OR UNIQUE CHARACTERISTICS: The orange color of
the larva, which carries over to the adult, is a very conspicuous feature of
this insect.

BASIS FOR STATUS CLASSIFICATION: The accuracy of Milne's identification, and thus the reliability of his Florida record, have never been confirmed.

RECOMMENDATIONS: The southern part of Florida should be searched for this colorful orange, black, and silver species.

PREPARED BY: John C. Morse, Department of Entomology, Clemson University, Clemson, SC 29634.

Butterflies and Moths

INTRODUCTION: The lepidopteran fauna of Florida is estimated to consist of over 3,000 species of moths and butterflies (J. B. Heppner, unpublished data). The diversity of Lepidoptera found in the state can be attributed to the variety of adjacent geographic regions that have donated species to the fauna, and to the isolation of the Florida peninsula in prehistoric times. The latter factor has resulted in the formation of some endemic species and races.

A small number of species in Florida are most closely related to groups centered in the southwestern United States and Mexico. These disjuncts are typically associated with xeric habitats such as the deep sand ridges and relict dunes of central Florida. Their presence in the state is a reminder of the vast changes in climate that have taken place since the beginning of the Pleistocene.

The tropical portions of the state extend from the Florida Keys and extreme southern mainland, northward along the coasts to about Tampa Bay on the Gulf and Merritt Island on the Atlantic side. These areas are inhabited by many species of West Indian origin. Most tropical species in Florida seem to have become established via chance dispersal from Cuba or the Bahamas, probably within the last 10,000 years. This process of dispersal and establishment is still taking place today, as evidenced by the high number of exotic species recorded from the state. Frank and McCoy (1992) list 52 species of Lepidoptera thought to be recent introductions to Florida. Some of the new arrivals have flourished while others persisted for but a short time before dying out. A few exotic species are known from single individuals or a small number of specimens that probably never established breeding colonies.

The majority of Florida's butterflies are widely distributed across much of the eastern United States. Some of these temperate species are limited to the panhandle, but many others have broad ranges throughout Florida. Whereas the panhandle and northern Florida have a strong Appalachian influence, the Florida peninsula is in many respects an extension of the Atlantic coastal plain.

The conservation of insects is a relatively new concept (Pyle, Bentzien, and Opler 1981); however, many of the same processes that affect vertebrate populations, such as habitat degradation and alteration, or the use of hazardous pesticides and herbicides, also affect invertebrates. Butterflies are integral

571

parts of food chains and also serve as pollinators of flowering plants. The decline of many species of Lepidoptera in recent times is cause for concern. Studies that have attempted to identify endangered or threatened Lepidoptera in various regions of the eastern United States include Shull (1981), Baggett (1982), Opler (1985), Shuey, Calhoun, and Iftner (1987), Shuey et al. (1987), Drewry (1989), Schweitzer (1989), Metzler and Lucas (1990), and Wood (1990). Covell (1990) gives a good account of the status of our knowledge of North American Lepidoptera. Baggett (1982) discussed the status of Lepidoptera in Florida and listed one endangered, two threatened, one rare, and three species of special concern, all but one of which were butterflies. Looking at the status of these same species in our current list, the Atala has changed from threatened status to a species of special concern, while the Florida leafwing and Bartram's hairstreak are now regarded as threatened.

Since 1982, our knowledge of butterflies in the state has increased, but is still limited. Even for a group as familiar as butterflies, some parts of Florida are virtually unexplored, and information on life histories and ecology of many species remains scanty. Unfortunately, there is no moth specialist available with the necessary information to write discussions for this volume. It is clear, however, that the most important way to protect rare and endangered Lepidoptera is through habitat protection. Scrubs, coastal habitats, wetlands, tropical hardwood hammocks, and tropical pinelands are in the most critical need of protection in Florida.

Most of the work in surveying and documenting the Lepidoptera of Florida has been and will continue to be done by amateur entomologists. Opler (1987) discusses the need for invertebrate surveys and the maintenance of data bases. We highly recommend increased funding for surveys and ecological and taxonomic studies of rare Lepidoptera, since even modest grants would spark considerable interest in such projects. Collection of specimens for scientific study is desirable and necessary to accurately document the distribution of Lepidoptera (Pyle 1984). Many species are so similar that the only means of identifying them is to dissect and examine the genitalia. Insects, including butterflies, are little affected by collecting activities, except for those species that are so restricted as to have population sizes of a few hundred individuals annually. The only species that are likely to be detrimentally affected by collecting in Florida are the Schaus' swallowtail and the Bahama swallowtail, and then only in years of low abundance.

Taxa appearing on rare and endangered species lists are sometimes "locked away" from interested naturalists and biologists by action of the permitting bureaucracy in state and federal agencies. In point of fact, these species need more study (including some sampling and collecting), not less! The Nature Conservancy has long recognized the importance of species surveys and actively solicits survey work to be done on its holdings in order to plan management strategies or monitor population levels of rare species. It is to be hoped that the State of Florida will continue a policy of promoting regular studies on the wide diversity of potentially threatened and actually endangered species within its boundaries.

Perhaps no other state in the eastern U.S. has experienced the increase in human population and loss of natural communities that Florida has endured during the last 10 years. We know of many populations of rare Lepidoptera that have been destroyed by human activities and some spectacular species are truly close to demise. Natural disasters such as hurricanes also pose a threat to local populations of butterflies. One of the most powerful storms of this century, Hurricane Andrew, devasted much of tropical southern Florida on 24 August 1992, and may have extirpated or severely impacted some of the species included in this list. We hope that the information presented below will call attention to species that are in danger of becoming extinct, and to the need to study the ecology of Florida's rare butterflies before they become endangered. The estimated resident population of Florida in 1992, some 13,470,000 people, is expected to increase 20% by the year 2002.

We gratefully acknowledge the help of the following people who contributed information on the Lepidoptera of Florida: Richard W. Boscoe, John V. Calhoun, Charles V. Covell, Jr., Mark Deyrup, Terhune S. Dickel, Douglas C. Ferguson, Richard M. Gillmore, Dale H. Habeck, Michael K. Hennessey, Leroy C. Koehn, Thomas M. Neal, Paul Opler, John Riggenbach, Stephen J. Roman, Dale F. Schweitzer, Jeffrey R. Slotten, and John Watts. The Southern Lepidopterists' Society also deserves much praise for its role in surveying the Florida fauna. In addition, the following people and agencies have done much to support the study of Lepidoptera in Florida: H. V. Weems, Jr., and John B. Heppner of the Florida Department of Agriculture and Consumer Services; James A. Stevenson, Dana Bryan, Renate Skinner, and Jeanne M. Parks of the Florida Department of Natural Resources; Robert M. Brantly, Don A. Wood, Brad Gruver, David Cook, Larry Lawrence, and Susan Cerulean of the Florida Game and Fresh Water Fish Commission; James A. Sanders and Richard W. Curry of the National Park Service; and David J. Wesley, Michael M. Bentzien, and Deborah Holle of the U.S. Fish and Wildlife Service. Jacqueline Y. Miller, Lee D. Miller, John B. Heppner, Jeffrey Lotz, and Vernon A. Brou kindly supplied photographs of the butterflies listed below.

PREPARED BY: Marc C. Minno and Thomas C. Emmel, Department of Zoology, University of Florida, Gainesville, FL 32611.

Class Insecta
Order Lepidoptera

INTRODUCTION: Approximately 160 species of butterflies of seven different families occur in breeding populations in Florida. Many butterflies are abundant and widely distributed throughout the state. Some ubiquitous species breed and flourish in urban lawns, gardens, and disturbed sites. Most butterflies, however, are closely associated with certain plants or habitats. Although butterflies are often a conspicuous part of our natural surroundings, in general, they are usually not as abundant as some other groups of insects such as ants, flies, or beetles.

The butterfly communities of Florida are changing in subtle ways. Whereas new species are becoming established in the state, particularly in south Florida, a few native species are declining, largely due to habitat destruction. We consider one-third of the fauna to be rare, based on species abundance and distribution within Florida. Only a few butterflies, mostly endemics with tropical affinities, are felt to be threatened or endangered in the state.

Invertebrates are just becoming recognized as valuable indicators of biodiversity (Wilson 1987), especially butterflies (Kremen 1992, Ehrlich 1992). Many of Florida's natural communities (especially pine flatwoods, scrubs, and sandhills) depend upon periodic fires in order to maintain biodiversity. Thus habitat maintenance requires the application of fire, frequently by prescription burning. However, little is known of the effects of fire on butterflies. Burning too frequently or during times when the eggs, larvae, or pupae are susceptible could eliminate some species from an area. If extirpated, rare species may not be able to recolonize a site due to large distances between populations and obstacles to dispersal such as roads, urban areas, and agricultural lands. Perhaps the best solution for managers of natural areas is not to burn entire tracts at once, but to attempt to develop mosaics of habitat with different fire histories.

Our maps of butterfly distributions may not be equivalent to the maps of many other invertebrates in this volume. Although there are species of butterflies that are rather inconspicuous, they are still more obvious and much more eagerly sought by a relatively large group of entomologists than are most other invertebrates. One result of this generally high interest in butterflies is that there are many more records for most species than for equally rare species of groups such as flies, or beetles or grasshoppers. Some of these records may not indicate that there is a breeding population in the area; this is easy to determine for some species, as we have indicated for some tropical butterflies, but impossible to determine for most species. A large number of records may be from breeding sites that no longer exist; in these cases of historical records one would need to visit each site, to see if the species, or at least its habitat, still persisted. There are two results of these problems: (1) There are very large numbers of records of some rare butterflies; this is one reason why we have a presence-absence triangle for each county rather than a triangle for each collection site; (2) The maps may give the impression that a particular species is widespread, even abundant, when the species is actually rare, perhaps confined to a special habitat that is rapidly being destroyed.

Major sources of information on the historical record, present distribution, and ecology of butterflies in Florida and adjacent areas include Klots (1951), Kimball (1965), Scott (1971, 1972), Brown and Heincman (1972), Harris (1972), Howe (1975), Riley (1975), Lenczewski (1980), Opler and Krizek (1984), Scott (1986a,b), Schwartz (1987, 1989), Minno (1992), and Minno and Emmel (1992).

PREPARED BY: Marc C. Minno, Department of Zoology, University of Florida, Gainesville, FL 32611.

Order Lepidoptera
FAMILY HESPERIIDAE

INTRODUCTION: This is the largest family of butterflies in Florida with over 65 species recorded (Gerberg and Arnett 1989). Hesperiids are characterized by the antennae, which are usually bent or hooked at the tip. The adults of many skippers are drab or similarly colored and are difficult to identify with field guides. The larvae of most species fold or tie leaves together to form shelters in which they hide. Three different subfamilies of the Hesperiidae are represented in Florida, the Pyrginae (broad-winged skippers), the Hesperiinae (branded skippers), and the Megathyminae (giant skippers). The Pyrginae frequently have a distinctive modification of the forewing in which a line of specialized scales used in the dissemination of pheromones during courtship lies covered by a membranous flap of the costal margin. Pyrginae larvae feed mostly on dicotyledonous plants, particularly legumes. Males of the branded skippers often have a conspicuous dark line or patch of specialized scales in the middle of the forewings. Their caterpillars feed mostly on grasses. The giant skippers are robust butterflies that bore into yucca stems and roots during the larval stages. None of the skipper butterflies occurring in Florida is considered to be endangered at this time, but two limited to the Florida Keys are threatened. Three other tropical skippers are treated as species of special concern and 17 mostly temperate species are listed as rare in Florida.

PREPARED BY: Marc C. Minno, Department of Zoology, University of Florida, Gainesville, FL 32611.

Threatened

Klots' Skipper

Euphyes pilatka klotsi L. Miller, Harvey, and J. Miller

DESCRIPTION: Klots' skipper is a medium-sized butterfly with black and golden-yellow wings above and brownish undersides. Males have a dark stigma across the upperside of each forewing. The golden patches are reduced to large spots in the females. The forewings range in length from 18 to 23 mm (0.7–0.9 in). Klots' skipper is darker than the typical race found on the mainland.

RANGE: Klots' skipper is found only in the lower Florida Keys. Miller, Harvey, and Miller (1985) list specimens from Big Pine Key, Sugarloaf Key, and Stock Island. The nominate race of *Euphyes pilatka* occurs sporadically on Key Largo and is locally abundant throughout much of Florida.

HABITAT: This race is found in tropical pinelands and sawgrass marshes at the edges of mangroves.

Klots' Skipper, *Euphyes pilatka klotsi* (courtesy of John B. Heppner). Male, dorsal view (*above*) and female, dorsal view (*below*).

Distribution of
Klot's skipper,
Euphyes klotsi.

LIFE HISTORY AND ECOLOGY: Females of Klots' skipper lay their eggs singly on the leaves of sawgrass (*Cladium jamaicense*). The larvae eat leaves and tie leaves together to form shelters. Adults visit flowers occasionally. Males perch near stands of the host plant to await receptive females with which to mate. Several generations are produced each year.

BASIS OF STATUS CLASSIFICATION: Klots' skipper is considered to be threatened because it is endemic to Florida and has a highly restricted range within the state. The species has lost habitat, as some pinelands with the host plant have been destroyed by urban development while other tracts have been protected from fire so long that the understory has been taken over by hardwoods.

RECOMMENDATIONS: Surveys are needed to determine the current distribution and abundance of this butterfly. Prescribed burning may be necessary to maintain pineland habitats for Klots' skipper.

PREPARED BY: Marc C. Minno and Thomas C. Emmel, Department of Zoology, University of Florida, Gainesville, FL 32611.

FAMILY HESPERIIDAE

Threatened

Rockland Grass Skipper

Hesperia meskei (W. H. Edwards) (Keys Population)

DESCRIPTION: The rockland grass skipper is a medium-sized hesperiid butterfly found in the lower Florida Keys. The upper sides of the wings are golden yellow with dark borders. Males have a dark stigma across each forewing. Females have less yellow above. The ventral hindwings are yellowish or greenish-yellow with a postmedial row of light-colored spots. The length of the forewings varies from 14 to 17 mm (0.5–0.7 in).

RANGE: The rockland grass skipper is known from Big Pine and Sugarloaf keys, and perhaps from the extreme southern mainland. Other subspecies of *Hesperia meskei* are found in the southeastern United States, including much

Distribution of the rockland grass skipper, *Hesperia meskei.*

Rockland Grass Skipper, *Hesperia meskei* (Keys population) (courtesy of John B. Heppner). Male, dorsal view (*above*), female, ventral view (*below*).

of peninsular Florida and the southern Great Plains. The southern Florida population represents a distinctive, but formally undescribed race.

HABITAT: This butterfly occurs in grassy tropical pinelands.

LIFE HISTORY AND ECOLOGY: The eggs are laid singly on grasses such as *Aristida purpurascens* (McGuire 1982). Larvae eat leaves and tie leaves together to make shelters. Although this species sometimes visits flowers, adults are more often found perching on grasses late in the afternoon. The adults have been found every month of the year.

BASIS OF STATUS CLASSIFICATION: The rockland grass skipper is listed as threatened because of its highly restricted range and low abundance. This butterfly was relatively common during the 1970s on Big Pine Key, but has not been seen there since 1985. Hurricane Andrew may have severely reduced *Hesperia meskei* populations on the southern mainland.

RECOMMENDATIONS: Surveys and ecological studies are needed to determine the current distribution, abundance, and habitat requirements of the rockland grass skipper. Prescribed burning of pinelands in the lower keys is necessary to maintain habitat for this butterfly. Managers should carefully assess the effects of fire on this species as well as on the Florida leafwing, and Bartram's hairstreak. These butterflies may require habitats of different post-burn age. Taxonomic studies are needed to determine the relationships in the *Hesperia meskei* group.

PREPARED BY: Marc C. Minno and Thomas C. Emmel, Department of Zoology, University of Florida, Gainesville, FL 32611.

                                                        FAMILY HESPERIIDAE

Rare
_____

Hoary Edge
Achalarus lyciades (Geyer)

DESCRIPTION: The hoary edge is a relatively large, dark brown skipper butterfly. The forewings range in length from 21 to 23 mm (0.8–0.9 in) and have a medial band of large golden spots. Some smaller spots lie near the apex. This skipper is similar to *Autochton cellus*, but the forewing band is more irregular and the undersides of the hindwings bear a distinctive whitish patch along the outer margin.

RANGE: This butterfly has been found in six counties in northern Florida. It occurs abundantly throughout much of the eastern United States.

HABITAT: Pinelands and the edges of hardwood hammocks are the usual places where the hoary edge occurs.

LIFE HISTORY AND ECOLOGY: Females deposit the eggs singly on leguminous herbs such as beggar ticks (*Desmodium* spp.). Larvae eat leaves

Hoary Edge, *Achalarus lyciades* (courtesy of John B. Heppner). Male,
ventral view.

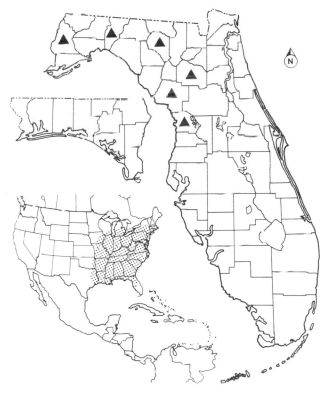

Distribution of the
hoary edge, *Acha-
larus lyciades.*

and fold or tie leaves together to form shelters. Overwintering takes place in the larval stage. Adults visit flowers and perch on low foliage. Two or three generations are produced each year.

BASIS OF STATUS CLASSIFICATION: The hoary edge is listed as rare because of its local distribution in Florida.

RECOMMENDATIONS: Surveys and ecological studies are needed to determine the current distribution, abundance, and habitat requirements of this butterfly in Florida.

PREPARED BY: Marc C. Minno, Department of Zoology, University of Florida, Gainesville, FL 32611.

FAMILY HESPERIIDAE

Rare

Textor Skipper
Amblyscirtes aesculapius (Fabricius)

OTHER COMMON NAMES: Cobweb little skipper, lace-winged roadside skipper.

DESCRIPTION: The textor skipper is a small, dark butterfly with a distinctive cobweb-like pattern of white lines on the undersides of the hindwings. The forewings range in length from 13 to 16 mm (0.5–0.6 in) and bear some small white spots. The fringes of the wings are checkered black and white.

RANGE: This species is known from 11 counties in northern Florida. The textor skipper is locally distributed throughout the southeastern United States.

HABITAT: The textor skipper occurs in the vicinity of cane brakes in hammocks and bottomland swamps.

LIFE HISTORY AND ECOLOGY: The eggs are laid singly on switch cane (*Arundinaria gigantea*). Larvae eat leaves and fold sections of leaves to make shelters. Overwintering takes place in the larval stage. Adults visit flowers and perch on foliage in the vicinity of switch cane. Several generations are produced each year.

BASIS OF STATUS CLASSIFICATION: The textor skipper is listed as rare because of its local distribution in Florida.

Textor Skipper, *Amblyscirtes aesculapius* (courtesy of John B. Heppner).
Female, ventral view.

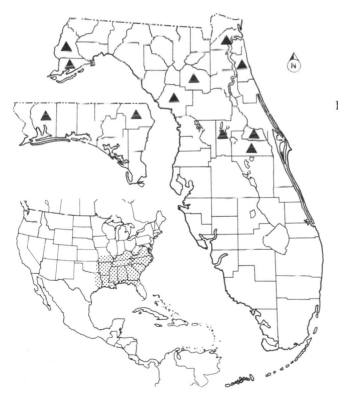

Distribution of the
textor skipper,
*Amblyscirtes
aesculapius.*

RECOMMENDATIONS: Surveys and ecological studies are needed to determine the current distribution, abundance, and habitat requirements of this skipper.

PREPARED BY: Marc C. Minno, Department of Zoology, University of Florida, Gainesville, FL 32611.

FAMILY HESPERIIDAE

Rare

Least Florida Skipper

Amblyscirtes alternata (Grote and Robinson)

OTHER COMMON NAMES: Dusky little skipper.

DESCRIPTION: The least Florida skipper is one of the smallest and most obscurely patterned butterflies in the state. The wings are black with lightly checkered fringes. The forewings range in length from 10 to 12 mm (0.4–0.5 in) and have a few vague spots. The undersides of the hindwings have a light gray flush.

RANGE: Although the least Florida skipper is known from 10 counties, mostly in the northern part of the state, its populations are usually highly localized and ephemeral. This butterfly occurs only in the southeastern United States, from eastern Texas to Virginia.

HABITAT: The least Florida skipper frequents pine flatwoods and sandhill ridges.

LIFE HISTORY AND ECOLOGY: The life history is unknown, but the larvae probably feed on grasses. Adults fly low to the ground and visit flowers occasionally. Finding more than one or two *Amblyscirtes alternata* in a single day is exceptional in Florida. Up to three generations are produced per year.

BASIS OF STATUS CLASSIFICATION: The least Florida skipper is listed as rare because of its localized distribution, low abundance, and seemingly short-lived populations.

RECOMMENDATIONS: Surveys and ecological studies are needed to determine the current distribution, abundance, and habitat requirements of the

Least Florida Skipper, *Amblyscirtes alternata* (courtesy of John B. Heppner). Male, ventral view.

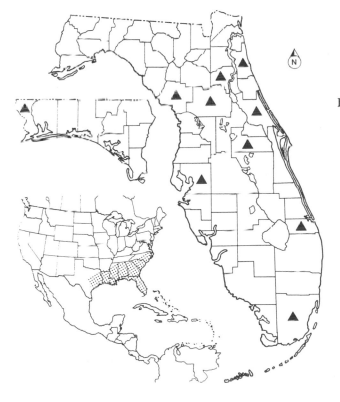

Distribution of the least Florida skipper, *Amblyscirtes alternata.*

least Florida skipper. The effects of fire on this highly localized species should be carefully examined. Managers of natural areas should not burn entire tracts that have populations of *Amblyscirtes alternata* or other rare Lepidoptera during a single year.

PREPARED BY: Marc C. Minno, Department of Zoology, University of Florida, Gainesville, FL 32611.

FAMILY HESPERIIDAE

Rare

Bell's Roadside Skipper
Amblyscirtes belli H. A. Freeman

DESCRIPTION: Bell's roadside skipper is a small dark butterfly with black and white checkered fringes. The forewings range in length from 13 to 14 mm (0.5 in) and bear a short row of small light spots. The undersides of the hindwings are dark with a faint postmedial band of light spots.

RANGE: This butterfly has been recorded from just three counties in northern Florida. Bell's roadside skipper is locally distributed from southern Indiana to northern Florida, west to Texas and Missouri.

HABITAT: The edges of hammocks near sandhill communities are where Bell's roadside skipper has been found in Florida.

LIFE HISTORY AND ECOLOGY: Very little is known of the natural history of this butterfly. Females lay the eggs singly on grasses, but the hosts used in Florida are unknown. The larvae eat leaves and tie leaves together to form shelters. Adults fly low to the ground. Several generations are produced each year.

BASIS OF STATUS CLASSIFICATION: Bell's roadside skipper is listed as rare due to its highly localized distribution in Florida.

RECOMMENDATIONS: Surveys and ecological studies are needed to determine the current distribution, abundance, and habitat requirements of this species.

PREPARED BY: Marc C. Minno, Department of Zoology, University of Florida, Gainesville, FL 32611.

Bell's Roadside Skipper, *Amblyscirtes belli* (courtesy of John B. Heppner).
Male, ventral view.

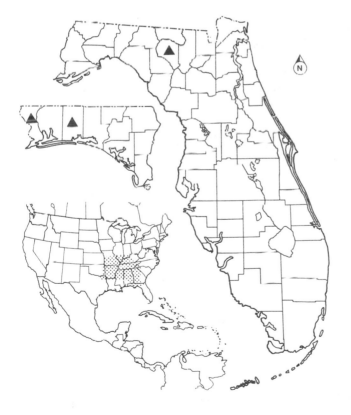

Distribution of
Bell's roadside
skipper, *Amblys-
cirtes belli.*

Rare

Pepper and Salt Skipper   *Amblyscirtes hegon* (Scudder)

OTHER COMMON NAMES: Greenish little skipper.

DESCRIPTION: *Amblyscirtes hegon* is a small blackish butterfly with checkered fringes and small white spots on the forewings, including a small spot in the cell. Forewing length varies from 11 to 13 mm (0.4–0.5 in). The undersides of the hindwings are grayish-green with small white spots.

RANGE: *Amblyscirtes hegon* occurs locally throughout much of the eastern United States. In Florida, this butterfly has been found only in Liberty County.

HABITAT: The pepper and salt skipper flies in grassy clearings within hammocks.

LIFE HISTORY AND ECOLOGY: The eggs are laid singly on grasses, but the hosts used in Florida are unknown. Adults fly low to the ground and occur in low abundance. All captures in Florida have been made during April and May.

BASIS OF STATUS CLASSIFICATION: The pepper and salt skipper is a rarely encountered butterfly, limited to the panhandle region of the state.

RECOMMENDATIONS: Surveys and ecological studies are needed to determine the current distribution, abundance, and habitat requirements of this species.

PREPARED BY: Marc C. Minno, Department of Zoology, University of Florida, Gainesville, FL 32611.

Rare

Roadside Skipper   *Amblyscirtes vialis* (W. H. Edwards)

OTHER COMMON NAMES: Black little skipper.

DESCRIPTION: *Amblyscirtes vialis* is a small (forewings range in length from 11 to 13 mm [0.5 in]) dark skipper. This butterfly bears few distinctive characteristics other than the checkered fringes, a few white spots near the tips of the forewings, and a blue-gray flush on the undersides of the hindwings.

RANGE: In Florida the roadside skipper has been found in only two counties in the panhandle. Although Kimball (1965) listed a few records of *Amblyscirtes vialis* from peninsular Florida, these appear to be based on misidentified specimens. This drab little butterfly is widely distributed, but local, elsewhere in North America.

HABITAT: This species flies in grassy clearings within hammocks and transitional areas between hammocks and pinelands.

LIFE HISTORY AND ECOLOGY: The eggs are laid singly on grasses. The host plants used in Florida are not known. Larvae eat leaves and tie leaves together to form shelters. Adults fly low to the ground. Several generations occur each year.

BASIS OF STATUS CLASSIFICATION: The roadside skipper is listed as rare because of its localized distribution in Florida.

RECOMMENDATIONS: Surveys and ecological studies are needed to determine the current distribution, abundance, and habitat requirements of this species.

Roadside Skipper, *Amblyscirtes vialis* (courtesy John B. Heppner). Male, ventral view.

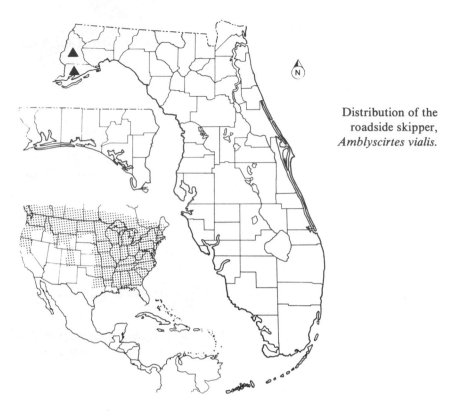

Distribution of the
roadside skipper,
Amblyscirtes vialis.

PREPARED BY: Marc C. Minno, Department of Zoology, University of Florida, Gainesville, FL 32611.

FAMILY HESPERIIDAE

Rare

Arogos Skipper

Atrytone arogos arogos (Boisduval and Le Conte)

OTHER COMMON NAMES: Brown-rim skipper.

DESCRIPTION: The Arogos skipper is a small, brownish butterfly. Forewing length ranges from 12 to 16 mm (0.5–0.6 in). There is a large golden-yellow patch on the upperside of the forewing in males, but females are mostly dark brown above.

Arogos Skipper, *Atrytone arogos arogos* (courtesy of John B. Heppner). Male, dorsal view (*above*) and female, dorsal view (*below*).

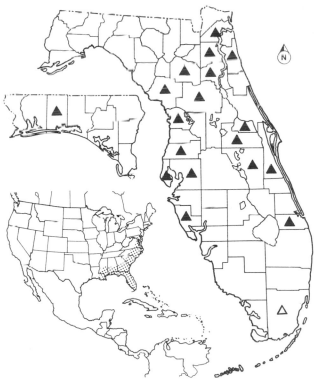

Distribution of the arogos skipper, *Atrytone arogos arogos.*

RANGE: This species ranges from central peninsular Florida north to New Jersey and west to Louisiana. Another race occurs in the Great Plains area. Although it has been reported from 19 counties in Florida, the adults occur in low abundance. Colonies are hard to find and seem to be short-lived.

HABITAT: In Florida, the Arogos skipper is found in pine flatwoods and sandhills.

LIFE HISTORY AND ECOLOGY: The eggs are laid singly on leaves of lopsided indiangrass (*Sorghastrum secundum*) and occasionally on *Andropogon* species. Larvae eat leaves and tie leaves together to form shelters. Partly grown larvae overwinter. The adults visit flowers such as thistle (*Cirsium horridulum*). Up to three generations occur per year.

BASIS OF STATUS CLASSIFICATION: The Arogos skipper is listed as rare because of its localized distribution and low abundance. Many of the known colonies in Florida have been destroyed by development. *Atrytone arogos arogos* appears to be declining in the eastern United States (D. F. Schweitzer, pers. comm.) and at present seems to be most numerous in Florida.

RECOMMENDATIONS: Surveys and ecological studies are needed to determine the current distribution, abundance, and habitat requirements of the Arogos skipper in Florida.

PREPARED BY: Marc C. Minno, Department of Zoology, University of Florida, Gainesville, FL 32611.

FAMILY HESPERIIDAE

Rare

Southern Dusted Skipper

Atrytonopsis hianna loammi Whitney

OTHER COMMON NAMES: Loammi skipper.

DESCRIPTION: *Atrytonopsis hianna loammi* is a medium-sized skipper with dark brown wings. The forewings range from 15 to 18 mm (0.6–0.7 in) in length and are marked with white spots. The undersides of the hindwings are dark brown with a flush of blue-gray along the outer margin and are dotted with white spots. Females have larger ventral white spots than males.

The relationship between this taxon and the typical race, which has greatly reduced white spots on the undersides of the hindwings, is uncertain. Although originally described as separate species, *Atrytonopsis loammi* and *Atrytonopsis hianna* are usually treated as geographical variants of a single species today.

RANGE: Although the southern dusted skipper has been found in many counties throughout Florida, this species is very local and usually occurs in low abundance. Its colonies seem to be short-lived. The range extends out-

Southern Dusted Skipper, *Atrytonopsis hianna loammmi* (courtesy of John B. Heppner). Male, ventral view (*above*) and female, dorsal view (*below*).

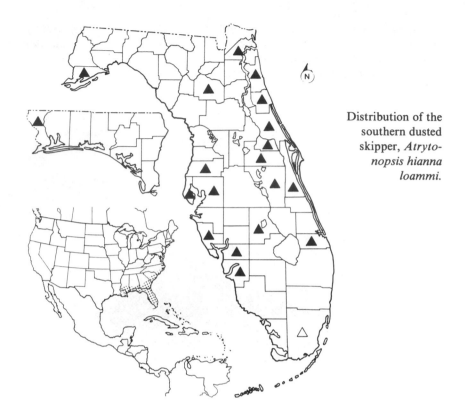

Distribution of the
southern dusted
skipper, *Atryto-*
nopsis hianna
loammi.

side of the state, in a narrow coastal band, west to Louisiana and north to
the Carolinas. The northern race is locally distributed in the eastern and mid-
dlewestern United States.

HABITAT: The southern dusted skipper is most often found in pine flatwoods.

LIFE HISTORY AND ECOLOGY: The females lay eggs singly on grasses.
The Florida hosts are not known, but the northern race uses *Andropogon*
species. Larvae eat leaves and tie leaves near the base of plant together to
form shelters. Overwintering occurs as partly grown larvae. Adults visit
flowers and perch on low foliage. Up to three generations occur per year.

BASIS OF STATUS CLASSIFICATION: The southern dusted skipper is
listed as rare because of the very local and ephemeral nature of Florida
populations.

RECOMMENDATIONS: Surveys and ecological studies are needed to determine the current distribution, abundance, and habitat requirements of
Atrytonopsis hianna loammi in Florida. Taxonomic studies are needed to

determine whether the southern dusted skipper is a race of *Atrytonopsis hianna* or a separate species.

PREPARED BY: Marc C. Minno, Department of Zoology, University of Florida, Gainesville, FL 32611.

Rare

Golden-Banded Skipper

Autochton cellus (Boisduval and Le Conte)

DESCRIPTION: *Autochton cellus* is a dark brown butterfly with a wide golden band across each forewing. The length of the primaries varies from 17 to 24 mm (0.6–1.0 in). The ventral hindwings are marked with broad dark bands.

Golden-Banded Skipper, *Autochton cellus* (courtesy of John B. Heppner). Male, dorsal view.

Distribution of the
golden-banded
skipper, *Autochton*
cellus.

RANGE: The golden-banded skipper has a disjunct range in northern Florida. This beautiful butterfly occurs in a few counties of the panhandle and also in the Gainesville area where limestone outcrops support diverse forests of broad-leaved trees. It is widely distributed, but local in occurrence, in the eastern United States. *Autochton cellus* is found in the southwestern United States, Mexico, and Central America as well (Burns 1984).

HABITAT: This species occurs in mesic hardwood hammocks and ravines.

LIFE HISTORY AND ECOLOGY: Females deposit the eggs singly or in small clusters on hog peanut (*Amphicarpa bracteata*) in shaded areas. Larvae eat leaves and fold and tie leaves together to form shelters. The pupae overwinter. Males perch in small clearings and sunspots to await receptive females with which to mate. Up to three generations occur each year.

BASIS OF STATUS CLASSIFICATION: The golden-banded skipper is considered to be rare in Florida due to its very local occurrence in just four counties.

RECOMMENDATIONS: Surveys and ecological studies are needed to determine the current distribution, abundance, and habitat requirements of this species.

PREPARED BY: Marc C. Minno, Department of Zoology, University of Florida, Gainesville, FL 32611.

FAMILY HESPERIIDAE

Rare

Caribbean Duskywing

Erynnis zarucco (Lucas) (Keys Population)

DESCRIPTION: The Caribbean duskywing is a medium-sized, dark skipper with some small white spots on the forewings. The primaries also have a pale patch at the end of the cell and range from 17 to 20 mm (0.7–0.8 in) in length. The keys population of *E. zarucco* has brown and white fringes on the hindwings rather than the uniform brown color of the mainland race. The fringes of some specimens, especially females, from the keys are nearly pure white. Although *E. zarucco* from the keys has sometimes been referred to subspecies *funeralis* (due to the white fringes), this butterfly appears to be most similar to Antillean populations. The coloration of the larvae of keys *E. zarucco* is also different from that of the mainland population.

RANGE: The Caribbean duskywing occurs in the lower Florida Keys, Cuba, Hispaniola, and Puerto Rico. Other races of *E. zarucco* occupy eastern North America, including most of Florida, and the western United States, Mexico, Central America, and South America (Burns 1964).

HABITAT: This butterfly is found in weed lots and disturbed sites.

LIFE HISTORY AND ECOLOGY: Eggs are deposited singly on the new growth of *Sesbania macrocarpa*. Large isolated plants sometimes will have dozens of eggs and larvae present. Larvae eat leaves and fold and tie leaflets together to make shelters. Adults are usually scarce. They fly low to the ground and visit flowers for nectar. This species has been found in the adult stage every month of the year. Urban development actually improves the habitat for this species as the host plant is patchily distributed in disturbed sites such as roadsides and weed lots as well as parking lots in the center of Key West.

Caribbean Duskywing, *Erynnis zarucco* (Keys population) (courtesy of John B. Heppner). Female, dorsal view.

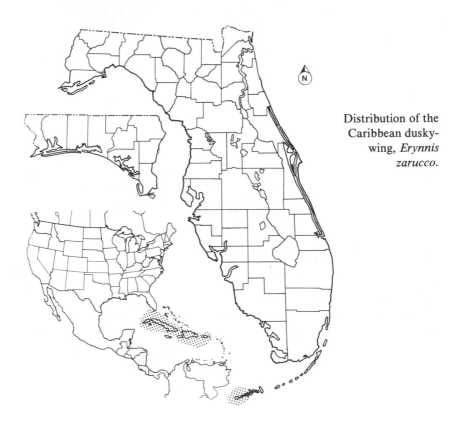

Distribution of the Caribbean dusky-wing, *Erynnis zarucco*.

BASIS OF STATUS CLASSIFICATION: The Caribbean duskywing is listed as rare because of its highly restricted range in Florida and low abundance.

RECOMMENDATIONS: Surveys are necessary to monitor the distribution and abundance of the Caribbean duskywing. Taxonomic studies are needed to determine the relationships within the *Erynnis zarucco* group. Ecological studies should also be conducted to identify the habitat requirements of this butterfly.

PREPARED BY: Marc C. Minno and Thomas C. Emmel, Department of Zoology, University of Florida, Gainesville, FL 32611.

FAMILY HESPERIIDAE

Rare

Berry's Skipper
Euphyes berryi (Bell)

OTHER COMMON NAMES: Florida sedge skipper.

DESCRIPTION: Berry's skipper is a medium-sized hesperiid (forewing lengths vary from 15 to 20 mm [0.6 to 0.8 in]) that is mostly dark brown with golden-yellow patches above. Males have a dark stigma across each forewing. The undersides are yellowish with pale veins.

RANGE: *Euphyes berryi* is known from only 12 counties throughout Florida. It is much less abundant outside of Florida, but its range extends along the coastal plain to North Carolina.

HABITAT: This skipper is found usually in wet prairies, marshes, and savannas with pitcher plants.

LIFE HISTORY AND ECOLOGY: Eggs are laid singly on the leaves of sedges, but the specific hosts have not been determined. Larvae eat leaves and tie leaves together to form shelters. The partly grown larvae overwinter. Adults visit flowers and may be rather abundant once a colony has been located, especially during the fall. Two generations occur each year.

BASIS OF STATUS CLASSIFICATION: Berry's skipper is listed as rare due to its very local occurrence. Some colonies in Florida are threatened by

Berry's Skipper, *Euphyes berryi* (courtesy of John B. Heppner). Male, ventral view (*above*) and female, ventral view (*below*).

or have been destroyed by urban development. Most of this species' range lies within Florida.

RECOMMENDATIONS: Surveys and ecological studies are needed to determine the current distribution, abundance, and habitat requirements of this species.

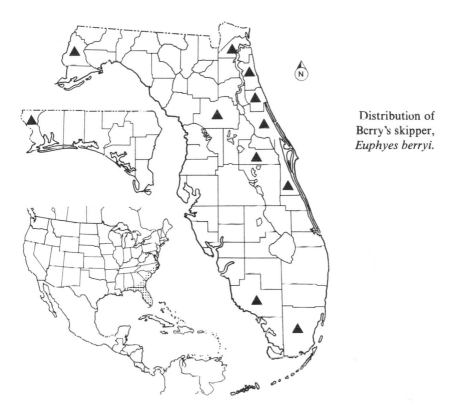

Distribution of
Berry's skipper,
Euphyes berryi.

PREPARED BY: Marc C. Minno, Department of Zoology, University of
Florida, Gainesville, FL 32611.

FAMILY HESPERIIDAE

Rare

Dion Skipper

Euphyes dion (W. H. Edwards)

OTHER COMMON NAMES: Eastern sedge skipper.

DESCRIPTION: The uppersides of the Dion skipper are blackish with
golden-yellow patches. The length of the forewings varies from 15 to 19 mm
(0.6–0.7 in). Males have a dark stigma across each forewing. The ventral

hindwings are reddish with a yellow streak from the base to the outer margin in both sexes. Shuey (1989) concluded that what had been considered a southern race or a separate species, *Euphyes alabamae*, is merely a dark form of the Dion skipper. Florida material is referred to as *E. alabamae* in the older literature.

RANGE: *Euphyes dion* is known from 11 counties in northern Florida. This skipper is locally distributed throughout much of the eastern United States.

Dion Skipper, *Euphyes dion* (courtesy of John B. Heppner). Male, dorsal view (*above*) and ventral view (*below*).

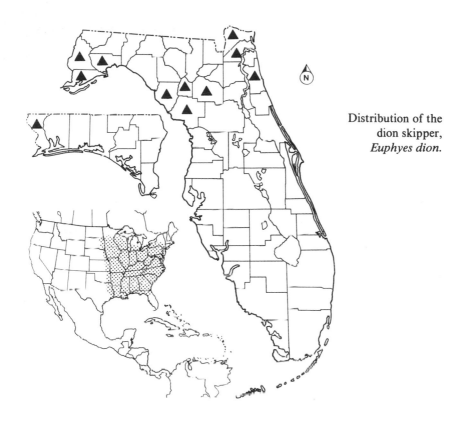

Distribution of the dion skipper, *Euphyes dion.*

HABITAT: It is found along the edges of swamps, wet prairies, and marshes.

LIFE HISTORY AND ECOLOGY: Eggs are laid singly on the leaves of sedges. Hosts in Florida have not been identified, but *Carex hyalinolepis* and *Scirpus cyperinus* are eaten elsewhere (Scott 1986). Larvae eat leaves and tie leaves together to make shelters. Overwintering occurs as partly grown larvae. Adults visit flowers readily and are most abundant in the fall. Two generations occur per year.

BASIS OF STATUS CLASSIFICATION: The Dion skipper is listed as rare due to its very localized distribution in Florida.

RECOMMENDATIONS: Surveys and ecological studies are needed to determine the current distribution, abundance, and habitat requirements of this species. The Dion skipper could be useful in evaluating the biological value or health of wetland habitats in Florida.

PREPARED BY: Marc C. Minno, Department of Zoology, University of Florida, Gainesville, FL 32611.

Rare

Duke's Skipper

Euphyes dukesi (Lindsey)

OTHER COMMON NAMES: Brown sedge skipper, scarce swamp skipper.

DESCRIPTION: Duke's skipper is a dark brown butterfly with diffuse light brown patches on the uppersides. The forewings range from 16 to 20 mm (0.6–0.8 in) in length. Males have a dark stigma across each forewing. The undersides of the hindwings are reddish with a yellow streak from the base to the outer margin. The taxonomic relationships between the Florida, Mississippi Valley, and midwestern populations are currently being studied by J. A. Shuey.

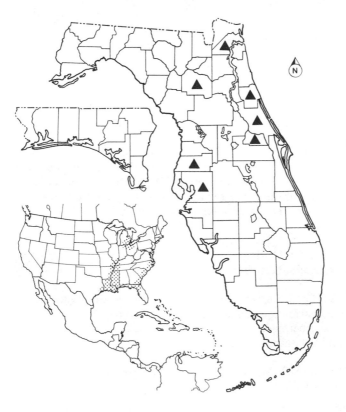

Distribution of
Duke's skipper,
Euphyes dukesi.

Duke's Skipper, *Euphyes dukesi* (courtesy of John B. Heppner). Male, dorsal view (*above*) and ventral view (*below*).

RANGE: This skipper occurs in northern and central Florida, the Mississippi Valley, the Upper Midwest, and along the Atlantic coastal plain.

HABITAT: Duke's skipper flies in shaded moist forests and swamps.

LIFE HISTORY AND ECOLOGY: Females deposit the eggs singly on the leaves of *Rhynchospora inundata*, a large sedge found in swamps. Larvae eat leaves and tie leaves together to form shelters. Tachinid flies often parasitize the caterpillars. Partly grown larvae overwinter. Adults fly low to the ground in shaded areas where the host plant grows. Males patrol patches of the food plant, searching for receptive females with which to mate. Flowers are occasionally visited for nectar. Two generations are produced per year.

BASIS OF STATUS CLASSIFICATION: Duke's skipper is listed as rare because of its very local occurrence in Florida. One of us (JVC) recently found colonies of this species near rapidly growing urban centers in Pasco and Hillsborough counties. Logging and the destruction of hydric forest communities for urban development have negatively impacted populations of Duke's skipper. The Florida Department of Environmental Regulation and other state agencies may allow developers to destroy some wetlands if they agree to build similar habitat elsewhere. However, Bernard Yokel (1991) notes that such mitigation does not work due to noncompliance by developers and weak enforcement of state laws. Further, it is unlikely that the specific environmental requirements of sensitive species, such as *Euphyes dukesi*, could be recreated by this process.

RECOMMENDATIONS: Surveys and ecological studies are needed to determine the current distribution, abundance, and habitat requirements of *Euphyes dukesi* in Florida. Known colonies should be monitored for fluctuations in population levels, especially in areas threatened by habitat alteration.

PREPARED BY: Marc C. Minno, Department of Zoology, University of Florida, Gainesville, FL 32611, and John V. Calhoun, Research Associate, Florida State Collection of Arthropods, P.O. Box 1269, Gainesville, FL 32602.

FAMILY HESPERIIDAE

Rare

_____

Common Sooty Wing
Pholisora catullus (Fabricius)

OTHER COMMON NAMES: Roadside rambler.

DESCRIPTION: *Pholisora catullus* is a small black skipper with small white spots on the forewings. The length of the forewings varies from 12 to 15 mm (0.5–0.6 in). The palps project conspicuously forward from the head in this species and are lightly colored below.

Common Sooty Wing, *Pholisora catullus* (courtesy of John B. Heppner).
Female, dorsal view.

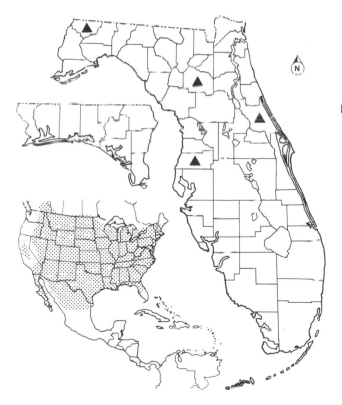

Distribution of the common sooty wing, *Pholisora catullus.*

RANGE: This species occurs over much of the United States, as well as southern Canada and northern Mexico. Despite its broad distribution, this butterfly has been found in only four counties in northern and central Florida.

HABITAT: This species is associated with cultivated fields and disturbed sites.

LIFE HISTORY AND ECOLOGY: The eggs are laid singly on the leaves of the host. The food plants used in Florida are unknown, but *Chenopodium* spp. and *Amaranthus* spp. are eaten in other parts of its range. One of us (JVC) recently found a colony of the common sooty wing associated with *Chenopodium ambrosioides* in Pasco County. The larvae eat leaves and fold and tie leaves together to form shelters. Mature larvae overwinter and pupate without further feeding in the spring. Adults fly low to the ground and visit flowers readily. Males patrol ecotone areas such as borders of taller vegetation and long fences. The wings are usually held to the sides rather than over the back when feeding or perching. Several generations are produced per year. Capman (1990) described the natural history of *Pholisora catullus* in central Illinois.

BASIS OF STATUS CLASSIFICATION: The common sooty wing is considered rare in Florida due to its very local distribution.

RECOMMENDATIONS: Surveys and ecological studies are needed to determine the current distribution, abundance, and habitat requirements of this species in Florida. The margins of pastures and cultivated fields should be checked for the presence of the common sooty wing, especially in late summer when adults are most abundant.

PREPARED BY: Marc C. Minno, Department of Zoology, University of Florida, Gainesville, FL 32611, and John V. Calhoun, Research Associate, Florida State Collection of Arthropods, P.O. Box 1269, Gainesville, FL 32602.

FAMILY HESPERIIDAE

Rare

Wild Rice Skipper

Poanes viator zizaniae Shapiro

OTHER COMMON NAMES: Broad marsh skipper, broad-winged skipper.

DESCRIPTION: The wild rice skipper is a medium-sized, brownish skipper with yellowish patches and spots above. Forewings range in length from 16 to 25 mm (0.6–1.0 in). The undersides are lighter brown with some yellowish spots and streaks.

RANGE: This butterfly ranges from the lower Mississippi Valley and along the Gulf and Atlantic coastal plains north to New England. A different subspecies occurs in the Great Lakes region. In Florida, the wild rice skipper is known from only six counties.

HABITAT: The wild rice skipper is usually found in close association with its larval host which grows along the margins of lakes and sluggish streams and rivers.

LIFE HISTORY AND ECOLOGY: The females deposit the eggs singly on the leaves of southern wild rice, *Zizaniopsis miliacea*. Larvae eat leaves and fold and tie leaves together to form shelters or hide in the leaf axils. Overwintering occurs as partly grown larvae. Adults fly within stands of the host but often readily visit flowers such as *Bidens alba* and *Pontederia cordata*. Two generations are produced per year. Although extremely local, this butterfly is often abundant, especially during the fall, where it does occur.

BASIS OF STATUS CLASSIFICATION: The wild rice skipper is listed as rare because of its very localized distribution in Florida.

Wild Rice Skipper, *Poanes viator zizaniae* (courtesy of John B. Heppner). Male, dorsal view.

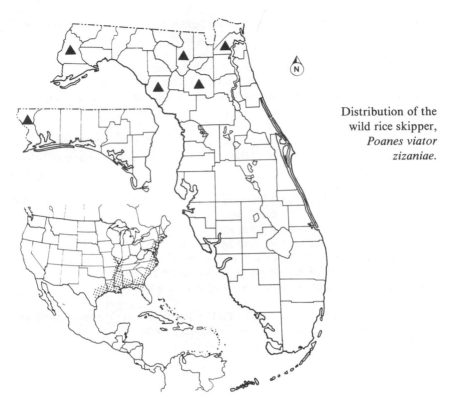

Distribution of the
wild rice skipper,
*Poanes viator
zizaniae.*

RECOMMENDATIONS: Surveys and ecological studies are needed to determine the current distribution, abundance, and habitat requirements of this species in Florida.

PREPARED BY: Marc C. Minno, Department of Zoology, University of Florida, Gainesville, FL 32611.

FAMILY HESPERIIDAE

Rare

Southern Swamp Skipper
Poanes yehl (Skinner)

OTHER COMMON NAMES: Yehl skipper.

DESCRIPTION: The southern swamp skipper has a forewing length ranging from 14 to 19 mm (0.6–0.7 in). The dorsal sides of the wings are dark brown with golden-yellow patches. Males have a dark stigma across the middle of the forewings. The ventral hindwings are light brown with a postmedial band of three white or yellowish spots interrupted by a yellow streak.

Southern Swamp Skipper, *Poanes yehl* (courtesy of John B. Heppner). Male dorsal view (*above*) and ventral view (*below*).

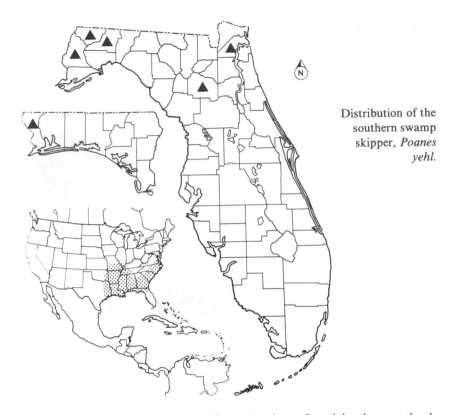

Distribution of the
southern swamp
skipper, *Poanes
yehl.*

RANGE: The southern swamp skipper has been found in six counties in northern Florida and occurs locally throughout much of the southeastern United States.

HABITAT: It occurs along the edges of hardwood hammocks and swamps.

LIFE HISTORY AND ECOLOGY: Female southern swamp skippers lay their eggs singly on the leaves of the host plant (probably switch cane, *Arundinaria gigantea*, M. Ricard, pers. comm.). In the laboratory, larvae eat the leaves of switch cane and fold and tie leaves together to form shelters. The young larvae overwinter. Adults readily visit flowers such as *Bidens alba*, and males perch in sunspots, small clearings, and forest edges. Two generations are produced per year. Adults are most numerous during the fall.

BASIS OF STATUS CLASSIFICATION: The southern swamp skipper is listed as rare because it is very local in distribution and is usually found in low abundance.

RECOMMENDATIONS: Surveys and ecological studies are needed to determine the current distribution, abundance, and habitat requirements of this species.

PREPARED BY: Marc C. Minno, Department of Zoology, University of Florida, Gainesville, FL 32611.

FAMILY HESPERIIDAE

Rare

Zabulon Skipper

Poanes zabulon (Boisduval and Le Conte)

OTHER COMMON NAMES: Southern dimorphic skipper, southern golden skipper.

DESCRIPTION: Males of the Zabulon skipper are golden-yellow above with dark brown borders. The ventral surfaces are light yellow with brown spots and margins. The females are black with some yellowish spots on the forewings. The length of the forewings varies from 14 to 17 mm (0.5–0.7 in).

RANGE: It is known from 15 counties in northern and central Florida and is widely distributed in the eastern United States.

HABITAT: This skipper occurs in grassy clearings in hardwood hammocks.

Zabulon Skipper, *Poanes zabulon* (courtesy of John B. Heppner). Male, dorsal view.

Distribution of the
zabulon skipper,
Poanes zabulon.

LIFE HISTORY AND ECOLOGY: Eggs of the Zabulon skipper are deposited singly on grasses, but the hosts used in Florida are unknown. The larvae eat leaves and fold or tie leaves together to make shelters. Overwintering occurs as partly grown larvae. The adults readily visit flowers. Males perch on foliage in sunspots, clearings, and forest edges. Two broods are produced per year.

BASIS OF STATUS CLASSIFICATION: Although the Zabulon skipper is locally abundant at some panhandle localities, this species is usually local and uncommon elsewhere in Florida.

RECOMMENDATIONS: Surveys and ecological studies are needed to determine the current distribution, abundance, and habitat requirements of this species.

PREPARED BY: Marc C. Minno, Department of Zoology, University of Florida, Gainesville, FL 32611.

Rare

Little Glassy Wing
Pompeius verna (W. H. Edwards)

DESCRIPTION: The little glassy wing is a small, dark brown skipper butterfly with some whitish apical and postmedial spots on the forewings. The spot located near the middle of the forewings is squarish and translucent. There is a medial row of faint spots on the undersides of the hindwings and the ventral surfaces have a purplish sheen. Males have a dark stigma in the center of the forewings. The length of the forewings varies from 12 to 17 mm (0.5–0.6 in).

RANGE: It is known from seven counties in northern Florida. The little glassy wing is widely distributed in the eastern United States.

HABITAT: It occurs along grassy trails and clearings in deciduous woods.

Little Glassy Wing, *Pompeius verna* (courtesy of John B. Heppner). Male, dorsal view (*above*) and female, dorsal view (*below*).

Distribution of the
little glassy wing,
Pompeius verna.

LIFE HISTORY AND ECOLOGY: The eggs of the little glassy wing are laid singly on grasses. The hosts in Florida have not been determined, but *Tridens flavus* is used elsewhere in its range. The caterpillars eat leaves and fold and tie leaves together to make shelters. Overwintering takes place as partly grown larvae. Adults fly low to the ground and visit flowers readily. Males perch in small clearings and sunspots. There are two generations each year.

BASIS OF STATUS CLASSIFICATION: Although *P. verna* may be abundant in some areas of the panhandle such as Torreya State Park, this butterfly is usually very local and uncommon in other areas of northern Florida.

RECOMMENDATIONS: Surveys and ecological studies are needed to determine the current distribution, abundance, and habitat requirements of this species.

PREPARED BY: Marc C. Minno, Department of Zoology, University of Florida, Gainesville, FL 32611.

Species of Special Concern

Zestos Skipper

Epargyreus zestos zestos (Geyer)

OTHER COMMON NAMES: Rusty skipper.

DESCRIPTION: The Zestos skipper is one of the larger hesperiids found in Florida. The forewings are brown with golden spots, and range in length from 26 to 30 mm (1.0–1.2 in). The undersides of the hindwings are reddish brown.

RANGE: The Zestos skipper once occurred on the southern Florida mainland and throughout the keys, but is now found mostly in the lower and middle keys. *Epargyreus zestos zestos* also occurs in the Bahamas, Puerto Rico, and Lesser Antilles. A different subspecies inhabits Great Inagua and Turks and Caicos islands (Clench and Bjorndal 1980).

HABITAT: It occurs along edges of tropical hardwood hammocks in the Florida Keys.

Zestos Skipper, *Epargyreus zestos zestos* (courtesy of John B. Heppner). Male, ventral view.

Distribution of the
zestos skipper,
*Epargyreus zestos
zestos.*

LIFE HISTORY AND ECOLOGY: The eggs are laid singly on the young leaves of *Galactia striata*. Larvae eat leaves and fold and tie leaves together to form shelters. Males perch on foliage along trails and clearings. The adults also perch on the undersides of leaves. Several generations are produced each year.

BASIS OF STATUS CLASSIFICATION: The Zestos skipper is listed as a species of special concern because of its diminishing range in Florida. This butterfly is still fairly abundant in the lower keys, but has disappeared from Biscayne National Park and the upper keys.

RECOMMENDATIONS: Surveys and ecological studies are needed to determine the current distribution, reasons for declining range, abundance, and habitat requirements of this species.

PREPARED BY: Marc C. Minno and Thomas C. Emmel, Department of Zoology, University of Florida, Gainesville, FL 32611.

Species of Special Concern

Florida Duskywing
Ephyriades brunneus floridensis Bell and Comstock

DESCRIPTION: The Florida duskywing is a dark, medium-sized skipper butterfly with some small white spots on the forewings. Males are mostly black and resemble *Erynnis zarucco*. Females are more contrastingly patterned than males and have a purplish iridescence.

RANGE: The Florida duskywing is found only in southern Florida. It is most abundant in the lower keys and pine islands in Everglades National Park, but is also present on Key Largo and in southeastern Dade County. Other subspecies of *E. brunneus* occur in the Bahamas, Cuba, Jamaica, and the Lesser Antilles.

HABITAT: It usually occurs in tropical pinelands.

Florida Duskywing,
*Ephyriades brunneus
floridensis* (courtesy
of John B. Heppner).
Male, dorsal view
(*above*) and female,
dorsal view (*below*).

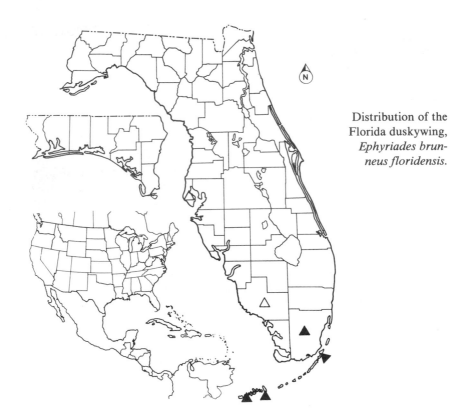

Distribution of the
Florida duskywing,
*Ephyriades brun-
neus floridensis.*

LIFE HISTORY AND ECOLOGY: The life history of the Florida duskywing has been described by Tamburo and Butcher (1955). The eggs are laid
singly on the leaves of shrubs in the Malpighiaceae. Locustberry, *Byrsonima
lucida*, is the native food plant, but the exotic Barbados cherry, *Malpighia
glabra*, is also eaten. Larvae feed on the leaves of the host and fold and tie
leaves together to make shelters. Adults visit flowers readily. The males patrol low to the ground. Several generations are produced each year.

BASIS OF STATUS CLASSIFICATION: The Florida duskywing is listed
as a species of special concern because it is an endemic with a restricted distribution. This butterfly is losing habitat as south Florida pinelands are being
destroyed by urban development at a rapid rate. Populations on the southern
mainland were probably greatly impacted by Hurricane Andrew.

RECOMMENDATIONS: Surveys are needed to monitor the distribution
and abundance of the Florida duskywing. Prescribed burning of pinelands is
necessary to maintain habitat for this species; however, land managers should
try to create mosaics of habitat with differing fire histories. Immature stages
of this and other butterflies will probably be destroyed by a fire, but adults
produced in nearby unburned tracts may benefit from the wealth of wild

flowers that frequently appear in the months after a fire has passed. Eventually, the host-plants in the burned site will be ideal for the growth of the larvae. Tropical pinelands should be protected from urban development, especially in the keys, and managed to benefit this butterfly.

PREPARED BY: Marc C. Minno and Thomas C. Emmel, Department of Zoology, University of Florida, Gainesville, FL 32611.

FAMILY HESPERIIDAE

Species of Special Concern

Mangrove Skipper

Phocides pigmalion okeechobee (Worthington)

OTHER COMMON NAMES: Batabano skipper.

DESCRIPTION: The mangrove skipper is one of the largest hesperiids in Florida. The forewings range in length from 25 to 33 mm (1.0–1.3 in). The adults are black with iridescent blue markings and cannot be confused with any other species in the state.

Mangrove Skipper, *Phocides pigmalion okeechobee* (courtesy of John B. Heppner). Male, dorsal view.

Distribution of the
mangrove skipper,
*Phocides pigmalion
okeechobee.*

RANGE: This skipper is found in coastal areas of south Florida and the keys. Other races occur in the Bahamas, Cuba, Cayman Islands, Hispaniola, Puerto Rico, Central and South America.

HABITAT: This butterfly is found usually in mangrove forests and salt marshes, but individuals sometimes fly along trails through tropical hammocks and in weed lots.

LIFE HISTORY AND ECOLOGY: The eggs are laid singly on the leaves of red mangrove (*Rhizophora mangle*). Larvae eat leaves and fold leaves to make shelters. Adults are powerful fliers and are readily attracted to flowers. As with some other tropical skippers, adults sometimes perch on the undersides of leaves. The mangrove skipper flies all year.

BASIS OF STATUS CLASSIFICATION: The mangrove skipper is listed as a species of special concern because it is a Floridian endemic that is closely associated with a protected plant, red mangrove.

RECOMMENDATIONS: Habitat protection will insure the survival of *Phocides pigmalion okeechobee* in Florida.

PREPARED BY: Marc C. Minno and Thomas C. Emmel, Department of Zoology, University of Florida, Gainesville, FL 32611.

Order Lepidoptera
FAMILY LYCAENIDAE

INTRODUCTION: Over 35 different kinds of hairstreaks (subfamily Theclinae) and blues have been found in Florida. Lycaenids are small butterflies that often have bright blue on the uppersides of the wings. The hindwings may have some reddish eyespots and thread-like tails, especially the hairstreaks. The slug-like caterpillars feed on buds, flowers, or the developing seeds of many kinds of plants. None of the lycaenids in Florida is currently endangered, but two are considered to be threatened, one is a species of special concern, and eight are rare. The rare species are mostly temperate butterflies that reach the southern limits of their ranges in Florida. The others are tropical species of West Indian affinity and are restricted mostly to the Florida Keys. Although *Mitoura sweadneri* Chermock is sometimes listed as a rare butterfly, it is omitted from this list. Sweadner's hairstreak is widely distributed, but of local occurence in northern Florida. The adults are short-lived and usually perch near the tops of cedar trees (the larval host), making them difficult to find. Although there has been widespread destruction of its usual coastal habitat, T. C. Emmel has successfully led preservation efforts designed to protect the host plant and coastal scrub habitat of Sweadner's hairstreak at the type locality in St. Augustine and St. Johns County, Florida.

PREPARED BY: Marc C. Minno, Department of Zoology, University of Florida, Gainesville, FL 32611.

FAMILY LYCAENIDAE

Threatened

Maesites Hairstreak
Chlorostrymon maesites (Herrich-Schäffer)

OTHER COMMON NAMES: Verde azul.

DESCRIPTION: The maesites hairstreak is a very small, brilliantly colored butterfly with short tails on the hindwings. The forewings range in length from 10 to 11 mm (0.4 in). The uppersides of the males are iridescent purple. Females are blue above. The wings are mostly bright green beneath with a reddish-brown patch at the base of the tails. The recently introduced St. Christopher's hairstreak (*Chlorostrymon simaethis*) is similar but larger and has a silvery band on the undersides of the wings.

RANGE: The maesites hairstreak is very locally distributed in the keys. Most specimens have been reported from Key Largo and Stock Island. Although the maesites hairstreak was historically known to occur in the Miami area, it has not been found on the mainland for many years. This species also inhabits the Bahamas, Cuba, Jamaica, Hispaniola, Puerto Rico, and Dominica (Johnson 1989).

HABITAT: It occurs along the edges of tropical hardwood hammocks and disturbed sites with leguminous trees.

LIFE HISTORY AND ECOLOGY: The eggs are laid singly on the flowers and buds of tropical trees in the Fabaceae such as *Albizia lebbeck* (R. Boscoe, pers. comm.). The caterpillars eat flowers, buds, and young seeds. Adults apparently spend most of their time in the forest canopy, but also visit flowers occasionally (Young 1937). Several generations are produced each year.

Maesites Hairstreak, *Chlorostrymon maesites* (courtesy of John B. Heppner). Male, ventral view.

Distribution of the
maesites hairstreak,
*Chlorostrymon
maesites.*

BASIS OF STATUS CLASSIFICATION: The maesites hairstreak is listed as threatened because of its highly restricted range in Florida. In addition, this butterfly has lost habitat due to urban development. The maesites hairstreak is usually considered to be a rare species throughout its range.

RECOMMENDATIONS: Surveys are needed to determine the current distribution and abundance of the maesites hairstreak. Preservation and management of tropical hardwood hammocks are necessary to conserve habitat for this species. Although Johnson (1989) considered the Florida population to be phenotypically similar to others in the Antilles, there are some distinctive features. Further taxonomic studies of the maesites hairstreak should be made.

PREPARED BY: Marc C. Minno and Thomas C. Emmel, Department of Zoology, University of Florida, Gainesville, FL 32611.

Threatened

Bartram's Hairstreak

Strymon acis bartrami (Comstock and Huntington)

DESCRIPTION: Bartram's hairstreak is a small grayish butterfly with two pairs of delicate tails on the hindwings. The forewings vary from 11 to 13 mm (0.5 in) in length. The undersides of the hindwings have a distinctive pattern of white spots and lines, plus a red eyespot at the base of the tails. *Strymon melinus* and *Strymon martialis* are similar, but have different ventral wing patterns.

RANGE: This pretty little butterfly is found only in southern Dade County, including Everglades National Park, and on Big Pine Key. Other subspecies occur in the Bahamas, the Greater Antilles, and the northern islands of the Lesser Antilles.

HABITAT: It occurs in open tropical pinelands with an abundance of the larval host plant.

LIFE HISTORY AND ECOLOGY: Females lay their eggs singly on the flowers of woolly croton, *Croton linearis*. The larvae feed on the flowers and leaves of the host. Adults frequently perch on woolly crotons and visit nearby flowers for nectar. Several generations are produced each year.

BASIS OF STATUS CLASSIFICATION: Bartram's hairstreak is listed as threatened because of its restricted distribution, low abundance, and recent loss of habitat. Thirty surveys, conducted between 23 May and 16 December 1988, found an average of 0.5 adults per hectare in pineland habitats of Everglades National Park and 0.3, 1.0, and 2.7 individuals per hectare at three locations on Big Pine Key (Hennessey and Habeck 1991). Hurricane Andrew may have severely impacted the mainland populations of this butterfly.

RECOMMENDATIONS: Additional surveys are needed to monitor the abundance and distribution of Bartram's hairstreak. Ecological studies should be conducted to identify its habitat requirements. Prescribed burning of pinelands may be necessary to maintain habitat for this species (Hennessey and Habeck 1991), but land managers should take care not to burn large tracts entirely, lest populations of Bartram's hairstreak and other rare butterflies be destroyed by the fire. Management of the remaining habitat in the keys and Everglades National Park should be carefully planned.

PREPARED BY: Marc C. Minno and Thomas C. Emmel, Department of Zoology, University of Florida, Gainesville, FL 32611.

Bartram's Hairstreak, *Strymon acis bartrami* (courtesy of the Allyn Museum).
Male, ventral view.

Distribution of Bartram's hairstreak,
*Strymon acis
bartrami.*

Rare

Eastern Tailed Blue

Everes comyntas comyntas (Godart)

DESCRIPTION: *Everes comyntas* is a small (forewing length: 9 to 13 mm [0.3 to 0.5 in]) blue butterfly with a pair of delicate tails on the hindwings. The uppersides are bright blue with an orange eyespot at the base of the tails. The ventral surfaces are white with black spots and two orange eyespots. Females have less blue above than males.

RANGE: This species ranges throughout much of the eastern and middle-western United States.

HABITAT: It occurs in old fields, roadsides and disturbed sites.

Eastern Tailed Blue, *Everes comyatas comyntas*? (courtesy of John B. Heppner). Male, ventral view.

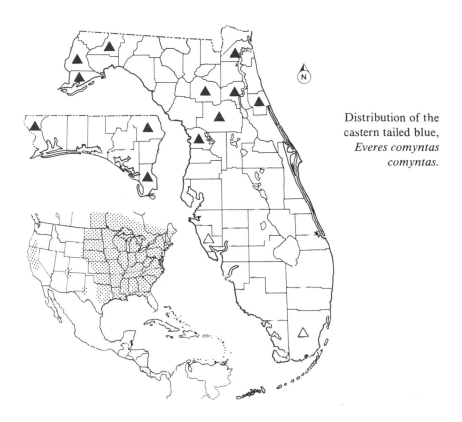

Distribution of the
eastern tailed blue,
*Everes comyntas
comyntas.*

LIFE HISTORY AND ECOLOGY: The eggs are laid singly on the flowers of leguminous herbs, but the hosts used in Florida are not known. The larvae eat flowers and young seeds. Overwintering takes place in the larval stage. Adults fly low to the ground and visit flowers for nectar readily. Several generations occur each year.

BASIS OF STATUS CLASSIFICATION: The eastern tailed blue is considered rare in Florida because it is very locally distributed.

RECOMMENDATIONS: Surveys and ecological studies are needed to determine the current distribution, abundance, and habitat requirements of *Everes comyntas* in Florida.

PREPARED BY: Marc C. Minno, Department of Zoology, University of Florida, Gainesville, FL 32611.

Rare

Coral Hairstreak

Harkenclenus titus mopsus (Hübner)

DESCRIPTION: The coral hairstreak is a small drab butterfly with a distinctive row of red spots along the outer margin of the hindwing. The forewings range from 12 to 18 mm (0.5–0.7 in) in length. Florida specimens tend to be relatively large.

RANGE: This butterfly occurs throughout most of the United States and southern Canada, but has been recorded from only two counties in Florida.

HABITAT: It is found along the edges of hardwood hammocks.

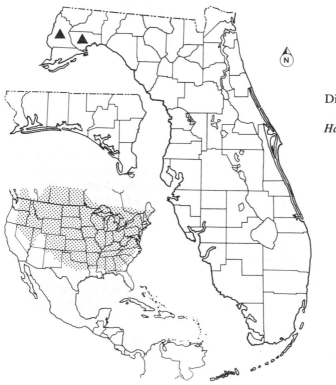

Distribution of the coral hairstreak, *Harkenclenus titus mopsus.*

Coral Hairstreak, *Harkenclenus titus mopsus* (courtesy of John B. Heppner). Male, dorsal view (*above*) and female, ventral view (*below*).

LIFE HISTORY AND ECOLOGY: The coral hairstreak lays its eggs singly on the twigs and buds of wild plums (*Prunus* spp.) and wild cherry (*Prunus serotina*) in the eastern United States. In Florida, a larva has been found on *Malus angustifolia* in April. The larvae feed on the leaves of the host. Over-wintering takes place in the egg stage. Adults are most frequently found at flowers. Only one generation is produced each year.

BASIS OF STATUS CLASSIFICATION: The coral hairstreak is considered to be rare due to its very restricted range in Florida.

RECOMMENDATIONS: Surveys and ecological studies are needed to determine the current distribution, abundance, and habitat requirements of this butterfly.

PREPARED BY: Marc C. Minno, Department of Zoology, University of Florida, Gainesville, FL 32611.

                                                    FAMILY LYCAENIDAE

Rare

Frosted Elfin

Incisalia irus (Godart)

DESCRIPTION: The frosted elfin is a small drab butterfly that lacks threadlike tails. The wings are dark brown above and light and dark brown, suffused with gray, below. The length of the forewings varies from 12 to 15 mm (0.5–0.6 in). The Florida population should belong to the southern race of the frosted elfin, *Incisalia irus arsace*, but there have been difficulties interpreting ecotypic and geographic variation within this species recently (Gatrelle 1991; Schweitzer 1992).

RANGE: It is found from the Great Lakes region to New England and southward to northern Florida. Thomas M. Neal first discovered this butterfly along a powerline near Camp Blanding in Clay County, Florida, during the spring of 1990. It has since been found at three separate sites in Clay County.

HABITAT: It is found in sandhills containing patches of the host plant.

LIFE HISTORY AND ECOLOGY: In Florida, adults of the frosted elfin are closely associated with sundial lupine (*Lupinus perennis*). The eggs are laid singly on the host flowers and young leaves. The caterpillars feed on the flowers, young seed pods, and occasionally leaves. There are two ecotypes of this butterfly throughout its range, one that feeds on sundial lupine (*Lupinus perennis*) and another that eats wild indigo (*Baptisia tinctoria*). Possibly, these ecotypes may represent sibling species (Schweitzer 1992). Overwintering takes place in the pupal stage. Adults frequently perch on or near the host and sip nectar from the flowers. Only one generation occurs each year, with adults appearing in April.

Frosted Elfin, *Encisalia irus* (courtesy of John B. Heppner). Male, ventral view.

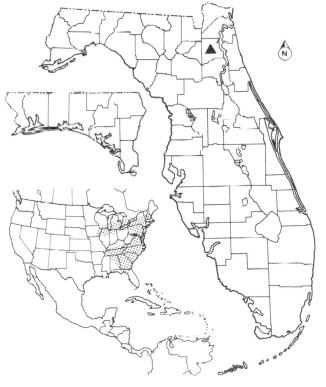

Distribution of the frosted elfin, *Incisulia irus.*

BASIS OF STATUS CLASSIFICATION: The frosted elfin is listed as rare because it is known from only a few colonies in Florida. One of the colonies has been partly destroyed by a housing development, but some disturbance may actually enhance the growth of the foodplant, which is shade-intolerant.

RECOMMENDATIONS: Surveys and ecological studies are needed to determine the current distribution, abundance, and habitat requirements of this butterfly in Florida. Clearing trees and creating modest soil disturbance benefits the lupine host plant and thereby the frosted elfin. Powerline corridors that are managed without the use of herbicides could provide prime habitat for the butterfly (D. F. Schweitzer, pers. comm.). Taxonomic studies are needed to determine the relationship of the Florida population to the lupine and wild indigo ecotypes and to the race, *I. irus arsace*.

PREPARED BY: Marc C. Minno, Department of Zoology, University of Florida, Gainesville, FL 32611.

FAMILY LYCAENIDAE

Rare

Eastern Pine Elfin

Incisalia niphon niphon (Hübner)

DESCRIPTION: The eastern pine elfin is a small (forewing length: 13-15 mm [0.5-0.6 in]) brownish butterfly that lacks tails. The coloration of the uppersides is variable. Males are typically dark brown, while females often have large fulvous patches above. The ventral surfaces are light and dark brown with jagged black and white lines.

RANGE: This elfin butterfly is locally distributed in the eastern United States and southern Canada. *Incisalia niphon* has been taken in only eight counties in northern Florida.

HABITAT: It occurs in upland areas with pines.

LIFE HISTORY AND ECOLOGY: The eggs are laid singly on new growth of pines (associated with sand pine, *Pinus clausa*, in Ocala National Forest). Larvae feed on the leaves of the host. Overwintering occurs in the pupal stage. Adults perch in the tops of pines and occasionally visit the flowers of wild plums (*Prunus* spp.) and *Lyonia* spp. for nectar or sip water from wet soil. The flight season is short, usually lasting two or three weeks in any single locality. February to May are the only months that the adults have been found.

Eastern Pine Elfin, *Encisalia niphon niphon* (courtesy of John B. Heppner).
Female, ventral view.

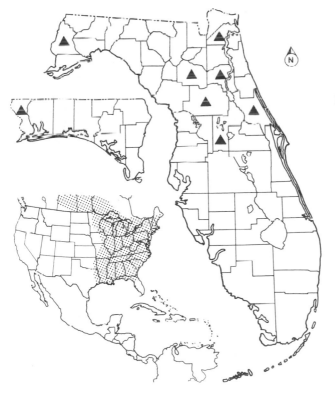

Distribution of the
eastern pine elfin,
*Incisalia niphon
niphon.*

BASIS OF STATUS CLASSIFICATION: The eastern pine elfin is classified as rare because of its very local distribution in Florida.

RECOMMENDATIONS: Surveys and ecological studies are needed to determine the current distribution, abundance, and habitat requirements of this species.

PREPARED BY: Marc C. Minno, Department of Zoology, University of Florida, Gainesville, FL 32611.

FAMILY LYCAENIDAE

Rare

Hessel's Hairstreak
Mitoura hesseli Rawson and Ziegler

OTHER COMMON NAMES: White cedar hairstreak.

DESCRIPTION: Hessel's hairstreak is a small, dark butterfly with two pairs of short tails on the hindwings. The dorsal surfaces are dark brown. Forewing length ranges from 12 to 13 mm (0.5 in). The undersides of the wings are brown and green with white spots and lines. Sweadner's hairstreak (*Mitoura sweadneri*) is similar, but the white lines are straighter. Florida individuals of Hessel's hairstreak are larger and somewhat different in appearance from northern specimens.

RANGE: *Mitoura hesseli* is found in close association with Atlantic white cedar, which has a spotty distribution from Maine to northern Florida. This butterfly has been found in only two counties of the Florida panhandle and is apparently absent from the white cedar stands in the Ocala National Forest area.

HABITAT: White cedar swamps are the habitat of Hessel's hairstreak.

LIFE HISTORY AND ECOLOGY: Females lay their eggs singly on leaves of Atlantic white cedar (*Chamaecyparis thyoides*). The green-colored larvae feed on the leaves of the host. Adults perch near the tops of white cedar trees and rarely visit flowers for nectar or the edges of mud puddles for moisture. The pupae overwinter. Two generations are produced per year. The adult flight period seems to last only a few weeks.

Hessel's Hairstreak, *Mitoura hesseli* (courtesy of John B. Heppner). Male, ventral view.

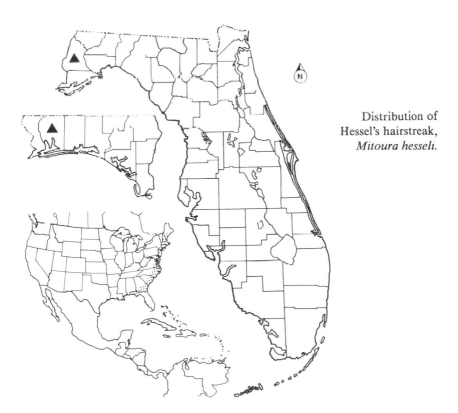

Distribution of Hessel's hairstreak, *Mitoura hesseli.*

BASIS OF STATUS CLASSIFICATION: Hessel's hairstreak has a very restricted distribution in the panhandle and is closely associated with the larval food plant.

RECOMMENDATIONS: Surveys and ecological studies are needed to determine the current distribution, abundance, and habitat requirements of this species. The white cedar swamps in the Apalachicola National Forest should be managed for the continued existence of colonies of Hessel's hairstreak. Surveys of Hessel's hairstreak populations are difficult to conduct due to the inaccessibility of the cedar swamps, variability in adult emergence, short adult life span, and preference for perching in the tops of the trees.

PREPARED BY: Marc C. Minno, Department of Zoology, University of Florida, Gainesville, FL 32611.

FAMILY LYCAENIDAE

Rare

King's Hairstreak

Satyrium kingi (Klots and Clench)

OTHER COMMON NAMES: Sweetleaf hairstreak.

DESCRIPTION: King's hairstreak is a small, dark butterfly with a pair of short and a pair of longer tails on the hindwings. The bases of the tails are marked by an orange eyespot and a blue patch on the ventral side. The undersides of the wings also have some broken black and white lines that form short bands. The length of the forewings varies from 14 to 17 mm (0.5–0.6 in). *Satyrium kingi* is intermediate in appearance between the striped hairstreak (*Satyrium liparops*), and the banded hairstreak (*Satyrium calanus*).

RANGE: It occurs locally in the southeastern United States and is known from four counties in the Florida panhandle.

HABITAT: King's hairstreak is usually found in ravines, moist hardwood hammocks, and occasionally white cedar stands.

LIFE HISTORY AND ECOLOGY: The eggs are laid singly on buds of horse sugar (*Symplocos tinctoria*). Overwintering occurs in the egg stage. The young larvae emerge in the spring and feed on the buds and leaves of the host. Adults perch on the leaves of trees and shrubs and occasionally visit flowers for nectar. King's hairstreak has been observed from mid-May to August in Florida.

King's Hairstreak, *Satyrium kingi* (courtesy of John B. Heppner). Female, ventral view.

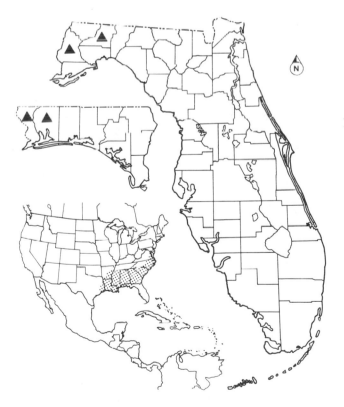

Distribution of King's hairstreak, *Satyrium kingi*.

BASIS OF STATUS CLASSIFICATION: King's hairstreak is considered rare because it is known from only four counties in the panhandle region.

RECOMMENDATIONS: Surveys and ecological studies are needed to determine the current distribution, abundance, and habitat requirements of this species.

PREPARED BY: Marc C. Minno, Department of Zoology, University of Florida, Gainesville, FL 32611.

FAMILY LYCAENIDAE

Rare

Striped Hairstreak

Satyrium liparops (Le Conte)

DESCRIPTION: The striped hairstreak is a small (forewing length: 13–17 mm [0.5–0.6 in]), dark butterfly with two pairs of tails on the hindwings. Undersides of the hindwings have a small blue patch and an orange eyespot near the base of the tails. The ventral surfaces also have some broken black and white lines which are relatively far apart. Two other hairstreaks may occur with *S. liparops* and have similar color patterns. King's hairstreak, *S. kingi*, also a rare species in Florida, has the ventral lines closer together, and in the banded hairstreak (*Satyrium calanus*), the lines converge to form a single postmedial row. Two subspecies of the striped hairstreak are represented in Florida. *Satyrium liparops liparops* has large patches of orange on the forewings. This race occurs in northern and central Florida, east and south of the panhandle. *Satyrium liparops strigosum* lacks the orange patches on the upperside of the wings and is found in the panhandle region of the state.

RANGE: *Satyrium liparops* has been reported from 11 counties in northern Florida. It is widely distributed in the eastern and midwestern United States and southern Canada.

HABITAT: It occurs on the edges of hardwood hammocks.

LIFE HISTORY AND ECOLOGY: The eggs are laid singly on twigs and buds of sparkleberry (*Vaccinium arboreum*) and hawthorns (*Crataegus* spp.). Overwintering takes place in the egg stage. The young larvae emerge in the spring and eat tender new leaves and flowers. Only one generation is produced each year. Adults fly during April and May and visit flowers or perch

Striped Hairstreak, *Satyrium liparops* (courtesy of John B. Heppner). Male, dorsal view (*above*) and ventral view (*below*).

in the foliage of trees. Like many other hairstreaks, the adults seem to be most active late in the afternoon and on cloudy days.

BASIS OF STATUS CLASSIFICATION: The striped hairstreak is considered to be rare because it occurs in very localized populations in only a few counties in the state.

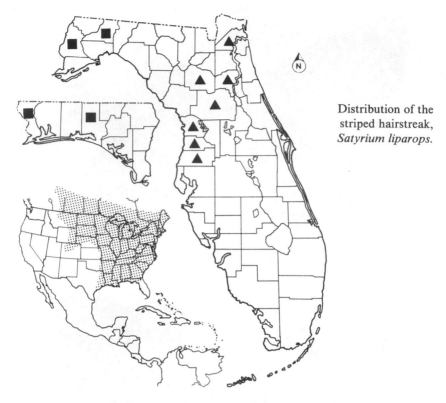

Distribution of the
striped hairstreak,
Satyrium liparops.

RECOMMENDATIONS: Surveys and ecological studies are needed to determine the current distribution, abundance, and habitat requirements of this
species.

PREPARED BY: Marc C. Minno, Department of Zoology, University of
Florida, Gainesville, FL 32611.

FAMILY LYCAENIDAE

Rare

Martial Hairstreak

Strymon martialis (Herrich-Schäffer)

OTHER COMMON NAMES: Blue-and-gray hairstreak, Cuban gray hairstreak.

DESCRIPTION: *Strymon martialis* is a small (forewing length: 13–16 mm
[0.5–0.6 in]), hairstreak butterfly with two pairs of tails on the hindwings.

The uppersides are bluish with black borders. The lower surfaces are light gray with a few dark lines and an orange eyespot near the base of the tails. Similar species include *Strymon melinus*, which has an orange eyespot on the upper and lower sides of the hindwings, and *Strymon acis*, which has two white spots near the base of the ventral hindwing.

RANGE: In Florida, the martial hairstreak is found in the keys and the southern mainland. This butterfly also occurs in the Bahamas, Cuba, Cayman Islands, and Jamaica.

HABITAT: It occurs near beaches, salt marshes, and the edges of tropical hardwood hammocks. Stray specimens sometimes turn up at flowers in weed lots.

LIFE HISTORY AND ECOLOGY: Females lay the eggs singly on the flowers of bay cedar (*Surianna maritima*) or the young leaves of Florida trema (*Trema micrantha*). Larvae eat flowers, developing fruit, and young leaves. Adults visit flowers (*Bidens alba* and *Lippia nodiflora*) and perch on or near host plants. This butterfly may be found in the adult stage during all months of the year.

BASIS OF STATUS CLASSIFICATION: The martial hairstreak is considered to be rare as it has a very limited range in Florida and is usually found in small, local populations.

Martial Hairstreak, *Strymon martialis* (courtesy of John B. Heppner). Male, ventral view.

Distribution of the martial hairstreak, *Strymon martialis.*

RECOMMENDATIONS: Surveys and ecological studies are needed to determine the current distribution, abundance, and habitat requirements of this species.

PREPARED BY: Marc C. Minno and Thomas C. Emmel, Department of Zoology, University of Florida, Gainesville, FL 32611.

FAMILY LYCAENIDAE

Species of Special Concern

Atala

Eumaeus atala florida Röber

OTHER COMMON NAMES: Coontie hairstreak.

DESCRIPTION: The atala is one of the most strikingly colored butterflies in Florida. The wings are black with iridescent blue spots and a red patch on the underside of the hindwings. The upper wings are black and iridescent green in males and iridescent blue in females. The abdomen is bright red. Forewing lengths range from 19 to 24 mm (0.7–1.0 in). It is uncertain whether or not the Florida population is sufficiently differentiated to be considered a separate race.

RANGE: This species is found in southern Florida, the Bahamas, and Cuba.

HABITAT: It occurs in tropical hardwood hammocks and pinelands in close association with the host plant. It also now uses some urban habitats such as gardens and nurseries where the food plant is grown as an ornamental.

LIFE HISTORY AND ECOLOGY: The eggs are laid in clusters on the new growth of coontie (*Zamia pumila*), and occasionally on related, exotic cycads. The larvae are aposematically colored bright red and yellow, and eat young leaves (Rawson 1961). Adults visit flowers readily and have a weak, moth-like flight pattern. Males perch on foliage at forest edges. Adults occur all year round. The atala has undergone several population booms and busts since the turn of the century in Florida. The species was feared extirpated in

Distribution of the atala, *Eumaeus atala florida*.

the early 1970s after the few known colonies died out. There were no reports of the atala in Florida over approximately an eight-year period. Then in the late 1970s, a single small colony was rediscovered in Miami. It is not known if this was a remnant of original Florida stock or an introduction from other Caribbean populations. Aided by conservationists, who moved immatures to new areas, the atala has reclaimed much of its former range. Ironically, this spectacular butterfly is now treated as a pest by some nurseries and gardeners, whose stock and ornamental plantings of coontie are defoliated or made unsightly by the caterpillars.

BASIS OF STATUS CLASSIFICATION: The atala is listed as a species of special concern because of its restricted distribution and cyclic fluctuations in abundance. This butterfly is currently known from more colonies on the mainland than were recorded before 1965, but the atala has lost habitat in the Florida Keys. Hurricane Andrew probably severely damaged populations of the atala in southern Dade County. During the 1970's, populations of the atala in Florida were in serious decline, prompting its listing in the first edition of this work as threatened. However, for unknown reasons, the atala has made a spectacular recovery and is now locally abundant in Palm Beach, Broward, and Dade counties.

RECOMMENDATIONS: Surveys are needed to monitor the distribution and abundance of the atala in Florida. Taxonomic studies should be conducted to determine if the current taxon is same as that present before 1965 and to define the relationship of *E. atala florida* to *E. atala atala*. Prescribed burning of pinelands may be necessary to maintain habitat for atalas in natural settings.

PREPARED BY: Marc C. Minno and Thomas C. Emmel, Department of Zoology, University of Florida, Gainesville, FL 32611.

FAMILY LYCAENIDAE

Species of Special Concern

Miami Blue

Hemiargus thomasi bethunebakeri Comstock and Huntington

DESCRIPTION: Males of the Miami blue are bright blue above. Females are also blue, but have a wide dark outer border, especially on the forewings, and a reddish eyespot on the hindwings. The undersides of both sexes have a similar pattern of spots with a pale postmedial patch and a reddish eyespot on the hindwings. The length of the forewings varies from 10 to 13 mm

(0.4–0.5 in). The ceranus blue (*Hemiargus ceraunus*) is similar, but has a different ventral pattern and flies close to the ground in open areas. The Cassius blue (*Leptotes cassius*) often occurs with *H. thomasi*, but has dark bars rather than spots on the undersides of the wings.

RANGE: The Miami blue is found in the Florida Keys and coastal areas of the southern mainland. Other races of *H. thomasi* occur in the Bahamas and Hispaniola.

HABITAT: This pretty little butterfly occurs at the edges of tropical hardwood hammocks.

LIFE HISTORY AND ECOLOGY: The eggs are laid singly on young pods of balloonvine (*Cardiospermum halicacabum*) and the flowers of leguminous trees. The caterpillars eat young seeds and flowers. Males frequently perch along trails and forest edges. The Miami blue is most abundant near disturbed hammocks where weedy flowers provide nectar. This species flies every month of the year in the Florida Keys.

BASIS OF STATUS CLASSIFICATION: The Miami blue is listed as a species of special concern because it is a Floridian endemic with a restricted distribution. This species is now rare on the southeastern mainland, but is still relatively common in the keys and may be locally abundant at Choko-

Miami Blue, *Hemiargus thomasi bethunebakeri* (courtesy of John B. Heppner). Male, ventral view.

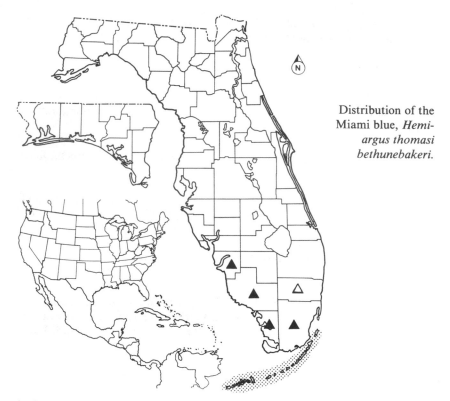

Distribution of the
Miami blue, *Hemi-
argus thomasi
bethunebakeri.*

loskee, Marco Island, and Sanibel Island. The Miami blue has suffered loss
of habitat due to urban growth.

RECOMMENDATIONS: Preservation of tropical hardwood hammocks as
well as nearby weedy areas with flowers is necessary to protect the Miami
blue from further decline.

PREPARED BY: Marc C. Minno and Thomas C. Emmel, Department of
Zoology, University of Florida, Gainesville, FL 32611.

Order Lepidoptera
FAMILY NYMPHALIDAE

INTRODUCTION. The Floridian Nymphalidae consist of the brush-footed
butterflies (subfamily Nymphalinae), satyrs and wood nymphs (Satyrinae),
leafwing butterflies (Charaxinae), hackberry butterflies (Apaturinae), passion-

flower butterflies (Heliconiinae), and milkweed butterflies (Danainae). The forelegs of adult nymphalids are greatly reduced in size, and thus they appear to have only four legs. Many species are brightly colored or have eyespots on the wings. The larvae may be spiny or smooth and often have a pair of horns on the top of the head. Only eight species are treated here, a threatened tropical species, three tropical species of special concern, and four rare temperate species that reach the southern limits of their ranges in Florida.

PREPARED BY; Marc C. Minno, Department of Zoology, University of Florida, Gainesville, FL 32611.

FAMILY NYMPHALIDAE

Threatened

Florida Leafwing

Anaea troglodyta floridalis Johnson and Comstock

DESCRIPTION: The Florida leafwing is a medium-sized, reddish butterfly with a pair of short tails on the hindwings. The forewings vary from 33 to 39 mm (1.3–1.5 in) in length. Males are mostly reddish above. Females are reddish with dark markings. The undersides of the wings are light brown and resemble dead leaves.

RANGE: The Florida leafwing occurs in rocky pinelands of southern Dade County and the lower keys. Most of its habitat in Palm Beach and Broward counties has been destroyed by urban development. Other races of *Anaea troglodyta* are found in the Greater Antilles and Mexico.

HABITAT: It occurs in tropical pinelands, usually near patches of the larval host plant.

LIFE HISTORY AND ECOLOGY: The eggs are laid singly on the leaves of woolly croton, *Croton linearis*. The larvae feed on the leaves and, unlike *A. andria* of northern Florida, do not build nests. Males perch on foliage at the edges of clearings. The adults sometimes feed on rotting fruit and dung, and can be found all months of the year.

BASIS OF STATUS CLASSIFICATION: The Florida leafwing is listed as a threatened species because it is a Floridian endemic with a highly restricted range. The species has lost habitat due to urbanization both on the mainland and in the keys. Surveys conducted in pineland habitats of Everglades Na-

Florida Leafwing, *Anaea troglodyta floridalis* (courtesy of the Allyn Museum).
Male, dorsal view.

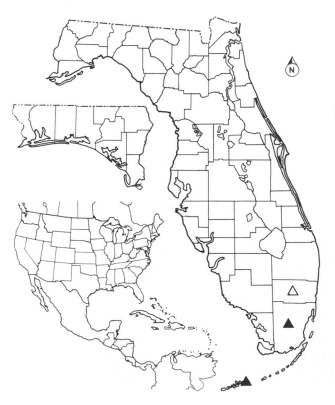

Distribution of the
Florida leafwing,
*Anaea troglodyta
floridalis.*

tional Park between 31 May and 16 December 1988 (N=29) and 1 March to 24 October 1989 (N=13) found an average of 6 and 1.4 adults per hectare, respectively. Similar studies at three locations on Big Pine Key in 1988 found averages of 5.8, 2.2, and 0.5 adults per hectare. Means of only 1.5 and 0.8 adults per hectare were obtained for sites on Big Pine Key in 1989 (Hennessey and Habeck 1991). The southern Dade County populations were probably severely impacted by Hurricane Andrew.

RECOMMENDATIONS: Surveys are needed to monitor the distribution and abundance of the Florida leafwing. Prescribed burning may be necessary to maintain the pineland habitat for this species, but land managers should avoid burning large tracts at one time. Creating mosaics of habitat with different fire histories should help to ensure that rare species will be not be eliminated by burning too frequently or during periods when the immature stages may be susceptible to fire. The remaining habitat in the keys should be preserved and properly managed for the continued existence of this interesting butterfly.

PREPARED BY: Marc C. Minno and Thomas C. Emmel, Department of Zoology, University of Florida, Gainesville, FL 32611.

FAMILY NYMPHALIDAE

Rare

Silvery Checkerspot

Chlosyne nycteis nycteis (Doubleday and Hewitson)

OTHER COMMON NAMES: Streamside checkerspot.

DESCRIPTION: The silvery checkerspot is named for the silvery ground color of the ventral hindwings. The uppersides are light orange-brown with black borders and lines. Each hindwing bears a row of small eyespots above and below. The forewings range in length from 18 to 24 mm (0.7–0.9 in).

RANGE: Only a few colonies of this butterfly are known to occur in Jackson County, Florida, near the Georgia border. The silvery checkerspot is a locally abundant species in the eastern and middle western United States.

HABITAT: The silvery checkerspot prefers moist meadows near streams.

LIFE HISTORY AND ECOLOGY: Females lay their eggs in clusters on leaves of the food plant. The hosts used in Florida are not known but com-

Silvery Checkerspot, *Chlosyne nycteis nycteis* (courtesy of John B. Heppner).
Male, dorsal view (*above*) and ventral view (*below*).

posites such as sunflowers (*Helianthus* spp.) are used elsewhere. The larvae
live communally in a web and eat the leaves of the host. Overwintering occurs as partly grown larvae. Adults fly low to the ground and visit flowers
readily. Two generations are produced per year.

BASIS OF STATUS CLASSIFICATION: The silvery checkerspot is listed
as Rare because of its restricted range in Florida.

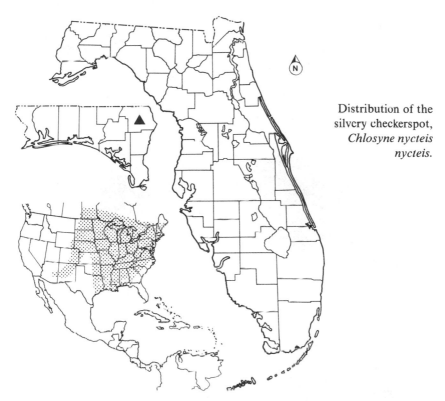

Distribution of the
silvery checkerspot,
*Chlosyne nycteis
nycteis.*

RECOMMENDATIONS: Surveys and ecological studies are needed to determine the current distribution, abundance, and habitat requirements of *Chlosyne nycteis* in Florida.

PREPARED BY: Marc C. Minno, Department of Zoology, University of Florida, Gainesville, FL 32611.

FAMILY NYMPHALIDAE

Rare

Mourning Cloak

Nymphalis antiopa antiopa (Linnaeus)

DESCRIPTION: The mourning cloak is a medium-sized (forewing: 36–46 mm [1.4–1.8 in]) butterfly with a distinctive color pattern. The wings are dark brown with an outer row of light blue spots on the uppersides and cream-colored margins.

Mourning Cloak, *Nymphalis antiopa antiopa* (courtesy of John B. Heppner).
Male, dorsal view.

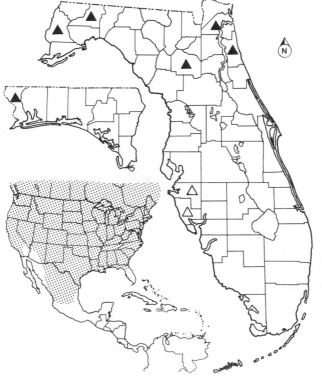

Distribution of the
mourning cloak,
*Nymphalis antiopa
antiopa.*

RANGE: *Nymphalis antiopa* has one of the broadest distributions known for a butterfly. This species is found in northern Mexico, most of the United States, Canada, Alaska, northern Asia, and most of Europe. In Florida, however, the mourning cloak has been found in only eight northern and central counties.

HABITAT: It is found along the margins of streams and other wetlands that support the host plant.

LIFE HISTORY AND ECOLOGY: Eggs are laid in clusters on the twigs of willows (*Salix* spp.). The black, spiny caterpillars eat willow leaves and live in groups until mature. Males often perch on or near the host plant. One generation is produced per year. Overwintering occurs in the adult stage. Fermenting fruit and trees with sap flowing from wounds are attractive to the adults.

BASIS OF STATUS CLASSIFICATION: The mourning cloak is listed as rare because of its very local occurrence and low abundance in Florida.

RECOMMENDATIONS: Surveys and ecological studies are needed to determine the current distribution, abundance, and habitat requirements of this butterfly.

PREPARED BY: Marc C. Minno, Department of Zoology, University of Florida, Gainesville, FL 32611.

FAMILY NYMPHALIDAE

Rare

Comma Anglewing
Polygonia comma (Harris)

OTHER COMMON NAMES: Hop merchant, comma.

DESCRIPTION: The comma anglewing is a medium-sized (forewing: 23–28 mm [1.0–1.1 in]) brush-footed butterfly with irregular wing margins. The dorsal surfaces of the wings are orange-brown with black spots and borders. The undersides are light brown with a silver comma mark in the middle of the hindwings. The only other similar species in Florida is the question mark, *Polygonia interrogationis*, which has a silver comma and period mark on the ventral hindwings.

Comma Anglewing, *Polygonia comma* (courtesy of John B. Heppner). Male, dorsal view (*above*) and ventral view (*below*).

RANGE: *Polygonia comma* is an abundant and widely distributed butterfly in the eastern United States, but has been found in only four counties of northern Florida.

HABITAT: It is found in moist hardwood hammocks.

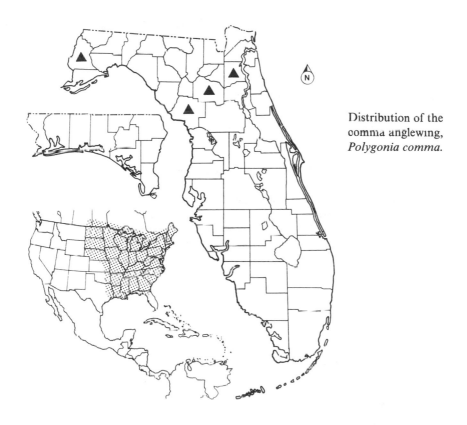

Distribution of the comma anglewing, *Polygonia comma.*

LIFE HISTORY AND ECOLOGY: The eggs are laid singly or in short strings on leaves of elms (*Ulmus* spp.). Nettles (*Urtica* spp.) and *Boehmeria cylindrica* may also be used in Florida. Larvae eat young leaves and fold and tie leaves together to form shelters. Overwintering occurs in the adult stage. At least two broods are produced each year. Adults often perch on foliage at forest edges and in sunspots and are easily attracted to fermenting fruit.

BASIS OF STATUS CLASSIFICATION: The comma anglewing is listed as rare in Florida because of its local distribution and low abundance. This butterfly has been found mostly as single specimens in bait traps in Florida.

RECOMMENDATIONS: Surveys and ecological studies are needed to determine the current distribution, abundance, and habitat requirements of this species.

PREPARED BY: Marc C. Minno, Department of Zoology, University of Florida, Gainesville, FL 32611.

Rare

Appalachian Eyed Brown

Satyrodes appalachia appalachia (R. L. Chermock)

OTHER COMMON NAMES: Woods eyed brown.

DESCRIPTION: The Appalachian eyed brown is a medium-sized (forewing: 22–27 mm [0.9–1.1 in]), light brown butterfly with a row of small eyespots near the outer margin of the wings above and below. *Satyrodes appalachia* is similar to the pearly eye (*Enodia portlandia*) but the latter species is larger and has a more contrasting pattern and violet shading on the undersides of the wings.

RANGE: *Satyrodes appalachia* has been reported from 12 counties in northern and central Florida; it is locally distributed in the eastern United States and reaches the southern limits of its range in Florida.

HABITAT: It occurs in swamps containing an abundance of the larval food plant.

Appalachian Eyed Brown, *Satyrodes appalachia appalachia* (courtesy of John B. Heppner). Male, ventral view.

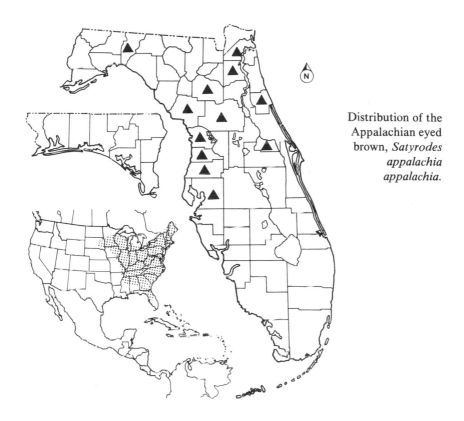

Distribution of the Appalachian eyed brown, *Satyrodes appalachia appalachia.*

LIFE HISTORY AND ECOLOGY: Eggs are laid singly on the leaves of horned beakrush, *Rhynchospora inundata* (Brown 1973c). Larvae eat leaves and overwinter in the middle instars. Adults fly low to the ground in close proximity to the host and are attracted to fermenting fruit baits. Two generations occur per year.

BASIS OF STATUS CLASSIFICATION: The Appalachian eyed brown is considered to be rare in Florida because of its very localized populations. Most of the known colonies have been discovered only in the last ten years. Locating new colonies and monitoring known populations has been difficult due to the inaccessibility of the swamps this butterfly prefers.

RECOMMENDATIONS: Surveys and ecological studies are needed to determine the current distribution, abundance, and habitat requirements of this species.

PREPARED BY: Marc C. Minno, Department of Zoology, University of Florida, Gainesville, FL 32611.

FAMILY NYMPHALIDAE

Species of Special Concern

Dingy Purplewing
Eunica monima (Stoll)

DESCRIPTION: Males of the dingy purplewing are dull purple above with a few white spots near the middle and apex of the forewing. Females are mostly brown instead of purple. The undersides of the hindwings are purplish-brown with some dark lines and a few eyespots. This species is similar to the Florida purplewing (*Eunica tatila tatilista*), but is smaller [forewings range from 16 to 24 mm (0.6–1.0 in)] and duller. The genus *Eunica* has recently been revised (Jenkins 1990).

RANGE: This butterfly occurs in southern Dade County, the Florida Keys, Cuba, Jamaica, Hispaniola, Puerto Rico, Central America, and South America.

HABITAT: The dingy purplewing prefers the canopy and edges of tropical hardwood hammocks.

Dingy Purplewing, *Eunica monima* (courtesy of John B. Heppner).
Dorsal view.

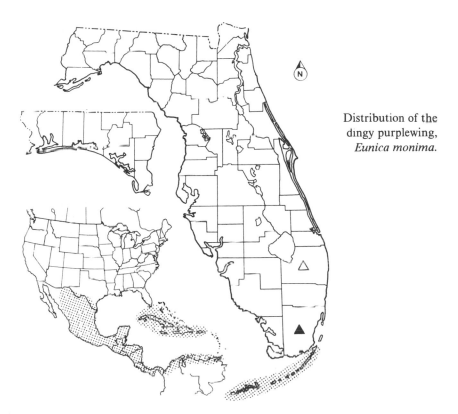

Distribution of the
dingy purplewing,
Eunica monima.

LIFE HISTORY AND ECOLOGY: Richard Boscoe has reared this species from gumbo limbo (*Bursera simaruba*) in south Florida (*News of the Lepidopterist's Society*, 1985, page 29). The larvae live in silk nests and eat young leaves. Adults perch in the forest canopy but will visit flowers and fermenting fruit. Several generations are produced each year.

BASIS OF STATUS CLASSIFICATION: Before the early 1980s, only a few specimens of the dingy purplewing, considered to be strays, were known from Florida. The dingy purplewing is now present in many areas of south Florida where it was formerly unknown. The abundance of this species seems to vary greatly seasonally and from year to year. The dingy purplewing is listed as a species of special concern because of its limited distribution and cyclic population fluctuations. Hurricane Andrew has probably severely impacted this species in Florida.

RECOMMENDATIONS: Surveys and ecological studies are needed to determine the current distribution, abundance, and habitat requirements of this butterfly.

PREPARED BY: Marc C. Minno and Thomas C. Emmel, Department of Zoology, University of Florida, Gainesville, FL 32611.

Species of Special Concern

Florida Purplewing

Eunica tatila tatilista Kaye

OTHER COMMON NAMES: Large purplewing.

DESCRIPTION: The Florida purplewing is a medium-sized tropical butterfly. Males are iridescent purple above with white spots on the forewings.
Females are shining blue rather than purple. The ventral pattern varies con-
siderably from a uniform gray to a complex pattern of white, gray, and black
patches, lines, and eyespots. The forewings vary from 22 to 31 mm (0.9–1.2
in) and are notched at the tip. Jenkins (1990) gives a more complete description of the color patterns.

RANGE: The Florida purplewing is found in southern Dade County, the
Florida Keys, Cuba, Jamaica, Hispaniola, Puerto Rico, and the Virgin Islands. Other races occur in Central and South America.

HABITAT: It occurs in tropical hardwood hammocks.

Florida Purplewing, *Eunica tatila talilista* (courtesy of John B. Heppner).
Male, dorsal view.

Distribution of the
Florida purplewing,
*Eunica tatila
tatilista.*

LIFE HISTORY AND ECOLOGY: Females lay their eggs singly on new growth of crabwood (*Gymnanthes lucida*). The larvae eat young leaves and do not make shelters. Adults fly along the edges of tropical hammocks as well as in the shade of the forest and frequently perch on tree trunks and branches. Fresh dung and fermenting fruit occasionally attract Florida purplewings. Adults fly every month of the year in the keys, but abundance varies greatly seasonally and between years.

BASIS OF STATUS CLASSIFICATION: The Florida purplewing is listed as a species of special concern due to its restricted range and cyclic population fluctuations in Florida. This butterfly has lost habitat, especially in the keys, due to urban development. The mainland and upper keys populations were probably severely impacted by Hurricane Andrew.

RECOMMENDATIONS: Surveys are needed to determine the current distribution, abundance, and habitat requirements of this species. The remaining tropical hardwood hammocks in the keys should be preserved.

PREPARED BY: Marc C. Minno and Thomas C. Emmel, Department of Zoology, University of Florida, Gainesville, FL 32611.

Species of Special Concern

Mangrove Buckeye

Junonia evarete (Cramer)

DESCRIPTION: Three species of buckeyes are found in Florida and all three may be found together on occasion in the keys. Some of these species have been treated in the literature as hybrids or seasonal forms. Turner and Parnell (1985) have correctly sorted out this taxonomic and nomenclatorial confusion. The mangrove buckeye (*Junonia evarete*) is the largest of the three species (forewings range in length from 24 to 32 mm [1.0–1.2 in]) and may be identified by the nearly equal size of the eyespots on the uppersides of the hindwings, the cream-colored forewing bar, and the brownish undersides. The Caribbean buckeye (*Junonia genoveva*) is smaller, the eyespots are similar in size, the forewing bar is pinkish, and the ventral hindwings are reddish and strongly patterned. The common buckeye (*Junonia coenia*) is similar to *J. genoveva*, but the eyespots are distinctly unequal, the forewing bar is white, and the ventral hindwings are not strongly patterned. Both the mangrove and common buckeye are native species. The Caribbean buckeye is thought to be a recently introduced butterfly.

Mangrove Buckeye, *Junonia evarete* (courtesy of John B. Heppner). Male, dorsal view.

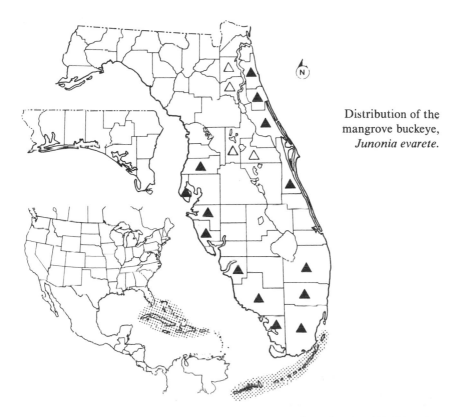

Distribution of the
mangrove buckeye,
Junonia evarete.

RANGE: This buckeye occurs in coastal areas of peninsular Florida, the Florida Keys, and throughout the Caribbean.

HABITAT: It is found in association with mangroves and salt marshes.

LIFE HISTORY AND ECOLOGY: Eggs are laid singly on the new growth of black mangrove (*Avicennia germinans*). The larvae eat the young leaves of the host. Males perch in open areas of salt marshes and mangroves and defend small territories against other males. Adults visit flowers occasionally. Several generations occur each year.

BASIS OF STATUS CLASSIFICATION: The mangrove buckeye is listed as a species of special concern because it has a restricted distribution in Florida and is closely associated with the host plant, which is a protected species.

RECOMMENDATIONS: Habitat conservation will ensure the survival of the mangrove buckeye in Florida.

PREPARED BY: Marc C. Minno and Thomas C. Emmel, Department of Zoology, University of Florida, Gainesville, FL 32611.

Order Lepidoptera

FAMILY PAPILIONIDAE

INTRODUCTION: The swallowtails are large colorful butterflies that usually have tails on the hindwings. The caterpillars feed on aromatic herbs and trees and have a fleshy, strong-smelling defensive gland, the osmeterium, behind the head. Most of the resident species in Florida are abundant and widely distributed. Two tropical species that are restricted to the Florida Keys are considered to be endangered.

PREPARED BY: Marc C. Minno, Department of Zoology, University of Florida, Gainesville, FL 32611.

FAMILY PAPILIONIDAE

Endangered

Bahama Swallowtail

Papilio andraemon bonhotei Sharpe

OTHER COMMON NAMES: Bahamas or Bahamian swallowtail.

DESCRIPTION: The Bahama swallowtail is a large black and yellow butterfly with two pairs of tails on the hindwings. The longer tails have a yellow spot centered in the black tip. The uppersides are mostly black with a yellow band. In addition to the yellow band, the hindwings bear a row of yellow marginal spots, an eyespot, and some blue shading. The ventral pattern is similar, except for a narrow orange patch on each hindwing. The giant swallowtail (*Papilio cresphontes*) and Schaus swallowtail (*Papilio aristodemus ponceanus*) are similar but differ in the size and arrangement of the yellow spots and bands. The Bahama swallowtail is the smallest of this trio (forewings range from 39 to 50 mm [1.5–2.0 in]).

RANGE: This swallowtail is found in the Bahamas and upper Florida Keys. Other races are found in the Greater Antilles. The Florida population may be distinct from those in the Bahamas.

HABITAT: It is found in tropical hardwood hammocks.

Bahama Swallowtail, *Papilio andraemon bonhotei* (courtesy of the Allyn Museum). Male, dorsal view

Distribution of the Bahama swallowtail, *Papilio andraemon bonhotei.*

LIFE HISTORY AND ECOLOGY: Females fly in hammocks and deposit the eggs singly on the upperside of the new growth of torchwood (*Amyris elemifera*) and occasionally on wild lime (*Zanthoxylum fagara*) and key lime (*Citrus aurantifolia*). The larvae eat only new growth when young, but can tolerate mature foliage when older. Males patrol along trails and forest edges. Flowers are visited occasionally for nectar. Adults are relatively short-lived (up to two weeks). Several broods are produced each year. This species varies in abundance seasonally and from year to year.

BASIS OF STATUS CLASSIFICATION: This butterfly has long been thought of as a temporary colonizer or accidental import from the Bahamas, but Brown (1973a,b) reported thriving populations of this species in Biscayne National Park. The Bahama swallowtail was listed as a federally endangered species in 1976. When a few status surveys failed to find any individuals (Loftus and Kushlan 1982), the butterfly was thought to have become extirpated from the United States and was taken off the federal list. However, Emmel and Minno (1988) have shown it to be resident in the upper Florida Keys, but it is very local and subject to wide variation in abundance. We are listing the Bahama swallowtail as endangered due to its very limited distribution and abundance in Florida. Hurricane Andrew has probably severely impacted this species within Biscayne National Park.

RECOMMENDATIONS: Surveys should be continued in order to monitor the abundance and distribution of the Bahama swallowtail. Taxonomic studies are needed to determine if the Florida population is distinct from those in the Bahamas. Tropical hardwood hammocks should be protected from development, especially on Key Largo, in order to preserve habitat for this butterfly.

PREPARED BY: Thomas C. Emmel and Marc C. Minno, Department of Zoology, University of Florida, Gainesville, FL 32611.

FAMILY PAPILIONIDAE

Endangered

Schaus Swallowtail

Papilio aristodemus ponceanus Schaus

DESCRIPTION: The Schaus swallowtail is a large dark brown and yellow butterfly with a pair of tails on the hindwings. Unlike the giant swallowtail (*Papilio cresphontes*) and the Bahama swallowtail (*Papilio andraemon bon-*

hotei) which occur in the same areas, the tails of the Schaus swallowtail are edged with yellow and lack a central yellow spot. A large rusty-orange patch is found on the underside of the hindwings, next to a postmedial row of blue spots. The length of the forewings varies from 40–58 mm (1.6–2.3 in).

RANGE: *Papilio aristodemus ponceanus* is found today only on islands within Biscayne National Park that have tropical hardwood hammocks and on Key Largo. It has not been seen on the mainland since 1924, when one individual was taken in Coconut Grove, south of Miami. Although this butterfly was apparently once relatively common in the Matecumbe keys, none have been found since the late 1940s. A few sightings have been reported from upper Matecumbe Key in recent times, but surveys have failed to detect any established populations southwest of Key Largo (Emmel and Minno 1988). Other subspecies of *P. aristodemus* occur in Cuba, Cayman Islands, the Bahamas, Hispaniola, and Puerto Rico.

HABITAT: The Schaus swallowtail occurs in tropical hardwood hammocks.

LIFE HISTORY AND ECOLOGY: Grimshawe (1940) and Rutkowski (1971) have reported on the life history and ecology of the Schaus swallowtail. Eggs are laid singly on the uppersides of the leaves of torchwood (*Amyris elemifera*) and rarely on wild lime (*Zanthoxylum fagara*). The larvae eat young leaves. Adults emerge at the beginning of the rainy season and may

Schaus Swallowtail, *Papilio aristodemus ponceanus* (courtesy of the Allyn Museum). Male, dorsal view.

Distribution of the
Schaus swallowtail,
*Papilio aristodemus
ponceanus.*

have a second brood toward the end of summer in some years (Brown 1976). Males patrol forest clearings and trails. Females spend most of their time within hammocks, searching for foodplants of proper quality on which to lay eggs. Both sexes visit flowers occasionally. Maximum lifespan of adults is three weeks. There is great variation in the abundance of this butterfly from year to year. The population status of the Schaus swallowtail has been monitored at irregular intervals by Covell and Rawson (1973), Brown (1973b), Covell (1977), and Loftus and Kushlan (1982, 1984). Through funding provided by the U.S. Fish and Wildlife Service, Florida Game and Fresh Water Fish Commission (Nongame Wildlife Program), the Elizabeth Ordway Dunn Foundation, and the duPont Fund, the population biology of the Schaus swallowtail has been investigated on an annual basis since 1984 (see Emmel and Minno 1988 for a review).

BASIS OF STATUS CLASSIFICATION: The Schaus swallowtail is a Floridian endemic limited to a small portion of the upper keys. Population levels fluctuate from a few hundred to several thousand individuals from year to year. It is one of the few swallowtails listed as globally endangered by the International Union for the Conservation of Nature and Natural Resources (Collins and Morris 1985). This butterfly is also listed as endangered by the

United States Fish and Wildlife Service. The populations within Biscayne National Park are likely to have been severely damaged by Hurricane Andrew.

RECOMMENDATIONS: Surveys should continue annually in order to monitor the abundance and distribution of the species. Tropical hardwood hammocks in the keys should be protected from development and mosquito spraying. Taxonomic studies are needed to determine the relationships of the Schaus swallowtail and its close relatives.

PREPARED BY: Thomas C. Emmel and Marc C. Minno, Department of Zoology, University of Florida, Gainesville, FL 32611.

Order Lepidoptera
FAMILY PIERIDAE

INTRODUCTION. The pierids are brightly colored butterflies that range in size from small to large. Two subfamilies are well-represented in Florida, the Pierinae (whites) and Coliadinae (sulphurs). The caterpillars are often green in color and feed on plants in the mustard or legume families. About 20 species of pierids have been recorded from the state. Five tropical species are listed as species of special concern.

PREPARED BY: Marc C. Minno, Department of Zoology, University of Florida, Gainesville, FL 32611.

FAMILY PIERIDAE

Species of Special Concern

Florida Statira Sulphur
Aphrissa statira floridensis (Neumoegen)

DESCRIPTION: Males of the Florida statira sulphur are lemon yellow with a pale yellow or whitish outer border on the uppersides of the wings. Females are pale yellow or whitish with a narrow black outer border and a small black spot at the end of the discal cell on the forewings. The length of the forewings ranges from 27 to 36 mm (1.0–1.4 in). In flight this species closely resembles cloudless sulphur (*Phoebis sennae*), which is a uniform lemon yellow.

Florida Statira Sulphur, *Aphrissa statira floridensis* (courtesy of John B. Heppner). Male, dorsal view (*above*) and female, dorsal view (*below*).

RANGE: The Florida statira sulphur occurs in coastal areas of the southern Florida peninsula as far north as Tampa Bay on the gulf coast and Palm Beach County on the Atlantic side. This species is strangely absent or sporadically present in the upper keys, although the host plant grows there. *Aphrissa statira* is widely distributed in Central America, South America, and the Caribbean.

HABITAT: It is found usually in coastal habitats, especially the edges of mangrove forests and along beaches.

LIFE HISTORY AND ECOLOGY: The Florida statira sulphur is closely associated with its larval host plant, coinvine (*Dalbergia ecastophyllum*). Females deposit the eggs singly on the new growth of this sprawling shrub or vine. The larvae feed on the young leaves of the host and rest exposed on the

Distribution of the Florida statira sulphur, *Aphrissa statira floridensis.*

plant. Adults are strong fliers, and visit red and yellow flowers readily. The Florida statira sulphur flies every month of the year.

BASIS OF STATUS CLASSIFICATION: The Florida statira sulphur is listed as a species of special concern because it is an endemic with a very limited range. This butterfly has lost habitat in recent times due to coastal urban development.

RECOMMENDATIONS: Surveys are needed to monitor the distribution and abundance of this species in Florida. Planting coinvine in coastal areas may help increase the breeding success of the Florida statira sulphur. The remaining habitat should be preserved.

PREPARED BY: Marc C. Minno and Thomas C. Emmel, Department of Zoology, University of Florida, Gainesville, FL 32611.

FAMILY PIERIDAE

Species of Special Concern

Florida White
Appias drusilla neumoegenii (Skinner)

DESCRIPTION: Males of this medium-sized butterfly are white with a narrow black border along the costal margin of the forewings. Females are also white, but have wider black borders, and are tinged with pale yellow. Both sexes have a shiny patch at the bases of the forewings above. Forewing length ranges from 24 to 34 mm (1.0–1.4). The great southern white (*Ascia monuste*) is similar, but the tips of its antennae are blue and this species usually flies close to the ground in open areas.

Florida White, *Appias drusilla neumoegenii* (courtesy of John B. Heppner). Male, dorsal view (*above*) and female, dorsal view (*below*).

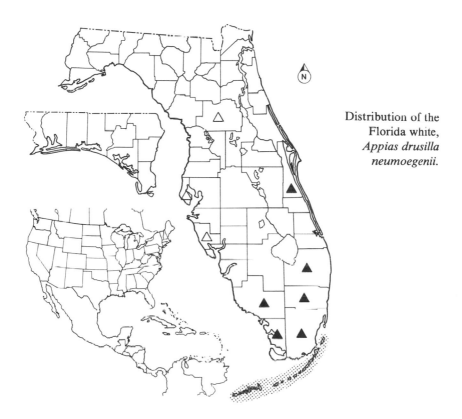

Distribution of the
Florida white,
*Appias drusilla
neumoegenii.*

RANGE: The Florida white is limited to the Florida Keys and coastal areas of the southern mainland. At least six other subspecies of *Appias drusilla* occur in the Caribbean and the nominate race is widely distributed in Central and South America.

HABITAT: It occurs in tropical hardwood hammocks.

LIFE HISTORY AND ECOLOGY: Chermock and Chermock (1947) briefly describe the immature stages of this butterfly. The eggs are laid singly on the new growth of guiana plum (*Drypetes lateriflora*) and limber caper (*Capparis flexuosa*). The larvae feed on young leaves and do not build shelters or nests. Males have a swift erratic flight and patrol hammock edges and upper canopy levels of the forest. Females search for host plants within the shade of hammocks. The adults often visit flowers for nectar and occur all months of the year. The Florida white undergoes fluctuations in abundance, but is often relatively numerous in the keys.

BASIS OF STATUS CLASSIFICATION: The Florida white is listed as a species of special concern because it is an endemic with a limited range and has lost habitat due to urban growth. Populations of this butterfly on the southern mainland and in the upper keys were probably severely damaged by Hurricane Andrew.

RECOMMENDATIONS: Surveys are needed to monitor the distribution and abundance of the Florida white. Tropical hardwood hammocks on the mainland and in the keys should be conserved.

PREPARED BY: Marc C. Minno and Thomas C. Emmel, Department of Zoology, University of Florida, Gainesville, FL 32611.

FAMILY PIERIDAE

Species of Special Concern

Bush Sulphur
Eurema dina helios Bates

DESCRIPTION: The bush sulphur is a small (forewing: 15 to 22 mm [0.6–0.8 in]), light orange or yellow butterfly with narrow black borders. Females are yellowish. Males are usually light orange, but a small percentage are yellow like the females. Several other similar *Eurema* species occur in Florida, but these are smaller or have much wider black borders than the bush sulphur.

RANGE: This sulphur occurs in Bahamas and southern Florida. Cuba, Jamaica, and Hispaniola have their own unique populations of the bush sulphur. In Florida, this species is found in just a few hammocks in southern Dade County that support the host plant.

HABITAT: It inhabits tropical hardwood hammocks.

LIFE HISTORY AND ECOLOGY: Eggs are laid singly on the new growth of *Alvaroda amorphoides*. The green caterpillars eat young leaves and rest exposed upon the plant. Adults fly at the edges of tropical hammocks and will fly into the forest if disturbed. Flowers are visited occasionally for nectar. Several generations occur each year.

BASIS OF STATUS CLASSIFICATION: The bush sulphur is listed as a species of special concern due to its limited range and close association with a single rare host. This butterfly is often abundant where it does occu.. Although many of the Dade County populations are located on public lands, Hurricane Andrew severely damaged these sites.

Bush Sulphur, *Eurema dina helios* (courtesy of John B. Heppner). Male, dorsal view.

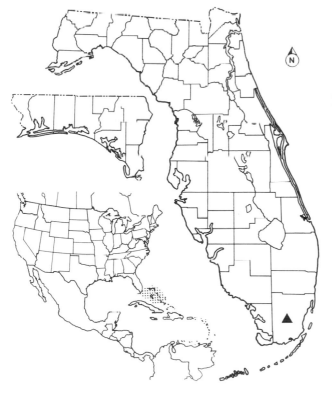

Distribution of the bush sulphur, *Eurema dina helios.*

RECOMMENDATIONS: Surveys are needed to determine if this species is still extant in Florida following Hurricane Andrew. If one or more colonies survived the storm, continued protection and intelligent management of the habitat will help to ensure the continued presence of the bush sulphur in Florida. Propagating and planting of the host plant may help increase the breeding success of this butterfly.

PREPARED BY: Marc C. Minno and Thomas C. Emmel, Department of Zoology, University of Florida, Gainesville, FL 32611.

FAMILY PIERIDAE

Species of Special Concern

Jamaican Sulphur

Eurema nise nise (Cramer)

OTHER COMMON NAMES: Blacktip sulfur, nisa or nise sulphur, mimosa yellow.

DESCRIPTION: The Jamaican sulphur is a small yellow butterfly with black borders. It closely resembles the common little sulphur (*Eurema lisa*), but may be distinguished by the narrower black borders and lack of a black spot in the discal cell of the forewings. The length of the forewings ranges from 14 to 16 mm (0.5–0.6 in).

RANGE: In Florida, the Jamaican sulphur is found in southern Dade County and the upper keys. It is also present in Cuba and Jamaica. Other races of *Eurema nise* occur in the Lesser Antilles, Central America, and South America.

HABITAT: It occurs in tropical hardwood hammocks.

LIFE HISTORY AND ECOLOGY: Eggs are laid singly on the new growth of *Lysiloma latisiliquum*. The caterpillars eat the young leaves of the host. Adults fly along trails and hammock edges, but retreat into the shade of forest if disturbed. This species undergoes large fluctuations in abundance. Colonies seem to persist only for a few generations before dying out. This butterfly probably occurs all months of the year, but most records are from the wet season, May through September. John Calhoun (1989) has summarized the available information on this species in Florida.

Jamaican Sulphur, *Eurema nise nise* (courtesy of John B. Heppner). Male, dorsal view.

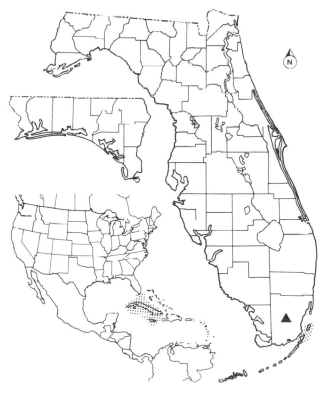

Distribution of the Jamaican sulphur, *Eurema nise nise.*

BASIS OF STATUS CLASSIFICATION: The Jamaican sulphur is listed as a species of special concern due to its highly restricted distribution, low abundance, and ephemeral nature. Remaining stands of tropical hardwood hammock in the keys and the southern mainland should be preserved. The southern Dade County hammocks where this butterfly has been observed in the past were severely damaged by Hurricane Andrew.

RECOMMENDATIONS: Surveys and ecological studies are needed to determine the current distribution, abundance, and habitat requirements of this species.

PREPARED BY: Marc C. Minno, Department of Zoology, University of Florida, Gainesville, FL 32611, John V. Calhoun, Florida State Collection of Arthropods, P.O. Box 147100, Gainesville, FL 32614, and Thomas C. Emmel, Department of Zoology, University of Florida, Gainesville, FL 32611.

FAMILY PIERIDAE

Species of Special Concern

Guayacan Sulphur
Kricogonia lyside (Godart)

OTHER COMMON NAMES: Lyside.

DESCRIPTION: The Guayacan sulphur is a small white butterfly with a yellow patch at the base of each forewing. Females are often a uniform light yellow. Individuals from other populations often have a black bar near the apex of the hindwing, but this form does not seem to occur in Florida. The length of the forewings varies from 18 to 27 mm (0.7–1.1 in).

RANGE: Upper Florida Keys, the Bahamas, Cuba, Jamaica, Hispaniola, Puerto Rico, Mexico, southwestern United States, Central America, and South America.

HABITAT: It is known on the edges of tropical hardwood hammocks.

LIFE HISTORY AND ECOLOGY: Nothing is known of the life history of this species in Florida, but Riley (1975) lists lignumvitae (*Guaiacum officinale*) as the host plant in the West Indies. The adults are usually found in low abundance during the summer (wet season). The flight is rather erratic. Adults readily visit flowers for nectar.

Guayacan Sulphur, *Kricogonia lyside* (courtesy of John B. Heppner). Male, dorsal view.

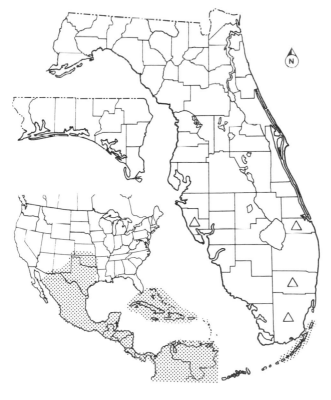

Distribution of the Guayacan sulphur, *Kricogonia lyside*.

BASIS OF STATUS CLASSIFICATION: The Guayacan sulphur is listed as a species of special concern because of its low abundance and restricted distribution in Florida.

RECOMMENDATIONS: Surveys and ecological studies are needed to determine the current distribution, abundance, and habitat requirements of this species.

PREPARED BY: Marc C. Minno and Thomas C. Emmel, Department of Zoology, University of Florida, Gainesville, FL 32611.

Flies and Mosquitos

INTRODUCTION: The order Diptera is a diverse group, but all of its adult members, except for a relatively small number of wingless species, have a single pair of wings, in contrast to the two pairs of wings found in other insect orders. The flies include almost 20,000 described species in North America north of Mexico, with thousands of species still undescribed. It is probable that several thousand species of flies occur in Florida, and this number must inevitably include a large number of rare or endangered species. Flies tend to be efficient in dispersal, and the group is not likely to provide as many examples of isolated endemic species as apterous groups such as spiders. On the other hand, some flies are fantastically specialized in their feeding habits or their microhabitat requirements. There are, for example, three species of flies (one undescribed) known only from the burrows of gopher tortoises, and two others confined to the water traps of pitcher plants.

Few flies, however, can be listed in this volume because our knowledge of geographic distribution is still rudimentary. Most of the rarest species are probably undescribed, and might even become extinct before they are recognized. Much of the work on flies in Florida has been concentrated on groups of medical importance; this explains why most of the species discussed below belong to families that have numerous blood-sucking species. It may seem strange to consider biting flies as rare or endangered, but it is likely that numerous innocuous insects are threatened by the same factors, especially habitat destruction, that threaten certain biting flies. Insects of medical importance may be particularly good indicator species. The best general taxonomic reference for Diptera is the profusely illustrated *Diptera Manual* (McAlpine, J. F. et al. 1981).

PREPARED BY: Mark Deyrup, Archbold Biological Station, Lake Placid, FL 33852.

Order Diptera
FAMILY PSYCHODIDAE

INTRODUCTION: Psychodidae, or moth flies, are small insects associated with damp or aquatic microhabitats. Identification is difficult, and there are undoubtedly undescribed species in the fauna of Florida.

PREPARED BY: D. G. Young, Department of Entomology & Nematology, University of Florida, Gainesville, FL 32611.

Status Undetermined

Sugarfoot Fly

Nemopalpus nearcticus Young

DESCRIPTION: *Nemopalpus nearcticus* adults are recognized chiefly by their hairy wings with distinctive venation, short mouthparts, long legs, and slender bodies. Other psychodid flies, especially phlebotomine sand flies, look like miniature *Nemopalpus*, but the phlebotomine females have two spermathecae instead of one, and the males have large spines on the styles of the genitalia, notably absent in *N. nearcticus*. In general appearance, *Nemopalpus* adults resemble dark mosquitos, but, unlike them, have mouthparts that are very short and not adapted for bloodsucking. Crane flies (family Tipulidae) occur in hardwood forests with *Nemopalpus*, but they have a V-shaped suture on their mesonota and the wings are devoid of setae. A detailed description of *N. nearcticus*, the only member of the subfamily Bruchomyiinae in North America, is given by Young (1974). The immature stages, presumably terrestrial and similar to phlebotomine larvae, have not been described.

RANGE: This fly is known only from the type locality (Sugarfoot Hammock, a mesic hardwood forest west of Gainesville, Alachua County, Florida).

HABITAT: During the day the adults rest in holes or crevices in the trunks of large trees. The larvae probably live in forest litter on the forest floor, at the base of large trees, or perhaps on tree trunks.

LIFE HISTORY AND ECOLOGY: Since the original description of this species in 1974, several specimens have been captured in June and July at Sugarfoot Hammock in flight traps or on tree trunks. Specimens are more common, however, in early September. The overwintering stage remains unknown. Preliminary laboratory rearings indicate a life cycle of about 60 days (egg to adult).

BASIS FOR STATUS CLASSIFICATION: Not enough information is available to classify this species. If the population is indeed restricted to the type locality, then *N. nearcticus* should be regarded as endangered.

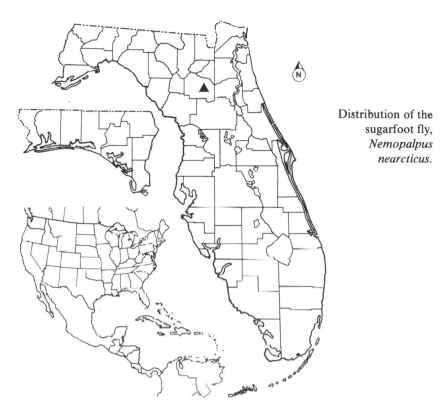

Distribution of the
sugarfoot fly,
*Nemopalpus
nearcticus.*

RECOMMENDATIONS: Further attempts should be made to find populations of the species in other hardwood forests. In the meantime, to prevent
the reduction or extinction of the only known population, the type locality
should not be disturbed or developed.

PREPARED BY: D. G. Young, Department of Entomology & Nematology,
University of Florida, Gainesville, FL 32611.

Order Diptera
FAMILY CULICIDAE

INTRODUCTION: The economic and medical importance of mosquitos has
stimulated the accumulation of a reservoir of entomological information un-
paralleled by that for any other insect family. Several comprehensive studies
(e.g., Carpenter & LaCasse 1955; King et al. 1960) treat the regional and national culicid fauna, including most of those species which I consider in this

chapter as rare or endangered in Florida. Breeland and Loyless (1983) have produced a useful key that permits specific identifications of most of the taxa mentioned herein, and Breeland (1982) provides an extensive bibliography for those Florida mosquito species which are rarely encountered elsewhere in the U.S.

In the preparation of this chapter I have made use of light trap records compiled from the 1940s through 1979 and maintained at the State of Florida's Office of Entomology in Jacksonville. These records have facilitated the examination of distribution patterns of most of Florida's 68 known culicid species. The limitations of this database include the absence of voucher specimens associated with records and the variation among species in their attraction to a New Jersey light trap.

The eight species selected as rare or endangered have been recorded from five or fewer of Florida's counties. None of these species is endemic to the state. Three species, *Aedes hendersoni*, *Orthopodomyia alba*, and *Wyeomyia smithii*, are widely distributed in temperate North America, and northern Florida represents the southernmost extent of their ranges. Three other species (*Culex mulrennani*, *Culex bahamensis*, and *Psorophora johnstonii*) are of West Indian origin, and the Florida Keys represent their northern distributional limit (Basham 1948; Pritchard et al. 1949). The seventh species, *Aedes thelcter*, is common in parts of Texas and additionally has been recovered in New Mexico, Oklahoma, and the Florida Keys. The last species, *Anopheles albimanus*, is broadly distributed in Central America and northern South America, and to the north reaches southern Texas and Florida.

Of these eight species, only *A. albimanus* has been recorded from as many as five Florida counties, but reproduction of this species is limited to the Florida Keys (Branch et al. 1958). Two other culicid taxa in Florida, *Culex atratus* and *Psorophora pygmaea* are also known from just five counties (Breeland 1982), but these latter two species probably breed in a wider geographic area than *A. albimanus* in Florida and, hence, are not considered herein as rare or endangered.

Some culicid species which were once collected from many Florida counties have not been reported recently. For example, *Anopheles georgianus* has been recorded from 10 Florida counties, but there are no published records anywhere in the Southeast for the past 35 years (Floore et al. 1976). Since it is unclear whether the absence of *A. georgianus* is due to undercollecting or an actual decline in its populations, this species has not been included in this compilation.

A single male of *Culex latisquama* was reported collected in 1906 in Lee County (Stone 1968), but the absence of any further records recommends the removal of this species from the Florida fauna.

Two culicid records new to Florida were documented in 1968, but as these species were most probably introduced by man, they are not included in this survey. *Aedes albopictus* is an Oriental container-breeder which likely arrived in the U.S. in rubber tires imported from Japan (Hawley et al. 1987); to date, in Florida it has been recorded only from Duval County. *Aedes bahamensis* is a West Indian species that also frequents artificial containers and has been captured in light traps and rubber tires in Broward, Dade and Monroe counties (Personal communication from Center for Disease Control, Fort Collins, Colorado, and G. F. O'Meara, Florida Medical Entomology Laboratory). If these two *Aedes* become established in Florida, their distributions may be expected to expand.

Since Florida currently spends $57 million annually for mosquito control, the conservation of selected mosquito species which could become human pests or disease vectors is liable to be inappropriate. Therefore, it would be a waste of space in this volume to provide recommendations concerning the preservation of any rare and endangered culicid species discussed in this chapter. As mentioned above, the chief value of these species may be as sensitive indicators of endangered habitats that harbor other species yet to be studied.

In the following accounts, if the original species descriptions are sparse or in obscure publications, I have cited supplementary references which provide greater descriptive detail. Dixinae and Chaoborinae, considered as subfamilies of the Culicidae by some authors (e.g., Balkin 1962), are not treated here.

I am grateful for the helpful comments of J. W. Knight, G. F. O'Meara, and T. J. Zavortink during the preparation of this chapter.

PREPARED BY: L. Philip Lounibos, Florida Medical Entomology Laboratory, 200 9th Street SE, Vero Beach, Fl 32960.

FAMILY CULICIDAE

Endangered

Central American Malaria Mosquito
Anopheles (*Nyssorhynchus*) *albimanus* Wiedemann

DESCRIPTION: This species is the only representative of the subgenus *Nyssorhynchus* occurring in the U.S. and the only anopheline in Florida with white bands on the hind tarsi. Breeland and Loyless (1983) provide keys for discriminating this species from other *Anopheles* in Florida. Published descriptions include Wiedemann (1820) and Faran (1980).

RANGE: This mosquito occurs north to Brownsville, Texas, south through Mexico and Central America, east to the Paria Peninsula of Venezuela, and west to Baja California and northern Peru. It is common in the Greater Antilles, the Bahamas, Cayman Islands, and Leeward Islands of the Lesser Antilles. In Florida it breeds in the Florida Keys. Other Florida records include

Distribution of the
Central American
malaria mosquito,
*Anopheles
albimanus.*

Dade and Broward counties, probably representing chance introductions at
these ports (Branch et al. 1958).

HABITAT: In middle America the immatures of this species have been recovered from potholes, drainage areas, spring seepages, borrow pits, and
ground pools (33%); ponds, lakes, dam spills, and reservoirs (16%); streams
and canals (21%); ditches (6%); swamps (6%); marshes (5%); and other habitats (13%) (Faran 1980).

LIFE HISTORY AND ECOLOGY: Throughout its range, *A. albimanus* is
an important vector of human malaria, being the principal transmitter in
most of Central America. Consequently, considerable information is available on its life history, summarized by Faran (1980).

BASIS FOR STATUS CLASSIFICATION: Pritchard et al. (1946) regarded
this species as native to the Florida Keys based on collection records from
1904 through 1945 (King 1937; Carpenter 1949; Carpenter et al. 1945). Later
light trap records authenticate the maintenance of breeding populations in
the keys through 1957 (Branch et al. 1958).

PREPARED BY: L. Philip Lounibos, Florida Medical Entomology Laboratory, 200 9th Street SE, Vero Beach, Fl 32960.

FAMILY CULICIDAE

Threatened

Bahamian Culex

Culex (Culex) bahamensis Dyar & Knab

DESCRIPTION: Adult females and larvae are similar in aspect to the southern house mosquito *Culex (Culex) quinquefasciatus*, but the two species are separable with the keys of Breeland and Loyless (1983). Published descriptions are found in Dyar and Knab (1906) and Carpenter and LaCasse (1955).

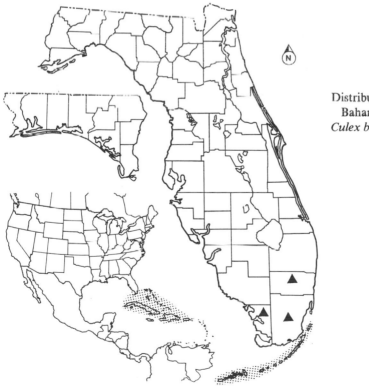

Distribution of the Bahamian culex, *Culex bahamensis.*

RANGE: This mosquito occurs in Florida (Monroe, Dade, and Broward counties) and the Greater Antilles.

HABITAT: The species is associated with temporary rain pools. In Jamaica, larvae have been found in coral rockholes near the sea, in shallow open pools in mangrove areas, and large artificial containers (Belkin et al. 1970).

LIFE HISTORY AND ECOLOGY: Very little known. Larvae have been found accompanying *Anopheles atropos* (Fisk 1939) and *Culex atratus* (Wirth 1945).

BASIS FOR STATUS CLASSIFICATION: Like *Culex mulrennani*, this mosquito requires more permanent limestone rain pools, which imposes limits on distribution and abundance.

PREPARED BY: L. Philip Lounibos, Florida Medical Entomology Laboratory, 200 9th Street SE, Vero Beach, Fl 32960.

FAMILY CULICIDAE

Threatened

Mulrennan's Culex

Culex (Melanoconion) mulrennani Basham

DESCRIPTION: This species is separable from five other members of this subgenus, which also occur in Florida, on the basis of the male genitalia and color pattern or scale arrangement on the pleural region of the thorax (Knight and Haeger 1971). A published description is found in Basham (1948).

RANGE: This mosquito occurs in the Florida Keys, Cuba, and Grand Cayman Island.

HABITAT: Larvae have been collected from a well and shallow depressions and solution holes in oolitic limestone.

LIFE HISTORY AND ECOLOGY: Unknown. This species has proven difficult to rear in the laboratory.

BASIS FOR STATUS CLASSIFICATION: It is probable that *C. mulrennani* and *C. bahamensis* require more permanent limestone rain pools than the sympatric but faster developing *A. thelcter* or *P. johnstonii*, which imposes a greater limit on the distribution and abundance of the two *Culex*.

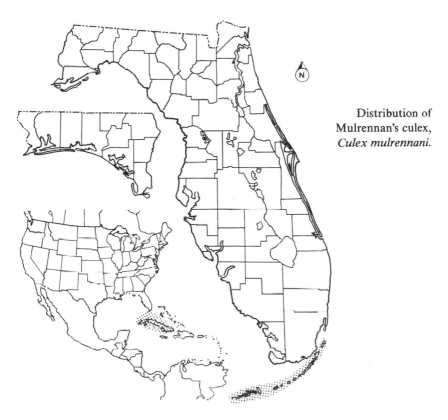

Distribution of
Mulrennan's culex,
Culex mulrennani.

PREPARED BY: L. Philip Lounibos, Florida Medical Entomology Laboratory, 200 9th Street SE, Vero Beach, Fl 32960.

FAMILY CULICIDAE

Rare

Keys Ochlerotatus

Aedes (Ochlerotatus) thelcter Dyar

DESCRIPTION: This species belongs to a large subgenus which includes at least four members (*Aedes atlanticus, A. sollicitans, A. taeniorhynchus,* and *A. tortilis*) that may occur in the same habitat. These five species of *Ochlerotatus* may be separated on the basis of adult scaling patterns and larval comb scales (Breeland and Loyless 1983). Published descriptions are found in Dyar (1918) and Arnell (1976).

Distribution of the
Keys ochlerotatus,
Aedes thelcter.

RANGE: This mosquito occurs in the Florida Keys, Rio Grande Valley of Texas, and southern New Mexico northeastward to central Oklahoma. It probably inhabits northeastern Mexico, but Arnell (1976) regards reports from Jalisco and Sinaloa as erroneous.

HABITAT: Larvae have been recovered in the Florida Keys from shaded rain-pool depressions in limestone in the transition zone between hardwood forest and black mangrove, in association with various mosquito species, including *Psorophora johnstonii* (Thurman et al. 1949).

LIFE HISTORY AND ECOLOGY: Very little known. Rapid larval development probably occurs after drought-resistant eggs hatch in response to rainfall. Adults are known to bite humans (Thurman et al. 1949). This species harbored the virus of Venezuelan equine encephalitis after an outbreak of this disease in Texas in 1971 (Sudia and Newhouse 1975).

BASIS FOR STATUS CLASSIFICATION: This mosquito is confined to temporary freshwater pools in oolitic limestone, habitats that are jeopardized by construction.

PREPARED BY: L. Philip Lounibos, Florida Medical Entomology Laboratory, 200 9th Street SE, Vero Beach, Fl 32960.

FAMILY CULICIDAE

Rare

Antillean Psorophora

Psorophora (Janthinosoma) johnstonii (Grabham)

DESCRIPTION: Adult females and fourth stage larvae of this mosquito are separable from other Florida *Psorophora* by means of keys in Breeland and Loyless (1983). Belkin et al. (1970) believed that the type form *johnstonii* from Jamaica may be a different species than that examined by Thurman et al. (1951) from Florida. Published descriptions are found in Grabham (1905) and Carpenter and LaCasse (1955).

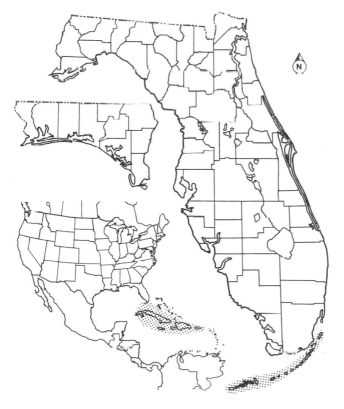

Distribution of the Antillean psorophora, *Psorophora johnstonii.*

RANGE: This mosquito occurs in the Florida Keys and the Greater Antilles.

HABITAT: It occurs in densely shaded, shallow, rain-filled depressions at the inner edge of the *Conocarpus* transition zone between hardwood forest and black mangrove. It has also been found in the Florida Keys among dead grass and leaves at the edges of a borrow pit and in deep sunlit potholes in oolitic limestone. This species is apparently not tolerant of brackish conditions (Thurman et al. 1951).

LIFE HISTORY AND ECOLOGY: Egg to adult development may be achieved within six days in nature. Males copulate with females in mating swarms, and females suck blood during the daylight. In the late 1940s, this species was a local pest in the Florida Keys (Thurman et al. 1951).

BASIS FOR STATUS CLASSIFICATION: In spite of past local abundance, the limestone-pothole habitat in the Florida Keys is threatened by development.

PREPARED BY: L. Philip Lounibos, Florida Medical Entomology Laboratory, 200 9th Street SE, Vero Beach, Fl 32960.

                                                        FAMILY CULICIDAE

Rare

North American Pitcher Plant Mosquito

Wyeomyia (*Wyeomyia*) *smithii* (Coquillett)

DESCRIPTION: This is the only species of mosquito whose larvae and pupae live in the fluid reservoir of *Sarracenia* pitcher plants. A southern race of *Wyeomyia smithii* was formerly classified as a distinct species, *Wyeomyia haynei*, by Dodge (1947), but Bradshaw and Lounibos (1977) argued on the basis of clinal characters and the absence of reproductive isolation between populations that there is but one species, *W. smithii*. This pitcher plant mosquito may be distinguished from two congeners in Florida, *W. mitchellii* and *Wyeomyia vanduzeei*, whose primary larval habitat is the bromeliad *Tillandsia utriculata*, on the basis of characters of larvae and adults (Breeland and Loyless 1983) and eggs (Frank et al. 1981). Published descriptions are found in Coquillett (1901) and Carpenter and LaCasse (1955).

RANGE: In Florida the range coincides with the distribution of the purple pitcher plant (*Sarracenia purpurea*) in the western panhandle region from

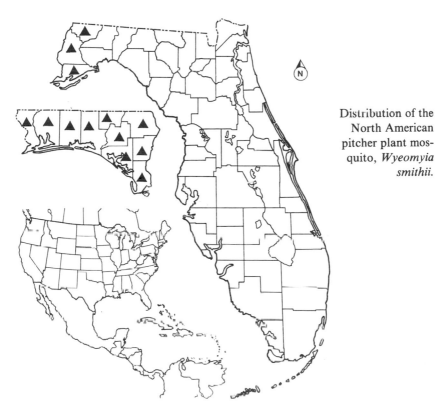

Distribution of the
North American
pitcher plant mos-
quito, *Wyeomyia
smithii.*

Escambia to Liberty counties. Outside of Florida, this species occurs from the Gulf Coast of the United States north to Labrador and west to Saskatchewan.

HABITAT: On the Gulf Coast the primary host plant of *W. smithii* occurs in wet pine savannahs and in the wet areas surrounding cypress domes and titi pocosins (McDaniel 1971). In these habitats, immature *W. smithii* may also be found in the leaves of *Sarracenia flava* and hybrids between *S. purpurea* and *S. flava, Sarracenia leucophylla, Sarracenia rubra* and *Sarracenia alata.* However, overwintering survivorship of *W. smithii* is higher in *S. purpurea* than in hybrid plants or leaves of *S. flava* (Bradshaw 1983).

LIFE HISTORY AND ECOLOGY: Adult female *W. smithii* from the Gulf Coast to the Carolina lowlands may take a blood meal, whereas individuals from elsewhere in its range are obligatorily autogenous (O'Meara et al. 1981). Gravid females are attracted by a water-soluble chemical to oviposit eggs singly in newly opened pitcher leaves (Istock et al. 1983). Larval development in *W. smithii* is density-dependent throughout the growing season (April-October) in Florida, and mosquito productivity in individual pitchers is positively correlated with prey capture success of the leaf (Bradshaw and

Holzapfel 1983, 1986). Larval diapause is induced by short autumn daylengths and development resumes in the spring in response to longer daylengths. The depth and stage of diapause are dependent on latitude of origin (Bradshaw and Lounibos 1977).

BASIS FOR STATUS CLASSIFICATION: The persistence of *W. smithii* in Florida is dependent on the integrity of populations of its host plant, *S. purpurea*, which was formerly considered threatened by disruption of its habitats in northern Florida.

PREPARED BY: L. Philip Lounibos, Florida Medical Entomology Laboratory, 200 9th Street SE, Vero Beach, Fl 32960.

FAMILY CULICIDAE

Status Undetermined

Cold-Hardy Orthopodomyia
Orthopodomyia alba Baker

DESCRIPTION: Larvae of this mosquito are separable from the sibling species *Orthopodomyia signifera*, which is widespread in Florida, by the absence of a sclerotized plate on the eighth abdominal segment. Minor setal and scaling differences separate adult females of the two species (Breeland and Loyless 1983). Although morphological differences are slight, a number of biological features, including cold-hardiness, distinguish *O. alba* from *O. signifera* (Copeland 1987). Published descriptions are included in Baker (1936) and Zavortink (1968).

RANGE: There are unconfirmed light trap records from Bay and Hillsborough counties. The general known range is New Mexico, Missouri, and New York south to Coahuila, Mexico, Texas, and Georgia.

HABITAT: Larvae occur in water-containing cavities in trees, especially in deep rot holes (Copeland 1987). This species is occasionally found in artificial containers.

LIFE HISTORY AND ECOLOGY: Adults are relatively unaggressive but will take blood from birds at night (Zavortink 1968). This species has recently been raised in the lab by Copeland (pers. comm.). Overwintering occurs in the larval stages, which are more cold-hardy than those of *O. signifera* (Copeland 1987).

BASIS FOR STATUS CLASSIFICATION: Too few collections have been made from treeholes, especially in the Florida panhandle, to determine the

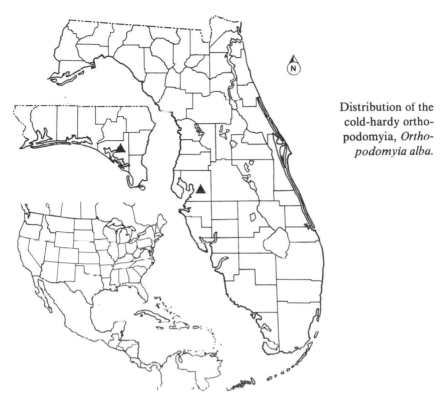

Distribution of the
cold-hardy ortho-
podomyia, *Ortho-
podomyia alba.*

prevalence of this species. Copeland (1987) found *O. alba* to be far more abundant in Indiana than previously assumed, more than five times as common as *O. signifera.*

PREPARED BY: L. Philip Lounibos, Florida Medical Entomology Laboratory, 200 9th Street SE, Vero Beach, Fl 32960.

FAMILY CULICIDAE

Status Undetermined

North American Canopy Treehole Aedes
Aedes (Protomacleaya) hendersoni Cockerell

DESCRIPTION: Adults are similar to those of *Aedes triseriatus*, a sibling species which is sympatric with *A. hendersoni* in much of its range and common throughout Florida. However, the scutum of *A. hendersoni* usually contains more silvery or white scales. Larvae of the two species are distin-

guished easily by the acus, which is detached from the sclerotized siphon in
A. hendersoni, and by the length of the anal papillae, which are longer than
the tenth segment in *A. hendersoni*. Published descriptions are included in
Cockerell (1918), Breland (1960), and Zavortink (1972).

RANGE: In Florida it is known only from a single specimen collected in
Leon County (Zavortink and Belkin 1979). General range includes eastern
coast of the U.S. to Oregon and southern Canada to northern Florida (Zavortink 1972).

HABITAT: The immature stages are found in rotted cavities of trees, especially holes above ground level (Scholl and Defoliart 1977; Sinsko and Grimstad 1977). In zones of sympatry *A. hendersoni* and *A. triseriatus* are
segregated by treehole type and height above ground (Copeland 1987).

LIFE HISTORY AND ECOLOGY: Extensive studies in the midwestern
U.S. have compared the life histories of sympatric *A. hendersoni* and *A.
triseriatus*. Although interspecific crosses will yield some hybrid offspring,
there is evidence for reproductive isolation (Truman & Craig 1968), and iso-
zyme electrophoresis provides unambiguous criteria for species separation
(Saul et al. 1977). In Indiana the two species differed in blood-meal hosts, *A.*

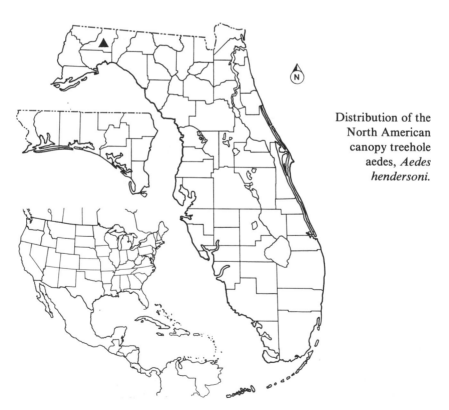

Distribution of the
North American
canopy treehole
aedes, *Aedes
hendersoni.*

hendersoni feeding mainly on raccoons and tree squirrels (Nasci 1982). Although both species are capable of transmitting LaCrosse (LAC) encephalitis virus, a potential human pathogen, *A. hendersoni* does so less efficiently (Grimstad et al. 1985), but its importance as a LAC host may depend on local blood-feeding habits (Nasci 1982).

BASIS FOR STATUS CLASSIFICATION: Too few collections have been made from canopy treeholes to estimate the prevalence of this species.

PREPARED BY: L. Philip Lounibos, Florida Medical Entomology Laboratory, 200 9th Street SE, Vero Beach, Fl 32960.

Order Diptera
FAMILY CHIRONOMIDAE

INTRODUCTION: The Chironomidae, or midges, include the familiar long-legged, non-biting flies that emerge in enormous numbers from lakes. The short mouthparts and lack of scales on the wings separate members of this family from the somewhat similar Culicidae (mosquitos). Most members of the family have aquatic larvae, often with specialized habitat requirements. It is probable that there are species restricted to major springs in Florida and to seeps or intermittent streams in north Florida. Some species are leaf miners, and there could easily be species with host-specific relationships with rare aquatic plants. It will probably be a long time before all the likely haunts of specialized midges are investigated, as the group is taxonomically difficult and the supply of taxonomists inadequate. The scarcity of information on Florida chironomids in no way reflects the ecological significance of the groups, as many species hold important positions near the base of the food chain in aquatic habitats.

PREPARED BY: Mark Deyrup, Archbold Biological Station, Lake Placid, FL 33852.

FAMILY CHIRONOMIDAE

Rare

North American Pitcher Plant Midge
Metriocnemus knabi Coquillett

DESCRIPTION: This is the only species of midge whose larvae and pupae live in the reservoir of *Sarracenia* pitcher plants, often in the company of the

North American pitcher plant mosquito (*Wyeomyia smithii*). Its close relative, *Metriocnemus edwardsi*, inhabits pitchers of *Darlingtonia californica*,
the cobra lily of western coastal United States. Published descriptions are included in Coquillett (1904) (adult) and Knab (1905) (larva and pupa).

RANGE: Similar to *Wyeomyia smithii*.

HABITAT: On the Gulf Coast, the primary host plant of *Metriocnemus*
knabi occurs in wet pine savannahs and in wet areas surrounding cypress
domes and titi pocosins.

LIFE HISTORY AND ECOLOGY: Larvae are found in the lower portions
of leaves amongst the insect carcasses upon which they feed (Fish and Hall
1978). Pupae occur individually in a gelatinous mass attached to the inner
leaf wall just above waterline (Knab 1905). Overwintering occurs in the larval stages, which diapause in response to decreasing autumnal daylengths
(Paris and Jenner 1959). Compared to many other species of chironomids,
M. knabi larvae are relatively intolerant to low oxygen concentrations, having evolved to live exclusively in the oxygen-rich sarcophagi of pitcher plants
(Cameron et al. 1977). By accelerating the breakdown of prey, *M. knabi* and

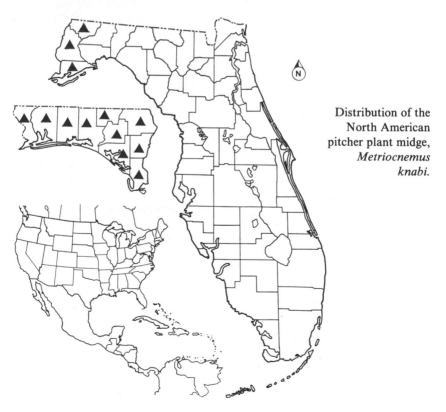

Distribution of the
North American
pitcher plant midge,
Metriocnemus
knabi.

W. smithii increase the availability of nitrogenous compounds required by *S. purpurea* (Bradshaw and Creelman 1984). The favorable exchanges of chemicals between the plant host and these dipterous inquilines led Bradshaw (1983) to describe the system as mutualistic.

BASIS FOR STATUS CLASSIFICATION: The persistence of this insect in Florida is dependent on the host pitcher plants.

RECOMMENDATIONS: Protect wet pine savannahs in the Florida panhandle that harbor populations of *S. purpurea*.

PREPARED BY: L. Philip Lounibos, Florida Medical Entomology Laboratory, 200 9th Street SE, Vero Beach, Fl 32960.

Order Diptera
FAMILY TABANIDAE

INTRODUCTION: Horseflies and deerflies seem all too common to most Floridians, but a large number of species are actually rather rare, and only seem abundant because humans or livestock are acting as powerful aggregants. Male horseflies and deerflies are not attracted to vertebrates; on the basis of records of males, there are a number of species that would be considered rare; none of these species is included below.

PREPARED BY: Mark Deyrup, Archbold Biological Station, Lake Placid, FL 33852.

FAMILY TABANIDAE

Rare

Florida Asaphomyian Tabanid Fly
Asaphomyia floridensis Pechuman

DESCRIPTION: This slender brown fly has an antennal style with five or six segments, and the scape and pedicel are each as long as wide; there is no trace of calli on frons. The wing has an appendix or bifurcation of the third longitudinal vein. Length is about 10 mm (0.4 in). Published description is found in Pechuman 1974.

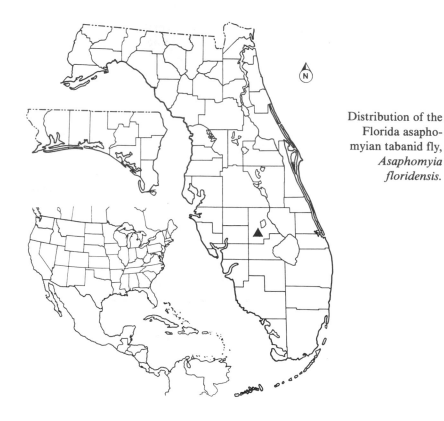

Distribution of the
Florida asapho-
myian tabanid fly,
*Asaphomyia
floridensis.*

RANGE: It is known only from Highlands County.

HABITAT: Adults occur in Florida scrub habitat.

LIFE HISTORY AND ECOLOGY: Small aggregations have been seen in the tops of low scrub oaks in early morning. Adults can occasionally be found on the underside of palmetto leaves. The mouthparts are unsuitable for biting, and it is possible the adult does not feed. Adults can be found in May through early July. The immature stages are unknown.

SPECIALIZED OR UNIQUE CHARACTERISTICS: This species has a very close relative in southeast Texas and appears to be an example of a western lineage with an isolated population in the sandy uplands of Florida.

BASIS FOR STATUS CLASSIFICATION: This species appears to be restricted to a few scrubs at the southern end of the Lake Wales Ridge, an area whose native habitat is rapidly disappearing.

RECOMMENDATIONS: Protect the scrub habitat of the southern Lake Wales Ridge.

PREPARED BY: L.L. Pechuman, Department of Entomology, Cornell University, Ithaca, NY 14853, and Mark Deyrup, Archbold Biological Station, P.O. Box 2057, Lake Placid, FL 33852.

FAMILY TABANIDAE

Rare

Little Panhandle Deerfly
Chrysops tidwelli Philip & Jones

DESCRIPTION: This small dark species about 6 mm (0.2 in) in size has the basal two segments of the abdomen yellow, the frontal callus yellow to brownish; the apical spot broad, nearly filling cell R4, and the hyaline triangle reaches R2 + 3. Legs are yellow except for dark distal half of fore tibiae. Published description is found in Philip and Jones (1962).

RANGE: A few specimens have been collected in Escambia and Santa Rosa counties.

HABITAT: This species occurs in areas of mixed sandhills and lowlands with small streams.

LIFE HISTORY AND ECOLOGY: The type specimen was taken from a horse. The male of this species is unknown. The flight season is relatively late, in July and August.

BASIS FOR STATUS CLASSIFICATION: The tabanids of Florida have received considerable study, and it appears that this species is very restricted in its range.

RECOMMENDATIONS: Protection of natural habitat with small unpolluted streams is necessary to preserve this species and any other similarly restricted animals.

PREPARED BY: L.L. Pechuman, Department of Entomology, Cornell University, Ithaca, NY 14853, and Mark Deyrup, Archbold Biological Station, P.O. Box 2057, Lake Placid, FL 33852.

Distribution of the
little panhandle
deerfly, *Chrysops
tidwelli.*

Order Diptera
FAMILY MYDIDAE

INTRODUCTION: This family includes the largest flies in Florida, and even uncommon species are so conspicuous that they are better represented in collections than many abundant flies. Some species with soil-dwelling larvae are likely to be restricted to special edaphic conditions. Females of some genera appear to be poor fliers, and inefficient dispersal could lead to recognizable local forms. The group has received little study, and we do not know whether there has been significant evolutionary divergence between populations.

PREPARED BY: Mark Deyrup, Archbold Biological Station, Lake Placid, FL 33852.

Status Undetermined

Black-Bearded Nemomydas

Nemomydas melanopogon Steyskal

DESCRIPTION: This is a relatively small species (12–14 mm [0.5-0.6 in]) long with clear wings, yellowish legs, and black hair on the central part of the face. *Nemomydes lara* is the female of *Nemomydas melanopogon*. A published description is found in Steyskal (1956).

RANGE: This fly is known from Lake, Putnam, Highlands, and Polk counties.

HABITAT: It is found in Florida scrub with open areas of bare sand.

Distribution of the black-bearded nemo-mydas, *Nemomydas melanopogon.*

LIFE HISTORY AND ECOLOGY: Adults have been collected in May through July. They have not been collected on flowers, and probably do not feed as adults. Larvae are unknown.

SPECIALIZED OR UNIQUE CHARACTERISTICS: There are several *Nemomydas* species in xeric areas of southwestern North America, and it is likely that *N. melanopogon* is an example of a western lineage isolated and persisting in scattered sandy uplands.

BASIS FOR STATUS CLASSIFICATION: This is an uncommon species with poor mobility, whose habitat is rapidly disappearing. Only one protected population is known.

RECOMMENDATIONS: This is one of a large number of species of organisms that appear to be dependent on open scrub areas in the interior of the Florida peninsula. A number of sites should be protected and managed to ensure survival of populations through their restricted geographic range.

PREPARED BY: Mark Deyrup, Archbold Biological Station, Lake Placid, FL 33852.

FAMILY MYDIDAE

Status Undetermined

Panhandle Nemomydas

Nemomydas jonesi (Johnson)

DESCRIPTION: *Nemomydas jonesi* is 16–17 mm (0.6 in) long, with clear wings, brown legs, and yellow hair in the central part of the face of the male. Published descriptions are found in Hardy 1950 and Steyskal 1956.

RANGE: This fly is known from Leon and Walton counties.

HABITAT: Considering the type locality (DeFuniak Springs), the habitat is probably sandhill.

LIFE HISTORY AND ECOLOGY: An adult was collected in June (Steyskal 1956).

BASIS FOR STATUS CLASSIFICATION: This is a relatively conspicuous fly, but only a few specimens are known. It is likely to be restricted to isolated sandhill areas in north Florida.

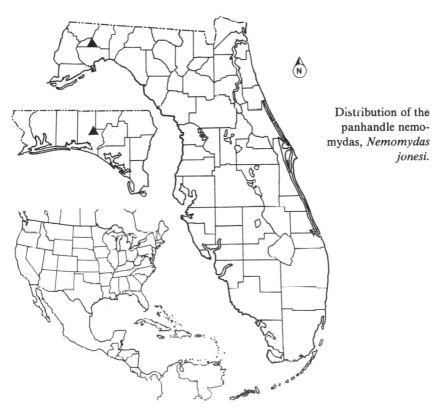

Distribution of the panhandle nemo-mydas, *Nemomydas jonesi.*

RECOMMENDATIONS: This species needs further study to determine its geographic range and habitat requirements.

PREPARED BY: Mark Deyrup, Archbold Biological Station, Lake Placid, FL 33852.

Order Diptera
FAMILY EMPIDIDAE

Species of Special Concern

Tortoise Burrow Dance Fly
Drapetis (Crossopalpus) sp.

DESCRIPTION: This species is rather large (1.75 mm [<0.1]) for the genus, with yellow legs and the antennal arista about as long as the width of the wing. Genitalic characters will probably be used to provide the best diagnosis of the species. There are many undescribed species in the subgenus *Crosso-palpus*, and it may be a long time before this species is described.

RANGE: This fly is known from Highlands County.

HABITAT: Adults occur in gopher tortoise burrows in the "twilight" areas back from the entrance and perhaps deeper in the burrow as well. The larvae might be predators attacking tiny arthropods in the burrows.

SPECIALIZED OR UNIQUE CHARACTERISTICS: The unusually long antennal arista might be an adaptation for the cave-like conditions in the burrow.

BASIS FOR STATUS CLASSIFICATION: This species is known only from gopher tortoise burrows. Since many empidids have specialized habitat requirements, and there are few if any local habitats that could substitute for a tortoise burrows, it seems likely that this species of fly belongs to the as-

Distribution of the
tortoise burrow
dance fly,
Drapetis sp.

semblage of obligate tortoise associates. This empidid is likely to share the fate of gopher tortoises.

RECOMMENDATIONS: Preservation of gopher tortoise populations in their natural range and habitats is probably necessary to preserve this fly. It is not known whether this fly is widely distributed within the range of the gopher tortoise.

PREPARED BY: Mark Deyrup, Archbold Biological Station, Lake Placid, FL 33852.

Order Diptera
FAMILY ANTHOMYIIDAE

INTRODUCTION: Anthomyiid flies are small blackish, brown, or gray flies, somewhat similar to houseflies in general appearance. Many species of anthomyiid flies are highly specialized in their larval food, which may be certain mushrooms, or one type of tissue of one plant, or a particular kind of accumulation of organic matter.

PREPARED BY: Mark Deyrup, Archbold Biological Station, Lake Placid, FL 33852.

FAMILY ANTHOMYIIDAE

Species of Special Concern

Tortoise Burrow Anthomyiid
Eutrichota gopheri (Johnson)

DESCRIPTION: This brownish fly is about 7 mm (0.3 in) long. It closely resembles a number of other sympatric species, and the most convenient diagnostic structural character is the shape of the male genitalia (Griffiths 1984). It appears to be the only medium-sized brownish fly that congregates in entrances of gopher tortoise burrows.

RANGE: This fly is widely distributed within the range of the gopher tortoise (Griffiths 1984).

Distribution of the tortoise burrow anthomyiid, *Eutrichota gopheri.*

HABITAT: The tortoise burrow is the only known habitat.

LIFE HISTORY AND ECOLOGY: This species probably feeds on tortoise dung (Hubbard 1896, Griffiths 1984). Adults are usually collected in spring.

BASIS FOR STATUS CLASSIFICATION: All evidence indicates that this species is completely restricted to gopher tortoise burrows and should share the status of its host.

RECOMMENDATIONS: Protect naturally occurring populations of gopher tortoises.

PREPARED BY: Mark Deyrup, Archbold Biological Station, Lake Placid, FL 33852.

Order Diptera
FAMILY ASILIDAE

INTRODUCTION: Asilid flies, usually known as robber flies, are elongate flies with bulging eyes and a stout, powerful, piercing beak. The larvae, as far as is known, are also predaceous. Adults of most species are not specialized in their prey requirements but may have special habitats, such as beaches or the trunks of fallen trees. Larvae may have more specialized habitat requirements. The robber flies of Florida are not well known, but there are a number of species confined to the state, and some of these are probably rare or local.

PREPARED BY: Mark Deyrup, Archbold Biological Station, Lake Placid, FL 33852.

FAMILY ASILIDAE

Threatened

Gopher Tortoise Robber Fly
Machimus polyphemi Bullington and Beck

DESCRIPTION: This black robber fly is 10.5 to 17.5 mm (0.4–0.7 in) long and has a dense covering of shining golden brown pollinosity (minute hairs); the thorax has a black stripe bisected by a pollinose band, the legs elongate for perching and for holding prey, eyes bulging, and the area between eyes concave. A published description is found in Bullington and Beck (1991). It is the only robber fly that lives in gopher tortoise burrows.

RANGE: This fly is known from northern Florida, southern Georgia, and Mississippi.

HABITAT: This robber fly is only known from the burrows of gopher tortoises (*Gopherus polyphemi*). Evidence suggests that it probably never leaves the burrow except for dispersal to other burrows.

LIFE HISTORY AND ECOLOGY: The larvae are unknown, but are probably predators of arthropods in gopher tortoise burrows. Adults occur in the burrow, no more than 1 m back from the entrance, and consume anthomyiid flies that also are associated with the burrows (Bullington and Beck 1991).

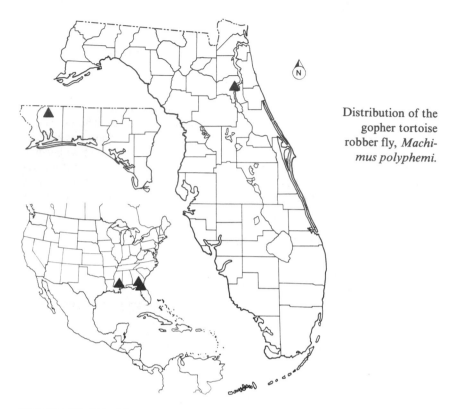

Distribution of the gopher tortoise robber fly, *Machimus polyphemi.*

SPECIALIZED OR UNIQUE CHARACTERISTICS: This species, along with two western species found in burrows of badgers, appears to be a specialized remnant of an ancient group of robber flies that were largely displaced in more common habitats by more advanced species (Bullington and Beck 1991).

BASIS FOR STATUS CLASSIFICATION: This species shares the status of its obligate host.

RECOMMENDATIONS: Preservation of this species depends completely on the persistence of healthy populations of the host.

PREPARED BY: Mark Deyrup, Archbold Biological Station, Lake Placid, FL 33852.

Ants, Bees, and Wasps

INTRODUCTION: The order Hymenoptera is a huge and diverse order that includes sawflies, ants, bees, and a great variety of "wasps." The group is so large, and the world supply of specialized taxonomists so small, that any given site in Florida is likely to yield many undescribed species. For this reason, species that are known from only a few sites are not particularly likely to be rare, but only poorly known. The group includes few species of medical importance and few crop pests, so survey work in Florida has proceeded slowly, with little economic incentive. There are undoubtedly many rare species in the state, but we will not be able to certify more than a small fraction for decades to come. Some Hymenoptera have specialized relationships with certain plants or prey upon host-specific phytophagous insects; rare or endangered plants may have hymenopterans that depend on them. Many species, especially ants and hunting wasps, make burrows or nests in the ground, and these species may be tied to particular soil types.

PREPARED BY: Mark Deyrup, Archbold Biological Station, Lake Placid, FL 33852.

Order Hymenoptera
FAMILY FORMICIDAE

INTRODUCTION: The Formicidae, or ants, provide most of our known examples of rare or endangered Hymenoptera. The chief reason for this is that Florida ants are comparatively well known, and it is possible to single out some apparently rare species. In addition, some species are known to be dependent on endangered habitats. Finally, ants are less efficient dispersers than most other Hymenoptera, a condition that can lead, over time, to reduced ranges or distinctly divergent populations on isolated islands of habitat. Although most ants have a winged dispersal phase, queens are usually heavy-bodied and land only a short distance from the parental colony.

713

Among ants, the number of colonies, not the number of individual ants, determines the abundance of a species. Isolated patches of habitat may have large numbers of individuals of habitat-specific ants, but the number of colonies may be small and the persistence of the species on the site much less certain than it appears.

The best general reference on ants is Hölldobler and Wilson (1990).

PREPARED BY: Mark Deyrup, Archbold Biological Station, Lake Placid, FL 33852.

FAMILY FORMICIDAE

Rare

Elegant Cone-Ant

Dorymyrmex elegans Trager

DESCRIPTION: Like other members of its genus, workers of this species have a conspicuous cone-shaped hump on the epinotum. Thorax, legs, and antennae are unusually elongate for genus; mesonotum flat in profile; color yellow. Queens and males are undescribed. Published description and keys to Florida *Dorymyrmex* (under the genus name *Conomyrma*) are found in Trager (1988) and Johnson (1989).

RANGE: This ant occurs on the Lake Wales Ridge in Highlands and Polk counties. A divergent population or closely related species occurs on the southern Brooksville Ridge in Citrus County.

HABITAT: It inhabits patches of open sand in sandhill and yellow sand phase of sand pine scrub, particularly in Paola, Astatula, and Lake soil types.

LIFE HISTORY AND ECOLOGY: The nest entrance is in open sand, surrounded by a conspicuous round crater-like mound in. The nest usually appears to have a single entrance. Workers are active both day and night, but seldom forage in bright sun. This species is probably almost completely predaceous. Males have been collected in October (Trager 1988), September, and June.

SPECIALIZED OR UNIQUE CHARACTERISTICS: The unusually gracile, "race-horse" appearance of this species is unique among North American species of *Dorymyrmex*. The adaptive significance of this body form is

Distribution of the
elegant cone-ant,
*Dorymyrmex
elegans.*

unknown. *D. elegans* has the most restricted distribution of any known Florida endemic ant.

BASIS FOR STATUS CLASSIFICATION: The yellow sand uplands where this species occurs are preferred for citrus, and few natural sites remain. *C. elegans* does not persist in heavily disturbed sites, nor can it survive in sites that are so overgrown with natural vegetation that no bare soil remains.

RECOMMENDATIONS: Protection and management of the remaining yellow sand habitats on the southern Lake Wales Ridge are necessary if this species and a number of associated organisms, such as the plants *Dicerandra* spp., are to survive. There are two protected populations.

PREPARED BY: Mark Deyrup, Archbold Biological Station, Lake Placid, FL 33852.

Rare

Silvery Wood Ant
Formica subsericea Say

DESCRIPTION: This ant represents a typical *Formica* in size and shape, but differs from the only other black *Formica* in Florida (*Formica arch-boldi*) by its silky appearance, caused by a dense covering of silvery pubescence. Published keys to the species are found in Creighton (1950); keys and description in Francoeur (1973).

RANGE: This ant is known from Quebec west to Manitoba, south to central Mississippi and northern Georgia (Francoeur 1973). In Florida, it is found in Liberty County, about 10 miles north of Bristol (Wilson and Francoeur 1974).

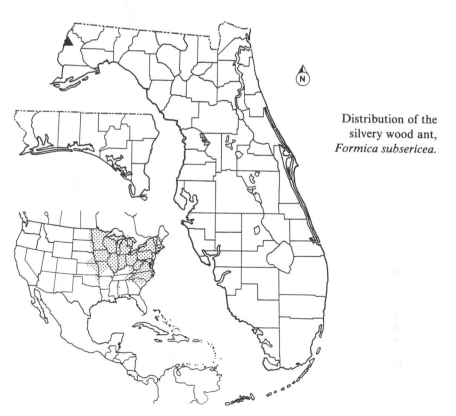

Distribution of the silvery wood ant, *Formica subsericea.*

HABITAT: It occurs in hardwood or mixed conifer forest. In Florida, it has been recorded from a hardwood forest on a white sand ridge (Wilson and Francoeur 1974).

LIFE HISTORY AND ECOLOGY: This is a conspicuous, diurnally active species that forages for insect prey. In the Florida population, the nests were dispersed in leaf litter and shallow cavities in the soil (Wilson and Francoeur 1974). Males were collected on 4 July in Florida (Wilson and Francoeur 1974).

SPECIALIZED OR UNIQUE CHARACTERISTICS: The Florida population is not a southern tongue of a contiguous distribution, but a true isolate far south of the nearest known population in northern Georgia (Wilson and Francoeur 1974).

BASIS FOR STATUS CLASSIFICATION: This is a conspicuous species that has not been found in other sites in northern Florida. The site itself is unusual in that it is a forest typical of bottomland growing on a white sand ridge (Wilson and Francoeur 1974). It is even possible that there is only one Florida population. The site has recently been cleared.

RECOMMENDATIONS: Any remnant at the site of the Florida population should be preserved; it should also be checked for other isolated populations of northern organisms.

PREPARED BY: Mark Deyrup, Archbold Biological Station, Lake Placid, FL 33852.

FAMILY FORMICIDAE

Rare

Desert Snapping Ant
Odontomachus clarus Roger

DESCRIPTION: Like other species of *Odontomachus*, this species has long, robust mandibles protruding forward. It differs from other members of the genus in the following combination of characters: gaster sparsely covered with fine appressed hairs, separated by at least one fourth their length; pronotum with several fine transverse striations posteriorly; petiolar node slightly rugose at sides, smooth in back. Published description and key to Florida species of genus are found in Deyrup et al. (1985).

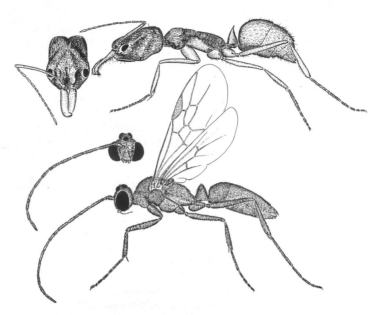

Desert Snapping Ant, *Odontomachus clarus* (courtesy of Mark Deyrup).

Distribution of the desert snapping ant, *Odontomachus clarus.*

RANGE: This ant occurs in Arizona, New Mexico, south Texas, and Mexico. In the eastern U.S. it is found on the Lake Wales Ridge in Highlands and Polk counties, and on the southern Brooksville Ridge in Citrus County.

HABITAT: It inhabits scrub and sandhill areas, either open or dense, in Florida.

LIFE HISTORY AND ECOLOGY: This species forages at night, or during the day under conditions of low light intensity. Nests are in sand, sometimes under fallen logs. Males fly on fall nights, with peaks of flight intensity associated with the full moon. The workers are generalist predators of arthropods; they subdue small prey with crushing snaps dealt by the ends of the mandibles, and larger prey are dismembered by the median shearing surfaces. The mandibles have a snapping device that allows them to suddenly release stored energy with such force that the mandibles, if they hit a solid object, can fling the ant into the air.

SPECIALIZED OR UNIQUE CHARACTERISTICS: This species is a particularly good example of an organism of southwestern origin now isolated on two old, high ridges, the Lake Wales Ridge and the Brooksville Ridge.

BASIS FOR STATUS CLASSIFICATION: The eastern population of *O. clarus* is confined to Lake Wales Ridge and southern Brooksville Ridge scrub and sandhill habitats, little of which remain in a natural state. It does not persist in disturbed habitats. There are only three protected populations.

RECOMMENDATIONS: Habitat preservation on the southern Lake Wales and Brooksville Ridges is needed to protect this and many other species.

PREPARED BY: Mark Deyrup, Archbold Biological Station, Lake Placid, FL 33852.

FAMILY FORMICIDAE

Rare

Jamaican Fungus Ant
Trachymyrmex jamaicensis (Andre)

DESCRIPTION: The large size (about 5 mm [0.2 in]), dark brown color, and dense covering of spines and tubercles distinguish this species from all other Florida ants. Florida specimens show significant differences from all

West Indian populations studied, and it is possible that the Florida population is a distinct species or subspecies.

RANGE: This ant is found in the West Indies, with a population in extreme south Florida.

HABITAT: It occurs in tropical hardwood hammocks.

LIFE HISTORY AND ECOLOGY: This species constructs nests with prominent turrets of stems and leaf fragments in shaded areas of tropical hammocks. Workers forage during the day, gathering vegetable matter, especially bits of flowers and caterpillar droppings. This material is carried to underground chambers, where it is modified to form the mushroom beds upon which the ants feed. The Jamaican fungus ant does not defoliate plants, as do some tropical species of *Atta* and *Acromyrmex*. A winged individual was collected in November.

SPECIALIZED OR UNIQUE CHARACTERISTICS: There is preliminary evidence that this ant may have been in Florida long enough to become morphologically distinct. It is the largest eastern fungus-growing ant.

BASIS FOR STATUS CLASSIFICATION: This species is abundant only on Elliott Key in Biscayne Bay National Monument. It is rare on several keys from Big Pine to Key Largo and has been seen once in Broward County and once in Martin County. It is possible that this species is susceptible to spraying for mosquitos, which could affect the ants directly or indirectly through the caterpillars that are important in providing pre-digested compost material for the fungus gardens. Its habitat is also disappearing over much of its range.

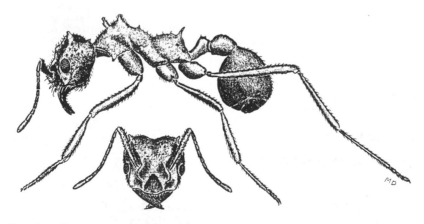

Jamaican Fungus Ant, *Trachymyrmex jamaicensis* (courtesy of Mark Deyrup).

Distribution of the
Jamaican fungus
ant, *Trachymyrmex
jamaicensis.*

RECOMMENDATIONS: Research is needed to identify the factors contributing to the rarity of this species. It seems suggestive that this species is abundant on Elliott Key, where there is almost no pesticide spraying. Aerial spraying should be regarded as a destructive practice in any area where preservation of native flora and fauna is a primary goal.

PREPARED BY: Mark Deyrup, Archbold Biological Station, Lake Placid, FL 33852.

FAMILY FORMICIDAE

Status Undetermined

Striate Aphaenogaster Ant
Aphaenogaster mariae Forel

DESCRIPTION: The worker ants have elongate legs and antennae, long narrow heads, and relatively large size (over 5 mm [0.2 in]). This species differs from other *Aphaenogaster* in having the anterior half of the gaster finely striate. Published keys are found in Creighton (1950).

RANGE: This species is known from New York west to Iowa, south to Florida. There are no known sites from Florida, but the type is from an unspecified Florida site.

HABITAT: It occurs in mixed hardwood forest (Wesson and Wesson 1940, Carter 1962).

LIFE HISTORY AND ECOLOGY: The biology of this species is almost unknown. Wheeler (1910) suspected that this species was a temporary nest parasite of some other species of *Aphaenogaster*, but this idea, which was based on the morphology of *A. mariae*, has never been confirmed. The rarity of this species throughout its range might give some flimsy support to this idea, since parasitic ant species often occur at low population levels. Nests have been seen in cavities and rotten stubs of live trees, which would make *A. lamellidens* the most probable host.

BASIS FOR STATUS CLASSIFICATION: Apparently, there have been no Florida records for more than a century. Like other species of *Aphaenog-*

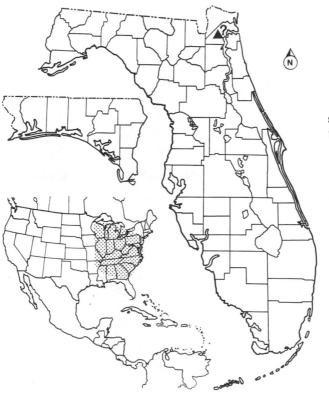

Distribution of the striate aphaenogaster, *Aphaenogaster mariae.*

aster, A. mariae is relatively large and should have been found by one of Florida's myrmecologists, including a graduate student who made a special study of the genus in north Florida (Carroll 1975). *A. mariae* may also be at the southern limit of its range in north Florida.

RECOMMENDATIONS: No recommendations are possible until this species has been rediscovered and its range and habitat identified.

PREPARED BY: Mark Deyrup, Archbold Biological Station, Lake Placid, FL 33852.

FAMILY FORMICIDAE

Status Undetermined

Yellow-Chested Cone-Ant

Dorymyrmex flavopectus

DESCRIPTION: Like other members of its genus, the worker of this species has a conspicuous cone-shaped hump on the epinotum. *D. flavopectus* is distinguished from other Florida species by the contrast between the orange thorax and the black head and gaster. Until the southeastern species were reviewed by Trager (1988), the name *flavopectus* was applied to more than one species. Published description and keys to southeastern species are found in Trager (1988), Johnson (1989).

RANGE: This species is known from Highlands, Lake, Marion, and Putnam counties.

HABITAT: It occurs in sand pine scrub, especially open stands of *Ceratiola ericoides*.

LIFE HISTORY AND ECOLOGY: This is a diurnal species occurring in the most open and sterile habitats of Florida scrub. It is absent from many apparently suitable sites. Where it occurs, it is usually a dominant species, apparently forming very large extended colonies. It is not known whether colonies of this species have multiple queens. Queens and males have been found in June.

BASIS FOR STATUS CLASSIFICATION: Although this species is locally abundant, it has strict habitat requirements. Not only does it need Florida scrub, a dwindling habitat, but it also requires that the scrub be managed so that there are persistent patches of bare sand. Further research may show that *D. flavopectus* should be placed in the rare category.

Distribution of the
yellow-chested
cone-ant, *Dory-
myrmex flavopectus.*

RECOMMENDATIONS: This is one of a complex of species, including several plants, that require open scrub with bare sand. The preservation of this ant is linked to that of many other interesting species.

PREPARED BY: Mark Deyrup, Archbold Biological Station, Lake Placid, FL 33852.

FAMILY FORMICIDAE

Status Undetermined

Pitted Myrmica Ant
Myrmica punctiventris Roger

DESCRIPTION: There is only one species of *Myrmica* known from Florida. It is distinguished from other Florida ants by the following combination of characters: thorax coarsely striate on sides; epinotal spines long and curved; gaster shining, with long hairs springing from small but distinct punctures.

RANGE: This ant occurs from Maine to Iowa, south to northern Florida. In Florida, it is known only from DeFuniak Springs in Walton County and Pine Barren in Escambia County.

HABITAT: It inhabits moist bottomland hardwood forests.

LIFE HISTORY AND ECOLOGY: Colonies in the Florida population occur in small cavities in heavy leaf litter; a queen was not found in every cavity. Workers are diurnal and conspicuous as they forage for insects among the dead leaves.

BASIS FOR STATUS CLASSIFICATION: This species is definitely not widespread in north Florida, and might be confined to a few sites. It has not been found in Torreya State Park or Florida Caverns State Park, both of which have relict populations of northern organisms. It is not known whether the Florida populations are highly disjunct (like *Formica subsericea* in Liberty County) or whether there are populations in southern Georgia.

Distribution of the pitted myrmica ant, *Myrmica punctiventris.*

RECOMMENDATIONS: More research is needed to establish the distribution of this species in Florida. There are preliminary indications that parts of Walton and Escambia counties have concentrations of isolated populations of invertebrates.

PREPARED BY: Mark Deyrup, Archbold Biological Station, Lake Placid, FL 33852.

FAMILY FORMICIDAE

Status Undetermined

Slave-Making Ant

Polyergus sp.

DESCRIPTION: Only one species of *Polyergus* is known from Florida. This species is distinguished from other Florida ants of the subfamily Formicinae by its long, sickle-shaped, finely serrate mandibles. Florida specimens have been referred to the species *P. lucidus* (Trager and Johnson 1985), but they probably represent an undescribed species (James Trager 1990, pers. comm.).

RANGE: The range is unclear, due to taxonomic uncertainties. In Florida it is known only from an isolated sandhill area in Alachua County and a sandhill area in Putnam County.

HABITAT: It has been found in turkey oak and longleaf pine sandhill, with sparse clumps of wiregrass and patches of gopher apple (Trager and Johnson 1985).

LIFE HISTORY AND ECOLOGY: (Condensed from Trager and Johnson 1985.) During late spring and summer raiding columns of this slave-maker emerge around 5:00-6:30 p.m. The raiders, about 25–50 strong, go to the nests of *Formica archboldi*, enter the nests, and return home bearing pupae of *F. archboldi*. When these pupae transform to adults, they do nest maintenance and brood care for the *Polyergus*. The *Polyergus*, with the help of their slaves, periodically relocate the nest, thus avoiding total depletion of the nearby colonies of *F. archboldi*. Queens and males flew 11:15–11:45 a.m. on hot, cloudless days in June and early July.

BASIS FOR STATUS CLASSIFICATION: The Florida population of *Polyergus* appears to be a distinct species. It may have an extraordinarily restricted range and, because of the low size of the effective breeding population, precarious prospects. On the other hand, it may be quite widespread in

Distribution of the
slave-making ant,
Polyergus sp.

the remaining sandhills of north Florida and even into adjacent states. If the latter is true, it is surprising that the species has not been seen elsewhere, as the raids are conspicuous events, even if they do occur after "working hours."

RECOMMENDATIONS: Further research is needed on the distribution and abundance of this species.

PREPARED BY: Mark Deyrup, Archbold Biological Station, Lake Placid, FL 33852.

Order Hymenoptera
FAMILY MUTILLIDAE

INTRODUCTION: Mutillids, or velvet ants, are solitary wasps whose larvae feed on mature larvae or pupae of solitary bees and wasps. Females are wingless, while the males are winged. Since long-range dispersal is difficult for females, and host species may be confined to a particular habitat, species of velvet ants could easily become restricted to small geographic areas. There is some evidence that this has occurred, as there is a confusing array of named subspecies but, in general, southeastern mutillids, even the rarely collected species, seem to be rather widely distributed. There are several Florida species that may be genuinely rare insects, but there is always the possibility that they are more elusive than rare. The single species listed as rare in this volume is very common in a small geographic area, making the absence of records from elsewhere more convincing.

PREPARED BY: Mark Deyrup, Archbold Biological Station, Lake Placid, FL 33852.

FAMILY MUTILLIDAE

Rare

Lake Wales Ridge Velvet Ant
Dasymutilla archboldi Schmidt and Mickel

DESCRIPTION: The female of this velvet ant is distinguished from other Florida velvet ants by the following combination of characters: conspicuous appressed silvery hairs on top of head; no protuberances on the posterolateral areas of head; scutellar scale narrow, hardly wider than long; posterior face of epinotum with small sparse tubercles, usually not clearly reticulate; tergites 2-5 with an apical band of silvery hairs, this band interrupted medially on tergite 2 by a patch of black hairs. Published descriptions are found in Schmidt and Mickel (1979), and Manley (1983, 1984).

RANGE: This species is found on Lake Wales Ridge in Highlands and Polk counties, and an isolated scrub in Osceola County.

HABITAT: It occurs in open sand pine scrub, including sand roads and firelanes.

LIFE HISTORY AND ECOLOGY: Within its restricted range, this is probably the most abundant velvet ant of open sandy uplands. Its hosts are unknown, but judging from the great size variation in adult *D. archboldi*, there are probably several species of hosts. This species is unusual among members of the genus *Dasymutilla* in that the male is consistently much larger than the female (Deyrup and Manley 1986).

Lake Wales Ridge
Velvet Ant, *Dasymu-
tilla archboldi*
(courtesy of Mark
Deyrup).

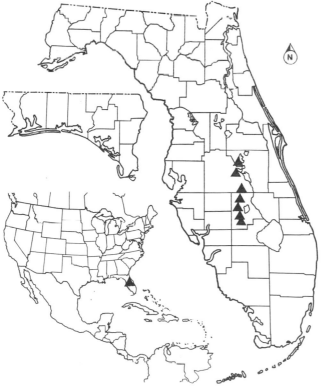

Distribution of the
Lake Wales Ridge
velvet ant,
*Dasymutilla
archboldi.*

BASIS FOR STATUS CLASSIFICATION: The restricted geographic range of this species and its dependence on a habitat that is rapidly disappearing automatically places this species in the "rare" category.

RECOMMENDATIONS: Good populations of this species occur on two protected sites (Archbold Biological Station and The Nature Conservancy Tiger Creek Preserve) that are managed to maintain the open habitats required. It is almost certain to be found in the Arbuckle State Forest.

PREPARED BY: Mark Deyrup, Archbold Biological Station, Lake Placid, FL 33852.

FAMILY MUTILLIDAE

Status Undetermined

Nocturnal Scrub Velvet Ant
Photomorphus archboldi Manley and Deyrup

DESCRIPTION: Only males are known. This velvet ant is distinguished from other Florida velvet ants by its whitish legs, pale reddish brown body color, and the shape of the metasternal and mesosternal processes. A published description is found in Manley and Deyrup (1987).

RANGE: This species is known from Highlands and Marion counties and probably occurs in the appropriate habitat elsewhere in inland Florida, especially Polk County.

HABITAT: It inhabits sand pine scrub.

LIFE HISTORY AND ECOLOGY: Males have been collected in Malaise traps (flight intercept traps) from April through October. This species, like other members of its genus, is active at night.

BASIS FOR STATUS CLASSIFICATION: This is a highly distinctive species that has not been found outside Florida, though velvet ants have been "popular" with insect collectors for decades. It is likely to be restricted to open scrub habitat, which is itself scarce, and could easily be missing from some scrub areas.

RECOMMENDATIONS: This species joins a long list of organisms that seem to be restricted to Florida scrub habitat, and would benefit from any

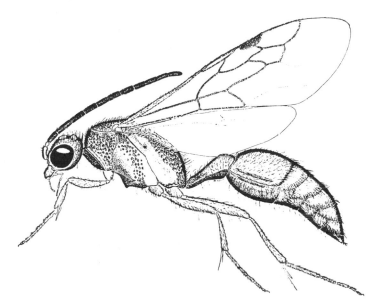

Nocturnal Scrub Velvet Ant, *Photomorphus archboldi* (courtesy of
Mark Deyrup).

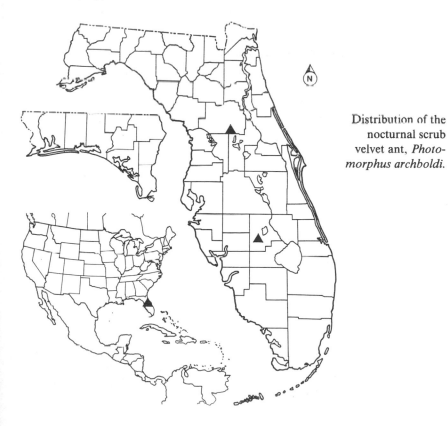

Distribution of the
nocturnal scrub
velvet ant, *Photo-
morphus archboldi*.

effort to preserve that habitat. More specific recommendations are impossible because we know nothing of the biological requirements of the species.

PREPARED BY: Mark Deyrup, Archbold Biological Station, Lake Placid, FL 33852.

Order Hymenoptera
SUPERFAMILY APOIDEA

INTRODUCTION: The Apoidea, or bees, are completely dependent on the pollen and nectar of plants, and it is not unusual to find species that are associated with a single genus or species of plant. In addition, some species are particular about nesting sites. For these reasons, one would expect that Florida's rich fauna of bees would include a number of documented examples of species that are rare and endangered, but, as usual with insects, the documentation is almost completely lacking. There are a number of species known from only one or a few sites, other species that probably have small southern range extensions into small areas of northern Florida, and others that seem confined to beach dune areas. As nobody has ever thoroughly studied the distribution of bees in Florida, we have only one species that can be listed below.

PREPARED BY: Mark Deyrup, Archbold Biological Station, Lake Placid, FL 33852.

Order Hymenoptera
FAMILY COLLETIDAE

Rare

Eastern Caupolicana Bee
Caupolicana electa (Cresson)

DESCRIPTION: About 20 mm (0.8 in) in length, this is one of the largest solitary bees in Florida. The thorax, legs, and first gastral segment are densely covered with golden-orange hair. The remainder of the gaster is black, typically with a narrow white band on segments 2-4. Published descriptions are found in Mitchell (1960) and Mitchner (1966).

RANGE: This bee occurs in the coastal plain from North Carolina to Florida and Alabama. In Florida it is known from Dade, Okaloosa, and Highlands counties.

HABITAT: It occurs in sand pine scrub.

LIFE HISTORY AND ECOLOGY: In Florida the adults appear in September. They are known to be active from about 3:00 p.m. to twilight and from about 8:00 a.m. to 10:00 a.m. Many individuals have been observed, and activity does not seem to occur at night or early morning. Only nectar-feeding individuals have been seen; the pollen host plant is unknown. Nectar hosts are *Seymeria pectinata*, *Dicerandra frutescens*, and *Trichostema suffrutescens*. This species is an efficient nectar robber, slitting flowers with a quick thrust of the sharp galeae.

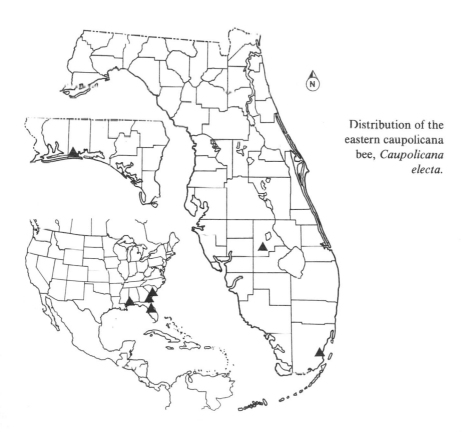

Distribution of the eastern caupolicana bee, *Caupolicana electa.*

BASIS FOR STATUS CLASSIFICATION: This species is known only from a few sandhill and scrub areas. It is a large and conspicuous insect that should have been noted by Florida hymenopterists if it were at all common. It is also vulnerable to Malaise traps, which have been set up in many sites in Florida, apparently without yielding any specimens of *C. electa*. Its habitat is also disappearing rapidly through much of the state. The Dade County record, for example, is from 60 years ago (Graenicher 1930), and it is extremely unlikely that the species persists in the Miami area.

RECOMMENDATIONS: The preservation and management of open sand pine scrub habitat is probably necessary for preservation of this species. Research aimed at identifying the pollen host and nesting site is needed if there is to be any directed conservation effort.

PREPARED BY: Mark Deyrup, Archbold Biological Station, Lake Placid, FL 33852.

Contributors

WRITERS

Arnfried Antonius, Florida Reef Foundation, P.O. Drawer 1468, Homestead, FL 33030.

Kurt Auffenberg, Florida Museum of Natural History, University of Florida, P.O. Box 117800, Gainesville, FL 32611-7800.

Robert S. Butler, U.S. Fish and Wildlife Service, 3100 University Boulevard South, Jacksonville, FL 32216.

John V. Calhoun, Florida State Collection of Arthropods, P.O. Box 147100, Gainesville, FL 32614-7100.

Jane E. Deisler-Seno, Corpus Christi Museum of Science and History, 1900 N. Chaparral, Corpus Christi, TX 78401.

Mark Deyrup, Archbold Biological Station, P.O. Box 2057, Lake Placid, FL 33852.

Sidney W. Dunkle,, Biology Department, Collins County Community College, 2800 East Spring Creek Parkway, Plano TX 75074.

G. B. Edwards, Florida State Collection of Arthropods, P.O. Box 147100, Gainesville, FL 32614-7100.

K. C. Emerson, 560 Boulder Drive, Sanibel, FL 32957.

Thomas C. Emmel, Department of Zoology, University of Florida, P.O. Box 118525, Gainesville, FL 32611-8525.

Richard Franz, Florida Museum of Natural History, University of Florida, P.O. Box 117800, Gainesville, FL 32611-7800.

Krista E. M. Galley, Department of Entomology, Cornell University, Ithaca, NY 14853.

Robert H. Gore, Naithloriendum Wildlife Sanctuary, P.O. Box 10053, Naples, FL 33941.

Walter C. Japp, Florida Marine Research Institute, 100 8th Avenue SE, St. Petersburg, FL 33701

L. Philip Lounibos, Florida Medical Entomology Laboratory, 200 9th St SE, Vero Beach, FL 32960.

William G. Lyons, Florida Department of Environmental Protection, Marine Research Laboratory, 100 Eight Avenue SE, St. Petersburg, FL 33701.

Barry D. Mansell, 2826 Rosselle Street, Jacksonville, FL 32205.

Samuel D. Marshall, Department of Zoology, University of Tennessee, Knoxville, TN 37996.

Marc C. Minno, Department of Zoology, University of Florida, P.O. Box 118525, Gaineville, FL 32611-8525.

Tom Morris, 2629 N.W. 12th Avenue, Gainesville, FL 32605.
John C. Morse, Department of Entomology, Clemson University, Clemson, SC 29634.
L. L. Pechuman, Department of Entomology, Cornell University, Ithaca, NY 14853.
William L. Peters, Laboratory of Aquatic Entomology, University P.O. 111, Florida A & M University, Tallahassee, FL 32307.
Roger W. Portell, Florida Museum of Natural History, University of Florida, P.O. Box 117800, Gainesville, FL 32611-7800.
Kevin S. Schindler, Florida Museum of Natural History, University of Florida, P.O. Box 117800, Gainesville, FL 32611-7800.
Paul E. Skelley, Florida State Collection of Arthropods, P.O. Box 147100, Gainesville, FL 32614-7100.
Micheal C. Thomas, Florida State Collection of Arthropods, P.O. Box 147100, Gainesville, FL 32614-7100.
Fred G. Thompson, Florida Museum of Natural History, University of Florida, P.O. Box 117800, Gainesville, FL 32611-7800.
Carol Mullinex Tibbets, Florida State Collection of Arthropods, P.O. Box 147100, Gainesville, FL 32614- 7100.
Thomas J. Walker, Department of Entomology and Nematology, University of Florida, P. O. Box 110620, Gainesville, FL 32611-0620.
H. K. Wallace (deceased), Department of Zoology, University of Florida.
Howard Weems, Florida State Collection of Arthropods, P.O. Box 147100, Gainesville, FL 32614-7100.
James D. Williams, National Biological Survey, 7920 N.W. 71st Street, Gainesville, FL 32606.
Robert E. Woodruff, Florida State Collection of Arthropods, P.O. Box 14700, Gainesville, FL 32614-7100.
David G. Young, 1324 SW 98th Street, Gainesville, FL 32601.

PHOTOGRAPHERS and ILLUSTRATORS

Ray Ashton, 611 NW 79th Drive, Gainesville, FL 32607.
Arnfried Antonius, Florida Reef Foundation, P.O. Drawer 1468, Homestead, FL 33030.
Kurt Auffenberg, Florida Museum of Natural History, University of Florida, P.O. Box 117800, Gainesville, FL 32611-7800.
Mark Deyrup, Archbold Biological Station, P.O. Box 2057, Lake Placid, FL 33852.
Sidney W. Dunkle, Biology Department, Collins County Community College, 2000 East Spring Creek Parkway, Plano, TX 75074.
G. B. Edwards, Florida State Collection of Arthropods, P.O. Box 147100, Gainesville, FL 32614-7100.
Thomas C. Emmel, Department of Zoology, University of Florida, P.O. Box 118525, Gainesville, FL 32611-8525
Shelley E. Franz, P.O. Box 1044, Melrose, FL 32666.
John B. Heppner, Florida State Collection of Arthropods, P.O. Box 147100, Gainesville, FL 32614-7100.

Horton H. Hobbs Jr., National Museum of Natural History, Washington, D.C. 20560.

William F. Loftus, South Florida Research Center, Everglades National Park, P.O. 279, Homestead, FL 33030

Barry D. Mansell, 2826 Rosselle Street, Jacksonsville, FL 32205.

Royal Ontario Museum (C. John McNeill, Director), 100 Queen's Park, Toronto 5, Ontario, Canada. (they hold the copyright for Wiggins' caddisfly book)

Paul E. Skelley, Florida State Collection of Arthropods, P.O. Box 147100, Gainesville, FL 32614-7100.

Michael C. Thomas, Florida State Collection of Arthropods, P.O. 147100, Gainesville, FL 32614-7100.

Fred G. Thompson, Florida Museum of Natural History, University of Florida, P.O. Box 117800, Gainesville, FL 32611.

James D. Williams, National Biological Survey, 7920 NW 71st Street, Gainesville, FL 32606

Thomas J. Walker, Department of Entomology, University of Florida, Gainesville, FL 32611-7800.

Robert E. Woodruff, Florida State Collection of Arthropods, P.O. Box 147100, Gainesville, FL 32614-7100.

Howard V. Weems, Florida State Collection of Arthropods, P.O. Box 147100, Gainesville, FL 32614-7100.

Literature Cited

CORALS AND SEA FANS

Almy, C. C., and C. Carrion-Torres. 1963. Shallow-water stony corals of Puerto Rico. Carib. J. Sci. 3:133-162.

Antonius, A. 1977. Coral mortality in reefs: A problem for science and management. Proc. 3rd Int. Coral Reef Symp., Univ. Miami, 2:623-681.

———. 1981. Coral reef pathology: A review. Proc. 4th Int. Coral Reef Symp., Univ. Philippines, Manila, 2:3-6.

———. 1985a. Coral diseases in the Indo-Pacific: A first record. P.S.Z.N.I.: Marine Ecology 6:197-218.

———. 1985b. Black band disease infection experiments on hexacorals and octocorals. Proc. 5th Int. Coral Reef Congr., Tahiti. Ant. Mus. EPHE, Moorea, 6:155-160.

Bayer, F. M. 1961. The shallow water Octocorallia of the West Indian region. Martinus Nijhoff, The Hague, 373 pp.

Colin, P. I. 1978. Caribbean reef invertebrates. T.F.H. Publications, Inc., Neptune, N.J., 512 pp.

Duarte Bello, P. P. 1960. Corales de los Arrecifes Cubanos. Edit. Acuario Nac., 85 pp.

Geister, J. 1972. Zur Oekologie und Wuchsform der Saulenkoralle *Dendrogyra cylindrus* Ehrenberg. Beobachtungen in den Riffen der Insel San Andres (Karibisches Meer, Kolumbien). Mitt. Inst. Colombo-Aleman Invest. Cient. 6:77-87.

Opresko, D. M. 1974. A study of the classification of the Antipatharia (Coelenterata: Anthozoa) with redescription of eleven species. Ph.D. thesis, Univ. Miami. 192 pp.

Roos, P. J. 1964. The distribution of reef corals in Curacao. Stud. Fauna Curacao 20:1-51.

———. 1971. The shallow-water stony corals of the Netherlands Antilles. Stud. Fauna Curacao 37:1-108.

Smith, F. G. W. 1948. Atlantic reef corals (second printing 1972). University of Miami Press, 164 pp.

Warner, G. F. 1981. Species descriptions and ecological observations of black corals (Antipatharia) from Trinidad. Bull. Mar. Sci. 31:147-163.

Wells, J. W. 1973. New and old Scleractinian corals from Jamaica. Bull. Mar. Sci. 23:16-58.

Wood, E. M. 1983. Corals of the world. T.F.H. Publications, Inc., Neptune, N.J., 256 pp.

Zlatarski, V. N., and N. Martinez Estalella. 1982. Les Scleractiniaires de Cuba. Bulgarian Academy of Sciences Press, Sofia, 472 pp.

Mollusks
MARINE BIVALVES

Johnson, C. W. 1890. Annotated list of the shells of St. Augustine, Fla. Nautilus 4(1):4–6.

―――. 1904. *Panopea bitruncata* Conrad. Nautilus 18(7):73–75.

―――. 1919. An old collecting ground revisited. Nautilus 33(1):1–8.

―――. 1929. Are certain marine pelecypods becoming locally extinct? Nautilus 42(3):82–86.

Johnson, M. C. 1956. A living specimen of the east coast geoduck from St. Augustine, Florida. Nautilus 69(4):121–123.

Pope, V. A. 1955 (1954). The geoduck clam in Florida. Quart. J. Florida Acad. Sci. 17(4):252.

Robertson, R. 1963. Bathymetric and geographic distribution of *Panopea bitruncata*. Nautilus 76(3):75–82.

FRESHWATER BIVALVES

Athearn, H. D. 1964. Three new unionids from Alabama and Florida and a note on *Lampsilis jonesi*. Nautilus 77(4):134–139.

Baker, F. C. 1898. The Mollusca of the Chicago area: The Pelecypoda. Chicago Acad. Sci. Bull. No. 3. 130 pp.

Bass, D. G. 1974. Ecological distribution of the introduced Asiatic clam, *Corbicula manilensis*, in Florida. Florida Game and Fresh Water Fish Commission, Tallahassee, Florida. 32 pp.

Branson, B. A. 1969. *Glebula* in Oklahoma. Sterkiana 36:22.

Burch, J. B. 1975. Freshwater unionacean clams (Mollusca: Pelecypoda) of North America. Malacological Publications, Hamburg, MI. 204 pp.

Burch, J. Q. 1944. Checklist of west American mollusks. Minutes, Conchological Club Southern California 38:18.

Butler, R. S. 1989. Distributional records for freshwater mussels (Bivalvia: Unionidae) in Florida and south Alabama, with zoogeographic and taxonomic notes. Walkerana 3(10):239–261.

Clarke, A. H. 1981. The tribe Alasmidontini (Unionidae: Anodontinae), part I: *Pegias, Alasmidonta*, and *Arcidens*. Smithsonian Contrib. Zool. No. 326. 101 pp.

Clench, W. J., and R. D. Turner. 1956. Freshwater mollusks of Alabama, Georgia, and Florida from the Escambia to the Suwannee River. Bull. Fl. St. Mus. 1(3):97–239.

Frierson, L. S. 1904. Observations on the genus *Quadrula*. Nautilus 17(10): 111–112.

―――. 1927. A classified and annotated check list of the North American naiades. Baylor University Press, Waco, Texas. 111 pp.

Fuller, S. L. H. 1974. Clams and mussels (Mollusca: Bivalvia). Pp. 215–273 in Hart, C. W., Jr., and S. L. H. Fuller, eds. Pollution ecology of freshwater invertebrates. Academic Press, New York. 389 pp.

Fuller, S. L. H., and D. J. Bereza. 1973. Recent additions to the naiad fauna of the eastern Gulf drainage (Bivalvia: Unionida: Unionidae). Assoc. Southeastern Biologists Bulletin 20(2):53.

Gordon, M. E. 1983. A pre-European occurrence of *Glebula rotundata* (Bivalvia: Unionidae) in Arkansas. Nautilus 97(1):42.

_____. 1984. First occurrence of *Anodonta suborbiculata* Say (Unionidae: Anodontinae) in Oklahoma. Southwestern Naturalist 29(2):233–234.

Heard, W. H. 1979. Identification manual of the freshwater clams of Florida. Florida Department of Environmental Regulation Technical Series 4(2). 82 pp.

Heard, W. H., and R. H. Guckert. 1971. A re-evaluation of the recent Unionacea (Pelecypoda) of North America. Malacologia 10(2):333–355.

Johnson, R. I. 1967. Additions to the unionid fauna of the Gulf drainage of Alabama, Georgia and Florida (Mollusca: Bivalvia). Breviora No. 270. 21 pp.

_____. 1969. Further additions to the unionid fauna of the Gulf drainage of Alabama, Georgia and Florida. Nautilus 83(1):34–35.

_____. 1970. The systematics and zoogeography of the Unionidae (Mollusca: Bivalvia) of the Southern Atlantic Slope Region. Bull. Mus. Comp. Zool. 140(6):263–450.

_____. 1977. Monograph of the genus *Medionidus* (Bivalvia: Unionidae) mostly from the Apalachicolan Region, southeastern United States. Occ. Pap. Mollusks 4(56):161–187.

_____. 1980. Zoogeography of North American Unionacea (Mollusca: Bivalvia) north of the maximum Pleistocene glaciation. Bull. Mus. Comp. Zool. 149(2):77–189.

Jorgenson, S. E., and R. W. Sharp, eds. 1971. Proceedings of a symposium on rare and endangered mollusks (naiades) of the U.S. U.S. Department of the Interior, Fish and Wildlife Service, Bureau of Sport Fisheries and Wildlife, Washington, D.C. 1–79.

Lea, I. 1863a. Descriptions of the soft parts and some embryonic forms of 143 species of Unionidae of the United States. Journ. Acad. Nat. Sci. Phila. 2(5):401–456.

_____. 1863b. Observations on the genus *Unio*. Vol. 9. Isaac Lea, privately published. Philadelphia. 180 pp.

_____. 1863c. Observations on the genus *Unio*. Vol. 10. Isaac Lea, privately published. Philadelphia. 94 pp.

_____. 1874. Observations on the genus *Unio* together with descriptions of new species in the family Unionidae, and descriptions of embryonic forms and soft parts, also, new species of Strepomatidae, Limnaeidae. Vol. 13. Philadelphia. 75 pp.

Ortmann, A. E. 1912. Notes upon the families and genera of the naiades. Annals Carnegie Mus. 8(2):222–365.

_____. 1914. Studies in Naiades. Nautilus 28(2):20–22.

_____. 1919. A monograph of the Naiades of Pennsylvania, part 3: Systematic account of the genera and species. Memoirs Carnegie Mus. 8(1). 385 pp.

_____. 1924. Notes on the anatomy and taxonomy of certain Lampsilinae from the Gulf drainage. Nautilus 37(4):137–144.

Schneider, R. F. 1967. Range of the Asiatic clam in Florida. Nautilus 81(2):68–69.

Schuster, G. A. 1988. Distribution of unionids (Mollusca: Unionidae) in Kentucky. Kentucky Department of Fish and Wildlife Resources, Project 2-437-R. 1099 pp.

Simpson, C. T. 1900a. Synopsis of the Naiades. Proc. Natl. Mus. Nat. Hist. 22:501-1044.

———. 1900b. New and unfigured Unionidae. Proc. Acad. Nat. Sci. Phila. 52:74-86.

———. 1914. A descriptive catalogue of the Naiades or pearly fresh-water mussels. Bryant Walker, Detroit, MI. 1540 pp.

Stansbery, D. H. 1971. A study of the growth rate and longevity of the naiad *Amblema plicata* (Say 1817) in Lake Erie (Bivalvia: Unionidae). American Malacological Union Annual Reports for 1970. 78-79.

Surber, T. 1915. Identification of the glochidia of freshwater mussels. Appendix 5 to the Report of the U.S. Commissioner of Fisheries for 1914, U.S. Bureau of Fisheries Document No. 813. 1-9.

Turgeon, D. D., A. E. Bogan, E. V. Coan, W. K. Emerson, W. G. Lyons, W. L. Pratt, C. F. E. Roper, A. Scheltema, F. G. Thompson, and J. D. Williams. 1988. Common and scientific names of aquatic invertebrates from the United States and Canada: mollusks. American Fisheries Society Special Publication 16. 277 pp.

van der Schalie, H. 1940. The naiad fauna of the Chipola River, in northwestern Florida. Lloydia 3:191-208.

Vidrine, M. F. 1985. Fresh-water mussels (Unionacea) of Louisiana; a zoogeographical checklist of post-1890 records. Louisiana Environmental Professional 2(1):50-59.

Walker, B. 1901. A new species of *Strophitus*. Nautilus 15(6):65-66.

———. 1905. List of shells from northwestern Florida. Nautilus 18(2):133-136.

Wright, B. H. 1897. New Unionidae. Nautilus 12(1):5-6.

———. 1899. New southern unios. Nautilus 13(2):22-23.

TERRESTRIAL SNAILS

Binney, W. G. 1885. A Manual of American Land Shells. Bull. U.S. Natl. Museum, vol. 28. 528 pp.

Craig, A. K. 1972. Observations on the arboreal snail *Orthalicus floridensis*. Quart. J. Florida Acad. Sci. 35(1):15-20.

———. 1974. Endangered species status of the south Florida tree snails. Unpublished report to the U.S. Fish and Wildlife Service. 12 pp.

Davidson, T. 1965. Tree snails, gems of the Everglades. National Geographic 127(3):372-387.

Jones, A. 1977. The Florida tree snail—*Liguus fasciatus* Müller. Unpublished report to the U.S. Fish and Wildlife Service. 7 pp.

Pilsbry, H. A. 1946. Land Mollusca of North America, vol. 2, part 1. Monograph of the Academy of Natural Sciences, Philadelphia. 520 pp.

Thompson, F. G. 1980. Proposed technical review draft of the recovery plan for Stock Island tree snail. Unpublished report to U.S. Fish and Wildlife Service. 5 pp.

Voss, R. S. 1976. Observations on the ecology of the Florida tree snail, *Liguus fasciatus* (Müller). Nautilus 90(2):65–69.

FRESHWATER SNAILS

Clench, W. J., and R. Turner. 1956. Freshwater mollusks of Alabama, Georgia, and Florida from the Escambia to the Suwannee River. Bull. Fl. St. Mus. 1:(3):97–239.

Dall, W. H. 1885. Notes on some Florida land and freshwater shells. Proc. U.S. Natl. Museum 8:256–257.

Goodrich, C. 1924. The group of *Goniobasis catenaria*. Nautilus 42(1):28–32.

Thompson, F. G. 1968. The aquatic snails of the family Hydrobiidae of peninsular Florida, University of Florida Press, Gainesville. 268 pp.

Crustaceans
AMPHIPODS

Bousfield, E. L. 1963. New freshwater amphipod crustaceans from Florida. National Mus. Canada, Natural History Pap. no. 18: 1–9.

Franz, R., J. Bauer, and T. Morris. 1994. Review of biologically-significant caves and their faunas in Florida and south Georgia. Brimleyana (20:1–109).

Holsinger, J. R. 1972. The freshwater amphipod crustaceans (Gammaridae) of North America. Environmental Protection Agency. U.S. Printing Office. 88 pp.

———. 1977. A review of the systematics of the holarctic amphipod family Crangonyctidae. Crustaceana Suppl. 5. viii+88 pp.

Shoemaker, C. R. 1941. A new subterranean amphipod of the genus *Crangonyx* from Florida. Charleston Museum Leaflet no. 16. 9 pp.

ISOPODS

Bowman, T. E., and B. Sket 1985. *Remasellus*, a new genus for the troglobitic swimming Florida asellid isopod, *Asellus parva*. Proc. Biol. Soc. Wash. 98(3):554–560.

Franz, R., J. Bauer, and T. Morris. 1994. Review of biologically-significant caves and their faunas in Florida and south Georgia. Brimleyana (20:1–109).

Maloney, J. O. 1939. A new cave isopod from Florida. Proc. U.S. Natl. Mus. 86(3057):457–459.

Steeves, H. R., III. 1964. The troglobitic asellids of the United States: The hobbsi group. Amer. Mid. Nat. 71:445–451.

DECAPODS

Abele, L. G. 1974. Taxonomy, distribution and ecology of the genus *Sesarma* (Crustacea, Decapoda, Grapsidae) in eastern North America, with special reference to Florida. Amer. Midland Naturalist 90(2):375–386.

Anonymous. 1990. Final listing rules: Squirrel Chimney cave shrimp (*Palaemonetes cummingi*). Endang. Sp. Tech. Bull. 15(7):6.

Beever, J. W., III, D. Simberloff, and L. L. King. 1979. Herbivory and predation by the mangrove tree crab *Aratus pisonii*. Oecologica (Berlin) 43:317–328.

Bouchard, R. W. 1978. Taxonomy, ecology, and phylogeny of the subgenus *Depressicambarus*, with the description of a new species from Florida and the redescription of *Cambarus striatus* (Decapoda, Cambaridae). Bull. Ala. Mus. Nat. Hist. 3:27–60.

Burgess, G. H., and R. Franz. 1978. Zoogeography of the aquatic fauna of the St. Johns River system with comments on adjacent peninsular faunas. Amer. Midl. Natur. 100(1):160–170.

Caine, E. A. 1978. Comparative ecology of epigean and hypogean crayfish (Crustacea: Cambaridae) from northwest Florida. Amer. Midl. Natur. 99(2):315–329.

Chace, F. A., Jr. 1954. Two subterranean shrimp (Decapoda: Caridea) from Florida and the West Indies, with a revised key to the American species. J. Wash. Acad. Sci. 44:318–324.

Dickson, G. W., and R. Franz 1980. Respiration rates, ATP turnover, and adenylate energy charge in excised gills of surface and cave crayfishes. Comp. Biochem. Physiol. 65A:375–379.

Dobkin, S. 1971. The larval development of *Palaemonetes cummingi* Chace (Decapoda: Palaemonidae) reared in the laboratory. Crustaceana 20:285–297.

Franz, R., J. Bauer, and T. Morris. 1994. Review of biologically-significant caves and their faunas in Florida and south Georgia. Brimleyana. (20:1–109)

———. and L. M. Franz. 1979. Distribution, habitat preference and status of populations of the Black Creek Crayfish, *Procambarus (Ortmanicus) pictus* (Decapoda: Cambaridae). Fla. Sci. 42(1):13–17.

———. and S. E. Franz. 1990. A review of the Florida crayfish fauna, with comments on nomenclature, distribution, and conservation. Fla. Sci. 53(4): 286–296.

———. and H. H. Hobbs, Jr. 1983. *Procambarus (Ortmannicus) leitheuseri*, another troglobitic crayfish (Decapoda: Cambaridae) from peninsular Florida. Proc. Biol. Soc. Wash. 96(2):323–332.

———. and D. S. Lee. 1982. Distribution and evolution of troglobitic crayfishes of Florida. Bull. Fla. St. Mus. 28(3):53–78.

Hartnoll, R. G. 1965. Notes on the marine grapsid crabs of Jamaica. Proc. Linnaean Soc. London 176(2):113–147.

Hobbs, H. H., Jr. 1942. The crayfishes of Florida. Univ. Fl. Stud. Biol. Sci. Ser. 3(2). 179 pp.

———. 1958. The evolutionary history of the Pictus group of the crayfish genus *Procambarus*. Quart. J. Florida Acad. Sci. 21:71–91.

———. 1971. A new troglobitic crayfish from Florida. Quart. J. Fla. Acad. Sci. 34(2):114–124.

———. 1981. The crayfishes of Georgia. Smithsonian Contrib. Zool. 381. i–vii, 1–549.

———. and R. Franz. 1986. New troglobitic crayfish with comments on its relationship to epigean and other hypogean crayfishes of Florida. J. Crustacean Biol. 6(3):509–519.

————. and R. Franz. 1990. A new troglobitic crayfish, *Procambarus (Ortmannicus) morrisi* (Decapoda: Cambaridae) from Florida. Proc. Biol. Soc. Wash. 104(1):55–63.

————. and R. Franz. 1992. *Procambarus (Ortmannicus) attiguus*, a new troglobitic crayfish (Decapoda: Cambaridae) from the Saint Johns River basin, Florida. Proc. Biol. Soc. Wash. 105(2):359–365.

————. and H. H. Hobbs III. 1991. An illustrated key to the crayfishes of Florida (based on first form males). Florida Scientist 54(1):13–24.

————, ————, and M. A. Daniel. 1977. A review of the troglobitic decapod crustaceans of the Americas. Smithsonian Contrib. Zool. no. 244. 183 pp.

————. and D. S. Lee. 1976. A new troglobitic crayfish (Decapoda, Cambaridae) from peninsular Florida. Proc. Biol. Soc. Wash. 89(32):383–392.

————. and D. B. Means. 1972. Two new troglobitic crayfishes (Decapoda: Astacidae) from Florida. Proc. Biol. Soc. Wash. 84(44):393–410.

Holthuis, L. B. 1959. The Crustacea Decapoda of Suriname (Dutch Guiana). Zool. Verhandl. (44):1–296.

Mohr, C. E., and T. L. Poulson. 1966. Life of the cave. McGraw-Hill Book Co., New York. 232 pp.

Morris, T. 1989. Biological studies at Wakulla Springs. Pp. 175–179 W. C. Stone, ed. The Wakulla Springs project. U.S. Deep Caving Team, Deerwood, MD.

Rathbun, M. J. 1918. The grapsid crabs of America. Bull. U.S. Natl. Museum 97: i–xxii, 1–461.

Relyea, K., and B. Sutton. 1973 (1974). Egg-bearing in the troglobitic crayfish, *Procambarus pallidus* (Hobbs). Fla. Sci. 36(2–4):173–175.

————. and B. Sutton. 1975. A new troglobitic crayfish of the genus *Procambarus* from Florida (Decapoda: Astacidae). Tulane Stud. Zool. Bot. 19(1–2):8–16.

————., D. Blody, and K. Bankowski 1976. A Florida troglobitic crayfish: biogeographic implications. Fla. Sci. 39:71–72.

Streever, W. J. 1992. Report of a cave fauna kill at Peacock Springs Cave System, Suwannee County, Florida. Fla. Sci. 55(2):125–128.

Warner, G. F. 1968. The larval development of the mangrove tree crab, *Agatus pisonii* (H. Milne Edwards), reared in the laboratory (Brachyrura, Grapsidae). Crustaceana, Suppl. 2:249–258.

Warren, R. D. 1961. The obligative cavernicoles of Florida. Fla. Speleol. Soc. Spec. Pap. no. 1.

Wood, D. A. 1991. Official lists of endangered and potentially endangered fauna and flora in Florida. Fla. Game and Fresh Water Fish Commission, unpubl. report. 23 pp.

Arachnids
SPIDERS

Brady, A. R. 1972. Geographic variation and speciation in the *Sosippus floridanus* species group (Araneae: Lycosidae). Psyche 79(1–2):27–48.

Edwards, G. B. 1978. Two new southern *Phidippus* (Araneae: Salticidae). Fla. Entomologist 61(2):77–82.

Gertsch, W. J., and N. I. Platnick. 1975. A revision of the trapdoor spider genus *Cyclocosmia* (Araneae, Ctenizidae). Amer. Mus. Novit. 2580. 20 pp.

————. 1980. The nearctic Atypidae. Amer. Mus. Novit. 2704. 39 pp.

Levi, H. W. 1977. The American orb-weaver genera *Cyclosa*, *Metazygia*, and *Eustala* north of Mexico (Araneae, Araneidae). Bull. Mus. Comp. Zool. 148(3):61–127.

McCrone, J. D. 1963. Taxonomic status and evolutionary history of the *Geolycosa pikei* complex in the southeastern United States (Araneae, Lycosidae). Amer. Midl. Natur. 70(1):47–73.

————. and H. W. Levi. 1964. North American widow spiders of the *Latrodectus curacaviensis* group (Araneae: Theridiidae). Psyche 71(1):12–27.

————. and K. J. Stone. 1965. The widow spiders of Florida. Arthropods of Florida and neighboring land areas, vol. 2. Florida Department of Agriculture, Division of Plant Industry, Gainesville.

Platnick, N. I., and M. U. Shadab. 1980. A revision of the spider genus *Cesonia* (Araneae: Gnaphosidae). Bull. Amer. Museum Nat. Hist. 165(4):337–385.

Reiskind, J. 1987. Status of the rosemary wolf spider in Florida. Univ. Fla. Coop. Fish. Wildl. Res. Unit. Tech. Rep. 28:1–13.

Richman, D. B. 1981. A revision of *Habrocestum* (Araneae: Salticidae) in North America. Bull. Amer. Museum Nat. Hist. 170:197–206.

Roth, V. D. 1985. Spider genera of North America. American Arachnological Society. Not paginated.

Wallace, H. K. 1942. A study of the *lenta* group of the genus *Lycosa* with descriptions of new species (Araneae, Lycosidae). Amer. Mus. Novit. 1185:1–21, 28 figs.

WHIP SCORPIONS

Mullinex, C. L. 1975. Revision of *Paraphrynus* Moreno (Amblypygida: Phrynidae) for North America and the Antilles. Occ. Pap. Cal. Acad. Sci. 116:1–80.

Muma, M. H. 1967. Scorpions, whip scorpions and wind scorpions of Florida. Arthropods of Florida and neighboring land areas, vol. 4. Florida Dept. Agric. 28 pp.

MILLIPEDES

Causey, N. B. 1957. *Floridobolus*, a new millipede genus (Spirobolidae). Proc. Biol. Soc. Wash. 70:205–208.

Insects
MAYFLIES

Berner, L., and M. L. Pescador. 1988. The mayflies of Florida. Revised edition. University Presses of Florida, Gainesville. xvi + 415 pp.

Edmunds, G. F., Jr., L. Berner, and J. R. Traver. 1958. North American mayflies of the family Oligoneuriidae. Ann. Entomol. Soc. Amer. 51:375–382.

————, and J. R. Traver. 1959. The classification of the Ephemeroptera 1. Ephemeroidea: Behningiidae. Ann. Entomol. Soc. Amer. 52:43–51.

Pescador, M. L. 1985. Systematics of *Pseudiron* (Ephemeroptera: Heptageniidae: Pseudironinae). Fla. Entomol. 68:432–444.

———— and W. L. Peters. 1980. A revision of the genus *Homoeoneuria* (Ephemeroptera: Oligoneuriidae). Trans. Amer. Entomol. Soc. 106:357–393.

Peters, W. L., and J. G. Peters. 1977. Adult life and emergence of *Dolania americana* in northwestern Florida (Ephemeroptera: Behningiidae). Intern. Rev. Geo. Hydrobiol. 62:409–438.

Traver, J. R. 1935. *In* J. G. Needham, J. R. Traver, and Yin-Chi Hsu, eds. The biology of mayflies with a systematic account of North American species, pp. 237–793. Comstock Pub. Co., Ithaca, NY.

DRAGONFLIES AND DAMSELFLIES

Bick, G. H. 1983. Odonata at risk in conterminous United States and Canada. Odonatologica 12:209–226.

————, and D. Sulzbach. 1966. Reproductive behavior of the damselfly *Hetaerina americana* (Fabricius) (Odonata: Calopterygidae). Animal Behaviour. 14:156–158.

Carle, F. L. 1979. Environmental monitoring potential of the Odonata, with a list of rare and endangered Anisoptera of Virginia, U.S. Odonatologica 8:319–323.

————. 1979. Two new *Gomphus* (Odonata: Gomphidae) from eastern North America with adult keys to the subgenus *Hylogomphus*. Ann. Amer. Entomol. Soc. 72:418–425.

————, and M. L. May. 1987. *Gomphus (Phanogomphus) westfalli* spec. nov. from the Gulf Coast of Florida (Anisoptera: Gomphidae). Odonatologica 16:67–75.

Corbet, P. S. 1963. A biology of dragonflies. Quadrangle, Chicago. 247 pp.

————. 1980. Biology of Odonata. Ann. Rev. Entomol. 25:189–217.

DeMarmels, J. 1984. The genus *Nehalennia* Selys, its species and their phylogenetic relationships (Zygoptera: Coenagrionidae). Odonatologica 13:501–527.

Donnelly, T. W. 1964. *Enallagma westfalli*, a new damselfly from eastern Texas, with remarks on the genus *Teleallagma* Kennedy. Proc. Entomol. Soc. Wash. 66:103–109.

Dunkle, S. W. 1981. The ecology and behavior of *Tachopteryx thoreyi* (Hagen) (Anisoptera: Petaluridae). Odonatologica 10:189–199.

————. 1989. Dragonflies of the Florida peninsula, Bermuda and the Bahamas. Scientific Publishers, Gainesville, Fla. 154 pp.

————. 1990. Damselflies of Florida, Bermuda and the Bahamas. Scientific Publishers, Gainesville, Fla. 148 pp.

————. 1991. Florida's dragonflies. Florida Wildl. 45(4):38–40.

————. 1992. Distribution of dragonflies and damselflies (Odonata) in Florida. Bull. Amer. Odonatology 1(2):29–50.

Hilder, B. E., and P. W. Colgan. 1985. Territorial behavior of male *Nannothemis bella* (Uhler) (Anisoptera: Libellulidae). Can. J. Zool. 63:1010–1016.

Johnson, C. 1961. Breeding behavior and oviposition in *Hetaerina americana*

(Fabricius) and *H. titia* (Drury) (Odonata: Agriidae). Canadian Entomol. 93:260–266.

———. 1962. A description of territorial behavior and a quantitative study of its function in males of *Hetaerina americana* (Fabricius) (Odonata: Agriidae). Canadian Entomol. 94:178–190.

———. 1963. Interspecific territoriality in *Hetaerina americana* (Fabricius) and *H. titia* (Drury) (Odonata: Calopterygidae) with a preliminary analysis of the wing color pattern variation. Canadian Entomol. 95:575–582.

———. 1972. The damselflies (Zygoptera) of Texas. Bull. Flor. State Mus., Biol. Sci. 16:55–128.

———, and M. J. Westfall, Jr. 1970. Diagnostic keys and notes on the damselflies (Zygoptera) of Florida. Bull. Flor. State Mus., Biol. Sci. 15:45–89.

Knopf, K. W., and K. J. Tennessen. 1980. A new species of *Progomphus* Selys, 1854 from North America (Anisoptera: Gomphidae). Odonatologica 9:247–252.

Lee, R. C. P., and P. McGinn. 1986. Male territoriality and mating success in *Nannothemis bella* (Uhler) (Odonata: Libellulidae). Can. J. Zool. 64:1820–1826.

McCafferty, W. P. 1979. Swarm-feeding by the damselfly *Hetaerina americana* (Odonata: Calopterygidae) on mayfly hatches. Aquatic Insects 1:149–151.

Moore, N. W. 1982. Conservation of Odonata-First steps towards a world strategy. Advances in Odonatology 1:205–219.

Needham, J. G., and M. J. Westfall, Jr. 1955. Manual of the dragonflies of North America (Anisoptera), including the Greater Antilles and the provinces of the Mexican border. Univ. Cal. Press, Berkeley. 615 pp.

Paulson, D. R. 1966. The dragonflies (Odonata: Anisoptera) of southern Florida. Ph.D. diss., Univ. Miami. 603 pp.

Schmidt, E. 1979. Approaches to a quantification of the decrease of dragonfly species in industrialized countries. Odonatologica 8:63–67.

Shiffer, C. 1985. Odonata. Pp. 91–161 *in* H. H. Genoways and E. J. Brenner, eds. Species of concern in Pennsylvania. Special Pub. Carnegie Mus. Nat. Hist. no. 11. 430 pp.

Walker, E. M. 1953, 1958. The Odonata of Canada and Alaska, vols. 1 and 2. Univ. Toronto Press. 610 pp.

———, and P. S. Corbet. 1975. The Odonata of Canada and Alaska, vol. 3. Univ. Toronto Press. 307 pp.

Westfall, M. J. 1965. Confusion among species of *Gomphus*. Quart. J. Fla. Acad. Sci. 28:245–254.

———. 1974. A critical study of *Gomphus modestus* Needham, 1942, with notes on related species (Anisoptera: Gomphidae). Odonatologica 3:63–73.

———., and K. J. Tennessen. 1979. Taxonomic clarification within the genus *Dromogomphus* Selys (Odonata: Gomphidae). Fla. Entol. 62:266–273.

Williamson, E. B. 1992. Libellulas collected in Florida by Jesse H. Williamson, with descriptions of two new species. Entomol. News 33:13–19.

GRASSHOPPERS AND THEIR ALLIES

Bland, R. G. 1987. Mating behavior of the grasshopper *Melanoplus tequestae* (Orthoptera: Acrididae). Fla. Entomol. 70:483–487.

Blatchley, W. S. 1920. Orthoptera of northeastern America with especial reference to the faunas of Indiana and Florida. Nature Publ. Co., Indianapolis. 784 pp.

Davis, W. T. 1914. Notes on Orthoptera from the east coast of Florida with descriptions of two new species of *Belocephalus*. J. N.Y. Entomol. Soc. 22: 191-199.

Franz, R., and S. E. Franz. 1989. Records for the rosemary grasshopper, *Schistocerca ceratiola* Hubbell and Walker, in north Florida. Fla. Entomol. 72:386-387.

Friauf, J. J. 1953. An ecological study of the Dermaptera and Orthoptera of the Welaka area in northern Florida. Ecol. Monogr. 23:79-126.

Gross, S. W., D. L. Mays, and T. J. Walker. 1989. Systematics of *Pictonemobius* ground crickets (Orthoptera: Gryllidae). Trans. Amer. Entomol. Soc. 115. 433-456.

Hebard, M. 1926. A revision of the North American genus *Belocephalus* (Orthoptera: Tettigoniidae, Copiphorinae). Trans. Amer. Entomol. Soc. 70:147-186, pls. 7, 8.

Hubbell, T. H. 1932. Revision of the *puer* group of the North American genus *Melanoplus*, with remarks on the taxonomic value of the concealed male genitalia in the Cyrtacanthacrinae. Univ. Mich. Mus. Zool. Misc. Pub. 23. 64 pp.

Love, R. E., and T. J. Walker. 1979. Systematics and acoustic behavior of scaly crickets (Orthoptera: Gryllidae, Mogoplistinae) of the eastern United States. Trans. Amer. Entomol. Soc. 105:1-66.

ROACHES

Atkinson, T. H., P. G. Koehler, and R. Patterson. 1990. Annotated checklist of the cockroaches of Florida (Dictyoptera: Blattaria: Blattidae, Polyphagidae, Blattellidae, Blaberidae). Fla. Entomol. 73:303-327.

Young, F. N. 1949. Insects from burrows of *Peromyscus polionotus*. Fla. Entomol. 32:77.

LICE

Emerson, K. C. 1972. Checklist of the Mallophaga of North American (North of Mexico), parts 1-4. Deseret Test Center, Dugway, UT.

Emerson, K. C., and R. D. Price. 1981. A host-parasite list of the Mallophaga on mammals. Misc. Publ. Entomol. Soc. Amer. 12(1):1-72.

BEETLES

Blatchley, W. S. 1920. Notes on the winter Coleoptera of western and southern Florida, with descriptions of new species. Can. Entomol. 52:42-46, 68-72.

Böving, A. G., & F. C. Craighead. 1931. An illustrated synopsis of the principal larval forms of the Order Coleoptera. Entomologica Americana, Brooklyn Entomol. Soc. 11:1-351.

Boyle, W. W. 1956. A revision of the Erotylidae of America north of Mexico (Coleoptera). Bull. Amer. Mus. Nat. Hist. 110(2):65–172.

Brach, V. 1976. Notes on the life history of *Onthophagus aciculatulus* (Scarabaeidae: Coprini). Fla. Entomol. 59(1):106.

Cartwright, O. L. 1939. Eleven new American Coleoptera (Scarabaeidae, Cicindelidae). Ann. Entomol. Soc. Amer. 32(2):353–364.

———. 1974. *Ataenius, Aphotaenius,* and *Pseudataenius* of the United States and Canada (Coleoptera: Scarabaeidae: Aphodiinae). Smithsonian Contrib. Zool. 154:1–106.

Choate, P. M. 1984. A new species of *Cicindela* Linnaeus (Coleoptera: Cicindelidae) from Florida, and elevation of *C. abdominalis scabrosa* Schaupp to species level. Ent. News 95:73–82.

———. 1987. Biology of *Ceratocanthus aeneus* (Coleoptera: Scarabaeidae: Ceratocanthinae). Florida Entomol. 70(3):301–305.

Dawson, R. W. 1922. New species of *Serica* (Scarabaeidae) V. J. N.Y. Entomol. Soc. 30:154–169.

———. 1952. New species of *Serica* (Scarabaeidae) IX. J. N.Y. Entomol. Soc. 60:65–89.

———. 1967. New and little known species of *Serica* (Coleoptera: Scarabaeidae) X. J. NY Entomol. Soc. 75:161–178.

Dillon, E. S., & L. S. Dillon. 1961. A manual of common beetles of eastern North America. Row, Peterson and Company, Evanston, Il. 884 pp.

Froeschner, R. C., and E. P. Meiner. 1953. The Languriidae and Erotylidae (Coleoptera) of Missouri with notes and keys. J. Kans. Entomol. Soc. 26:18–25.

Galley, K. E. M. 1990. A revision of the genus *Selonodon* Latreille (Coleoptera: Cebrionidae). M.S. thesis, Cornell Univ., Ithaca, NY. x + 137 pp.

Horn, G. H. 1862. Descriptions of some new North American Coleoptera. Proc. Entomol. Soc. Philadelphia 1:187–188.

Hovore, F. T., R. L. Penrose, and E. F. Giesbert. 1978. Notes on North American Cerambycidae. Entomol. News 89:95–100.

Howden, H. F. 1952. A new name for *Geotrupes (Peltotrupes) chalybeus* LeConte, with a description of the larva and its biology. Coleopterists Bull. 6:41–48, 8 figs.

———. 1954. Habits and life history of *Mycotrupes,* with a description of the larva of *Mycotrupes gaigei. In* A. L. Olson, T. H. Hubbell, and H. F. Howden, eds. The burrowing beetles of the genus *Mycotrupes.* Misc. Publ. Mus. Zool. Univ. Mich. 84:52–56, figs. 65–74.

———. 1961. New species and a new genus of Melolonthinae from the southeastern United States (Coleoptera: Scarabaeidae). Can. Entomol. 93:807–812.

———, and P. Vaurie. 1957. Two new species of *Trox* from Florida (Coleoptera, Scarabaeidae). Amer. Mus. Nov. 1818:1–6.

———. and S. Endrodi. 1966. Five new species of *Cyclocephala* Latreille from North and Central America (Coleoptera: Scarabaeidae). Can. Entomol. 98:295–302.

Hubbard, H. G. 1894. The insect guests of the Florida land tortoise. Insect Life 6:302–315.

Jerath, M. L. 1960. Notes on larvae of nine genera of *Aphodiinae* in the United States (Coleoptera: Scarabaeidae). Proc. U.S. Natl. Mus. 111:43–94.

Kalisz, P. J., and E. L. Stone. 1984. Soil mixing by scarab beetles and pocket gophers in north-central Florida. Soil Sci. 48:169–172.

Knull, J. N. 1946. The long horned beetles of Ohio (Coleoptera: Cerambycidae). Ohio Biol. Survey, Bull. 39, vol. 7, no. 4:133–354.

———. 1948. A new genus and species of Cerambycidae with notes. Ohio J. Sci. 48:82–83.

———. 1949. New Coleoptera with notes (Elateridae, Buprestidae and Cerambycidae). Ohio J. Sci. 49:102–104.

———. 1956. A new species of *Typocerus* from Florida. Ohio J. Sci. 56:388.

Lago, P. K. 1991. A survey of arthropods associated with gopher tortoise burrows in Mississippi. Entomol. News 102:1–13.

Lampert, L. L., Jr. 1977. Notes on *Aneflomorpha delongi* (Champlain and Knull) (Coleoptera: Cerambycidae). Coleop. Bull. 31:82.

Linell, M. L. 1895. New species of North American Coleoptera of the family Scarabaeidae. Proc. U.S. Natl. Mus. 1096:721–731.

Linsley, E. G. 1962a. The Cerambycidae of North America, part 2. Univ. California Publ. Entomol. 19:1–102.

———. 1962b. The Cerambycidae of North America, part 3. Univ. California Publ. Entomol. 20:1–188.

———. 1963. The Cerambycidae of North America, part 4. Univ. California Publ. Entomol. 21:1–165.

———. 1964. The Cerambycidae of North America, part 5. Univ. California Publ. Entomol. 22:1–197.

Moore, J. C. 1953. The fox squirrel in Florida, variation and natural history. Ph.D. dissertation, Univ. of Florida, Gainesville. 202 pp.

Peck, S. B., and H. F. Howden. 1985. Biogeography of scavenging scarab beetles in the Florida Keys: post pleistocene land bridge islands. Can. J. Zool. 63:2730–2737.

Potts, R. W. L. 1945. A key to the species of *Cremastocheilini* of North America and Mexico (Coleoptera, Scarabaeidae). Bull. Brooklyn Entoml. Soc. 40:72–78.

———. 1976. New species of North American *Anomala* (Scarabaeidae: Anomalinae). Pan-Pacific Entomologist 52:220–226.

———. 1977a. Revision of the Scarabaeidae: Anomalinae 2. An annotated checklist of *Anomala* for the United States and Canada. Pan-Pac. Entomol. 53:34–42.

———. 1977b. Revision of the Scarabaeidae: Anomalinae. 3. A key to the species of *Anomala* of America north of Mexico. Pan-Pac. Entomol. 53:129–134.

Schwarz, E. A. 1878. The Coleoptera of Florida. Proc. Amer. Phil. Soc. 17:353–472.

Skelley, P. E. 1988. Pleasing fungus beetles of Florida (Coleoptera: Erotylidae). M.S. thesis, University of Florida, Central Science Library, Gainesville, FL. 172 pp.

———. and M. A. Goodrich. 1989. A redescription of *Ischyrus dunedinensis* Blatchley (Coleoptera:Erotylidae) with a key to the species of *Ischyrus* of America, north of Mexico. Coleop. Bull. 43:349–354.

———. and R. E. Woodruff. 1991. Five new species of *Aphodius* (Coleoptera: Scarabaeidae) from Florida pocket gopher burrows. Florida Entomol. 74(4): 517–536.

Thomas, M. C. 1991. Rediscovery of *Romulus globosus* (Coleoptera: Cerambycidae). Insecta Mundi 5:127–128.

Turnbow, R. H., Jr., and F. T. Hovore. 1979. Notes on Cerambycidae from the southeastern U.S. (Coleoptera). Entomol. News 90:219–229.

Vaurie, P. 1956. *Diplotaxis* of the eastern United States, with a new species and other notes (Coleoptera, Scarabaeidae). Coleop. Bull. 10:1–9.

Woodruff, R. E. 1960. Suppression of the genus *Roplisa* Casey with notes on the United States species of *Trigonopeltastes* Burmeister (Coleoptera: Scarabaeidae). Fla. Entomol. 43:139–145.

———. 1973. The scarab beetles of Florida (Coleoptera: Scarabaeidae), part 1. The Laparosticti (Subfamilies: Scarabaeinae, Aphodiinae, Hybosorinae, Ochodaeinae, Geotrupinae, Acanthocerinae). Florida Department of Agriculture, Division of Plant Industry, Arthropods of Florida and Neighboring Land Areas 8:1–220.

———. 1982a. Arthropods of gopher burrows. Pp. 24–48 in R. Franz and R. Bryant, eds. The gopher tortoise and its sandhill habitat. Proc. 3rd Ann. Mtg. Gopher Tortoise Council, Tall Timbers Research Station, Tallahassee, Florida.

———. 1982b. Rare and endangered Scarabaeidae of Florida. Pp. 84–102 in R. Franz, ed. Rare and endangered biota of Florida. Invertebrates. Vol. 6., University of Florida Press, Gainesville.

———. and B. M. Beck. 1989. The scarab beetles of Florida. (Coleoptera: Scarabaeidae). Part 2. The May or June Beetles (Genus *Phyllophaga*). Florida Dept. of Agriculture, Division of Plant Industry, Arthropods of Florida and Neighboring Lands Areas 13:1–226.

CADDISFLIES

Armitage, B. K. 1983. Diagnostic atlas of the North American caddisfly adults, I. Philopotamidae. Caddis Press, Athens, AL. 99 pp.

Banks, N. 1903. Some new neuropteroid insects. J. N.Y. Entomol. Soc. 11:236–243.

———. 1905. Descriptions of new Nearctic neuropteroid insects. Trans. Amer. Entomol. Soc. 32:1–20, plates 1–2.

———. 1907. Descriptions of new Trichoptera. Proc. Entomol. Soc. Wash. 8:117–133, pls. 8,9.

Blickle, R. L. 1961. New species of Hydroptilidae (Trichoptera). Bull. Brooklyn Entomol. Soc. 56:131–134.

———. 1962. Hydroptilidae (Trichoptera) of Florida. Florida Entomol. 45:153–155.

———. 1979. Hydroptilidae (Trichoptera) of America north of Mexico. Bull. New Hampshire Agric. Expt. Sta. 509:1–97.

———. and D. G. Denning. 1977. New species and a new genus of Hydroptilidae (Trichoptera). J. Kans. Entomol. Soc. 50:287–300.

———, and W. J. Morse. 1957. New Hydroptilidae from New Hampshire. Bull. Brooklyn Entomol. Soc. 52:48–50.

Bowles, D. E., and M. L. Mathis. 1989. Caddisflies (Insecta: Trichoptera) of mountainous regions in Arkansas, with new state records for the order. J. Kansas Entomol. Soc. 62:234–244.

Bueno-Soria, J. 1981. Estudios en insectos acuaticos de Mexico I. Trichoptera (Leptoceridae). Cinco nuevas especies de *Oecetis* McLachlan. Folia Entomol. Mex. 49:103-120.

———, and O. S. Flint, Jr. 1978. Catálogo sistimático de los tricópteros de Mexico (Insecta: Trichoptera), con algunos registros de Norte, Centro y Sudamérica. An. Inst. Biol. Univ. Na. Autón. México 49, Ser. Zoología (1):189-218.

Daigle, J. J., and J. D. Haddock. 1981. The larval description and ecological notes of a caddisfly, *Nectopsyche tavara* (Ross), from the central Florida refugium (Trichoptera: Leptoceridae). Pan-Pac. Entomol. 57:327-331.

Denning, D. G. 1947. Hydroptilidae (Trichoptera) from southern United States. Can. Entomol. 79:12-20.

———. 1948. Description of eight new species of Trichoptera. Bull. Brooklyn Entomol. Soc. 43:119-124.

———. and R. L. Blickle. 1972. A review of the genus *Ochrotrichia* (Trichoptera: Hydroptilidae). Ann. Entomol. Soc. Amer. 65:141-151.

Deyrup, M. 1990. Arthropod footprints in the sands of time. Florida Entomol. 73:527-538.

Edwards, S. W., and C. R. Arnold. 1961. The caddis flies of the San Marcos River. Texas J. Sci. 13:398-415.

Etnier, D. A. 1965. An annotated list of the Trichoptera of Minnesota, with description of a new species. Entomol. News 76:141-151.

Flint, O. S., Jr. 1964. The caddisflies (Trichoptera) of Puerto Rico. Univ. Puerto Rico Agr. Expt. Sta., Rio Piedras, Tech. Paper 40.

———. 1968. The caddisflies of Jamaica (Trichoptera). Bull. Inst. Jamaica Sci. Ser. 19:1-68.

———. 1971. Studies of Neotropical caddisflies. 12: Rhyacophilidae, Glassosomatidae, Philopotamidae, and Psychomyiidae from the Amazon Basin (Trichoptera). Amazoniana 3:1-67.

———. 1972. Studies of Neotropical caddisflies. 13: The genus *Ochrotrichia* from Mexico and Central America (Trichoptera: Hydroptilidae). Smithsonian Contrib. Zool. 118:1-28.

Garono, R. J., and D. B. MacLean. 1988. Caddisflies (Trichoptera) of Ohio wetlands as indicated by light-trapping. Ohio J. Sci. 88:143-151.

Gordon, A. E. 1974. A synopsis and phylogenetic outline of the Nearctic members of *Cheumatopsyche*. Proc. Acad. Nat. Sci. Phila. 126:117-160.

———. 1984. The Trichoptera of Florida: A preliminary survey. Pp. 161-166 *in* J. C. Morse, ed. Proceedings of the 4th International Symposium on Trichoptera, Clemson, South Carolina, 11-16 July 1983, Dr. W. Junk Publishers, The Hague, Series Entomologica 30. 486 pp.

Haddock, J. D. 1977. The biosystematics of the caddis fly genus *Nectopsyche* in North America with emphasis on the aquatic stages. Amer. Midl. Nat. 98:382-421.

Hamilton, S. W. 1986. Systematics and biogeography of New World *Polycentropus sensu stricto* (Trichoptera: Polycentropodidae). Ph.D. dissertation, Clemson University, Clemson, SC. 257 pp.

Harris, S. C. 1986a. Hydroptilidae (Trichoptera) of Alabama with descriptions of three new species. J. Kans. Entomol. Soc. 59:609-619.

————. 1986b. New species of caddisflies (Trichoptera) from Alabama. Proc. Entomol. Soc. Wash. 88:30–41.

————. 1990. Preliminary considerations on rare and endangered invertebrates in Alabama. J. Alabama Acad. of Sci. 61:64–92.

————, and B. J. Armitage. 1987. New Hydroptilidae (Trichoptera) from Florida. Entomol. News 98:106–110.

————, and P. K. Lago. 1990. Annotated checklist of the Rhyacophiloidea and Integripalpia (Trichoptera) of Alabama. Entomol. News 101:57–66.

————, P. K. Lago, and J. F. Scheiring. 1982. An annotated list of Trichoptera of several streams on Eglin Air Force Base, Florida. Entomol. News 93:79–84.

————, ————, and P. E. O'Neil. 1984. Trichoptera of the Cahaba River system in Alabama. Entomol. News 95:103–112.

————, ————, and R. W. Holzenthal. 1982. An annotated checklist of the caddisflies (Trichoptera) of Mississippi and southeastern Louisiana. Part 2: Rhyacophiloidea. Proc. Entomol. Soc. Wash. 84:509–512.

————. P. E. O'Neil, R. V. Chandler, M . F. Metee, and E. J. McCullough. 1983. Biological and hydrological impacts of surface mining for federal minerals on the Tyro Creek watershed, Alabama. Phase I. Premining—aquatic baseline information. U.S. Dept. of Interior, Bureau of Land Mgmt., University, AL. 98 pp.

Holzenthal, R. W. 1982. The caddisfly genus *Setodes* in North America (Trichoptera: Leptoceridae). J. Kans. Entomol. Soc. 55:253–271.

————, and R. W. Kelley. 1983. New micro-caddisflies from the southeastern United States (Trichoptera: Hydroptilidae). Fla. Entomol. 66:464–472.

————, S. C. Harris, and P. K. Lago. 1982. An annotated checklist of the caddisflies (Trichoptera) of Mississippi and southeastern Louisiana. Part 3: Limnephiloidea and conclusions. Proc. Entomol. Soc. Wash. 84:513–520.

Kelley, R. W. 1981. New species of *Oxyethira* (Trichoptera: Hydroptilidae) from the southeastern United States. J. Ga. Entomol. Soc. 16:368–375.

————. 1984. Phylogeny, morphology and classification of the micro-caddisfly genus *Oxyethira* Eaton (Trichoptera: Hydroptilidae). Trans. Amer. Entomol. Soc. 110:435–463.

————. 1985. Revision of the micro-caddisfly genus *Oxyethira* (Trichoptera: Hydroptilidae). Part 2: subgenus *Oxyethira*. Trans. Amer. Entomol. Soc. 111:223–253.

————, and J. C. Morse. 1982. A key to the females of the genus *Oxyethira* (Trichoptera: Hydroptilidae) from the southern United States. Proc. Entomol. Soc. Wash. 84:256–269.

Kingsolver, J. M., and H. H. Ross. 1961. New species of Nearctic *Orthotrichia* (Hydroptilidae, Trichoptera). Trans. Ill. State Acad. Sci. 54:28–33.

Lago, P. K., and S. C. Harris. 1983. New species of Trichoptera from Florida and Alabama. Ann. Entomol. Soc. Amer. 76:664–667.

————, and ————. 1987a. The *Chimarra* (Trichoptera: Philopotamidae) of eastern North America with descriptions of three new species. J. N.Y. Entomol. Soc. 95:225–251.

————, and ————. 1987b. An annotated list of the Curvipalpia (Trichoptera) of Alabama. Entomol. News 98:255–262.

————, R. W. Holzenthal, and S. C. Harris. 1982. An annotated checklist of the caddisflies (Trichoptera) of Mississippi and southeastern Louisiana. Part 1: Introduction and Hydropsychoidea. Proc. Entomol. Soc. Wash. 84:495-508.

Lake, R. W. 1984. Distribution of caddisflies (Trichoptera) in Delaware. Entomol. News 95:215-224.

Longridge, J. L., and W. L. Hilsenhoff. 1973. Annotated list of Trichoptera (caddisflies) in Wisconsin. Wisc. Acad. Sci. Arts Letters 61:173-183.

Milne, L. J. 1934. Studies in North American Trichoptera. Privately printed, Cambridge, MA. 1:1-19.

————. 1936. Studies in North American Trichoptera. Privately printed, Cambridge, MA. 3:56-128, 2 plates.

Morse, J. C. 1975. A phylogeny and revision of the caddisfly genus *Ceraclea* (Trichoptera, Leptoceridae). Contrib. Amer. Entomol. Inst. 11(2):1--97.

————. 1990. *Nyctiophylax barrorum* (Trichoptera: Polycentropodidae), a new species from Alabama. J. Kans. Entomol. Soc. 63:133-137.

————, J. W. Chapin, D. D. Herlong, and R. S. Harvey. 1980. Aquatic insects of Upper Three Runs Creek, Savannah River Plant, South Carolina. Part 1: Orders other than Diptera. J. Ga. Entomol. Soc. 15:73-101.

————, and R. W. Holzenthal. 1984. Trichoptera genera. Pp. 312-347 in R. W. Merritt and K. W. Cummins, eds. An Introduction to the Aquatic Insects of North America, 2nd edition. Kendall/Hunt Pub. Co., Dubuque, IA. 722 pp.

Nielsen, A. 1948. Postembryonic development and biology of the Hydroptilidae. Kgl. Danske Videnskab. Selskab. Biol. Skrifter 5:1-200, pls. 1-3.

Noyes, A. A. 1914. The biology of the net-spinning Trichoptera of Cascadilla Creek. Ann. Entomol. Soc. Amer. 7:251-272.

Parker, C. R., and J. R. Voshell, Jr. 1981. A preliminary checklist of the caddisflies (Trichoptera) of Virginia. J. Ga. Entomol. Soc. 16:1-7.

Resh, V. H. 1976. The biology and immature stages of the caddisfly genus *Ceraclea* in eastern North America (Trichoptera: Leptoceridae). Ann. Entomol. Soc. Amer. 69:1039-1061.

Roeding, C. E., and L. A. Smock. 1989. Ecology of macroinvertebrate shredders in a low-gradient sandy-bottomed stream. J. N. Amer. Benthol. Soc. 8:149-161.

Ross, H. H. 1938. Lectotypes of North American caddis flies in the Museum of Comparative Zoology. Psyche 45:1-61.

————. 1941. Descriptions and records of North American Trichoptera. Trans. Amer. Entomol. Soc. 67:35-126, pls. 1-13.

————. 1944. The caddis flies, or Trichoptera, of Illinois. Bull. Ill. Nat. Hist. Surv. 23:1-326.

————. 1947. Descriptions and records of North American Trichoptera, with synoptic notes. Trans. Amer. Entomol. Soc. 73:125-168, plates 2-8.

————. 1959. The relationships of three new species of *Triaenodes* from Illinois and Florida (Trichoptera). Entomol. News 70:39-45.

————, J. C. Morse, and A. E. Gordon. 1971. New species of *Cheumatopsyche* from the southeastern United States (Hydropsychidae, Trichoptera). Proc. Biol. Soc. Wash. 84:301-306.

————. and D. C. Scott. 1974. A review of the caddisfly genus *Agarodes*, with descriptions of new species (Trichoptera: Sericostomatidae). J. Ga. Entomol. Soc. 9:147–155.

———. and J. B. Wallace. 1974. The North American genera of the family Sericostomatidae. J. Ga. Entomol. Soc. 9:42–48.

Roy, D., and P. P. Harper. 1975. Nouvelles mentions de trichoptères du Québec et description de *Limnephilus nimmoi* n. sp. (Limnephilidae). Can. J. Zool. 53:1080–1088.

———, and P. P. Harper. 1979. Liste préliminaire des trichoptères (insectes) du Québec. Ann. Soc. Entomol. Québec 24:148–172.

Scheiring, J. F. 1985. Longitudinal and seasonal patterns of insect trophic structure in a Florida sand-hill stream. J. Kans. Entomol. Soc. 58:207–219.

Schmid, F. 1980. Les insectes et arachnides du Canada, partie 7: Genera des trichoptères du Canada et des États adjacents. Agric. Can. 1692:1–296.

Ulmer, G. 1906. Neuer Beitrag zur Kenntnis aussereuropaeischer Trichopteren. Not. Leyden Mus. 28:1–112.

Unzicker, J. D. 1968. The comparative morphology and evolution of the internal female reproductive system of Trichoptera. Ill. Biol. Monogr. 40:1–72.

———, V. H. Resh, and J. C. Morse. 1982. Trichoptera. Pp. 9.1–9.138 in A. R. Brigham, W. U. Brigham, and A. Gnilka, eds. Aquatic Insects and Oligochaetes of North and South Carolina. Midwest Aquatic Enterprises, Mahomet, IL. 837 pp.

Vaillant, F. 1965. Les larves de Trichopteres hydroptilides mangeuses de substrat. Proc. Twelfth Inter. Congr., Entomol., London. 165.

Weaver, J. S., III. 1988. A synopsis of the North American Lepidostomatidae (Trichoptera). Contrib. Amer. Entomol. Inst. 24:1–141.

———, J. A. Wojtowicz, and D. A. Etnier. 1981. Larval and pupal descriptions of *Dolophilodes (Fumonta) major* (Banks) (Trichoptera: Philopotamidae). Entomol. News 92:85–90.

Wiggins, G. B. 1977. Larvae of the North American Caddisfly Genera (Trichoptera). Univ. of Toronto Press. 401 pp.

———. 1984. Trichoptera. Pp. 271–311 in R. W. Merritt and K. W. Cummins, eds. An Introduction to the Aquatic Insects of North America, 2nd edition. Kendall/Hunt Pub. Co., Dubuque, IA. 722 pp.

Wood, J. R., V. H. Resh, and E. M. McEwan. 1982. Egg masses of Nearctic sericostomatid caddisfly genera (Trichoptera). Ann. Entomol. Soc. Amer. 75: 430–434.

BUTTERFLIES

Anonymous. 1992. Florida population map. Kiplinger Washington Editors, Inc. Washington D.C. Map 4-0990-4A.

Baggett, H. D. 1982. Lepidoptera. Pp. 72–81. In R. Franz (ed.). Rare and endangered biota of Florida. Volume Six, Invertebrates. University Presses of Florida, Gainesville. 131 pp.

Brown, C. H. 1976. A colony of *Papilio aristodemus ponceanus* (Lepidoptera: Papilionidae) in the upper Florida Keys. J. Ga. Entomol. Soc. 11:117–118.

Brown, F. M., and B. Heineman. 1972. Jamaica and its butterflies. E. W. Classey Limited, London. 478 pp.

Brown, L. N. 1973a. Populations of a new swallowtail butterfly found in the Florida Keys. Fla. Naturalist, April, p. 25.

_____. 1973b. Populations of *Papilio andraemon bonhotei* Sharpe and *Papilio aristodemus ponceanus* Schaus (Papilionidae) in Biscayne National Monument, Florida. J. Lepid. Soc. 27:136–140.

_____. 1973c. A population of *Lethe appalachia* (Satyridae) from west central Florida. J. Lepid. Soc. 27:238–239.

Burns, J. M. 1964. Evolution in skipper butterflies of the genus *Erynnis*. Univ. Calif. Publ. Entomol. 37. iv + 216 pp.

_____. 1984. Evolutionary differentiation: differentiating golden-banded skippers-*Autochton cellus* and more (Lepidoptera: Hesperiidae: Pyrginae). Smithsonian Contrib. Zool. no. 405. 38 pp.

Calhoun, J. V. 1989. Observations of *Eurema nise* in Florida. S. Lepidop. News 11:35–36.

Capman, W. C. 1990. Natural history of the common sooty wing skipper, *Pholisora catullus* (Lepidoptera: Hesperiidae), in central Illinois. Great Lakes Entomol. 23(3):151–157.

Chermock, R. L., and O. D. Chermock. 1947. Notes on the life histories of three Floridian butterflies. Can. Entomol. 79:142–144.

Clench, H. K., and K. A. Bjorndal. 1980. Butterflies of Great and Little Inagua, Bahamas. Ann. Carnegie Mus. 49:1–30.

Collins, N. M., and M. G. Morris. 1985. Threatened swallowtail butterflies of the world. In IUCN Red Data Book. IUCN, Gland, Switzerland, and Cambridge, U.K. 401 pp.

Covell, C. V., Jr. 1977. Project Ponceanus and the status of the Schaus swallowtail (*Papilio aristodemus ponceanus*) in the Florida Keys. Atala 5:4–6.

_____. 1990. The status of our knowledge of the North American Lepidoptera. Pp. 211–230 *in* Kosztarab, M., and C. W. Schaefer (eds.). Systematics of the North American Insects and Arachnids: Status and needs. Va. Agric. Exp. Sta. Infor. Ser. 90-1, Virginia Polytechnic Institute and State University, Blacksburg.

_____. and G. W. Rawson. 1973. Project Ponceanus: A report on first efforts to survey and preserve the Schaus swallowtail (Papilionidae) in southern Florida. J. Lepid. Soc. 27:206–210.

Drewry, G. (ed.). 1989. Endangered and threatened wildlife and plants; animal notice of review. Federal Register 54:554–579.

Ehrlich, P. R. 1992. Population biology of checkerspot butterflies and the preservation of global diversity. Oikos 63:6–12.

Emmel, T. C., and M. C. Minno. 1988. Habitat requirements and status of the endemic Schaus' swallowtail in the Florida Keys. Final report, Florida Game and Fresh Water Fish Comm., Tallahassee. 202 pp.

Frank, J. H., and E. D. McCoy. 1992. The immigration of insects to Florida, with a tabulation of records published since 1970. Florida Entomol. 75:1–28.

Gatrelle, R. R. 1991. The taxonomic implications of the discovery of *Incisalia irus* in Florida. News of the Lepid. Soc. July/August (4):57–58.

Gerberg, E. J., and R. H. Arnett, Jr. 1989. Florida Butterflies. Natural Science Publications, Inc., Baltimore, Maryland. 90 pp.

Grimshawe, F. M. 1940. Place of sorrow: The world's rarest butterfly and Matecumbe Key. Nature Magazine 33:565-567, 611.

Harris, L., Jr. 1972. Butterflies of Georgia. University of Oklahoma Press, Norman. 326 pp.

Hennessey, M. K., and D. H. Habeck. 1991. Effects of mosquito adulticiding on populations of non-target, terrestrial arthropods in the Florida Keys. Final Report, U.S. Fish and Wildlife Service and University of Florida Cooperative Wildlife Research Unit, Gainesville, Florida. 68 pp.

Howe, W. H. (ed.). 1975. The butterflies of North America. Doubleday and Co., Inc., Garden City, NY. 633 pp.

Jenkins, D. W. 1990. Neotropical Nymphalidae VIII. Revision of *Eunica*. Bull. Allyn Mus. 131:1-177.

Johnson, K. 1989. Revision of *Chlorostrymon* Clench and description of two new austral neotropical species (Lycaenidae). J. Lepid. Soc. 43:120-146.

Kimball, C. P. 1965. The Lepidoptera of Florida. Florida Dept. of Agriculture, Gainesville. Arthropods of Florida 1. 363 pp. + 26 pls.

Klots, A. B. 1951. A field guide to the butterflies of North America east of the Great Plains. Houghton Mifflin Co., Boston. 349 pp.

Kreman, C. 1992. Assessing the indicator properties of species assemblages for natural areas monitoring. Ecological Applications 2:203-217.

Lenczewski, B. 1980. Butterflies of Everglades National Park. National Park Service, South Florida Research Center, Homestead. Report T-588. 110 pp.

Loftus, W. F., and J. A. Kushlan. 1982. The status of Schaus' swallowtail and the Bahama swallowtail butterflies in Biscayne National Park. National Park Service, Everglades National Park. Report M-649. 18 pp.

――――― and ―――――. 1984. Population fluctuations of the Schaus swallowtail (Lepidoptera: Papilionidae) on the islands of Biscayne Bay, Florida, with comments on the Bahamian swallowtail. Fla. Entomol. 67:277-287.

McGuire, W. H. 1982. New oviposition and larval hostplant records for North American *Hesperia* (Rhopalocera: Hesperiidae). Bulletin of the Allyn Museum 72:6 pp.

Metzler, E. H., and V. P. Lucas. 1990. An endangered moth in Ohio, with notes on other species of special concern (Lepidoptera: Saturniidae, Sphingidae, Notodontidae and Arctiidae). Ohio J. Sci. 90:33-40.

Miller, L. D., D. J. Harvey, and J. Y. Miller. 1985. Notes on the genus *Euphyes*, with description of a new subspecies (Lepidoptera: Hesperiidae). Fla. Entomol. 68:323-335.

Minno, M. C. 1992. Lepidoptera of the Archbold Biological Station, Highlands County, Florida. Florida Entomol. 75:297-329.

―――――, and T. C. Emmel. 1992. Butterflies of the Florida Keys. Scientific Publishers, Gainesville. 168 pp.

Opler, P. A. (ed.). 1985. Invertebrates. Pp. 79-165. *In* H. H. Genoways and F. J. Brenner (eds.). Species of special concern in Pennsylvania. Special Publ. Carnegie Mus. Nat. Hist. No. 11. 430 pp.

———. 1987. Invertebrate surveys in North America are necessary. Wings, Spring 1987. pp. 8–10.

———. and G. O. Krizek. 1984. Butterflies east of the Great Plains. Johns Hopkins University Press, Baltimore. 294 pp.

Pyle, R. M. 1984. The Audubon Society handbook for butterfly watchers. Charles Scribner's Sons, New York. xiv + 274 pp.

———, M. Bentzien, and P. Opler. 1981. Insect conservation. Ann. Rev. Entomol. 26:233–258.

Rawson, G. W. 1961. The recent rediscovery of *Eumaeus atala* (Lycaenidae) in southern Florida. J. Lepid. Soc. 15:237–244.

Riley, N. D. 1975. A field guide to the butterflies of the West Indies. William Collins Sons & Co., London. 224 pp.

Rutkowski, F. 1971. Observations of *Papilio aristodemus ponceanus* (Papilionidae). J. Lepid. Soc. 25:126–136.

Schwartz, A. 1987. The butterflies of the Lower Florida Keys. Milwaukee Pub. Mus. Contrib. Biol. Geol. no. 73. 34 pp.

———. 1989. The butterflies of Hispaniola. University of Florida Press, Gainesville. 580 pp.

Schweitzer, D. F. 1989. A review of category 2 Insecta in USFWS regions 3, 4, 5. Report to the U. S. Fish and Wildlife Service, Newton Corners, MA, pp. 81–143, Order Lepidoptera.

———. 1992. Comments regarding *Erynnis persius persius* and *Incisalia irus*. Ohio Lepidopterist 14:21–23.

Scott, J. A. 1970 (1971). A list of Antillean butterflies. J. Res. Lepid. 9:249–256.

———. 1972. Biogeography of Antillean butterflies. Biotropica 4:32–45.

———. 1986a. The butterflies of North America. Stanford University Press, Stanford, CA. 583 pp.

———. 1986b. Distribution of Caribbean butterflies. Papilio (New Series). 3:1–26.

Shuey, J. A. 1989. The morpho-species concept of *Euphyes dion* with a description of a new species (Hesperiidae). J. Res. Lepid. 27:160–172.

———. J. V. Calhoun, and D. C. Iftner. 1987. Butterflies that are Endangered, Threatened, and of Special Concern in Ohio. Ohio J. Sci. 87:98–106.

———. E. H. Metzler, D. C. Iftner, J. V. Calhoun, J. W. Peacock, R. A. Watkins, J. D. Hooper, and W. F. Babcock. 1987. Status and habitats of potentially endangered Lepidoptera in Ohio. J. Lepid. Soc. 41:1–12.

Shull, E. M. 1981. Indiana state records and notes on some rare and endangered Lepidoptera (1972–1980). Proc. Indiana Acad. Sci. 91:309–312.

Tamburo, S. E., and F. Butcher. 1955. Biological studies of the Florida dusky wing skipper and a preliminary survey of other insects on Barbados Cherry. Fla. Entomol. 38:65–69.

Turner, T. W., and J. R. Parnell. 1985. The identification of two species of *Junonia* Hubner (Lepidoptera: Nymphalidae): *J. evarete* and *J. genoveva* in Jamaica. J. Res. Lepid. 24:142–153.

Wood, D. A. 1990. Official lists of endangered and potentially endangered fauna and flora in Florida. Florida Game and Fresh Water Fish Commission, Tallahassee. 23 pp.

Uobel, B. 1991. Florida Naturalist 64:i.

Young, F. N. 1937. Notes on the occurrence of *Strymon maesites* (Herrick-Schaffer) in Florida (Lepid.: Lycaenidae). Entomol. News 48:80–81.

FLIES AND MOSQUITOS

Arnell, J. H. 1976. Mosquito studies (Diptera, Culicidae) XXXIII. A revision of the *scapularis* group of *Aedes (Ochlerotatus)*. Contrib. Amer. Entomol. Inst. 13:1–144.

Baker, F. C. 1936. A new species of *Orthopodomyia*, *O. alba* sp. n. (Diptera, Culicidae). Proc. Entomol. Soc. Wash. 38:1– 7.

Basham, E. H. 1948. *Culex (Melaniconion) mulrennani*, a new species from Florida. Ann. Entomol. Soc. Amer. 41:1– 7.

Belkin, J. N. 1962. The mosquitoes of the South Pacific (Diptera, Culicidae). U. of California Press, Berkeley. 576 pp.

——, S. J. Heinemann, and W. A. Page. 1970. Mosquito studies (Diptera, Culicidae). XXI. The Culicidae of Jamaica. Contrib. Amer. Entomol. Inst. 6:1–458.

Bradshaw, W. E. 1983. Interaction between the mosquito *Wyeomia smithii*, the midge *Metriocnemus knabi*, and their carnivorous host, *Sarracenia purpurea*. Pp. 161–189 *in* J. H. Frank & L. P. Lounibos (eds.). Phytotelmata: terrestrial plants as hosts for aquatic insect communities. Plexus, Medford, NJ.

——, and C. M. Holzapfel. 1983. Life cycle strategies in *Wyeomyia smithii*: seasonal and geographic adaptations. Pp. 167–185 *in* V. K. Brown and I. Hodek (eds.). Diapause and life cycle strategies in insects. W. Junk, The Hague.

——, and C. M. Holzapfel. 1986. Geography of density-dependent selection in pitcher-plant mosquitoes. Pp. 48–65 *in* F. Taylor & R. Karban (eds.). The evolution of insect life cycles. Springer-Verlag, New York.

——, and L. P. Lounibos. 1977. Evolution of dormancy and its photoperiodic control in pitcher-plant mosquitoes. Evolution 31:546–567.

——, and R. A. Creelman. 1984. Mutualism between the carnivorous purple pitcher plant and its inhabitants. Amer. Midl. Nat. 112:294–304.

Branch, N., L. Logan, E. C. Beck, and J. A. Mulrennan. 1958. New distributional record for Florida mosquitoes. Fla. Entomol. 41:155–163.

Breeland, S. G. 1982. Bibliography and notes on Florida mosquitoes with limited distribution in the United States. Mosquito Syst. 14:53–72.

——, and T. M. Loyless. 1983. Illustrated keys to the mosquitoes of Florida. Florida Department of Health and Rehabilitative Services, Jacksonville.

Breland, O. P. 1960. Restoration of the name, *Aedes hendersoni* Cockerell, and its elevation to full specific rank (Diptera, Culicidae). Ann. Entomol. Soc. Amer. 53:600–606.

Bullington, S. W., and A. F. Beck. 1991. A new species of *Machimus loew* (Diptera: Asilidae) from burrows of *Gopherus polyphemus* (Testudines: Testudinidae). Ann. Entomol. Soc. Amer. 84:590–595.

Cameron, C. J., G. L. Donald, and C. G. Paterson. 1977. Oxygen fauna relationships in the pitcher plant *Sarracenia purpurea* L. with reference to the chironomid *Metriocnemus knabi* Coq. Car. J. Zool. 55:2018–2023.

Carpenter, S. J. 1949. Collection of a fourth instar larva of *Anopheles albimanus* at Boca Raton Field in 1944. J. Econ. Entomol. 42:834.

———, R. W. Chamberlain, and J. F. Wanamaker. 1945. New distribution records for the mosquitoes of the southeastern states in 1944. J. Econ. Entomol. 38:401–402.

———, and W. J. LaCasse. 1955. Mosquitoes of North America (north of Mexico). U. of California Press, Berkeley.

Cockerell, T. D. A. 1918. The mosquitoes of Colorado. J. Econ. Entomol. 11:195–200.

Copeland, R. S. 1987. Habitat segregation and life history patterns of the Culicidae of treeholes in northern Indiana. Ph.D. thesis, U. of Notre Dame.

Coquillett, D. W. 1901. Three new species of Culicidae. Can. Entomol. 33:258–260.

———. 1904. Several new Diptera from North America. Can. Entomol. 36:10–12.

Dodge, H. R. 1947. A new species of *Wyeomyia* from the pitcher plant (Diptera, Culicidae). Proc. Entomol. Soc. Wash. 49:117–122.

Dyar, H. G. 1918. New American mosquitoes (Diptera, Culicidae). Insec. Inscit. Menstr. 6:120–129.

———, and F. Knab. 1906. The larvae of Culicidae classified as independent organisms. J. NY Entomol. Soc. 14:169–230.

Faran, M. E. 1980. Mosquito studies (Diptera, Culicidae). XXXIV. A revision of the Albimanus Section of the subgenus *Nyssorhynchus* of *Anopheles*. Contrib. Amer. Entomol. Inst. 15:1–215.

Fish, D., & D. W. Hall. 1978. Succession and stratification of aquatic insects inhabiting the leaves of the insectivorous pitcher plant, *Sarracenia purpurea*. Amer. Midl. Nat. 99:172–183.

Fisk, F. W. 1939. New mosquito record from Key West, Fla. J. Econ. Entomol. 30:8–15.

Floore, T. G., B. A. Harrison, and B. F. Eldridge. 1976. The *Anopheles (Anopheles) crucians* subgroup in the United States (Diptera: Culicidae). Mosquito Syst. 8:1–109.

Frank, J. H., G. A. Curtis, G. W. Erdos, and E. A. Ellis. 1981. On the bionomics of bromeliad-inhabiting mosquitoes. VIII. The flotational structure of *Wyeomyia vanduzeei* eggs. (Diptera: Culicidae). J. Med. Entomol. 18:337–340.

Grabham, M. 1950. Notes on some Jamaican Culicidae. Can. Entomol. 37:401–411.

Griffiths, G. C. D. 1984. Anthomyiidae. Part 2, no. 4, vol. 8, pp. 409–600 *in* G. C. D. Griffiths (ed.). Flies of the Nearctic region. Schweizerbart, Stuttgart.

Grimstad, P. R., C. E. Garry, and G. R. DeFoliart. 1974. *Aedes hendersoni* and *Aedes triseriatus* (Diptera: Culicidae) in Wisconsin: characterization of larvae, larval hybrids, and comparison of adult and hybrid mesoscutal patterns. Ann. Entomol. Soc. Amer. 67:795–804.

———, S. L. Paulson, and G. B. Craig. 1985. Vector competence of *Aedes hendersoni* (Diptera: Culicidae) for LaCrosse virus and evidence of a salivary-gland escape barrier. J. Med. Entomol. 22:447–453.

Hardy, D. E. 1950. The nearctic Nomoneura and Nemomydas (Diptera: Mydaidae). Wasmann. J. Biol. 8:9–37.

Hawley, W. A., P. Reiter, R. S. Copeland, C. B. Pumpuni, and G. B. Craig. 1987. *Aedes albopictus* in North America: probable introduction in used tires from northern Asia. Science 236:1114–1116.

Hubbard, H. G. 1986. The insect guests of the Florida land tortoise. Insect Life 6:302–315.

Istock, C. A., K. Tanner, and H. Zimmer. 1983. Habitat selection by the pitcher-plant mosquito, *Wyeomyia smithii*: behavioral and genetic aspects. Pp. 191–204 in J. H. Frank & L. P. Lounibos (eds.). Phytotelmata: Terrestrial plants as hosts for aquatic insect communities. Plexus, Medford, NJ.

King, W. V. 1937. On the distribution of *Anopheles albimanus* and its occurrence in the United States. S. Med. J. 30:943–946.

———, G. H. Bradley, C. N. Smith, and W. C. McDuffie. 1960. A handbook of the mosquitoes of the southeastern United States. U.S. Department of Agriculture Handbook no. 173.

Knab, F. 1905. A chironomid inhabitant of *Sarracenia purpurea, Metriocnemus knabi*. Coq. J. NY Entomol. Soc. 13:69–73.

Knight, J. W., and J. S. Haeger. 1971. Key to adults of the *Culex* subgenera *Melanoconion* and *Mochlostyrax* of eastern North America. J. Med. Entomol. 8:551–555.

Kondratieff, B. C., and J. L. Welch. 1990. Nemomydas of southwestern United States, Mexico, and Central America (Diptera: Mydidae). Proc. Entomol. Soc. Wash. 92(3):471–482.

McAlpine, J. F., B. V. Peterson, G. E. Shewell, H. J. Tesky, J. R. Vockeroth, and D. M. Wood, eds. 1981, 1987. Manual of Nearctic Diptera. Vols. 1–2. Agriculture Canada Monograph 27–28. 1332 pp.

McDaniel, S. T. 1971. The genus *Sarracenia* (Sarraceniaceae). Bull. Tall Timbers Res. Sta. 9:1–36.

Nasci, R. S. 1982. Differences in host choice between the sibling species of tree-hole mosquitoes *Aedes triseriatus* and *Aedes hendersoni*. Amer. J. Trop. Med. Hyg. 31:411–415.

O'Meara, G. F., L. P. Louinbos, and R. A. Brust. 1981. Repeated egg clutches without blood in the pitcher plant mosquito. Ann. Entomol. Soc. Amer. 74. 68–72.

Paris, O. H., Jr., and C. E. Jenner. 1959. Photoperiodic control of diapause in the pitcher plant midge, *Metriocnemus knabi*. Pp. 601–624 in R. B. Withrow (ed.). Photoperiodism and related phenomena in plants and animals. Amer. Assoc. Adv. Sci., Publ. no. 55, Washington, DC.

Pechuman, L. L. 1974. Two new Tabanidae from southeastern United States (Diptera). J. N.Y. Entomol. Soc. 82:183–188.

Philip, C. B., and C. M. Jones. 1962. New North American Tabanidae. XV. Additions to records of *Chrysops* in Florida. Fla. Entomol. 45:67–69.

Pritchard, A. E., E. L. Seabrook, and J. A. Mulrennan. 1949. The mosquitoes of the Florida Keys. Fla. Entomol. 30:8–15.

———, ———, and M. W. Provost. 1946. The possible endemicity of *A. albimanus* in Florida. Mosquito News. 6:183–184.

Saul, S. H., M. J. Sinsko, P. R. Griamstad, and G. B. Craig. 1977. Identification of sibling species, *Aedes triseriatus* and *Aedes hendersoni* by electrophoresis. J. Med. Entomol. 13:705-708.

Scholl, P. J., and G. R. Defoliart. 1977. *Aedes triseriatus* and *A. hendersoni*: vertical and temporal distribution as measured by oviposition. Environ. Entomol. 6:355-358.

Sinsko, M. J., and P. R. Grimstad. 1977. Habitat separation by differential vertical oviposition of two treehole *Aedes* in Indiana. Environ. Entomol. 6:485-487.

Steyskal, G. C. 1956. The eastern species of *Nemomydas* Curran (Diptera: Mydaidae). Occ. Pap. Mus. Zool. Univ. Mich. 573:1-5.

Stone, A. 1968. A new mosquito record for the United States. Proc. Entomol. Soc. Wash. 47:199-210.

Sudia, W. D., and V. F. Newhouse. 1975. Epidemic Venezuelan equine encephalitis in North America: a summary of virus-vector-host relationships. Amer. J. Epidem. 101:1-13.

Thurman, E. B., J. S. Haeger, and J. A. Mulrennan. 1949. The occurrence of *Aedes (Ochlerotatus) thelcter* Dyar in the Florida Keys. Mosquito News 9:171-172.

_____, _____, and _____. 1951. The taxonomy and biology of *Psorophora (Janthinosoma) johnstonii* (Grabham 1905) Ann. Entomol. Soc. Amer. 44:144-157.

Truman, J. W., & G. B. Craig. 1968. Hybridization between *Aedes hendersoni* and *Aedes triseriatus*. Ann. Entomol. Soc. Amer. 61:1020-1025.

Wiedemann, C. R. W. 1820. Diptera exotica. Kiliae. 244 pp.

Wirth, W. W. 1945. The occurrence of *Culex (Melanoconion) elevator* Dyar and Knab in Florida, with keys to the *Melanoconions* of the United States. Proc. Entomol. Soc. Wash. 47:199-210.

Young, D. G. 1974. Bruchomyiinae in North America, with a description of *Nemopalpus nearcticus* n. sp. (Diptera: Psycodidae). Fla. Entomol. 57:109-113.

Zavortink, T. J. 1968. Mosquito studies (Diptera, Culicidae) VIII. A prodrome of the genus *Orthopodomyia*. Contrib. Amer. Entomol. Inst. 3:1-221.

_____. 1972. Mosquito studies (Diptera, Culicidae). XXVIII. The New World species formerly placed in *Aedes (Finlaya)*. Contrib. Amer. Entomol. Inst. 8:1-206.

_____, and J. N. Belkin. 1979. Occurrence of *Aedes hendersoni* in Florida. (Diptera, Culicidae). Mosquito News 39:673.

ANTS, BEES, AND WASPS

Carroll, J. F. 1975. Biology and ecology of ants of the genus *Aphaenogaster* in Florida. Unpublished Ph.D. dissertation, University of Florida. 177 pp.

Carter, W. G. 1962. Ant distribution in North Carolina. J. Elisha Mitchell Sci. Soc. 78:150-204.

Creighton, W. S. 1950. The ants of North America. Bull. Mus. Comp. Zool. 104. 585 pp.

Deyrup, M., and D. D. Manley. 1986. Sex biased variation in velvet ants (Hymenoptera: Mutillidae). Fla. Entomol. 69:327-335.

———, J. C. Trager, and N. Carlin. 1985. The genus *Odontomachus* in the southeastern United States (Hymenoptera: Formicidae). Entomol. News 96:188–195.

Francoeur, A. 1973. Revision taxonomique des especes nearctiques du groupe fusca, genre *Formica* (Formicidae, Hymenoptera). Mem. Soc. Entomol. Quebec 3. 316 pp.

Graenicher, S. 1930. Bee fauna and vegetation of the Miami region of Florida. Ann. Entomol. Soc. Amer. 23:153–174.

Hölldobler, B., and E. O. Wilson. 1990. The Ants. Belknap Press of Harvard Univ. Press, Cambridge. 732 pp.

Johnson, C. 1989. Taxonomy and diagnosis of *Conomyrma insana* (Buckley) and *C. flava* (McCook) (Hymenoptera: Formicidae). Insecta Mundi 3:179–194.

Manley, D. D. 1983. Description of apparent males of *Dasymutilla archboldi* from Florida (Hymenoptera: Mutillidae). J. Ga. Entomol. Soc. 18:252–255.

———. 1984. An easily used character for identification of *Dasymutilla archboldi* Schmidt and Mickel. (Hymenoptera: Mutillidae). J. Ga. Entomol. Soc. 19:228–229.

———, and M. Deyrup. 1987. A new species of *Photomorphus* (Hymenoptera: Mutillidae) from Florida. J. Entomol. Sci. 22:57–60.

Mitchell, T. B. 1960. Bees of the eastern United States. Vol. I. N. C. Agric. Exp. Sta. Tech. Bul. 141. 538 pp.

Mitchner, C. D. 1966. The classification of the *Diphlaglossinae* and North American species of the genus *Caupolicana* (Hymenoptera: Colletidae). Univ. Kans. Sci. Bull. 46:717–751.

Schmidt, J. O., and C. E. Mickel. 1979. A new species of *Dasymutilla* from Florida (Hymenoptera: Mutillidae). Proc. Entomol. Soc. Wash. 81:576–579.

Trager, J. C. 1988. A revision of *Conomyrma* (Hymenoptera: Formicidae) from the southeastern United States, especially Florida, with keys to the species. Fla. Entomol. 71:11–29.

———, and C. Johnson. 1985. A slave making ant in Florida: *Polyergus lucidus* with observations on the natural history of its host *Formica archboldi* (Hymenoptera: Formicidae). Fla. Entomol. 68:261–266.

Wesson, L. G., and R. G. Wesson. 1940. A collection of ants from south central Ohio. Amer. Midl. Nat. 24:89–103.

Wheeler, W. M. 1910. Ants: their structure, development and behavior. Columbia University Press, New York. 663 pp.

Wilson, E. O., and A. Francoeur. 1974. Ants of the *Formica fusca* group in Florida. Fla. Entomol. 57:115–116.

Index

Note: Numbers in *italic type* denote maps; numbers in **bold type** denote illustrations.

765